AF334432

GLOBALIZATION AND EUROPEAN INTEGRATION

GLOBALIZATION AND EUROPEAN INTEGRATION

ARNO TAUSCH AND PETER HERRMANN

Nova Science Publishers, Inc.
Huntington, New York

Senior Editors: Susan Boriotti and Donna Dennis
Office Manager: Annette Hellinger
Graphics: Wanda Serrano
Information Editor: Tatiana Shohov
Book Production: Cathy DeGregory, Jonathan Rose, Jennifer Vogt and Lynette Van Helden
Circulation: Ave Maria Gonzalez, Ron Hedges, Andre Tillman

Library of Congress Cataloging-in-Publication Data
Available upon request.

Includes bibliographical references and index.
ISBN 1-56072-921-X

Copyright © 2001 by Nova Science Publishers, Inc.
227 Main Street, Suite 100
Huntington, New York 11743
Tele. 631-424-6682.   Fax 631-425-5933
e-mail: Novascience@earthlink.net
Web Site: http://www.nexusworld.com/nova

Printed in the United States of America

Arno Tausch, Associate Visiting Professor, Department of Political Science,
Innsbruck University, Austria

and

Peter Herrmann, Department of Applied Social Studies,
University of Cork, Ireland

CONTENTS

LIST OF ABBREVIATIONS AND CONCEPTS (FUNCTIONAL TERMS)

a - constant in multiple regression analysis (statistics)

ACDA - Arms Control and Disarmament Agency (United States Department of State)

ASEAN - Association of Southeast Asian Nations

$b_{1,2,3}$ - coefficients in multiple regression analysis (statistics)

BSE - bovine spongiform encephalopathy

capability poverty measure (CPM-value) (UNDP, 1996. The measure weights unattended births, underweight children, and female illiteracy. It is regarded by the UNDP as a direct measure of absolute poverty)

capitalism - our definition of capitalism is based on Samir Amin (1997): private property, wage labor, production of commodities, agricultural revolution, exponential growth

CEEC-7 - The following 7 Central and East European countries: Bulgaria, Czech Republic, Hungary, Poland, Romania, Slovak Republic, Slovenia

CEFTA - Central European Free Trade Area (as of 1.9.1995, Czech Republic, Slovak Republic, Poland, Hungary)

CIS - Community of Independent States (in the ex-USSR)

CO_2 - carbon dioxide

deforestation rate(UNDP, 1993-95; World Bank, 1995; World Resources Research Institute).- The index measures annual rates of deforestation in the 1980s in percent. Because of missing data, a number of countries had to be coded by the LDC average or the OECD average

destabilization index - (coded according to Weltalmanach, 1995. The indicator codes all those countries as '1' (destabilized), that have entries about serious armed internal or external conflict in 1994. The rest is coded as '0'

df. - degrees of freedom (statistics)

DYN HD - growth of life expectancy over time

DYN - variables, measuring growth (economic growth, human development *et cetera*)

e - Eulers number (2.7...)

EC - European Community, after the Amsterdam Treaty: EU

economic growth - 80-93, pc. and year (UNDP, 1996)

ECU - European Currency Unit

Employment - (UNDP, 1994) labor force as percent of total population

ENCONS - energy consumption per capita

EO/AA - equal opportunity and affirmative action laws in the United States of America

ethno-linguistic fractionalization index, mid-1960s - (Bornschier/Heintz, 1979, based on Taylor/Hudson). Ethnic discrimination is thought to be the purest form of a 'distribution coalition'

ethno-warfare - (Gurr, 1994) magnitude of ethno-political conflict. The scores are country sums of the squared roots of the deaths (in 10s of thousands) from ethno-political conflict 1993-94 plus refugees (in 100s of thousands). Countries with no entries according to Gurr's main research results, 1994, are coded as '0'

EU membership years - (Fischer Weltalmanach, 1995, 1996)

EU - European Union (per 1.9.1995 15 member states)

EXCEL - a computer software for, amongst others, calculating statistics

export processing zones (Bailey et al., 1993) - The variable codes the number of export processing zones per country at the beginning of the 1990s

F - F-test-value in multiple regression analysis

F - productivities

forest area per total land area (UNDP, 1993-95) - In contrast to the above indicator, that measures flows, this measure rather captures stocks of already existent forest destruction. Agricultural land per total land area has to be taken into consideration as an independent variable, because else the regression equations would be biased by a desert-factor

GDP - Gross Domestic Product

gender empowerment measure (GEM) (UNDP, 1995.) - The index weights seats held by women in parliament, the percentage share of women and managers, the share of women in the professional and technical workforce, and the share of women in total earned income

gender-related development index (GDI) (UNDP, 1995) - dimension female life chances. This index was developed by the UNDP especially for the 1995 women's conference in Beijing. The index weights the share of earned income for females and males, the gender-specific life expectancies, the gender-specific adult literacy rates, and the gross primary, secondary and tertiary enrollment ratios. It ranges theoretically from 0.0 to 0.999, with Sweden (0.919) at the top of the international scale, and Afghanistan (0.169) at the bottom. Since there unfortunately no were no data for Dominica, Grenada, Antigua, Seychelles, Saint Lucia, Saint Vincent, Saint Kits, Belize, South Africa, Oman, Jordan, Gabon, Solomon Islands, Sao Tome, Congo, Rwanda, Bhutan, Angola, Mauritania, Somalia, Gambia, Germany and Israel, we had to substitute these missing values with averages for the socio-economic groups concerned: a) the industrialized democracies (gender development index average 0.87) b) developing countries with a Human Development Index above 0.6 (in our 123 nations analysis: Barbados to Tunisia, gender development index average 0.721) c) developing countries with a Human Development Index from 0.599 to 0.389 (Oman to Egypt, gender development index average 0,542) d) developing countries with a Human Development Index under 0.388 (except for the very least developed countries; Kenya to Sierra Leone; gender development index average 0.33) and e) the very least developed countries Benin, Guinea Bissau, Chad, Mali, Niger, Burkina Faso and Sierra Leone with a gender development index of 0.2. This procedure can be regarded only as a first approximation and should be substituted in future research

GNP - Gross National Product

government consumption per GDP, 1990 (UNDP, 1993/94)

government expenditures per GNP, 1991 (UNDP, 1993/94; UNICEF, Regional Monitoring Report, 1, 11, 1993, see Cornia, 1993; World Resources Research Institute)

greenhouse index, 1989 (greenhouse index per 10 million people, UNDP, 1994. The greenhouse index measures the net emissions of three major greenhouse gases: carbon dioxide, methane and chlorofluorocarbons. The index weights each gas according to it's heattrapping quality in carbon dioxide equivalents and expresses them in metric tons of carbon per capita) - dimension environmental quality/degradation

HD(I) - Human Development (Index), combining life expectancy, adult literacy, combined enrollment ratios, and real GDP per capita

HDR - *Human Development Report,* document, published each year by the UNDP

human development index (HDI) (UNDP, 1994). The index combines life expectancy, adult literacy rate, combined enrollment, and real GDP.

IBM - International Business Machines, international manufacturer of computer hard- and software

ILO - International Labor Office

IMF - International Monetary Fund

income distribution (Moaddel, 1994. The measure focuses on the share of the top 20percent in total incomes in over 80 countries. Wherever possible, Moaddel's data were updated by World Bank WDR, 1994, 1995 and 1996)

increase in life expectancy 1960-90 (calculated from UNDP, 1993/94 via a regression procedure, predicting 1990 life expectancy on 1960 life expectancy, and then taking the residuals as growth rates) - dimension redistribution and human development

increase/decrease of fertility rates 1960-90 (UNDP, 1993/94)

inflation 93 - (UNDP, 1996)

LDCs - less developed countries

LEX - life expectancy

life expectancy at birth as an indicator for the quality of past social policy, 1990 (UNDP, 1993/94 and World Bank, WDR, 1994)

LN PCI - natural logarithm of per capita income

Ln - natural logarithm

M - Imports

main telephone lines per 100 population (UNDP, 1996)

mean years of schooling of the population aged 25 and > (UNDP, 1993 and 1994)

mezzogiorno - 'South' (from the Italian language), a term, more and more used to describe a periphery (like the one in Southern Italy)

migration dependency (UNDP, 1993) - net worker remittances per GNP/GDP at the beginning of the 1990s

military expenditures per GDP (UNDP, 1996)

MNC penetration index - penetration by transnational capital, weighted by population and capital stock, mid-1970s (Bornschier/Heintz, 1979, based on OECD)

MNC - Multinational Corporations

n - sample size

NAFTA - North American Free Trade Area

natl - .natural logarithm

NATO - North Atlantic Treaty Organization

NO_X - nitrogen

O_2 - oxygen

OECD - Organization of Economic Co-operation and Development

PCI - per-capita-income

percent labor force participation ratio (UNDP, 1996)

percent of the labor force in agriculture (UNDP, 1996; Fischer Weltalmanach, 1996)

percent of the labor force in industry (see: labor force agriculture)

π – number π (3.14...)

population density total number of inhabitants, divided by the surface area of a country - Due to the skewness of the indicator, the squared root (population density$^{\wedge.50}$) had to be taken (calculated from UNDP, 1993/94)

PPP - purchasing power parity

PSL - Polish Peasant Party

R^2 - total variance explained

RGP - linear standard regression procedure of the EXCEL 5.0 program

RKP - non-linear standard regression procedure of the EXCEL 5.0 program

Rpp - real purchasing power parity

S.J. - Jesuits Fathers (Catholic Church)

SO_2 - sulfur-dioxide

social security benefits expenditure as percent of GDP in the era of the evolving contemporary Kondratieff cycle, 1985-90 (UNDP, 1994) -. Social security benefits expenditures include here the compensations for the loss of income for the sick and the temporarily disabled; payments to the elderly, the permanently disabled and the unemployed; they also include family, maternity and child allowances and the cost of welfare services. The UNDP data collection is based on ILO sources

state sector size (gov. expenditures per GDP; UNDP 1996; Weltalmanach, 1995, 1996; World Resources Institute)

structural heterogeneity - (labor force share in agriculture divided by product share of agriculture; see labor force data)

terms of trade index 1987-90 (UNDP, 1994, Weltalmanach, 1994, based on UN)

TNC - Transnational Corporations

trade dependency index - exports plus imports as percent of GDP 1990 (UNDP, 1993/94)

UK - United Kingdom

UN ECE - United Nations Economic Commission for Europe

UN membership years (Weltalmanach, 1996, 1995)

UN(O) - United Nations (Organization)
UNDP - United Nations Development Program

UNICEF - United Nations Children's Fund

USA - United States of America

USSR - former Union of Soviet Socialist Republics

violation of civil rights, 1991 - (Stiftung, 1993/94, based on Freedom House, combining freedom of religion, the press, freedom of assembly and association, freedom of trade unions, the right to property and equality before the law)

violation of political rights index, 1991 - (Stiftung, 1993/94, based on Freedom House, combining free elections, role of the elected parliament in political decision making, party competition, protection of minorities)

voivodship - Polish province. The country had 49 voivodships; whose number was reduced to 16 by the regional reform 1999

vulnerability of a nation in terms of the expansion of the new international division of labor, 1990 (share of women in the national labor force) (UNDP, 1993/94)

WDR - *World Development Report,* document, published each year by the World Bank

world political threats to a country, to be measured by the percentage of armed forces per population. Some neo-liberals maintain that world political threats increase the growth potential of a nation. Due to the skewness of the indicator, the natural logarithm ln (MPR+1) has to be taken (calculated from UNDP, 1993/94; see also: Weede, 1985)

X - Exports

x - independent variable(s)

y - dependent variable(s)

years of Communist Rule (Autorenkollektiv; Weltalmanach)

years of membership in the United Nations (coded from Weltalmanach, 1995)

LIST OF TABLES

LIST OF GRAPHS

LIST OF MAPS

FOREWORD (1)

This joint Austrian and Irish study is the outcome of empirical research on the development and decay tendencies of the capitalist world economy since the early 1980s and the role, that Europe will play in these constellations. In a way, it continues the socio-liberal re-reading of dependency theory, presented by Arno Tausch in *'Towards a Socio-Liberal Theory of World Development'*, published together with Fred Prager in 1993 with Macmillan.

Over these years we came to the conclusion that the logic of capitalist world development changes with the ups and downs of longer Kondratieff cycles, and that different periods of hegemony and of world political constellations, connected with these Kondratieff cycles, in turn give rise to different constellations of world economic ascent and decline.

We owe a lot to Samir Amin, Giovanni Arrighi, Chris Chase Dunn, Luigi Scandella and Jadwiga Staniszkis, who helped us with their contributions to further advance the theoretical viewpoints presented here. At the same time, the issue of transnational integration and tendencies for national disintegration, so clearly presented by Osvaldo Sunkel over a quarter of a century ago, emerged with full force during the last years.

Nova Science publishing house in Huntington in New York again has shown to us, that it is today one of the main voices in academic publishing in the English-speaking world, interested in a cross-cultural dialogue with the European East after the transformation. No Huntingtonian inter-cultural warfare, but learning from the sometimes painful experiences of newly capitalist societies in Eastern Europe and the former Soviet Union. So, our thanks go to Frank Columbus and his team in Huntington, New York.

We would also like to thank colleagues both in the academic world and in Government, in Austria, in the Irish Republic, in Poland, and in our EU partner countries. Gary Gabriel, Matthew Kahane and Jerzy Skuratowicz from the United Nations were absolutely helpful in the gathering of materials for this manuscript - in fact, it is understood to be a way of saying thanks to the UNDP for all the materials that we received from them. Without the UNDP, this book would never have been written.

The Vienna Institute for International Economic Comparisons and its director, Professor Michael Landesmann, have provided us with valuable materials and discussion inputs. Their analyses were always clear and concise, and more often than not against the mainstream. Final - and ultimate - thanks go to our families.

I, Arno Tausch would like to say here thanks to Krystyna, my beloved wife, without her inspiration I would not have written my part of this text.

From my, Peter Herrmann's side, I want to thank the students at the University College of Cork, Department of Applied Social Studies. Their desire to learn about the theoretical foundations of what they can see in the reality and read in the newspapers as well as their desire to take practice and with this the opportunities to change political and personal practice as criterion to check the validity of any theoretical approach had been a challenge for me to rethink again and again my arguments.

Arno Tausch and Peter Herrmann
Vienna and Cork, June 2001

FOREWORD (2) AND EXECUTIVE SUMMARY

The present book, the outcome of our analytical work over the last years, owes a lot to debates about the capitalist world system, that were carried out in the 1980s and 1990s. Those, that hoped that world trade and open financial markets will shift incomes in favor of the poor, must now recognize that - however we look at the figures - there is a tendency towards rising poverty on a global scale, especially after the Asian crash of 1997. Here and there, there were positive signs - like the leveling off of the incidence of poverty, measured by the 2 $ World Bank concept, in the Middle East and in Eastern Europe and the ex-USSR, and in China. But as M. Lundberg and B. Milanovic recognized in their contribution on the World Bank's *PovertyNet* Website, there is overwhelming evidence nowadays that world economic openness is to the detriment of the poorest 20%. The cumulative effect was a huge upsurge in the number of poor people in the Third World from around 2.7 billion people in 1996 to 2.8 billion people in 1998:

World Poverty: people living on less than 2 $ per day and capita

	E Asia + Pacific	Eastern Europe +Central Asia	Latin America	Middle East and North Africa	South Asia	Sub Saharan Africa	China
1987	299,9	16,3	147,6	65,1	911	356,6	752,4
1990	284,9	43,8	167,2	58,7	976	388,2	799,5
1993	271,6	79,4	162,2	61,7	1017,8	427,8	764,2
1996	236,3	92,7	179,8	60,6	1069,5	457,7	627,6
1998	260,1	92,9	182,9	62,4	1095,9	474,8	632,1

Source: World Bank, World Development Report, 2000

The evolution of world poverty 1987 - 1998

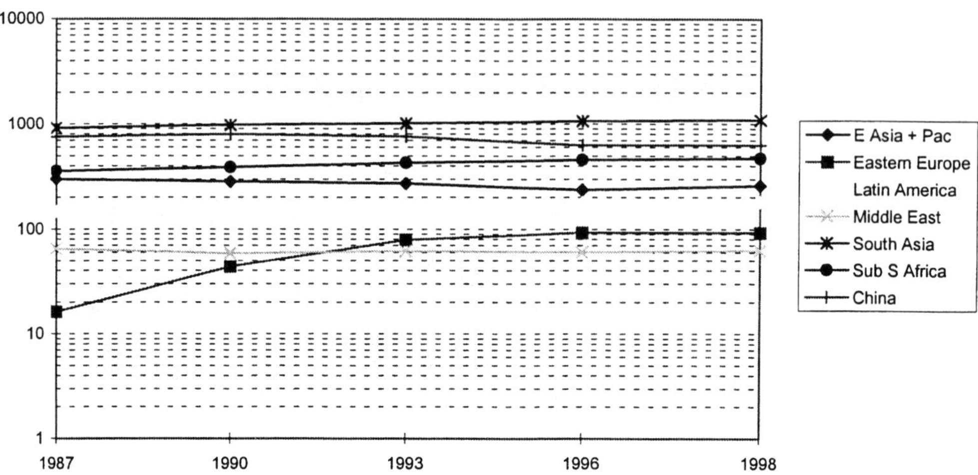

Global Second and Third World Poverty

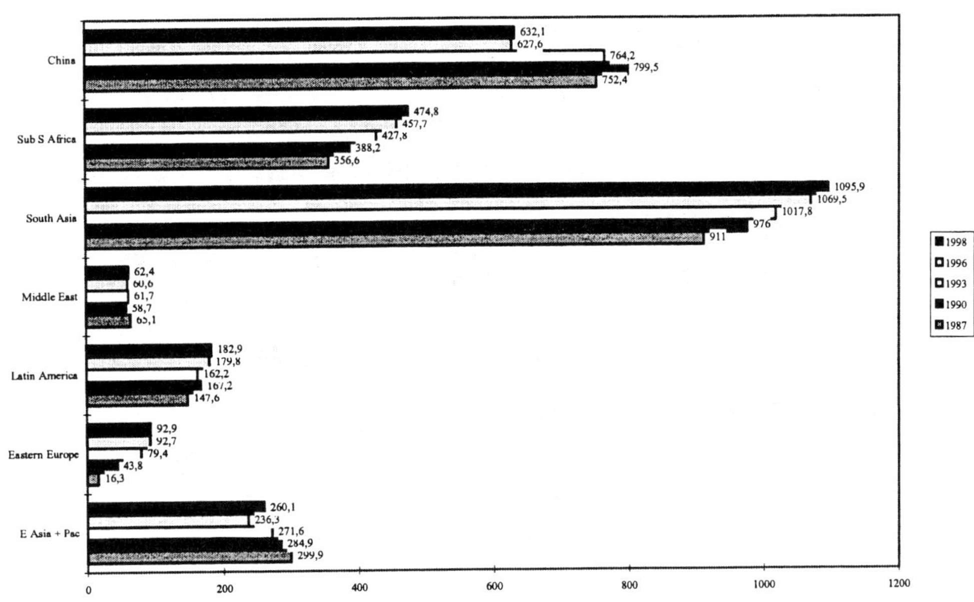

The absolute number of poor people in the Second and Third World

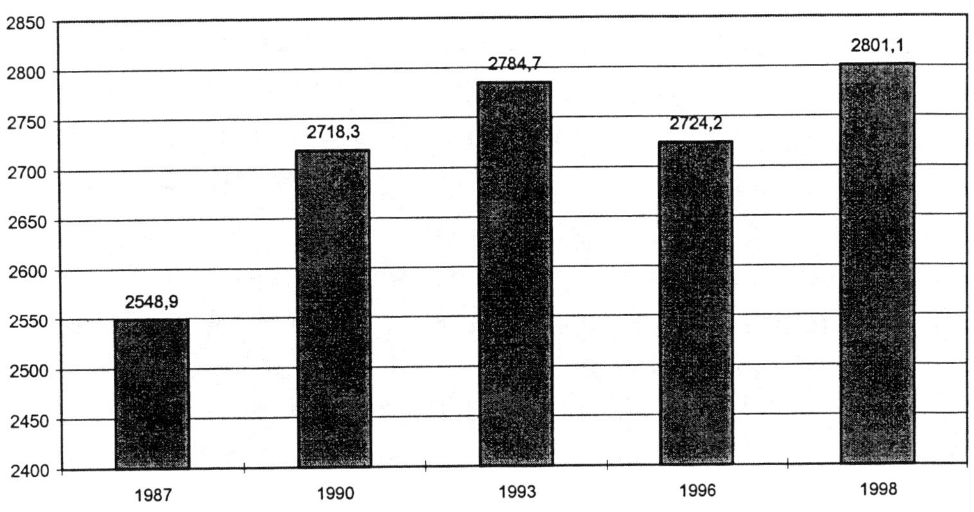

The increase/decrease in the number of poor in the Second and Third World

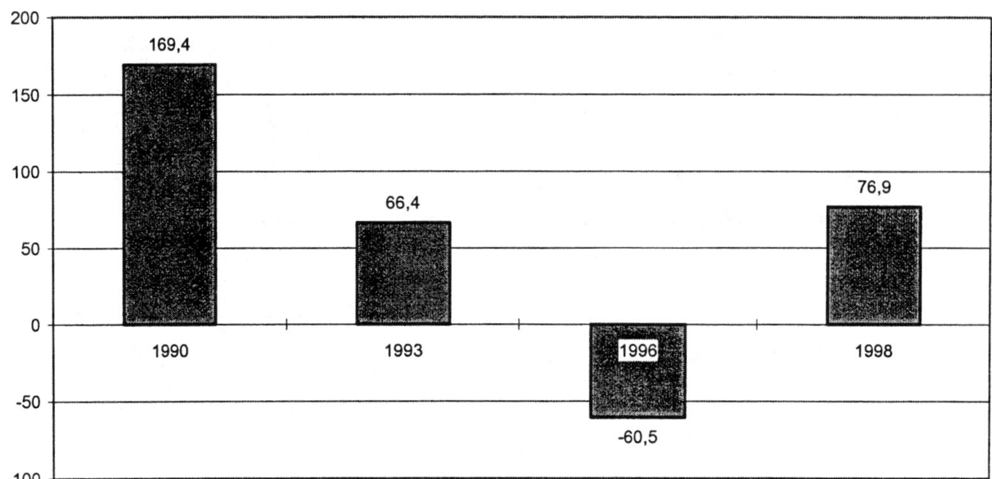

The transformation depression - or call it 'the process of creative destruction' - was so severe, that only Poland had a higher real GDP in 1997 than back in 1989, as the following graph tries to show:

Graph 0.1: The success or failure of the transformation process

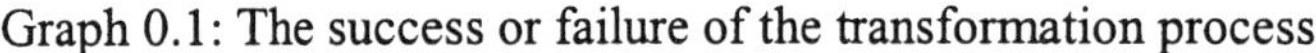

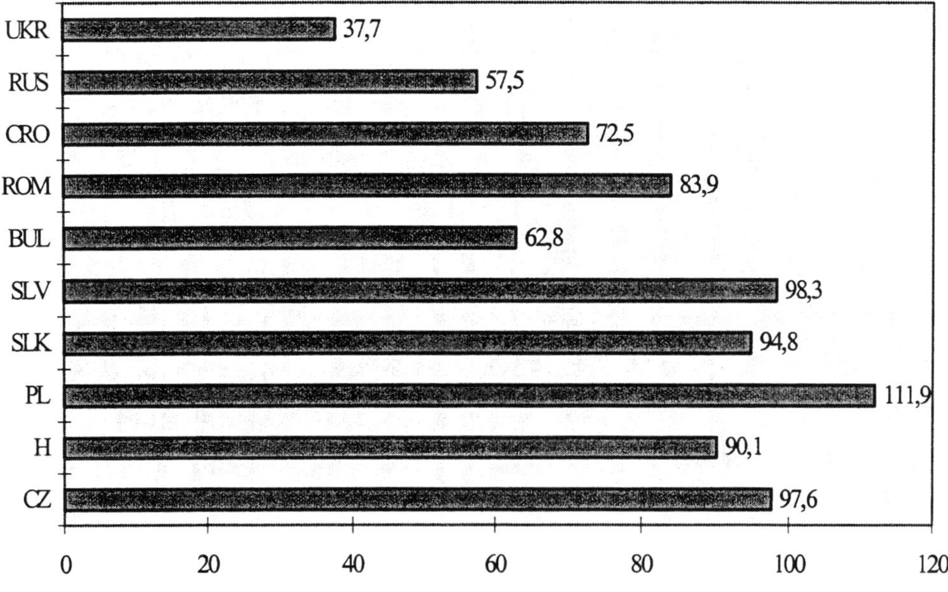

Legend: our own compilations from Podkaminer, *et al.,* 1998. East European GDP 1997 in percent of East European GDP in 1989 in real terms

In reality, there is no catching-up process of the European East with the countries of the Western part of the continent, while some of the net contributors to the European Union budget, like Austria, threaten also to fall below the EU average in the long run and thus will be caught in the same relative downward spiral of dependent capitalism the further you move eastwards on the European continent, away from the Atlantic:

Graph 0.2: projections for the real income gap between the accession countries and the EU

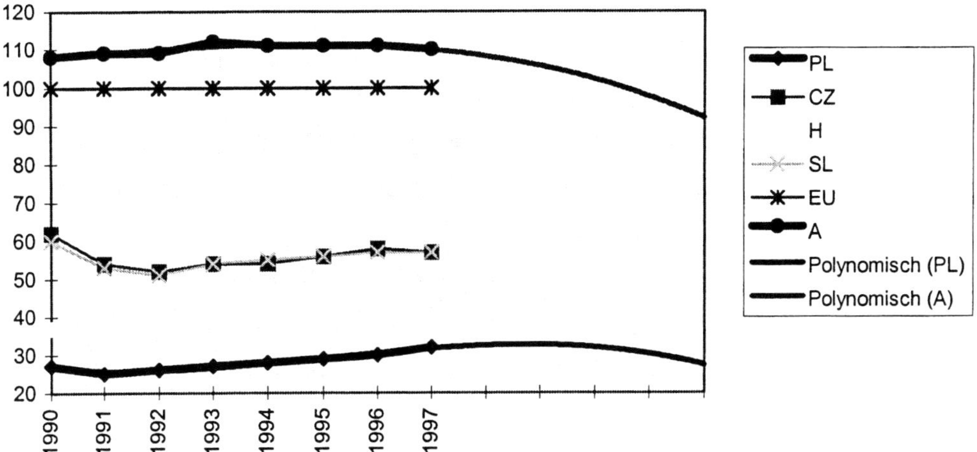

Legend: our own trend-line projections from Podkaminer *et al.,* 1998. Real income projections of various European regions in percent of the EU average

It is the simultaneous occurrence of the transformation process, European monetary union, eastward extension, globalization, structural reform of the Union, all at the same time, which calls for a systematic and long-term perspective which is empirically valid, politically feasible and conceptually forward-looking.

Despite all the progress towards a civil society, towards market reforms, and above all, towards democracy, dark clouds hang again over the horizons, here and there, that should be seriously watched indeed. In addition to Eastern Europe's long-standing debt-problem, post-transformation current account balances in percent of the GDP, as well as overall trade balances (in $ bn) point again in a downward direction, in a way resembling the 1970s in the region. The main external balances for the CEEC-7 countries (Czech Republic, Hungary, Poland, the Slovak Republic, Slovenia, Bulgaria, Romania) are:

Table 0.1: An Andre Gunder Frankian picture of the transformation process of the CEEC-7 countries

	CEEC-7 TRADE BALANCE	GROSS DEBT	CURR ACCOUNT BALANCE
1994	-10,482		
1995	-16,299		
1996	-28,628		-3,70%
1997	-28,53		-4,10%
1998	-31,45		-4,80%
Total	**-115,389**	**116,9**	

Current account balance in Millions of US $, 1996-2000:

	1996	1997	1998	1999	2000	2001	Total 1996-2001
Estonia				-316	-300	-350	-966
Latvia				-631	-600	-600	-1831
Lithuania				-1194	-1200	-1150	-3544
Bulgaria	82	427	-61	-663	-700	-700	-1615
Croatia	-858	-2434	-1554	-1395	-1300	-1400	-8941
Poland	-3264	-5744	-6901	-11700	-13500	-13700	-54809
Romania	-2571	-2338	-2968	-1303	-1500	-1600	-12280
Slovakia	-2098	-1953	-2059	-1080	-1150	-1400	-9740
Slovenia	39	37	-4	-581	-350	-250	-1109
Czech R	-4292	-3211	-1335	-1058	-1300	-1400	-12596
Hungary	-1678	-981	-2298	-2076	-2300	-2500	-11833
Yearly Total	-14640	-16197	-17180	-21997	-24200	-25050	**-119264**

Legend: our own compilations from Bank Austria, Report, 1, 1997 and CEE Report, 1/2000; and Podkaminer, *et al.,* 1998. Absolute values of the current account balances in East Central Europe until 2001. The lowest data series are cumulated values for the entire region.

If world-wide social science could learn something from the work of the Egyptian social scientist Samir Amin, it is the critical consciousness of the relevance of the current account balance as the main indicator of the external - or if you wish - 'dependency' situation of a country. The Vienna Institute for International Economic Studies analyses and projects the following ratios of the current account balances per GDP in the transformation countries:

Graph 0.3: current account balances in Eastern Europe, 1996 - 1999

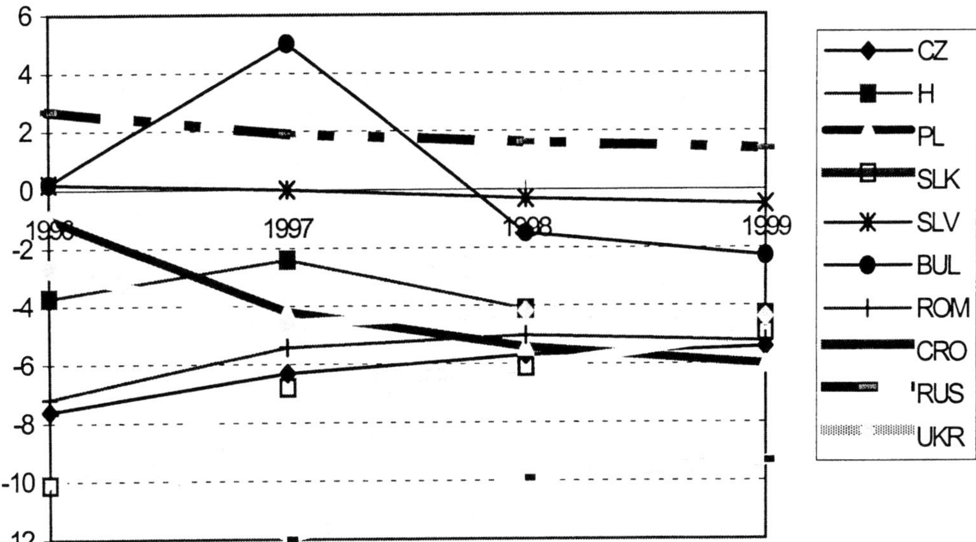

Legend: our own compilations from Podkaminer, *et al.*, 1998. Current account balances in percent of GDP in the different countries of East Central Europe

The problems are huge, not to say overwhelming, especially when we also consider the amount of unemployment, that was created by the transformation process. In some countries, unemployment decreased, while in others, it even increased over time (on the Balkans, in the Czech Republic and in the Ukraine):

Graph 0.4: unemployment in Eastern Europe, 1996 and 1997

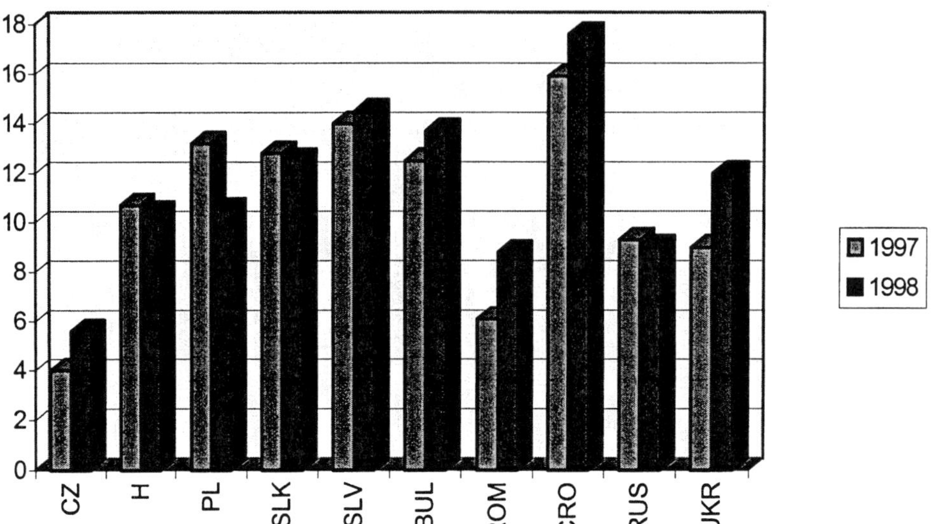

Legend: our own compilations from Podkaminer et al., 1998 and *Business Central Europe,* March 1998. Unemployment rates in the different countries of East Central Europe in percent of the total workforce (labor market service data)

A systematic application of our contemporary and empirically testable knowledge to the basic issues of European integration is, we feel, more necessary than ever before. After the end of the Cold War, a good part of world-systems oriented research, as the main body of knowledge today, that deals with the future perspectives of the world system, turned to historic and long-term aspects of the evolution, the rise and fall of empires and earlier civilizations, with an unspoken question in mind: what will happen to the contemporary Rome, the United States, the last remaining superpower, whose hegemony is now based, more than ever before, on the power of electronics, communication, information mobility, and the production - and monopolization - of knowledge. Authors like Christopher Chase-Dunn and Andre Gunder Frank have taught us all over the last years important insights into the structure, the rise and decline of major civilizations. Keeping in mind all these important questions of the future of the waning capitalist civilization (Schumpeter perhaps more forcefully than even Marx believed in the waning of capitalism), the question-writing, and thus the plan for this research documentation, was oriented towards the present and future role of Europe in the whole set-up. And yet, considering the European malaise, America's hegemony will still last for quite some time (let us risk the prediction: a Kondratieff cycle), while Europe's peripherization will increase. The task of European Monetary Union and eastward extension of the European Union could not come at a worse time. Long-term evidence, based largely on Goldstein's data series (see Chapter 3) suggests that the world economy is characterized by very strong cyclical fluctuations of the Kuznets type (18-22 year fluctuations) and Kondratieff type (40-60 year fluctuations), and that by around 2004 or 2005, at the latest, we will have quite a strong recession in Europe again, while the first years of European Monetary Union will be characterized by considerable capital inflows:

Graph 0.5: the long economic cycles in the capitalist world economy, 1740 - 1997

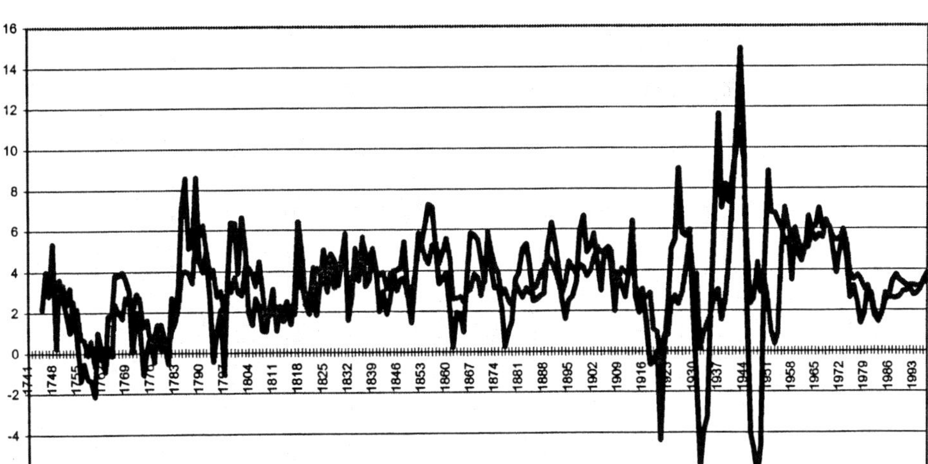

Legend: estimates about the economic growth rates in the capitalist world system from 1740 onwards, based on 5 and 10-year moving averages, calculated from Goldstein's data, augmented by data from the IMF, the UN ECE, IFRI and the World Bank for the post-1975 period; see Chapter 3 for the details

We use the macro-quantitative method of studying the conditions for the rise and fall of nations to arrive at our conclusions, based on the systematic study of development in the post-1980s. The choice of the time period is not arbitrary: we believe, that transnational capitalism is a cyclical process, and that in the post-1980s years, new social patterns for the rise and decline of nations have emerged, that need to be studied.

In Chapter 1 we outline present-day tendencies of globalization, and come to the conclusion, that a growing proportion of the people of our globe are faced by economic, social, personal, and ecological insecurity. In Chapter 2 we present an outline of the major theories that explain the rise and decline of nations: the world-system/dependency model, the socio-liberal reform model, and the neo-liberal model. Chapter 3 presents the methods of this study, both in a cross-national as well as in a time-series, cycle-oriented sense. The major ideas about the interdisciplinary nature of the development concept, and the development functions used in this study, are presented, as well as evidence about the cyclical fluctuations, that force us to make a particular choice of the time period used. The end-result of our methodological exercise is also a qualification of the old debate about the historical nature of social science: each cycle (Kondratieff cycles of about 40-60 years duration) has its own 'laws' of development, and macroquantitative results about, say, the presumed causes of rapid social development or stagnation in the late 1960s, the 1970s and very early 1980s correspond to another logic (a B-phase in the Kondratieff cycle), than, say, results about post-war development from 1945 to 1965 (the A-phase of the *'fordist'* cycle from, say, 1932 - 1982) or results from 1980 onwards (the A-phase of the present new cycle of flexible specialization), or results from, say, the 1880s to 1914 (the A-phase of the *'enlargement of participation'* cycle). Our ideas coincide here with those of Samir Amin, Giovanni Arrighi, and Volker Bornschier. Since development is a multidimensional process, we study in Chapter 4 (Chapter 9, Chapter 10) the conditions for the rise and decline of 123 (134) nations on up to 19 indicators of development, that range from the traditional concept of economic growth to social, ecological, and political security. It is shown that TNC penetration (UNCTAD-concept of FDI per GDP) is again one of the main long-term stumbling blocs for development, short-term spurts of growth notwithstanding. Yet there are important qualifying processes that intervene here - the early or late rise of a country to nationhood, and thus - the position in the international system, that very much works like a 'distribution coalition', and also the relative achievements of feminism over the last decades, which are threatened to be wiped out with a vengeance by the new and latest phases of global capitalism. Chapter 5 and 6 qualify our results on the ecological dimension and further highlight the tendency of global capitalism to produce a sexist pattern of inequality on a global scale. Chapter 7 is dedicated to the philosophical dimensions of our notion of 'development' - as a follow-up to the preceding two Chapters.

Chapter 8 takes up the challenge of Huntington's counter-model of development in the 1980s and beyond, that is based on the concept of the evolving threat of a 'clash of civilizations'. We can show, that - if anything - there should be a link-up between those, thriving for a sustainable future in the 'West' and those in the Islamic and Orthodox world, who care for the environment. Under proper consideration of the factors of globalization, Islamic or Orthodox cultures are not an impediment to development.

Chapter 9, - the main Chapter of this introductory and study textbook in terms of political conclusions - offers what we call a 'labor perspective' on European integration. It analyses the continued trend towards peripherization in East Central Europe, it offers detailed results about these trends from a variety of studies on Poland in a regional perspective as well as from the transformation countries in general, and it shows the limits of the process of European integration. OECD country stagnation, depressingly enough, is caused by three factors - democratic age, state sector expenditures, and years of membership in the European Union. Precisely because of that, the Union needs again and again extensions, that only partially can remedy her in-built fundamental weaknesses.

In Chapter 10, we finally offer a pessimistic picture on international mobility and the process of migration, that is part and parcel of what Samir Amin called 'the five pillars of international inequality'.

Chapter 11 is a final, theoretical debate about the future role of social movements in a United Europe.

Not that you believe, that this research documentation is Euro-centric: again and again, it being attempted to show, how the forces of global capitalism structure nowadays European realities. What has been Osvaldo Sunkel's prediction more than 25 years ago?

'...The advancement of modernization introduces, so to speak, a wedge along the area dividing the integrated from the segregated segments (...) The effects of the disintegration of each social class has important consequences for social mobility. The marginalized entrepreneur will probably add to the ranks of small or artesanal manufacture, or will abandon independent activity and become a middle class employee. The marginalized sectors of the middle class will probably form a group of frustrated lower middle class people trying to maintain middle class appearance without much possibility of upward mobility and terrorized by the danger of proletarization. The marginalized workers will surely add to the ranks of absolute marginality, where, as in the lower middle class, growing pools of resentment and frustration of considerable demographic dimension will accumulate (...) Finally, it is very probable that an international mobility will correspond to the internal mobility, particularly between the internationalized sectors (...) The process of social disintegration which has been outlined here probably also affects the social institutions which provide the bases of the different social groups and through which they express themselves. Similar tendencies to the ones described for the global society are, therefore, probably also to be found within the state, Church, armed forces, political parties with a relatively wide popular base, the universities etc.' (Sunkel, 1972: 18-42).

More than 25 years after Sunkel's essay about transnational integration and national disintegration, parts of the periphery might be underway towards a partial redistribution and a partial re-integration of their marginal sectors, while polarization increases in Europe. This generalized hypothesis is also supported by our analysis of employment data, which, limited as they are, show, that while the South(especially Latin America, South Asia) made at least some headway, parts of the 'North' (and that, as usual, includes the very 'down under South' of

Australia, New Zealand, and partially also Argentina, as correctly predicted by Wheelwright and his school a quarter of a century ago) has declined. Thus, our predictions are again not too far from those of Samir Amin (1997):

Map 0.1: income inequality in the world system

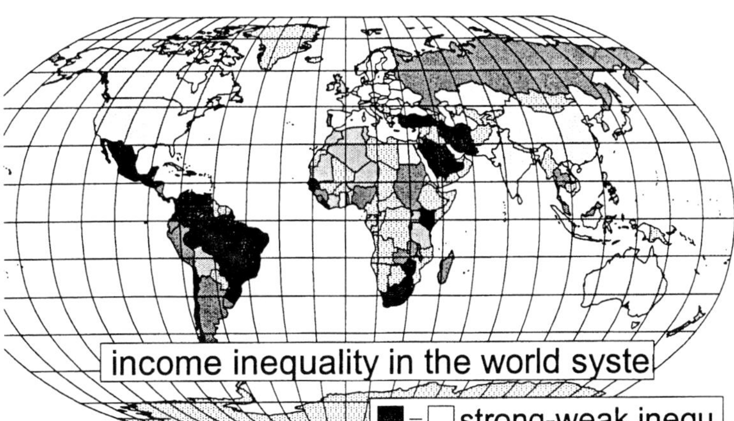

Legend: EXCEL 7.0 graph from World Bank WDR 1996 data (Table 5) and Moaddel, 1994. The darker, the higher the income inequality rates. Throughout this work, zebra-type colors indicate: missing values.

Map 0.2: capitalism and inequality growth/decline in the world system

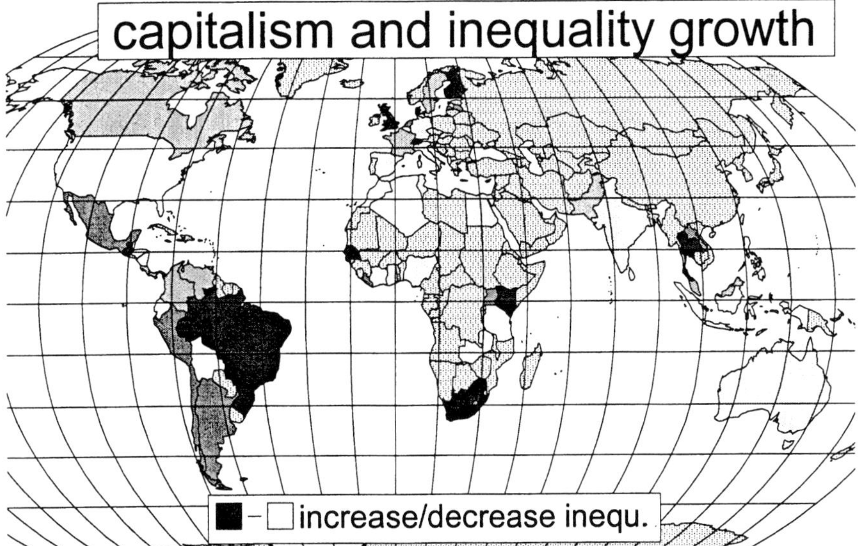

Legend: income distribution changes as measured by the 10 year standardized growth/decline in the share of the top 20% in total incomes. Calculated from World Bank, WDR, 1996 and Moaddel, 1994, using EXCEL 7.0. The darker, the higher income inequality growth. Throughout this work, zebra-type colors indicate: missing values.

The real basis of rising inequality in the capitalist world system is the fact, that globalization changed the power relationships between capital and labor to a dramatic extent. For every increment of 1% to the GNP of the countries of the world per year, there is only an annual increment of 0.63% to the real earnings of dependent labor throughout the period 1980-92/93. Our following Graph shows these latest available UNDP statistics on economic growth and real earnings growth, 1980-92/93 p.a.:

Graph 0.6: economic growth and real earnings growth, 1980-92/93

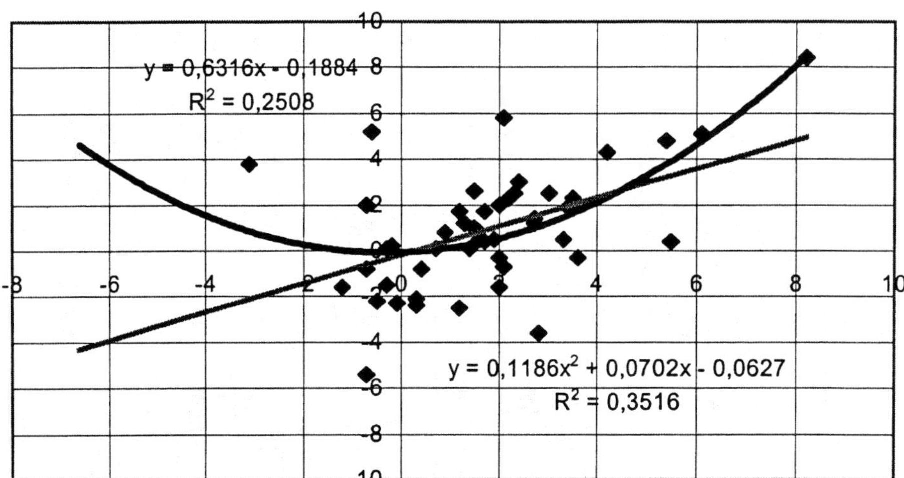

Legend: our own compilations from UNDP, Human Development Report, 1996. For the choice of countries, see sample Chapter 10 (n = 134 nations). X-axis: economic growth 1980-93 p.a.; y-axis: real earnings growth during the same period p.a.

There is mounting evidence, focused on in this research documentation, about the limits of the process of European integration as a strategy of world economic ascent. Euro-optimists, like professor Werner Weidenfeld in his article in *Neue Zuercher Zeitung* (10.07.1998), maintain that the Union will soon comprise every 7th state in the world, that the Union is about to crown its success of its internal market with European monetary union, and the Union concentrates within its borders around half of world trade and ¼ of world product. Half a billion (500 million) inhabitants will share among each other the fruits of the integration process. Our view, developed in Chapter 9 of this research documentation, is much more somber: while it is true, that the Union could re-distribute between its center and its periphery between 1960 and 1994, this process will practically come to a halt with European monetary union and eastward expansion. And Europe again falls behind, at least in relative terms, to other capitalist centers, like the United States of America, due to a process of the becoming 'South', a partial *mezzogiorno-zation*, of the whole of Europe. Connected with it is the rise of the shadow economy, distribution coalitions, organized crime and spread of the Mediterranean criminal transnational corporations to the whole of Europe:

Graph 0.7: relative GDP per capita income gaps within the European Union and between the European Union and the United States of America (expressed in real 1987 $ at current exchange rates)

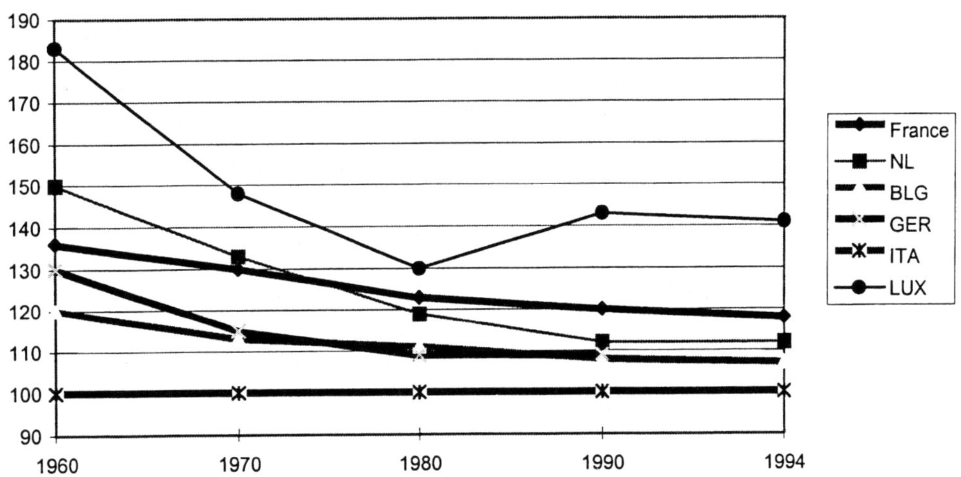

Legend: real GDP per capita of the founding members of the European Union in percent of the **Italian GDP** per capita for 1960, 1970, 1980, 1990, and 1994. In the 1950s, Italy was by far the poorest country of the Union. Our data are from UNDP, Human Development Report, 1997. They refer to the UNDP data series on GDP per capita in 1987 real $ since 1960, and were calculated from the original tables for the purpose of this research documentation. The empirical values for the above graphical presentation are:

	1960	1970	1980	1990	1994
France	136	130	123	120	118
NL	150	133	119	112	112
BLG	120	113	111	108	107
GER	130	115	109	109	
ITA	**100**	**100**	**100**	**100**	**100**
LUX	183	148	130	143	141

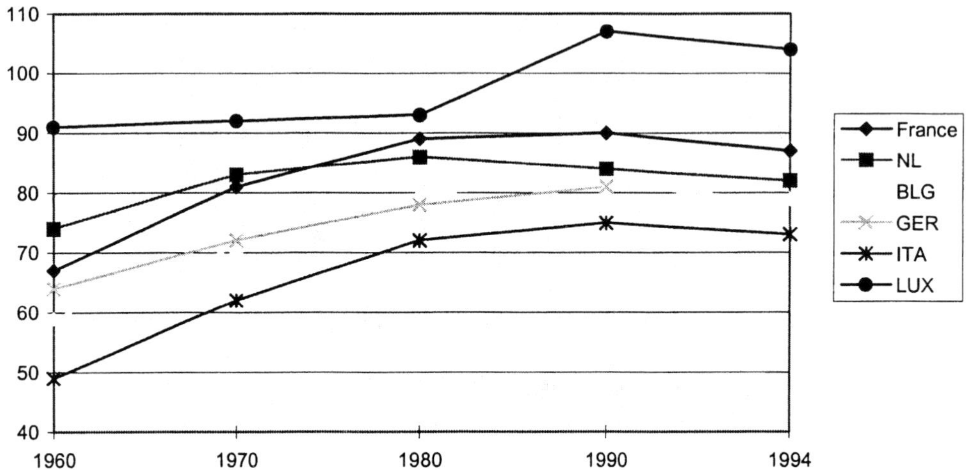

Legend: real GDP per capita of the founding members of the European Union in percent of the **US GDP** per capita for 1960, 1970, 1980, 1990, and 1994. Our data are from UNDP, Human Development Report, 1997. They refer to the UNDP data series on GDP per capita in 1987 real $ since 1960, and were calculated from the original tables for the purpose of this research documentation. The empirical values for the above graphical presentation are:

	1960	1970	1980	1990	1994
France	67	81	89	90	87
NL	74	83	86	84	82
BLG	59	71	80	81	79
GER	64	72	78	81	
ITA	49	62	72	75	73
LUX	91	92	93	107	104
USA	**100**	**100**	**100**	**100**	**100**

The amount of problems of the Italian *mezzogiorno,* in particular, are truly staggering: among its 21 million inhabitants, unemployment among the young is now approaching 50 percent. Fewer than a quarter of the young people between the age of 15 and 29 are in the official workforce. Ever since Italy was united and monetary union between the North and the South was introduced, unity concealed diversity. Rampant poverty, crime and corruption, but also the heroic attempts of the local population to continue living under such strenuous circumstances, characterize the scene. The 182 km Palermo-Messina highway took more than 20 years to build, and 50 kilometers are still unfinished, the final viaduct half-ready for perhaps eternity. In Porto Empedocle, the government poured millions into a gigantic chemical plant, that never started work. The new Catania hospital was never opened, the swimming pool in Nuoro in Sardinia was closed down soon after opening *(The European,* 426, 20-26 July 1998, p. 8-12). The *bizzo,* the protection money, paid by the majority of enterprises to the large transnational criminal enterprises, is but the tip of the iceberg of market distortions and economic waste.

There is a partially optimistic, and a partially pessimistic implication for the transformation countries of Eastern and Central Europe. They can be optimistic, because a host of societal problems definitively becomes easier after the 'turning points', expressed in terms of already achieved human development levels. Most of the reform countries are well beyond these 'crisis points', and for that reason alone, the **European center cannot close its frontiers to the East.** The 'turning points' for these problems are:

adjustment problems in the world economy   0.5
avoiding deforestation   0.75
avoiding destabilization and wars   0.425
avoiding ethno-warfare   practically linear
civil rights performance   0.3
controlling refugee inflows   0.5
gender development   practically linear
gender empowerment   0.7
general life expectancy   practically linear
growth potential   0.4
income redistribution   0.5
maternal mortality reduction   practically linear
political rights performance   0.2
poverty reduction   practically linear
protection of the national forest area   0.9
reducing corruption   0.55

However, there is another, a more somber side of development, which we discuss in Chapter 7 of this introductory and study textbook. A host of problems increase, rather than decrease with 'development', and we think we are justified, when we speak about 'decay' rather than development:

divorce rates increase in a linear fashion
drug crimes grow exponentially
green house emissions increase after 0.5 HDI
homicides grow practically in a linear fashion
increases in life expectancy diminish after 0.4 HDI
municipal waste increases in a strong way
prisoners per population increase after 25000 $ PPP income
rape increases strongly after 20000 $ PPP income
road accidents increase dramatically after 22000 $ PPP income
suicide (male and female) increase in a linear fashion

These are the tramps of capitalist post-industrial civilization as such. Peripheries and semi-peripheries in addition are threatened by unequal exchange and unequal specialization in the international division of labor. In some stagnant societies, strong wage labor organizations could - temporarily - prevent real earnings from falling, but these victories are short-lived and often at the price of long-run stagnation and inflation. Graph 0.8 now shows the influences of socio-economic variables on development in the 1980s and the 1990s: global capitalism increases the internal contradictions in the world system, and indeed, there is a process of transnational integration and national disintegration:

Graph 0.8: the determinants of development in 123 countries of the world system with comparable data, 1980s and 1990s

a)   the influences of MNC Penetration (UNCTAD measure) on development

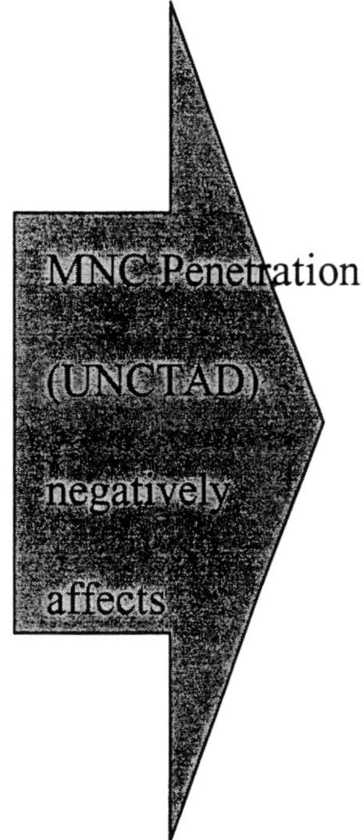

* adjustment
* growth
   dyn life expectancy
* reduction greenhouse em.
* political rights
* civil rights
* human development (HDI-Index)
* gender development
* gender empowerment
* life expectancy
* reduction maternal mortality
* present-day forest coverage
* avoidance of rapid deforestation
* human capital formation (mean years of schooling)
* full employment (labor force participation rate)
* avoidance of poverty (CPM-measure)
* avoidance of inequality (share of top 20%)

Legend: see Table 4.1, Chapter 4. The graph symbolizes the empirical results of Table 4.1 (significant predictors in multiple regressions), keeping initial development levels (and sometimes also: agricultural area) constant.

Only MNC penetration influence on life expectancy increases over time is not significant at the 5% level; but long-established nationhood, another dependency indicator (Amin, 1997), takes over the effect of MNC penetration, which is still significantly and negatively affecting life expectancy increases, even in this equation. In addition, militarization is another very significant predictor

b) other negative influences

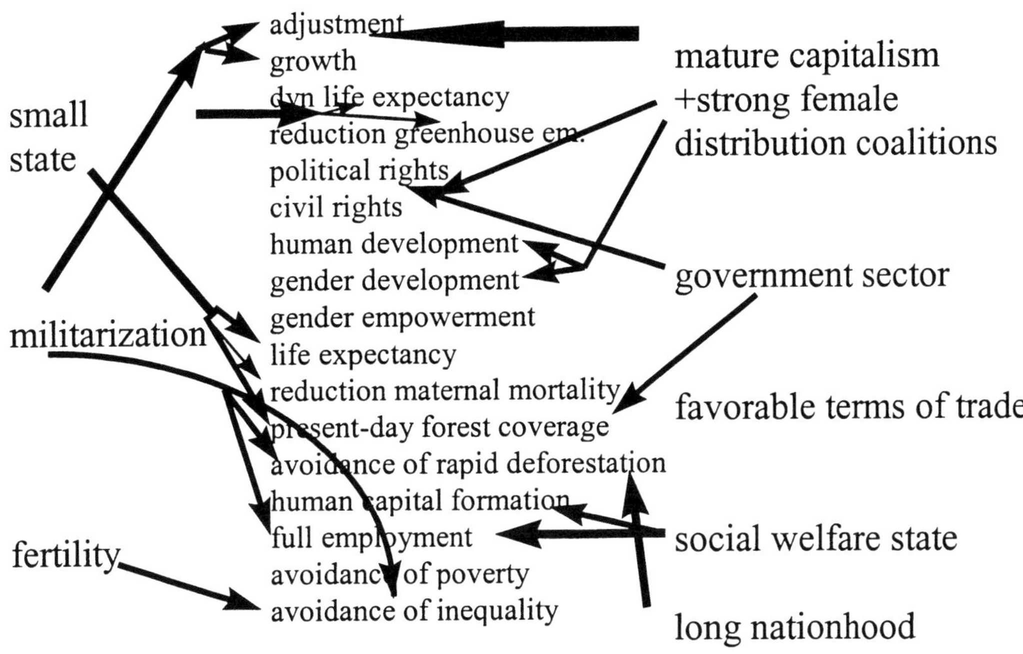

c) positive influences

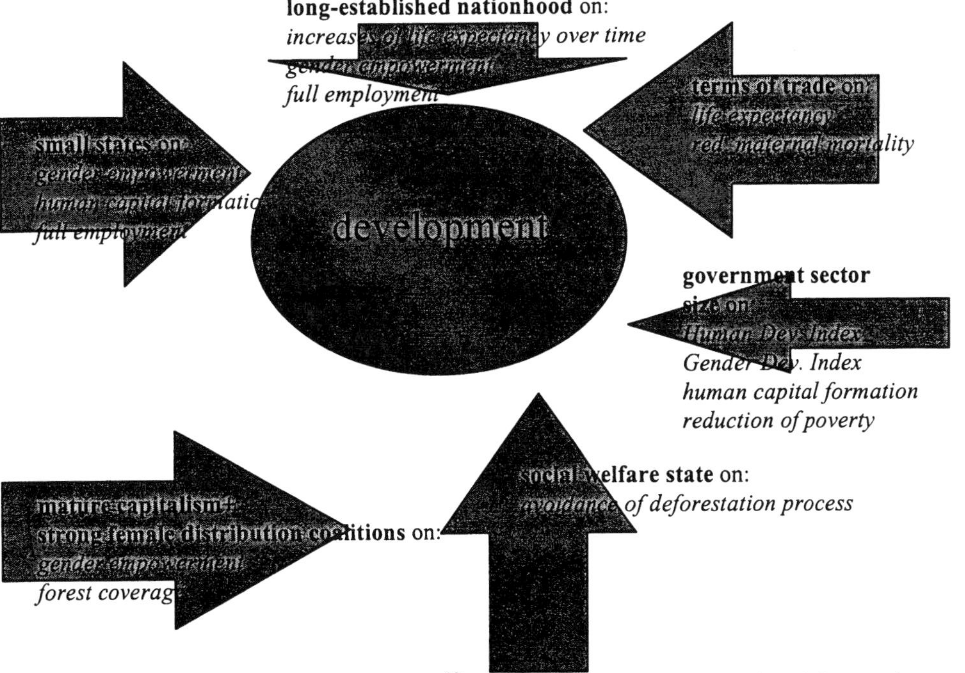

Legend: the determination coefficients ($R^{\wedge 2}$) of the main empirical results of this study are the following:

human capital formation	88
gender development	87,1
human development	87
gender empowerment	82,2
life expectancy	77,4
dyn life expectancy over time	75,7
maternal mortality rates	72,3
CPM-poverty measure	65,1
civil rights violations	60,1
political rights violations	56,8
employment (LFPR)	55,1
economic growth	44,2
greenhouse gas emissions	42,4
adjustment (see Chapter 3)	37,8
annual deforestation rate	34,5
forest coverage	30,3
share of top 20% in total incomes	25,2

These contradictory tendencies are to blame for what we fear will be the long-run and slow erosion of the international order, that is characterized by the cycles, so aptly described by Joshua Goldstein, already more than 10 years ago (Goldstein, 1988; see also: Chapter 3). The partial re-peripherization of the 'North' and 'far South' is accompanied by partial increases in human rights violations and more exclusive patterns of government in these former zones of prosperity in the world system. The 'Southernization' of the 'North' in the economic sphere is partially accompanied by 'southernization' in the political sphere. Suffice to say here, that in Europe we experienced the largest civil rights violations since the Second World War, and that unemployment in Germany reached Weimar proportions (10.9%; IFRI, 1998).

Map 0.3: human rights violations in the world system

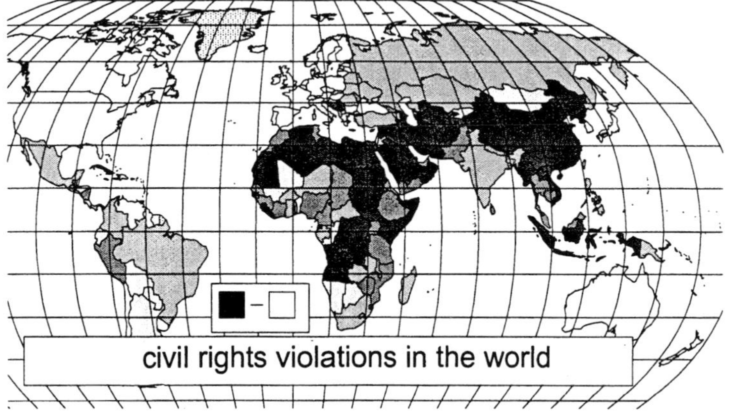

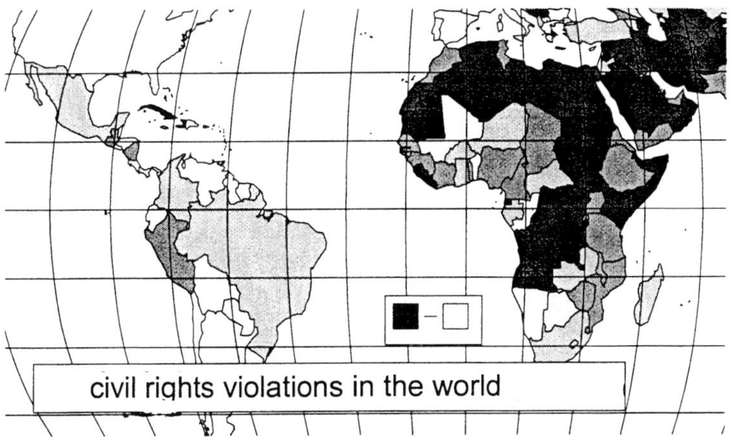

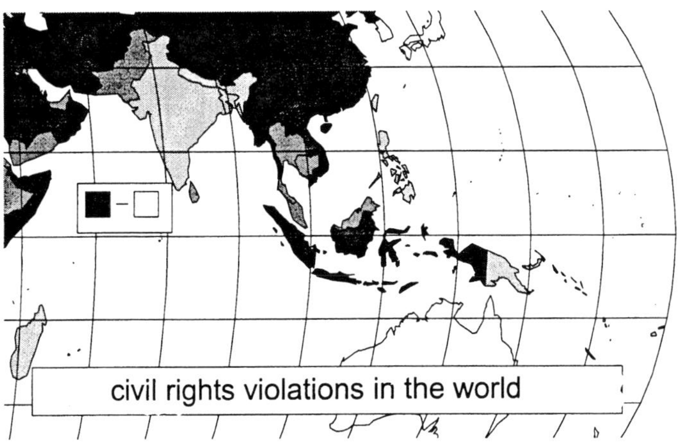

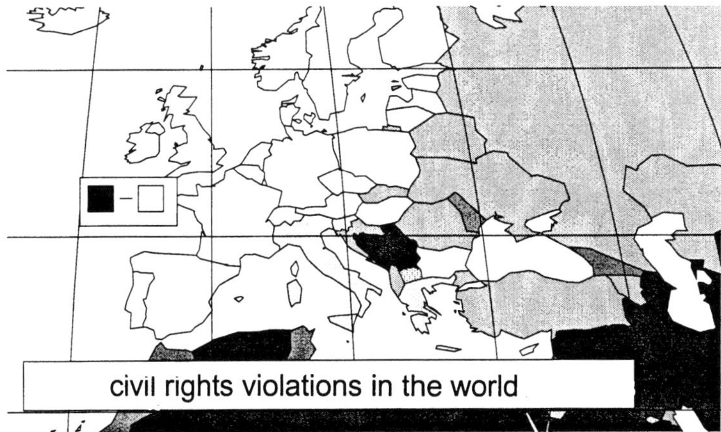

Legend: our own compilations from Freedom House Sources/Stiftung Entwicklung und Frieden, 1996, and EXCEL 7.0 map system. The darker, the more severe human/civil rights violations are at the same time, the narco-economy establishes itself as the most dynamic core of world capitalism; in effect threatening the very existence of 'civil society'.

Map 0.4: international narcotics control priority areas

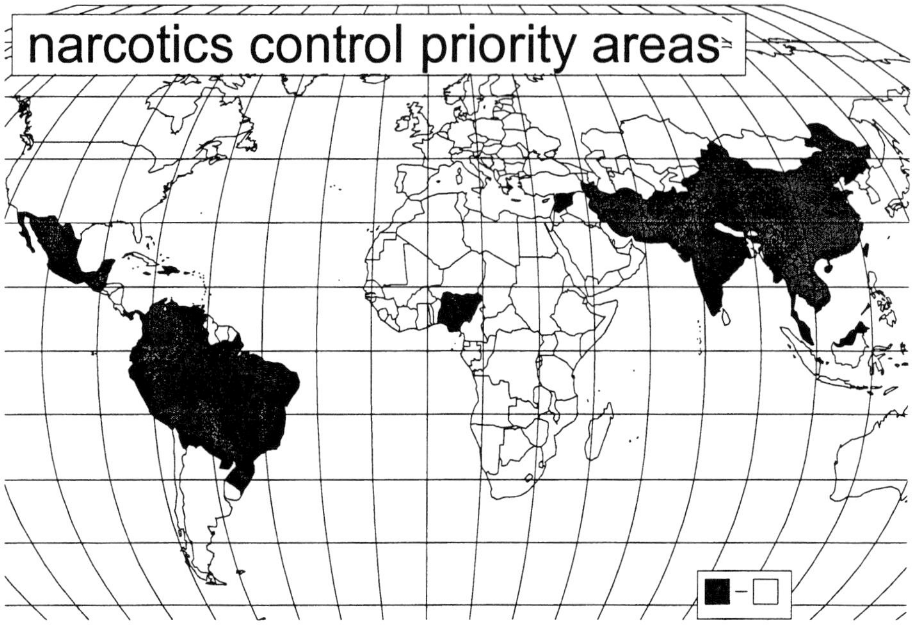

Source: EXCEL 7.0 map on the basis of US Department of State (1996), *'International Narcotics Control Strategy Report'*, March. The dark regions in our Map are the US Dep of State Drug Control priority areas.

Europe thus faces three very important decisions about the future: east-ward expansion of the European Union, European monetary union, and the structural internal reform of the Union. Faced with these decisions, an intellectual battle rages across the continent between euro-skeptics and integrationists, between federalists and nationalists, between centralists and regionalists. World systems research and development research provides radical, fascinating and novel answers to these old controversies. What is the evidence of cross-national quantitative research?

Political disintegration could go hand in hand with economic disintegration. The realities of semi-periphery and periphery capitalism are, that dependency and market imperfections interact. Thus many of the past controversies between dependency theory and neoclassical economics are simply futile and rather a question of language and not of substance. Take again the example of Central and Eastern Europe. Official current accounts show that the region lost over half a decade more than $bn 100 *(Warsaw Voice,* April 20, 1997: 12; see also, Table 0.1 above). The East European new democracies are on their way towards 'Latinamericanization' - viz. towards rising debts and negative current account balances. Call it *tequila* effect, *caipirinha* effect or what you like - the negative current account balances are there again with a vengeance. Amin (1997) has maintained, that this will be the most likely outcome of the world economy for the region of East-Central Europe for the next decades. The Maastricht fundamentalism of the up-to-now ruling constellations in Western Europe will make matters worse, while post-communist liberal 'neo-corporatism' - like in Poland after 1993 - at least avoided some of the harshest contradictions of neo-monetarism (like in Poland before 1993) or neo-Stalinism (like in Belarus) alike. Chase-Dunn and Hall, 1995, are correct in pointing out the long-term detrimental effects of cultural patterns of dependency in determining a far larger portion of 'internal' developments than is suggested by most measures of 'direct' dependency. In Poland - as a careful reading of the international press will suggest us -, car imports amounted to $4 billion, a fact, that is traditionally hidden in most aggregate statistics published on that country. The trade balance deficit increased from $6.2 billion in 1995 to $14.2 billion in December 1999:

Trade balance ($bn)	Latest	As of	Year ago
Bulgaria	-1.1	11-99	-0.3
Croatia	-3.5	12-99	-3.8
Czech Republic	-0.2	2-00	-0.1
Estonia	-0.2*	2-00	-0.1
Hungary	-0.2	1-00	-0.2
Latvia	-0.1	1-00	-0.1
Lithuania	-0.1	1-00	-0.1
Poland	-14.2	12-99	-13.7
Romania	-1.9	1999	-3.5
Russia	4.0	1-00	1.7
Slovakia	-0.1	1-00	-0.1
Slovenia	-1.4	12-99	-1.1

*Preliminary **end of previous year

Source: Business Central Europe, http://www.bcemag.com/

An entire army of experts assures us that there is no need for concern yet. Amin (1997) correctly pointed out that international development bureaucracies seem to be inclined towards optimistic assessments, when already debt-driven development patterns set in. But the Polish foreign trade deficit for agriculture and food alone came to $1.2 billion, in many ways reflecting the advancement of the *car + meat* culture so popularized in western TV serials. At the same time, a large portion of the population (> ¼) still works in agriculture, and public transport is marginalized by state intervention into the economy. Another structural feature is the difficulty of the Polish economy to sustain a high level of exports. The prevalence of raw materials and partially processed goods in exports contributes to a worsening of the terms of trades. Copper, coal and coke all were cheap - and are being exported to the world market, while Polish state funds are used to maintain that structure - to the detriment of the relative availability of funds for human capital formation, science, health, environmental protection, public transport and technological development, made in Poland. Powerful 'internal' workers coalitions coexist and even connive with the state class management to maintain the extractive sector. The inflow of cheap and - in the case of the EU - highly subventioned - goods from the outside has given unexpected competition to Polish firms, which are driven out from the market. Domestic demand grows much more rapidly than domestic production; indeed, the **growth** rate of production has dropped from +12.1% to +8.5%. The import absorption of foreign capital, as *Warsaw Voice* has shown, is also considerable: foreign capital in Poland was responsible for 42.4% of Polish imports, and 70 percent of the negative trade balance (the TNCs in Poland contributed to only 32.4% of exports). The negative trade and current account balance - also a result of the not sufficiently far enough trade liberalization policy of the European Union increased over the years, with the exception of Russia:

Current-account balance ($bn)•	Latest	As of	Year ago
Bulgaria	-0.5	10-99	-0.3
Croatia	-0.6	9-99	-0.9
Czech Republic	-0.2	9-99	-0.5
Estonia	0.0	9-99	-0.1
Hungary	-2.1	1999	-2.3
Latvia	-0.1	9-99	-0.1
Lithuania	-0.8	1999	1.3
Poland	-11.7	1999	6.9
Romania	-0.9	11-99	-2.3
Russia	14.6	9-99	-4.4
Slovakia	-0.8	9-99	-1.5
Slovenia	-0.5	11-99	0.0

Source: our own compilations from http://www.bcemag.com

An insufficient part of the economy - and of course here we disagree with conventional world system theories - is under the discipline of a real market, which is, by the very inflexibility that such a structure creates, a powerful motive to maintain a relatively high exchange rate of the Zloty, favoring easy and cheap imports, thus continuing the downward long-term circle of dependency. But, one might argue, this is the class-relation set-up of semi-peripheral capitalism. In such a synthesis of neoclassical and dependency perspectives of development constraints in a country like Poland, internal inequalities - in Poland mainly regional and sector inequalities - will not be missing. Income distribution data on a global level show (see above and appendix), that large areas of the world are dominated by medium to high inequality, and that inequality decreased in some countries, but increased in others - especially in the former socialist countries after the transformation, in Sub-Saharan Africa, and in industrialized nations themselves. Our estimates about world-wide internal income inequalities are:

Table 0.2 income inequality in the world system (top 20%)

Country code	share of income/consumption richest 20% to poorest 20%
Slovakia	*2,600*
Belarus	2,900
Austria	**3,200**
Japan	3,400
Czech Republic	*3,500*
Sweden	3,600
Belgium	3,600
Finland	3,600
Denmark	3,600
Norway	3,700
Luxemburg	3,900
Egypt	4,000
Rwanda	4,000
Italy	4,200
Slovenia	*4,200*
Romania	*4,200*

Lao People's Dem. Rep.	4,200
Pakistan	4,300
Bulgaria	*4,400*
Hungary	*4,500*
Germany	4,700
Ukraine	4,800
Bangladesh	4,900
Ghana	5,000
Canada	5,200
Korea, Rep. of	5,200
Lithuania	*5,200*
Poland	*5,300*
Latvia	*5,300*
Burundi	5,300
Spain	5,400
Greece	5,400
Sri Lanka	5,400
Netherlands	5,500
Uzbekistan	5,500
France	5,600
Viet Nam	5,600
Indonesia	5,600
Mongolia	5,600
India	5,700
Switzerland	5,800
Jordan	5,800
Portugal	5,900
Nepal	5,900
Moldova, Rep. of	6,000
Algeria	6,100
Israel	6,200
Jamaica	6,200
Côte d'Ivoire	6,200
Ireland	6,400
United Kingdom	6,500
Estonia	*6,700*
Tanzania, U. Rep. of	6,700
Ethiopia	6,700
Cambodia	6,900
Australia	7,000
Morocco	7,000
Uganda	7,000
Mozambique	7,200
Guyana	7,400
Mauritania	7,400
Guinea	7,400
Kyrgyzstan	7,500

Senegal	7,500
Thailand	7,600
Yemen	7,600
Turkmenistan	7,800
Tunisia	7,800
China	7,900
Turkey	8,200
Trinidad and Tobago	8,300
Bolivia	8,600
United States	8,900
Uruguay	8,900
Ecuador	9,200
Saint Lucia	9,300
Philippines	9,700
Kenya	10,000
Burkina Faso	10,000
Madagascar	10,200
Peru	11,600
Malaysia	12,000
Gambia	12,000
Russian Federation	12,200
Mali	12,200
Dominican Republic	12,500
Papua New Guinea	12,600
Nigeria	12,700
Costa Rica	13,000
Zambia	13,000
Nicaragua	13,100
Venezuela	14,400
Panama	14,700
Zimbabwe	15,600
Mexico	16,200
El Salvador	16,600
Honduras	17,100
New Zealand	17,400
Chile	17,400
Colombia	20,300
Niger	20,500
Lesotho	21,500
South Africa	22,300
Swaziland	23,900
Brazil	25,500
Paraguay	27,100
Guinea-Bissau	28,000
Guatemala	30,000
Central African Republic	32,500
Sierra Leone	57,600

Sources: see above and Appendix.

What is the evidence of our cross-national quantitative research?

- The process of globalization did not level-off the differences in wealth and well-being between the different regions of the world, especially between Europe and the Mediterranean southern periphery of Europe. Far from granting a real free trade regime, Europe has petrified existing patterns of the division of labor between the centers and the peripheries. Poverty, unemployment, homelessness and other negative social phenomena become more and more relevant, not just for periphery and semi-periphery countries, but for the former centers in Europe themselves. We are evidencing a peripherization of the European landmass, while the countries of the Western Pacific and the Eastern Indian Ocean are the future centers of world capitalist development.

- Europe is characterized by the very mix of conditions, which, on a world-wide scale, block against rapid economic growth. Too little national savings, privileged home-markets for idle and saturated European transnational corporations and the European continental powerful banks, migration instead of innovation, excessive government consumption, political distribution coalitions - also regarding gender conflict lines - which try to get via political means what they cannot achieve on the world markets anymore, the continued practicing of traditional patterns of national defense, based on conscription, are precisely the mix that explains 44.2% of stagnation from 1980 world-wide, without resorting to capital investments and other intra-economic explanations of growth. The 134 nation study on growth in world society, mentioned above, again underlines these points. What would be the answer against this process what in the Dutch language has been so aptly termed *Verluderung?* A slim, socially just state, which enhances savings, deters distribution coalitions, subjects the European transnationals to the discipline of the market, instead of pouring down the sink billions of ECU's in terms of subvention money, ending up more often than not in the pockets of the shadow economists of our times, would be among the pre-requisites of a real reform of the European Union structures and an adequate answer to the question about the place of Europe in the world. 14 of the most important 19 development dimensions in the world system are being negatively determined nowadays by MNC penetration. The capitalist world economy is in addition characterized by strong 18-22 year cycles (Kuznets cycles) and 40-60 year longer waves (Kondratieff waves), which again are shown to be relevant on the basis of new calculations, based on Joshua Goldstein's previous research. As the visual inspection of the scatterplots would suggest, the 18th Century and the early 19th Century would tend towards Kuznets cycles, while from the 19th Century onwards, the Kondratieff fluctuations are more pronounced. But the more detailed statistical analysis of available data shows that Kuznets cycles and Kondratieff cycles interact in the world economy to this day. Cycles and their logic, and not so much grand designs of conference diplomacy, will determine the future place of Europe in the world economy. Precisely, because the Union is presently a protective club shielding away market influences from European transnationals, banks, and distribution coalitionists, Europe's upswing is belated, and the Maastricht-induced stagflation threatening to coincide with the next major Juglar cycle trough, to be expected in 2004 or 2005 at the latest, will make our stagnation even worse. Political stability, under such circumstances, in the Mediterranean and in other countries becomes a question mark.

- Subventions, mass migration and distribution coalitions mean structural conservation and environmental decay at the same time. Since environmental strain cycles coincide with world economic swings, it is to be expected that any real future European recovery will increase the environmental problems on the European continent, still increased by the transport-intensity of

EU-development patterns, connected with the subvention system. **Physical mobility** of labor is the key de-facto concept of the past policies of the Commission in Brussels, while **information mobility** is being hindered by local and national telephone monopolies, and the absence of privatization in transport, especially roads.

- The eastward expansion of the Union - especially the second wave - will have to face up to the dilemmas of modernization in the environment of past rapid urbanization (what world system scholars have termed the urban bias in world development), little efficient state-directed mass communication and belated demographic transitions in much of the Balkans and the former Soviet Union, if not the former Warsaw Pact in general. Modernization and structural adjustment in the post-1989 set-up is bound to fail in the East if it is not accompanied by a massive real inflow of foreign resources. The semi-democratization in much of the region, that set in after 1989, is much more dangerous than the full rule of dictatorship or full democracy. Money laundering and fluctuations in the terms of trade are additional important determinants of the growth prospects of the reform countries.

- Modernization, globalization, and East-ward expansion of the Union might increase existing cleavages in the countries of the East, if they are not accompanied by a deep structural change in favor of the up to now underprivileged sectors and strata. Many of the lessons of neo-classical economists about Southeast-Asia from 1945 to around 1995 can be repeated here in an East European context. The discrimination against exports by import substitution strategies, effective currency overvaluations, privileges and wage inflexibility in the monopolistic sectors, and finally and overarching all these phenomena, a conspicuous contempt of urban elites against the countryside and a deep urban bias of development have created a structure, where the political and social divisions between the different parts of countries have increased. It is shown in this study with regional multivariate analyses from Polish election data 1993 to 1997, that electoral results are heavily determined by these regional and world economic aspects, while other theories fail to capture the dynamics of socio-political cleavages in the new democracies of the East.

- Euro-sclerosis at the heart of the Union of presently 15 nations is a reality. Take any indicator of economic illness in the relatively stable Western democracies today - unemployment, lack of economic growth, insufficient human development: it will be neatly determined by just three variables:

1. - age of democracy within world politically guaranteed boundaries
2. - size of the state sector, like central government expenditures per GDP
3. - years of membership in the European Union

- Instead of causing stable long-term economic growth, the Union rather causes what might be termed *'the Belgium syndrome'*. Relatively young democracies, like Poland or the Czech Republic, Hungary or Slovenia, will still benefit for a few years from the positive effects of early membership; but the positive initial effects will disappear with the workings of the *really existing Union* in the long run.

So, what then is the prescription? For Arrighi (1995), there seems to emerge the imperative of organizing the international community anew around the axis of the East Asian/North American archipelago, gravely shattered by *le crash* of fall 1997, implicitly hoping for democratization spin-offs along this axis. Arrighi seems to advance the viewpoint that such a *'world community'* controlled capitalism would still be better than the rule of chaos and war. This analysis will be of course sharply contended by those who think that Asia's days have gone. But people as far apart as Andre Gunder Frank and Jeffrey Sachs agree on the hypothesis, that Asia's troubles must be seen in the context of its long-term upsurge. It still might be, that the race towards the EURO rocked the boat in favor of Europe and in disfavor of Asia for a short while; but wait and see: the true high seas for the European common currency boat will be coming only by around 2002 or 2003, when the effects of the common currency under neo-monetarist conditions will become fully visible.

For us, Europeans, the lectures of the empirical study of contemporary changes in world capitalism are twofold: one is more medium-term, the other long-term: the real empowerment of the European Parliament *('no taxation without representation')*, a full-fledged European Constitution, a European Government, a European more slender and socially just state, European federalism in the member countries, free periphery access to the markets of goods of the center, and also more decisive efforts in human capital formation (in the framework of privatization of Universities and other institutions of higher learning). Thus, only a kind of socio-liberal United States of Europe would be able to overcome the present impasse of the Union. The European Parliament, preferably as a two-chamber system, should have one chamber representing the electorate according to population weight, the other chamber representing the then former member nations of the Union (say, 5 deputies for each member nation). There must be also a European Judiciary, a clear federal structure, a strong subsidiarity down to the smaller entities and regions, and finally, an economic policy, based on a basic social minimum income, a negative income tax, a radical downsizing of all the other state sector influence, and a certain *Canadization* of migration policy (orderly and limited legal chances of immigration) *et cetera.*

To learn form the historic *East Asian Space-of Flows* (Arrighi, 1995) above all suggests that heeding the advice of contemporary economics, learning its lessons from East Asia from 1945 to around 1995 in such areas as corporate strategy, labor market organization, international trade and migration, would be more advantageous than to be trapped again by the fatal conceit of a thinking along the lines of the territorial control, alas by democratic methods this time, a democratic economic space, *Lebensraum.* And Germany, in particular, at the decisive time, seems to forget that the main imperatives of world system ascent are economic and not territorial - now in the wider, European Union sense. Such advice unheeded, eastward European Union expansion could dismally fail, made all the worse by the negative effects of ongoing Maastricht austerity. Thus the time is ripe for a socio-liberal alternative to orthodox etatism and neo-conservatism alike.

On a long-term basis, though, only a socio-liberal world state will be able to overcome the intrinsic instabilities of the capitalist nation system, that has (un)governed the world since 1450. Today's problems are too global to be left to a (supra)national state. And at any rate, transnational capitalism rings the bell to all attempts at national regulation for the next 50 or 100 years, and its earth and labor consuming civilization will be doomed as all the other civilizations before it in the rhythm of 250 to 300 years of ascent and decline, from the days of Egypt and Mesopotamia onwards (Chase-Dunn and Hall, 1997).

From whichever angle we approach those facts as we presented them above, we will not arrive at a contemplative picture. This is the case seen from both the countries which are – without having been systematically prepared and without having had the opportunity to do it on their own – teared into the process of globalization and for those countries that are basically the moving forces. Starting from here, we cannot even attempt to draw a picture for a better world. Nevertheless – and without approaching the matter by putting the gloss over –, there is a glimmer of hope at the end of the tunnel. This is based on two momentums.

* The one is the predicament, which arises for the so-called developed countries and especially for the member countries of the European Union. Up to a certain point it had been possible to build national success stories – under headings as economic growth, wealth, social market economy, social justice but as well cultural diversity, tolerance, advanced education and training and others – on the foundation of the exploitation of the countries of the so-called third world. It had been very simple "exchange" – success here paid by systematically withholding opportunities of development for the other countries. However, it is getting increasingly obvious that this strategy reached the limits. Externalization of costs, striving for economic success on the back of others is not getting morally reprehensible. Moreover, the western world

is now challenged by consequences of the own – intended and unintended – action. This advantage of "unrecognized export of social issues" tips now over into the requirement to repay for the shortcoming and carelessness of the past.

This is most visible in regard of migration. The patterns of migration reflect very much the past strategies – to some extent just turning previous trends back; to some extent continuing these trends in a different setting. Portugal is an example for both these trends – turning back and continuation. A recent article, which looks at Portugal's shift from being a country of emigration to becoming a country of immigration, mentions four momentums that characterize the pattern of immigration.

- The lack of highly qualified migrants coming into the country – surely not least a reflection of the history and the politics to keep Portugal as one of the rural backyards of Europe.
- A high share of migrants is coming from previous Portuguese colonies.
- The ongoing absence of migrants coming from the near regions of North Africa – Muslims stay away and continue in a specific way their resistance against the early Portuguese conquest.
- The settlement of the migrants in only a few large urban areas – a reflection of the general urban pattern of capitalist development *(see for qualitative data on the migration flows in Portugal Schmidt-Fink, 2000: 17 f.).*
- Second, we are working in an extremely contradictious field – and here we are concerned with fundamental antagonisms of the process of modernization rather than with "single issue" contradictions. Speaking of fundamental contradictions is on the one hand concerned with those inherent in capitalist development, but moreover it is at the very same time employing the contradiction of modernization and modernity. To mention the most important of these contradictions we want briefly point at the following.
- Even if class relationships never had been as easy as they had sometimes been interpreted, this is today even more the case. Social class interests are still the basis for the structuration of current societies. However, in the context here we are concerned with the national classes, the same classes in different countries and the different classes in different countries. This complex multi-layered pattern – which is permanently present, even if at times dormant – makes it easily possible to play interests around nationality off against class interests.
- Another contradiction – to some extent just an expression of the one mentioned before – is the one between actions against different horizons in regard of time – medium and long term interests are more and more taken consciously into consideration as part of developing economic and political strategies.
- A crucial challenge exists in balancing the contradictious field of regional, namely EUropean interests versus the monopolistic, worldwide oriented interests of the capitalist block, as it is represented by the TNCs. Even in political terms the later take always part in the negotiations. However, this is both the contradiction between regional and truly international interests and between economic and political interests. Interestingly, the representatives of the economic block are reaching further in regard of the political dimension – they are global players on the foundation of being "global thinkers". One could now formulate the other point of view from the parliamentary perspective – far reaching political approaches and limited economic power and as well limited global impetus are characterizing the politicians' views.
- Especially the current economic status is characterized by the contradicting interests of productive capital on the one hand side and capital in the sphere of circulation on the other side. The latter is divided in – on the one hand – the financial capital and – on the other side – the interest in services. The latter, again, is especially tricky and contradictious in itself insofar as explicitly not-for-profit aspects, common goods and the like are included. This causes special problems either for the service providers – if they agree upon the fact to produce market goods under non-market conditions – or it causes problems for the users of some services as far as they are forced to accept non-market services as market-commodities.

◆ Another important aspect is concerned with the ever increasing integration of the structures of acquiring the existing knowledge; on the other hand the capabilities of action are getting increasingly negatively effected by processes of differentiation, which undermine the development of complex and strategically elaborated action.

History never repeats itself. However, what happens is a kind of reinforcing reintegration which makes place for at least part of the previously – and still suppressed, excluded and disadvantaged parts of the world. This is concerned with the spatial regional, namely the integration of the interest of countries of the so-called Third World. Furthermore, it is concerned with the inclusion of social groups and interests in political action. We are concerned with a process of regaining capability of action. Of course, this is a very painful process because some groups will loose power or will have less power than they currently have. Thus, it is a contradictious process. – As *Frederick Engels* highlighted 'We make our history ourselves, but, in the first place, under very definite assumptions and conditions. Among these the economic ones are ultimately decisive. But the political ones, etc., and indeed even the traditions which haunt human minds also play a part, although not the decisive one.' *(Engels, 1890)*

Necessarily we have to come back now on the previous remarks on NGOs – the last resort of action. Since and insofar the prevailing economic and political systems are not in the position to resolve the conflicts – simply because they lost ground and are fetters for further action – they have to give power away. This is what we mentioned as process of bringing society back to the fore. Citizenship, civil action are gaining a pronounced meaning – as we said above *decision making is getting more and more concerned with trying to control unintended consequences of previous action; freedom of action and opportunities for action are abolished and localized or regionalized – a question of space, but as well one of time and "sociality"*.

Especially we highlight what we call the last resort and go a little bit beyond the issue of NGOs to ask *if we are on the way to any kind of a globalizes citizenship or a responsible and sustainable European citizenship?* – Asking these questions – and attempting to give answers – implies already some optimism. We are strongly suggesting that such optimism is not based on a voluntaristic worldview. Rather this is an optional worldview, taking into account the fact that is behind the *Marxian* quote given above; i.e. it is the people who make their history; but we have to be well aware of the limits of power

We find empirical evidence for an increasing importance of globality not just in regard of markets but as well in regard of citizenship or responsibility. Even if it is a contradictory process, we can see this development in connection with two issues. The one is – to some extent at least – a top-down process. The United Nations and the Council of Europe are a kind of classical examples in this regard – they have an extensive strategy of including non-governmental organizations in their policy development processes. Besides the usual openness for lobbying procedures we find a formally elaborated system of accreditations, negotiations and decision making structures. The institutions of the European Union, in particular the European Commission is as well concerned with enhancing and signaling openness for the interests of civil society organizations. Hearings, open fora, specialized "NGOs" (or supporting selected NGOs in an extensive way), established from above and act as mediators (as for example EAPN, the Platform of social NGOs and others) have to be mentioned here *(cf. Herrmann, 1998 a)*.

In both cases, this brings us to the issue of multidimensionality as it draws attention to the necessity of acting in various – connected – dimensions, namely

a) the inherent injustices of capitalism.
b) the price of the Western lifestyle, including not least
   ◆ the commodification as it is especially currently visible in the trend to a "service based society" respectively the dominance of service providing industries
   ◆ "depowerment" of people, actually an unintended effect, which counteracts modernization by its own means – we described it as breaking apart of capacities of appropriation (increasing knowledge etc.) and decreasing opportunities to utilize it.
c) the social and cultural resources of the so-called Third World.

Anyway, we should not overlook the dangers. Surely, civil society is part of the solution; but we should not forget that they are part of the problem as well: they are in many cases based on social inequality (acting with the aim to reproduce it) and in many cases they succeed in doing so – in fighting in an elitist way for particularistic interests. Furthermore, they are part of the problem as they enforce and enhance processes of differentiation in the bad sense of disguising class conflicts, increasing soci(et)al complexity, making sustainable action nearly impossible.

Following this approach consequently further we come to the conclusion that speaking of empowerment of NGOs and enhancing politics by "civilizing the policy process" on the one hand and – on the other side – empowering the so called Third-World-countries has to go hand in hand. In fact, we are employed by two sides of a single coin. Conversely, this has drastic consequences for the two dimensions already mentioned. On the one hand the idea of civil-society-organizations has to be developed as understanding them as entities with a specific focus, nevertheless permanently in a conscious, intended communication, mediation and tuning with their immediate social setting as well as with society in general. On the other hand – with view on the developing world – they have to be included as "countries" rather than as "states". In other words, it has to be guaranteed that participation and empowerment is not reduced on the elite of these countries and thus refurbishes national – economic, social and political – inequalities and extends unproductive tensions.

This is the main consequence for the European Pathway as we propose it here – linking the regional EU and the global development together. If this shall be successful, the condition is, however, to base this strategy on an enlightenment-based understanding of modernization. Thus, a European pathway combines developing own, "internal" strength with an approach of integration not as absorption and not at all as subordination. Instead, integration of others is nothing less than an expression and enhancement of own openness.

So, our predictions for Europe are mixed: Sunkel's scenario, at least in part, offers a key to our future. Capitalist globalization can only be answered by global democratization strategy. Whether or not this will be already too late in terms of the environmental destruction, that makes our planet's future more and more dangerously similar to that of planet Mars' history, or not, only history can tell.

Chapter 1

GLOBALIZATION, ENVIRONMENTAL DECAY AND SEXISM IN THE CAPITALIST WORLD SYSTEM

Arno Tausch

Associate Visiting Professor, Department of Political Science,
Innsbruck University, Austria

1) INTRODUCTION

The conservative-liberal paradigm, that shaped politics and economics after the fall of Communism in Europe, seems to have reached its limits, while the predictions of world society paradigms - starting with Karl Polanyi - gain in relevance. Is capitalism, at the very moment, when it seemed to triumph over the communist rival, unable to integrate the new territories of the East (Chase-Dunn and Hall, 1997), thus producing anew the tensions between the centers and the semi-peripheries that, in the end, historically were so instrumental in the rise of historical communism? Or is the *'real existing capitalist order'*, by the very socio-political set-ups and alliances it produces, at least not able to overcome phenomena of monopoly, distribution coalitions, and institutional age, that lead to impoverishment and dependence in wide parts of our globe? And is capitalism, although in theory open to reform, de-facto unable to do so at the expense of its own long-term survival capability?

Sunkel first proposed in his *'Transnational capitalism and national disintegration (in Latin America)'* the still provocative thought that transnational investment and integration might go hand in hand, under certain conditions, with an increasing relative social polarization between rich and poor in the host countries of the evolving transnational system and on the international level. At that time, Sunkel said:

'The interpretation so far advanced suggests that the international capitalist system contains an internationalized nucleus of activities, regions and social groups of varying degrees of importance in each country. These sectors share a common culture and 'way of life', which expresses itself through the same books, texts, films, television programs, similar fashions, similar groups of organization of family and social life, similar style of decoration of homes, similar orientations to housing, building, furniture and urban design. Despite linguistic barriers, these sectors have a far greater capacity for communication among themselves than is possible between integrated and marginal persons of the same country who speak the same language (...) Modernization implies the gradual replacement of the traditional productive structure by another of much higher capital intensiveness (...) On the one hand, the process of modernization incorporates into the new structures the individuals and groups that are apt to fit into the kind of rationality that prevails there; on the other hand, it expels the individuals and groups that have no place in the new productive structure or who lack the capacity to become adapted to it. It is important to emphasize that this process does not only prevent or limit the formation of a national entrepreneurial class, as indicated by Furtado, but also of a national middle class (...) and even a national working class. The advancement of modernization introduces, so to speak, a wedge along the area dividing the integrated from the segregated segments (...) In this process, some national entrepreneurs are incorporated as executives into the new enterprises or those absorbed by the TRANCO (i.e. transnational corporations), and others are marginalized; some professionals, forming part of the technical staff and the segment of employees are incorporated, and the rest are marginalized; part of the qualified labor supply and those that are considered fit to be upgraded are incorporated, while the remainder are marginalized.

The effects of the disintegration of each social class has important consequences for social mobility. The marginalized entrepreneur will probably add to the ranks of small or artesanal manufacture, or will abandon independent activity and become a middle class employee. The marginalized sectors of the middle class will probably form a group of frustrated lower middle class people trying to maintain middle class appearance without much possibility of upward mobility and terrorized by the danger of proletarization. The marginalized workers will surely add to the ranks of absolute marginality, where, as in the lower middle class, growing pools of resentment and frustration of considerable demographic dimension will accumulate (...) Finally, it is very probable that an international mobility will correspond to the internal mobility, particularly between the internationalized sectors (...) The process of social disintegration which has been outlined here probably also affects the social institutions which provide the bases of the different social groups and through which they express themselves. Similar tendencies to the ones described for the global society are, therefore, probably also to be found within the state, church, armed forces, political parties with a relatively wide popular base, the universities etc.' (Sunkel, 1972: 18-42).

Globalization since 1980 negatively affected the lives of around 1.5 thousand million people on earth, whose per-capita incomes were lower than in earlier decades. These 1.5 thousand million people live in around 100 countries; while 15 nations experienced rapid capitalist development over the last decade. Among the world's desperate nations, 43 countries had a per-capita income which was lower - in real terms - than that of the 1970s (UNDP, 1996, 1999)

More than ever before, economic growth tended to be concentrated in some regions of the world system, most notably East and Southeast Asia and the Pacific, while other regions tended to be excluded. Map 1.1 shows the tendencies of economic growth in the world system since 1980:

Map 1.1: economic growth in the world system since 1980

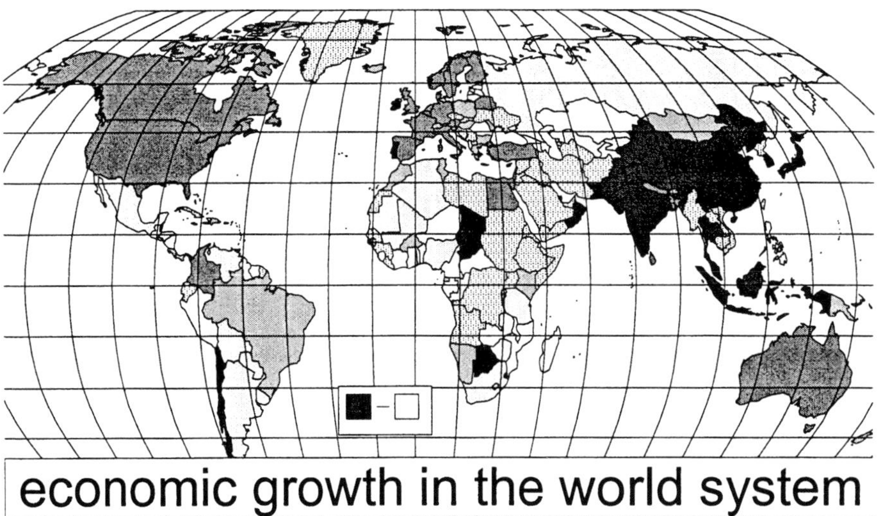

Source: EXCEL 7.0 graph from UNDP (1996) data

Not only the world's South, but also the extreme North seems to be put at increasing risks. And now, after the Asian crash, even those 15 'emerging markets' are put at risk, with only the USA remaining as the last 'capitalist miracle'. Among the nations, that reached their present-day real per capita income level already back in the 1980s, we find - perhaps to our surprise - the *northern democracies* Canada, Finland, and Iceland, among a total of 31 nations. In all, these three OECD democracies, 7 'other Asian' nations, 14 Arab countries, 20 Eastern European and CIS countries, 22 Latin American countries and 35 countries of Sub-Saharan Africa were, in per capita terms - richer in earlier decades. China, India, 20 OECD democracies, 2 Arab countries, 12 Latin American and Caribbean countries and 8 Sub-Saharan African nations, together with 21 'other Asian countries', increased their per-capita income over the last decades (UNDP, 1996-99). In the developing countries, despite the increases in life expectancy over 1960-93, the specter of poverty is still overwhelming. 1.3 billion people are to be classified as poor, 800 million people do not eat enough food, and 500 million are chronically malnourished. Each year, 20 million hectares of tropical forests are degraded or completely cleared; there are now 11 million refugees in the developing countries, and entire regions are affected by destabilization and war, most notably the lake region of East-Central-Africa, wide areas of Central Asia, and some countries of West Africa.

The relative polarization effects along the welfare borders of the world, which happen to be the outward borders of the economic integration zones, drawn up by the rich countries, are the first basic conflict that confronts the process of transnational integration, and especially European integration today. The second basic conflict is the tendency towards increasing social exclusion in the trasnationally integrated core areas and in the semi-peripheries and peripheries themselves. Suffice to look at contemporary Mexico after NAFTA to find preliminary evidence that speaks in favor of Sunkel and against the optimistic predictions of the integrationists. In the words of contemporary journalists:

Le Monde Diplomatique for April 97 reported the latest research into the incredible pace of the concentration of Capital. This is leading *to what Le Monde calls a "A Global Government of the Multinationals"*.

It reports that, Eastern Europe and the Former Soviet Union have been "colonised" in the name of "the glories of the free market" and that, inspite of 41 million unemployed in the advanced capitalist countries, "the manufacturing industries worldwide (excepting those of China) only operate at 70-75% of their capacity". "The top 200 companies are conglomerates whose planetary activity cover all sectors without distinction, the primary, secondary and tertiary, the grand agricultural exploiters, the manufacturers, financial services, commerce, etc. Geographically they are divided between ten countries: Japan (62), the United States (53), Germany (23), France (19), Britain (11), Switzerland (8), South Korea (6), Italy (5) and the Low Countries (1)." Their turnover at 7,850 trillion dollars was equal to 30% of world GNP in 1995. Le Monde Diplomatique explains that in reality the concentration is even greater than the figures indicate.
For example the world's number one company Mitsubishi owns five companies in the top 200. Their empire pays 37% of the funds of the Liberal Democratic Party of Japan thus completely corrupting the political system. In South Korea, 6 of whose companies leapt into the top 200 between 1985 and 1995, Daewoo the largest, now has a turnover of over $ 52 billion (US), ahead of Unilever and Nestle. The largest 30 company groups in South Korea have a turnover over 4/5ths of the country's GNP. These companies support the, "ruthlessly repression of the working class and the liquidation of the rights of the individual", says the report. Such dictatorial concepts pervade in the older centres of world capital as well. The Director General of Nestle, Helmut Maucher presides over the European Round Table of Industrialists, the elite club of 47 companies. "An implacable opponent of the European Social Chapter, he is an militant fighter for the flexibility of work, like all the members of this caste". Le Monde Diplomatique explains that the "Global Government of the Multinationals" is run by "Totalitarian Structures". This latest evidence of the increasing concentration of wealth and their dictatorial hold on political and economic life, comes after the shocking United Nations Human Development Report 1996. This revealed that, "the assets of the world's 358 billionaires exceed the combined annual incomes of countries with 45% of the world's people." (p2) The UN Report showed that the idea that, "the only way to finance growth

would be by channeling the initial benefits into the pockets of rich capitalists"...has ..." been disproved by recent evidence of a positive correlation between economic growth and income equality"...(p6) If there is not a radical shift towards egalitarianism and control of the major corporations in the interests of working people, then the predictions of the UN, of a "world gargantuan in its excesses and grotesque in its human and economic inequalities", will become a terrible reality. Trade Unionists and Socialists worldwide must make it their responsibility to combine together through computer networks which will link the unions in the largest 200 companies together. In this way we can act to defend the workers, protect the environment and the consumers. Unions monitoring the activities of these companies will be able to shatter their "Totalitarian Structures", establishing in their place direct democratic control over decision making processes through worldwide workers' councils.
(WNR Editorial 28-4-97) heiko@easynet.co.uk

Having lived and worked in Eastern Europe one cannot but remember the important lessons of dependency and world system research for an understanding of what surrounds us. Income poverty has spread to a third of the population of the region - 120 million people below the poverty line of \$4 a day (UNDP, 1997). As we shall analyze in more detail in Chapter 9, the pressure towards peripherization in Eastern Europe builds up, thus vindicating the more pessimistic prognosis voiced by Samir Amin (1997) about the 'Latin Americanization' of Eastern Europe:

Graph 1.1a: The Amin hypothesis about the Latin Americanization of Eastern Europe. Current account balances from 1992 onwards in the region

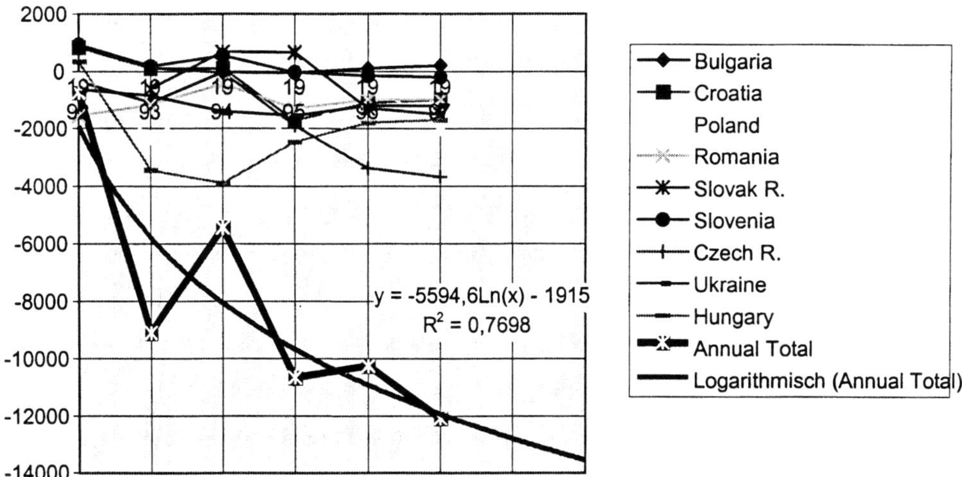

Development aid from the CEEC

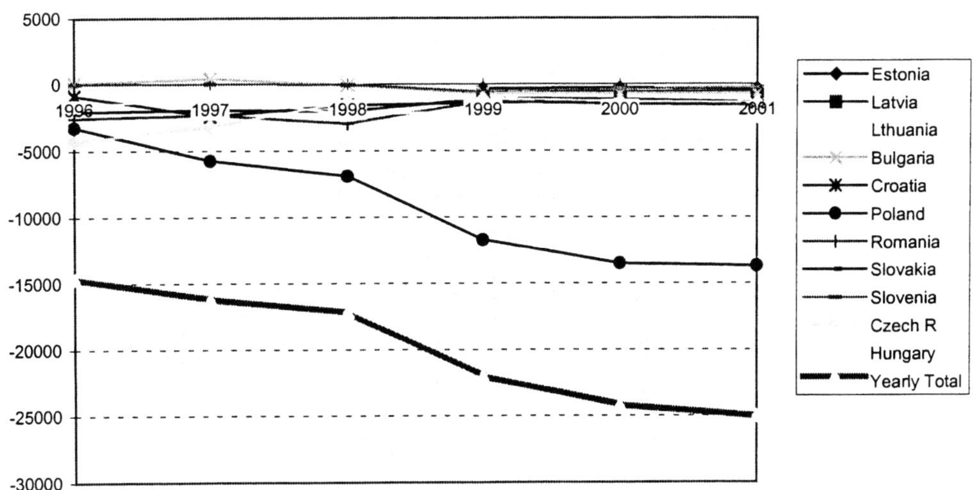

Legend: our own compilations from Bank Austria, Report, 1, 1997 and CEE Report, 1/2000.
Absolute values of the current account balances in East Central Europe until 2001. The lowest line
in the lower graph symbolizes the cumulated values for the entire region.

The successive crises - or let's term them abysses - that shattered entire continents since the
1980s, shifting the burden of misery from Latin America to Africa, Asia and Russia, brought
home to the world and to millions and millions of human beings, that their livelihoods are
determined by the ups and downs of the world market and the forces of the international economy.
Europe, that has launched a common, single currency, is characterized by a process of non-
convergence of wages and incomes, that finally could accelerate centrifugal political tendencies,
as long as the structures of unequal exchange are not overcome.

Unequal exchange is the most visible aspect of an international economy, that is based on
inequality and social polarization. It is understood to be a process, by which always more and
more labor in the periphery and semi-periphery has to be used to buy a constant or diminishing
amount of products of the centers. Workers in a poorer country in 2000 have to work a week to
buy, say, an imported medicine, next year it will be 2 weeks. Unequal exchange can be measured
by calculating the difference between the real, internal purchasing power of a country and the
'international' exchange rate of the currency, and weighting the exports of a given country by this
factor. In the late 1990s, the periphery lost more than 1000 million $ per year due to this process.
The importance of unequal exchange has risen dramatically over the years, and is increased by the
workings of the international financial system.

The relevance of this can be shown in the following tables for East Central Europe:

Average monthly wages ($)	Latest	As of	Year ago
Bulgaria	109.0	12-99	114.0
Croatia	656.0	11-99	689.0
Czech Republic	394.0	12-99	435.0
Estonia	**302.0**	**12-99**	**276.0**
Hungary	396.0	12-99	399.0
Latvia	243.0	12-99	na
Lithuania	280.6	12-99	287.9
Poland	**459.0**	**1-00**	**451.0**
Romania	92.0	1-00	138.0
Russia	**85.0**	**12-99**	**74.0**
Slovakia	297.0	12-99	332.0
Slovenia	1003.0	12-99	1073.0

*Preliminary **end of previous year

Only Estonia, Poland and Russia had rising real international wages, although economic growth was positive in Bulgaria, Estonia, Hungary, Poland, Slovakia and Slovenia. In other words: Bulgarian, Hungarian, Slovak and Slovene wages could have risen in the absence of unequal exchange. Only Latvia and Lithuania had a fairly constant international exchange rate, while the other countries' currencies drifted downwards:

GDP real growth (%)	Latest	As of	Year ago
Bulgaria	2.5	1999	3.5
Croatia	-2.0	1999	2.5
Czech Republic	-0.2	1999	-2.3
Estonia	1.9	12-99	-0.7
Hungary	4.4	1999	4.9
Latvia	-1.3	9-99	5.4
Lithuania	-4.8	6-99	5.1
Poland	4.1	1999	4.8
Romania	-3.2	1999	-5.4
Russia	1.7	1999	-4.6
Slovakia	1.9	1999	4.4
Slovenia	3.7	1999	3.9

*Preliminary **end of previous year

Exchange rate/$	Latest	As of	Year ago
Bulgaria	2.0	3-00	1.8
Croatia	8.0	3-00	7.0
Czech Republic	36.8	3-00	34.8
Estonia	16.1	3-00	14.3
Hungary	265.3	3-00	233.1
Latvia	**0.6**	**3-00**	**0.6**
Lithuania	**4.0**	**3-00**	**4.0**
Poland	4.0	3-00	3.9
Romania	20.000	3-00	14.054
Russia	28.4	3-00	23.5
Slovakia	42.9	3-00	40.7
Slovenia	208.8	3-00	174.5

*Preliminary **end of previous year

Certainly, the work of the Hungaro-Austrian Karl Polanyi provided already a clear vision of the problems facing the world economy and facing Europe at the beginning of the new millenium. Later world system theories, that picture the capitalist world economy as a single, conflict-producing mechanism that evolved in cycles of economics and war since around 1450, and that is characterized by a relative stability of a division of the world into centers, semi-peripheries and peripheries, necessarily started also from the assumption, that there is an unequal exchange between the centers, and the peripheries, that transfers in some fashion or another the surplus of the labor in the peripheries to the centers. Economists like the Argentinian Raul Prebisch foresaw its devastating force in international relations. Overnight, entire generations saw their incomes and savings halved or worse during the Asian and Russian financial crisis, and there is more to come of that in the world economy in the future.

'Emerging markets' under such circumstances become an almost Orwellian misnomer; instead, we should speak of *'submerging markets'*, allowing for the fact, that more than five hundred million people in such 'emerging markets' around the globe suffer from the severest recession since the Great Depression in the 1930s. The world since 1960 - hardly ever studied in the totality of it's growth process - resembles much a marathon race, where most of the participants stumble on their way or even race backward or wildly search for a direction which they lost underway. The old Greek mythology of the original tales telling the story of the race to Marathon come to one's mind, and certainly the (re)appearance of a God Pan - a human capital oriented development - would be a comfort to most of our thirsty runners, exhausted by a race which they can never finish, which resembles much more the tread mill of Sisyphos than a race.

Only a very small number of countries - mainly the centers and a few exceptions in the periphery - followed the 'normal' path of having the lowest real per capita income in 1960, and the highest in 1995. There was an alarming trend of wide regions of our globe having their lowest historical income value over the last 4 decades in 1989 or even later. A very fortunate and small number of countries achieved their highest GNP per capita in 1995, while others have to realize that they were better off ten, fifteen, or even twenty years from now. Untold human misery, human rights violations, and raped minorities and environments are but the consequence of this process of unequal development that continues and deepens, as we entered the new Century.

Europe, especially if it were to continue the process of Eastern enlargement without tackling the fundamental consequences of unequal exchange would be paramount to risk the failure of the whole process. Wages in the East melt like the snow of winter in the spring sunshine under the impact of currency fluctuations:

	Latest	Year ago	absolute change in US $ over 1 year	relative change (in %)	today's wages relative to Portugal (777$=100)	number of years, in which at the current speed of change the level of Portugal today would be reached
Bulgaria	111	112	-1	-0,9	14,3	never
Croatia	624	673	-49	-7,3	80,3	never
Czech Republic	356	374	-18	-4,8	45,8	never
Estonia	286,9	265,5	21,4	8,1	36,9	61 years
Hungary	324	322	2	0,6	41,7	755 years
Latvia	238	211,8	26,2	12,4	30,6	43 years
Lithuania	270,5	n.d.			34,8	
Poland	459	421	38	9	59,1	35 years
Romania	125	157	-32	-20,4	16,1	never
Russia	67	71	-4	-5,6	8,6	never
Slovakia	273	293	-20	-6,8	35,1	never
Slovenia	953	1024	-71	-6,9	122,7	level of Portugal reached, but wages are falling again

Source: our own calculations from Business Central Europe, *http://www.bcemag.com/*

Wage earners from the non-export-oriented sectors in the West of the continent, confronted by increased social polarization, and third-worldization under the pressure of the process of the new international division of labor, become opposed to the European extension project, just as the export sector workers and farmers in the European Eastern semi-periphery, confronted by falling earnings for their labor, measured in current world market exchange rates. Exchange rates and internal buying powers at purchasing power parity rates drift apart, and the differences increase, instead of decreasing.

In the entire region of Eastern Europe, income poverty increased at an alarming speed between 1988 and 1994 - from 4% to 32% of the total population. 62% of all Russian children and 34% of the aged are poor; the suicide rate increased by more than 50% and the homicide rate more than doubled against 1989. 9.6% of all people are not expected to survive to age 40, 38% of Russians are living below the World Bank absolute world poverty line of a dollar a day, and the Human Development Index has fallen, compared to 1993 (UNDP, 1997). The poorest 20% have an income of 881 $ per capita and year in terms of real purchasing power, while the richest 20% have 12804 $ per capita and year (UNDP, 1997). Under these circumstances, the implementation of the *Acquis Communautaire* in the social field in the whole of East Central and Eastern Europe will become a very urgent necessity.

Transnational corporations and their foreign investments are the cornerstone of the international system, as Osvaldo Sunkel so correctly foresaw in his penetrating analysis a quarter of a century ago. The outward stock of foreign direct investments of 39000 parent firms in their 270000 affiliates reached $2.7 trillion in 1995. The gross product of foreign affiliates amounted to 8.7% of home country GDP in the countries of the European Union in 1991, the last year with available data. In North America this ratio stood at 6.4%, in the LDCs at 6.5%, and in Central and Eastern Europe at 1.3%. On a world level, the TNCs control 6.4% of the world gross domestic product. The sales of foreign affiliates amounted to 116% of the total of world exports of goods and non-factor-services in 1982; this ratio now has risen to 127.9% (UNCTAD, 1996). For ages, economists have warned repeatedly against the danger of such a monopoly capitalism. Kalecki and Rothschild should be specially mentioned in this context here. An ever larger proportion of world trade is nothing but trade between the affiliates and headquarters of transnational corporations. In recent years, there has been a massive inflow of Western capital into the region of East Central Europe, but this inflow increased the social contradictions of development:

Foreign direct investment ($bn) (end 1999)

Bulgaria	2.8
Croatia	2.5
Czech Republic	15.6
Estonia	2.3
Hungary	19.7
Latvia	2.1
Lithuania	2.0
Poland	38.9
Romania	6.4
Russia	10.3
Slovakia	1.7
Slovenia	2.6

The international system, in addition, is not only a system of social and economic polarization, it is also a system of recurring international long-run tensions, that erupt along these socio-economic conflict lines. Ever since the days of Akerman's pioneering study, published with Macmillan's before the Second World War, social scientists have studied by quantitative methods the connection between economic long cycles and major wars, among them Modelski, 1987, and Goldstein, 1988. We should not forget here, as Luigi Scandella has reminded us recently, that long cycles form part and parcel of social scientific debates since their first discovery by Hyde Clark in 1847, to be followed by W. S. Jevons (1884), Alexander Israel Helphand (1901), J. Van Gelderen (1913), J. Lescure (1914), and the Russian Marxist M. I. Tougan-Baranovski, who was Kondratieff's teacher. Akerman's received a dangerous counterpoint by Siegfried von Ciriacy-Wantrups study, published in Berlin 1936, on *'Agrarkrisen und Stockungsspannen - Zur Frage der Langen Welle in der wirtschaftlichen Entwicklung'*. Ciriacy maintains that war is not the consequence, but the cause of economic upsurges - a theory, perfectly fitting with the official German spirit of the time (1936). However, Ernst Wagemann already showed in his study on *'Struktur und Rythmus der Weltwirtschaft: Grundlagen einer weltwirtschaftlichen Konjunkturlehre'* (Berlin, 1931), that the real tensions in the world system arise out of the unequal spread of capitalist growth on a world scale, between what he calls the old capitalist countries with high densities of capital and labor, the neo-capitalist countries, where capital and labor are 'relatively scarce', the semi-capitalist nations with abundant labor and scarce capital, and the non-capitalist nations. Migration, foreign investment and technical innovations all swing along the long cycles, and the flows of migrations and investments are caused by the economic differences between the four mentioned categories (for a more detailed literature survey, see Scandella, 1998). Inequality, and not homogenization, characterize the international system.

International tension has characterized the world system since 1450 in ups and downs, that have led the world to three catastrophic world wars (Goldstein, 1988). Whether there is room for optimism now, after the end of the so-called Cold War, will be finally decided, among other factors, by the growing tension between the human species and the environment. Each day, 140 species are condemned to extinction; the CO2-content in the atmosphere is 26% higher than at the beginning of the industrial age; the earth surface was warmer in 1990 than at any point since the middle of the 19th century, when measurements began; each year, a forest area of the world as big as Finland is being destroyed, and each year, another Mexico is being added to the world's population (World Watch Institute Report, 1992). Winter temperatures in 1997/98 in most of North America and Europe were the mildest for ages.

Rather than predicting the **end of history**, the **acceleration of history** - might loom ahead. Our work shows that there is strong evidence to believe that transnational capitalist penetration in the end leads to disintegration, and conflict, and not towards integration and peace. We use up to 19 indicators of social change since 1980 to show precisely that. Sunkel foresaw then, from the viewpoint of his structural economic theory, many of the problems that seem to beset the post-1989 world. At the time of writing this analysis, South Asia is plunged into a nuclear arms race, drug lords dominate de facto a number of countries south of the 23rd parallel and north of the 23rd southern parallel, civil wars and refugee crises dominate the international headlines of stations like BBC and CNN, which present to their listeners more than the usual parochial and limited information that is in reality so common today around the globe. Instead of heralding a better and more peaceful future, recent tendencies might imply:

(i)   an ever greater ecological danger for the future of our globe, stemming mainly from the rapid depletion of the ozone layers, now also over the northern hemisphere
(ii)   the rapid destabilization of large parts of West and Central Africa, which in turn might increase the migratory pressure to Europe and North Africa, which
(iii)   in turn might finally bring to an end the present regime of 'West Rome'

A look at UNDP and UNCTAD statistics gives us a more than alarming picture of the reality of transnational integration and national, economic, social, ecological, and spiritual disintegration. In 1993, 76% of the stock of world-wide foreign direct investments were still anchored in the old industrialized countries, and only 23% in the developing countries. 40% of all investment flows between 1990 and 1994 went to the LCD's, 4/5 of which to the top ten among the semi-industrialized or newly industrialized nations (China, Singapore, Argentina, Mexico, Malaysia, Indonesia, Thailand, Hong Kong, Taiwan and Nigeria). European leadership towards growth for the European East in an ecologically sustainable way would be one of the main tasks of rebuilding the world-economy. Between 1990 and 1994, the share of the 'triad'(US+CND; Japan; EU) in world GNP rose from 50.3% to 50.7%; the share of the rest of Asia rose from 17.2% to 23.1%, while the participation of Eastern Europe and the ex-USSR in the world economy was nearly wiped out and reduced to half in less than a decade - from 10.9% to 5.3% of world GNP. Will Europe be able to lead the East to growth, or will - what a bleak, though nonetheless realistic scenario, the stagnation of the East between 1990 and 1994 become the future of the West of the continent (our compilations from Stiftung, 1993, and 1996)?

The wealth gaps between the rich center in Europe and the surrounding peripheral and semi-peripheral areas are part of the economic, ecological and social history over the last 500 years. They continue to exist today, and if anything, have deepened since the 1980s. In terms of most wealth indicators, as calculated by the UNDP, the East (Eastern Europe and the former USSR) and the southern rim of Europe (the Arab world), are as distant from 'us', the European Union, as the 'Haves' and the have-nots are divided from each other at any welfare border around the world, be it on the shores of the Rio Grande or across the China Sea. However, it would be wrong to be misled by wealth statistics alone. In terms of life expectancy, only 7% separate Poland, say, from Austria, while in terms of real purchasing power, the differences are estimated to be 1:4. But wealth differences create political tensions of their own, and wealth and consumption differences lead to 'catch-up' processes, with a structurally unbalanced development in the semi-peripheral and peripheral societies resulting in the end. Thus, from ancient societies onwards, wealth and consumption differences have lead towards a polarized form of development in peripheral societies (Chase-Dunn and Hall, 1997).

At the same time, the population balance, and the balance of military forces shifts in favor of the poorer nations, that surround the rich man's land, the European Union, beset by a growing number of internal problems, like unemployment, drugs, crime, environmental decay, and aging populations. The following calculation from UNDP-data, 1995, shows the dramatic character of the welfare gap at the outer borders of the Union:

	East-West-gap	North-South-gap
	for the European Union, by around 1995	
real purchasing power	1:3.5	1:4
life expectancy	1:1.12	1:1.22
share of world industrial GNP	1:8.5	-
defense expenditures	1:6.1	1:1.8
population potential, 2000	1:0.9	1:1.3
military personnel	1:1.8	1:1
total GDP	1:9	-

The East's challenge to the aging north-west is its population and thus migration potential, its high military personnel ratio, but the East's unease number one is its low share in world total GDP and industrial GNP. The South's challenge in military terms has been building up over recent years, combined with a rapid population growth and still existing large-scale poverty. Let us hope and work for peace in the Middle East; but if that is not achieved quickly, and development in the Arab world does not reach down to the poorest strata, centuries of unequal exchange, foreign rule and neglect could combine with the archaic weight of religious tradition - then the *Dar al harb,* the world of war and disbelief will be held responsible for 80 million illiterates, for the 73 million poor, for the 12% of resources, spent on arms, for the scarcity of water that affects 55% of the Arabs. If the balance will not be achieved by political and economic means within the next 25 years, then migration and the military expansion of the desperate nations will attempt to redress the balance. This scenario is all the more likely, since migration pressure from the decaying center of Africa will start to push northwards in the coming years. With real purchasing power parity rates, the gaps are today:

Japan - East Asia (excl. China)	1:2.6
Europe - Eastern periphery	1:3.5
Europe - South	1:4
North America - Latin America	1:4.1

The professional political optimism of our times in Europe holds, that after overcoming the transformation crisis, Europe will re-unite and catch up with the competing market economic centers. Another vision might hold though that the inability of the East to find a proper niche in the world market might spill over to the West of the continent. Social scientific thought in the long-term policy planning and development research tradition - in Austria of Otto Bauer, Karl Polanyi, Joseph Alois Schumpeter, or Kurt Rothschild, would dare to ask, whether or not the crisis and final collapse of communism, in the end, is the product of the one and single movement in world economic dynamics away from the European landmass and the Euro-Atlantic region towards the Pacific. GDP real growth, p.a., from 1986-95 was:

Asia	+7.3%
LCD's in the Middle East and Southern Europe	+3.7%
Latin America	+2.6%
USA	+2.5%
Japan	+2.5%
EU	+2.4%
Africa	+2.4%
Eastern Europe	-1.9%
CIS	-4.2%

Source: Stiftung Entwicklung und Frieden, 1996

Re-reading Osvaldo Sunkel's penetrating analysis, one is struck by the parallels between the Latin America of yesterday and the Eastern Europe of today. One of the most recurrent predictions of structuralists as Osvaldo Sunkel, or Raul Prebisch, would be that a country, specializing in investment goods and other manufactures has a much better chance for long-run and stable development than nations, specializing in raw materials and semi-finished products. Samir Amin and other critics of the Union have maintained, that the structure of trade relations with the outer rim of the Union favors unequal specialization, and prolongs the periphery's trade in raw materials and semi-finished products. Just that that seems to have been the case from 1980 to 1992:

Graph 1.1b: Structural dependence of the European East

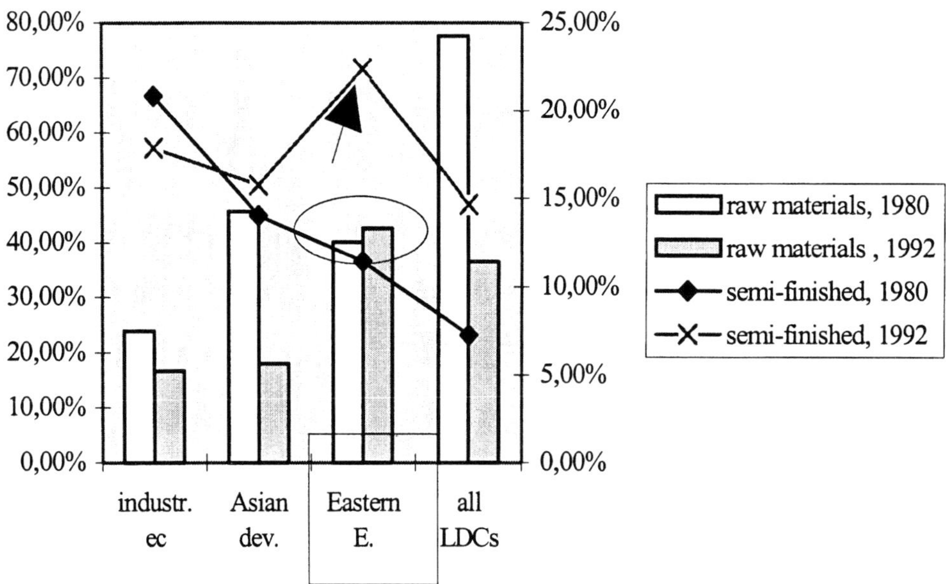

Legend: right-hand scale: percentage share of semi-finished products in total exports; left-hand scale: percentage share of raw materials per total exports. Source: our own compilations from Stiftung Entwicklung und Frieden, 1996

While other regions could advance and received a fairer share of the world market, Eastern Europe was increasingly marginalized at the very hour of liberation in 1989. More and more, there seems to be a 'legal' and a parallel illegal core of the world economy. What the legal economy cannot redress, the illegal economy will. The Mafias around the world have a turnover of more than $ 500 thousand million a year alone from the narcotics' trade. Each year, $ 85 thousand million in drug profits are 'laundered' through the financial markets. The new, speculative character of the global market economy dictates, that even legal transnationals have to earn much of their profits from speculation on the international financial markets. With that, the basic instability of the international system increases (UNDP, 1994, 1995; Stiftung Entwicklung und Frieden, 1996). Among the most powerful groups, threatening the very fabric of legal society in western countries today, are the following large illegal transnational corporations (with their estimated turnover)

La Costa Nostra	(USA)	100 thousand million $
Colombian cartels	(Colombia)	15 thousand million $
Italian organized crime	(Italy)	100 thousand million $
Cosa Nostra		
Camorra		
n'drangheta		
Sacra Corona Unita		
Yakuza	(Japan)	120 thousand million $

(Source: our compilation from Raith, 1995). For an update, see also: Christian de Brie, Thick as Thieves, *Le Monde Diplomatique,* April 2000: *http://www.monde-diplomatique.fr/en/*

Newcomers, like the Russian, Albanian and Turkish Mafia groups, and formally regional groupings, like the Chinese Triads, are expanding rapidly as well into the core areas of the world-wide market. By the year 2020, the expansion of these and other criminal corporations will be not a threat, but a reality, practically subverting entire states of even the developed capitalist centers (Raith, 1995). The logic of accumulation of these large, transnational criminal corporations seems nowadays to reflect the growing weight of 'flexible specialization', while the earlier, post-1932 model reflected 'corporatist structures' (Behan, 1996). The 'neo-corporatist' structure of the classic Sicilian Mafia of Salvatore *'Toto'* Riina is more and more superseded by flexible newcomers like the Camorra and the drug cartels of Latin America and Eastern Europe. In terms of profits, the Asian gangs seem to be on the ascent. Indeed, a relevant issue for future world systems research: the interaction between long economic and civilization cycles and patterns of the criminal underworld. The question cannot be neglected any longer by world system research: in the 1970s and 1980s, reported crimes increased worldwide by 5% *per annum,* in the US alone, there are now 2 million victims of violent crime every year (UNDP, 1997). The rise of crime is going parallel with the destruction of the family. Killings of minors increased in many developing countries by more than 40% in the 1990s. A third of married women in the developing countries are battered by their husbands during their lifetime. Dowry deaths in India are put at least at 5000 a year. In the US, every year nearly 3 million children are reported to be victims of abuse and neglect. 75 million children in the developing world are working in slavery, prostitution and hazardous conditions; among these 1 million girls, mostly in Asia, are forced into prostitution each year. In the OECD countries, there are now annual 129000 reported adult rapes; the prison population has increased from 80 to 88, there are now 4.8 intentional homicides, committed by male persons per 100000 inhabitants, and 1020 annual road deaths per 100000 inhabitants. The suicide rate is at 21 (males) and 7 (females); 34 annual divorces per 1000 couples are registered. The oligopolistic structure of late capitalism is now superseded by a kind of *'Dreigroschenopera'* capitalism, begging the question of the very nature of capitalist elites that Schumpeter raised in the 1940s.

The core of the transnational economy, Sunkel observed, used to be the legal transnational corporation and the legal transnational bank. From 1991 to 1993, the following growth rates were observed:

world GDP	+1.6%
world trade	+3.1%
world-wide stock of FDI	+8.0%
sales of the foreign affiliates of transnational corporations	+20.0%

Source: our own compilations from Stiftung Entwicklung und Frieden, 1996

More than $ 1300 thousand million are shifted around each day by way of international financial markets. The cumulative debt of the developing countries reaches the staggering proportion of $ 1945 thousand million, and grew in 1998 to $ 2600 thousand million dollars:

Graph 1.2: The debt crisis of the world periphery

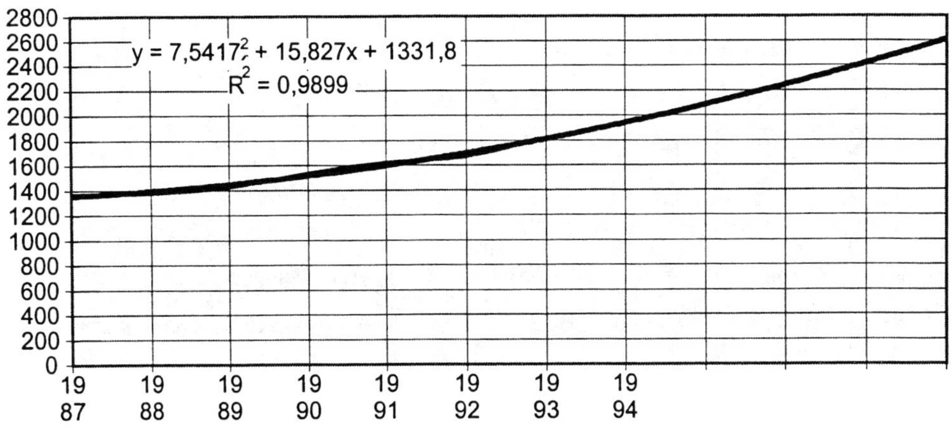

Legend: our own compilations from Stiftung Entwicklung und Frieden, 1996. Cumulated and projected values of total Third World debt, 1987 - 1998

The problem of international development, to a large extent, is also the problem of underdevelopment and poverty, in which a large part of the malnourished children of this world grow up - 11 - 19 countries, which, in addition, have to shoulder a large part of the world refugee problem as well:

Table 1.1: The 11 - 19 main crisis points in the world system

	refugees in thousands	malnourished children in millions
Iran	2495	1,6
Philippines	3	3
Indonesia	2	8,8
China	**288**	**19,3**
Vietnam	5	4,4
Myanmar	**0**	**2,3**
Pakistan	**1480**	**9,4**
India	**260**	**61,8**
Nigeria	5	7
Bangladesh	**199**	**11**
Ethiopia	248	4,7
Rest LDCs	6805	23,6

Country	estimated number of poor people according to the capability-poverty-measurement-scale
Mexico	14,6
Brazil	15,2
Turkey	12,1
Thailand	11,7
South Africa	11,8
Philippines	18,4
China	**204,9**
Iran	17,9
Algeria	12,7
Indonesia	79,4
Morocco	12,8
Egypt	23,4
Pakistan	**73,9**
India	**530,6**
Tanzania	10,6
Zaire	17,3
Nigeria	57,8
Bangladesh	**89,5**
Ethiopia	36
Rest	172,3

Source: our own calculations from UNDP, 1996. Figures for South Asia are printed in bold letters

The incomes of more than a billion people have fallen below levels first reached 10, 20, sometimes 30 years ago (UNDP, 1997-99). Between 1987 and 1993 the number of people with incomes of less than $1 a day increased by almost 100 million to 1.3 billion, and the number appears to be growing in every region except East and South-East Asia and the Pacific. In the past year, the Human Development Index dropped in 30 countries (UNDP, 1997). The share of the richest 20% in world incomes rose from 70% to 85%, with the differences between these two rising from 30:1 to 61:1 in 1991, to reach 78:1 in 1994 (UNDP, 1997). The share of the poorest 20% of the world's people in global income now stands at 1.1%, down from 2.3% in 1960. Even in the developed core countries of the world economy alone, 80 million people are categorized as poor with less than $14.40 a day in 1985 PPP$ (the US poverty line), and at least 30 million are homeless. In the United States of America, 47 million people have no health insurance. In Eastern Europe, the introduction of 'turbo'-capitalism brought about 9 million extra deaths, caused by violence and the sharp increase in cardiovascular diseases. In the Federal Republic of Germany alone, 900000 people are homeless, 10% of the total workforce have no job, and 7.5 million are poor *(Orientierung, 60, 1996: 204; IFRI, 1998; NZZ, 11, 1999)*. Between 1989 and 1996 the number of billionaires - world-wide - increased from 157 to 447. The net wealth of the richest 10 individuals on our planet is 1.5 time greater than the total annual income of all the least developed countries of our globe with 534.2 million inhabitants. The richest single individual in Mexico had a bigger wealth than the annual income of 17 million of his compatriots. 200 billionaires doubled their assets from 1994 to 1998 to more than $ 1 trillion. **Nowadays, the assets of the world top 3 billionaires are more than the combined GNP of the 600 million people living in the least developed countries on earth (UNDP, 1999).**

Nollert (1990), based on Berry et al., has shown, that the share of the bottom 60% in world consumption, after due consideration to income distribution within the nations of the world, is 11.9%, while the share of the top 10% is 50.5%. The wave of the world recession - or as we prefer to say, the Kondratieff B-phase - first hit Africa in the 1970s, and rolled on to hit Latin America and the Arab world in the 1980s and Eastern Europe in the 1990s. Even in the highly industrialized countries, capitalist development became more and more

(i) **jobless**: in the countries of the European Union in 1993, there were 16.86 million unemployed people, and in 2000, 18 million people. In the industrial countries as a whole, there are 30 million people out of work, and in Eastern Europe and the former USSR, 15 million people (UNDP, 1999).

(ii) **ruthless**: global GNP grew by 40%, but the number of poor grew by 17%. In the European Union, the ratio between the richest 20% and the bottom 20% is now 7.5 in France, 9.6 in the UK, 7.1 in Denmark, 5.8 in Germany, and 6.0 in Italy. Each year, damage to forests due to air pollution leads to economic losses of about $35 billion - about the annual GDP of Hungary.

(iii) **voiceless**: human and political rights performance on a global scale has deteriorated in many countries according to the well-known *Freedom House* data series (Stiftung, 1997); even in the countries of the European Union, the following performances in 1996 were below the maximum value '1', in the Spanish and British case under the weight of the fight against regional, primordial terrorism in the Basque country and in Northern Ireland

Belgium	2
France: civil rights	2
Germany: civil rights	2
Great Britain: civil rights	2
Greece: civil rights	3
Irish Republic: civil rights	2
Italy: civil rights	2
Northern Ireland-political rights	3
Northern Ireland-civil rights	4
Spain: civil rights	2

The poorest 40% in the EU countries receive only 18% of total incomes. Women receive on average only 2/3 of the income of males; and hold only 12% of parliamentary seats

(iv) **rootless**: 10000 cultures of humans and millions of species are on the verge of disappearance world-wide; local human dialects, cultures and accents disappear also in Europe at a rapid pace. Nationality conflicts and regional conflicts have increased in many countries over the last decade. Low-quality satellite TV more and more substitutes national TV output; the transnational economy dominates more and more domains of radio, TV, and the press. Even in EU countries, nationally made films amount from just only 2% (Greece) to 34.9% (France) of all films shown in cinemas. The US film industry holds a market-share of 2/3 or ¾ and more. The US exports more than 120000 hours of television programming a year to Europe alone (UNDP, 1997-99). At the same time, social deviance increases in the age of rootless growth or stagnation. In the European Union, there were 77 prisoners per 100 000 people in 1987; now there are 87. The intentional homicide rate is Union-wide 7.7 per 100 000. In the Netherlands it is 14.8 per 100.000 inhabitants. 44% of all male EU adults smoke (women: 25%), alcohol consumption is 9.6 litters per capita and year, and the male cancer rate is 235, the female cancer rate is 171 Union-wide. Television takes up now some 40% of the free time of the average American, and participation in voluntary associations such as the Red Cross has declined by 25-50%. The basic networks, necessary for the functioning of democracies, are on the retreat around the globe. Trade Union membership rates declined in the Netherlands from 39% in 1978 to 25% in 1991; from 30% to 15% in the USA et cetera. In the Union as a whole, trade union membership declined from 37% in 1970 to 33%; in Austria and in many other countries, the decline was even more dramatic (from 62% to 46%). Nearly 130000 women are reported annually to be raped in the industrial countries.

(v) **futureless**: annual fresh water withdrawals amount to 862 m^3 in the Union. Commercial energy use in oil equivalents is 3588 kg per capita in oil equivalents, and each year, the Union produces 15.13% of the world's greenhouse gas emissions, 3373 metric tons of heavy metal from nuclear reactors, and 48220 tons of hazardous highly-toxic waste. The average Union citizen produces 399 kg of municipal waste a year, and recycles only 45% of his or her paper and 52% of his or her glass. 2 million people are already affected with HIV.

Instead of an end of history, global or regional anarchy in countries like Afghanistan, Albania, Angola, Burundi, Georgia, Kampuchea, Liberia, Mozambique, Rwanda, Somalia, Sudan, Tajikistan, and Yemen, seems to be likely. A global financial crash cannot be ruled out entirely. In a very brilliant commentary, Rudi Dornbusch thinks that repetitions of the Mexican crisis - or rather Peso disaster for the world economy - are likely again and again (Dornbusch, in *Business Week,* November 25th , 1996). Recent experience in Brazil, Indonesia, Malaysia, the Philippines and Thailand, where the negative current account balance went out of proportion, underlines his point. The ghosts of this *'tequila effect'* or *'caipirinha-effect'* walk around Eastern Europe, too.

The capacity of the US to act as a global policeman under such circumstances is severely constrained by the secular balance of trade deficit of the US economy, not being offset by an enough positive balance of services and payments. America's current account deficit reached the staggering amount of $bn 411.6 in 2000 *(Bilan du Monde,* 2000). Indeed, the outflow of hegemonic capital after each hegemonic period is a well-known phenomenon and in the end explains very well, why American capital today will have no tendency to restore the US economy at home. The comparative characteristics of hegemonic decline were always, Chase-Dunn and Hall teach us, secular balance of payment deficits. America is no different from Britain, the Netherlands, Genova and Venice before in the history of the world economy.

Hundreds of millions of human beings are unemployed or under-employed on a world scale. Even in a highly social-policy-oriented country like Austria, which ranks 16 among the 174 nation list of human development, net earnings from profits and property are now 29.4% of national income, the state withdraws and has a share of 27.7% in net national income, and net total wages are down to 43.3% (Federal Ministry of Labor and Social Affairs, Social Report Austria, 1995, and UNDP, 1999). This tendency for relative wages to fall in relation to profits, property and the state, seems to be universal. There are reliable income distribution data available from 68 countries. In 29 nations, the ratio of the top 20% to the bottom 20% exceeds 10 to 1; in 17, 15 to 1; and in 9, 20 to 1. The 1998 HDR of the UNDP estimates the most glaring contradictions of the inequality in consumption the world over. The additional annual cost to achieve universal access to basic educational services in all developing countries would be 6 billion US $; the annual expenditures for cosmetics in the USA is 8 billion US $; water and sanitation for all in the Third World would require 9 billion $ annually, while ice cream consumption in Europe is 11 billion $ annually. The annual expenditures necessary for basic health and nutrition in the Third World are 13 billion $, while pet food consumption in the USA is 17 billion $ and cigarettes in Europe 50 billion $ (UNDP, HDR, 1998). Government subsidies in agriculture, energy, water, and road transport total US $ 700-900 billion annually, and they considerably increase inequalities further. At the same time, a considerable percentage of people is thrown into poverty by the workings of the process of globalization:

Graph 1.3: Poverty data for the European Union (poverty threshold is 50% or below of average consumer expenditures on a Union-wide level) and the Human Development Index

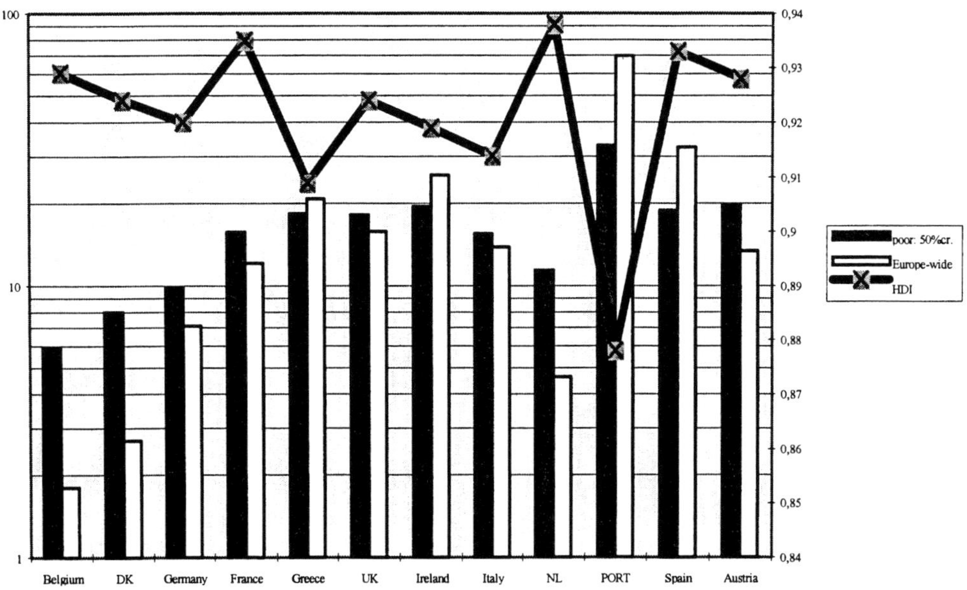

Source: comparative European Union poverty data, as compiled by the Austrian Federal Ministry of Labor, Vienna. Left-hand scale (bars): percentage of people, considered to live in poverty; right-hand scale (line): Human Development Index (UNDP).

The notion of full employment, once the objective of economic policy making, together with monetary stability, economic growth, social justice, ecological and external equilibrium, is a thing of the past. At the same time, dependency ratios are sharply rising, so that the percentage of people world-wide engaged in productive work is stagnating or even falling.

2) THE THEORETICAL FRAMEWORK: WHAT CAN POLICY-MAKERS KNOW ABOUT ASCENT AND DECLINE IN THE WORLD ECONOMY?

Dependency and world system theory hold, that poverty and backwardness in poor countries are caused by the peripheral position that these nations have in the international division of labor. Ever since the capitalist world system evolved, there is a stark distinction between the nations of the center and the nations of the periphery. Cardoso summarized the quantifiable essence of dependency theories as follows:

(i)   there is a financial and technological penetration by the developed capitalist centers of the countries of the periphery and semi-periphery

(ii)   this produces an unbalanced economic structure both within the peripheral societies and between them and the centers

(iii)   this leads to limitations on self-sustained growth in the periphery

(iv)   this favors the appearance of specific patterns of class relations

(v)   these require modifications in the role of the state to guarantee both the functioning of the economy and the political articulation of a society, which contains, within itself, foci of inartuculateness and structural imbalance (Cardoso, 1979)

Already the classics of political economy provided a framework of quantifiable dependency theory. Let us recall that for Marx and his labor theory of value, total product consists of constant capital, c, variable capital (labor), v, and surplus, s. Rate of surplus value, s', the organic composition of capital, q, and the profit rate, p, are hence:

$$(2.1)\ P = c + v + s$$

$$(2.2)\ s' = s/v$$

$$(2.3)\ q = c/(c+v)$$

$$(2.4)\ p = s/(c+v); \text{ hence, after some transformations:}$$

$$(2.5)\ p = s'(1-q)$$

Class relationships of a rising power of labor in the centers determine, that, in the end, long-term fluctuations notwithstanding, cheaper raw materials and exploitation of the periphery become one of the cornerstones of a strategy to halt the fall in the profit rate. Among others, mass migration, unequal exchange, and a new international division of labor are key elements to increase, at least temporarily, s'. Kalecki adapted political economy to the age of monopolization. Let gross production be P, W are wages, M are the payments for raw materials. The monopolization factor is $_k$. We are in a sit.uation of less than full employment. Costs for wages, W, and raw materials M, are multiplied by a factor of $_k$ ($_k > 1$) to arrive at prices. The gross value of production of an enterprise is thus

$$(2.6)\ P = {_k} * (W + M)$$

(2.7) if M/W denote the terms of trade, $_j$, between the raw material producing sector of the economy and the rest, then we arrive for the determination of the share of wages, $_w$, by the following formula: $_w = 1/(1+(_k-1)*(_j+1))$

A rising degree of monopolization in the leading center countries over time determines, that, in order to keep the share of wages at least constant, a rising exploitation of the raw material producers sets in to offset the balance. There is a massive, internationally published evidence that speaks in favor of dependency theory. Kalecki and Rothschild are vindicated by contemporary developments in transformation economies: transfer pricing alone costs - according to Polish Treasury experts - the Polish economy 8 billion Zlotys a year (approximately $bn 2.29; *Zycie*, 92, 20th of April, 1998: 15). Former Finance Minister Balcerowicz now reckons that consumption rises twice as fast as productivity, and Planning Chief Kropiwnicki thinks that the high trade deficit threatens macro-economic stability *(Rzeczpospolita*, 91, 18th - 19th April 1998: 9).

The almost unlimited number of empirical studies on peripheral capitalism and development on a world level in the B-phase of the Kondratieff cycle from 1965 onwards go back, in a way, to the classic essay, published by Johan Galtung in the spring issue of the *Journal of Peace Research* a quarter of a century ago (Galtung, 1971). For Galtung, income inequality, and hence, relative poverty in the nations of the world system is linked to trade partner concentration of the peripheral country and a trade structure, that relies on the exports of raw materials and the imports of finished products. Bornschier, Chase-Dunn, and their school later on reformulated the argument: not only income inequality, but also long term economic growth are being negatively determined by dependency from transnational capital, to be measured by a weighted share of transnational investment penetration per economic and social size of the nation. Later essays extended the argument to other indicators of human well-being and the environment as well as democratic stability.

Other formulations of dependency insisted on 'unequal exchange' which, according to one such formulation, hampers development if double factorial terms of trade of the respective country are < 1.0 (Raffer, 1987, Amin, 1975). Labor in the export sectors of the periphery is being exploited, while monopolistic structures of international trade let the centers profit from the high prices of their exports to the world markets in comparison to their labor productivity. Since double factorial terms of trade are simply net barter terms of trade weighted by productivities (F) of X, exports, and M, imports, the formula

(2.8) $((P_X * F_X)/(P_M*F_M)) = 1$ denotes the conditions of 'equal' exchange as opposed to unequal exchange:

(2.9) $((P_X * F_X)/(P_M*F_M)) = < 1.0$ while nations with

(2.10) $((P_X * F_X)/(P_M*F_M)) = > 1.0$ are the countries that benefited from unequal exchange.

Empirical support for Raffer's reformulation of the theory of unequal exchange is overwhelming. **Since the early 1970s the least developed countries have suffered a cumulative decline of 50% in their terms of trade.** If terms of trade in 1987 are 100, the 1994 values indicate:

Sub-Saharan Africa	95
South Asia	97
East Asia	104
South-East Asia and Pacific	94
Latin America and Caribbean	96
least developed countries	91
Industrial countries	104

For the developing countries as a whole, terms of trade losses between 1980 and 1991 amounted to $bn 290 (UNDP, 1997). Real commodity prices were 45% lower than in 1980 and 10% lower than the lowest prices during the Great Depression, 1932 (UNDP, 1997). Interest rates for credits of the developing world were in effect four times as high as those charged on rich countries during the 1980s. Goods from the developed countries enjoyed much greater tariff reductions in the Uruguay Round than those from developing countries - 45% compared with 20-25%. The least developed countries face tariffs that are 30% higher than the global average (UNDP, 1997). Tariff escalation forces developing countries into primary commodities, whose real prices are declining. For developing countries, tariffs will be higher for final products. The discrimination of LDC textile exports continues, while subsidies to agriculture in the rich countries keep world prices low and exclude the Third World from the food markets of the rich countries. It confronts domestic food producers in the poorer countries with cheap food imports, which reduce the incentives for local food production and destroy the livelihoods of millions of peasants (UNDP, 1997). This is the real crisis of agriculture in Africa, but it also affects agriculture in East Central Europe. We Westerners tend to think of Polish agriculture in terms of backwardness, but we underestimate the peripherization, that we impose by our subventions and trade barriers on Eastern European agriculture, and in the long run, also on employment in the under- and semi-developed regions of the East.

By a reduction of agricultural subsidies by just 30%, LDCs could earn an extra $bn 45 a year. Unequal access to trade, labor and finance costs the periphery up to $bn 500 a year, 10 times the amount of the yearly overall international foreign assistance (UNDP, 1997, 1992). Intellectual property rights increase the price of technology, while the USA in the 19th Century and Japan in the 20th Century enormously benefited from the free flow of ideas (UNDP, 1997).

Skepticism about the expanding world order, dominated by the transnationals, as a tool for achieving stable market-oriented development persisted, the neo-liberal transformation literature in the wake of the earthquake of the revolution of the year 1989 in Eastern Europe and the breakdown of communism notwithstanding (Aslund, 1992; Sachs, 1993). The fall of the Berlin Wall is a good testing ground for various theories of development and social decay: what really happens, if 'capitalism' has 'its way'?

Giovanni Arrighi proposed in his provocative analysis of the *'Long 20th Century'* (1995) the thought that the logic of accumulation on a world-scale is governed by the ups and downs in the succession of regulation and de-regulation, starting from the Venetian (regulatory) and Genoese (deregulated) era of capitalism, followed by the Dutch (regulatory) and British (deregulated) era, and the US hegemony, which - after 1945 - was a regulatory model. From the late 1970s, however, we witness, Arrighi's argument goes on, again the renewed rise of a deregulated model of world capitalism. The often bemoaned end of the Keynesian era has its real basis, Arrighi's argument goes, in the shifting accumulation pattern of world capitalism. We agree with Arrighi that the rise of financial capitalism and the decline of productive capitalism are always connected to major shifts in the location of the centers of world capitalism, first from Venice to Genoa, followed by the shift from Genoa to Amsterdam, from Amsterdam to London, from London to New York, and from there on to the capitalist archipelago of East Asia of yesterday, perhaps to be followed by South Asia today (Arrighi, 1995). Arrighi also introduced the important notion, that there is a certain coexistence in the time-perspective between the 'different logics', so that elements of the waning and elements of the emerging order might coincide for years. Arrighi's sequential model of world capitalism is also a historic interpretation of the old Marxist notion of financial expansion - > material expansion- >financial expansion *(MCM')*, and as such radically challenges the notion of 'unchanging' general laws of rise and decline. Following Arrighi, we postulate that regulatory strategies might have been well compatible with growth under the rise of the Venetian, Dutch, and American era, while at the time of the rise of 'deregulation', such deregulatory strategies and not 'big government' will be conducive to economic growth.

There were dozens of articles being published on these 'laws' of development in world society, with the quantitative dependency argument perhaps most clearly having been stated by Bornschier and Chase Dunn in 1985. Their widely received book still can be considered as the quantitative *canon* or *summa* of arguments about the workings of domination and dependence in the capitalist world economy put forward over the years by such different authors in such different countries at such different points of time as Herb Addo (before his untimely death in Trinidad); Samir Amin (now Senegal); Volker Bornschier (Switzerland); Fernando Henrique Cardoso (now the president of his home-country, Brazil); Christopher Chase-Dunn (USA); Armando Cordova (Venezuela); Steffen Flechsig (Neue Bundeslaender); Andre Gunder Frank (presently USA); Folker Froebel, Juergen Heinrichs and Otto Kreye (Germany); Walter Goldfrank (USA); Björn Hettne (Sweden); Otmar Hoell (Austria); George Kent (Hawaii, USA); Kimmo Kiljunen (Finland); Kari Levitt-Polanyi (Canada); Kunibert Raffer (Austria); Robert Ross (USA); Kurt Rothschild (Austria); Dieter Senghaas (Germany); Robert Stauffer (Hawaii, USA); Jadwiga Staniszkis (Poland); Hanns-Albert Steger (Germany); Osvaldo Sunkel (Chile); Henryk Szlajfer (now Poland's OSCE Ambassador in Vienna); Immanuel Wallerstein (USA); Edward L. Wheelwright (Australia), being joined by the quantitative debate in such journals as *American Journal of Sociology, American Political Science Review, American Sociological Review, Social Forces,* and many others.

The basic questions that we formulate are then:

a) do these 'laws' still hold and are they still in force after the world went through the recession of the late 1970s and early 1980s?

b) do these 'laws' still hold for new phenomena, like social, ecological, and human development, as well as gender disparities, that more and more become an intrinsic part of the capitalist world system, and that, better than economic growth, express ascent and decline in world society today?

c) is capitalism a transitory stage in the evolution of humankind, with a rise and demise, as suggested by Chase-Dunn and Hall in their comparative study about the ups and downs of entire civilizations over the last 10000 years? Is the contemporary stage of capitalism to be interpreted then within this larger framework?

The second *'Great Transformation'* of our century, that from socialism back to the world-wide market economy, can be seen in the perspective of the specific globalization aspects inherent in the writings of Karl Polanyi: a Polanyian world view would hold, that authoritarian socialism in Eastern Europe crumbled like the old Hapsburg empire back in 1918, under pressure of the world market, that democracy had a chance in the region, as it had from 1918 onwards, but that this new chance, as the one in 1918, is now being at stake. For followers of the globalization school, Polanyi's anthropology in a way foresaw the destabilization, the nationalist warfare, the unemployment, the international conflict, the social decay, and the more than 9 million excess mortality cases since the transformation in the whole of Eastern Europe and the former USSR, as UNDP studies, available on the Internet, so aptly put it. These phenomena also, the argument goes on, imply why in the East the lessons of 'critical' development theory should remain on the agenda. Political turmoil continues in some regions of Eastern Europe and the former USSR more than 10 years after the transformation, and transnational crime from the East and the South has become a very serious negative factor in international relations. In terms of real income growth over time, practically only Poland had up to now a successful transformation from socialism to capitalism, while all the other nations of the East have fallen behind (WERI, 1997). Indeed, it is even plausible that the old big-power rivalries will continue under the new banner of culture and nationalism. Only four of the seventeen countries that adopted democracy during the Kondratieff cycle B-phase between 1915 and 1931 could save democracy; and today, freedom in the world is again on the retreat while violence and repression is on the increase. At the end of 1993, only 57.5%, that is, 107 out of 186 UN member countries had competitive elections and various guarantees of political and human rights (Lipset, 1994: 1).

Small nations in the world economy might find it difficult to get access to bigger markets. That is one of the main themes of dependency theory. Where dependency theory differs from later world system research, is its relative neglect of the role and trajectory of the centers. In Western Europe, unemployment and early retirement rose dramatically, while in the USA there was a considerable withdrawal from the labor force into crime, to be followed today by working poverty and the creation of 13.5 million jobs (Wood, 1994). The institutional greater flexibility of wage labor in the US still allowed for a better employment creation record than in Western Europe, with both major regions of developed capitalism being affected by trans-border migration and a growth of the shadow economy. The South's official exports of manufactures to the developed countries have meanwhile risen to $ 250 thousand million a year, and the developed countries' and East's industrial labor intensive base shrinks rapidly. That there is a new international division of labor seems to be increasingly out of the question. The cumulative effect of the expansion of trade in manufactures and services with the South reduced the demand for unskilled labor in the developed countries and the East relative to skilled labor. In the developed countries, this amounts to a 20 percent reduction in the relative demand for unskilled labor (Wood, 1994). Transnational capital and its tendency to re-deploy the sites of production world-wide is seen by the theories of neo-dependency and international division of labor as the basic underlying cause of the crisis in the developed countries themselves (Froebel et al., 1977-86; Ross and Trachte, 1990; Tausch and Prager, 1993). Wage and personnel side costs in industry per hour in a country like the Federal Republic of Germany *(alte Bundeslaender)* or Sweden exceed those in the United States of America by a ratio of approximately 2:1, those in a country like Turkey by a ratio of 6:1 (Weltalmanach, 1995: 989-990). Automatization, work robots, rationalization and personnel reduction are the answer of capital *vis-à-vis* the high labor costs in industry in some leading industrialized countries.

Neo-dependency and world system schools (which in terms of development theory never reached the originality of dependency approaches, see Tausch and Prager, 1993) would fear, that the most recent tendencies of world capitalism will strongly work against high female employment and create female unemployment, and they would especially expect two hypotheses to hold (i) transnational capital marginalizes female labor power (ii) the dynamics of growth turn away from those countries, where women still have a strong position on the labor market. The measurement scale, compatible with such hypotheses, would be the share of women in total employment and its trade-off with growth rates. The new indicator series, first developed by the UNDP for the UNO-Women-Conference in Beijing 1995, provide a further testing ground for the different feminist social theories of world development.

Our main operationalization of the concept of dependence will consist of MNC penetration, measured by the UNCTAD-time series on the share of inward FDI stock in gross domestic product from 1980 to 1994, and it will also consist of the more traditional indicators of dependency, like terms of trade or trade dependency. The main theoretical expectation of the refined globalization model in the tradition of Cardoso can still be summarized as follows:

(2.10a) **structural imbalance of the development process** (like high polarization of income distribution, insufficient human development, political or human rights violations) = constant + b_1 * **MNC penetration** index + b_2 * **trade dependency** index - b_3 * **terms of trade** index

while 'classic' small state theories and early macroquantitative studies of development in addition would expect:

(2.10b) **economic growth** = constant - b_1 * **MNC penetration** index - b_2 * **trade dependency** index + b_3 * **terms of trade** index

The presentation of the liberal and socio-liberal counterpositions to the dependency approach will be rather condensed: the basic problem of institutional reform in the less developed part of the world economy is the creation of a market economy, based on private property in the framework of democracy. Over recent years, the liberal doctrine challenged the near dominance of globalization-paradigms in international social science that was evident in the late 1970s and the early 1980s. From the viewpoint of critical development thinking, Griffin forcefully presented the points to be conceded to the 'deregulation' perspective recently (Griffin, 1996). Market imperfections in the banking and labor market sectors must be abolished; human capital formation - in short, 'investment in people', must take a priority. Seen in such a way, there is no real contradiction between dependency theory and a socio-liberal model, as Griffin and Tausch/Prager have extensively shown.

First of all, **there is** a certain **structural similarity** between many of the arguments from **dependency theory and liberal development theory,** once you 'translate' one theoretical language into the other and vice versa. As the *Economist* paper put it so aptly on October 26, 1996:

> 'although some investment can be financed by foreign money, high savings rates will be needed to pay for the accumulation of capital and thus to boost growth rates'

For a true liberal economist, dependency is a special situation of the typical constraints, caused by a policy of import substitution and export discrimination. Policies, that create double deficits (huge current account balance deficits + large state sector budget deficits) and discriminate against internal savings, will lead to a high propensity to import foreign capital, often still aided by *de-iure* or *de-facto* policies that prevent enterprise creation and savings mobilization. The growing peripherization of Europe should be mentioned in this context. Neo-classical economists would agree with *'dependentistas'* in their critique of import substitution strategies, and - hence - the discrimination against exports to the benefit of the urban sector and to the detriment of rural society. The basic argument of such a sophisticated version of the neo-liberal school further runs as follows: in world politically stable countries with long recognized international borders, narrow distribution coalitions emerge in the wake of too big a state sector influence, and they will thwart growth perspectives and bring about stagnation and unemployment. High *real* appreciation of the national currency (Poland + 9% 1990-94) declining private savings rates (Poland: 12.4% growth rate of *private consumption),* inadequate investments in the tradable sector, low export growth rates compared to imports, high official *current account balance deficits* per GDP (estimated by some economists to be unsustainable when half the numerical value of the *export growth rate* or bigger), a growing reliance on short-term capital flows and large currency exposures are all too well known to both neo-classical economics and dependency theories alike (Dadush and Brahmbhatt, 1995). Export growth in the European Union 1980-1993 was only 87 percent of import growth (UNDP, 1996).

In addition, the state and its economic activities (EU: central government expenditure per GDP 43 percent, USA: 24 percent) will be most harmful in older democracies due to the unhalted workings of the mechanism of narrow distribution coalitions. For liberals and partially converted neo-Marxists like Griffin alike, double-deficits also are a key towards understanding the distortions on the capital markets. These distortions, the argument goes, are just as important as rigidities on the labor market in blocking economic growth (Griffin, 1996: 146). Measured in terms of central state sector expenditures per total GNP, the average European Union country today is more 'socialist' than most former communist states. Even in the UK, after years of conservative rule, 39.9% of GNP in 1994 was controlled by the central government in London, a figure, which does not include expenditures by government in the broader sense in the municipalities *et cetera*. Thus, the British Government is bigger in relative size to the economy than the government of the Czech Republic, about the size of Poland in 1997, and bigger than the government in Estonia, Belarus, and Croatia (UNDP, 1999). True liberals would not preclude, that distribution coalitions indeed foster situations, where imported capital plays a predominant role in an economy.

What might be politically valid for old democracies like New Zealand or the United States, does not necessarily hold true for a young democracy like Spain after Franco or Poland after the downfall of communism.

Neo-liberal cross-national studies of growth and development tended to conceptualize 'systems age' or 'age of democracy' by the number of years, that a polity enjoyed without changes to the externally recognized borders and in the framework of the establishment of free and competitive elections to the legislative chamber(s) (Weede, 1985-1992). Our operationalization of the concept of system's age is sometimes also the concept of the strength of international distribution coalitions: *'years of United Nations membership of a state'*, to account for the 'internationally recognized' position of a country in the international community. It must be emphasized however, that an interpretation along the lines of Samir Amin's dependency theory is also possible: for Amin, the distinctive feature between the center and the periphery, *inter alia*, is the early development of a bourgeois state. Thus, the power position as a distribution coalition broker in the international system is being measured:

(2.11a) **stagnation** = constant + b_1 * **age of the international post-war system participation** + b_2 * **national state sector influence** (like state sector expenditures per GDP)

or, on a world-scale:

(2.12b) **stagnation** (in the countries of the world system) = constant + b_1 * *chance for distribution coalitions to arise* (years of UN membership) + b_2 * *state sector influence* (like state sector expenditures, **government consumption** per GDP or share of **public investment** per total investment) - (b_3 * **proper internal and external conditions for the defense of democracy** (a firmly entrenched democratic system and a stable integration into the Western security zone)) - b_4 * **cultural preconditions** (like the Huntington Index)

Linnemann and Sarma developed a model, whereby the linkages between external and internal constraints further underline the basic similarity between neo-liberal and dependency approaches. Let **CA** denote the current account balance, NFP net factor payments, NTR net transfers, C consumption, I gross domestic investments, S gross domestic savings, T government revenue, G government expenditure, X, exports, M, imports, **NFA** net foreign assets, **DS** foreign debt, K reserves, L liabilities, let $_{DYN}$ symbolize growth, GDP gross domestic product, GNP gross national product, let the subscript $_g$ denote government, $_p$, the private sector, $_f$ foreign countries, so we have

(2.12c) **CA** = (GDP + NFP + NTR) - (C + I)

(2.12d) **CA** = (C + S) - (C + I)

(2.12e) **CA** = ((C_g + S_g) - (C_g + I_g)) + ((C_p + S_p) - (C_p + I_p))

(2.13f) (T - G) + (S_p - I_p) = (X + NTR + NFP) - (M)

(2.14g) (T - G) + (S_p - I_p) = $_{DYN}$ **NFA**

(2.14h) $_{DYN}$ **DS** = $_{DYN}$ K + L - I_f - **CA**

Privatizing rapidly public enterprises might lead reform countries - given rigidities of supply - even to higher inflation rates, while the effects of the liberalization of prices and the cut-back on government subventions will be only a more short-term improvement in the current account balance. Reconstruction makes necessary investments which by far exceed savings, and hence, the current account balance will deteriorate again.

Ever since the classical political economy of J.S. Mill, socio-liberal reformers have maintained the compatibility of social reform and market economic/capitalist growth. The official social doctrine of the Christian Churches, in Latin America especially the Catholic Church, in some aspects uses similar arguments - from Pope Leo XIII to John Paul II, with liberation theology at any rate advancing the viewpoint of non-violent salvation and liberation, justice and community (Brackley SJ, 1996: 117). In a world, where structural adjustment, Maastricht and other similar concepts dominate the scholarly horizon, at least in the West, liberation theology, with its emphasis on the two millenia old beatitudes of the Sermon of the Mount, on *Yahweh*, the God of the poor, and the Hebrew concepts of *hendiadys* (steadfast living-kindness) and *sedeq* (justice for the oppressed) turns development theory on its head (Brackley SJ, 1996: 129). The rich literature of liberation theology draws parallels between the LDCs today and landlessness, debt, unemployment, heavy taxes, hunger and malnutrition suffered by the mass of the people in Galilee two thousand years ago. It is a conscious effort at re-discovering the social commitment of these traditions; non-violent protest movements, that empower *people*, are certainly corresponding to the spirit of liberation theology and the Judeo-Christian gospel (Brackley, 1996: 153-155). The Catholic Church *magisterium* (official teaching) has been more in line with traditional, 'top' to 'bottom' visions of the state and of organizations as actors, delivering and inter-mediating goods and services *in favor* of the poor, although Vatican pronouncements were also very frank and forwardlooking in defending landless laborers and the poor in general (see especially John Paul II, 1988, 1991a and 1991b).

Already in his famous macro-economic model, Nicholas Kaldor explained the conditions of growth of a capitalist economy in the postwar-period: mass demand. If mass demand is seriously undermined by the process of globalization, we are back to the long-term stagnation traps of 19th Century capitalism. Let total product Y be the sum of wages, W, and profits, P, let there be the identity between savings and investments, I = S, and let us divide the savings rate S into savings out of workers' incomes and out of profits, and let savings of workers Sw be proportional to wages and savings of profit income recipients Sp be proportional to profits, we arrive at the final, but still tautological formulation, that profits are a function of investments:

(2.13) Y = W + P

(2.14) I = S

(2.15) S = Sw + Sp

(2.16) Sw = sw * W

(2.17) Sp = sp * P

(2.18) P/Y = f (I/Y)

At given propensities to save out of profits and wages, the profit rate is a function of investments. On the way to a model of the real economy in the postwar period, Kaldor now says, that real wages have to be above subsistence wages, the profit rate must not fall below a certain minimum, the share of profits is institutionally determined at least at a certain minimum, and the capital output ratio must not be influenced by the profit rate. Only these conditions, Kaldor thinks, assure that the clear causal relationship between investment and profits holds. Else, especially, when wages fall down to the subsistence level, the Keynesian mechanism to guarantee full employment will not be in force anymore, output will be limited by available capital, and not by labor, and finally, the classic and not the Keynesian adjustment mechanism will be in operation: the surplus, available for investment, determines investments, and not investments savings.

Capitalism must have a long-term interest in wages in order to survive. This is also the reason, why, of lately, there is a growing concern in the international press about the effects of globalization on mass demand. There are common denominators for a reform-oriented social policy program: a leading variable, of interest to this school, will be social security benefits expenditures per GDP in the contemporary period. The social insurance program experience index measures the social security experience of a nation during the earlier Kondratieff cycle as a precondition for contemporary growth.

Some authors in the tradition of this 'social policy approach', summarized in a statement by Nancy Birdsall from the World Bank before the delegates of the Social Committee, UN General

Assembly, October 19th, 1992, would also expect a very strong negative relationship between development performance and population growth. Throughout his academic and political life, Myrdal emphasized this point of development theory, thought to be so important for the structure of labor markets, income distribution, and economic growth. Apart from that, human capital formation and the patterns of human ecology and the use of scarce natural resources, all connected with the population issue, are of relevance for this approach (Tausch and Prager, 1993). The anti-natalist view, however, is not shared by the mainstream of Catholic social reform thinking.

The liberal corporatist school, an important sub-school, which draws its experience from the post-war development of countries like Sweden or Austria, treats the combination of world economic openness (trade dependency index) with a democratic political regime (for example a low index of violations of civil and political rights) as an ideal mix, conducive towards political compromise and a partial alliance between capital, wage labor and the state. It expects positive trade-offs between world economic openness, democracy and social policy on the one hand and economic and social performance on the other hand. Katzenstein was most prominent to formulate such a theory (1984); others, most notably Schmidt, 1986, and Munoz, 1982, followed suit. According to the social policy approach, markets always need the element of existing and functioning social safety nets. Rent seeking is a reality, but it is a process that in the end redistributes incomes upwards and wastes economic resources. By concentrating social policy on the real needy and poor sectors of society, an impetus can be created to cut government expenditures in other areas.

By way of summary, a social and ecological reform theory would expect at least:

(2.4) **pace and level of development** = constant - b_1 * **increase** of **fertility** rates 1960-90 (UNDP, 1993/94) + b_2 * **social insurance program experience index** (or **social security benefits** expenditures as % of GDP) + b_3 * **share of women in the membership of national legislature or other measures of gender development** - b_4 * **total fertility rate** - b_5 * **share of richest 20% in total incomes** + b_6 * **trade dependency index**

3) THE INTERNATIONAL ENVIRONMENT IS BASICALLY UNSTABLE. A SURVEY OF THE CONTEMPORARY RESEARCH METHODS FOR THE STUDY OF INTERNATIONAL SOCIAL POLICY SINCE 1989

International social science since the mid-1960s studied patterns of international social policy in a cross-national perspective. This movement towards retrievability of research results, based on statistical analysis with internationally available and recognized data, which was initiated, amongst others, by the late Karl Wolfgang Deutsch from Harvard University, had important implications for international social policy. It allowed for the rigorous testing of hypotheses, contested in the political arena in an often passionate fashion.

The methodological innovation of this introductory and study textbook is mainly the combination of cross-national development research with research about cyclical trends in the world economy. Cyclical trends in the world economy are certainly not absent from a very long tradition of scholarship in political economy, beginning with Kuznets and Schumpeter. The very logic of industrial processes and basic innovations, as well as the societal models, connected with them, would suggest to build cyclical fluctuations into more general theories of development (Amin, 1997). Blast furnaces and other important components of the industrial process, too, have a certain life-cycle, comparable with the Juglar and Kuznets cycle, just as technical innovations are scattered in a non-random fashion along time, coinciding with the Kondratieff cycle (Bornschier, 1988; for a very comprehensive summary Scandella, 1998). There are, as we already said, short term instabilities of 3 to 5 years (Kitchin cycles), 8-11 years (Juglar cycles), 18-22 years (Kuznets cycles), and longer, 40-60 year Kondratieff waves. The following dating scheme could be suggested in the light of the Schumpeterian theory tradition (Scandella, 1998). Global capitalism since 1740 has the following Kuznets cycles:

1741-1756; R^2 = 23. 5%
1756-1774; R^2 = 36. 1%
1774-1793; R^2 = 34. 8%
1793-1812; R^2 = 39. 7%
1812-1832; R^2 = 16. 4%   *1. Kondratieff*
1832-1862; R^2 = 25. 7%
1862-1885; R^2 = 36. 3%   **2. Kondratieff**
1885-1908; R^2 = 56. 2%
1908-1932; R^2 = 44. 2%   *3. Kondratieff*
1932-1958; R^2 = 19. 1%
1958-1975; R^2 = 68. 8%   *4. Kondratieff*
1975-1992; R^2 = 66.2%   *5. Kondratieff*

Our attempt to estimate the determinants of world economic and social development **from 1980 onwards** tries to be based in this tradition. The UNDP Human Development Reports, our main new data source, emerged over the years as one of the leading socially relevant data collections for cross-national research; the wealth of data contained in them shows concern for the global environment and for social decay and by far exceeds in quality other comparable products on the market today. The choice of the time period corresponds to the Kondratieff-type long cycle theories, that are presented below.

Our data sources for the study of this latest phase in the evolution of transnational capitalism relied at least in part also on Fischer Weltalmanach; Nohlen; Seager and Olson and Stiftung Entwicklung und Frieden, which are excellent data handbooks for the study of international relations. Some data were also cross-checked with Tausch, 1993, 1994; UNECE; UNICEF (Cornia, 1993 and 1994); and the World Bank *WDR* and other sources. Our main sample of 123 nations comprised all the countries for which the UNDP reports economic growth rates and life expectancies at two different periods. The countries of the ex-USSR are not being included for reasons of data limitations, while other 'real socialist' or ex-'real socialist' nations, like China and Hungary, at any rate integral parts of the conceptualizations of the capitalist world economy today, do form part of our investigation.

Our leading, but not exclusive indicator of the process of dependence and globalization is the UNCTAD version for the old MNC (multinational corporation) penetration indicator of a country in the present Kondratieff-cycle. The MNC-penetration-concept was first contained in the very widely used publication by Bornschier and Heintz, reworked and enlarged by Ballmer-Cao and Scheidegger, later on widely popularized by the book publication Bornschier/Chase Dunn, 1985, and used throughout the world in quantitative research. Their emphasis then was on MNC investments, 1967 and 1973, weighted by population and total capital stock. The UNCTAD MNC penetration indicator based on the concept of the share of FDI stock is defined in terms of total host-country GDP.

The more dependent a country is in the system of the world-wide market economy, the greater will be the penetration of its economy by transnational capital. Dependency theories (Cardoso/Faletto, 1971) hold, that the countries of the periphery were integrated into the world-economy in the following sequence of events:

(i)   *desarrollo hacia exterior* (development to the outside)
(ii)   *desarrollo hacia adentro* (inward-looking development)
(iii)   *transnacionalizacion de los mercados internos* (internationalization of the internal markets)

Starting from the late 1950s, the transnational system increasingly dominates the industrialization process of the periphery and the semi-periphery (phase iii). The penetration of the host countries by transnational investment becomes the most important scientific yardstick of dependency (Bornschier/Chase-Dunn, 1985).

To these phases in the evolution of the international division of labor, one would have to add:

(iv)   financial capitalism and globalization

as the latest stage of center-periphery relationships during the 1980s and 1990s.

Cycle time plays an important role in our approach. Above, we already hinted at Arrighi's thought, that the logic of accumulation on a world scale shifts along time, and that we again witness during the 1980s and beyond a deregulated phase of world capitalism with a logic, characterized - in contrast to earlier regulatory cycles - by the dominance of financial capital. Arrighi further teaches us that even a century can be a 'short run' in the evolution of world capitalism. There are *signal crises* of world capitalism, and there are *terminal crises* of the world system, like the great crash of the early 1340s, which marked the beginning of the Genoese age, the 1560s, which marked the beginning of the Dutch era, the 1750s and 1760s, which marked the beginning of the British era, and the 1930s, which were the terminal crisis of British world capitalist dominance. Regulation can be successful, like after 1560, and 1930, and deregulation can be successful, like after 1340, 1760, and - most probably - the 1980s (compiled from Arrighi, 1995). Macroquantitative research about the determinants of world development has to be conscious about the time horizon, in which the research design is situated. Bornschier (1988) found out that state sector expenditures in 21 western democracies correlate with economic growth in the following fashion:

1950-60 $r = + .41$
1960-75 $r = - .07$
1974-77 $r = - .72$

(Bornschier, 1988: 309)

For the period 1980-93, the correlation was:

1980-93 $r = -.02$

(our own calculation from UNDP, HDR, 1997 (growth rate of GNP); World Resources Institute (state sector size, around 1980); cross-checked with Fischer Weltalmanach, 1998 (state sector). In the world of transformation (nine countries with complete data on state sector size (UNDP, 1997) and economic growth (Economist, The World in 1998; Fischer Weltalmanach, 1998), the best fit between central state sector size and growth was $y = 0,0034x^3 - 0,3334x^2 + 10,388x - 99,014; R^2 = 0.3227$)

Thus, the growth efficiency of public expenditures has drastically declined over the 1970s, to be indecisive today. If the post-war period was regulatory, the post-1968 period was decidedly anti-regulatory, to achieve a level of non-determination today (Arrighi, 1995; Bornschier, 1988). Studies about world development throughout the entire period 1960 - 1998 might be misleading, because the time period would reflect the 'logic' of the waning 'regulatory' cycle, the economic global crisis of the 1970s and the early 1980s, and the ascent of financial capitalism and the East Asian archipelago of the early 1990s, which today might have reached its first limits. Thus, the beginning of the 1980s serve as our 'cutting point'.

The long cycle literature, largely overlooked by macroquantitative development studies, tells us, why there is a recurrent pattern of instability in the social orders both at the level of national society as well as at the level of the international system. It also explains the often puzzling aspect, how different studies, using different time perspectives, reach different results. Long cycles, to be explained by at least 13 different types of theories, by themselves are quite a strong argument in the debate about the long-run viability of the world-wide market economy: the recurrence of cycles, depressions and wars was thematically portrayed, amongst others, by Scandella (1998), Goldstein (1988), Bornschier and Suter (1992), Bornschier (1988, expanded and updated English version 1996) and Arrighi (1995).

The intense controversy about cycles should only be mentioned briefly here; for the policy-maker perhaps more important is the fact, that after the economic crisis of 1825, the stock exchange collapse of 1873, the Black Friday of 1929 and the world recession starting in 1973/75, world capitalism has experienced quite severe downswing-phases, that hit with elementary weight especially the countries of the periphery and the semi-periphery. The *Kondratieff cycles* of approximately *40-60 years duration* and the Kuznets cycles, 18-22 years long, are especially relevant for our understanding of the ups and downs of world economics and politics: our data series, constructed from Goldstein's original data, is explained quite markedly by the application of the Kondratieff and Kuznets-cycle hypotheses, even when there are no data filtering or smoothening operations being performed. And thus, we have to disagree in one fundamental aspect with Chase-Dunn and Grimes, 1995: Kondratieffs exist, especially when you filter out the very short-term Kitchin cycle. And add to this the lagged movement of world prices and interest rates, which are part and parcel of the cycle structure (Scandella, 1998). Among the main theories, that explain these Kondratieff cycles, the following schools stand out (Bornschier and Suter, 1992):

(i)   economic factor theories, that again have to be broken down into the sub-categories of innovation theories, capital accumulation theories, sector theories, and terms of trade approaches

(ii)   socio-cultural factor theories, that explain from the viewpoint of quantitative and historical sociology the long cycles by the social structure of accumulation, by the modes of regulation (regulatory approaches), by technological styles, by employment processes, by social inequality trends, by social movements and conflicts, by cycles of order, or by societal structural change

(iii)   hegemonic cycle theories in the quantitative international relations school, that link Kondratieff cycles to international instability, war and peace.

For Bornschier's sociology of the long cycle, there are the following phases

(i)   upswing
(ii)   prosperity
(iii)   prosperity-recession
(iv)   crisis
(v)   temporary recovery
(vi)   depression

The question is not to choose between Kondratieff and Kuznets cycles. The research strategy should integrate these two concepts by properly applying more long-term moving averages that filter the shorter-term fluctuations. Our starting point are the two well-known data series on industrial production growth in the world economy 1740-1975 by J. Goldstein (1988):

Let X_{tn+1} be the index value of world production for $tn+1$; X_{tn} index value of world production for tn

$$(3.1.1) \% DYN = \frac{X_{tn+1}}{X_{tn}} - 1$$

Post-1975 data on OECD country economic growth: UN ECE; Fischer Weltalmanach, see Tausch, 1994. X is the time axis. Pre-1975 data are world industrial product growth estimates.

The approximately 20-year Kuznets cycles, that emerge from Goldstein's data, can be neatly shown by 6th-order polynomial regression estimates, based on the above described data series (see above). Now we update the evidence, that led Goldstein to the conclusion that the capitalist world systems tends continuously towards wars and violent conflicts. The international system is characterized according to him by

global war → world hegemony of the dominant power → de-legitimization of the international order → de-concentration of the global system → global war *et cetera*

The duration of these phases of the international order is approximately one Kondratieff cycle, so the unit of time of the international system can be symbolized by the expression 1_K.

Graph 3.1: the tendencies of the capitalist world economy towards Kondratieff cycles

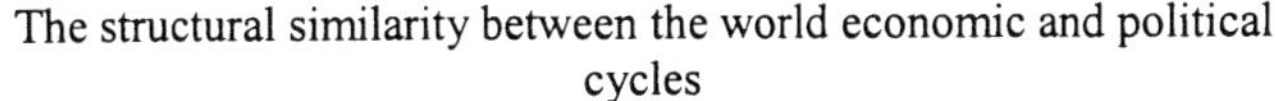

The structural similarity between the world economic and political cycles

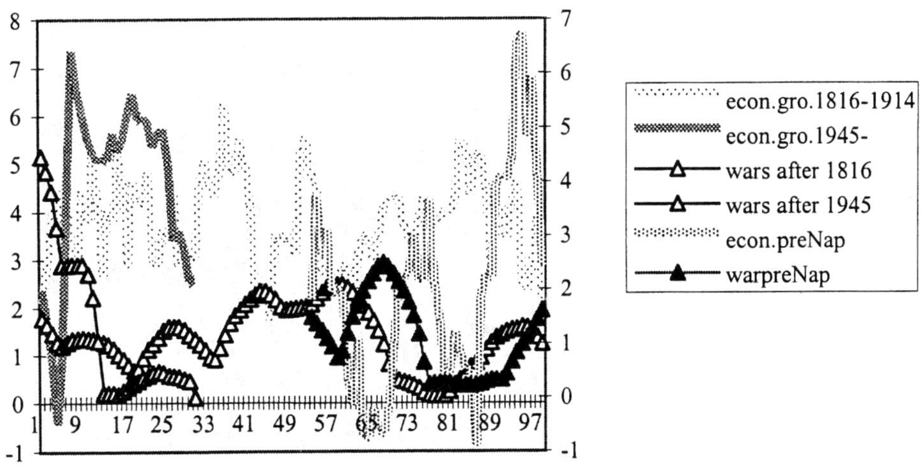

Economic growth (left hand scale) and war intensity (right-hand scale) in the world economy. Moving 9-year averages, calculated with EXCEL 5.0 from Goldstein's original data.

The tendency towards war in the capitalist world economy, 1495-1975

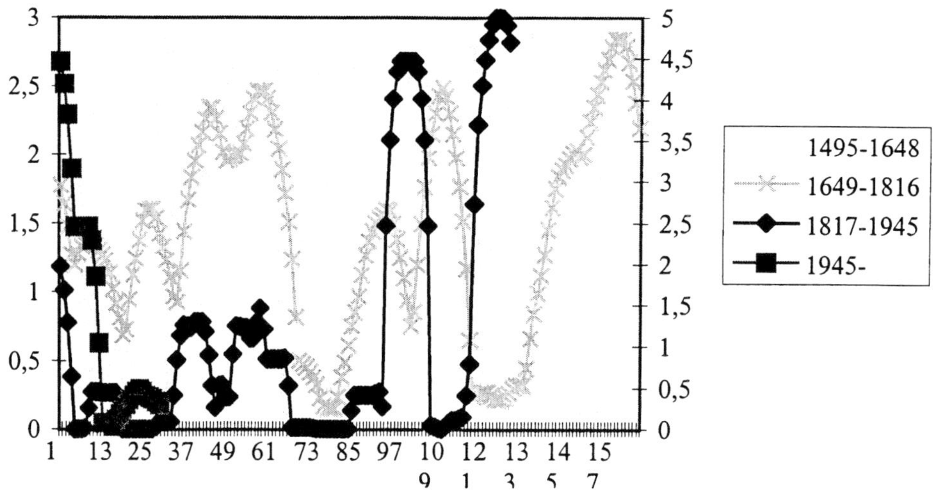

War intensity = Nat. logarithm from (1 + battle fatalities from great-power wars $^{0.10}$)

At a time of major shifts in world politics and economics, it is no wonder that systematic studies in the evolution of the international order have gained ground. Arrighi's main hypotheses (1995) differ from those of Goldstein. Goldstein's quantitative approach (1988 ff.) concentrates on the major power confrontations as the 'watershed' in international relations. Ample empirical evidence supports both Arrighi's and Goldstein's theories. The recurrence of major power wars in the capitalist world economy from 1495 to the present is one of the most intriguing features of the international system. Each world political cycle up to now corresponded to a '*W*'-pattern of untransformed annual battle fatalities from major power wars in thousands. The war cycle 1495-1648 is a polynomial expression of the 6th order; R^2 is 91.7%; 1649-1816 yields an R^2 of 33.6%; while a polynomial expression of the 6th order explains 50.1% of war intensity 1817-1945. The x-axis in our graph is the number of years after the end of the major power wars, i.e. 1648, 1816, and 1945. The same, deadly function explains 49.5% of annual battle fatalities in thousands from 1946 to 1975.

The starting point to our analysis of Kondratieff cycles is Goldstein's untransformed data series about economic growth since 1740. Since 1975, we used UN ECE Economic Survey of Europe, IFRI data (world GDP growth) and IMF World Economic Outlook data (for OECD country growth as a proxy for world development):

Graph 3.2: Kondratieff cycles, based on *9 year moving averages*

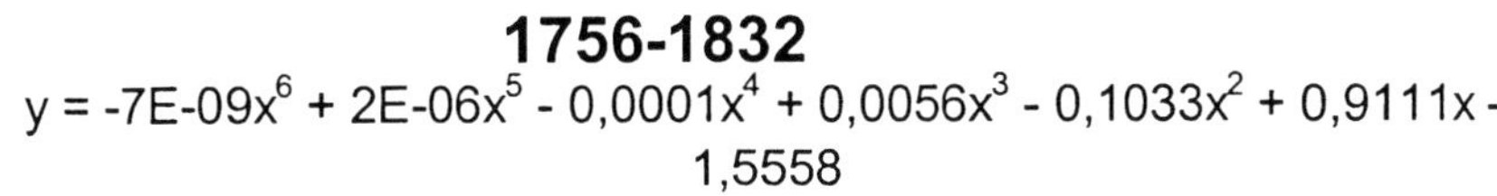

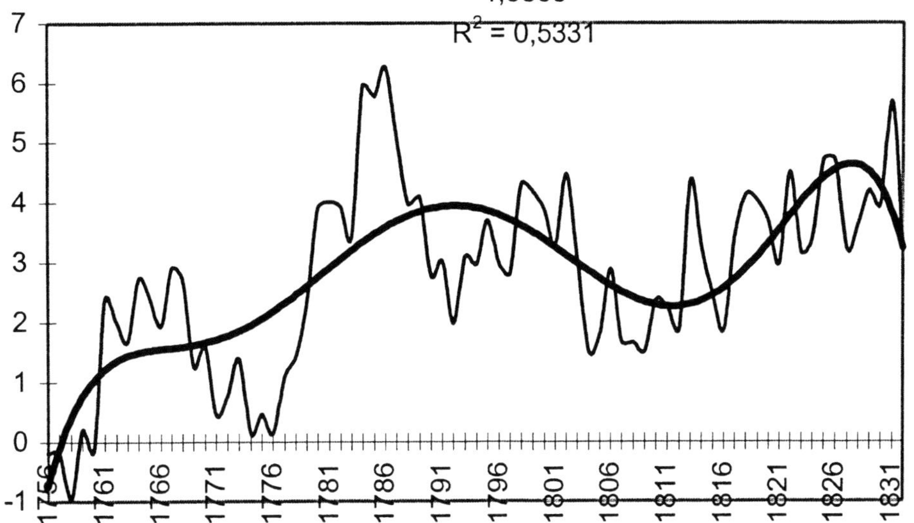

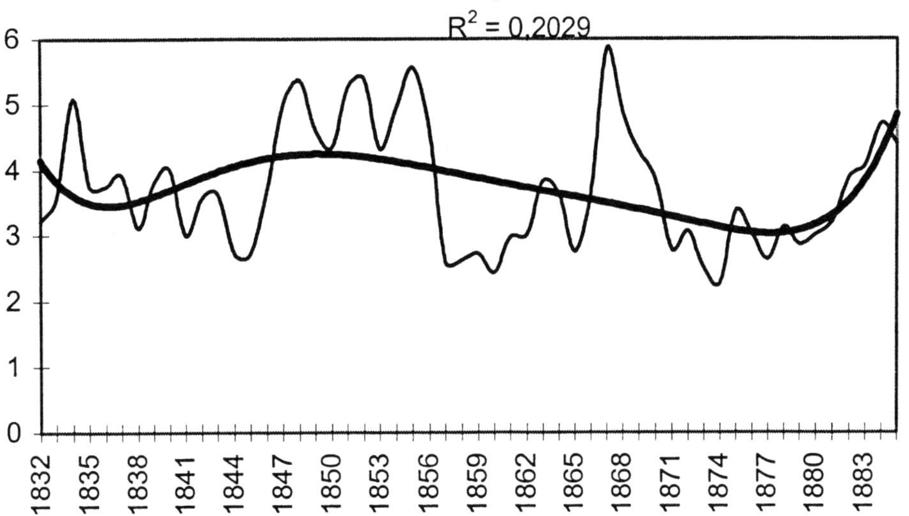

1885-1932

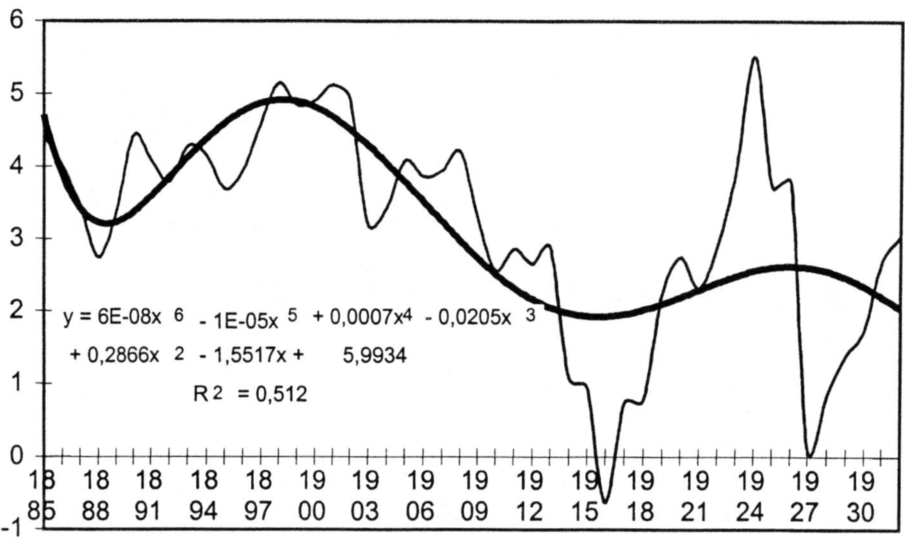

1932-1982

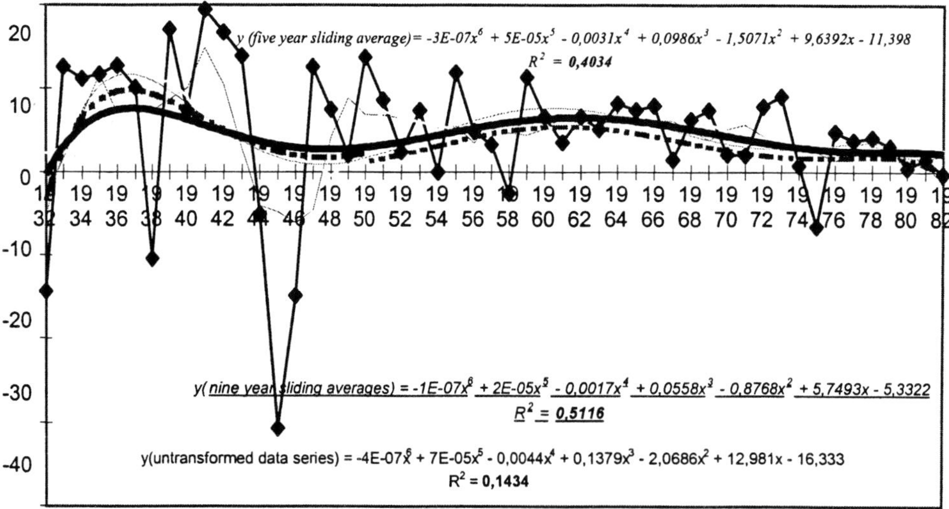

Legend: economic growth rates in the world system, as being estimated from Goldstein's data series

If we let the postwar-cycle end with 1975, the functions have the following shape:

1932 - 1975

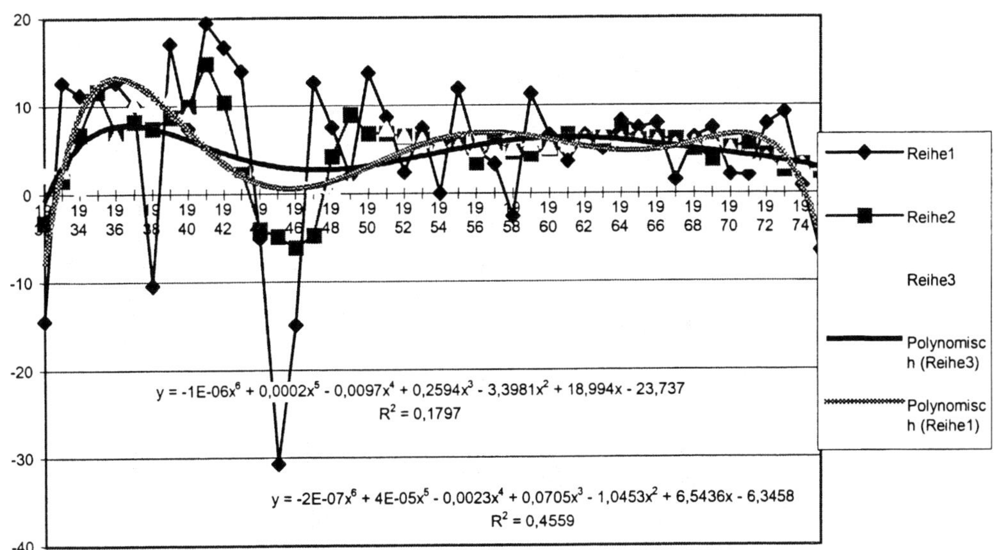

Legend: data about the severity of the depression in 1975 differ according to the data source used.

The stylized Kondratieff-function could have the following form:

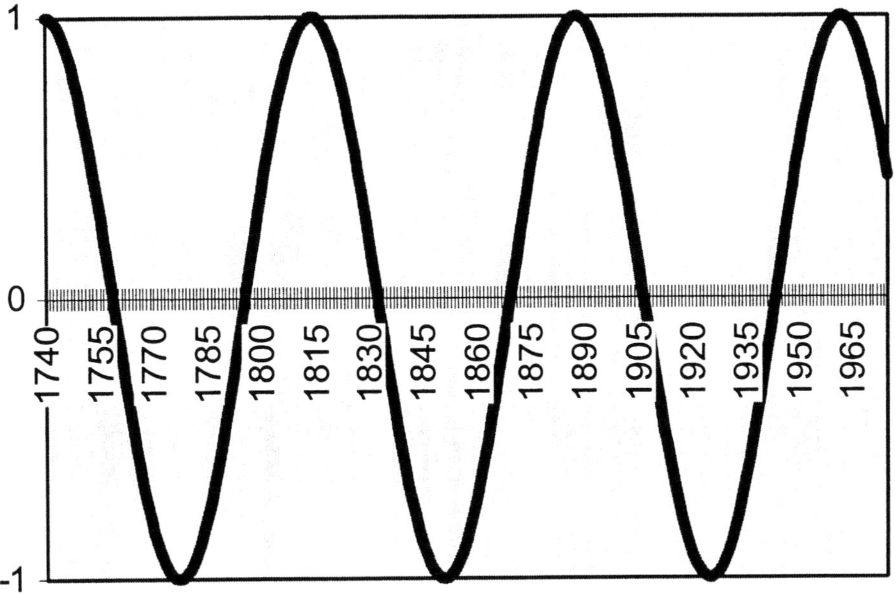

Source: our own compilations, using a cosine function (1740 = 0; 1741 = 0,85; 1742 = 0,85 + 0,85 etc.). Economic growth in the world system since 1740; adapted from Goldstein, 1988 and UN ECE/Fischer Weltalmanach, current issues. 5 and 10-year moving averages and the trend lines for these two data series

In his new overview of Kondratieff cycle theories, Luigi Scandella re-interprets economic theories, like the Phillips curve and the Fisher equation, in the light of the long-cycle literature and arrives at the conclusion, that **price levels** and **interest rates** fluctuate as well in the above described way, with a time-lag of 5 to 10 years between production and price levels and again between price levels and interest rates. Thus the way is open for important further empirical research, since historic price level data are far more complete than historic production data.

Throughout this work, the following statements hold:

> Regression coefficients at the level of error probability < or = 5% are printed in **bold** type. The following further conditions do hold:

> Concepts: growth always refers to per capita income growth in real terms, if not specified otherwise

> Time period: 1980s and beyond (if not specified otherwise)

> Missing values: **mean substitution**, if possible, by known values for the economic or geographic region (like: countries with low human development, excluding India *et cetera)*

It should be explained here, what is meant under the term 'structural adjustment': the empirical measurement (and not normative concept) of adjustment compares the GNP per capita growth rates in two subsequent periods with a regression-based residual analysis. In other words: we try to answer the empirical, and not normative question, which countries accelerated economic growth compared to the earlier cycle, and which countries adapted badly to the new conditions. Our measurement concept compares growth rates predicted for the period of the new Kondratieff cycle (post 1980/82)$(^\wedge Y_i)$ upon knowledge of the performance during the earlier Kondratieff B-phase (1965-80) with the actual growth rates Y_i during the new Kondratieff cycle from 1980/82 onwards:

$$(3.2a)\ \textbf{adjustment}_{i} = Y_{i_{tn}} - {}^{\wedge}Y_{i_{tn}}$$
$$Y = \text{economic growth}$$
$$Y_{tn} = a + b_1 * Y_{tn\text{-}1}$$

Changes in the underlying logic of ascent and decline in the world economy will be especially observable at a time of comparison between the logic of a waning Kondratieff cycle and the emerging laws of a new cycle. Thus, adjustment will be a theoretically especially relevant phenomenon.

Next, we should deal with the trade-off between development level and performance. Policy planning must, in order to avoid spurious results, under any circumstances properly specify such trade-offs. Poor countries increase rapidly their average life-expectancy or economic growth and they quickly reduce their income inequality; *prima vista* there will be a spurious and very high, but absolute non-sense correlation between, say, the number of shanty-town dwellers per total population and life expectancy increases. The reduction of the infant mortality rate, the acceleration of growth or the redistribution of income over time will all dramatically and positively be influenced by the number of people still living in shanty towns. If we do not properly specify development level as an intervening variable, our results will be biased extremely.

The curve-linear function of growth, being regressed on the natural logarithm of development level and its square, is sometimes called the *'Matthew's effect'* following Matthew's (13, 12):

'For whosoever hath, to him shall be given, and he shall have more abundance: but whosoever hath not, for him shall be taken away even that he hath'

Social scientists interpreted this effect mainly in view of an acceleration of economic growth in middle-income countries *vis-à-vis* the poor countries and in view of the still widening gap between the poorest periphery nations *('have-nots')* and the *'haves'* among the former Second and Third World (Jackman, 1982):

(3.2b) economic growth/adjustment success $= a_1 + b_1 * \ln (PCI_{tn-1})\text{-}b_2 * (\ln(PCI_{tn-1}))^2$

The same function is also applied to income inequality, following a famous essay published by S. Kuznets in 1955. Redistribution gets underway after 1000 $ per capita income is reached; the share of the richest 20% diminishes from approximately 55% to around 40%. Growth and adjustment accelerate with redistribution. In general terms, we explain development performance by the following standard multiple cross-national development research equations:

(3.2c) **development performance** $_{\text{1980-mid 1990s}}$ $= a_1 + b_1 *$first part curvilinear function of development level $_{\text{by around 1980}}$ - $b_2 *$second part curvilinear function of development level $_{\text{by around 1980}}$ - $b_3... *$**MNC penetration** (UNCTAD) and other dependency indicators $_{\text{mid 1980s}}$ - $b_4... *$state sector influence indicators$_{\text{mid 1980s}}$ + $b_5... *$social reform indicators $_{\text{mid 1980s}}$ - $b_6... *$ distribution coalition prone environment indicators$_{\text{mid 1980s}}$ + $b_7... *$political feminism indicators $_{\text{mid 1980s}}$

In each of the 19 equations, MNC penetration forms part and parcel of the predictor variables. In addition, our growth equation (GNP per capita income growth in real terms) starts from the following predictors:

(3.2d) growth $= a_1 + b_1 * \ln (PCI_{tn-1}) - b_2 * (\ln(PCI_{tn-1}))^2 - b_3 *$MNC penetration (UNCTAD) $_{\text{mid 1980s}}$ + $b_4 *$social security expenditures per GDP$_{\text{mid 1980s}}$ - $b_5 *$fertility rate $_{\text{mid 1980s}}$ - $b_6 *$ UN membership years + $b_7 * \%$women in parliament $_{\text{mid 1980s}}$ + $b_8 *$female share of the labor force $_{\text{mid 1980s}}$ - $b_9 *$trade dependency $_{\text{mid 1980s}}$ - $b_{10} *$military personnel rate $_{\text{mid 1980s}}$ - $b_{11} *$state sector expenditures $_{\text{mid 1980s}}$

Reformists would hold that social security expenditures, women in parliament, and female employment, together with low fertility rates, are indicators of social reform, while liberals would clearly interpret UN membership years as enhancing the existence of distribution coalitions, while military personnel and state sector expenditures are to be interpreted as indicators of a strong state sector influence. In our equations, adjustment, ethno-warfare, gender development, gender empowerment, growth, human development, human rights violations, labor force participation, mean years of education, political rights violations, and the UNDP-CPM-poverty measure are all explained by an equation, analogue to 3.2d. For the equations determining forest coverage, deforestation rates, and the destabilization/war indicator we had to add '% of land area used by agriculture' as an additional control variable in order to take abundance or scarcity of agricultural land and its influences on development into account.

Now, we should turn to basic human needs satisfaction and hence, life expectancy: it is very difficult to arrive at valid propositions about social conditions and development as a dependent variable on the basis of income distribution data alone. There are comparable World Bank income distribution data for only 65 countries, while basic human needs satisfaction data are available from many more countries. Studies about the determinants of basic human needs satisfaction, and hence, poverty were written in the 1990s (Stokes and Andreson, 1990; Tausch and Prager, 1993; furthermore: Moon and Dixon, 1992; Ragin and Bradshaw, 1992, just to mention a few). The idea to link life expectancy to energy consumption levels or dollar income levels, that is to say, to patterns of civilization, that exploit mother earth and lead to the self-destruction of life chances of the human species, is still somewhat revolutionary, although there has been quite an extensive debate among different researchers from the ILO, the World Bank and other researcher institutions, most notably Goldstein, 1985b and Russett, 1983b, on the proper specification of the development-basic-human-needs trade-off. Among the decision makers of our time, US vice-president Gore formulated such 'green' philosophical apprehensions in the most stringent fashion (Gore, 1994). It is difficult to design a single indicator of the civilisational *malaise* constituted by the environmental crisis caused by the industrial mode of production. But the energy consumption-life expectancy trade-off offers a very clear, mathematical expression. The prime success measure of a society should be, how much energy can be saved in achieving a given quantity of life of the population and to avoid premature death. The limited resources of our planet, so clearly foreseen by Polanyi, dictate, that as little as possible energy is being used. The social demands and moral convictions of civilizations dictate, that premature death should be avoided. Thus, eco-social reasoning taking into account the performance scores of the energy consumption-life expectancy trade-off would hold, that the energy consumption of a society should be minimized and life expectancy maximized. One formulation of this position, reported in Tausch and Prager, 1993, that contains a reference to the extensive earlier debate at the World Bank and at the ILO, arrived at the conclusion that using very common deviates of the natural constants e (2.7) and π (3.14159...) reproduce this important trade-off in an optimal fashion, although most other published mathematical formulations boil down to similar strong curve-linear functions. It is also imperative to consider the effect of already achieved levels of life expectancy on the subsequent life expectancy increase: a poor society with, say, 40 years life expectancy will find it easier to expand the well-being of the population to 50 years average life expectancy than a society that already reached the level of a 75 year-average.

To avoid problems of collinearity, increases in life expectancy over time are being calculated by differences in logarithms 10, *i.e.*

$$(3.3)\ \text{DYN LEX} = ((\log_{10}(\text{LEX}_{tn}) - \log_{10}(\text{LEX}_{tn-1})) * 100$$

Let *LEX* denote life expectancy or other basic human needs indicators, *PCI* per capita incomes, *ENCONS p.c.* energy consumption rates per capita and year in kg oil equivalent, and *DYN* rates of increases of basic human needs satisfaction. On a world scale and for different groups of countries, levels of human development and increases in terms of human development, reductions in infant mortality *et cetera* will always **significantly** correspond to the following function and the first derivative:

$$(3.4)\ \text{LEX} = a + b_1 * (\text{ENCONS p.c.})^{(1/(e^2))} - b_2 * (\text{ENCONS p.c.})^{\ln(\pi)}$$

$R^2 = 72.4\%$; $F = 157.63$; $df. = 120$; α (one-tailed) $5\% > 1.289$

$$(3.5)\ \text{DYN LEX}_{(tn)} = a - b_1 * \text{LEX}_{(tn-1)}\ +-$$

$$b_2 * (\text{PCI})_{(tn-1)}^{((1/(e^2))-1)} - b_3 * (\text{PCI})_{(tn-1)}^{((\ln(\pi))-1)}$$

$R^2 = 69.8\%$; $F = 91.85$; $df. = 120$; α (one-tailed) $5\% > 1.289$

predictors b_2 and b_3 only: $R^2 = 43.3\%$; $F = 45.89$; $df. = 120$; α (one-tailed) $5\% > 1.289$. Formulation also possible with ENCONS p.c., but the PCI data series is more complete

Based on UNDP (1993) data for all the countries that report economic growth rates for the periods 1965-80-90, equation (3.4) explains 72.4% of total variance of life expectancy; equation

(3.5) - even without life expectancy in 1960 as an additional control variable - explains 45.9% of total variance.

Equation (3.2) can also be applied to human development, the world gender issues and democratization:

(3.6a) human development or gender development or gender empowerment = a_1 - b_1* ln (PCI_{tn-1}) + b_2* $(\ln(PCI_{tn-1}))^2$

or

(3.6b) political rights violations or civil rights violations = a_1 + b_1* ln (PCI_{tn}) - b_2* $(\ln(PCI_{tn}))^2$

Human development, and the growing participation of women in society, are a clearly rising function of achieved development level, while political and civil rights violations decrease along the course of development. No result is weaker than roughly 2/5 of variance explained; and all results show - *per se* - an optimistic perspective for human development, gender justice and democratization: the human development index, the gender development index, the gender empowerment index (ranging from 0.0 to 0.999 each), political rights violations and civil rights violations (ranging from 1.0 to 7.0) are all to be represented as a function of achieved development level in 1990 (expressed in purchasing power parity rate). For the calculation of the gender empowerment (GEI) function, the following procedure to estimate missing data was followed: means of country groups with available data were taken to substitute missing values. The following groups were used: industrial countries (UNDP definition, 1993; GEI = 0.56); developing countries with a higher human development index (UNDP 1993 list - Barbados through to Saint Lucia; GEI = 0.391); developing countries with medium human development (UNDP 1993 list - Turkey through to El Salvador; GEI = 0.347); developing countries with low human development (UNDP 1993 list - Maldives through to Sierra Leone; GEI = 0.27). The following statistical properties of the functions hold:

human development index	R^2 = 82.4%; F = 281.0
gender development index	R^2 = 80.1%; F = 240.8
gender empowerment index	R^2 = 60.0%; F = 90.0
political rights violations	R^2 = 38.0%; F = 36.8
civil rights violation	R^2 = 40.0%; F = 39.9

(3.6a) might be formulated, however, by function (3.6b), applying model (3.4). The function is:

(3.6b) Human Development Index = a + b_1 * (real purchasing power p.c.)$^{(1/(e^2))}$ - b_2 * (real purchasing power p.c.)$^{\ln(\pi)}$

The income inequality equation starts out from the well known Kuznets-curve, and uses militarization and fertility as additional control variables.

4) TNC DEPENDENCE IS CAUSING LONG-TERM STAGNATION

Following equation 3.2c and 3.2d we now establish for 19 development indicators, that TNC-dominated development pressures societies towards higher income inequality, and less development. Women, especially, become marginalized, a trend, which is still enhanced by the growing tendency towards a new international division of labor. In Europe, where the legacy of politically established feminism is still relatively strong, state expenditures are being used to redress the balance, but the struggle is an uphill one against the tendencies of contemporary globalization. Feminism will become over the years the big loser in the redistribution of world political and economic resources.

High MNC penetration becomes one of the main blocks against further long-term ascent in the world economy, spurts of short-term growth notwithstanding (see also Chapter 2). We have already stated, that for a true liberal economist, dependency is a special situation of the typical constraints, caused by a policy of import substitution and export discrimination. Policies, that create double deficits (huge current account balance deficit + large state sector budget deficits) and discriminate against internal savings, will lead to a high propensity to import foreign capital.

Neo-classical and of course *dependencia* theorists would admit, that gender discrimination is a typical violation of the assumptions of a functioning market economy. The neo-classical remedy would consist in creating better market access for the underprivileged groups. Without question, the gender issue is one of the most typical instances of such a market imperfection under 'capitalism'. The solution, especially in Europe, has been to remedy this imperfection with huge programs of state expenditures. But state expenditures in excess of revenues, together with a deficit in the balance on the current account, are a good receipt for increasing the share of foreign capital in the national economy. The *circle* continues.

Government consumption in the EU was 19% already in 1992, and will still increase with the eastward expansion of the Union and the rising unemployment problem. Tax revenue was on average only 38% of GNP - in contrast to the 50.9% of GNP, spent by the national government. EU-imports were 23% of GNP, while EU-exports only 22% of EU-GNP. By 1992, the average deficit per EU-GNP was 10%. In such a situation, the inflow of foreign capital, including that of dubious legality, will become an economic necessity. Indirect taxes play an overwhelming role in European finances, and indirect taxes are a growth-inhibiting structure of their own (Tausch/Prager, 1993). By the beginnings of the 1990s, the penetration of MNC in the European Union economies in terms of total manufacturing employment was quite considerable.

The cross-national results about the effects of globalization

In our empirical analysis, as we already explained in our methodological section above, we included the proper specifications for development levels and other trade-offs affecting processes of development. For example, it would be senseless to predict life expectancy increases without properly taking into account earlier, achieved levels of life expectancy; and it would be senseless to talk about deforestation rates and coverage of a country with woodlands, not knowing how much of the total area is taken up by agricultural land. Dependency from the transnational corporations both in 1973 and in 1985 significantly and fairly constantly blocks development. The data outprints of Table 4.1 reiterate again the well-known dependency and neo-classical results in the tradition of Bornschier, Chase-Dunn, Dadush and Brahmbatt, even for the new time period and the new indicators of world development, published by the UNDP. To judge from Table 4.1, the world after 1980 seems to be a neat repetition of the well-known scholarly *Weltbild,* that emerged from the writings of Volker Bornschier and Chris Chase-Dunn during the 1980s, and to which we referred to above. Our findings suggest, that MNC penetration in the present Kondratieff cycle period again significantly blocks adjustment, growth, increases of life expectancy, the political and human rights record, the human development index, and the gender development index, the gender empowerment index, the life expectancy, a reduction of maternal mortality, and the protection of the world forests.

In addition, income inequality (the share of top 20% of income earners in 81 countries according to Moaddel's data base, enlarged by WDR World Bank data, 1994) is also well explained by the penetration of multinational corporations in the host countries, and is - in contrast to Weede's earlier findings - nowadays significantly enhanced and not lessened by militarization. Almost as a footnote to these arguments, one can add, that terms of trade have a significant effect in the expected direction on the process of maternal mortality:

Table 4.1: The effects of dependency (FDI stock per total GDP in the host countries) and world development - data for the 1980s and beyond

	MNCP85	Govex	Trade Dep	social sec	UN-membery	Women Parl	Women %LF	ln PCI	ln PCI^2	ln(MPR+1)	Fertility Rate	Constant
adjust-ment	-0,758	-0,717	0,1956	-4,491	0,0169	-0,05	-0,045	0,1354	0,0044	-0,042	0,0092	27,36
65/80/93	0,1563	0,7946	0,2894	4,3203	0,0211	0,0329	0,0181	0,0512	0,0064	0,0188	0,014	16,516
	0,3777	**2,2049**										
	6,1235	111										
	327,46	539,62										
t-Test	**-4,847**	-0,902	0,6757	-1,039	0,8025	-1,53	**-2,483**	2,643	0,6865	**-2,228**	0,661	

	MNC PEN85	Govex	Trade Dep	social sec	UN-membery	Women Parl	Women %LF	ln PCI	ln PCI^2	ln(MPR+1)	Fertility Rate	Constant
growth	-0,907	-0,281	0,0954	-3,147	0,0144	-0,063	-0,038	0,1416	0,0086	-0,04	0,0145	23,795
1980-93	0,1551	0,7885	0,2872	4,2869	0,0209	0,0327	0,0179	0,0508	0,0063	0,0187	0,0138	16,389
	0,4425	**2,1879**										
	8,0108	111										
	421,8	531,33										
t-Test	**-5,846**	-0,356	0,3322	-0,734	0,6895	**-1,922**	-2,104	2,7849	1,3644	**-2,116**	1,0498	

	LEX 1960	1 der e-funct	1 der π-func	MNCP85	Viol Civ Rits	Trade Dep	Terms Trade	UN-membery	Women Parl	Women %LF	ln(MPR+1)	Constant
DYN	1,3468	-0,05	-0,033	-0,028	0,0147	-0,006	0,0599	0,0348	-0,497	-25,58	-0,292	27,108
LEX	0,7823	0,0201	0,03	0,0179	0,0157	0,0062	0,171	0,0137	0,7032	6,6478	0,0353	2,5246
	0,7565	**2,1702**										
	31,349	111										
	1624,1	522,79										
t-Test	1,7215	-2,509	-1,115	*-1,578*	0,9382	-0,903	0,3502	**2,528**	-0,707	**-3,847**	**-8,265**	

	e-func Encon	π-func Enc	MNCP85	Viol Civ Rits	Trade Dep	Terms Trade	pub invest	Women Parl	Women %LF	ln(MPR+1)	Fertility Rate	Constant
green house index	0,0107	0,0514	0,0016	-0,002	-0,003	-3E-04	0,0001	0,0116	-0,001	2E-05	0,0249	0,0823
	0,0152	0,0681	0,0018	0,0025	0,0013	0,0013	0,0005	0,0129	0,0011	4E-06	0,0798	0,2998
	0,4238	0,1787										
	7,4227	111										
	2,606	3,5427										
t-Test	0,7035	0,7549	*0,882*	-0,742	**-2,351**	-0,26	*0,254*	0,901	-0,901	**4,328**	0,3121	

pol rights	MNCP85	Govex	Trade Dep	social sec	UN-membery	Women Parl	Women %LF	ln PCI	ln PCI^2	ln(MPR+1)	Fertility Rate	Constant
viola-tions	0,5633	1,3303	0,0892	-1,74	0,0046	0,0561	0,0209	-0,11	0,0057	0,0133	0,0032	6,9943
	0,1083	0,5504	0,2005	2,9926	0,0146	0,0228	0,0125	0,0355	0,0044	0,013	0,0097	11,441
	0,568	1,5273										
	13,266	111										
	340,4	258,92										
t-Test	**5,2024**	**2,4168**	0,4451	-0,582	0,3158	**2,4594**	**1,6653**	-3,098	1,2994	1,0218	0,3327	

	MNCP85	Govex	Trade Dep	social sec	UN-membery	Women Parl	Women %LF	ln PCI	ln PCI^2	ln(MPR+1)	Fertility Rate	Constant
civil rights viola-tions	0,3549	1,4809	0,0051	-0,535	-0,002	0,0361	0,0275	-0,098	0,002	-0,008	0,0014	4,4396
	0,084	0,4268	0,1554	2,3205	0,0113	0,0177	0,0097	0,0275	0,0034	0,0101	0,0075	8,871
	0,601	1,1843										
	15,203	111										
	234,53	155,67										
	4,2269	**3,4698**	0,0328	-0,231	-0,21	**2,0412**	**2,8337**	-3,566	0,5888	-0,748	0,184	

Human Development Index	MNCP85	Govex	Trade Dep	social sec	UN-membery	Women Parl	Women %LF	ln PCI	ln PCI^2	ln(MPR+1)	Fertility Rate	Constant
	-0,095	0,1544	0,0047	0,0402	-1E-04	-0,003	-4E-04	0,0009	-2E-04	0,0006	0,0005	0,4008
	0,0079	0,04	0,0146	0,2177	0,0011	0,0017	0,0009	0,0026	0,0003	0,0009	0,0007	0,8321
	0,8695	0,1111										
	67,224	111										

9,125	1,3697										
-12,08	**3,8562**	0,3237	0,1845	-0,106	*-1,589*	-0,426	0,3348	-0,716	0,663	0,6949	

MNCP85	Govex	Trade Dep	social sec	UN-membery	Women Parl	Women %LF	ln PCI	ln PCI^2	ln(MPR+1)	Fertility Rate	Constant
-0,071	0,0814	-0,008	0,1812	0,0009	-0,002	-2E-04	0,0022	-2E-04	0,0004	0,0007	-0,072
0,0058	0,0294	0,0107	0,1597	0,0008	0,0012	0,0007	0,0019	0,0002	0,0007	0,0005	0,6107
0,8705	0,0815										
67,801	111										
4,9568	0,7377										
Gender Development Index											
-12,36	**2,7703**	-0,706	1,1346	1,1746	**-1,809**	-0,23	1,1382	-0,707	0,5363	1,285	

MNCP85	Govex	**Trade Dep**	**social sec**	UN-membery	Women Parl	Women %LF	ln PCI	ln PCI^2	ln(MPR+1)	**Fertility Rate**	Constant
-0,021	0,0038	0,015	-0,177	0,0014	0,0055	0,0007	0,0023	-1E-04	5E-05	0,0006	0,8051
0,0041	0,0208	0,0076	0,1129	0,0006	0,0009	0,0005	0,0013	0,0002	0,0005	0,0004	0,4317
0,8216	0,0576										
46,465	111										
1,6974	0,3686										
Gender Empowerment Index											

MNCP85	Govex	Trade Dep	social sec	UN-membery	Women Parl	Women %LF	ln PCI	ln PCI^2	ln(MPR+1)	**Fertility Rate**
-5,089	0,1813	**1,9835**	*-1,57*	**2,5954**	**6,364**	*1,537*	1,7252	-0,895	0,1112	*1,644*

e-func Encon	π-func Enc	MNCP85	Viol Civ Rits	Trade Dep	Terms Trade	Constant	Life Expectancy
0,0387	0,0082	-1,41	0,0046	-4E-04	17,262	25,561	
0,0356	0,0138	0,3021	0,0303	1E-04	1,58	5,1809	
0,7737	5,009						
66,116	116						
9953,2	2910,5						
1,0862	0,5931	**-4,668**	0,1524	**-3,766**	**10,925**		
Life expectancy							

e-func Encon	π-func Enc	MNCP85	Viol Civ Rits	Trade Dep	Terms Trade	Constant		Maternal Mortality
-1,564	-0,247	22,606	-0,05	0,0129	-551,3	1655,5		
1,158	0,4491	9,8139	0,9842	0,0032	51,33	168,31		
0,7231	162,73							
50,487	116							
8E+06	3E+06							

e-func Encon	π-func Enc	MNCP85	Viol Civ Rits	Trade Dep	Terms Trade
-1,351	-0,55	**2,3034**	-0,051	**4,0413**	**-10,74**

	MNCP85	Govex	Trade Dep	social sec	UN-membery	Women Parl	Women %LF	ln PCI	ln PCI^2	ln(MPR+1)	Fertility Rate	%agland	Constant
% forest area	-0,451	-2,685	-11,86	-2,419	34,205	0,5247	0,6685	-0,072	-0,385	-0,06	0,1344	-0,193	-85,86
	0,1307	1,4212	7,0959	2,5719	38,418	0,1874	0,2954	0,1607	0,4696	0,0565	0,1678	0,127	147,29
	0,3029	19,589											
	3,9827	110											
	18339	42211											
t-Test	**-3,447**	**-1,889**	**-1,672**	-0,941	0,8903	**2,7998**	**2,2632**	-0,447	-0,819	-1,057	0,8006	-1,521	

	MNCP85	Govex	Trade Dep	social sec	UN-membery	Women Parl	Women %LF	ln PCI	ln PCI^2	ln(MPR+1)	Fertility Rate	%agland	Constant
annual deforest	0,0127	0,0805	-0,653	-0,223	3,2788	0,0047	-0,002	0,0077	-0,058	0,0049	-0,001	-0,007	-11,43
	0,0064	0,0696	0,3473	0,1259	1,8803	0,0092	0,0145	0,0079	0,023	0,0028	0,0082	0,0062	7,2093
	0,3446	0,9588											
	4,8196	110											
	53,166	101,12											
t-Test	**1,979**	1,1567	**-1,879**	-1,774	**1,7437**	0,5142	-0,166	0,9756	-2,503	**1,7661**	-0,148	-1,053	-1,586

MNCP85	Govex	Trade Dep	social sec	UN-membery	Women Parl	Women %LF	ln PCI	ln PCI^2	ln(MPR+1)	Fertility Rate	%agland	Constant

	MNCP85	Govex	Trade Dep	social sec	UN-membery	Women Parl	Women %LF	ln PCI	ln PCI^2	ln(MPR+1)	Fertility Rate	%agland	Constant
ethno	0,0102	0,1021	0,5162	-0,038	0,4516	0,0119	0,0318	0,023	-0,043	-1E-03	-0,017	0,0002	-2,072
warfare	0,0108	0,1178	0,5883	0,2133	3,1854	0,0155	0,0245	0,0133	0,0389	0,0047	0,0139	0,0105	12,213
	0,1152	1,6242											
	1,1933	110											
	37,776	290,19											
t-Test	0,9403	0,8667	0,8773	-0,179	0,1418	0,765	1,2968	1,7257	-1,092	-0,208	-1,226	0,0144	
destab./	0,0022	0,0166	0,0792	-0,029	0,4441	0,0021	-0,001	0,0074	-0,013	-8E-04	0,001	-0,002	-1,842
war	0,0026	0,0279	0,1392	0,0504	0,7534	0,0037	0,0058	0,0032	0,0092	0,0011	0,0033	0,0025	2,8885
	0,1319	0,3841											
	1,3929	110											
	2,4667	16,233											
t-Test	*0,876*	0,5952	*0,569*	-0,579	0,5895	0,5772	*-0,193*	2,36	-1,38	-0,689	0,309	*-0,853*	

	MNCP85	Govex	Trade Dep	social sec	UN-membery	Women Parl	Women %LF	ln PCI	ln PCI^2	ln(MPR+1)	Fertility Rate	Constant
mean y	-0,821	1,1775	0,5406	-6,526	0,02	-0,009	-6E-04	0,0817	-0,008	-0,012	-0,013	26,224
of edu-	0,0871	0,4429	0,1613	2,4078	0,0118	0,0184	0,0101	0,0286	0,0035	0,0105	0,0078	9,2048
cation	**0,8799**	1,2288										
	73,939	111										
	1228,1	167,61										
t-Test	**-9,419**	**2,6589**	**3,3519**	**-2,711**	**1,7038**	-0,487	-0,055	2,8626	-2,385	-1,178	-1,647	

	MNCP85	Govex	Trade Dep	social sec	UN-membery	Women Parl	Women %LF	social sec	ln PCI^2	**ln(MPR+1)**	Fertility Rate	Constant
employ-	-1,729	1,3969	2,0486	-31,17	0,3784	0,1233	-0,05	-0,07	0,0436	-0,153	-0,06	156,76
ment	0,4309	2,1905	0,7978	11,909	0,0581	0,0908	0,0498	0,1412	0,0175	0,0519	0,0385	45,529
	0,5513	6,078										
	12,397	111										
	5037,6	4100,6										
t-Test	**-4,012**	0,6377	**2,5678**	**-2,617**	**6,5094**	1,3583	-1	-0,493	2,4854	**-2,939**	-1,565	

	MNCP85	Govex	Trade Dep	social sec	UN memy	Women Parl	Women %LF	ln PCI	ln PCI^2	ln(MPR+1)	Fertility Rate

cpm	5,6962	-9,65	-1,156	8,4534	-0,131	-0,029	0,0247	-1,711	0,0388	-0,14	-0,078	16,497
mea-sure	0,9599	4,9936	2,1929	31,463	0,1232	0,2494	0,1189	0,8804	0,0376	0,1178	0,0805	115,66
	0,6509	12,162										
	14,917	88										
	24270	13016										
t-Test	**5,934**	**-1,933**	-0,527	0,2687	-1,06	-0,117	0,2078	-1,944	1,0332	-1,186	-0,973	

	MNCPen85	ln PCI	ln PCI^2	ln(MPR+1)	Fertility Rate	constant
inequality	1,660219	-5,34162	-2,13994	31,8547	0,12603	-73,7864
share top	0,65447	3,456306	1,019608	15,49074	0,070035	59,09442
20%	**0,252326**	7,897908				
	4,92722	73				
	1536,726	4553,517				
t-Test	**2,53674**	-1,54547	-2,09879	**2,05637**	**1,799521**	

Legend: as in all EXCEL 5.0 outprints in this work, first row: unstandardized regression coefficients, second row: standard errors, last row: t-Test. The values immediately below the standard errors are R^2 (third row, left side entry), *F,* and degrees of freedom (fourth row).

The above materials strongly support dependency theory. There are 19 variables and processes of development measured here. 14 variables are explaining different aspects of development. MNC penetration **significantly** and negatively affects 15 of the 19 dimensions reported, the rest - life expectancy increases, the greenhouse index, ethno-warfare, and the existence of war and political destabilization in a country, are still affected in a fashion, as predicted by our theory, but not significantly.

MNC penetration also increases significantly poverty, as measured by the new UNDP 1996 CPM poverty measure. International system participation age - or early statehood - is an important control variable in the whole process of the explanation of post-1982 growth and development/stagnation. It significantly enhances the increase of life expectancy over time, gender empowerment, and the educational and employment record of a given country (the strong points of long established nations), while it significantly fails to block the deforestation process, especially due to the divergence between professed ideals and dire realities in the long-established nations in Latin America and in Eastern Europe.

Terms of trade have a significant effect in the expected direction on the process of maternal mortality, and life expectancy. The most important further results are:

(i) **militarization** is one of the main development blocks in the period after 1980, with 5% significant results for adjustment, growth, employment, income redistribution, the greenhouse effect, and further notable effects on the two deforestation indicators. The main theoretical thrust of our new results with MNC penetration during the 1980s points, however, in the following further directions:

(ii) **fertility** is negatively related to redistribution, employment and human capital formation, but there is a perhaps somewhat surprising *ceteris paribus* positive effect on gender empowerment, mainly due to the relatively good gender empowerment performance of countries with a relatively higher historical fertility rate like Barbados, Bahamas, China,

Ireland etc., whose gender empowerment is higher than that of nations with a historically low birth rate like France

(iii) The **small and open economies** in world society tend towards gender political power sharing and towards a better employment situation. A world economically open society with a high proportion of foreign trade per total product is more likely to have - *ceteris paribus* - a lower greenhouse-index. To further support the predictions about the positive effects of trade dependency on growth, developed by Katzenstein, one should emphasize also the positive effects on human capital formation and employment. But trade dependency works as a classic transmitter of mechanisms of dependency by the effects it wields on life expectancy, maternal mortality, and the coverage of a nation with forests.

(iv) **Government** activity is not significantly related to adjustment and growth; but a government-controlled economy decreases the political and human rights performance. On the other hand, strong, and not weak government, enhances the human development index, the gender development index, the human capital formation record of a nation, and government significantly reduces the amount of poverty measured by the new UNDP CPM-measure and de-forestation. The strength - or rather burden here - of the **social welfare** state has a **negative effect on employment**, and it has a **negative** effect on **human capital formation** (mean years of education).

(v) **Established feminism** (representation of women in parliaments and in the work force) emerges as the **main loser of the world economic changes that have taken place since the 1980s.** States with a high feminist power base were performing relatively well on the forest protection front; but even the gender development index could not be affected in an upward direction by established feminism; and *ceteris paribus,* states with a well-developed feminist power base were performing very badly regarding adjustment, growth, life expectancy increases, political and civil rights performance, and the human development index.

5) THE CONTRADICTIONS OF THE PROCESS OF THE GLOBAL ENVIRONMENTAL DESTRUCTION, TO WHICH EUROPE AS ONE OF THE MAIN REGIONS OF WORLD INDUSTRY AND TRAFFIC, DISPROPORTIONATELY CONTRIBUTES

Over the years, there has emerged a new sub-field of development and transformation theory, that is sensitive to the concerns of 'the new social movements' around the globe (Bello, 1989; Friberg, 1988; UNDP, 1993, 1994; Woehlke, 1987, 1993). The situation of women and the situation of the environment emerge as prime issues of development (Benard and Schlaffer, 1985; Betz and Bruene, 1995; L. R. Brown, 1992; Dubiel, 1993; Frank and Fuentes-Frank, 1990; Leggett, 1991; Saffioti, 1978; Seager and Olson, 1986). Cross-national analysis about economic and social preconditions and the quality of the environment are relatively new (Beckerman, 1992; Shafik and Bandyopadhyay, 1992).

Environmental disintegration

In the former or continuously communist countries of Eastern Europe and the USSR-successor-states, environmental quality poses indeed one of the main concerns of development planning nowadays (World Resources Institute, 1992). Eastern Europe's transformation could be again seen as a testing ground for various growth paradigms and strategies. The globalization argument would emphasize, that, contrary to the optimistic expectations about an improvement in the environmental situation due to the new presence of transnational capital, the adoption of an energy-consuming 'US-style'- model would mean a significant long-term increase of various emissions.

The global atmospheric carbon dioxide concentration increased from 280 ppm in pre-industrial times to 315.8 in 1959, to stand at 354 in 1990. World carbon dioxide emissions increased from 6.002 thousand millions of metric tons in 1950 to 21.863 thousand millions of metric tons in 1989. In 1995, CO_2 emissions reached 23.1 thousand millions of metric tons (Fischer Weltalmanach, 1997). The United States are responsible for 4.88 thousand millions of tons, followed by China (2.67 thousand millions) and Russia (2.1 millions), followed by Japan (1.09 millions), Germany (0.88 thousand millions), India (0.77 millions) (Graph 5.1)

Graph 5.1: CO_2-emissions in the world system (1995)

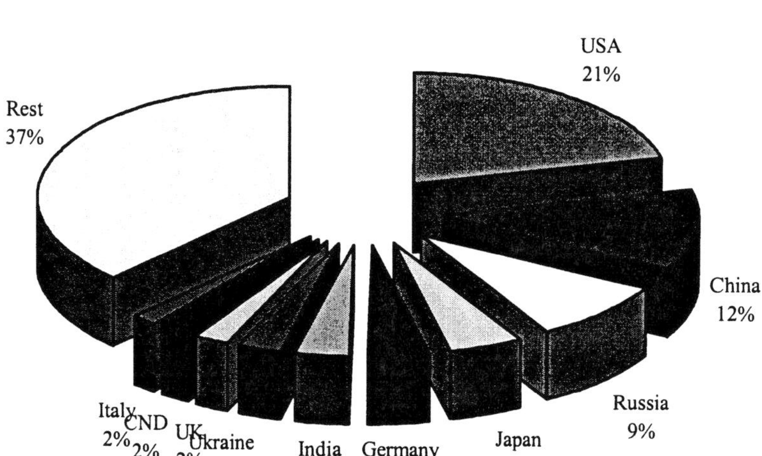

Source: our own calculations, based on Fischer Weltalmanach, 1997, based on Carbon Dioxide Information Centre. The graph shows the percentage share of major polluters in total world CO_2 emissions.

Over the last 100 years, the earth's temperature rose by 0.6 degrees; from 1970 to today, the rise was 0.3 degrees. The earth's temperature will rise by a further 3.5 degrees until 2100, if contemporary emission trends continue (Stiftung, 1996). The most probable scenario, according to the Intergovernmental Panel on Climate Change (IPCC), reaches the conclusion that an increase of +2 °C on a global level and a rise of the sea-level by 50 cm is very probable (Fischer Weltalmanach, 1997: 1122). Severe storms, droughts, and other catastrophes would be the immediate consequence. In terms of the average temperature for the three decades 1961-90, 1995 presented an increase of +0.4 °C (Fischer Weltalmanach, 1997: 1122, based on Hadley-Center, 1996). From 1910 to the end of the Second World War, there was a thirty year increase in temperatures, to be followed by two troughs around 1950 and 1968 and a continuous rise since the end of the 1970s (Fischer Weltalmanach, 1997: 1122).

Over the last 160000 years, there has been a close correlation between carbon-dioxide concentrations and changes in the world temperature (Gore, 1994; Leggett, 1991). Roughly, a change of +- 100 ppm carbon dioxide historically led to a change of +- 12.5 degrees Celsius. From 1750 to today, carbon dioxide emissions amount to 800 thousand million tons of CO_2. Although the temperature change factor might be smaller, and a rise by 100 ppm CO_2 might lead to a temperature rise of 1.1 degrees, the heating of the atmosphere in the coming decades will be enormous:

Graph 5.2 Charles D. Keeling's data series from Mauna Loa - atmospheric concentrations of greenhouse and ozone-depleting gases, 1959-90, and the trend for the next 60 years

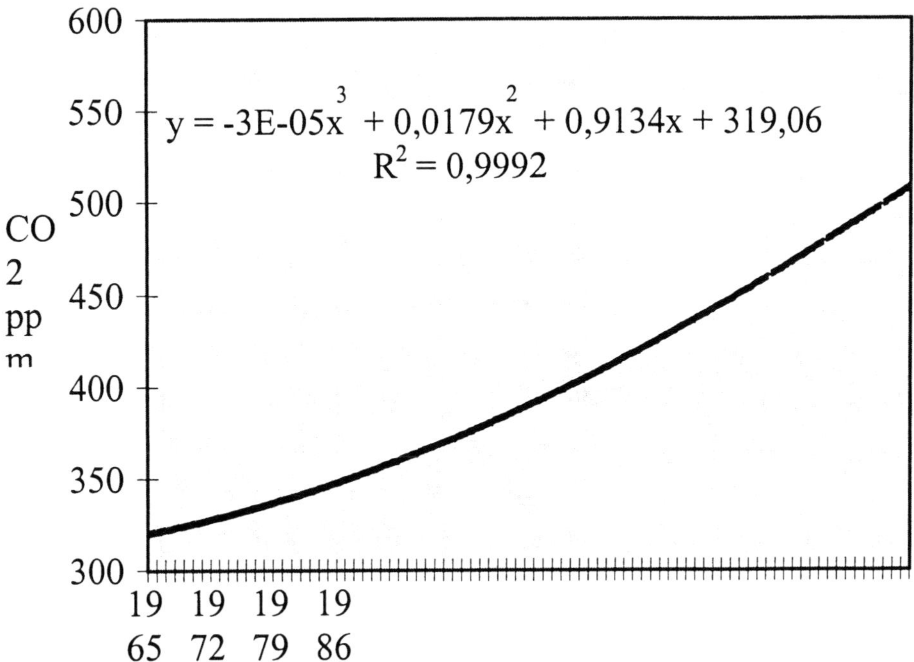

Legend: CO_2-concentration on Mauna Loa, Hawaii, measured in particles per m^3 Our own calculations from D. Keeling's data, Scripps Institution of Oceanography, World Resources Institute, 1992, using the trend-line extrapolation of the EXCEL 5.0 program (3-order polynomial expression).

Desertification, storms, flooding in many parts of the world, as well as famine and droughts could be the results of these recent increases in carbon dioxide levels and are indeed already a reality in many parts of the world. There were 16 major disasters in the 1960s, 29 in the 1970s, and 70 in the 1980s. Natural disasters now strike 120 million people each year (UNDP, 1997). Since 1967, 1.3 million people died from droughts, 800000 in cyclones, 600000 in earth quakes and 300000 in floods (UNDP, 1994). The last time, that a carbon dioxide concentration as high as around 300 ppm was reached in the earth's history, was around 130000 before our time; from that moment onwards, global temperatures and carbon dioxide concentration ratios fell to 20000 before our time, when a level of just 180 ppm was reached. And again, the poor have to pay the bill: Bangladesh produces only 0.3% of global greenhouse emissions but could see its land area shrink by 17% due to global warming (UNDP, 1997).

An important question is, whether or not the recurrence of major floods and hurricanes in our age is coincidental or connected to global warming. In the summer of 1997, Europe again was hard-hit by extensive floods, just as in summer 1996. In 1996, the Netherlands were hardest hit, and in 1997, Poland and the Czech Republic. Apart from the social aspects of these disasters, which bring to the surface the vulnerability of the social structures of people living in poverty, there are severe ecological implications. The delicate long-standing oscillations in the velocity and temperature of Oceanic currents intervene. Precisely this delicate balance seems, one could tentatively argue, to have been upset now in a fundamental way: already in 1991 it was discovered that the velocity of the Gulf stream northeast of Iceland decreased by 80%, thus affecting the equilibrium between the salt-content of the Oceanic waters, the velocity of Oceanic circulation, and the cold winds from the North Pole (Gore, 1994). A huge, powerful current usually carries warm water from the vicinity of Florida to the coast of Ireland before turning westward, cooling, sinking, and going back south near Labrador. Deep-lying parcels of unusually warm water move continually through that pipeline, alternating with cooler ones, along with the rhythm of sun-spot activity. Each parcel takes about 20 years to travel from the tropics, around the North Atlantic circuit to Labrador. Sea-surface temperatures rise and fall in concert with the movement of these parcels *(New York Times,* March 18th, 1997). Since the 1970s, the North Atlantic oscillation and a similar oscillation in the Pacific have made the continents of the Northern hemisphere unusually warm, during winter and spring *(New York Times,* March 18th, 1997). 'El Nino', that vast pool of unusually warm surface water that comes and goes every few years in the eastern tropical Pacific, and first discovered around Christmas by Peruvian fishermen 200 years ago, is a similar phenomenon *(Los Angeles Times,* May 16th, 1997), that, in the past, was followed each time by 'La Nina', the corresponding pool of cold water in the rhythm of two to seven years *(NY Times,* June 3rd, 1997):

> In their search for convincing evidence of global warming, scientists have been puzzling over shifting tree lines in the Sierra Nevada, dying coral in the Caribbean, melting alpine glaciers, and seasonal temperatures so extreme that the 10 warmest years of the past century have occurred in the last 15 years.
> When malaria-infected mosquitoes recently turned up in New Jersey and tropical microorganisms were discovered poisoning shellfish as far north as Monterey, climate experts were quick to wonder whether they had detected evidence of climate changes.
>
> In each case, pests once confined to the world's hottest regions appeared to be moving into new territory--evidence, perhaps, of formerly cool zones warmed by greenhouse gases.
>
> Now some researchers believe that they have detected the distinctive signature of global warming in the infamous Pacific Ocean current known as El Nino, a seasonal upwelling of warm seawater that has been implicated in disastrous droughts, torrential rains, killing heat waves and other distortions of the daily weather from Southern California to South Africa.
>
> The El Nino current arises from the dance between order and chaos as the ocean and the atmosphere interact to balance the Earth's thermal energy. It is the heart of a complex system called the El Nino Southern Oscillation, which is so delicate that even a subtle alteration in temperatures can affect its seesaw, annual rhythms.
>
> Global warming should make El Nino effects stronger and more frequent, said Kevin Trenberth of the National Center for Atmospheric Research in Boulder, Colo. And, as if to prove his point, the most recent El Nino, which some scientists say lasted from 1990 through 1995, is the longest in 130 years of record-keeping (Los Angeles Times, May 16th, 1997)

The emerging pattern seems easy to predict: milder and drier winters in Alaska, Canada, and the Pacific Northwest, cooler in the Southeastern United States and wetter in the US Southwest. Powerful west-to-east winds across the Atlantic bring more oceanic warmth to Northern Europe and Asia, making for milder winters there. Northern Europe gets more precipitation, while Southern Europe and the Middle East less. Until now, the oscillations in Oceanic currents caused ups and downs in world weather cycles, causing a shift of the westerly winds to the European South, making Northern Europe much colder and drier and bringing more warmth and precipitation to Mediterranean Europe, Africa and the Middle East. The Medieval warm period and the Little Ice Age were all - current opinion goes - a consequence of previous such oscillations *(New York Times,* March 18th, 1997). The question is of course, whether or not we're in for a more secular change, that seems to be directing towards more hurricanes in the Southeastern US, more torrential summer rains in Europe, and Western Latin America, and more droughts in many other parts of the world, among them Australia and many parts of Asia. It might also well be that the 'peaks' in the common re-occurrence of the *'El Nino'* phenomenon get larger, up to five years *(Los Angeles Times,* May 16th, 1996). Several meteorologists, among them Timothy Barnett at the Scripps Institution of Oceanography, rule out the connection between *'El Nino'* and global warming, however. Their arguments say that similar prolonged *El Ninos* were observed during 1911 to 1915, and that volcanic eruptions, deep-sea thermal events or the 11 to 22 year sun-spot cycle may cause the phenomenon. Indeed, they'd argue that up to 50% in global temperature rise since 1900 must be attributed to a rising sunspot activity, and not to Carbon Dioxide levels *(LA Times, ibidem).* Fairly safe predictions estimate however, that up to a third of the world's glaciers will melt away over the next decades, together with a 2-6 degrees Fahrenheit rise in average surface temperature and a rise in the sea levels up to three feet during the next 100 years *(LA Times, ibidem).* Such huge fresh water supplies from the Antarctic to the South-east Pacific, and from Greenland and the Arctic to the North Atlantic would in turn explain, why less salt water submerges and becomes colder in the process, moving southward along North Americas coastline. However, there seems to be rising consensus that severe hurricanes will continue to develop in the Atlantic arena over the next years *(New York Times,* June 3rd, 1997). The hurricanes are facilitated by the warming up of the tropical zones of the Atlantic, but expected to be kept in check at least in part by the *El Nino* phenomenon. The coincidence of the cold *La Nina* in the Pacific and higher Sea surface temperatures in the tropical Atlantic, which have risen since 1955 in almost continuous fashion, would however combine to create terrible hurricanes that will hit the Eastern USA in the not too distant future *(NY Times, ibidem).* It should be recalled, that wet weather and low pressure areas in Africa's Sahel zone are at the root of hurricane embryos, kept in check by high-level westerly winds blowing from the Eastern tropical Pacific, and caused by *El Nino (NY Times,* June 3rd, 1997). One plausible hypothesis is of course:

One of the most powerful indicators, according to the new study by Dr. Saunders and Andrew R. Harris, climate scientists at University College London in Britain, is the Atlantic sea-surface temperature. Their statistical analysis found that while most of the relevant factors were indeed favorable for hurricane development in the banner year of 1995, the dominating influence was the unusually warm ocean. The temperature in the region where hurricanes develop was 1.2 degrees Fahrenheit above the 1946-1995 average, a record. The development region was 0.36 of a degree warmer than average last year and is about 0.9 of a degree warmer now. This, said Dr. Saunders, presages another active season. His study appeared in the May 15 issue of the journal Geophysical Research Letters.

The researchers suggest that warmer seas cause more water to evaporate from the surface. With evaporation, latent heat is released in the atmosphere, and the researchers believe that this is what imparts more energy to the embryonic storms coming out of Africa, making it more likely that they will develop into hurricanes. "It seems that this is a stronger effect that any other mechanism, like El Nino or the monsoon in the western Sahel," Dr. Saunders said.

The question, he said, is whether the rising sea temperature is a natural expression of the climate system's variability, independent of any influence from a warming atmosphere. Dr. Gray, for his part, says he believes the warmer ocean temperature is "a manifestation of a major change in North Atlantic ocean circulation." Stately currents in the North Atlantic undergo periodic shifts on decadal time scales. Dr. Gray said he believed that a new pattern was in place, and that it was likely to presage a decade or two of above-average hurricane activity.

"This is the greatest fear we have," he said, "that we're entering a new era. I believe we are." (New York Times, June 3rd, 1997)

In the northern hemisphere, regions north-east of the warming Ocean regions receive above than average rainfalls, while in the southern hemisphere, regions south-east of the *'El Nino'* area receive the highest rainfalls. On the western shores of the Pacific and the Atlantic, severe droughts can develop during the summers, in regions as far apart as North Korea, Australia, and Eastern Canada. Severe storms are to be expected in countries or regions like Western Mexico, Peru, and Chile *(Reuters, North America News Report,* July 15th, 1997). World poverty and environmental degradation in marginal lands are closely inter-linked with such phenomena. During the last *El Nino,* which happened in 1982-83, hundreds died in Peru in flood and landslides, and tens of thousands were left homeless:

> Chicago--Jun 27--The current El Nino has been one of the fastest growing El Nino weather events this century, and sea surface temperatures are expected to continue rising into the fall and winter, Smith Barney weather analyst Jon Davis said in a special report. Pacific Ocean surface temperatures began to rise at the beginning of the year and have continued to climb at a steady pace ever since, Davis said in an El Nino update.
>
> "The increase in SSTs during the past 6 months has been the most dramatic of any 6-month period since the late 1970s," he said. "In fact, this is one of the most dramatic warmings over such a short period of time this century."
>
> The La Nina--colder-than-normal water temperatures in the Pacific-- ended in March, with the 1995-96 event lasting a little more than 2 years. By early May, sea surface temperatures had risen enough to declare an El Nino event. The continued rise in those temperatures in the past 6 weeks has been enough to classify the event as moderate, with current temperatures about 1.5 degrees Celsius above normal.
>
> "If the current rate of change continues at the same magnitude, the El Nino event will be ranked as a strong one within a matter of months," Davis said.
>
> (...) Areas that normally see dryness and heat during El Nino events include China, India, Southeast Asia--Indonesia, Malaysia, Thailand, Philippines--and Australia.
>
> The problems in Asia mostly are due to a lack of irrigation caused by poor summer and fall rains. Australia also typically sees very dry conditions in El Nino years.
>
> "The more that SSTs in the Pacific warm up, the more likely it is for a major drought during the spring and summer (Oct-Feb) across the continent," Davis said.
>
> Along with these potential problem areas, the weather event could cause difficulties in South Africa during that region's corn planting season in October and November.
>
> (...) The strengthening of the event decreases the chances of an active hurricane season in the Gulf of Mexico and Atlantic, Davis said (...)
>
> If the sea surface warming continues into the fall and winter as expected, a warmer 1997-98 winter could result in Canada, the US and Europe, he said. (Bridge World Markets News, at http://www.dialogselect.com)

More than 500 million poor people live on marginal lands in the Sahel and in the upper regions of the Andes and the Himalayas. Their main preoccupation will not be with the price of commodities that you can sell, but with survival as such. Dry lands are the home to 1.5 billion people on earth. Conflicts between farmers and herders are proliferating in Africa and in Asia (UNDP, 1997). The tragic events in Rwanda and Burundi cannot be separated from two processes a) these conflicts b) the structure of land intensive raw material exports, like coffee growing, imposed by the structures of world tariffs and world trade, on Africa (Amin, 1994). The water supply per capita in developing countries today is only a third of what it was in 1970. More than 55% of the people in the Arab world suffer from serious water shortages. Over the past 50 years, 65 million hectares of productive land have become desert globally (UNDP, 1997).

World pollution is even a clear statistical function of the ups and downs of the longer swings in the world economy, most notably the Kuznets cycle and the Kondratieff cycle. The World Resources Institute has provided information on the basis of the Carbon Dioxide Information Analysis Center about CO2 emissions in the world from 1950 onwards. The growth rates of CO2 consumption clearly correspond to the Kondratieff and Kuznets cycle analysis about economic growth, which we introduced in Chapter 3.

Graph 5.3: CO_2 emissions and their growth rates from 1950 onwards

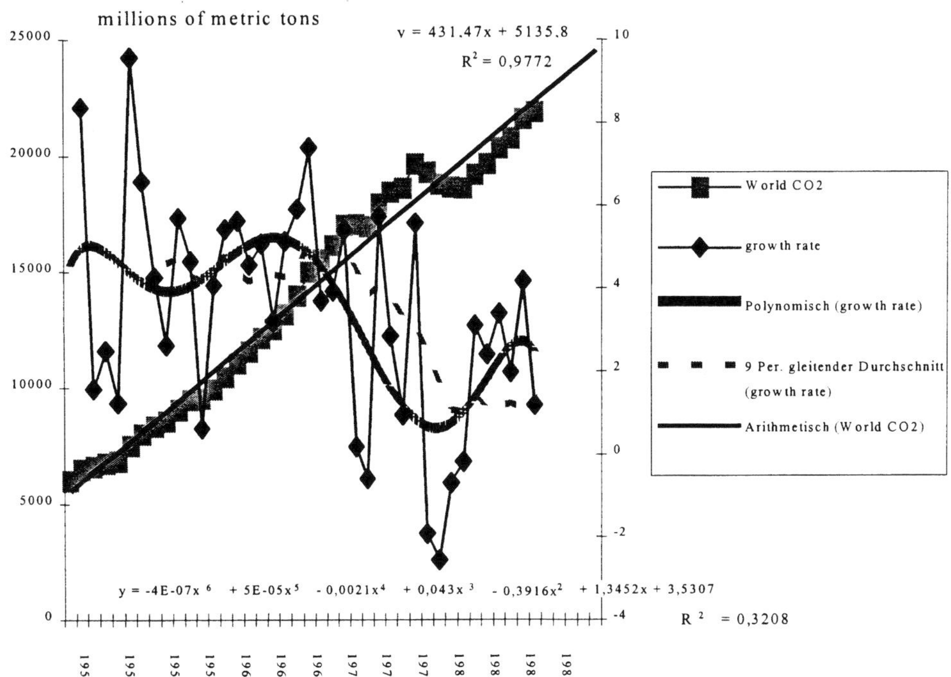

Legend: World CO_2 emissions from fossil fuel consumption and cement manufacture, 1950-89. Left hand scale: emissions in millions of metric tons per year; right-hand scale: growth rates of these emissions. The graph shows also the polynomial expression (6th order) of these growth rates, as calculated by EXCEL 5.0, as well as the gliding averages on a 9-year basis. The dark line is the linear regression trend of CO_2 emissions, projected for 5 consecutive periods

About 700 million people, mainly women and children, inhale indoor smoke from burning biomass fuel. Air pollution causes losses of $bn 35 a year in Europe, costing farmers $bn 4 in Germany and $bn 2 in Poland. The smoke-stack landscape of north-central Europe, that ranges from Northern England, via Belgium, northern France, north-eastern Germany to Poland, the Czech Republic, Slovakia, the Ukraine and other parts of east-central Europe presents a high concentration of SO_2 emissions, rapid defoliation and scarce water resources. Table 5.1 and Map 5.1-5.2 now summarize the most important environmental and social indicators for the region before or during the start of the transformation process. Defoliation and forest destruction in turn increase the probability of flooding, because the water masses, pouring down with the rains, cannot be properly soaked into the earth anymore:

Table 5.1: environmental quality in Eastern Europe and the former USSR in comparison to the US, the UK, France, (West) Germany, Sweden and Austria

Country	Environmental degradation indicator			
	CO_2	SO_2	NO_X	% forest defoliation (moderate to severe)
	per capita emissions (tons) (in industry)			
Albania	3.04	15.6	2.8	-
Bulgaria	11.87	114.6	16.7	24.9%
former CS	14.47	178.9	60.7	33.0%
East Germany	-	313.3	42.6	16.4%
Hungary	6.05	115.2	24.5	12.7%
Poland	**11.54**	**103.3**	**39.1**	**31.9%**
Romania	9.16	8.6	16.8	-
former Yug.	5.61	69.6	8.0	22.6% (Slovenia)
former USSR	-	32.4	14.6	35.0% (Kaliningrad oblast)
USA	**19.68**	**83.2**	**79.6**	-
UK	9.89	62.1	43.9	28.0%
France	6.38	27.1	30.1	-
W-Germany	10.48	24.2	48.4	15.9%
Sweden	7.0	25.9	35.4	12.9%
Austria	6.82	16.3	27.7	4.4%

Source: our own compilations from World Resources Institute, 1992

Map 5.1: defoliation in Central and Northern Europe's forests

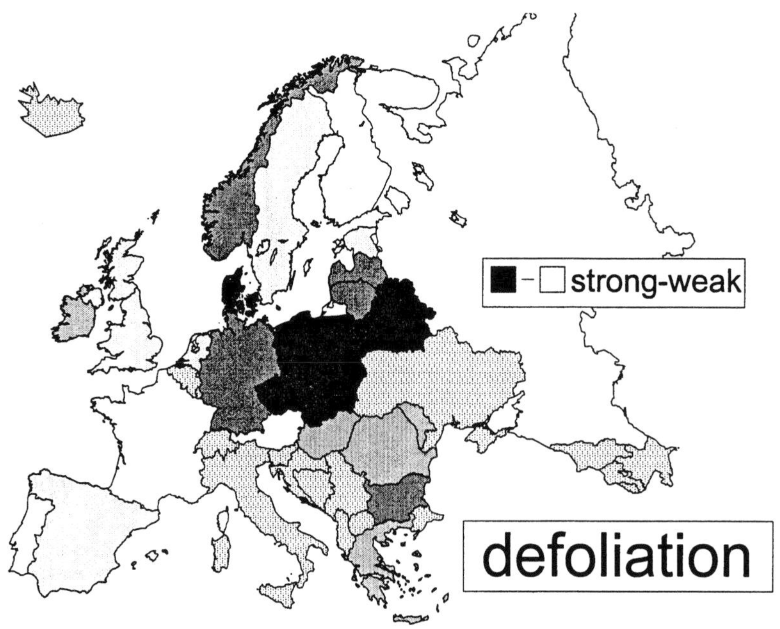

Source: Polish Central Statistical Office, 1996, *Ochrona Srodowiska.* The darker, the stronger the defoliation process

Map 5.2: internal renewable water resources per capita

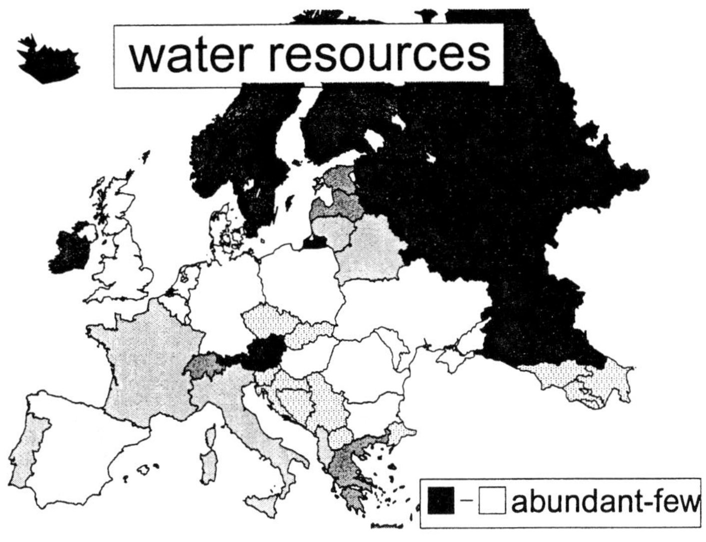

Source: EXCEL 7.0 graph, based on UNDP 1996 data and Fischer Weltalmanach. The lighter, the more severe is water scarcity already.

The short-run prediction thus points towards more severe flooding in Eastern Europe over the next years, to be followed by desertification. Forests have the unique capacity of attracting rainfalls by emitting terpenes (C_5H_8) and dimethylsulphides (Gore, 1994).

Deforestation in Eastern Europe and the former USSR is already more severe than in most parts of Western Europe. Defoliation is a more than serious problem in North-Central Europe, where water scarcity is also extending. To this we must add, that in a country like Poland environmental concerns do not receive the priority that they should receive. Only 34% of the population is served by waste water treatment plants (EU average 70%); municipal waste services reach only 55% of the population (EU average: 96%; our own compilations from UNDP, 1995). The basic argument of a globalization-oriented explanation of environmental quality on a world scale (Launer, 1992; Woehlke, 1987) would run as follows: dependent growth not only leads to social strains and imbalances, with all its economic dynamics that it might initiate at the same time; it also means a further strain on the natural resources and the environment by the energy-, space-, forest- and individual-traffic intensive life-style that capitalism, especially in its North American variety, brings about. Although some forest-, energy- and emission-saving might be the initial consequence of the introduction of more modern and western technologies, the basic problem of dependent and polarizing development would remain on the agenda. Profit-oriented growth between unequal partners will always, globalization theory argues, lead to forms of 'unequal exchange'. Concretely, the world-wide market economy and the new international division of labor will (i) transfer energy and pollution intensive industries to the countries of the periphery and the semi-periphery (ii) industrial waste from the centers will be increasingly attempted to be deposited in those regions (iii) export-intensive industrialization and the debt crisis will mean an almost reckless use of remaining natural resources, especially forest areas, for export purposes to earn badly needed foreign cash, or to destroy forests to gain land for tropical and sub-tropical export agriculture. International tourism (including its 'soft-body'-component), air traffic, individual traffic and the 'western' lifestyle, that begins with the plastic bag, ranging over well-known soft drinks - preferably from the tin-can - to equally well-known western TV-serials, will in the end more than negatively compensate the initially positive contributions, that economic transformation, market mechanisms and the recession of the 1980s will have meant for the countries of the periphery and the semi-periphery of Eastern Europe and the countries of the South in terms of the environment. Poland produces today more waste per inhabitant already (1500 kg per year) than Spain, Italy, France, the UK or Germany (1021 kg) *(Wprost,* 20.09. 1995: 52). Poland might have new factories for paper recycling with western technology, but the raw material - old paper - is being imported from Western countries, because there is no recycling and Poles have to throw old newspapers into the dustbin, for lack of proper recycling boxes in most parts of major Polish cities. Turn-key paper recycling factories in Poland, this is no joke, built by Western capital after the transformation, are now importing old paper from the European Union countries, because in Poland there is too few recycling (direct communication from the representative of a major Austrian enterprise in Poland to the author). Privatization of garbage collection is not so much on the agenda as the privatization of heavy industry - who cares, after all, about the mountain of waste, that is created by dependent capitalist development?

In addition, regional development authorities throughout Eastern Europe and in other semi-peripheral regions will hope to attract foreign buying power in exchange for local property rights in environmentally still undamaged regions. Insert here what you like: Caribbean island coasts, still untouched regions in Eastern Europe, like the Mazurian lakes, the Tatra mountains, *et cetera.* They will share the fate - dependency theory would tell us - of the sell-out on the Spanish Mediterranean coast, wide areas of the Austrian Alps and many other places in Europe. In other zones, unabated deforestation will develop, not unlike many Third-World countries. Unequal environmental exchange will increasingly affect (semi)peripheral regions in greater geographical distance from the centers; mass tourism to the tropical zones of the world will cause a tremendous increase in air-pollution from air-traffic that these 'island get-aways' bring about. For these reasons, environmental indicators are so negatively determined by transnational penetration. An important control variable in our analysis of the deforestation process is the percentage of total land, devoted to agriculture. On the one hand, it allows for the fact, that large regions of the world are affected by a growing desertification; on the other hand, this control variable duly considers the negative effect, that the expansion of world agriculture had on the world's woodlands in a historic perspective.

It is hard to construct a single indicator of the environmental situation of a country. The following indicators are being used widely: the *greenhouse index* per 10 million people, *energy consumption per capita,* and the *annual rate of deforestation.* A fourth indicator, per capita *carbon dioxide emissions,* is also available. The greenhouse index measures the net emissions of three major greenhouse gases: carbon dioxide, methane and chlorofluorocarbons. The index weights each gas according to its heattrapping quality in carbon dioxide equivalents and expresses them in metric tons of carbon per capita. Energy consumption, on the other hand, refers to commercial forms of primary energy - petroleum (crude oil, natural gas liquids, and oil from non-conventional sources), natural gas, solid fuels (coal, lignite, and other derived fuels), and primary electricity (nuclear, hydroelectric, geothermal, and other) - all converted into oil equivalents. Energy consumption refers to domestic primary energy supply before transformation to other end-use fuels and is calculated as indigenous production plus imports and stock changes, minus exports and international marine bunkers. The use of firewood, dried animal excrement, and other traditional fuels is *not* taken into account for lack of international comparative data. Energy consumption per capita can be considered as perhaps the most important single indicator of the factors, that lead to global environmental degradation. The two environmental indicators have a very high positive correlation with each other. The third indicator, annual rate of deforestation or total forest area (under proper consideration of arable land per total land), is connected with the first and the second process in a complex fashion. For the future of the world environment, deforestation is the most alarming contemporary process of environmental degradation. Forest burning directly leads to a greatly increased CO_2 emission; deforestation reduces the world's future capacity to produce oxygen and to adapt to increasing CO_2 levels. To put it into a drastic comparison with medicine: the patient suffers from cancer on the **left** lung *(the green house-effect),* but the doctors decide to extract the still functioning **right** lung (the world-wide CO_2 --> O_2 photosynthetic regenerative capacity of the world's tropical forests). Due to the destruction of the outer ozone-layer of the earth, this fatal process will still be increased. **Each second, a rainforest area as large as a football field, is being demolished on purpose (Launer, 1992).**

Among the factors, leading to deforestation, the export-oriented economy, the use of tropical wood in the world paper and furniture industry, and the burning of wood for cooking and heating purposes are the three most commonly mentioned factors. A great number of scholars, among them Leggett et al., 1991, tried to bring deforestation rates systematically into a causal relationship with the kind of dependent capitalist growth, analyzed amongst others by Bornschier and Chase Dunn, 1985. The creation of large plantations in Latin America for meat exports to the United States of America is often causally linked in the literature to the problem of deforestation (Launer, 1992). Brazil's supposed role is of special importance here, because Brazil still has a share of 27.5% of the world's tropical forests. Indonesia's year-long wood-export drive has often been mentioned as the most paradigmatic case of the influence of the capitalist world economy on the rapid disappearance of the world's forests. The role of the peasantry in dependent capitalism was also often mentioned in this context. Extensive tropical agriculture, implanted by 500 years of dependent development, described by the Peruvian Marxist José Carlos **Mariateguí** in his classic *'7 Essays',* and later on analyzed by Feder, 1972, is thought to be one of the main factors leading to the alarming rates of deforestation. Small scale peasants - the *dependencia* argument runs - are evicted throughout the countries of Latin America, Africa, Asia and the Pacific from their meager holdings by the land-hungry process of dependent agricultural capitalism for the sake of export-oriented breeding for meat production and tropical export crops. Language and cultural barriers have prevented Mariateguís work from becoming known to a larger audience (and if anything, most social scientists today will know him only from the lamentable fact that the Peruvian terrorist group *Sendero Luminoso* usurped his name by calling itself *Partido Comunista del Peru del Sendero Luminoso del Pensamiento **de José Carlos Mariateguí;*** i.e. the Comunist Party of Peru of the Shining Path of the Thinking of **José Carlos Mariateguí**). But Mariateguís analyses of the workings of tropical agriculture are a superb and masterly piece of social scientific analysis of the crisis conditions of our world at the turn of the millenium, with its confrontation between the industrial center and the tropical agricultural periphery, which more and more resembles the conditions of the decline and fall of Ancient Rome (Chase-Dunn and Hall, 1997).

What is already commonplace in the former 'Third World' could become a rule of the day also in the former 'Second World'. Forests are being cut down not only in Indonesia and in Northern Borneo at an amazing speed, but also in the *Warmia* region of the Mazurian lakes in Poland and in other parts of Eastern Europe. Forest cutting for export purposes, disregarding the social and ecological rights of the local populations could serve, a *dependencia*-minded argument could maintain, the short-term profit interests of the old and new export-oriented elites.

6) GENDER DISCRIMINATION AND SEXISM IN WORLD CAPITALISM

Europe must not only come to terms with the environmental destruction, to which it contributes disproportionately on a global scale, Europe must also lead the way in bringing about a lean and socially just state at the same time. Social justice, by and large, means gender justice today (UNDP, 1995). The eastward expansion of the Union will further increase this problem dimension.

Faced by the marginalization of women on the labor markets due to the workings of globalization, Europe is tempted to spend its way out to maintain its position in a global context. The eastward expansion of the Union will mean, that millions of up to now economically marginalized women will become citizens of the Union, whose fate has to be taken care of by Brussels at least in some way.

Aggregate societal data suggest that after the transformation, the situation of women in Eastern and Central Europe did *relatively* deteriorate in many ways (Cornia, 1993, 1994). Since Cornia's very telling research results are easily available internationally, it might suffice here to quote some aggregate UNDP data to further illustrate our point. Our aggregate data show, how difficult a relatively rapid integration of the more traditionalist, rural and in many ways backward East into the European Union could become. Only the Czech Republic is socially by any means on a comparable level with the more highly developed countries of Western Europe:

Table 6.1: The marginalization of women, social devastation and decay in former communist countries of Central and Eastern Europe in comparison to the European Union countries

Indicator	CS	H	BUL	PL	ROM	ALB	EU
maternal mortality per 100000 live births	14	21	40	15	210	100	**9**
sulfur and nitrogen emissions per capita	239	141	-	141	-	-	**74**
Rapes per 100000 women	12	31	21	19	-	-	**17**
homicides by men per 100000	1.3	3.5	4.0	2.5			**1.6**
prisoners per 100000 inhabitants	-	142	160	204	-	-	**59**
suicides by men per 100000	30	58	23	24	13	-	**19**
total health expenditure as % of GDP	5.9	6.0	5.4	5.1	3.9	-	**8.2**
mean years of schooling female population >25y.	8.6	9.9	6.4	7.8	6.7	5.2	**9.9**
mean years of schooling male population >25y.	9.8	9.7	7.6	8.5	7.5	7.2	**10.3**
tertiary graduates as % of population of normal graduate age	11.8	6.4	6.4	6.6	2.2	1.7	**12.6**
average age of women at first marriage	22.2	22.4	21.1	22.8	21.1	20.4	**25.1**
% of seats in parliament occupied by women	9%	7%	13%	9%	3%	6%	**13%**
human development index rank on the world scale	**27.**	**31.**	**48.**	**49.**	**72.**	**76.**	-

Source: our own compilations from UNDP (HDR, 1994). The world rankings of the EU countries on the human development index were in that year:

Sweden	*4.*
France	6.
NL	9.
UK	10.
Germany	11.
Austria	12.
Belgium	13.
DK	15.
SF	16.
LUX	17.
IRE	21.
Italy	22.
Spain	23.
Greece	25.
Portugal	**42.**

Gender empowerment, as it is known, combines parliamentary seats, held by women, the share of women in the total number of administrators and managers in a country, the share of women in the professional and technical workforce, and the share of women in earned income (UNDP, 1996). Table 5.3 shows the performance of the transformation countries in comparison to Western democracies:

Table 6.2: gender empowerment

CND	0.685
USA	0.645
Japan	*0.445*
NL	0.646
NOR	0.786
SF	0.710
France	*0.437*
SW	0.779
Spain	*0.490*
Australia	0.590
BLG	0.580
Austria	0.641
NZ	0.685
CH	0.594
UK	0.530
DK	0.718
GER	0.654
IRE	0.504
ITA	0.593
GRE	*0.370*
ISR	*0.485*
HUN	**0.507**
POL	**0.431**
BUL	**0.486**

Source: our own compilations from UNDP, 1996

Eastern Europe, finding itself at the absolute lower middle range of the continuum between backward and 'modern' societies, characterized by the values of education as an end in itself, self-realization outside traditional role patterns, associated with child-bearing and the family, control of male aggressive behavior and a developed social welfare system, socially belongs much more to the countries, still (semi-)characterized by traditional role patterns. In the industrialized world, countries as different as Japan, France, Israel and Greece also have a gender empowerment index lower than 0.500. They all have in common a certain secondary role of women in public life, as compared to the real world leaders in terms of emancipation, like the Protestant democracies in Scandinavia, the Netherlands and Canada. The unquestionable advances in the relative role of women, that were evident throughout the region before the year 1989, came to a grinding halt after the transformation. With the background of the general poverty levels, sketched above, the socially disruptive dimension of this conflict becomes evident.

For the political economy of the world system, interesting research questions arise out of such tendencies. Does the market economy, especially in its dependent variety, in the end really marginalize women further, or does the (re)advent of full-fledged capitalism bring about a marked improvement in the social situation of women? There emerge very interesting results on the situation of women from our empirical investigations in Table 4.1.

Three measures are used to further test the relationship between globalization and gender-related human development. One is maternal mortality, the second is the UNDP gender-related development index, the third is the gender empowerment measure. The first and the third index are more distribution-oriented than the second indicator. Each year, 290 women per 100000 live births lose their lives in the moment of giving birth. What is the ultimate moment of happiness in a life for woman and man, to experience in togetherness the advent of a newly-born life, becomes the ultimate pain for millions of mothers around the world. They lose their lives due to the structural violence existing in the world system, they lose their lives in their ultimate moment of loneliness while giving birth, desolated and marginalized by a social order on the global level that produces more and more commodities, services and pollution but that forgets about the poor backyards, shanty towns and desolate clinics in the world poverty belts. The distribution conflict evident in the health sector, often under constraints from 'structural adjustment programs', has a real, deadly consequence for them. In the industrialized countries of the OECD, maternal mortality is 11 per 100000. That is to say, at the global level there is an 'excess mortality' of **279 women per 100000 live births,** considering the progress in medicine reached at the level of the western democracies. In Eastern Europe, maternal mortality already reaches 66 per 100000 live births, and in the developing countries, 420. All three indicators of the female *situation de la vie* are being significantly blocked by MNC penetration (see Table 4.1).

Our results indicate that dependency is by far the most important determinant of maternal mortality, and that the two dependency-related indicators: *terms of trade* and *trade dependency* co-determine the process of maternal mortality in the world system. Our results also indicate that gender empowerment and gender development are significantly and negatively influenced by MNC penetration.

7) DEVELOPMENT OR DECAY?

More and more, the promise of growth that is inherent still in almost any government or other official international document on a world scale, is being challenged by the knowledge, that development under present conditions means decay. The world system scholar Richard K. Moore commented on the World Systems Network on my idea to speak about a theory of decay, and not a theory of development (<wsn@csf.colorado.edu>, 4th of August, 1997):

> The biosphere is decaying - being polluted from all directions – and various kinds of collapse are just waiting to happen, the question is only one of timing. The environmental movement itself is decaying, removing the main counter pressure to biosphere decay.

> The nation-state system is being intentionally led to decay by the neoliberal forces of globalization. Social services are being systematically dismantled, governments are being bankrupted, privatization/laissez-faire has become the effective religion of the day, and national sovereignty is being dismantled economically, politically, and militarily (...)

From everything, we have said, it should be clear that in theological/philosophical terms, we neither share - in the words unpublished words of scholar Alberto Moreira from Brazil (1997), - in the *'colonization of the realms of life'* nor in the temptation to declare the *'bankruptcy of modernity'*. We cannot give up authentic conquests of modernity in the various fields of social life, that are in the service of the poor. We are sent straight back to the search for the human factor, for the integrity of being, that is the counterpoint to anxiety, alienation, solitude, the feeling of void and lack of meaning, which, according to Moreira, are the fruit of a life spent as isolated subjects surrounded by multitude of lifeless objects. Great masters of humanity, such as Buddha, St. Francis, the Polish Jewish doctor Janusz Korczak, who went with his children to the concentration camp, or the 19th Century French-Peruvian feminist Flora Tristan, or all these martyrs of faith during the totalitarian dictatorships of our Century, like Otto Neururer, a Tyrolean parish priest, murdered by the Nazis during the Second World War, all have shown a way beyond the civilization of commodities and power, and that this deficit in humanity cannot be compensated even by the greatest amount and abundance of things possessed (Moreira, 1997). Such philosophical reservations are not in vain. The social anomalies that accompany 'growth' are increasing on a world scale, making the very notion of 'growth' as the expression of *'having'* instead of *'being'* questionable more than ever before. The overweight consumer, buying an automobile and driving it down the next 200 meters for his shopping, increases more the real GDP of a society than the same person after his 'conversion' to buy a bicycle at less than 10% the price of his car (and by diligently using it thus probably avoiding a heart attack).

The following UNDP indicators for the western democracies (Canada through to Malta, 34 countries) were used to show the relationship between real GDP per capita in purchasing power parity rates and social and ecological anomaly:

- *prisoners per 100000 inhabitants*
- *intentional homicides by men per 100000 people*
- *drug crimes per 100000 people*
- *reported adult rapes (thousands)*
- *injuries and deaths from road accidents per 100000 people*
- *suicides per 100000 people, male and female*
- *divorces per 1000 couples*
- *municipal waste in kg per person and year*

Having more increases the contradictions of modern society in an often linear way; viz. more prison inmates, more murderers, more drug criminality, more sexual violence, more traffic accidents, more suicide, more unhappy marriages, and more waste. Above, we hinted at the ecological disasters, that the capitalist civilization and its philosophical twin brother, 'real socialism', brought or brings about on a global scale. Now it is to be shown, that development does not bring necessarily about *happiness*, but more often than not, *social decay*:

Graph 7.1: Theories of development or theories of decay? Purchasing power and social decay in 34 developed western democracies

prisoners

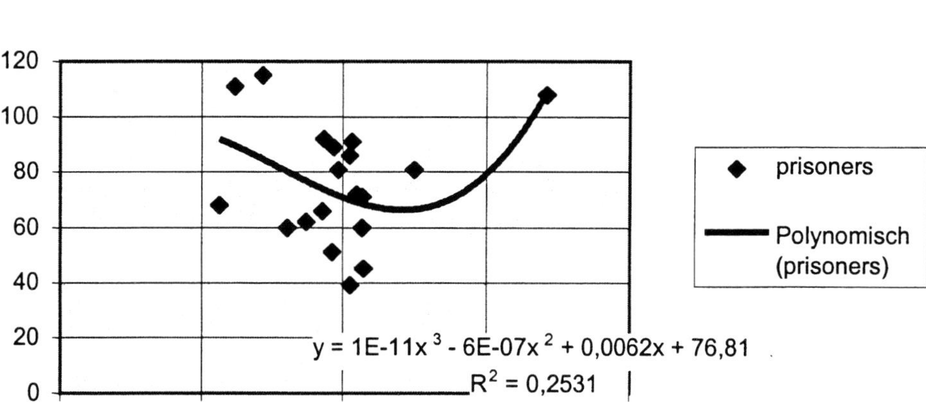

$$y = 1E\text{-}11x^3 - 6E\text{-}07x^2 + 0,0062x + 76,81$$
$$R^2 = 0,2531$$

Legend: in this and in the following graphs, the x-axis symbolizes purchasing power parity rates in real US $, while the y-axis is a UNDP-indicator of social decay per total population

homicides

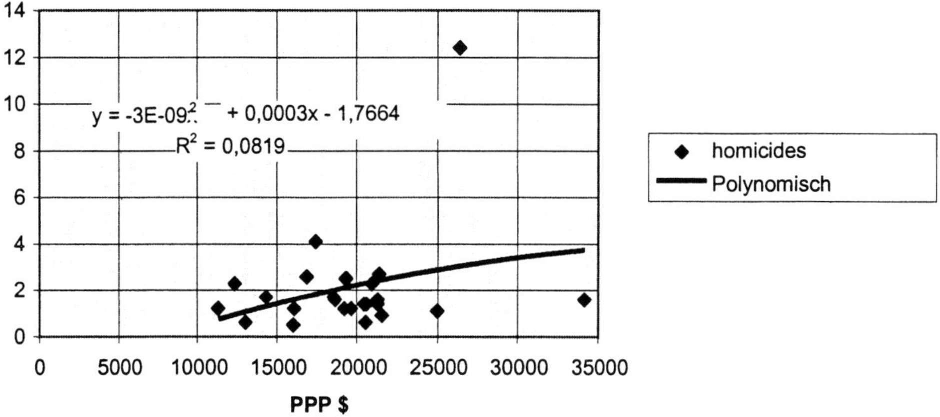

$$y = -3E\text{-}09x^2 + 0,0003x - 1,7664$$
$$R^2 = 0,0819$$

drug crimes

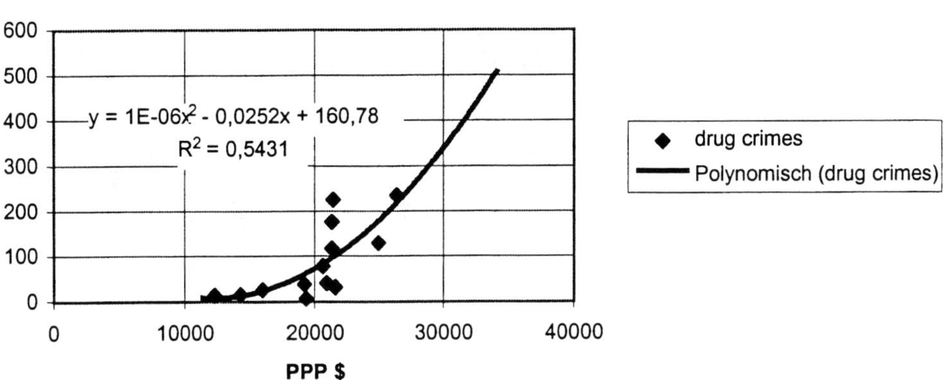

rape

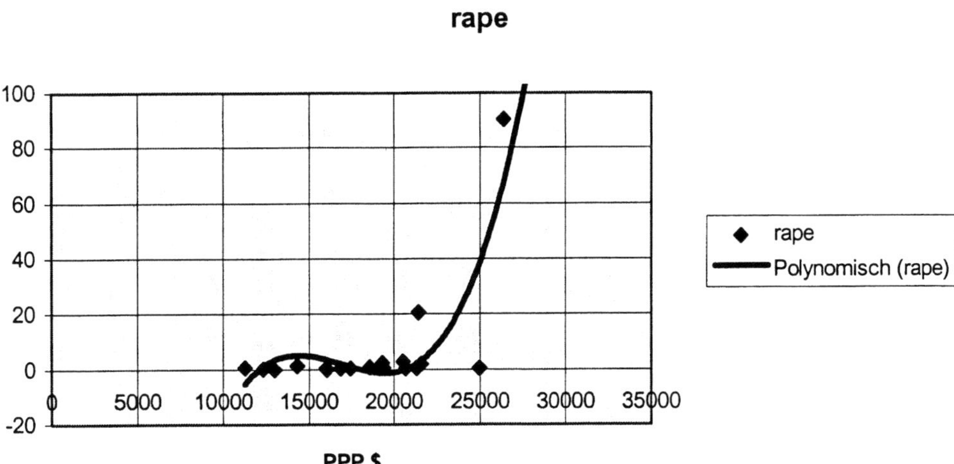

 Arno Tausch

road accidents

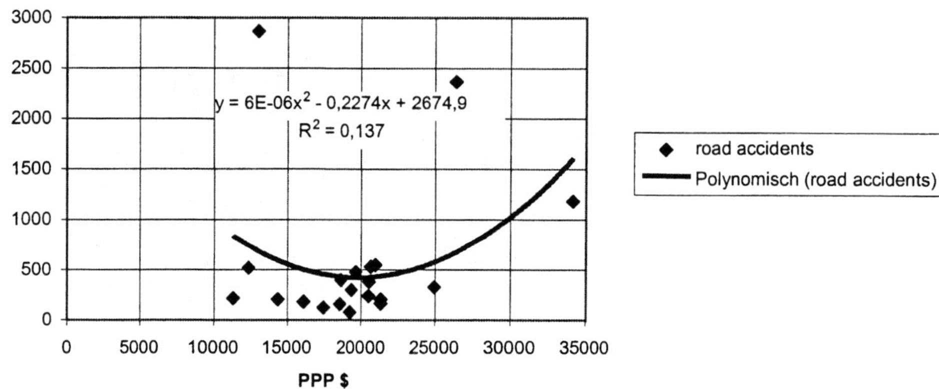

male suicide

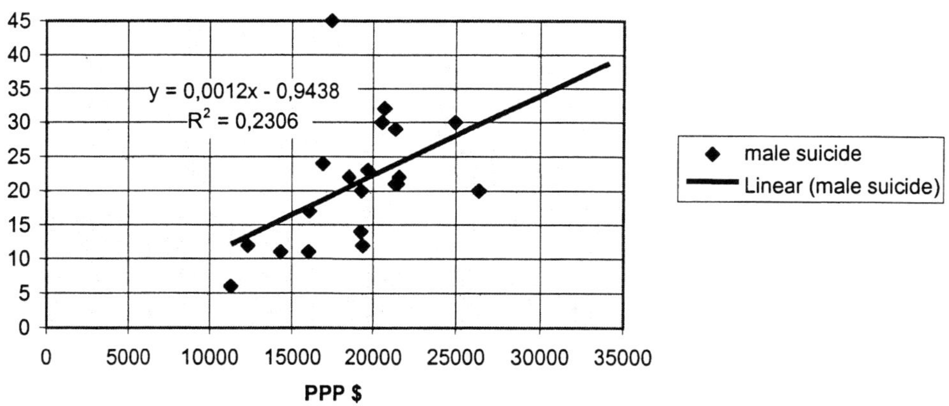

female suicide

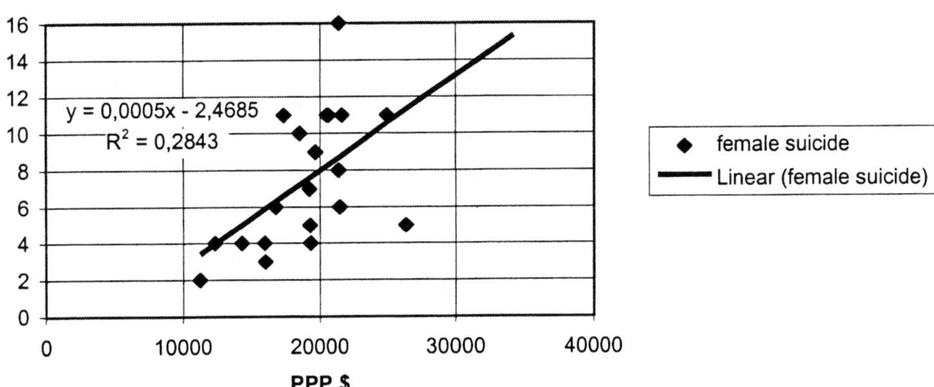

divorce rate

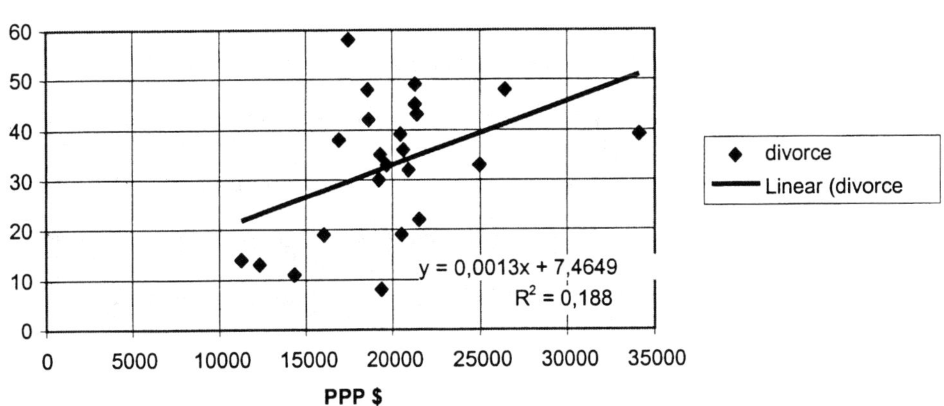

municipal waste

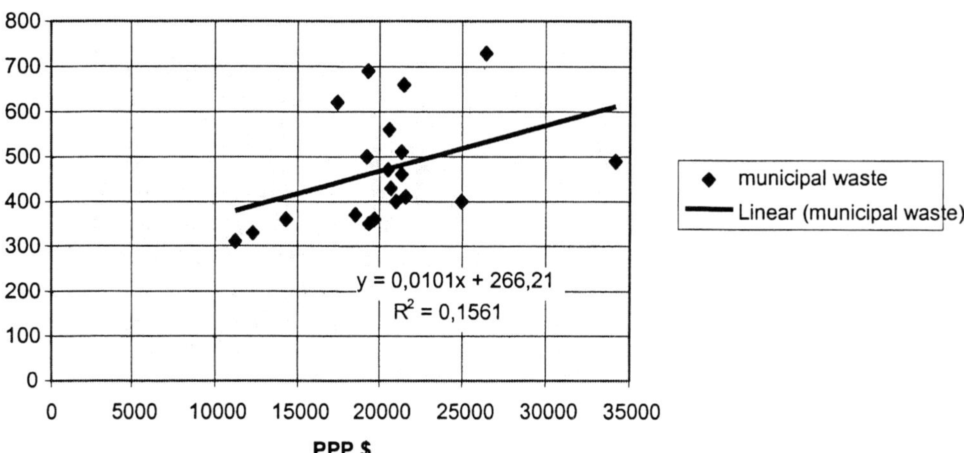

Thus, we are confronted with the limits of development, the central objective of the economy-dominated attempts at transnational integration.

Chapter 2

INSTABILITY OF THE TRANSFORMATION PROCESS

Arno Tausch

Associate Visiting Professor, Department of Political Science,
Innsbruck University, Austria

8) THE INSTABILITY OF THE TRANSFORMATION PROCESS

About two-third of the world's people now live under relatively pluralistic and democratic regimes. Does history end there? Since 1980, nearly 85 elections were held in East and South-East Asia. In Sub-Saharan Africa (since 1990 30 multiparty elections), Latin America (since 1974 150 elections) and in the Arab world (since 1990 22 general elections) democracy - in the formal sense - seems to have strengthened. Thus, the democratic experience of Eastern Europe after 1989 seems to be a general trend. But is it all really so? The long-run tradition of a bourgeoisie national state is the *differentia specifica* between the centers and the peripheries (Amin, 1997). Nationalism will continue to receive a powerful impetus from the contradictions of globalization. One important more recent theory (Huntington) holds, that cultural dividing lines increasingly achieve relevance; and even could threaten to endanger the transformation project to build up a stable, market oriented western democracy on the ruins of communism.

To those, accustomed to the dialogue about international politics as a *'dismal science'* it will be no surprise to learn about international research results regarding genocide and mass murder in this century (Rummel, 1994, 1995). 218 repressive regimes (141 state regimes and 77 quasi-state and group regimes) from 1900 to 1987 have killed nearly 170 million of their own citizens and foreigners - about four times the number of people killed in domestic and international wars during that same period. Among the mass murderous regimes of this century, totalitarian communism alone is accountable for more than 100 million deaths (Rummel, 1994, 1995). Power kills; democracy is the general method of non-violence, says Rummel: but what happens, if democracy and non-violence are seriously undermined by ethno-political conflict? After the horrors of the Holocaust and the Second World War, the following victimization of mostly civilians stand out in contemporary history:

Graph 8.1a: Victims of mass murder

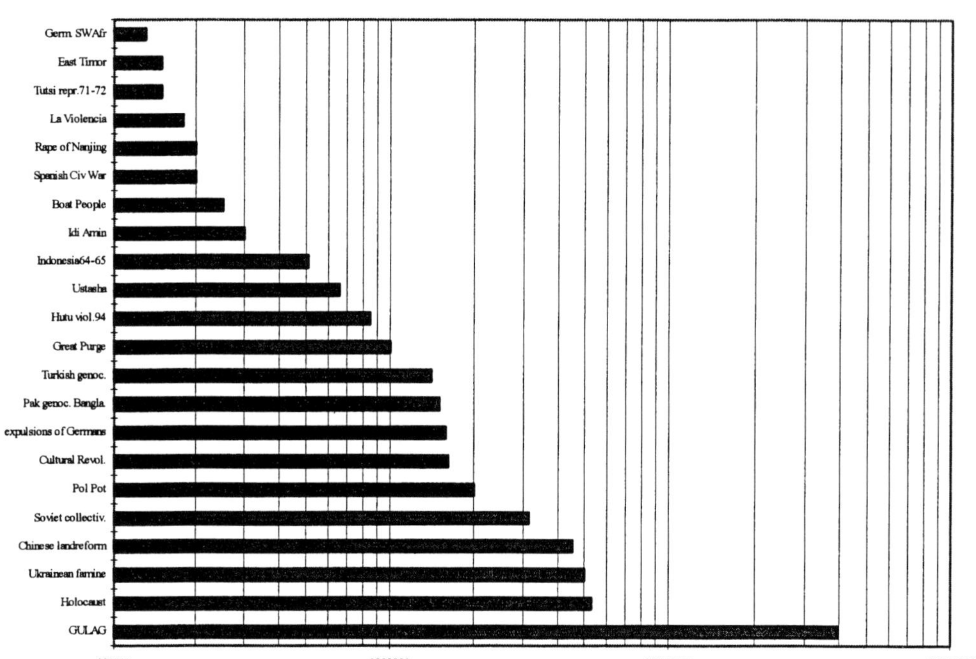

Legend: victims of totalitarian regimes since 1900. Source: our own compilations from Stiftung Entwicklung und Frieden, 1996, based on Rummel, 1994. The statistical tables, contained in Rummel's website (*http://www.freedomnest.com)* about the **victims of democide and repression in history** are:

Chinese Infanticide 1971-	110
Soviet Union	61,9
All Wars, 30BC-19AD	40,5
Wars 1900-	38
Communist China	35,2
Old China (-1900)	33,5
Mongols 1300 - 1400	29,9
Chinese Leap Forward	27
Nazi Germany	20,9
African Slavery	17,3
American Indians	13,8
Nationalist China	10,1
Japan (1936-45)	5,9
Old India (-1800)	4,5
Chinese guerrilla (1923-49)	3,5
other 20th Century murderers	2,8
Old Iran (-19th Century)	2
Ottoman Emp.(-19th Century)	2

Pol Pot	2
Turkey 1909-18	1,9
Communism in Vietnam 1945-87	1,7
North Korea	1,7
Poland (1945-48)	1,6
Old Japan (-19th Century)	1,5
Pakistan (1958-87)	1,5
Mexico (1900-20)	1,4
Tito (1944-87)	1,1
Old Russia (-19th Century)	1
Crusades 1095-1272	1
Zarist Russia 1900-17	1
Aztecs	1
Atatürk 1919-23	0,9
Chinese Warlords (1917-49)	0,9
UK 1900-87	0,8
Portugal 1926-82	0,7
Indonesia 1965-87	0,7
Spanish Inquisition 1500-1700	0,35
French Revolution	0,263
Albigensian Crusade (1208-1249)	0,2
Witch Hunts (1400-1600)	0,1
Grand Total (regimes and repressions 1-40)	**482,113**

Rummel's research on democide and war poses very intricate questions to the very nature, that we world system researchers see our role as social scientists:

„Political scientists almost everywhere have promoted the expansion of government power. They have functioned as the clergy of oppression" (Rummel, 1998: http://www.freedomnest.com)

In absolute terms, we get the following distribution of democide and other victims of politics in history:

(1) Marxism in the 7 most brutal comunist regimes of the world since 1917 (USSR, China, Vietnam, North Korea, Cambodia, Poland, Yugoslavia)	135,7
(2) Chinese Infanticide 1971 onwards	110
(3) Old Asia	91,3
(4) all wars in history	78,5
(5) the victims of the expansion of the capitalist world economy: Africans and Latin American Indians	47,9
(6) National Socialism	20,9
all others (482 million victims minus the victims of regimes 1-7)	15
(7) 3rd world dictatorships-1900 onwards	10,16

Legend: our own calculations from Rummel's website

Graph 8.1b now shows the distribution of the victims of mass murder by regime and repression type:

Graph 8.1b: victims of mass murder

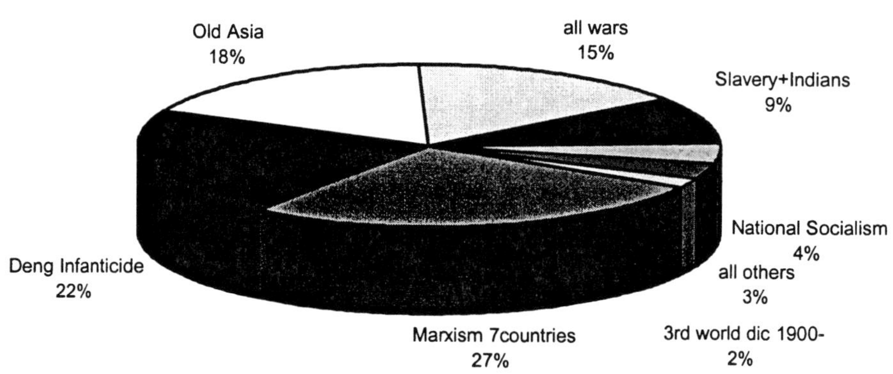

Legend: our own calculations from Rummel, see above

Who will be the groups that most violently are going to challenge the logic of accumulation on a global scale? Does capitalist globalization, that process of unequal and uneven development, in the end cause the cultural conflicts in the world system, as globalization theories would maintain (Axtmann, 1995)? Among the most murderous regimes of our waning 20th Century, which killed 169.2 million people from 1900 to 1987, only **2 belonged to the capitalist center -** the UK as a retreating colonial power, and Germany (see below), which might be termed as a semi-semi-periphery, and not a proper center at the time of the onset of the National Socialist threat (Pommerania, Eastern Prussia), **while 37 others were countries of the periphery and the semi-periphery. Peace and survival on earth will be determined to a great degree, whether or not democratic, and not authoritarian 'reform' models will take hold. Both German Nazism and Communism in the 7 leading most repressive Marxist regimes of the world since 1900, in between them share already 31% of estimated violent deaths in history, to which one should add the 22%, comprised by China's infanticide (Rummel, 1998, website).** But the unspeakable terror of Nazism stands out in terms of its **singularity** because of the **time factor** (millions of people killed per regime year in power), the **inescapability of terror factor** (no victim of the Shoah could save herself or himself by becoming a member of the Party), and the **inclusiveness of terror** (number of victims per population group under de-facto rule).

Ethno-nationalistic conflicts, terrorism and war were to break out along the real 'earthquake line' in today's international system, the great dividing line **between the cultures**. That is at least what Samuel Huntington, Harvard professor of political science and for many years one the closest advisers of successive United States governments on matters of international security and military policy, has maintained in his contributions. Our counter-thesis is that the cultural conflict lines might overlap more and more with the conflict lines between centers and peripheries,

Huntington tries to offer a socio-cultural explanation to the question, where Europe's frontier will be finally drawn. Are there clear empirically observable tendencies in development performance according to the classification, suggested by Huntington, of the basic underlying socio-cultural patterns of a given country, distinguishing the Orthodox and Islamic regions of the world economy as the least compatible with the logic of market-oriented development? The following graph shows the probable borders of the European Union by around 2008 - they do not exactly overlap, but well coincide with the Huntington map. The two remaining Baltic states, the Ukraine, the present EU-member Greece and the future member Cyprus and the rest of former Yugoslavia could become the zones, where the spheres of influence between the Protestant and Catholic Western and Orthodox Eastern Europe will be most fiercely contested:

Map 8.1: The European Union - 2008

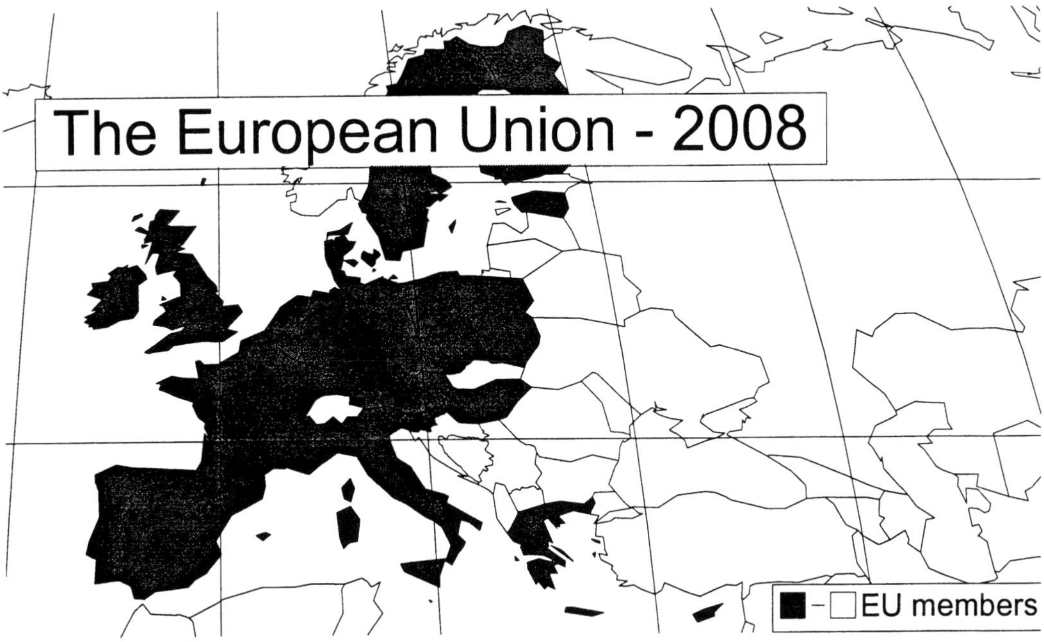

Legend: a successful EU extension scenario, based on the '5 + 1' model, including the Czech Republic, Slovenia, Poland, Hungary, Estonia, and Cyprus (from West to East)

Professor Huntington's thesis is not at all abstract and has - however we view it - a vital importance for the future of the European Union. From Marseilles to Algiers, from Madrid to Rabat, from Rome to Tunis or Sofia, from Athens to Bucharest or Cairo, from Vienna to Kiev or Ankara or Teheran geographical distances are smaller or about equal as the distances from these European Union cities to the Canary Islands, the Irish Republic, northern Scotland or northern Scandinavia or other remoter parts of the already existing Union. The migration pressures from Eastern Europe and the population explosion on the southern rim of the Mediterranean will increase. In 30 years, the population balance on the southern rim of Europe will have dramatically shifted. The southern border of Europe already is and will even more so become a border between relatively wealthy developed societies and societies, that are threatened by overpopulation, scarcity of resources, and poverty. By the year 2015, 371.8 million people will live in the 19 countries of the Arab world alone. The facts of underdevelopment in the Arab world are lamentable enough:

armed forces	2,257,000
malaria per 100.000	125
military expenditures as % of combined educ and health expenditures	108
terms of trade (1987=100)	91
adult literacy male	67,2
life expectancy	63,5
TBC per 100.000	60,5
infant mortality rate	55
adult literacy female	44,2
contraceptive prevalence	37
without access to sanitation	30
female share in total incomes	21,4
without access to safe water	21
% children underweight	17
people not surviving age 40	14
without access to health	13
% children low-weight at birth	11
school drop-out rate at grade 5	7
CO2 emissions per capita (tons)	3,7
health expenditure per GDP	2,9
human development index	0,636
internet users per 1000	0,2
GDP per capita fall 1980-1990 in 1987 PPP$	-1101
current account balance in $	-15,395,000

Source: our own compilations from UNDP, HDR, 1998

These tendencies are all the more notable, because eastward expansion of NATO and the EU is not synchronic, and the most probable outcome would leave open an entire geographical corridor from Russia and Belarus right through to Switzerland. While Ireland, Sweden, Finland, and Austria are the four neutral EU members, the Slovak Republic - left out - would provide a corridor through the European heartland - from Kiew to Geneva. The most realistic scenario is of course Huntington's borderline between western Christianity (Catholics and Protestants) on the one hand and Orthodox Christianity and Islam on the other hand in Europe. Huntington's European eastern border rather would look like the following:

Map 8.2: Huntington's border of the EU, 2008

Legend: Huntington's theory, applied to the eastern border of the European Union. Scandinavia, the Baltic States, Poland, the Czech and Slovak Republics, Hungary, Slovenia and Croatia are seen as part of the West; while the rest of Eastern Europe belongs to the Orthodox or Islamic heritage.

The still existing high concentration of development problems and population dynamics in the immediate vicinity of Europe over the next 30 years will dramatically change the shape of international politics, economics and migratory pressures in the region.

Huntington's theory of course can be challenged from the perspective of dependency theory. A dependency-oriented explanation of underdevelopment would hold, that the *'Huntington factor'* is in reality disappearing, whenever we control for MNC penetration. Thus MNC penetration, and not 'the Huntington factor' or *'Islam'* are responsible for the semi-peripherization of the Arab world. The main result of our own investigation will be that the Huntington factor only plays a certain role when we do not control for the amount of MNC penetration; however, if we do consider MNC penetration properly, the effects become indeed weaker or are even the reverse.

The(in)validity of Huntington's culture conflict approach on a world level

However forceful Huntington's theory might seem to be at first sight, we can consider it to be falsified by our investigations. While Lipset and Weede seem to be inclined to regard Confucianism as a growth precondition, Huntington's theory is more pessimistic and foresees a joint rising world cultural challenge against the dominant centers by Islam and Orthodoxy. The important element for the test of Huntington's theory seems to be the *joint* interaction of Islam and or Orthodoxy, classified under his index. The Huntington-Index might be thus the mere reflection of this underlying geographical and world economic peripherization, that jointly affects the Orthodox and the Islamic world. This joint peripherization would cast a large shadow on the prospects for market-economic reform in Russia, Romania, Bulgaria, and the 'Federal Republic of Yugoslavia'.

Enough of ideologies. Let the hard facts speak. The Huntington-index of the clash of civilizations (Huntington-Index countries = 1, other countries = 0), is used here as an important control variable in macro-sociological explanations of world development:

Table 8.1: The influence of Huntington's index on development performance at the level of world society

	MNC PEN73	Govex	Trade Dep	social sec	Huntington-1	Women Parl	Women %LF	ln PCI	ln PCI^2	ln(MPR+1)	Fertility Rate	Constant
adjust-ment	-0,761	-1,491	0,125	-3,538	0,048	-0,058	0,83	0,133	0,01	-0,024	-0,004	21,47
	0,188	1,029	0,349	5,208	0,029	0,04	0,806	0,06	0,007	0,022	0,002	19,93
	0,301	2,649										
	4,341	111										
	335,1	779,1										
t-Test	**-4,035**	-1,449	0,359	-0,679	1,684	-1,46	1,03	**2,193**	1,353	-1,08	**-1,989**	

	MNC PEN73	Govex	Trade Dep	social sec	Huntington-1	Women Parl	Women %LF	social sec	ln PCI^2	ln(MPR+1)	Fertility Rate	Constant
growth	-0,944	-0,625	0,167	-4,228	0,021	-0,084	0,209	0,138	0,015	-0,038	-0,003	26,73
	0,165	0,9	0,305	4,558	0,025	0,035	0,706	0,053	0,007	0,02	0,002	17,45
	0,409	2,319										
	6,997	111										
	413,8	596,8										
t-Test	**-5,723**	-0,694	0,546	-0,928	0,844	**-2,426**	0,296	**2,616**	2,311	**-1,956**	-1,645	

	LEX 1960	1 der e-funct	1 der π-func	MNC PEN73	Viol Civ Rits	Trade Dep	Terms Trade	Huntington-1	Women Parl	Women %LF	ln(MPR+1)	Constant
DYN	0,811	-0,025	-0,038	0,984	0,013	0,001	-0,049	2E-04	-0,706	-29,49	-0,299	26,79
LEX	0,885	0,024	0,031	0,708	0,017	0,006	0,173	0,002	0,742	6,961	0,037	2,724
	0,737	2,257										
	28,23	111										
	1582	565,3										
t-Test	0,916	-1,054	-1,216	**1,391**	0,793	0,238	-0,282	0,147	-0,952	**-4,237**	**-7,993**	

	MNC PEN73	Govex	Trade Dep	social sec	Huntington-1	Women Parl	Women %LF	ln PCI	ln PCI^2	ln(MPR+1)	Fertility Rate	Constant
pol rights viola-tions	0,536	1,045	0,079	-1,473	0,02	0,06	1,002	-0,103	0,004	0,009	5E-04	5,987
	0,108	0,588	0,199	2,976	0,016	0,023	0,461	0,035	0,004	0,013	0,001	11,39

	MNC PEN73	Govex	Trade Dep	social sec	Huntington-1	Women Parl	Women %LF	ln PCI	ln PCI^2	ln(MPR+1)	Fertility Rate	Constant
	0,576	1,514										
	13,68	111										
	344,9	254,4										
t-Test	**4,973**	**1,778**	0,399	-0,495	*1,193*	**2,663**	**2,175**	-2,992	0,939	0,713	0,453	
(headers)	MNC PEN73	Govex	Trade Dep	social sec	*Huntington-1*	**Women Parl**	**Women %LF**	ln PCI	ln PCI^2	ln(MPR+1)	Fertility Rate	Constant
civil rights	0,354	1,21	-0,015	-0,074	*0,002*	0,037	0,571	-0,087	8E-04	-0,011	-9E-04	3,205
violations	0,086	0,468	0,159	2,372	*0,013*	0,018	0,367	0,028	0,003	0,01	8E-04	9,077
	0,586	1,206										
	14,28	111										
	228,7	161,5										
	4,121	**2,582**	-0,093	-0,031	*0,177*	**2,027**	**1,554**	-3,15	0,244	-1,115	-1,041	
HDI	MNC PEN73	Govex	Trade Dep	social sec	*Huntington-1*	**Women Parl**	Women %LF	ln PCI	ln PCI^2	ln(MPR+1)	Fertility Rate	Constant
	-0,095	0,173	0,006	0,02	*-5E-04*	**-0,003**	-0,033	7E-04	-2E-04	7E-04	6E-05	0,488
	0,008	0,043	0,015	0,217	*0,001*	**0,002**	0,034	0,003	3E-04	9E-04	8E-05	0,832
	0,871	0,111										
	67,9	111										
	9,137	1,358										
	-12,04	**4,018**	0,392	0,092	*-0,38*	**-1,72**	-0,986	0,26	-0,598	0,736	0,808	
	MNC PEN73	**Govex**	Trade Dep	social sec	*Huntington-1*	**Women Parl**	Women %LF	ln PCI	ln PCI^2	ln(MPR+1)	Fertility Rate	Constant
	-0,071	0,101	-0,006	0,16	*6E-04*	-0,002	-0,032	0,002	-1E-04	4E-04	8E-05	0,026
	0,006	0,031	0,011	0,159	*9E-04*	0,001	0,025	0,002	2E-04	7E-04	6E-05	0,608
	0,873	0,081										
	69,29	111										
	4,971	0,724										

Gender Development Index

	MNC PEN73	Govex	Trade Dep	social sec	Huntington-1	Women Parl	Women %LF	ln PCI	ln PCI^2	ln(MPR+1)	Fertility Rate	Constant
	-12,38	**3,232**	-0,609	1,008	*0,692*	**-2,021**	-1,311	1,096	-0,58	0,568	1,401	
(headers)	MNC PEN73	Govex	**Trade Dep**	social sec	*Huntington-1*	**Women Parl**	Women %LF	ln PCI	ln PCI^2	ln(MPR+1)	Fertility Rate	Constant
	-0,02	0,016	0,015	-0,184	*0,001*	0,005	-0,018	0,003	-2E-04	-6E-05	4E-05	0,866
	0,004	0,023	0,008	0,114	*6E-04*	9E-04	0,018	0,001	2E-04	5E-04	4E-05	0,437
	0,818	0,058										
	45,46	111										

	MNC PEN73	Govex
	1,691	0,375

Gender Empowerment Index

	MNC PEN73	Govex	Trade Dep	social sec	Huntington-1	Women Parl	Women %LF	ln PCI	ln PCI^2	ln(MPR+1)	Fertility Rate
	-4,882	0,7	**2,019**	-1,606	*1,868*	**6,039**	-1,006	1,946	-0,958	-0,117	1,015

	MNC PEN73	Govex	Trade Dep	social sec	Huntington-1	Women Parl	Women %LF	ln PCI	ln PCI^2	ln(MPR+1)	Fertility Rate	%agland	Constant
% forest	-0,391	-1,834	-5,294	-2,078	*28,24*	0,334	0,689	-10,99	-0,366	-0,082	0,107	0,008	-63,58
area	0,128	1,408	7,606	2,559	*38,26*	0,211	0,293	5,918	0,46	0,055	0,164	0,014	146,8
	0,313	19,45											
	4,173	110											
	18940	41610											
t-Test	**-3,043**	-1,303	-0,696	-0,812	*0,738*	1,584	**2,353**	-1,856	-0,797	-1,495	0,654	0,564	

	MNC PEN73	Govex	Trade Dep	social sec	Huntington-1	Women Parl	Women %LF	ln PCI	ln PCI^2	ln(MPR+1)	Fertility Rate	%agland	Constant
annual	0,015	0,091	**-0,646**	**-0,22**	*3,273*	0,008	0,001	0,278	-0,054	0,003	-0,004	3E-04	-11,53
deforest	0,006	0,07	0,377	0,127	*1,898*	0,01	0,015	0,294	0,023	0,003	0,008	7E-04	7,281
	0,336	0,965											
	4,643	110											
	51,87	102,4											
t-Test	**2,324**	1,306	**-1,712**	**-1,732**	*1,724*	0,748	0,099	0,946	-2,367	1,181	-0,511	0,511	

	MNC PEN73	Govex	Trade Dep	social sec	Huntington-1	Women Parl	Women %LF	ln PCI	ln PCI^2	ln(MPR+1)	Fertility Rate	%agland	Constant
ethno	0,009	0,098	0,218	-0,059	*0,91*	0,016	0,032	0,511	-0,032	-0,002	-0,02	-0,001	-3,323
warfare	0,011	0,118	0,638	0,215	*3,207*	0,018	0,025	0,496	0,039	0,005	0,014	0,001	12,3
	0,109	1,63											
	1,116	110											
	35,59	292,4											
t-Test	0,816	0,83	0,342	-0,275	*0,284*	0,884	1,292	1,031	-0,823	-0,391	-1,444	-0,985	

	MNC PEN73	Govex	Trade Dep	social sec	Huntington-I	Women Parl	Women %LF	ln PCI	ln PCI^2	ln(MPR+1)	Fertility Rate	%agland	Constant
destab./	0,002	0,029	0,073	-0,033	0,535	-6E-04	-0,002	-0,048	-0,008	-0,001	-2E-04	-4E-04	-1,938
war	0,003	0,028	0,153	0,052	0,771	0,004	0,006	0,119	0,009	0,001	0,003	3E-04	2,959
	0,095	0,392											
	0,965	110											
	1,78	16,92											
t-Test	0,885	1,02	0,477	-0,633	0,693	-0,151	-0,28	-0,399	-0,883	-1,078	-0,049	-1,55	

Legend: our own calculations with EXCEL 4.0 and 5.0. As in all EXCEL 5.0 outprints in this work, first row: unstandardized regression coefficients, second row: standard errors, last row: t-Test. The values immediately below the standard errors are R^2 (third row, left side entry), *F,* and degrees of freedom (fourth row).

The Huntington Index, under control for MNC penetration, is even significantly and positively related to adjustment and gender empowerment; and the only negative significant effect is the influence on deforestation. Traditional forms of globalization are responsible for the process of stagnation in the world periphery and semi-periphery. So, our empirical investigation can be regarded as supporting the concerns of the environmentalists in the Orthodox and the Islam world, but not as a support to Huntington's theory. And this is quite another matter.

The return of dictatorship? Towards understanding the process of ethno-political conflict and the world-wide refugee problem

In 1989 we heard the prophecy of the 'end of history'. Instead of talking about the end of history, we might be faced with the acceleration of history. Deadly ethno-political conflicts continue to beset the world. In the international system, wars are of course not new; 16 of all the 21 wars with more than a million deaths in history happened during the 20th Century. From 1945 to 1992 more than 25 million people died in wars or as a direct consequence of wars (Stiftung Entwicklung und Frieden, 1997). Civilians have to pay an ever larger price for these wars; the tendency has been rising steadily and in 1990, already 90% of all war victims were civilians. The number of *international* refugees according to the most narrow definitions increased world-wide from 7.8 million in 1982 to 13.2 million according to the strictest criteria in 1996. To these numbers, one would have to add 3.4 million refugee-like situations of people in foreign countries and 23.5 million internal refugees. All together, there were at least *43 million refugees* classified according to *various categories* around the world in 1991 *(op. cit.: 184-185)*. But estimates of the real number of refugees reach as high as 500 million on a global scale (Datta, 1993).

Ethno-political conflicts are among the most vicious forms of international and domestic conflicts. Over 40% of the states of the world have more than 5 major ethnic groups within their borders, with at least one of them facing permanent discrimination (UNDP, 1994). There were 10 major ethnic conflicts in Europe, 6 in the Middle East, 28 in Asia, 23 in Africa, 3 in Latin America during the period 1993-94 (Gurr, 1994). These 50 lethal conflicts produced almost 4 million deaths and displaced 26.8 million people as refugees (Gurr, 1994: 351). It would be wrong, though, to assume that there are necessarily centrifugal tendencies in the international system as such that will still further extend these types of conflicts like bush-fires. Rather, Gurr in his far-reaching empirical work proposes to start from the hypothesis, that the collapse of the communist bloc is only partly to blame for the increase in ethno-political violence, since 54% of all ethno-political conflicts were started before 1987. Since the 1990s, already existing conflicts have tended to intensify, but the spreading of conflicts, Gurr argues, could be avoided. Contention for power, struggle for indigenous rights and ethno-nationalism were the main causes of these conflicts. Huntington's thesis about the clash of civilizations receives a considerable qualification from Gurr's empirical work: only 4 of the ethno-political conflicts correspond to the traditional left-right ideological struggle; while 18 are motivated by civilisational struggles (Gurr, 1994: 357). *Although ethno-political conflict intensified after the end of the Soviet Union, it would be wrong to blame the first process on the second. The disintegration of the Soviet Union only increased an already existing tendency in world society.* Power shifts, the emergence of new states, and revolutions still play an important role in the determination of conflict. *But, according to Gurr, it would be wrong to assume, that the fragmentation tendency of the world system were to continue indefinitely.* Rather, the most likely scenario will be an increase in communal contention about access to power in the weak and heterogeneous states in Africa. Secessionist conflicts outside Africa and the former communist bloc even declined in intensity over the years (Gurr, 1994: 364). Map 8.3 shows the Gurr-Index on a world scale:

Map 8.3: ethno-political conflict in the world system

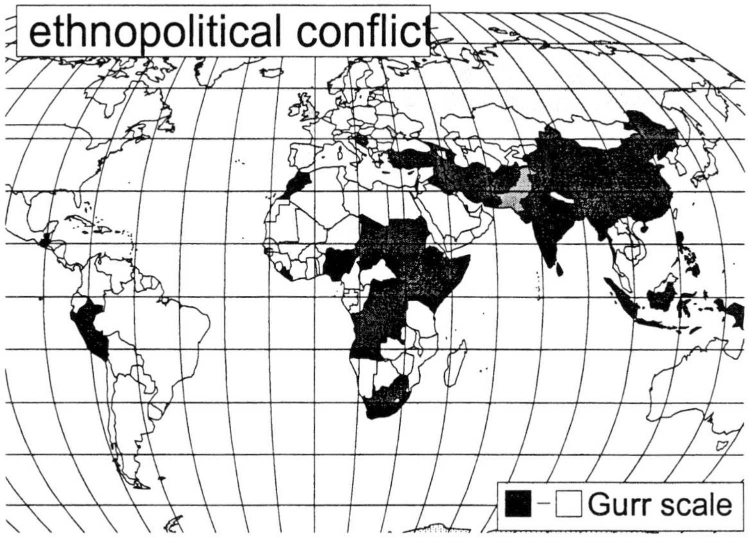

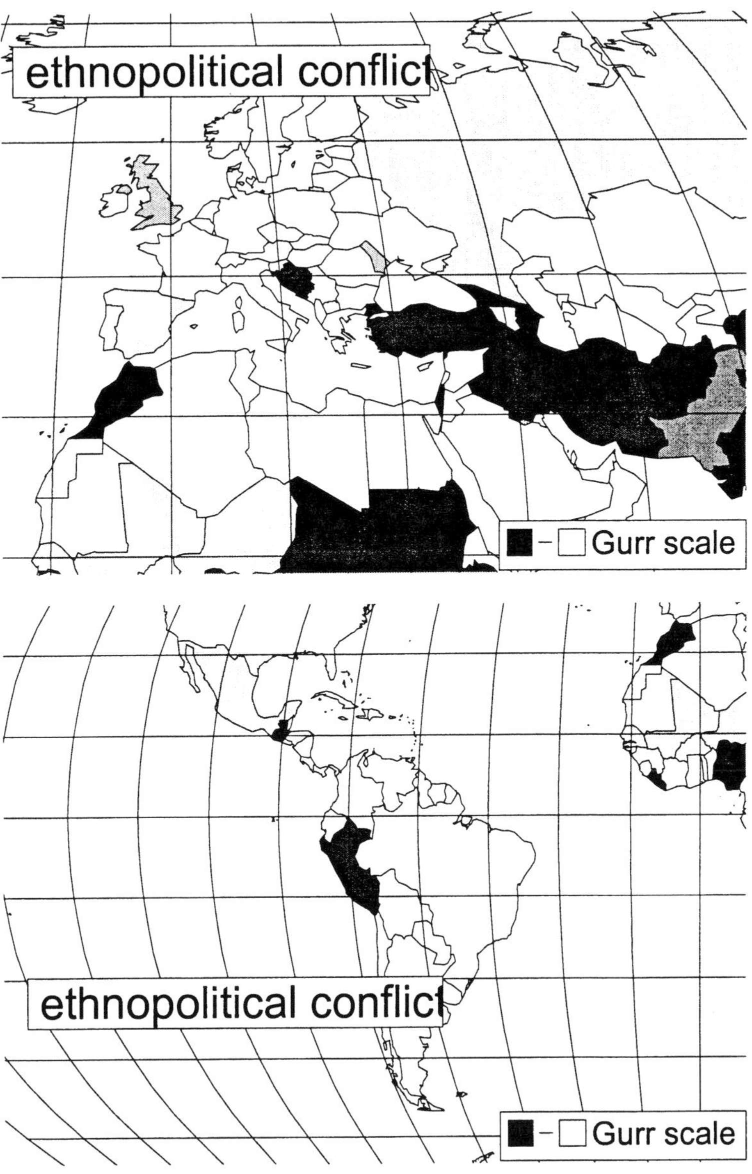
ethnopolitical conflict
■ – □ Gurr scale
ethnopolitical conflict
■ – □ Gurr scale

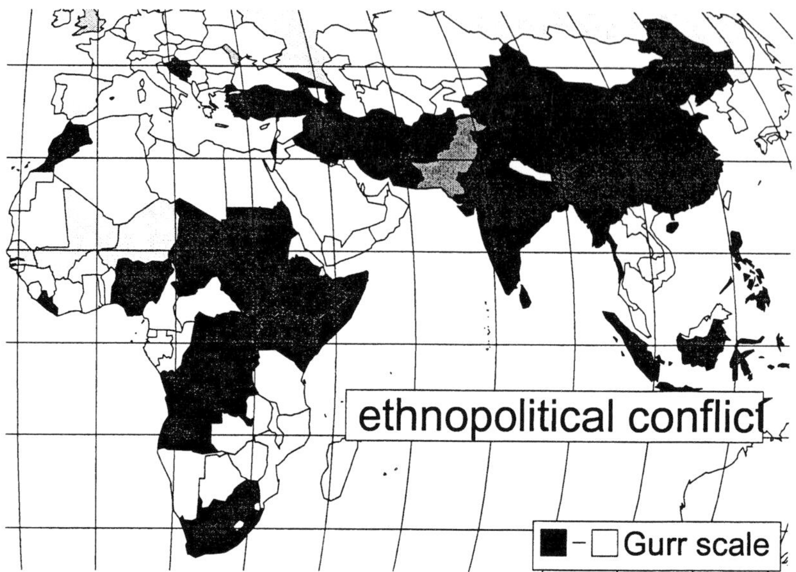

Legend: Gurr (1994) and EXCEL 7.0 map program, as applied to Gurr's original data (Gurr, 1994: 369-375. The Gurr scale - magnitude of ethno-political conflict - is the squared root of the sum of deaths (in 10s of thousands) plus refugees (in 100s of thousands) from ethno-political conflicts 1993-1994. The darker, the more severe the ethno-political conflict.

Macroquantitative evidence on these processes is very difficult to construct and collect, as long as data collection and data reporting is so deficient in many of the new states of the East and continues to be so in the South as well. Thus, our model can be called only a preliminary test of the Deutsch/Huntington approach to ethno-political conflict and had to start with a few available data series that render themselves at least partially to the testing of the general patterns of the new realities of ethno-political conflict around the world. Our predictors included indicators of dependency (aggregate net transfers, that is to say, inflows that are greater than outflows due to international exploitation), of the liberal approach to development (political and human rights violations versus respect), and of the social-policy approach (mean years of schooling, adult literacy rate, human development index, the fertility rate and its change as an indicator of the process of demographic change). The Deutsch/Huntington school however regards alphabetization as an indicator of social mobilization, and hence as a threat to stability.

Our following analysis shows, that the threat to democracy in the semi-periphery and the periphery continues. Superficially, it seems to be, that similar conditions at different times produce similar theories and empirical results: during the emergence of the many new states in the 'Third World' in the early 1960s, more pessimistic versions of modernization theory gained ground. With the contemporary problems of democracy in the former 'Second World', the stability question of the newly emerged or liberated states cannot be separated from such modernization theory dimensions anymore. In the model, that we propose, the chain of causation, underlying the empirical trends, is related to, but not completely patterned according to modernization theories. For Huntington, instability always was determined by social mobilization *(SM)*, which works in the direction of instability *(IST)*. This is at least the consistent interpretation, that Weede (1985) has proposed, and which we follow here.

Deutsch was even more radical than Huntington in expressing the idea that development is a threat to stability. His clearly formulated mathematical formula for political stability expects a positive trade-off between government sector size, income concentration and stability on the one hand and a negative trade-off between social mobilization, level of development and stability on the other hand (Deutsch, 1960/66). Let L denote alphabetization, *pol* the rate of participation of people in politics, which in developed societies could be substituted by v, voter participation; in many societies also by *ve*, the percentage of people, entitled to vote; let y_{10} denote the share of the richest 10% in total incomes, y the per capita income, and *g*, the state sector. S_t, stability, is then equal to

(8.1) $S_t = (g / L * pol) * (y_{10} / y)$

The tragedy in former Yugoslavia could be regarded in many ways as a paradigmatic case, to be explained at least in part by Deutsch's theory. The Deutsch/Huntington school would believe that, however legitimate the issue of transformation from the communist political and economic system in that country might have been, the strategy to cling to communist regional power while opening up the country to the world market was the real and final reason for the break-out of the conflict. And seen in such a respect, this has important lessons for the rest of the region as well.

In fact, Yugoslavia in the 1980s held many world or at least European records in economic and social policy, that seem to be forgotten more and more in the futile debate about early international recognition of Slovenia, Croatia and Bosnia as the alleged main cause for the subsequent tragedy. At first inspection, Yugoslavia should have become a real miracle of neo-liberal economic transformation in the 1980s after the ethno-heterogeneous state class model of the 1970s came to a grinding halt. Malicious social scientists might dig out some day these old journal and book contributions, praising the old leadership for what it had achieved in the name of the market, the international financial institutions, and in the name of economic theory. *Amen.* We refrain from that: *errare humanum est.* Yugoslavia attempted the most-far-reaching neo-liberal transformation strategy in the region; and for that reason alone its experience should be carefully studied elsewhere: (i) Yugoslavia had the most rapid urbanization rate of all European countries from 1960 to 1990 (3.2% per annum). In fact, urban population doubled from 28% to 56% in just thirty years. This enormous potential and challenge of social mobilization was coupled with (ii) a very rapid process of economic transformation and a disappearance of the central state. Yugoslavia recorded the highest rate of gross domestic investment of all countries of the world with complete World Bank WDR data for 1988 and also the highest gross domestic savings rate for the same year. With a savings rate of 2/5 of the national income, Yugoslavia should have been well underway towards self-sustained growth. At the same time, however, the central government in Belgrade reduced in accordance with many international advisors and in a very radical fashion (iii) its role in national economic affairs to almost non-existence. Yugoslavia again holds a world record here, this time for having trimmed down the size of the national total government expenditure as percentage of GNP from 1972 - from 21.1% to 7.5% in 1988. It was the most radical economic transformation from socialism to dependent regional nationalism ever to have been recorded throughout the period of the end of communism in the world; because in no former communist country had there been such a deliberate attempt to reduce the share of the federal government below the 10%-mark. Leszek Balcerowicz also wants to reduce the state sector to 10%. Not even in Pinochet's Chile such a radical cure has been attempted.

In both relative and in absolute terms, Yugoslavia was a megaperformer of a kind of regional post-communist IMF-adapted adjustment. The price of the strategy was very clear, but many will shrug their shoulders and ask: *so what?* The price of the medicine is well-known from many countries now and in a way was also paid in most of the other countries of the region: absolute poverty - according to World Bank *World Development Report* figures 1990 - increased in the crucial years between 1978 and 1987 from 17% of the population to 25% of the population, and earnings per employee fell by 1.4% annually from 1980 to 1987. Still, household income distribution (iv) was still relatively egalitarian, with the highest 20% controlling just 42.8% of total incomes, and thus not tying the rich closely enough to their political system, so that they would be prepared to fight and die for it, while at the same time impoverishing the poor in absolute terms. All the necessary preconditions for instability, as predicted by Karl Deutsch more than 30 years ago, were present: and to complete the checklist for an absolutely assured crash in the light of Deutsch's nation-building theory, the country had recorded a fairly rapid economic growth rate in the period preceding the stagnation and disaster course of the 1980s; GDP growth stood at 6.0% in the period between 1965 and 1980 and was again in fact the highest economic growth rate in Europe.

The present study on the basis of a sample of 99 countries with complete data on transfers and ethno-political violence includes countries of the periphery and the semi-periphery, and nearly all newly-formed states of the former world of communism. There, the Gurr-Index of ethno-political conflict *(EP)* is significantly pushed upwards on the one hand by the degree of development of the productive forces. Lamentably enough, adjusted per capita income *(PCI)* increases, and not decreases ethno-political conflict in world society. This result confirms Deutsch's approach and rejects the still more optimistic vision of the trade-off between stability and development level, expressed by Huntington. The dialectic of the situation is further complicated by the fact, that countries, in order to avoid the stability trap of ethno-political conflict, have to undergo an early demographic and/or social and cultural transition; without that, the tendency towards ethno-political conflict even more increases. High fertility is related to subsequent high income concentration, low fertility to subsequent low income concentration (Tausch and Prager, 1993). With high fertility rates *(FR)* - or plausibly, a poorly developed mass communication system -, no reductions in the level of ethno-political conflict can be achieved. Deutsch furthermore believed, that especially in a crisis government sector size increases stability. Huge per capita aggregate net transfers, that is to say, inflows that are greater than outflows, decrease the level of ethno-political strife; while repressive states *(REPRESS)* are less prone to ethno-political conflict than full scale democracies. Thus stability-oriented 'Keynesianism' in the periphery is today being substituted by the 'Tiananmen formula': repression + capital inflows. There are some elements, that further qualify Deutsch's theory further: social mobilization (alphabetization) has no visible effect on instability:

Table 8.2: The determination of the Gurr-Index of ethno-political conflict in the periphery and semi-periphery

	unstandardized regression coefficient	t-value	significant at 5%-level
transfers per capita	**-0.74**	**-2.06**	**yes**
political rights violations	**-0.60**	**-2.65**	**yes**
human development index	-0.51	-0.64	no
repressiveness of the security apparatus	+6.22	+0.59	no
population density^0.50	+0.04	+0.02	no
adult literacy rate	-0.03	-0.87	no
mean years of schooling	+0.02	+0.16	no
ln PCI	**+0.91**	**+3.65**	**yes**
ln PCI^2	2.56	+0.25	no
historical fertility rate	+0.34	+2.76	yes
failure of demographic transition	-0.00	-1.26	no

Legend: regression coefficients, T-test and significance. The sample was based on n = 99 countries with complete data; R^2 = 32.5%; F = 3.81; 87 degrees of freedom. 5% of ethno-political strife is being determined by our model. Net transfers mean, that inflows are greater than outflows due to international exploitation.

We should go back here once more to our Yugoslav example. Yugoslavia, by all its strenuous efforts to achieve a capitalist transformation, produced little in terms of real foreign capital inflows. Net private direct investments were 0 for the year 1988; while it relied - like Jordan and Egypt - to a heavy degree on the earnings of its labor force abroad. Although fertility rates were reasonably low by overall standards in the 1980s, Yugoslavia still was a relatively traditional society especially in terms of media exposure, thus still weakening the link between 'modernity' and the 'state' on the hand and 'the village' and later on the urban misery on the other hand, precisely at a time, when mass communication would have been necessary to hold society together. Again, Karl Wolfgang Deutsch predicted how important mass communication can become for stabilization, and how dangerous it is to neglect it. There were only 197 TV-sets per 1000 people in 1988-89; and only a daily newspaper circulation rate of 100 per 1000 people was achieved at the end of the old Yugoslavia in 1988-89. Thus, only Albania had a lower television density in Europe; and only Spain and Portugal had a worse newspaper circulation on the European continent. Combined, Yugoslavia had the worst media density in Europe. And do not forget, that the combined indices still hide the regional diversities between, say, rich Slovenia and the rural regions of Bosnia. Thus, traditional forms of communication were much stronger than the mass media, controlled by the party and the state, at a time, when great economic hardships hit the population and the state abandoned its role on the economic stage, thus unable to function politically in the end.

The frightening scenario emerging from this analysis is, that indeed a 'Yugoslavia' could re-appear at least under the following conditions in ethnically heterogeneous former communist countries

(i) a rapid urbanization process preceding transformation

(ii) coupled with great efforts to redirect economic resources towards economic growth

(iii) under the condition of a neo-liberal program to abolish large part of the former state economic influence on the economy

(iv) with little real resource flows coming in from the capitalist centers

(v) while at the same time, democracy only partially having been restored and

(vi) modern patterns of social behavior and/or mass communication, typical for a Western developed democracy, not yet fully developed

To make perhaps matters worse still, Yugoslavia, by not being a member of the European Union, could not send entire families of guest workers abroad for residence; and hundreds of thousands of youngsters - including the fighting generations of the war of the 1990s - were raised by the grandparents instead, who still kept alive the memories of the atrocities of the Second World War and the immediate post-war-periods, both characterized by repression and mass-murder. Yugoslavia again holds a European record - it was the European society with the highest worker remittances from abroad. The postwar guest-worker generation, which in many ways communicated much better with fellow Yugoslav nationalities than the parent generation, left the children behind to be raised in poor and backward villages, saving for all these private beautiful new homes. During the long winter nights, the tales of terror and atrocities, that characterize Yugoslav 20th Century history, were most probably rekindled by the grandparents in the minds and hearts of the young generation. Did one ever notice, that precisely the *'adversaries''* new houses were later so viciously being bombarded and burnt systematically to ruins during the long war of Yugoslav disintegration? The children, raised by their grandparents, in reality must have missed their far-away parents tremendously, and the children most probably began to hate their absent parents for having them deserted. *'Our son always wept so terribly when we departed after the holidays',* an unnamed Yugoslav mother told us once, standing here for hundreds of thousands of Yugoslav parents. But you hardly will hate your own parents, rather, you will project the hatred against 'the' others - **'them'**, the 'opponents', the Albanians, the Bosnian Muslim, the Croats, the Serbs (named alphabetically), *et cetera,* who stand in the way **to fully grasp the fruits of modernization.** The preconditions for the disaster were thus already present; to make matters worse, the reforms of the regime came too late and never stopped short of steering a middle-course between guided democracy and repression. Thus, condition (vii) for the repetition of the Yugoslav tragedy anywhere else in the region could be a future migration regime of the European Union, that continues to separate migrants from their families and leaves children alone abroad.

Country risk analysis

This is the answer to the first question of 'country risk' analysis, the causes of instability. The lack of an early demographic transition (FAILURE DEM) and the degree of development (LN PCI) increase, while political rights violations and capital transfers significantly decrease the Gurr-Index of ethno-political conflict on a global level. Other indicators of social or political mobilization however fail to support other aspects of either Huntington's or Deutsch's theory. It should be noted, that there are *insignificant* predictors whose direction of influence cannot be explained by the conservative aspects of the Deutsch/Huntington tradition: the human development index and adult literacy rate, *ceteris paribus,* even decrease the level of ethno-political conflict, while mean years of schooling slightly increase the level of ethno-political conflict. The velocity of change in fertility rates also has no significant influence on the Gurr index.

In order to stabilize the newly-formed countries of the semi-periphery and the periphery, whose instability increases with the level of development, and which initially makes, say, Laos less prone to conflicts as Russia or the Ukraine, the following significant processes intervene:

* *the real transfers from the centers of the world-wide market economy*
* *the continuing or newly formed power monopoly of a dictatorial group*
* *an early demographic transition*

China received 11 thousand million $ of net foreign direct investment in 1992 alone, and 45,3 thousand million $ in 1997. Brazil received 16,3, Mexico 12,1, Singapore 10, Argentina 6,3, Russia 6,2 and Poland 5,0 thousand million $. In relation to the practically predetermined fertility rate and the size of the per-capita-income, a government in a semi-transformation country seems to be able to respond to the threats of ethno-political conflict by only two processes nowadays: by trying to attract foreign capital inflows and by preventing a further political democratization. In one word, the *'Tiananmen strategy'.*

Aggregate **net transfers**, that is to say, inflows that are greater than the outflows due to international exploitation, are **lowest** in countries with civil rights violations very much in excess of political rights violations and in countries with a **high human** development index; a *relatively* repressive state machinery in an environment of already begun political reforms and a high human development index are conducive to low inflows or even real outflows of capital.

The trap for the countries of Orthodox Eastern Europe and the former USSR could not be worse in this context: they are **low priority areas for transnational capital.** *Political reform has begun decisively even in countries, where civil rights violations are much higher than political rights violations, and because human development and thus also social expectations to the investor are higher than in the communist rest of Asia and in other (non-communist) dictatorships. Nothing, what has been written by political scientists in the 1960s, 1970s and 1980s has to be revoked in this context: semi-repressive regimes are more prone to instability and stagnation than full democracies and full dictatorships; and international capital flows react accordingly.*

It seems worthwhile to reflect a while on the historical lessons of pre-war Europe for today's transformation strategies. Quantitative evidence about the Great Depression already suggests the fatal connection between the economic slump of the 1930s and the totalitarian Right's rise to power:

Graph 8.2: The Kondratieff cycle and instability in the Weimar Republic of pre-war Germany: the long economic swing and the Nazi vote

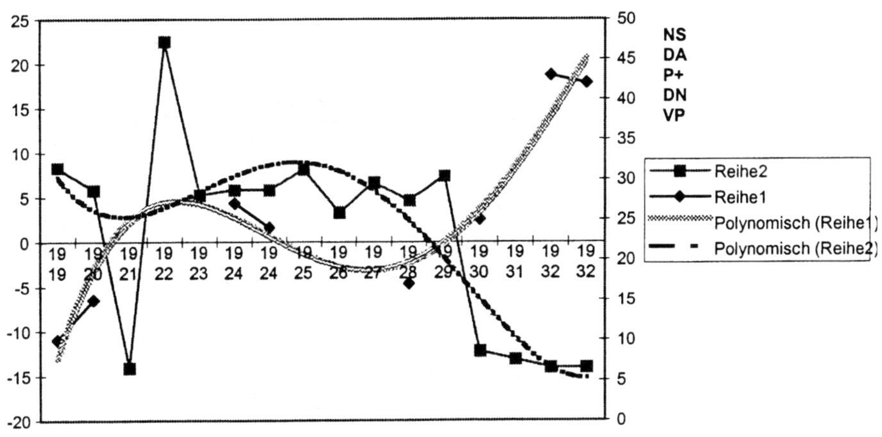

Legend: NSDAP + DNVP votes in Weimar general elections in % of the total vote (shady trend line; right-hand scale); economic growth or recession in the entire capitalist world system (left-hand scale, dotted trend line). Sources: Stephens, 1989; Goldstein, 1988, our own calculations

If anything, the application of cyclical world-economic long swing data to the political history of the Weimar Republic also shows, how the radicalism on the left fluctuated with the ups and downs of the world economy:

Graph 8.3: Weimar - radical right and left

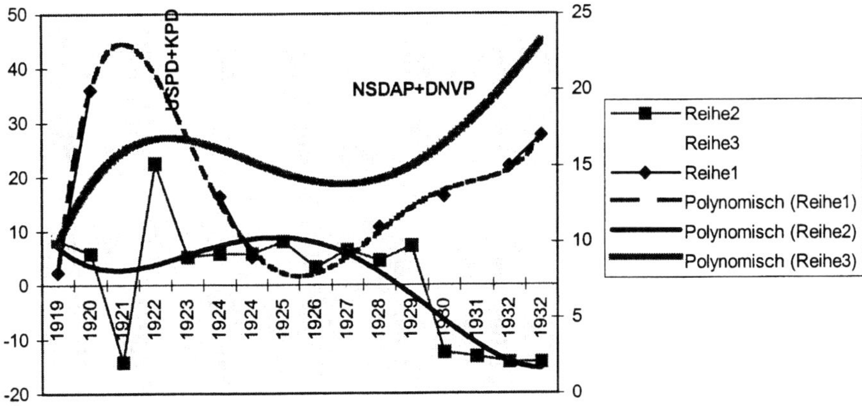

Legend: economic growth on the world level (left hand-scale, dark line); right-wing radicalism in Germany during the Weimar Republic (left-hand scale, shady trend-line) and left radicalism in Germany during the Weimar Republic (right-hand scale, dotted trend-line). Sources: see above

The trend-data from Weimar also show, how, under the impact of a world economic recession, it is the liberal societal center whose voter support most rapidly dwindles, while radicalism increased and the Catholic Center Party approximately could hold its position:

Graph 8.4: Weimar and the end of the liberal center

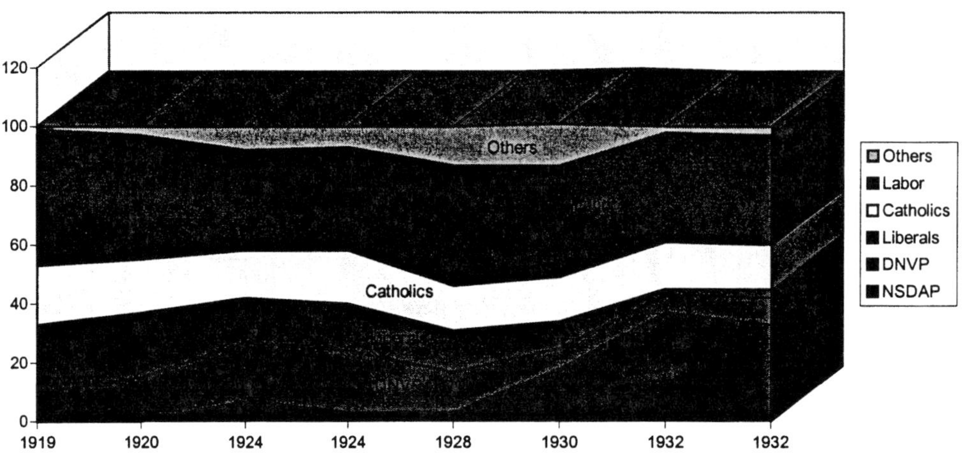

Legend: the share of the different Weimar parties in the total vote from 1919 to 1932. Sources: see above. Catholics and Labor remain practically stable throughout the depression, while the other parties, the liberal and the national right contribute to the rise of the NSDAP.

What, then, is *'the beef'* of this comparison for today? The resilience of semi-peripheral democracies against world economic shocks has certain limits, and the likelihood of a renewed breakdown of democracy in countries like the Ukraine, Bulgaria, Romania, or Russia cannot be ruled out altogether. This is especially relevant, when we think about the possibly disastrous effects of long-term European stagnation under European Monetary Union on the 'outs' in East Central Europe (Friedman, 1997; Watzal, 1997). It is an irony of the day, that the neo-liberal Nobel laureate Milton Friedman compared the *EURO* project with the gold-standard and thus renewed the warnings of Karl Polanyi, written more than half a Century ago: first declining prices, but after 1896 rising prices, sharp fluctuations. A more thorough analysis of Polanyi's text (1944) will show the close connection that this author established between democratic instability and monetary orthodoxy in the countries of the European eastern semi-periphery.

For the moment, the world economy seems to prefer the environment of low human development, where political repression is still high enough not to warrant any 'excess repressiveness' of the state security apparatus to control via infringements on the level of civil rights the destabilization, brought about by the lowering of the rate of political repression in heterogeneous countries. **Net transfers, that is to say, inflows that are greater than outflows due to international exploitation, in turn determine to a large extent the chances of a country in the semi-periphery and periphery for social development.** The empirical relationship is drastic enough to be mentioned here: life expectancy, that single, best, and most reliable indicator of the social situation of a country, is being determined by the well-known e/π-function on the basis of real income in purchasing power, introduced in Tausch/Prager, 1993, and net transfers. Almost 4/5 of life expectancy in the (semi)periphery are thus being determined; net transfers are the predictor of life expectancy, whose unstandardized regression coefficient is 5 times bigger than the standard error of the estimate.

Further support to our interpretations is given by the last two regression equations in Table 4.1. *Thus, the countries of the periphery and the semi-periphery today are at the mercy of transnational capital flows: they are at the mercy of transnational capital politically, because inflows of capital stabilize ethno-political conflict potential, and they are the mercy of transnational capital socially, because inflows determine to a large extent and directly the life expectancy of the populations - from Wladiwostock to Hanoi, from Riga to Tirana.*

Whether or not democracy in Eastern Europe can survive the transformation shocks, will depend to a large extent also on the kind of world economic relationships that the West is offering to the new democracies. Real transfers out of Weimar Germany, as Frank and Fuentes/Frank have correctly remarked, destabilized German democracy in the pre-war years to a considerable extent. The predictions of the *Economist Intelligence Unit* for the share of the current account balance per real GDP up to the year 2001 show, that in the Czech Republic, Hungary, and Poland, **considerable deficits will characterize the transformation process for years to come:**

Graph 8.5: current account balances per GDP, 1997 - 2001

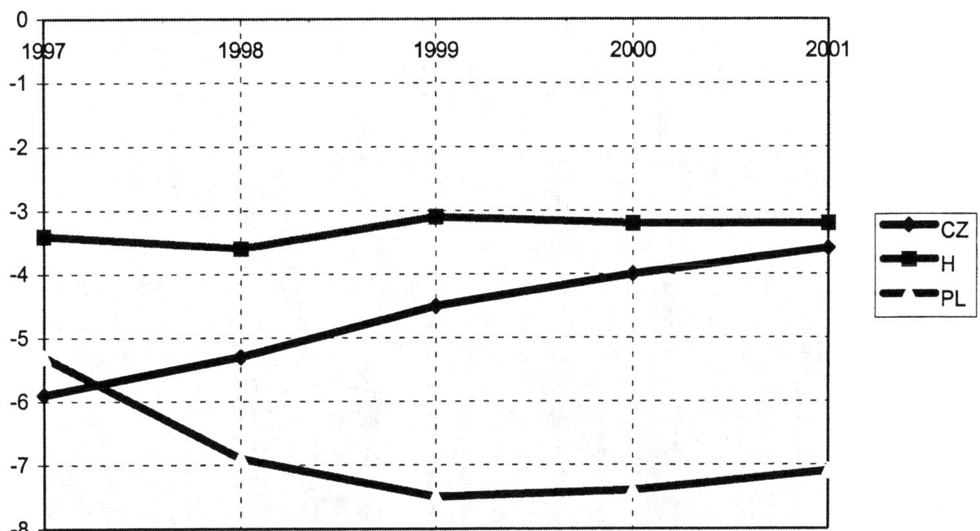

Legend: projections about current account balances per GDP in East Central Europe; based on our own compilations from *Business Eastern Europe,* February 23, 1998, Dialog Select Information System

On a world scale, **democratic** transformation of former communism has been combined with long-term growth success practically only in **Slovenia** and **Poland,** while the 'Asian' authoritarian transformation strategy still seems to offer some tangible benefits in comparison to semi-authoritarian dependent capitalism in most of the former USSR:

Table 8.3: economic growth and political rights violations in (ex)communist nations

CZE	-2,3	1
EST	-6,1	1
HUN	-1,3	1
LIT	-4,5	1
POL	*0,5*	*1*
SLO	*0,6*	*1*
BUL	-3,7	2
LET	-7,9	2
MON	0	2
RUM	-3,2	2
SLK	-2,2	2
MOL	-11,1	3
RUS	-5,9	3
UKR	-9,5	3
ALB	2,1	4
CRO	2,2	4
GEO	-17,1	4
KIR	-5,9	4
MAC	-7,9	4
ARM	-13	5
AZE	-15	6
BLR	-5,2	6
CAM	5,2	6
KAZ	-8,2	6
CHI	10,1	7
LAO	6,1	7
TAD	-11,3	7
TUR	-6,2	7
UZB	-1,7	7
VIE	7,2	7

Legend: our own compilations from *Le Monde (1998)*, *'Bilan du Monde, Edition 1998'*. Paris: *Le Monde*, and Stiftung Entwicklung und Frieden (1998).

The relationship between authoritarianism and economic growth in former communism is a fairly constant one, with a significant curve-linear trade-off indicating that stagnation is worst at middle democracy levels:

Graph 8.6: the non-linear trade-off between levels of democracy and economic growth in former communism

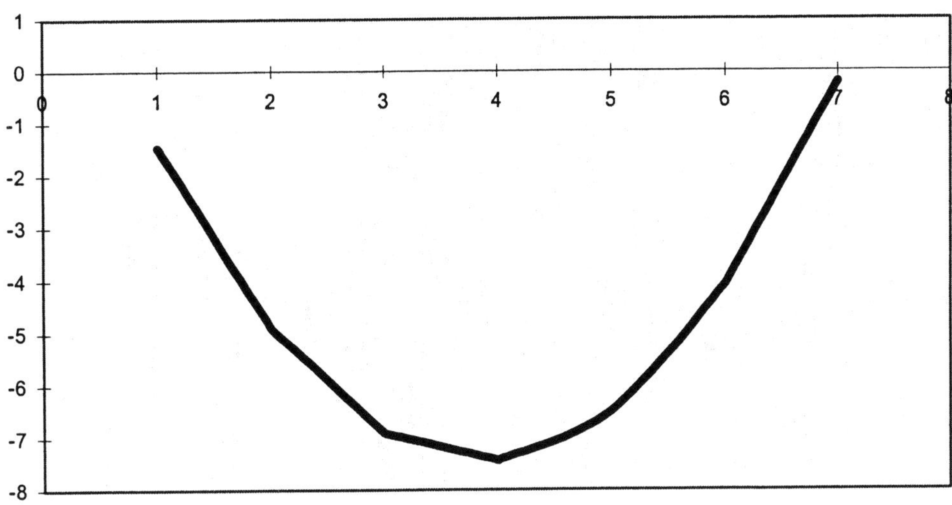

Legend: economic growth (left hand scale) and violations of political rights (x-axis). Economic growth is worst at middle levels of political transformation. The equation is:

$$(8.2) \text{ growth} = a + b_1 * \text{POL RIGHTS VIOL} - b_2 * \text{POL RIGHTS VIOL}^{2}$$

unstandardized c.	0,733344948	-5,659918882	3,475900038
standard error	0,31115839	2,560208118	4,181824728
R^2	**0,17706894**		
F/degrees of freedom	2,904776351	27	
t-Test	2,356822028	-2,21072609	

Legend: As in all EXCEL 5.0 outprints in this work, first row: unstandardized regression coefficients, second row: standard errors, last row: t-Test. The values immediately below the standard errors are R^{2} (third row, left side entry), F, and degrees of freedom (fourth row).

The stability of the transformation process will also depend, to a large extent, on the ability of the Eastern economies to recover economic growth. In Table 8.4, 8.5 and in Graph 8.7 we show April 1998 data about unemployment, growth, and inflation, as well as the discount rate, the budget deficit (surplus) per GDP, debt per GDP, foreign direct investment per GDP, and the current account balance per GDP. Latest tendencies are documented as well. Countries, whose performance has worsened, are printed in **bold** letters:

Table 8.4: unemployment, growth, and inflation in the transformation countries, 1998 - 2000

	Unemployment	Growth	Inflation
BUL	13,7	-7,4	383,1
CRO	17,6	5	5,3
CZE	5,6	1	13,1
EST	3,9	9	14,2
HUN	10,4	4	17,6
LAT	6,7	6	6,4
LIT	7,2	5	6,6
POL	10,5	7	13,7
ROM	8,8	-6,6	132,1
RUS	9	1,3	10,1
SLK	12,5	6,5	7,6
SLV	14,5	2,9	9,1

GDP real growth (%)	Latest	As of	Year ago
Bulgaria	**2.5**	**1999**	**3.5**
Croatia	**-2.0**	**1999**	**2.5**
Czech Republic	-0.2	1999	-2.3
Estonia	1.9	12-99	-0.7
Hungary	**4.4**	**1999**	**4.9**
Latvia	**-1.3**	**9-99**	**5.4**
Lithuania	**-4.8**	**6-99**	**5.1**
Poland	**4.1**	**1999**	**4.8**
Romania	-3.2	1999	-5.4
Russia	1.7	1999	-4.6
Slovakia	**1.9**	**1999**	**4.4**
Slovenia	**3.7**	**1999**	**3.9**

*Preliminary **end of previous year

Inflation (%). year-on-year	Latest	As of	Year ago
Bulgaria	**9.1**	**2-00**	**-1.8**
Croatia	**4.6**	**1-00**	**3.4**
Czech Republic	**3.7**	**2-00**	**3.4**
Estonia	3.2	1-00	4.6
Hungary	**9.8**	**2-00**	**9.4**
Latvia	3.4	2-00	na
Lithuania	0.8	2-00	1.9
Poland	**10.4**	**2-00**	**5.6**
Romania	**55.7**	**2-00**	**32.5**
Russia	28.9	1-00	96.9
Slovakia	**15.5**	**2-00**	**6.9**
Slovenia	**8.1**	**2-00**	**5.6**

*Preliminary **end of previous year

Unemployment (%)	Latest	As of	Year ago
Bulgaria	**18.1**	**2-00**	**13.2**
Croatia	**20.8**	**1999**	**18.6**
Czech Republic	**9.7**	**2-00**	**8.3**
Estonia	**5.6**	**2-00**	**4.8**
Hungary	9.6	1999	9.6
Latvia	**14.5**	**2-00**	**9.7**
Lithuania	**11.2**	**3-00**	**8.5**
Poland	**13.9**	**2-00**	**11.9**
Romania	**12.2**	**2-00**	**11.8**
Russia	12.3	2-00	14.1
Slovakia	**19.5**	**1-00**	**16.3**
Slovenia	13.3	1-00	14.5

*Preliminary **end of previous year

Source: *Business Central Europe,* April 1998 - April 2000, our own compilations

Graph 8.7: East Central Europe at the hour of boom?

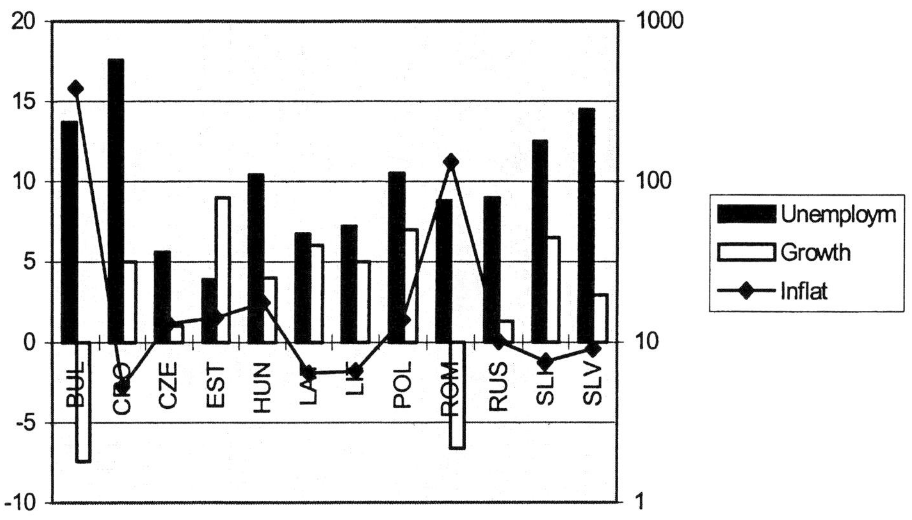

Legend: unemployment and growth (left hand scale); inflation (right hand, logarithmic scale) in East Central Europe. Source: *Business Central Europe,* April 1998

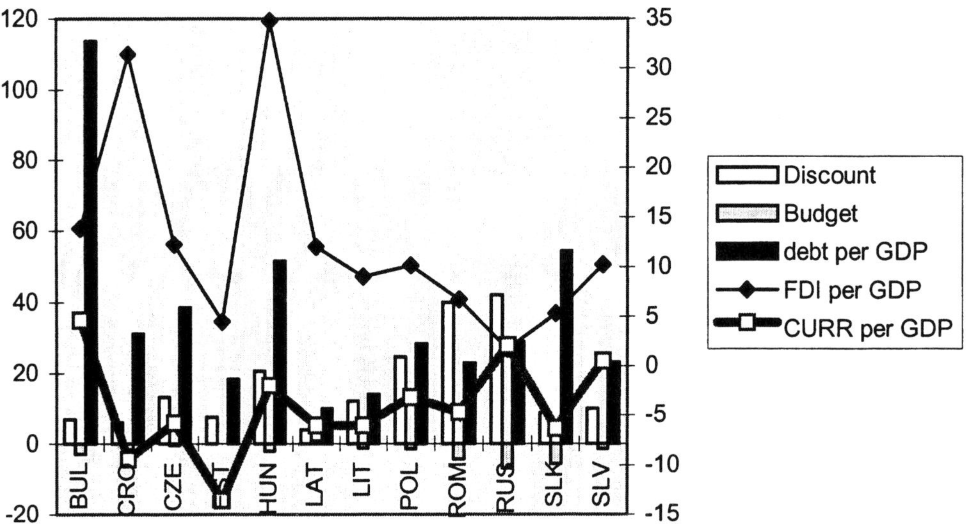

Legend: debt per GDP, discount rate (left hand scale); all other variables (right hand scale); Source: see above

Table 8.5: The discount rate, the budget deficit, debt ratios, investment penetration and current account balance deficits in East Central Europe

	Discount rate	Budget deficit	debt per GDP	FDI per GDP	CURR per GDP
BUL	6,8	-2,9	113,8	13,8	4,6
CRO	5,9	-1,6	30,9	31,4	-9,4
CZE	13	-0,5	38,5	12,2	-5,8
EST	7,4	-0,1	18,2	4,5	-13,6
HUN	20,5	-2,1	51,6	34,8	-2
LAT	4	0,7	10	12	-6
LIT	12	-1,3	14	9	-6
POL	24,5	-1,4	28,2	10,1	-3,2
ROM	40	-4,5	22,8	6,7	-4,7
RUS	42	-6,8	28,9	1,7	2,1
SLK	8,8	-5,7	54,2	5,3	-6,3
SLV	10	-1,5	23,1	10,2	0,5

Source: our own compilations from *Business Central Europe,* April 1998

Poland and the other EU member candidates are confronted with the problem, that their economic performance with 10% unemployment or more, during a world economic cycle peak, is that of a usual center country during a milder recession. Unemployment can soar up again to 15% or more, if the seas of international business cycles become rougher again. Our data series on the basis of Goldstein (see Chapter 3) clearly shows this. In addition, the 7-11 year Polish Juglar business cycle had its last trough in April 1990 (WERI, 1997: 152), and before that in 1980/83, and Poland will certainly enter a Juglar cycle B-phase and then a Juglar cycle trough. In addition, yet another swing from the 18-22 year Kuznets cycle, that had its last trough internationally by around 1975, might combine with the next local Juglar cycle trough to produce quite a strong recession after the boom of the 1990s, especially in America, but also in Europe:

Graph 8.8: Kuznets-cycles in the world system, 1756 - 1997

1741-1756

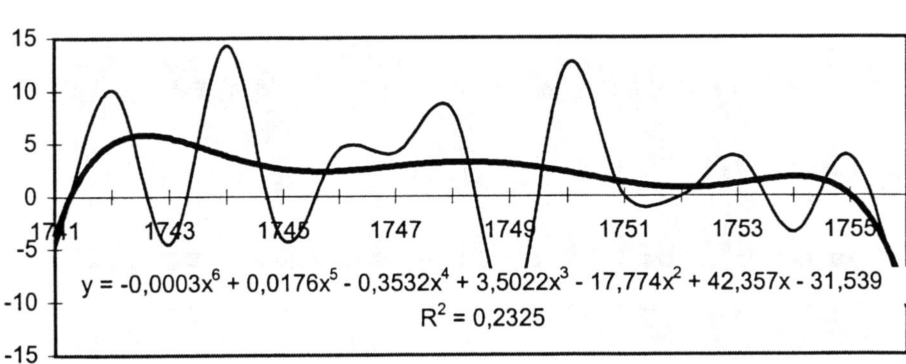

1756-1774

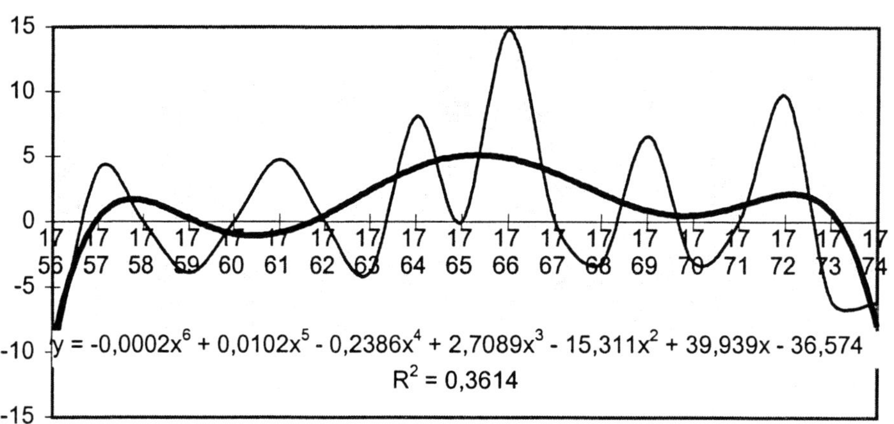

1774-1793

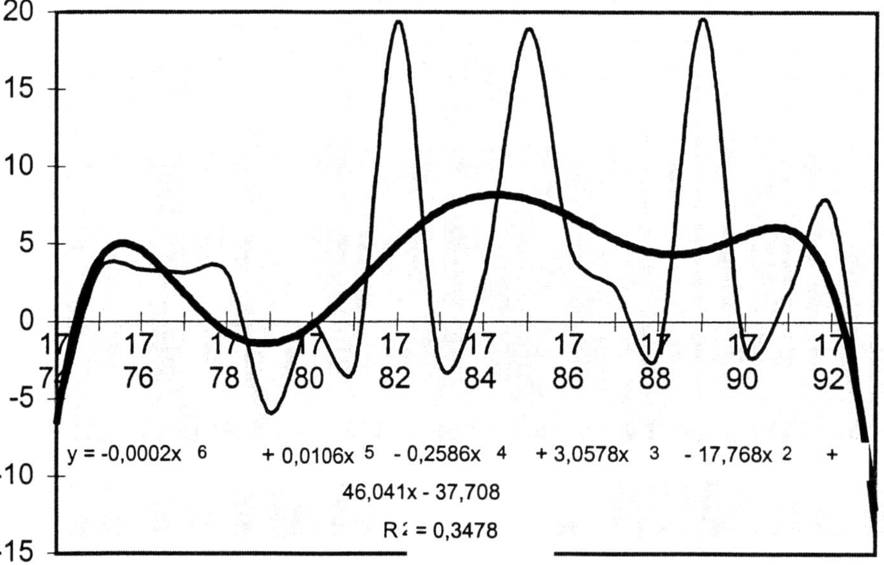

1793-1812

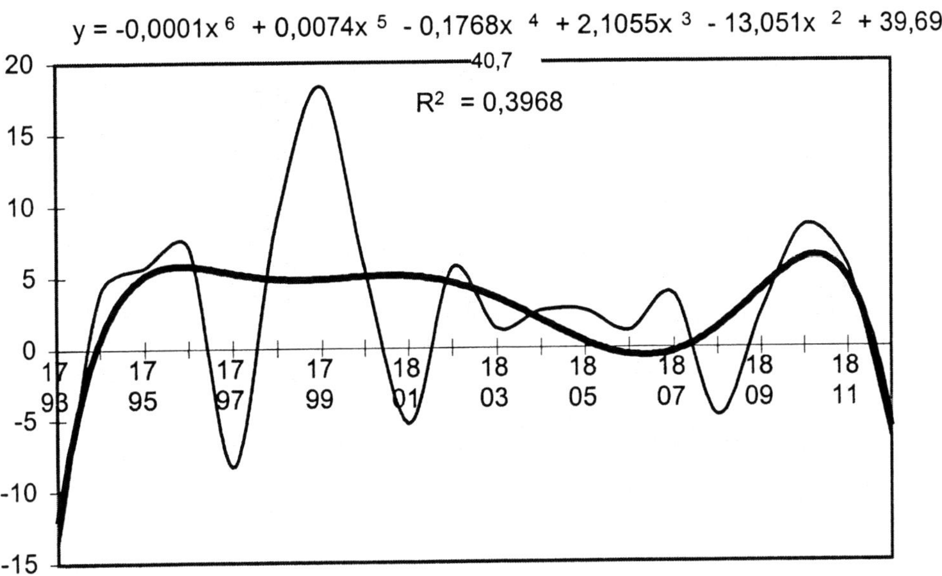

1812-1832

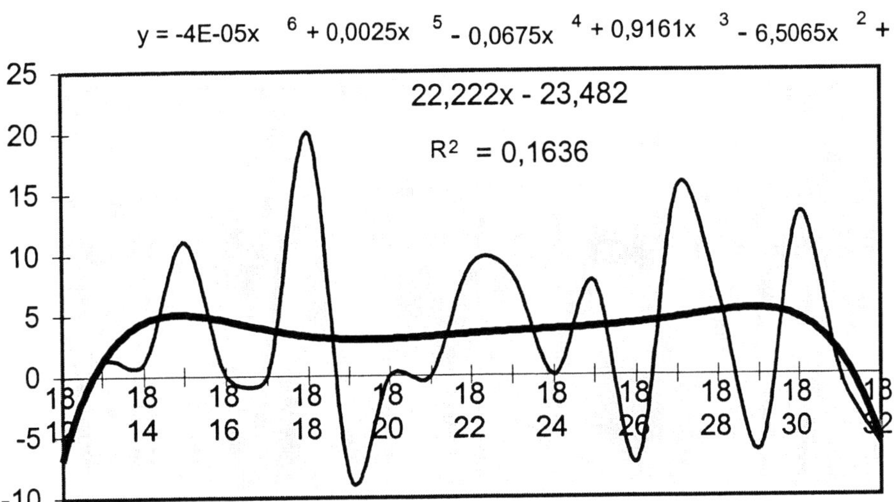

1832-1862

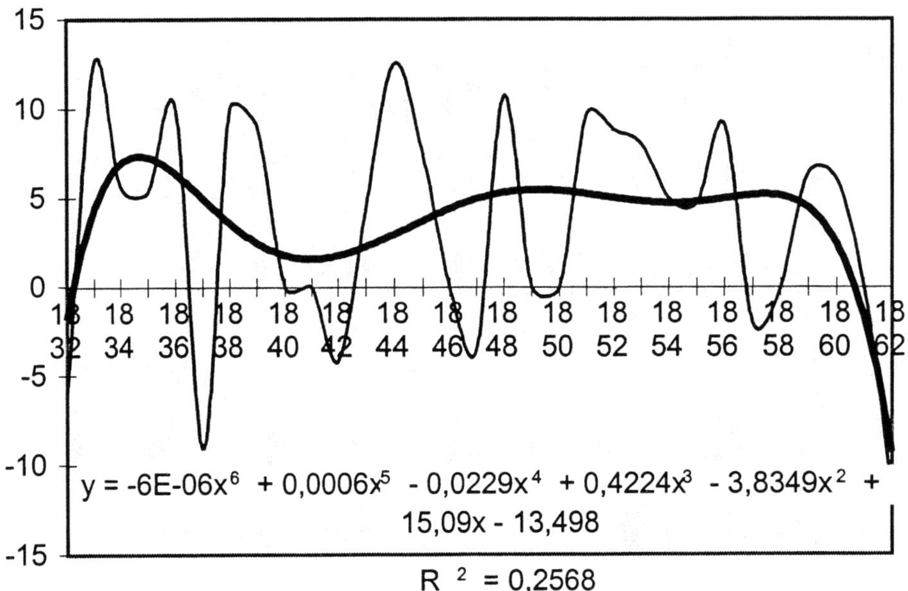

$$y = -6\text{E-}06x^6 + 0{,}0006x^5 - 0{,}0229x^4 + 0{,}4224x^3 - 3{,}8349x^2 + 15{,}09x - 13{,}498$$

$$R^2 = 0{,}2568$$

1862-1885

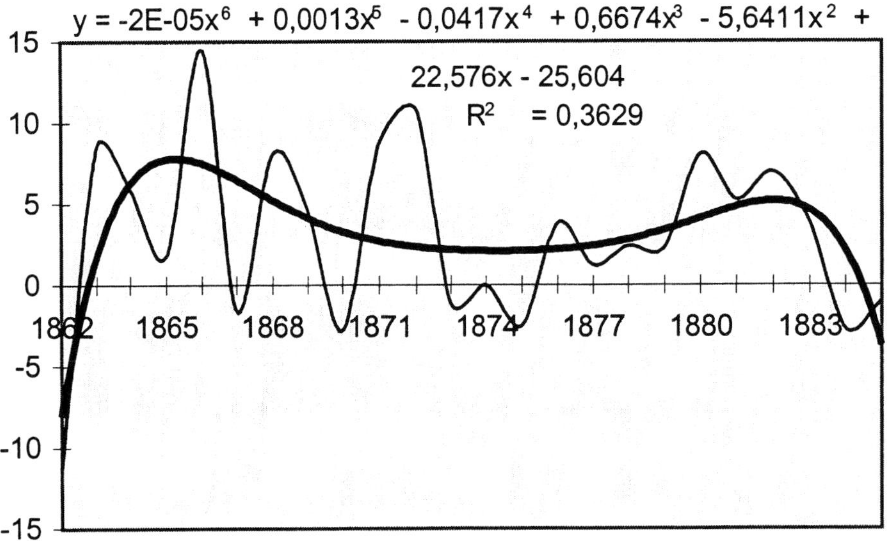

$$y = -2\text{E-}05x^6 + 0{,}0013x^5 - 0{,}0417x^4 + 0{,}6674x^3 - 5{,}6411x^2 + 22{,}576x - 25{,}604$$

$$R^2 = 0{,}3629$$

1885-1908

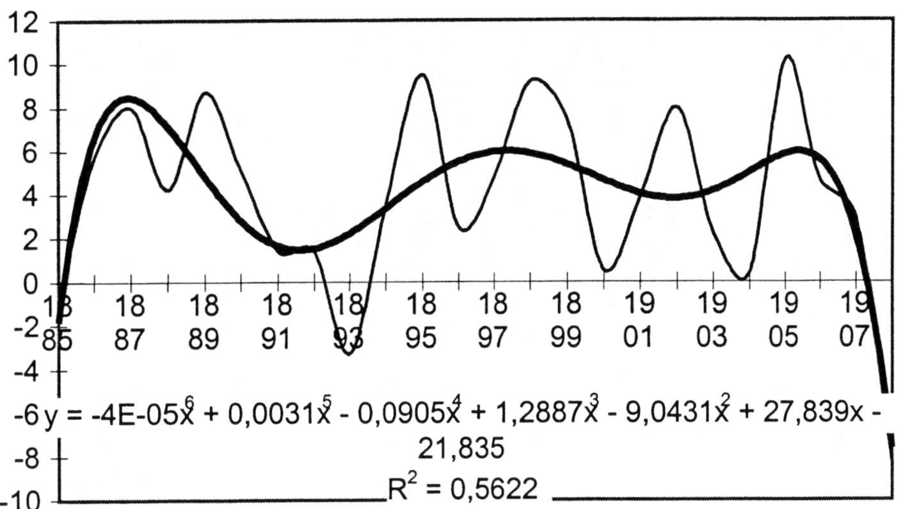

1908-1932

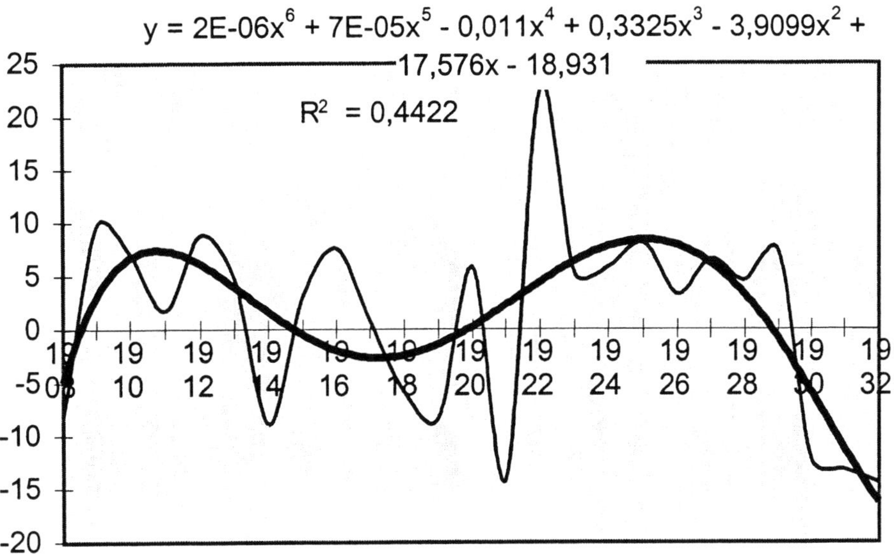

1932-1958

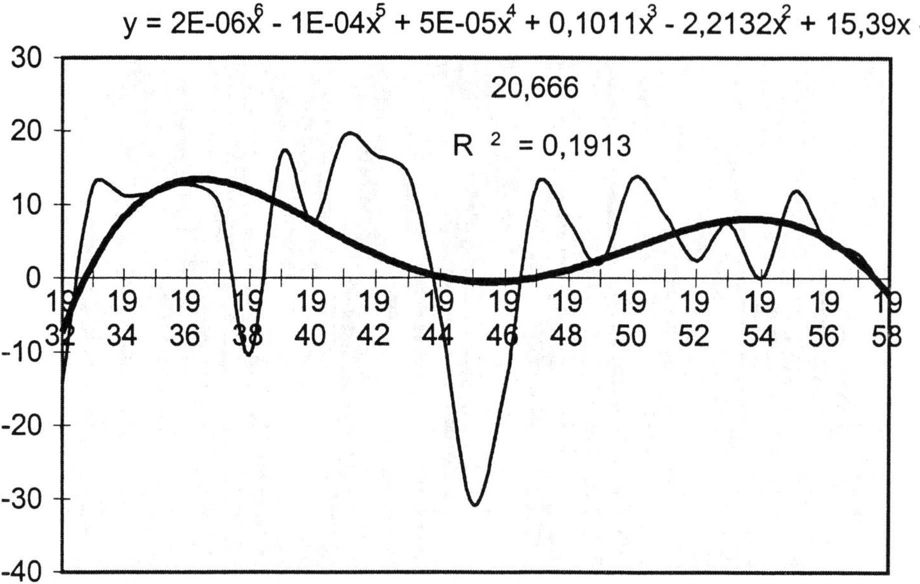

1958-1975

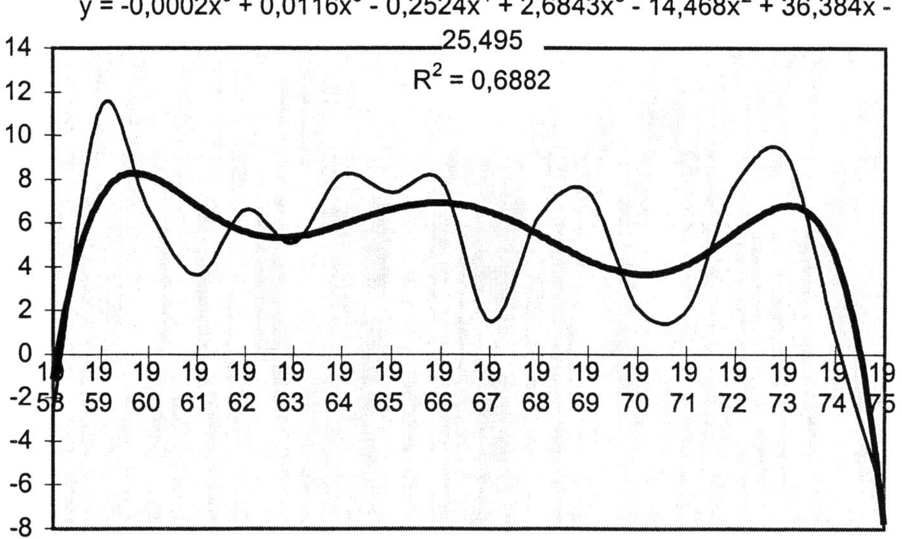

1975 - 1992 (estimate 1)

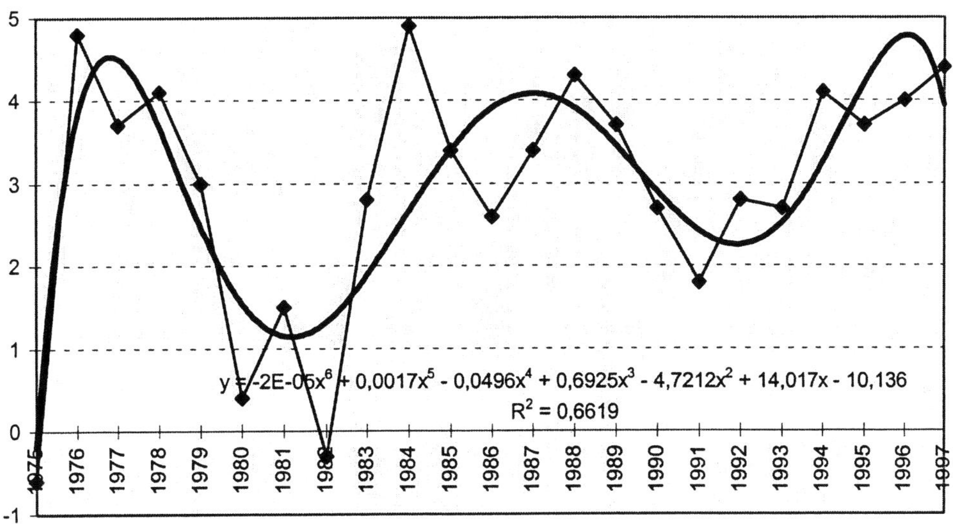

estimate 2

1975-1997

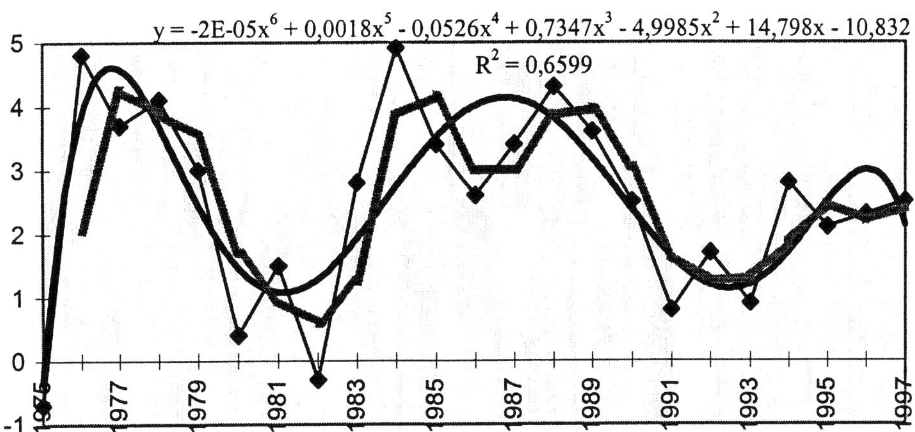

Legend: EXCEL multiple regressions, based on 'insert trend lines'; the data are the original, un-transformed growth rates of capitalist world production, according to Goldstein, 1988, as calculated in Chapter 3. The data series about industrial country GDP growth 1975 - 1997 is from UN ECE *(Economic Survey of Europe)*, IFRI and IMF sources *(World Economic Outlook)*. In the last graph about growth in the period 1975 - 1998, we also show 2-year sliding averages. The difference between the two data series lies in the assumption about economic growth in the 1990s. (1) is based on IFRI; (2) is based on IMF

The data series about Polish unemployment suggest, that the peak of employment and the trough of unemployment was reached by around November 1997, and that unemployment increased again after that. Apart from business cycle considerations, also structural factors have to be taken into account, like the restructuring of heavy industry and the demographic dynamics of a baby boom generation, entering the labor market:

Graph 8.9: Polish unemployment 1996 - 1999

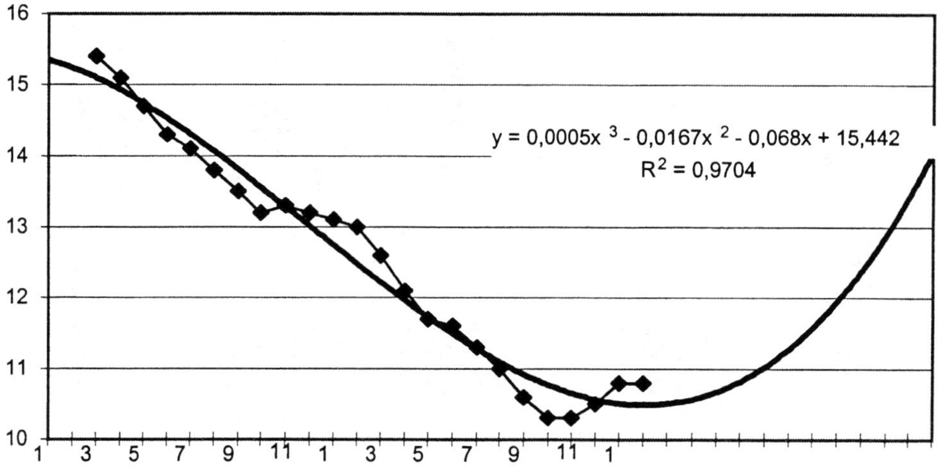

Legend: unemployment in Poland over the last 24 months. Our own calculations, based on G.U.S., 1996-98, Statistical Bulletin, various issues

Formal employment in the economy has quite dramatically shrunk during and after the transformation recession, only to recover later on:

Graph 8.10: Polish employment in 1000 persons from 1950 to 1996

Legend: employment in Poland since 1965. Based on our own compilations from G.U.S., *Rocznik Statystyczny Pracy*, 1997

With 13.9% unemployment in Poland in February 2000, we believe, that the EU-accession countries will be confronted in a few years by **mounting, and not by declining unemployment rates.**

What are the employment policy pre-conditions for the coming years on a European level (see also Chapter 9)?

Europe 1a: **Iceland, Norway, Estonia**: very low unemployment, as yet no *morbus bruxellicus,* coastline location

Europe 1b: **Russia**: still low open unemployment, because the transformation process gets underway only by now. Trade unionism is very weak

Europe 2a: **Austria, Switzerland, the Czech Republic,** (no or very recent *morbus bruxellicus,* wage felxibility through strong corporatism still guaranteed), **Netherlands**: *long morbus bruxellicus,* but wage flexibilty now guaranteed by very strong liberal elements. Liberal elements will have to increase, the longer *morbus bruxellicus* lasts

Europe 2b: **Britain, Portugal, Lithuania** (run-away investment by big transnationals, high wage flexibility achieved by application of neoliberal capitalism; new international division of labor very strongly felt)

Europe 3a: **Sweden, Denmark, Ireland:** threat of unemployment was very strong in the 1980s, now liberal concepts applied; strong investments in human capital formation and knowledge-based industries

Europe 3b: **Latvia, Hungary, Rumania:** transformation process underway; countries have already a high potential of urban-rural disparities; with EU-integration, unemployment could rise considerably

Europe 4: **Italy, France, united Germany, Slovakia, Poland, Finland:** structural transformation from heavy industry to knowledge-based industries not yet completed, historically strong urban-rural inequalities; strong trade-unionism in the cities, high concentration of wealth, low flexibility of wages on the part of the elite of workers who have a secure job; structurally increasing left-right political cleavages. Danger, that high unemployment will increase, if no decisive reforms in the direction of knowledge-based information society are realized. Poland's and Slovakia's luck: a long stagnation, followed partially by a shadow-economy-driven growth period. With *morbus bruxellicus,* the problems will increase.

Europe 5: **Spain, Belgium, Slovenia, Croatia, Yugoslavia, Bulgaria:** negative weight of old-fashioned industrial structures even larger, combined with the most pressing need to go for knowledge-based industries and better human capital formation. Spain's case could be less dramatic, with better employment chances for women, especially in the North-western, Central and Southern regions. Belgium, the geographical center of the EU, best symbolizes the *morbus bruxellicus*

Map 8.4: Unemployment in Europe

Legend: unemployment rates in Europe. The graph is based on our own compilations from Polish Central Statistical Office, Poland Quarterly Statistics, 3, 1997. The darker, the more severe is the unemployment situation

Semi-peripheral capitalism in Poland also means, that both real wages (as a sign of the political strength of the organized sector's labor movement) and labor accidents (as a strong sign of the political and social weakness of labor in the unorganized sectors, but also as a sign of the social neglect, that exists in heavy industry during boom years) rise with the ups of the business cycle. A Polish recession will strongly increase the pressure of organized labor in the organized, formal sectors in the political system, to proceed with wage demands. Our following statistical materials are based on G.U.S., *Rocznik Statystyczny Pracy,* and on *Business Central Europe:*

Graph 8.11: Real wage rate and labor accidents in the Polish economy, 1985 - 1996

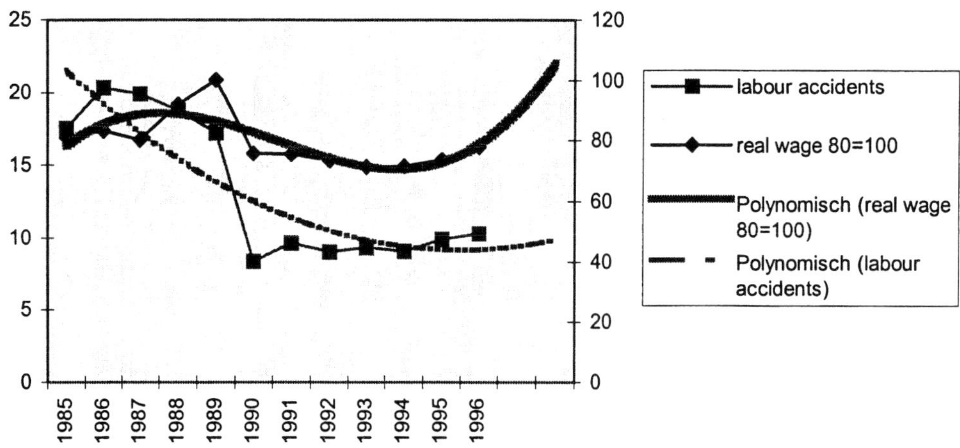

Legend: right-hand scale: real wages (1980 = 100); left-hand scale: deadly labour accidents per 1000 employees and year. Source: our own compilations from Glowny Urzad Statystyczny (1997) 'Rocznik Statystyczny Pracy' Warszawa: G.U.S.

Another factor of instability is the glaring deviation of the growth of international currency reserves from the tendencies in the current account balance (see also, Chapter below). In Eastern Europe, Poland and Hungary are the biggest outlayers, suggesting, that gray-sector money flows into these economies. In Poland, this influx is reckoned by Italian police sources to be at the pace of 100000 $ an hour *(Polityka,* 16, 1998): **Money laundering** will however **greatly increase for some time to come**, especially in Poland, Slovenia and Estonia, where economic conditions are relatively good and EU-membership is just around the corner:

	Curr ac/GDP	**reserves/GDP**	**curr account (per GDP) growth**	**reserves (per GDP) growth**
BULG	3,8	22,1	3,8	-4,5
CROA	-11,9	13	-7,2	-0,1
CZECH	-0,6	21	5,1	-5,5
ESTO	-2,2	17,8	0,1	-0,4
HUNG	-0,9	21,6	0,4	2,6
LATV	-9,3	13	-3,3	-1
LITH	-11,1	12,2	-2,2	-0,5
POLA	-2,1	17,8	-0,4	2,4
ROMA	1,1	6,9	0,3	-0,1
RUSS	0,4	3,5	-2,3	-0,5
SLOK	-7,2	16,9	-0,3	-0,7
SLOV	0	18,9	0	1,4

Legend: data from Business Central Europe, July, August 1998

Both stocks and flows of current accounts and reserves per GDP each seem to indicate, that Poland indeed is a 'special case', where unaccountable inflows dominate the realities of the financial markets:

Graph 8.12: Current account balances and international reserves in East Central Europe - without and with outlayers

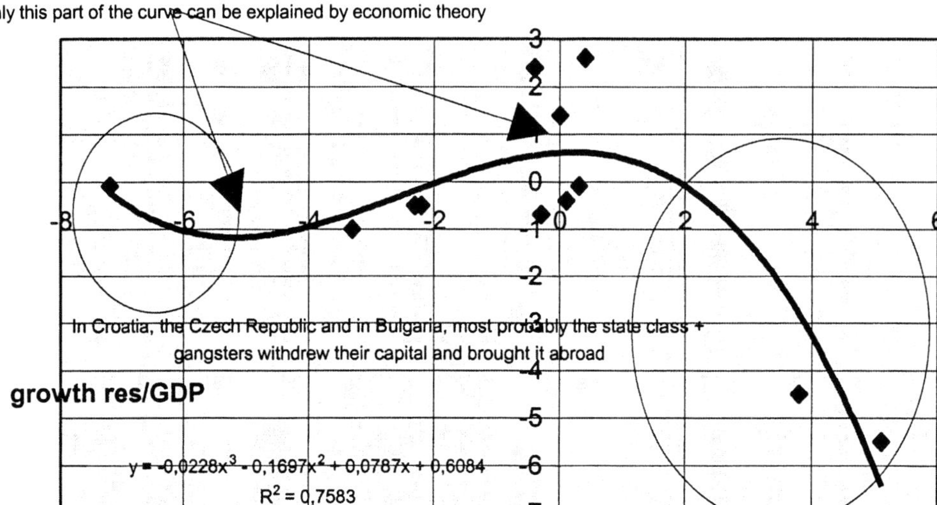

Legend: growth rates of the current account balance per GDP (x-axis) and growth rates of the international reserves per GDP (y-axis); calculated from *Business Central Europe,* July, August 1998

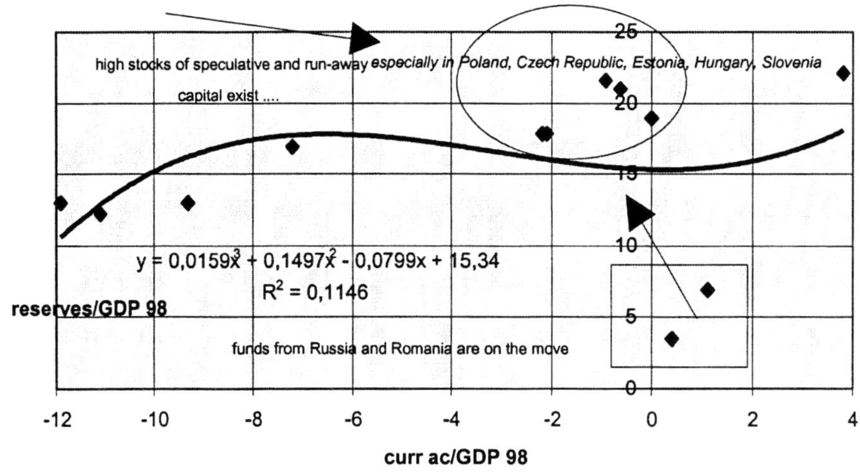

Legend: current account balance per GDP (x-axis) and international reserves per GDP (y-axis); calculated from *Business Central Europe,* July, August 1998

At the same time, social decay continues - even during boom years, as for example the following data about housing construction from the region suggest:

Table 8.6: Housing construction in Eastern Europe and the former USSR

Romania	+ 5%
Slovenia	+ 0%
Hungary	-15%
Croatia	-33%
Macedonia	-40%
Turkmenistan	-42%
Russia	-43%
Poland	-55%
Belarus	-55%
other countries	-55% to -93%
(Czech Republic -72%; Estonia -82%)	

Housing construction: dwellings completed, percentage change 1996 over 1991. Our own compilations from G.U.S., Poland Quarterly Statistics, 3, 1997.

Finally, we should note that by the very same process of radical neo-liberal transformation, the state undermines its own base of existence. If we take general government data for Poland into account, and not just central government data, we find that the following scenario, above described, is the most probable: the share of general government in the GDP sinks, and with it the share of expenditures for police, internal security, and human capital formation, while the general government deficits will grow in the long run.

Graph 8.13: General government share and deficit in Poland, 1992 - 1997, in percent of GDP

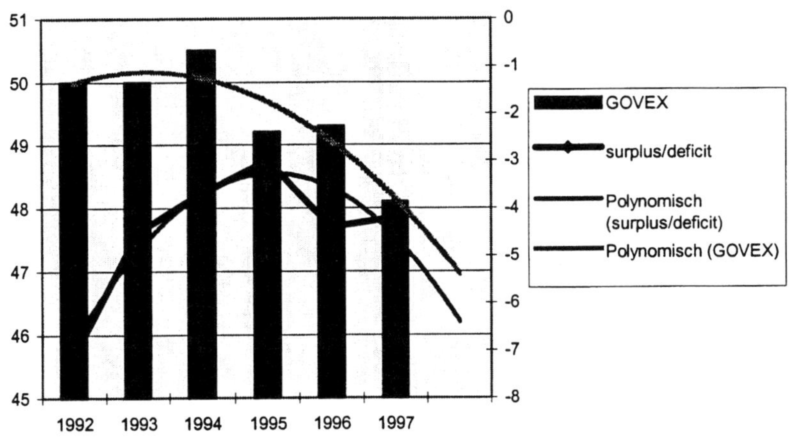

Legend: Polish government expenditures per GDP (columns, left hand scale) and Polish central government surplus/deficits (line, right hand scale) and the trend lines since 1992. Source: our own compilations and estimates from Polish Central Statistical Office, various publications, and from the systematic analysis and evaluation of articles from the Polish Press at *Rzczeczpospolita* archive *(http://www.rzczeczpospolita.pl)*

Our prediction of rising budget deficits in several EU-accession countries is not too far off the mark, as the following materials show, although only Latvia is at present past the Maastricht 3%:

Budget balance (% of GDP)	Latest	As of	Year ago
Bulgaria	**-1.4***	**1999**	**1.3**
Croatia	-.7*	1999	-0.9
Czech Republic	**-1.7***	**1999**	**-1.4**
Estonia	**-2.8**	**1999**	**-0.3**
Hungary	-0.3*	1999	-5.4
Latvia	**-3.8**	**1999**	**0.8**
Lithuania	**-2.3**	**1999**	**-1.6**
Poland	**-2.3***	**1999**	**-2.1**
Romania	-2.6	1999	-2.8
Russia	5.7	2-00	2.2**
Slovakia	-1.8*	1999	-2.6
Slovenia	**-1.1***	**1999**	**-1.0**

*Preliminary **end of previous year

Source: our own compilation from Business Central Europe, op. cit.

In terms of political stability, a strong state is necessary. This is the lesson of Karl Deutsch's stability theory. As far as these research results are concerned, they are rather in the tradition of the gloomy description of the conditions of democracy in the semi-periphery in the 1920s, written by Karl Polanyi more than 50 years ago. Will - in contrast to then - the world-wide market economy save Eastern European democracy?

Transnational crime as a global actor

A cynic could say: an economically realistic staging of a G-8 conference would have to invite today the *cupolas* of transnational crime. In terms of world economic power, international drug traffic alone is more powerful than states like Spain, Russia, or Canada (our own calculations from Raith, 1995, UNDP, 1994). International illegal flight capital prefers certain economic and social conditions; and in turn, it will contribute to changing the socio-economic conditions of its host countries. To investigate the effects of international capital flights on the host countries concerned, we have developed a simple macro-quantitative model. Using standard international economic indicators from Fischer Weltalmanach, we understand money laundering to be the excess international currency reserves, which are unaccounted for by the following data in a multiple regression equation. A surplus means, a country most probably is a heaven for the money launders; while a minus indicates the opposite.

(8.3) money laundering =

	population	GNP per capita	growth 80-93	dyn food production	food imports	raw material exports	fertilizer consumption	curr account	debt service	terms of trade	dyn energy production	dyn energy consumption	constant
predic-tion	687,85	1,38	-7,018	-6,349	-0,819	1,0837	1,7616	-12,26	1058,8	-98,17	1,6636	10,68	-1245
currency	335,4	107,28	56,63	37,213	0,2119	1,0991	34,449	127,9	536,44	447,15	0,4484	4,5276	6542,9
reserves	0,7034												
	9,8829	50											
t-test	**2,051**	0,0129	-0,124	-0,171	**-3,86**	0,986	0,0511	-0,096	**1,974**	-0,22	**3,71**	**2,359**	

Legend: as in all EXCEL 5.0 outprints in this work, first row: unstandardized regression coefficients, second row: standard errors, last row: t-Test. The values immediately below the standard errors are R^2 (third row, left side entry), *F*, and degrees of freedom (fourth row). Data based on Fischer Weltalmanach, 1997

To assess, in turn, the effect of money laundering on growth, we worked with the following data matrix:

Table 8.7: Money-laundering and its destructive effects on the national economy:

	population	GNP per cap	growth 80-93	dyn food prod	food imp	raw mat exp	fertilizer cons	curr account	debt service	terms trade	money laund
Egyp	56,4	660	2,8	1,3	24	67	3392	1566	14,9	99	6873,6
Algeria	26,7	1780	-0,8	1,2	29	97	123	361	76,9	95	-1638,2
Argen	33,8	7220	-0,5	-0,3	5	68	78	-7452	46	116	-1256,7
Ethio	53,6	100	-1,8	-1,2	6	96	95	-183	9	67	-1857
Bangla	115,2	220	2,1	-0,1	15	18	1032	243	13,5	94	-3065
Benin	5,1	430	-0,4	1,9	25	70	82	-52	5,9	133	1949,3
Boliv	7,1	760	-0,7	0,7	9	81	58	-495	59,4	78	-529
Braz	156,4	2930	0,3	1,2	10	40	608	-637	24,4	97	22358,5
Burun	6	180	0,9	-0,3	18	70	34	-26	36	52	-2734,3
Chile	13,8	3170	3,6	1,9	6	81	849	-2093	23,4	104	-524,2
China	1178,4	490	8,2	3	3	19	3005	-11609	11,1	101	-2670,6
Costa R	3,3	2150	1,1	0,7	8	67	2354	-470	18,1	94	-6627,4
Cote Iv	13,3	630	-4,6	-0,1	19	83	132	-1229	29,2	79	-790,3
Dom Rep	7,5	1230	0,7	-0,9	16	47	694	161	12,1	130	381,3
Ecuad	11	1200	0	0,6	5	92	380	-360	25,7	90	-1905,8
El Sal	5,5	1320	0,2	0,7	15	52	1073	-77	14,9	88	-3019,4
Gabon	1	4960	-1,6	-1,4	17	97	11	-269	6	106	-6344,3
Ghana	16,4	430	0,1	0,3	10	77	38	-572	22,8	65	-1217,9
Guatem	10	1100	-1,2	-0,5	11	70	833	-687	13,2	93	-1290,6
Hondu	5,3	600	-0,3	-1,3	11	86	210	-393	31,5	73	615,7
India	898,2	300	3	1,5	5	29	720	-315	28	96	-259,2
Indon	187,2	740	4,2	2,2	7	47	1147	-2016	31,8	90	1351
Jamaica	2,4	1440	-0,3	1	14	34	973	-182	20,1	109	-3438,7
Camer	12,5	820	-2,2	-1,9	15	86	30	-638	20,3	77	702,1
Kenya	25,3	270	0,3	-0,4	8	71	410	153	28	81	-200,5
Colom	35,7	1400	1,5	1	8	60	1032	-2220	29,4	68	246
Congo	2,4	950	-0,3	-1,5	19	97	118	-507	10,8	98	437,9
S-Korea	44,1	7660	8,2	0,5	6	7	4656	384	9,2	100	-693
Laos	4,6	280	2,1	-0,2	33	96	42	-13	9,6	90	387
Madag	13,9	220	-2,6	-1,5	11	81	25	-167	14,3	68	1371,7
Malaw	10,5	200	-1,2	-4,2	8	94	434	-143	22,3	86	4244,7
Malay	19	3140	3,5	4,3	7	35	1977	-2103	7,9	99	9940,5
Mali	10,1	270	-1	-0,9	20	92	103	-103	4,5	102	1200,2
Maroc	25,9	1040	1,2	2,3	17	43	326	-525	31,7	114	-1408,3
Mauri	1,1	3030	5,5	0	13	34	2512	-92	6,4	108	-6459,2
Mex	90	3610	-0,5	-0,9	8	47	653	-23393	31,5	99	-601,6
Nep	20,8	190	2	1,2	9	16	391	-195	9	97	-5203,7
Nica	4,1	340	-5,7	-2,7	23	93	246	-457	29,1	94	1695
Niger	8,6	270	-4,1	-1,8	17	98	4	-29	31	105	1819,7
Nigeria	105,3	300	-0,1	2,1	18	98	175	2268	28,9	99	311,2

	population	GNP per cap	growth 80-93	dyn food prod	food imp	raw mat exp	fertilizer cons	curr account	debt service	terms trade	money laund
Pak	122,8	430	3,1	1,2	14	14	1015	-3327	24,7	100	-7258,4
Pan	2,5	2600	-0,7	-1,2	10	84	476	70	3,1	87	-1382,5
Pap	4,1	1130	0,6	-0,2	17	89	308	495	30,2	91	-967,1
Para	4,7	1510	-0,7	1,3	11	83	96	-492	14,9	112	-5875,9
Peru	22,9	1490	-2,7	-0,4	20	83	216	-1768	58,7	90	2438,1
Philip	64,8	850	-0,6	-1,3	8	24	540	-3289	24,9	117	1732,6
Poland	**38,3**	**2260**	**0,4**	**0,7**	**11**	**40**	**811**	**-3698**	**9,2**	**95**	-1086,5
Port	9,8	9130	3,3	2,6	12	17	813	947	19,3	104	3197
Roman	*22,8*	*1140*	*-2,4*	*-2,4*	*14*	*24*	*423*	*-1162*	*6,2*	*111*	4733,1
Zambia	8,9	380	-3,1	-0,3	8	99	160	-471	32,8	98	2707,6
Zimb	10,7	520	-0,3	-3	18	64	481	-116	31,1	89	561,3
Sri Lank	17,9	600	2,7	-1,8	16	28	964	-381	10,1	86	2054,3
Sudan	26,6	400	-0,2	-2,2	19	99	72	-1446	5,4	91	-931,8
Tans	28	90	0,1	-1,3	6	85	137	-408	20,6	85	2134,4
Thai	58,1	2110	6,4	0	5	28	544	-6928	18,7	103	10516
Trinid	1,3	3830	-2,8	-0,6	15	66	801	122	23,8	92	-6794
Tunes	8,7	1720	1,2	1,5	8	25	223	-912	20,6	100	-5093,5
Turk	59,6	2970	2,4	0,3	6	29	702	-6380	28,3	109	-5097,7
Ugan	18	180	1,9	0,3	8	100	1	-107	143,6	49	-415,7
Hung	*10,2*	*3350*	*1,2*	*-0,7*	*6*	*32*	*292*	*-4262*	*38,8*	*102*	825,2
Urug	3,1	3830	-0,1	0,3	8	57	608	-227	27,7	114	-4631,9
Venez	20,9	2840	-0,7	0,2	11	86	874	-2223	22,8	93	6139,1
CAfriR	3,2	400	-1,6	-1	19	56	5	-21	4,8	91	0

This yielded the following results, explaining almost 65% of economic growth:

(8.4) money laundering and economic growth

dyn food prod	food imp	raw mat exp	fertilizer cons	curr account	debt service	terms of trade	money laundering	lnGNP	ln GNP^2	constant
0,160315	-2,43436	1,86E-06	-0,00958	0,004269	-4,6E-05	**0,001343**	**-0,02796**	-0,02825	0,513553	11,36795
0,172427	2,366866	4,77E-05	0,01811	0,012305	6,88E-05	**0,000313**	**0,010356**	0,042082	0,164342	7,91605
0,6475										
9,552412	52									
0,929751	-1,02852	0,039072	-0,52907	0,346949	-0,66766	**4,295231**	**-2,69961**	-0,67126	3,124894	t-test

Legend: as in all EXCEL 5.0 outprints in this work, first row: unstandardized regression coefficients, second row: standard errors, last row: t-Test. The values immediately below the standard errors are $R^{\wedge 2}$ (third row, left side entry), F, and degrees of freedom (fourth row).

The Matthew's effect, terms of trade, and money laundering explain significantly economic growth in the world periphery and semi-periphery from the 1980 onwards. 64.8% of total variance is accounted for by our model. Contrary to the myth, that - however morally detestable, such a shadow economy is beneficial for economic growth-, the opposite holds.

Another way to look at the problem would be via the international corruption index, ranging from 0 (high corruption) to 10 (low corruption), that is now calculated for 52 countries *(Polityka, Warsaw, 32, 1998: 35)*. First of all, corruption is a typical inverted U-shaped function of overall development level, namely:

Graph 8.14: Corruption as a function of overall development - the Human Development Index and the absence of Corruption Index

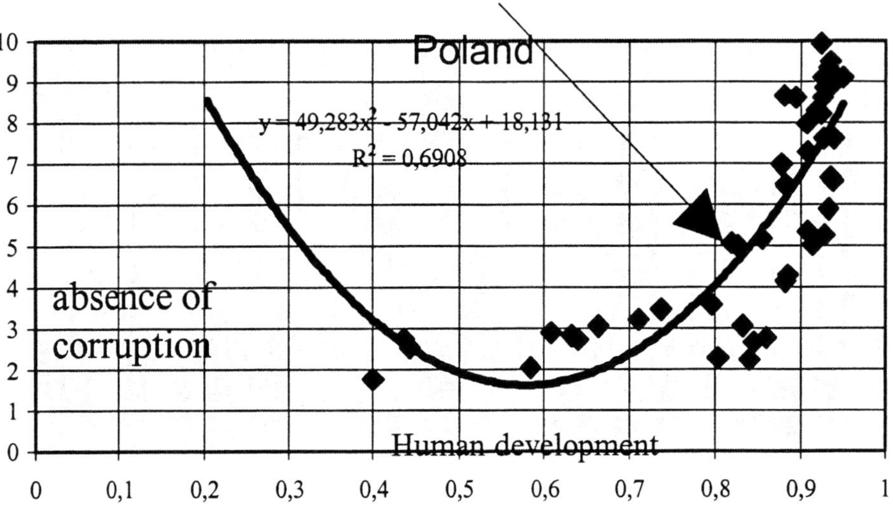

Legend: Human Development Index (x-axis, ranging from 0 to 1) and the absence corruption, as measured by the Transparency International survey (y-axis, ranging from 0 (absolute corruption) to 10 (absolute rule of law)). The Graph shows that Poland's and Hungary's performance are a normal consequence of their still relatively low level of human development, but that they already have 'the worst behind them', while countries in Latin America and in the European Union, like Italy, Belgium, Greece, leave much to be desired in their performance, and still have an excessive level of corruption, as compared to their development level. Source: our own compilations from the data base of Chapter 9 of this work and from *Polityka, 32, 1998: 34 - 35*.

The above hypothesis about the inverted U-shaped pattern of the increase/decrease in corruption levels can be further specified. Endemic corruption, it seems, is the consequence of a number of factors of the development and decay process in the world system, among others the upward push, that corruption receives from excessive military outlays and high population growth. The U-shaped pattern of corruption is again shown to be relevant here, while foreign capital penetration has no significant effect on corruption patterns:

(8.5) factors affecting corruption

UN memb.y	mean y scho	absoluteGNP	FDI per GDP	Years of Comm	population gr	state sector	%labor force	ln PPP	ln PPP^2
1,5787	0,0243	-0,0255	0,7965	-13,311	**0,099**	0,0375	0,2197	**-0,035**	**0,045**

corruption	6,6604	0,1057	0,0551	0,6243	11,867	0,0397	0,0248	0,3411	0,0182	0,0174
	0,853									
	14,753	33								
t-Test	0,237	0,2303	-0,4627	1,2759	-1,1217	**2,489**	1,5117	0,6441	**-1,907**	**2,613**

agr.shareGP	MILEX	HDI	constant
-0,0003	**0,263**	0,0046	50,698
0,0002	0,1285	0,0154	52,183
-1,2912	**2,047**	0,3014	0,9715

Legend: as in all EXCEL 5.0 outprints in this work, first row: unstandardized regression coefficients, second row: standard errors, last row: t-Test. The values immediately below the standard errors are R^2 (third row, left side entry), F, and degrees of freedom (fourth row).

Thus, it seems to be certain that corruption levels in the transformation countries will decrease, while arms imports, connected with NATO-membership, will push corruption levels upwards for some time to come.

Chapter 3

A LABOR PERSPECTIVE ON SOME BASIC ISSUES OF EUROPEAN INTEGRATION

Arno Tausch
Associate Visiting Professor, Department of Political Science,
Innsbruck University, Austria

9) A LABOR PERSPECTIVE ON SOME BASIC ISSUES OF EUROPEAN INTEGRATION

The pressures of globalization pose very intricate questions for the future of the European continent in the world economy. The optimistic version holds, that with NATO and EU extension, security is increased in the East of the continent, while the ups and downs of transformation produce tangible results for the great majorities of the population, stabilizing young democracies. Eastward expansion of the European Union will enhance growth and stability, while European Monetary Union will enhance Europe's chances the international economy. Institutional reform of the Union will proceed, leading to a region of prosperity, peace and stability on the old continent. Monetary Union will end competitive devaluation circles, it will stabilize employment and growth, and will strengthen the European position in the long run.

At this stage, some general points should be permitted, that try to advance what I call here a *'labor movement perspective'* on some of the basic problems of the future of European integration, but which, I concede, are also very well compatible with a thorough liberal critique of some of the basic assumptions of current European integration. Opinion in Europe among circles that identify themselves with *'labor'* and with the *'new social movements'* of the 1980s is at best divided over future integration policy, including the speed of EU eastward extension, while in America Wall Street and business is apprehensive or critical about the Union, and the left in North America largely overlooks the potential benefits of a successful European Union for the world economy. Researchers from the South, most notably Samir Amin (1997), have written committed, critical, alternative agendas for European integration. European success is necessary for an alternative agenda in world society. Gernot Koehler and the present author developed their own agenda of global Keynesianism and European integration recently (Koehler/Tausch, 2000).

To continue and develop this tradition, we start from the assumption that eastward expansion of the Union still could fail, because East European democracies become more ungovernable under the pressure of the world market; institution reform could fail, because the EU is - under the dominance of big-business and big agriculture lobbying - a stagnation-prolonging mechanism, and European Monetary Union could fail, because international capital is more and more a narco-capital that shifts around the world. Thus, this Chapter is meant to be a provocation, but it is meant as an honest provocation written by a committed European. Precisely because the present author believes in the political imperative of a social and politically United Europe, which could become an important factor of international peace and stability, east-west and north-south cooperation, trade and conflict management, a thorough critique of the 'real existing Union' must be allowed

The Chapter deals with the issues in a macro-quantitative fashion, trying to explain the performance of the countries of the world economy, of eastern and western Europe by their sets of initial policy-conditions. It presents evidence, based on UNDP and UNCTAD data series. It will be shown that

a)   'dependent' development in the East, under classic assumptions, increases rather than decreases internal relative cleavages and contradictions

b)   years of European Union membership, under present circumstances, are a prime development constraint, i.e. the Union is dynamic enough only for young members; while the way, it functions, increases the societal power of mighty distribution coalitions

c)   only the maintenance of some kind of 'social element', like education, a fair share of agriculture, will guarantee long-term economic and political stability in the long run. The growth strategy of the 'social element' of human capital formation and world political *detente* is to be combined with the liberal element of a slender and efficient state. Seen in such a way, the growth perspectives for Eastern Europe are considerable

d)   the *EMU*, under classic Maastricht assumptions, will further increase the gaps between the North and the semi-periphery in Europe

We present here some of the first cross-national tests of the transformation policy failure or success since the end of Communism in Europe in 1989. What are the lessons to be drawn from our knowledge about world societal ascent and decline?

The eastward expansion of the European Union

No one seriously doubts the necessity of world political security and market access for East Central Europe. Our view of EU eastward expansion is more somber: the end result should not be the *re*-peripherization of the Eastern half of the continent, that was all too familiar for the region during the capitalist development from the Long 16th Century to 1939. Thus, a perspective is taken up again, that is a classic theme of especially Polish sociology, especially in the works of Jadwiga Staniszkis. The average incidence of poverty in Eastern Europe - as defined by a daily income of $4 or less (measured in 1990 PPP$) - increased sevenfold between 1988 and 1994, from 14 million to more than 119 million. In Russia, over 60% of all children live below the poverty line. 66% of all Russians below the poverty line have jobs. Only 40% of workers were paid in full and on time (UNDP, 1997). The incidence of chronically malnourished children in Russia rose from 9% to 14% since 1992. The life expectancy of Russian males has fallen in five years to 58 years - in fact, it is lower than that of India today (61.1) (UNDP, 1997). 9 Eastern European reform states accumulate a negative current account balance to the tune of around $bn 10 every year. The basic hypothesis of this Chapter is that the East of the European continent is threatened by Latin-americanization (Amin, 1997), and that a socio-liberal transformation alternative would soon have to be found. That this is not just *dependendista* propaganda, we read from a commentary from the Polish Press:

> "In order to reduce the foreign trade deficit, it is necessary to export more highly processed goods, which for the time being account for a mere 5 percent of the value of Polish exports," Professor Urszula Plowiec said as the presented the annual report of the Institute of Business Cycles and Prices on Poland's economic policy.

According to the authors of the report, the influence of the state on foreign economic policy of the country is declining and the economy is becoming increasingly dependent on interna- tional organizations, such as the European Union, the World Trade Organization or the OECD.

The report suggests that the state has not been doing enough to promote the growth of exports. In particular, the state should support exporters by financing export insurance policies and guaranteeing export loans. "In highly developed countries, up to 50 percent of exports are insured, compared to 1.5 percent in Poland," one speaker pointed out.

One of the most serious foreign economic policy flaws, according to the Institute, is the lack of coordination between the opening up of the market and the restructuring of the economy. The reduction of import duties on manufactured goods was not accompanied by the adoption of protective clauses serving the protection of domestic manufacturers from excessive imports, including subsidized ones or ones offered at dumping prices.

The Institute estimates that customs protection of the Polish market was reduced by up to 60 percent in the years 1995-97. (Based on 7-8 June 1997 issues of Gazeta Wyborcza No. 131, p. 23; Dziennik Prawa i Gospodarki No. 51, p. 5).

Following the radical perspective, so brilliantly exposed by Claude Julien in *Le Monde Diplomatique* September 1996 and by Samir Amin (1997), the question cannot be how well countries like Poland adapted a blueprint, (for example, contained in the famous White Paper of the *European Commission (1995))*, but what contradictions, cleavages and conflicts arose within Eastern Europe and between Eastern Europe and the old West European centers in the process of globalization and the expansion of the market order into Eastern Europe after 1989. Or to put the problem in Osvaldo Sunkel's terms: Eastern Europe saw a slow rise in the share of the gross product of foreign affiliates as a ratio to home country GDP (from 0.0% in 1982 to 1.3% in 1991), while the market-power of the transnational corporations saw to it, that the sales of foreign affiliates dominated an ever-growing share of the exports of goods and non-factor-services of the transition countries (the share went up from 0.9% in 1982 to 22.8% in 1993). The successive Governments of Poland - like the other governments of the region - have done a lot in the right directions for preparing the country for Union membership, but the framework of a semi-periphery country in the world economy creates pressures and instabilities which largely co-determine the social policy outcomes. Published social scientific evidence (UNDP, *1996, 1997 Human Development Report Poland)* suggests, that the following basic and real conditions for Polish social policy still exist - the spurt of economic growth notwithstanding - ((i) to (ix) all UNDP data). These conditions also explain the shifting cultures of protest voting in Poland - Tyminski in 1991, SLD and PSL in 1993, AWS in 1997 and who knows in 2000 and 2001, when the next presidential and parliamentary elections are due:

(i) the number of employed in Poland is still smaller by 2.4 million persons in comparison with the end of 1989
(ii) the growth of employment in the private sector did not yet fully compensate the job losses in the public sector after 1989
(iii) 800000 to 1.1 million Poles work in the 'hidden economy'
(iv) there was a long-term decline in the outflow from unemployment to official work in relation to the total outflow, suggesting that the hidden economy, illegal foreign labor, and other forms of existence compensated for the losses:

Graph 9.1: Unemployment in Poland - total outflows and outflows to work, 1990-1995

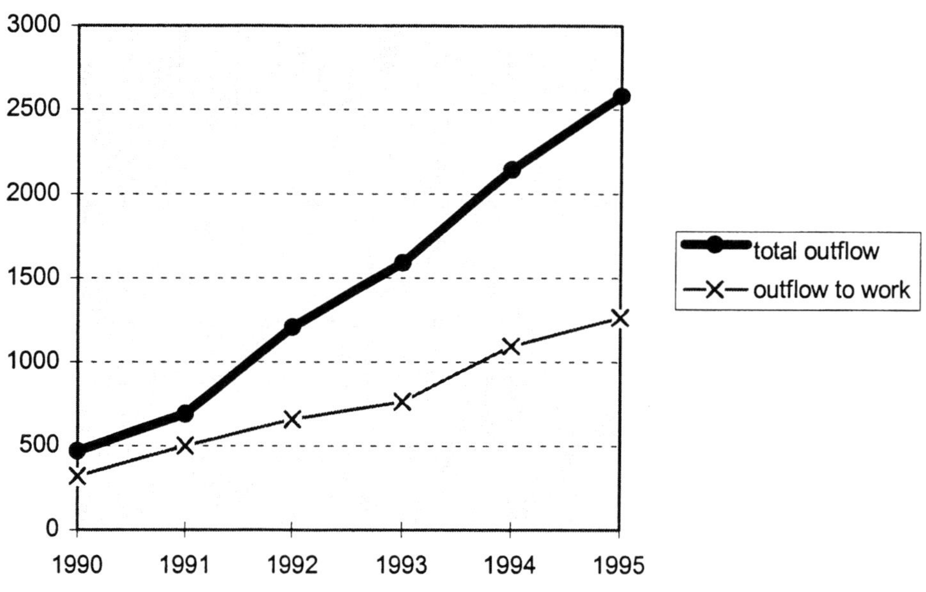

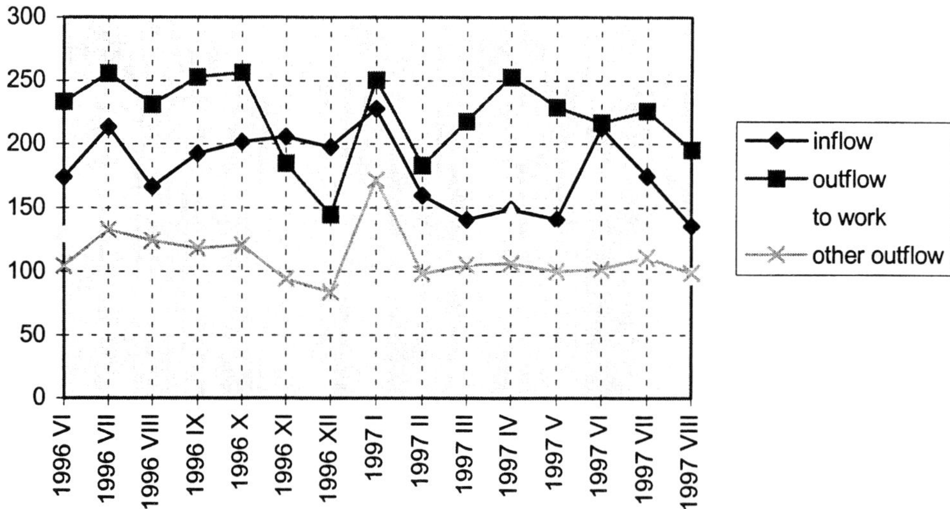

Legend: labor market statistics in Poland. Inflows to unemployment, outflows from unemployment (total, to work, and other outflow) in thousands of persons. Compiled from Central Statistical Office, *Statistical Bulletin,* September 1997

(v) youth unemployment remains very high and is in fact over 30%

(vi) 280000 persons are totally discouraged from looking for any kind of work, a trend which is exacerbated by the ever more stringent requirements to receive unemployment benefits

(vii) hidden unemployment on the farms also amounts to a large number of affected people, in all 450000 to 690000 persons. The total rural underclass comprises more than 5 million people

(viii) social insurance benefits paid from the national budget consume now 1/6 of the total GDP. By 2020, the number of pensioners will increase by yet another 3 million from 9 million persons to 12 million beneficiaries

(ix) several studies suggest, that the social policy frame of reference for the disabled persons in Poland is still not satisfactory (UNDP, 1996). There are over 4000000 disabled persons in Poland. 60% of them only have the most basic educational level, making this group of people even more vulnerable on the labor market. The majority of disabled persons in Poland is professionally inactive. In 1995, the unemployment rate of disabled persons in the cities was 28.1%, while in the countryside it was only 6.2%. Young disabled male persons under 24 years of age have an unemployment rate of more than 50% (UNDP, 1996: 88). Almost 43% of the households of disabled persons assert that they can only afford the cheapest food and clothing. Over half are indebted and have difficulties with the repayment of debts. As many as 43% assert that they lack means for basic medicines and treatment. 85% of all disabled feel themselves excluded from the means of public transportation. Pollution and low access to medical care in the countryside determine, that 39% of all disabled persons live in the villages.

There are widely differing estimates about poverty in Eastern Europe. Our own view is that a policy of investment in human capital could fairly quickly redress the existing imbalances, and at the same time help the country to avoid double deficits and a rising dependence from foreign capital.

What way out from the transformation trough, from poverty and dependence a country should choose? The debate about Eastern European reconstruction seems to be dominated by several fallacies. The **first fallacy** would concern the famous hypothesis about the *'market economy without adjective nouns'* as an engine of a successful transformation process. Following the logic, already proposed by Adamczyk, 1992; Angresano, 1994 and Jenkins, 1987, a de-facto policy of mass demand maintenance might have been better adapted to survive the transformation shocks and might - in the end - have been even more profitable for large-scale TNC investment than the real 'shock therapy strategies'. The **second fallacy** concerns the workings of foreign capital in the region and in the development process. Simple macro-economic reasoning would already demonstrate, that a sound economy, based on dynamic export-growth and huge positive trade and service balances, tends to be an overall capital exporter and not a capital importer. However, to paraphrase current bankers' language, Eastern Europe wants historic East Asian growth rates at African savings rates. The result is of course, *neo-classics* and *dependentistas* will agree, increased foreign capital imports in a relatively backward economic structure. The rest already has been described by Gunnar Myrdal in full detail. The macro-economic need for high net foreign investment, hence the predominance of foreigners investing at home as compared to the investments of nationals abroad on the enterprise level, precisely arises, when either export-led growth is insufficient or import-substitution strategies are in force or both. Everything that has been said over the last thirty years about globalization can also be interpreted in terms of a radical neo-classic critique of import-substitution policies and insufficient export-oriented strategies (Ernst, 1973). The East, hoping to attract foreign capital to the detriment of the relative share of the developed countries, in world investment flows must ask itself, whether or not low labor costs are a necessary let alone a sufficient condition to attract foreign capital.

The 9 most promising reform countries increased their total debt from 101 billion $ in 1992 to 127.2 billion $ in 1995. The present author thus expected all along a renewed East European debt cycle as entirely likely. The latest debt data from the international financial press are:

Gross foreign debt ($bn)	Latest	As of	Year ago
Bulgaria	9.0	1-00	9.7**
Croatia	**8.8**	**6-99**	**8.5***
Czech Republic	22.6	6-99	23.3**
Estonia	0.2	11-99	0.3**
Hungary	**25.0**	**6-99**	**23.0**
Latvia	0.4	2-00	0.4**
Lithuania	2.4	1-00	na
Poland	31.6	10-99	33.2
Romania	8.2	11-99	9.2**
Russia	**143.8**	**6-09**	**130.8**
Slovakia	10.3	8-99	11.9**
Slovenia	**5.3**	**6-99**	**4.9***

*Preliminary **end of previous year

Source: *Business Central Europe,* op. cit. Countries, whose names are printed in **bold** letters, had a worsening debt performance over time

The right wing in Poland contends - not without justification -, that the left which governed Poland from 1993 to 1997, incurred a trade balance deficit to the tune of 22 billion $ since taking power to the end of their regime. That their own policy of unilateral opening of markets, 1989 - 1993, contributed to the process, is another matter. In fact, one could even argue that there was no such thing as Western aid to the East at the early stages of the transformation, especially to some transformation economies in Europe. Talks about the Marshall plan were relatively belated on May 28, 1997 50 years after the original; in fact, such a plan - and its philosophy - would have been necessary years ago. Regimes that received real net transfers were the (former) 'real socialist' regimes of various Marxist or 'real socialist' denominations in the South and in the (former) USSR, but not all the transformation economies of Eastern Europe. Western protectionism, transfer pricing and other monopoly practices are to be held partially responsible for the fact, that aggregate net transfers to the East (after due consideration of interests paid for Western Banks, donors and profits, paid out to investors) were sometimes negative (our own compilations from Vienna Institute for International Economic Comparisons; World Bank, WDR (1994), HDR UNDP, 1994, and *Business Central Europe,* July 1997). Although later data (World Bank, WDR, 1996) seemed to suggest a certain reversal in the trends of the international division of labor within Europe, it is pretty certain that the whole region, from 1990 to 1995, received only 15% of all total investment inflows to the tune of $1640 thousand million (World Bank, WDR, 1996). The World Development Report 1996 clearly stated:

'One might have expected huge imports of capital, both private and official, to participate in financing the costly economic and political transformation (...) However, except for the former East Germany (i.e. $700 thousand million), CEE and the NIS have not absorbed a great deal of foreign capital - either private investment flows or official external assistance (...) Between them the countries of CEE and the NIS absorbed 15 percent of total capital flows to developing and transition countries (...) Net resource inflows are much lower and even negative to some countries, once debt service and capital flight are taken into account. Capital flight from Russia alone has been estimated at some $50 billion (i.e. thousand million) for 1992-95, although part of this represented capital exported through Russia from other NIS (...) In 1994, FDI to CEE and the NIS was only $6.5 billion (i.e. thousand million), equivalent to the total received by Malaysia and

Thailand (...) The Visegrad countries received fully three-quarters of the total, whereas many other countries in the region are still all but untouched by foreign investment (...) All in all, then, transition has not absorbed a large slice of global capital flows (...) Aid under the Marshall Plan after World War II averaged 2.5 percent of the incomes of the recipient countries at the time. Total official disbursements to the CEE economies, which have generally progressed furthest in their reforms, accounted on average for about 2.7 of their combined GDP in 1991-93. Under-recording of GDP in these economies may bias this ratio upward, but on this measure Marshall Plan disbursements were not materially larger (...) The Marshall Plan did, however, embody a larger grant element, and it was much more generous relative to the donor economy's income, at 1.5 percent of U.S. GDP.' (World Bank, World Development Report, 1996: 136 and 10)

Thus, there is a certain evidence on a de-facto de-capitalization of the transition countries during their vital hour of transformation:

Table 9.1: The Amin hypothesis about the Latin Americanization of Eastern Europe. Current account balances from 1992 onwards in the region

	1992	1993	1994	1995	1996	1997	Country Total
Bulgaria	-361	-1098	-32	-43	100	200	-1234
Croatia	823	104	103	-1712	-1100	-1000	-2782
Poland	-269	-2329	-944	-2299	-400	-2000	-8241
Romania	-1564	-1174	-428	-1292	-1000	-1000	-6458
Slovak R.		-601	665	646	-1300	-1500	-2090
Slovenia	926	192	540	-36	-150	-200	1272
Czech R.		115	-50	-1892	-3400	-3700	-8927
Ukraine	-621	-854	-1396	-1545	-1200	-1200	-6816
Hungary	324	-3455	-3911	-2480	-1800	-1700	-13022
Annual Total	-742	-9100	-5453	-10653	-10250	-12100	**-48298**

Legend: CEEC 7 comprises the Czech Republic, Hungary, Poland, the Slovak Republic, Slovenia, Bulgaria, and Romania. From: Vienna Institute for International Economic Comparisons, Monatsberichte des Oesterreichischen Instituts fuer Wirtschaftsforschung, 5, 1997

Although earlier studies, among them Chase-Dunn, 1982, Szlajfer, 1977 and Tausch, 1985, already stressed the world-market dependent character of 'real socialism', the flow of direct foreign investments increased significantly only after the fall of the Berlin Wall in 1989. Russia and Hungary received the lion's share of western capital flows to the East. *Business Central Europe* estimated, that Poland ranks fifth in terms of per-capita foreign direct investment stock in the region, surpassed by Hungary, Slovenia, the Czech Republic, and Estonia. The FDI stock as percentage of GDP in 1994 was already 5.1%, while in Brazil it was 8.0%. **Poland even paid aggregate net transfers to the West during the Solidarity years 1989-1993.** And here, the **third fallacy** about post-1989 reconstruction arises: **some Eastern countries were at the crucial time of the political transition in an increasingly precarious position *vis-à-vis* the centers of the transnational economy,** just like the predecessor regimes in the region in the 1920s and 1930s and the countries of the periphery today. Aggregate net transfers are understood as aggregate net resource flows minus interest payments on long-term loans and remittance of all profits. Aggregate net resource flows are the sum of net flows on long-term debt (excluding use of IMF credit), plus official grants (excluding technical assistance) and net foreign direct investment. That is to say, Poland (just as Hungary), in reality, were **de-capitalized by the world economy, when** the new elites in power would have needed Western support most urgently (World Bank, WDR, 1994). As we will show below, the workings of the transnational economy did probably contribute to the political cleavages and to the downfall of the Solidarity government in 1993. The yearly de-capitalization amounted to 27 million $. The share of foreign investment per total GDP, i.e. the value of the index, what Bornschier and Mueller (1988) call *foreign property'*, was anywhere around 8.5% for the overall Polish economy in 1995 (UNCTAD, 1996). In terms of the employment effects, one finds that transnational capital now controls the most important modern, dynamic consumer goods sectors; 2.7% of the total labor force and 6.8% of all workers and employees in industry work for international firms. The private sector is dominated to a still larger degree by foreign firms; 16% of the labor force in private industry in fact works for foreign firms. The following materials document the share of the FDI inflows in GDP in various *'emerging markets'*

FDI ranked by Share of GDP, 1995

	Share of GDP (%)	Share of total investment (%)
Hungary	9.3	46
Malaysia	6.9	21
China	5.5	13
Chile	4.6	18
Indonesia	2.3	8
Nigeria	1.7	11
Poland	1.6	10
Argentina	1.4	8
Thailand	1.4	3
Mexico	1.2	5
Greece	0.9	4
Brazil	0.5	3

Source: EIU, *China Market Atlas*, 1997. Documented by John Henley et al. in *http://www.man.ac.uk/idpm/ppm_wp7.htm*. See also the recent paper by Leon Zurawicki at: *http://adam.mgmt.umb.edu/journal/fashionrev.html*

The **fourth fallacy** concerns the effects of 'dependent development' on the host countries. **The employment effects of transnational investments were over- the socially polarizing effects of transnational investments underestimated.** Regional concentration of development increases, and with that the political cleavages of a basically still semi-peripheral society. Even for the case of China, the World Bank WDR 1996 states:

'FDI to China was $33.8 billion (i.e. thousand million) in 1994, second only to flows to the United States. However, a substantial portion consisted of domestic funds recycled as foreign investment to take advantage of fiscal concessions' (World Bank, WDR, 1996: 136)

A Polish regional case study

Poland's position in the world is first of all confronted by the fact, that *since 1989 all her neighbors have changed* - only the Baltic seacoast has remained the same. East Germany to the East has disappeared and has been reunited with West Germany, Czechoslovakia to the South has separated into the Czech and the Slovak Republics, and to the East, the USSR dissolved - leaving the Ukraine, Belarus, Lithuania, and Kaliningrad *oblast,* pertaining to Russia, behind. The development effort of the West in such a world politically highly sensitive region - and especially TNC investment - is concentrated around the rich centers of Poland, like Warsaw, Gdansk, Katowice, Krakow, Poznan and Wroclaw. A similar picture arises from the other transformation countries. The poor rural regions of Poland are almost totally neglected by foreign capital; some run-away industries are growing up in the western regions, bordering the Federal Republic of Germany. From Central Statistical Office data we estimate, that the difference between the richest and the poorest voivodship is for:

infant mortality	1:1.9
inhabitants per doctor	1:3.4
inhabitants per hospital bed	1:2.3
telephones per inhabitants	1:3.5
cancer death rate	1:1.7
unemployment	1:4.1
investment per capita	1:4.2

Legend: our own compilations from Polish Central Statistical Office data

The transformation after 1989 destroyed more than 3 million jobs in the public sector and more than 150 000 jobs in private agriculture, mainly in the East and the North of the country; in comparison to that, the performance of private national and or foreign capital in creating jobs has been more than modest from 1989 to 1994:

	1989	**1994**	**growth/decl.**
public sector	9277,8	5878,4	-3399,4
private agric.	3898,7	3744,9	-153,8
foreign cap.	130,4	228,1	97,7
other priv sec.	4082,5	4881,8	799,3

Source: our own calculations from G.U.S. Rocznik Statystyczny Pracy 1995

In a way, development of capitalism in Poland meant first and foremost an increase of the reserve army - and of the second economy, amounting to 43% of the Polish GDP (Economist, *The World in 1998).* Statistics from the Polish press indicate the following distribution of foreign direct investment in Poland in 1997, which today reaches almost $bn 40, i.e. 24.7% of Polish GDP:

Graph 9.2: MNC investments in the Polish economy

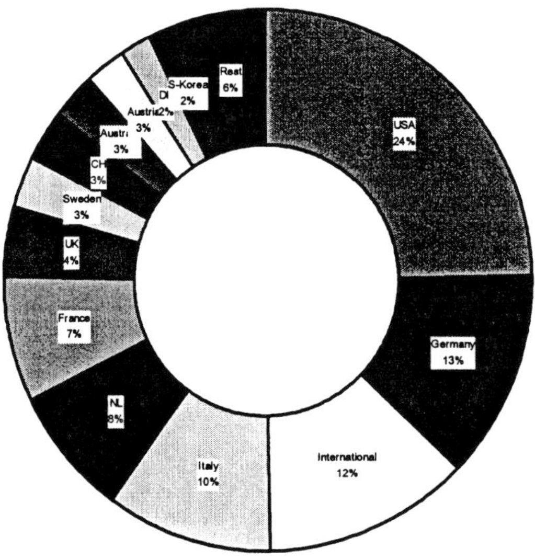

Legend: stock of MNC capital by country of origin

Legend: breakdown of foreign investors in percent. Source: our own compilations from Polish Agency for Foreign Investment (PAIZ), for December 1996, as published in *Okecie Airport Magazine,* April 1997, 4: 5

Poland was hit by the worst floods in human memory during summer 1997. The most dynamic regions of the country, around Wroclaw and further to the North-west, but also in Upper Silesia, were devastated by the flood waters. The consequences were far-reaching, insofar as the psychological impact on the population, that was about to gain the first real fruits of transformation, was very negative and long-lasting. The floods, furthermore, have exposed many of the weaknesses of the administrative centralist structure in such fields as environmental policy, sewage disposal, garbage collection, and infrastructure. International and Polish press reports suggest that basic initiatives by neighborhood committees emerged in the South and South-west under the impression of prime ministerial arrogance, rotting animal corpses and broken sewage pipes, thus challenging again the 'centralist' authority of the Polish state, perhaps marking the beginning of yet another 12 to 14 year cycle of protest and dissatisfaction, that is so typical of Polish history since the re-founding of the Polish state within today's borders in 1944/45 (1956, 1968 - 1970, 1980 - 1983). It is interesting to note, that there is a vague temporal correlation of this Polish protest cycle with the Kuznets and or Kondratieff cycle troughs since 1945 in the periphery (with the western troughs in the years 1958, 1975, 1981). Although the Polish economy seems to be still in full swing again for the moment, the relationship of trust between the governed and the government tilted against the latter in the September election of 1997, and the foreign balances of the economy point in a downward direction. Again, as in 1989, a triumphant labor movement, Solidarity, is supposed to push through an austerity course while in government. Such a Polish political tango could remind us, if a lot goes wrong, rather of Argentina in the 1960s, 1970s, and 1980s. Regional unemployment in Poland is relatively stable and is a clear indicator of the semi-peripheral character of the country in the world economy:

Graph 9.3: unemployment in Poland - regional aspects

Legend: unemployment rate 1993 (x-axis) and unemployment rate 1996 (y-axis), based on G.U.S. statistics on unemployment in the 49 voivodships of Poland.

The multiple regression to explain the residuals from the above Graph works with the following variables taken from the Polish Central Statistical Office and from the daily Polish Press:

- *big estates per total land*
- *employment in agriculture*
- *employment in foreign capital enterprises per total employment*
- *employment in mixed enterprises per total employment*
- *external migration per total population*

- *female excess infant mortality rates (based on regression residuals of male on female infant mortality rates in the different voivodships of the country). Voivodships are said to have an excess female infant mortality, when the regression residual is positive)*
- *human development index*
- *industrial employment*
- *industrial waste*
- *private land per total land*
- *real GDP per capita*
- *religious practice*
- *urbanization*
- *voting data on a voivodship level for all the elections and referenda since 1993, compiled from the Polish dailies*
- *wage level*

During the post-communist years, there was a clear 'political' economy of castigating the opposition strongholds and handing out benefits to one's own political folk:

equation (9.1) the rise or fall of unemployment in Poland 1993/97:

religious pract	ext migr/pop	PSL	private land	peasants	big estates	SLD	real gdp pc	HDI-Index	for cap pen	mixed cap pen	2tour Walesa	
-0,005	0,33	**-2,422**	0,649	4E-05	0,126	**-0,097**	0,05	**-0,033**	-0,083	-0,002	**0,076**	-0,501
0,047	0,603	0,979	10,43	5E-04	0,088	0,036	0,048	0,018	0,067	0,006	0,043	8,071
0,45												
2,453	36											
-0,105	0,547	**-2,47**	0,062	0,079	1,429	**-2,71**	1,04	**-1,91**	-1,244	-0,378	**1,756**	constant

religious pract	ext migr/pop	PSL	private land	peasants	big estates	SLD	real gdp pc	HDI-Index	for cap pen	mixed cap pen	2tour Walesa

Note: as in all EXCEL 5.0 outprints, first rows are unstandardized regression coefficients, second rows are standard errors of the estimate, the third row shows the value for R^2 of the whole equation and the standard deviation of the estimate for y; the fourth row are the F-value and the degrees of freedom of the whole equation; the fifth row shows the sum of squares of the regression and the sum of square of the residuals.

In Tausch (1997) it was shown that the post-communist SLD clearly emerged in the period 1993-95 as a party in regions with a high amount of environmental damage, and in rural regions with low industrialization and excessive sexist patterns of mortality. According to the World Bank WDR 1999/2000, **carbon dioxide damage costs Poland annualy 1.7% of its GDP, after Romania one of the highest values anywhere in the world.**

The post-communists clearly lost in 1993 and 1995 in terms of electoral support due to a higher penetration of a region by foreign capital. The radical right, not represented in the Sejm between 1993 and 1997, was especially strong in regions of low urbanization, industrialization and high external, poverty-driven migration. In 1997, this potential increased dramatically, especially in the aftermath of the Papal visit to Poland and the flood

disaster, which, many people believe, was managed very badly during the first few days by the Central Government in Warsaw. With the disintegrative tendencies of the right-wing-liberal-trade-unionist coalition, formed after the 1997 election, on the increase, this protest potential will shift to other, populist formations like Mr. Lepper's Peasant League in the years to come.

Urban, less traditionally catholic, and less private-peasantry-oriented and less big landholding areas were far more attractive to transnational capital than the traditional Polish countryside, while joint ventures prefer urban low-wage areas of Poland, also characterized by the absence of a numerically strong private (and conservative) peasantry. The main results of the above analysis also hold for the constitutional referendum of May 25th 1997. The results are a neat reproduction of the second round of the presidential elections in 1995, as is to be shown from the following graph:

Graph 9.4: The regionally constant pattern of voting in Poland - the second round of the presidential elections in 1995 as a determinant of the 'NO'-vote in the constitutional referendum of May 25th 1997:

Walesa vote 95/referendum vote 97

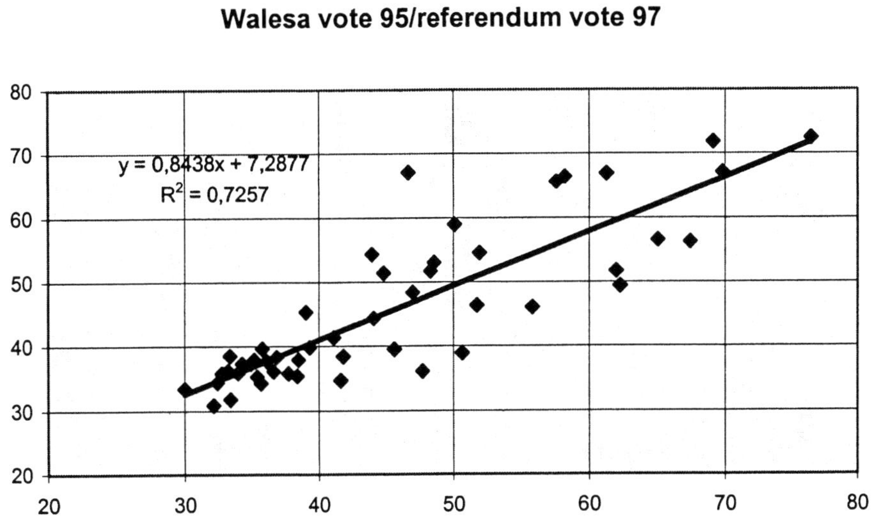

Legend: the Walesa-vote 1995 (x-axis) and the constitutional vote 1997 (y-axis) as dependent variables, based on the 49 voivodships of Poland. Our own compilations from the official election/referendum results, as published in the daily Polish Press.

The 1997 referendum again showed the political cleavages of the country: the catholic, foreign-capital penetrated regions voting with the political right, while the semi-peripheral regions of the Northwest and Northeast, characterized by big landholding before 1918, voting with the political left. However, the time perspective reveals another tendency. **The AWS-Solidarity alliance in the fall 1997 parliamentary elections could relatively increase its vote in regions, characterized by big landholding before 1918, and also in regions, characterized by paternalistic patterns of excess female infant mortality rates. These are the regions, where dependent development has the biggest contradictions. Precisely there, the left showed its weaknesses well before the election of the 21st of September 1997, when four years of left government in Poland ended:**

Table 9.2: the determinants of the 1997 referendum on the constitution

Variables	religious pract	ext migr/pop	industr waste	private land	peasants	big estates	fem exc inf m	real gdp pc	HDI-Index	for cap pen	mixed cap pen	constant
NO-Vote	6,896	-6,435	65,98	-0,002	-0,004	-0,357	0,105	0,056	-1E-04	0,049	0,951	-22,77
1997	3,614	6,955	63,42	0,002	0,005	0,202	0,197	0,106	7E-05	0,042	0,215	44,31
	0,674											
	6,96	37										
t-test	**1,908**	-0,925	1,04	-0,902	-0,665	**-1,77**	0,534	0,526	-1,402	1,174	**4,432**	-0,514

increases/decreases of the anti-SLD-protest vote in %

Variables	religious pract	ext migr/pop	industr waste	private land	peasants	big estates	fem exc inf m	real gdp pc	HDI-Index	for cap pen	mixed cap pen	constant
increase	-3,67	-4,801	-2,089	-4E-04	-0,002	0,322	0,635	3E-04	1E-04	-0,074	-0,187	-12,11
decrease/ protest	3,554	6,841	62,38	0,002	0,005	0,198	0,193	0,104	7E-05	0,041	0,211	43,58
	0,742											
	9,654	37										
t-test	-1,032	-0,702	-0,033	-0,179	-0,37	**1,622**	**3,286**	0,003	1,424	**-1,8**	-0,887	

Legend: our own compilations from the above mentioned data. Anti-SLD-protest vote: 1995 presidential election vote for Lech Walesa; 1997 'NO' at the constitutional referendum. As in all EXCEL 5.0 outprints in this work, first row: unstandardized regression coefficients, second row: standard errors, last row: t-Test. The values immediately below the standard errors are R^2 (third row, left side entry), F, and degrees of freedom (fourth row).

The 1997 general election, in turn, repeated the results of the referendum and the 1995 general election. Both large political camps show a very surprising degree of homogeneity:

Graph 9.5: Voting 1995 and 1997

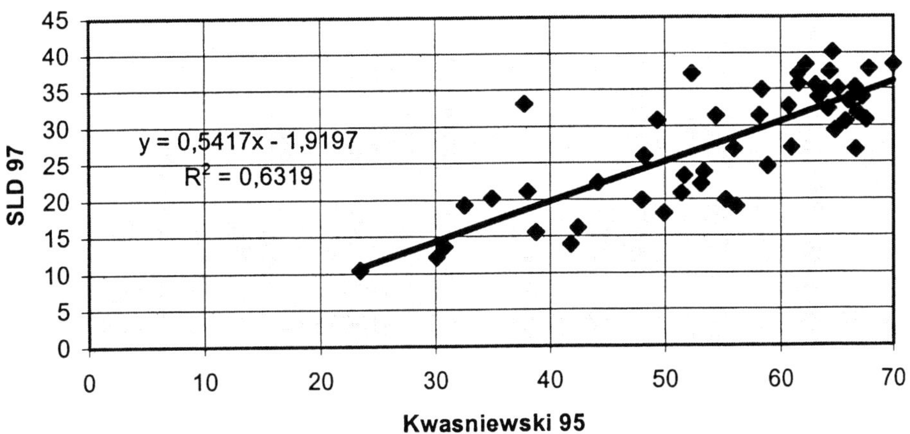

Legend: Walesa vote, 1995 (x-axis) and AWS-vote, 1997 (y-axis), based on the 49 voivodships of Poland.

Legend: the Kwasniewski vote (1995) (x-axis) and the SLD vote (1997) (y-axis), based on data about political performance in the 49 voivodships of Poland.

The Solidarity-led AWS was especially strong in regions with mixed foreign capital presence, while the post-communist SLD had the following significant factors working in favor or against it:

positive influences on the SLD vote:

- percentage of employment in agriculture
- share of big estates per total agricultural area
- Human Development Index

negative influences on the SLD vote:

- religious practice

- female excess mortality rates
- foreign capital employment
- mixed capital employment

The SLD as the party of the 'modernizing state class' could still - relatively - hold its place in regions with high human development and in the typical northern agricultural zones, characterized before 1939 by *Junker* German big landholding, although a great number of their potential voters stayed at home, thus increasing the voter abstention rate; whereas the left-wing defeat in the traditional small-scale peasantry regions of the East and South-east was almost total. These regions are characterized by high female excess infant mortality rates and by traditional religious patterns. The SLD also significantly lost in the 'modern' regions with high foreign capital and mixed capital presence.

Table 9.3: the 1997 general election in Poland

Variables	religious pract	ext migr/pop	industr waste	private land	peasants	big estates	fem exc inf m	real gdp pc	HDI-Index	for cap pen	mixed cap pen	constant
AWS	4,797	4,317	30,485	-0,001	-0,006	-0,255	-0,077	0,0713	-3E-05	0,02	0,8388	-7,098
	3,3637	6,4739	59,032	0,0022	0,005	0,1877	0,1829	0,0984	6E-05	0,0387	0,1998	41,239
	0,556											
	4,22	37										
t-test	1,4261	0,6668	0,5164	-0,502	-1,111	-1,359	-0,42	0,7242	-0,497	0,5187	**4,199**	-0,172
Variables	religious pract	ext migr/pop	industr waste	private land	peasants	big estates	fem exc inf m	real gdp pc	HDI-Index	for cap pen	mixed cap pen	constant
SLD	-4,251	3,4467	-51,91	0,0011	0,007	0,2615	-0,257	-0,034	7E-05	-0,071	-0,512	85,714
	2,0753	3,9943	36,421	0,0013	0,0031	0,1158	0,1129	0,0607	4E-05	0,0238	0,1233	25,443
	0,773											
	11,454	37										
t-test	**-2,05**	0,8629	-1,425	0,7979	**2,245**	**2,257**	**-2,27**	-0,563	**1,766**	**-3**	**-4,15**	3,3688
Variables	religious pract	ext migr/pop	industr waste	private land	peasants	big estates	fem exc inf m	real gdp pc	HDI-Index	for cap pen	mixed cap pen	constant
inc S	-4,018	14,117	-19,34	-2E-04	-0,006	0,2304	0,2147	0,0072	0,0002	-0,083	0,0997	-24,18
	3,5634	6,8583	62,537	0,0023	0,0053	0,1989	0,1938	0,1042	7E-05	0,0409	0,2116	43,688
	0,364											
	1,9257	37										
t-test	-1,127	**2,058**	-0,309	-0,078	-1,149	1,1583	1,1081	0,069	**2,509**	**-2,03**	0,4712	-0,553

	religious pract	ext migr/pop	industr waste	private land	peasants	big estates	fem exc inf m	real gdp pc	HDI-Index	for cap pen	mixed cap pen	constant
incr SLD	0,7107	9,9122	-40,32	0,0007	0,0063	0,0413	-0,625	0,0736	2E-05	-0,043	-0,082	-5,751
	1,9507	3,7544	34,234	0,0013	0,0029	0,1089	0,1061	0,0571	4E-05	0,0224	0,1159	23,916
	0,8702											
	22,541	37										
t-test	0,3644	**2,64**	-1,178	0,562	**2,149**	0,3796	**-5,89**	1,2903	0,5802	**-1,93**	-0,705	-0,24
	religious pract	**ext migr/pop**	industr waste	private land	**peasants**	big estates	**fem exc inf m**	real gdp pc	HDI-Index	**for cap pen**	mixed cap pen	constant

Legend: our own calculations from the above mentioned variables and the election results, as reported by *http://www.prokom.pl,* the web-site of a Polish electronics company, managing the calculation of the official results for the Polish Government. As in all EXCEL 5.0 outprints in this work, first row: unstandardized regression coefficients, second row: standard errors, last row: t-Test. The values immediately below the standard errors are R^2 (third row, left side entry), *F,* and degrees of freedom (fourth row).

Thus, still 2/3 up to ¾ of Polish voting are being determined by the structural characteristics of social policy and the insertion of Poland into the capitalist world economy. On the other hand, 71% of TNC employment and 38% of joint venture employment per total employment are explained by our equations:

Table 9.4: the political ecology of foreign capital attraction to the different regions in Poland, 1993

Explan. Var. of/ region	employment for multinat. corporations explains *(ceteris paribus)* 1993:	Joint ventures
	employment in TNCs	joint ventures
wage level		-
Catholicism migration	-	
ecological crisis private land	-	-
traditional employment in agriculture big landholding	-	
patriarchical structures		
industrial employment		
urbanization	+	+
R^2	71%	38%

Source: Our own calculations (EXCEL 4.0 multiple regression IBM PS 2 notebook N51 SX) from C.S.O. data

Polish unemployment is a typical phenomenon of low-wage regions with either high pollution or high agricultural employment. Foreign capital does contribute to a better employment record, but the effect is not significant. The effect on life expectancy is even negative, although not significant. We again use the standard functions for life expectancy determination. Thus, the societal expectations created by globalization are not met:

equation (9.2) **unemployment in Poland** = 26.02 - **4.18 * wage level** - 1.50 * religious practice - 0.06 * outward migration + **0.24 * industrial waste** - 0.00 private land + **0.58 * employment in agriculture** - 0.08 * big estates + 0.04 * excess mortality + 0.00 * industrial employment - 0.02 urbanization - 0.15 * foreign capital penetration *(t*-value 1.5911) - 0.003 mixed capital penetration

$$R^2 = 73.39\%; F = 8.27; df. = 36; \alpha \text{ (one-tailed) } 5\% > 1.69$$

External migration, the well-known function of income level and human development, and the level of urbanization co-determine life expectancy in Poland. On the other hand, there is a really perverse negative determination of life quality variables, like life expectancy and infant mortality, by the number of doctors per voivodship, indicating the gross inefficiencies of the health system of the country:

Table 9.5: human development on a regional level in Poland, as being determined by socio-political processes

life expectancy in Poland =

gdp^1/e^2	gdp^ln(p)	religious pra	ext mig/pop	industr waste	private land	peasants	big estates	fem exc inf m	ind.employm	urbanisation	for cap pen	mixed cap	constant
0,25896	-0,9082	-0,0069	-0,0322	-0,0002	-0,021	-0,0046	0,00597	-3E-06	-0,0028	0,04318	-6E-05	3,45214	62,2839
0,23142	0,4564	0,01614	0,01467	0,00035	0,0138	0,02232	0,00741	4,8E-06	0,00259	0,01309	9,6E-05	4,52338	12,6892
0,70286	0,47696												
6,36843	35												
18,8341	7,96228												

gdp^1/e^2	gdp^ln(p)	religious pra	ext mig/pop	industr waste	private land	peasants	big estates	fem exc inf m	ind.employm	urbanisation	for cap pen	mixed cap pen	
1,119	**-1,9898**	-0,4305	**-2,1946**	-0,4549	-1,5236	-0,2052	0,80583	-0,6114	-1,0641	**3,29921**	-0,6334	0,76318	constant

life expectancy in Poland as determined by health policy data =

doctors per pop		hospital beds	
-0,053	0,0547		72,862
0,0159	0,0216		0,5609
0,1947	0,6849		
5,5621	46		
5,2182	21,578		
-3,333	**2,5321**		t-test
doctors per pop		hospital beds	

infant mortality in Poland =

gdp^1/e^2	gdp^ln(p)	religious pra	ext mig/pop	industr waste	private land	peasants	big estates	fem exc inf m	ind.employm	urbanisation	for cap pen	mixed cap pen	constant
-0,1869	-2,2702	0,13882	-0,0374	0,00096	-0,0412	0,07048	-0,0257	-2E-05	0,00162	0,00825	0,00011	-8,46	32,2124
0,87801	1,73163	0,06122	0,05565	0,00132	0,05235	0,08467	0,02813	1,8E-05	0,00981	0,04965	0,00037	17,162	48,1437
0,29022	1,80963												
1,10082	35												
46,864	114,616												

gdp^1/e^2	gdp^ln(p)	religious pra	ext mig/pop	industr waste	private land	peasants	big estates	fem exc inf m	ind.employm	urbanisation	for cap pen	mixed cap pen	
-0,2129	-1,311	**2,26768**	-0,6722	0,73093	-0,7865	0,83243	-0,9137	-0,987	0,16531	0,16618	0,29755	-0,493	constant

infant mortality in Poland as determined by health policy data =

doctors per pop		hospital beds	
0,0836	-0,059		10,5
0,0414	0,0563		1,4601
0,0945	1,7829		
2,3993	46		
15,254	146,23		
2,0201	**-1,049**		t-test
doctors per pop		hospital beds	

Legend: as in all EXCEL 5.0 outprints in this work, first row: unstandardized regression coefficients, second row: standard errors, last row: t-Test. The values immediately below the standard errors are R^2 (third row, left side entry), F, and degrees of freedom (fourth row).

Religious practice - as an indicator of the absence of modernization in a particular region - was in the 1990s lamentably enough one the more robust indicators of regional infant mortality rates in Poland, while the concentration of doctors in a region does practically nothing to increase life expectancy. The trade-off between religious practice and infant mortality could be interpreted in a non-causal way, however, since religious practice and infant mortality are both characteristics of peripheral regions in Poland:

Graph 9.6: the number of doctors and life expectancy in Poland

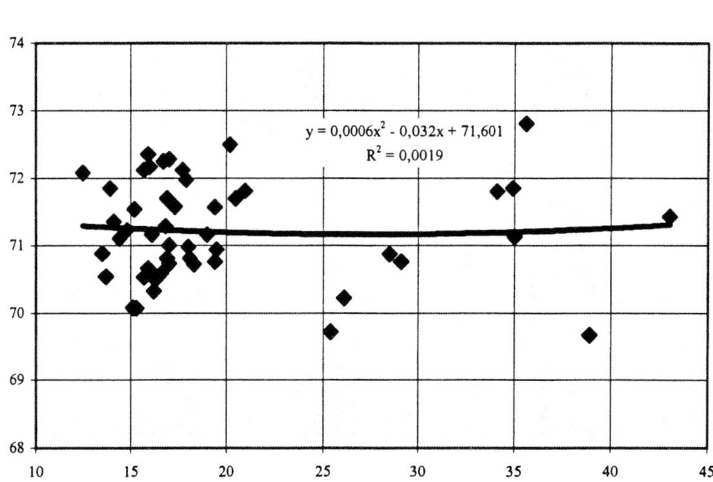

Legend and source: number of doctors per 10000 population (x-axis) and life expectancy at birth, measured in years (y-axis) for the 49 Polish voivodships. Our own calculations from regional development statistics, contained in Rocznik Statystyczny, 1996, Polish Central Statistical Office

Life expectancy is also being negatively, but not significantly, determined by foreign capital penetration. The negative trade-off, well known from cross-national policy planning and development research (Tausch and Prager, 1993), can be shown to be existing for the transformation country Poland, although the long-term negative effects of mass foreign migration on the health situation of the population in the 'guest worker export periphery' Poland are stronger than those of the direct foreign capital penetration. Here we should recall, how a guest-worker economy, in the end, can destroy the social fabric of the sender-country (see also: Chapter 10). Environmental decay is related to the general life expectancy situation in Poland, but the directly observable statistical effect is weak and below the usual significance levels, because the other intervening variables, like the social and biological stress of a guest-worker economy, are stronger. It will be expected, that especially cardiovascular-vascular diseases increase under the pressure of migration and family separation. The typical urban/rural cleavages, so well-known from policy planning and development research about the capitalist periphery (Lipton, 1977), again emerge to be relevant for the post-communist capitalist periphery. Urbanization is a positive significant determinant of life expectancy. Infant mortality rates, however, are being mainly determined by traditionalist socio-cultural patterns that express themselves in religious practice rates. Our equations explain over 70% of life expectancy and over 29% of infant mortality rates.

Again, it is being confirmed that dependent capitalism creates growth and employment only to some extent, but that its effects on the social sphere are contradictory and connected to socially long-run disintegrative tendencies. *Ceteris paribus,* the control of foreign capital over overall employment is even slightly negatively related to life expectancy at the voivodship regional level. Our results about Poland should also be seen in the more general context of our results about the transformation dynamic of Eastern Europe.

Up to now, the leading elites did not question the basic principles of Western integration. Political constellations might arise, which will be more nationalistic in orientation, reflecting the peripheral role that Poland still plays in the world economy, especially when Poland should suffer a crisis like other emerging market economies suffered in 1997. Yet it would be wrong to portray the protest against the **contradictions** of state-class dominated, centralist, dependent capitalism, that is growing in strength in Poland, as only a backward and fundamentalist reaction against the **'benefits of Western integration'**. As Jadwiga Staniszkis has shown already for the old, 1991-1993 parliament, 100 members of parliament were at the same time members of the boards of various, state-class dominated companies (Staniszkis, 1998). By mid-1998, 17% of the assets of the 500 largest companies in Poland were in foreign hands, another 8% were in the ownership of mixed capital, the state controlled 26% directly, and another 6% via the national investment funds, while Polish private capital owned only 43%. Again and again, the Polish and the international press link some of these private entrepreneurs to shady business dealings, and their enterprise history back to the days of the communist institutions in Poland in the late 1980s. In addition, the **power of illegal foreign capital inflows is enormous; Italian crime groups** alone (we mentioned this already above) are estimated to **launder 100000 $ an hour in Poland** (see *Polityka*, 16).

A Staniszkiean picture of the Polish political landscape would look like the following: the present set-up of the centralist state, dominated by the state class, mainly recruited from the banking sector and foreign trade companies, in alliance with transnational capital, which has remained relatively stable since 1989, is challenged on various fronts, and not only by the nationalists at the URSUS tractor works and from the catholic right-wing radio station *'Radio Maryja'*:

- by a growing **regionalist movement**, which is also a reaction in the context of the effects of flood waters on Poland's South. Not all manifestations of regionalism need to be 'backward-looking'
- by a growing **environmentalist movement**
- by a new generation of the labor movement, that is demonstrating especially against the lack of **safety at work**. An appalling number of major industrial accidents remind us of the fact, that *'the cage'* of the *'Polish tiger'* often releases poisonous gases, or that parts of the cage crumble and bury miners
- the protest movement in the state sector, especially in the **health sector**
- to this one has to add the crisis of the **education sector** and
- the disintegration effects of 'westward integration' on **Polish agriculture,** brought about by large-scale imports of highly subsidized EU-produced food, with whose price level and economies of scale Polish agriculture cannot compete

It is thus no wonder, that according to a standard random-sample poll by the usually very reliable social scientific public opinion research institute CBOS, mentioned in the Polish press, only 21% of Poles consider their country as a full democracy, while 32% see it on the way to democracy, and a staggering 35% consider Poland to be still un-democratic *(Polish News Bulletin,* British and American Embassy, Warsaw, 27th calendar week, 1998).

The Eastern part of Europe and the long Kondratieff wave: historical evidence

Just as during the world depression of the 1930s, democracy could not survive in the region (Polanyi, 1944), today the danger arises, that instability and not democratization will triumph in the end especially on the Balkans and in the countries of the former USSR in the long run. The turning points in the long economic waves between the ascents and decline phases (B-phases) were always the beginnings of political decay in the region as well, while the ascent phases were associated with authoritarian modernization; time-lags between the Western cycle and the Eastern semi-periphery and periphery have to be admitted (Tausch, 1997). The *decisive-kairos*-years are:

1509
1539
1575
1621
1689
1756
1835/42
1884
1933
1975/1982

Source: our own compilations from Goldstein and our own data interpretations after 1740, based on Goldstein. It should be recalled, that there is another tradition - based on Braudel - to view the cycle, that begins in 1689, as ending in 1747, to be followed by a 1747 - 1790 cycle, and a 1790 - 1848 cycle (for a debate about these issues, see especially Amin, 1997).

The logic of the Kondratieff waves from 1756 onwards are given as follows:

Table 9.6: The logic of the Kondratieff waves in the world economy since 1756

social process	cycle 1756-1835/41
basic project	*defeudalization*
prosperity reform	compulsory education, conscription; American and French Revolution; Joseph II (Austria)
mid-cycle conflict	wars of the French Revolution, Napoleonic wars Poland: 1807 Duchy of Warsaw
technological change	
basic industrial projects	steam engine (end 18th century) 'Spinning Jenny' (J. Stargreave, 1770)
new technologies emerging during prosperity recession	steam locomotive 'Puffing Billy'(W. Hadley, 1813)
Unresolved problem	freedom of association
crisis of the model	revolution 1830 Poland: rebellion 1830/31
international regime	
A-phase	British naval dominance (George III)
B-phase	'congress of Vienna'-regime
dominant economic theory	A. Smith, 1776
political economy of world system	D. Ricardo, 1817

social process	cycle 1835/42-83	1884-1932	1933-75/81
basic project	*freedom of market and enterprise*	*enlargement of participation*	*welfare state, corporatism*
prosperity reform	freedom of association	social security, parliamentarism	educational reform, civil rights, emancipation of women
mid-cycle conflict	wars and civil wars Poland: revolution 1863/64	Eastern Europe: Revolution 1905	Vietnam war, world student rebellion 1968 strikes, terrorism Polish Winter 1970
technological change			
basic industrial inputs and technological projects	railway, steamship	steel, electricity, electric motor	oil, synthetics, automobile
new technologies emerging during prosperity recession	steel	petrochemicals	chips
unresolved problem	enlargement of participation	relationship capital, labour, state	basic income environment unequal exchange
crisis of the model	revolution 1871 Poland: socialist movement 1880s	revolution 1917 Poland: strikes peasant uprisings 1936/37	contestation of the model from 1968 onwards Poland: Summer 1980
international regime			
A-phase	liberal world trade	mercantilism	Bretton Woods
B-phase	-"-	hypermercantilism	neo-protectionism
dominant economic theory	J. St. Mill, 1848	A. Marshall, 1890	J.M. Keynes, 1936
political economy of world system	K. Marx, 1867	R. Hilferding, 1910	K. Polanyi, 1944

The danger is of course, that the Cold-War structure will be substituted by a new power rivalry between the former members of the winning coalition of World War II:

Hegemonic wars in the world system from 1495 onwards.

Table 9.7: hegemonic cycles in the world economy since 1450

Role in War	Thirty Years War	Napoleonic	WW I+II
losing hegemonic contender	Hapsburgs	France	Germany
new hegemony	Netherlands	Britain	USA
newly emerging challenger: economically decimated member of winning coalition	France	Germany	China+Russia
past contender for systemic hegemony, joining the war effort of the winning coalition	Sweden	Hapsburgs Portugal	France

The former hegemonic contenders slowly slide into an acceptance of their status in the international system. The real power struggle erupts already soon after the great hegemonic war, and through the ups and downs of the history of the system evolves slowly into the hegemonic challenge. Seen in such a way, not 1989, but Korea and Vietnam could become rather the benchmarks of the future W-structure of conflict in the international arena. For the foreign policies of the European Union, it is also important to notice the following tendency: German-Russian alliances tend to happen during depressions, and they break up during the economic upswings of the world system, when, especially during waning hegemonies, conflicts over spheres of influence set it (Amin, 1997, partially based on Bergesen):

- *Khol + Gorbi/Boris 1985 ff.*
- *Rapallo 1922*
- *Bismarck's Three Emperor Alliance 1873*
- *Holy Alliance 1815*
- *Alliance Russia-Germany 1764*
- *Nordic War 1700-1721*

The relationship of the Kondratieff and Kuznets cycles with Russian history is the following:

Table 9.8: World economic cycles and internal instability in Russia since Ivan the Terrible

	Reforms
KONDRATIEFF OR KUZNETS DOWNSWING	Perestroika, Lenin's NEP, Great Reforms 1861, Katharinas Assembly 1775
	Nobility's Victory 1730, Split of the State Church 1653, Boris Godunow 1598-1605
	Repressive Modernization
KONDRATIEFF OR KUZNETS UPSWING	Joseph Stalin, Imperialistic Expansion and Repressive Industrialization at the end of 19. th century Nikolas the Gendarme of Europe, Elisabeth's expansionist policy, Peter the Great, Michael III, Ivan the Terrible

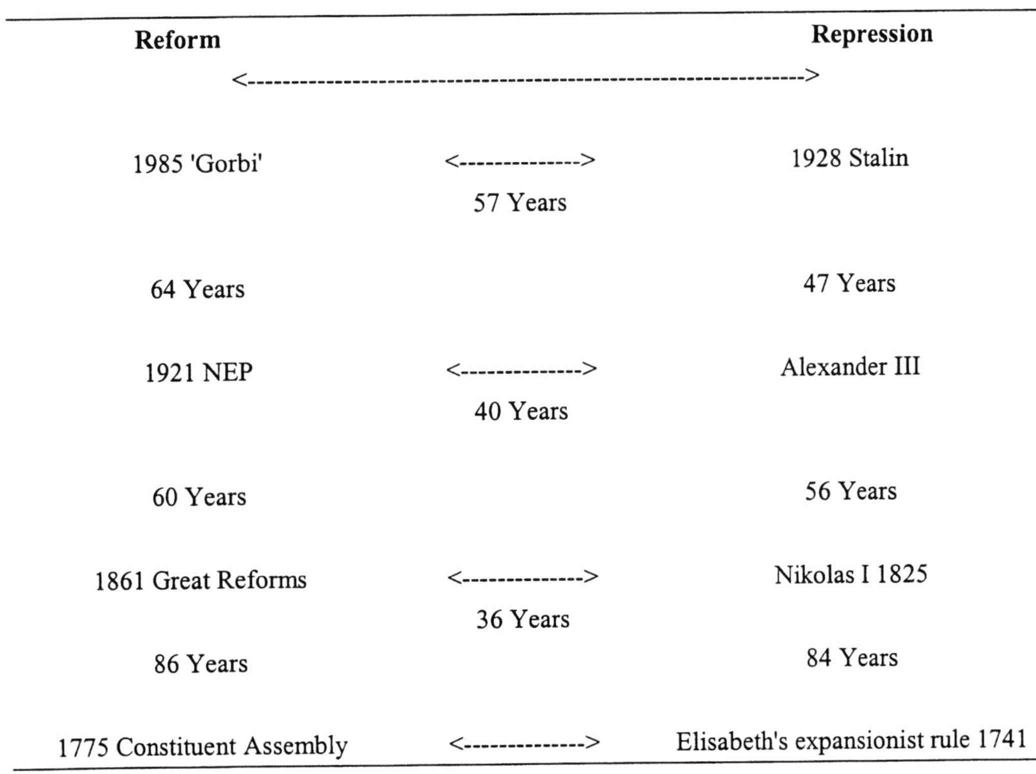

34 Years

45 Years   52 Years

1730 Victory of Nobility   <--------------->   Peter I 1689
                                          41 Years

77 Years   76 Years

Church Split 1653   <-------------->   Michael III 1613
                                          40 Years

55 Years   48 Years

Boris Godunow 1598   <--------------->   Iwan's 'Oprichina' 1565
                                          33 Years

Average periods of Russian history:

Perestroika   <-------------->   authoritarian modernization
                                          40 Years

64.5 Years   60.5 Years

Seen in such a way, there is little that the West seems to be able to do to stabilize democracy in Russia. However, the return of East Central Europe towards a 'middle of the road' and sensible philosophy - whatever the color of the government (Orenstein, 1996) - seems to be an urgent necessity, after the ups and downs of central planning and 'the central market principle'.

Transformation success or failure - the macroquantitative evidence

Practically, only Poland recovered its pre-transformation real income level of 1990 (Fischer Weltalmanach, 1998: 1019). Our analysis from the world of transformation shows, that a rapid privatization is not in itself a precondition of a more rapid socio-economic development, and that a policy oriented towards human development and democracy will be successful, while extreme egalitarianism also has certain growth limits in the region (Osteuropa-Institute Munich, *Working Paper* 186 (GDP growth, privatization); Stiftung Entwicklung und Frieden (Political Rights Violations, based on Freedom House); UNDP, 1995 (urbanization, Human Development Index); Fischer Weltalmanach (GNP per capita)). In good Aristotelian tradition, the truth is thus - again - in the middle. The multiple regression results from the available data are given below. The first test generally supports a socio-liberal interpretation of the Matthew's effect:

Table 9.9: The determinants of economic growth in the transformation countries

	privatization	Pol Rights violations	urbanization	ln (GNP)	ln(GNP)^2	HDI	Constant
econ growth	-23,53855	-2,007199	51,691191	-1,265286	-2,739098	0,6255463	-132,3854
	145,43797	10,124597	139,62757	0,4348674	5,155963	0,346291	514,0504
	0,594606						
	3,666841	15					
t-test	-0,161846	-0,19825	0,3702076	**-2,90959**	-0,531249	**1,806418**	

Note: as in all EXCEL 5.0 outprints, first rows are unstandardized regression coefficients, second rows are standard errors of the estimate, the third row shows the value for R^2 of the whole equation and the standard deviation of the estimate for y; the fourth row are the F-value and the degrees of freedom of the whole equation; the fifth row shows the sum of squares of the regression and the sum of square of the residuals. The sixth row is the t-test, calculated from row (1) and (2)

59.5% of growth in the world of transformation are explained by our equation. **Thus, it emerges that the best strategy would be a policy of thorough-going reform, that assured a high human development index and a fair amount of political and civil liberties**. A socio-liberal reading of such experiences is also supported by the second analysis. The region seems to be beset by an excessive amount of egalitarianism, that becomes a stumbling block against long-run economic growth, **when the share of the top income earners in total incomes falls below 35%,** when **taxes** - compared to development level - are **very** high, and when the **social services consume** a percentage of total expenditures, that is already comparable to the most advanced welfare states in the world. The reform of social security thus becomes an all-important necessity.

The share of the richest 20% in total incomes in the region, with the notable exception of Russia, is even lower than the respective share in most developed welfare democracies, like Sweden, Finland, the Netherlands, Denmark, and Norway, or - for that matter - in the market economies of Asia. Tax rates per total income in Eastern Europe **skyrocket** and **savings** are generally **low**, as materials from the World Bank WDR, 1996 for the former or continuously communist countries show by international comparison. Up to a certain point, social security expenditures of the state stabilize mass demand and contribute to economic growth. High inequality rates, like in Brazil, where the top income earners received 67.5% of total incomes in 1989, are certainly growth-inhibiting as well (Tausch/Prager, 1993). But when income differentiation is below a certain limit - as in some countries of Eastern Europe and the former USSR - also negative consequences arise. The egalitarianism of movements like *Solidarnosc* might have its deep roots in East European history, but economically, it is counter-productive beyond a certain point. East European and transformation country inequality is positively related to economic growth, and it lowers unemployment; while transnational investment dependence brings about higher inequality and - ceteris paribus - it does not alleviate unemployment due to the capital intensity of most investments. For Eastern Europe, the choice is not the one between Latin American inequality rates (towards which Russia seems to be heading) and the former communist egalitarianism; rather the choice is the one between continuing present rates of egalitarianism (like in Belarus) at the price of stagnation or to opt for distribution and growth patterns like in the more egalitarian developing countries of East Asia before 1997. **Foreign capital penetration only insignificantly contributes to the employment record, but significantly increases transformation country income inequality. Economic growth in the transformation countries is influenced significantly by two processes: political freedom and economic incentives, large enough, to overcome the vested egalitarianism of the communist years.** There is little, that foreign aid will be able to do to maintain growth in the more advanced countries of the region or to shorten the transformation recession in the laggard countries of Eastern Europe. Aid dependence - beyond a certain point - rather seems to contribute to the stagnation path of the laggard countries. The internationally comparable economic and social data from the *World Development Report* 1996 by the World Bank make our point for the transition economies very clear. Poland, with its spurt of economic growth often termed the 'European tiger', achieved a per-capita-income in internationally comparable $ of 8430 $, with economic growth now amounting to 4.1%. Unemployment is 13.9%, ingflation 10.4%, and industrial ouput grew by 16.3%. The trade balance in March 2000 amounted to $bn -14.2, and the gross foreign debt to $bn 31.6 (GDP at 157.0). On the positive side for Poland, official development assistance amounted in 1994 to 2.0% per GNP, the highest value for all the transformation countries in Europe with complete data except Albania, and foreign investment amounted to $bn 38.9 (http://www.bcemag.com/). But the 27% of population, who live from agriculture, just receive 6% of the total GNP - an expression of the perennial structural heterogeneity of Polish society, that characterizes the country from the Long 16th Century onwards. The empirical cross-national evidence is presented below:

equation (9.3) economic growth =

Gini inequality	political repr.	civil rights violations	ln (GNP)	(ln(GNP))^2	constant
10,91358546	-162,8188826	-0,722897795	0,116576987	-11,0941545	607,4708743
2,711016139	39,90219401	0,98220757	0,764921232	10,11245772	148,4162944
0,6951136					
4,103838325	9				
4,025643853	**-4,080449376**	-0,735992897	0,152403911	-1,097077962	t-test
Gini inequality	political repr.	civil rights violations	ln (GNP)	(ln(GNP))^2	constant

equation (9.4) GINI income inequality =

pol rights violations	civil rights violations	FCAPPen	lnGNPpc	lnGNP^2	constant
-0,018992718	0,176971676	**0,004611249**	-0,020469912	0,006726173	0,061751233
0,025122747	0,324494352	0,002916141	0,028052902	0,020223575	1,016901378
0,504766872					
2,24235225	11				
-0,755996872	0,545376754	**1,581284635**	-0,729689648	0,332590687	
pol rights violations	civil rights violations	FCAPPen	lnGNPpc	lnGNP^2	

equation (9.4) unemployment rate =

GINI inequality	pol rights violations	civil rights violations	GNP per capita	FCAPPen	constant
-0,218971053	0,000392913	-1,528791364	-0,907559915	-17,56078807	19,53812103
0,183471851	0,000686046	2,166180602	1,418759587	14,50565314	6,935047266
0,56989396					
2,385014466	9				
-1,193485827	0,572720543	-0,705754341	-0,639685485	-1,210616847	T-test

GINI inequality	pol rights violations	civil rights violations	GNP per capita	FCAPPen

Source: our own calculations with EXCEL 5.0 multiple regression routine from the above mentioned data. As in all EXCEL 5.0 outprints in this work, first row: unstandardized regression coefficients, second row: standard errors, last row: t-Test. The values immediately below the standard errors are R^2 (third row, left side entry), F, and degrees of freedom (fourth row).

Eastern Europe cannot be 'saved' by external means or by external means alone. The mobilization of savings and exports, a clear-cut policy of human capital formation and technology, and various other reforms would achieve much more lasting effects than transfers - even on a scale like in East Germany (estimated at $bn 700 since 1990).

The World Bank has developed a *liberalization index,* which measures the extent to which policies supporting liberalized markets and entry of new firms prevailed. The index is a weighted average of estimates of liberalization of domestic transactions (price liberalization and abolition of state trading monopolies), external transactions (elimination of export controls and taxes, substitution of low to moderate import duties for import quotas and high tariffs, current account convertibility), and the entry of new firms (World Bank, WDR, 1996). The weights on these components are 0.3, 0.3, and 0.4, respectively. Our equation now summarizes our final research results about the transformation success/failure in Eastern Europe and the former USSR:

equation (9.6) economic recovery in Eastern Europe and the former USSR:

privati-zation	**Pol Rights Violations**	ln (GNP)	ln(GNP)^2	HDI	NET FLOWS	DEV ASS	*Liberali-zation*	Constant
0,536737	-6,757594	-0,988263	-4,253716	18,634372	-274,6279	4,6616276	0,932771	1024,9646
5,2836872	2,9991756	1,9402744	167,95219	13,84864	197,52304	5,844472	0,6182559	727,345
0,5709663								
2,1625809	13							

privati-zation	**Pol Rights Violations**	ln (GNP)	ln(GNP)^2	HDI	NET FLOWS	DEV ASS	Liberalization
0,1015838	**-2,253151**	-0,509342	-0,025327	1,3455741	-1,390359	0,7976131	*1,5087134*

Source: our calculations from the above Tables on the basis of the EXCEL 5.0 multiple regression program. As in all EXCEL 5.0 outprints in this work, first row: unstandardized regression coefficients, second row: standard errors, last row: t-Test. The values immediately below the standard errors are R^2 (third row, left side entry), F, and degrees of freedom (fourth row).

The indicators, which affect transformation in a significant and positive direction (at 10% error probability) are **liberalization and the freedom from political repression. Foreign aid is only marginally efficient in promoting growth, while a policy of human development has a positive effect on growth, and net inflows -** *ceteris paribus* **- even a negative effect. Thus it has been established again, how important it is for the transformation countries to carry on with political transformation and reform.** Without political pluralism, economic transformation will definitely fail. Our results, by and large, confirm the conventional UNDP wisdom on the transformation process, already expressed in the UNDP 1992 and 1993 *Human Development Report.* Confronted with the **'market frenzy'** of the early transformation years, our results do not explicitly contradict, but they do correct much of the conventional neo-classical wisdom prevailing at that time. Finance Minister Balcerowicz spoke in 1998 and 1999 about his plans to reduce the state sector in Poland to just 10% of the national product - but even in one of the remaining market economy 'superstars' Chile we have a central government share of 21%, and only in some developing countries, like Guatemala and Myanmar, we reach such proportions. In the USA, the central government share was 22% in 1997, to which we have to add the often powerful economic influence of the other federalist entities (UNDP, HDR 1999).

Measures aimed at maintaining and building up democracy and human development are just as important as the fight against local monopolies, expressed in the liberalization index. Privatization, external development assistance and capital inflows, under due consideration of these factors, are not **so** important as these, more immediate goals, which find their ultimate aim, above all, in the rule of law.

Our analysis of the trajectory of the transformation countries should be concluded by an assessment of the realistic possibilities for EU-eastward expansion. On the one hand, Western Europe should avoid illusions about its own weak position in the world economy. Germany's tragedy always seems to be a *'sandwich'* position between the dominant centers of maritime capitalist accumulation and the temptation to squeeze the East European *'hinterland'* in order to be able to challenge the world hegemonic leaders (Arrighi, 1995). Wait a moment: this is not anti-German talk by an Austrian, but a sincere preoccupation about the future political economy of that former European work bench, that now occupies only rank 14 of the world-wide human development index scale, whose unemployment rate reaches 4.3 million people, and that has 11% of its people dying before their 60th birthday(UNDP, 1999). After the integration experiment of the *new Laender,* that under Kohl's 1:1 exchange conditions ruined eastern exports and cost DEM bn 150 to 200 a year, Germany continues to pay up to 70% of the European Union entire budget and will risk to pay another DEM bn 150 to 200 a year for European Monetary Union (Watzal, 1997). Germany's current account balance after German unification, and even more so after European Monetary Union, could and can only increase at the expense of the East European current account balance - a potential of economic nationalism and conflict in the new European house after 1989. The sharp world political conflict over spheres of influence in Eastern Europe between Germany and Russia, that is predicted by world system theories during each world economic upswing, threatens to become a reality again under such circumstances. And that is the situation, with which we are already presented: Germany comes out from its current account deficit, while America's balance deteriorates further and Japan will recover. A trilateral split of the world economy into three major currency blocks will be the most likely outcome under such circumstances:

Graph 9.7a: current account balances in the capitalist world economy in % of GDPs

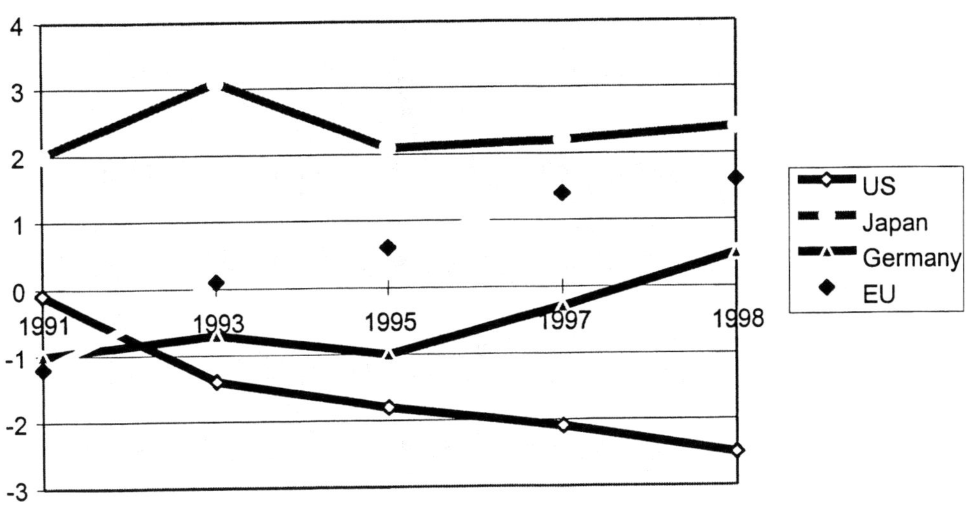

current accounts in % of GDP

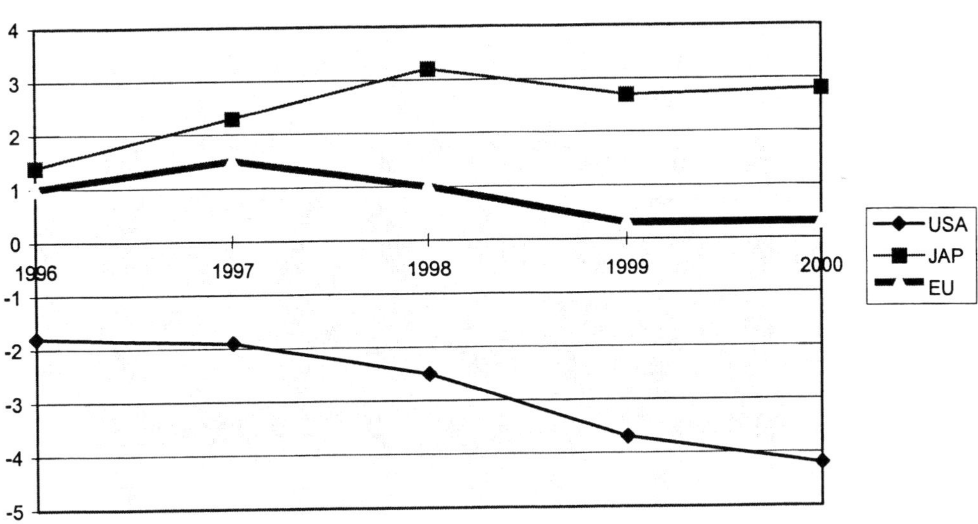

Legend: current account balances in % of the GDP since 1991. Our own compilation from Le Monde (1998 - 2000), *'Le Bilan du Monde'* Paris: Le Monde

Secondly, the environmental strains, already existing in the Union, will increase. But thirdly, and above all, eastward expansion of the Union will be first and foremost a test of Europe's ability to stand by its commitment towards democracy on the European continent. A small number of nations - in terms of the current account balance - are becoming again the winners of the international system, while a great number of other nations (in our map in lighter shades) are the losers of international exchange. Our map summarizes the tendencies of the current account balance in the world system:

Map 9.1: current account balance in the world system

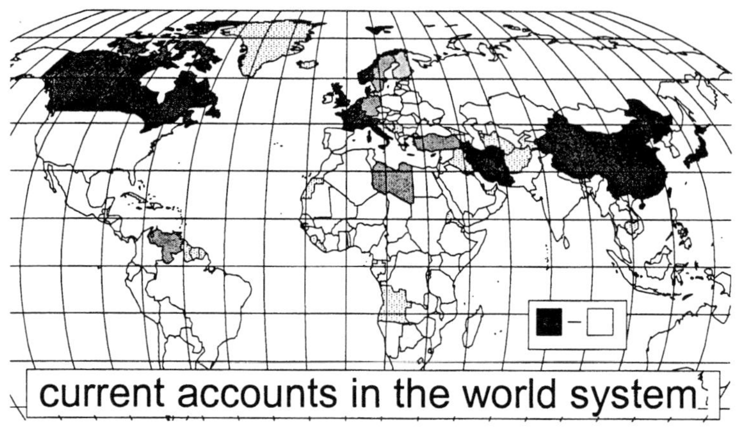

Source: our own compilations from Fischer Weltalmanach, 1997 and EXCEL 7.0 maps. The darker, the higher the positive current account balance.

A well-designed policy of Eastern European integration into the Union, that stresses the elements of democracy, savings mobilization, liquidation of local monopolies (also for the sake of the environment!) and early market access for the East Europeans in the agricultural sectors, could be successful; **however, this policy would imply, that the European center itself adapts rapidly to the contemporary challenges.** Eastern Europe's case during the negotiations with Brussels will be, that at present, its overall social performance is not worse than that of the European Union periphery. Poland, the Czech Republic and Slovenia have still a relatively favorable growth record, and the democracy scores are as good as those in Italy and Greece. The question is, however, how many more European peripheries the 'real existing Union' can reasonably afford. Considering the negative current account balance tendencies and the pressure that they exert in the direction of a *'weak state'*, I think it is most likely that the negative part of the Barta and Richter-scenario (1996) about the integration process of the East European new democracies into the European Union will come true:

(i)   the fragile domestic CEEC markets will be exposed to unrestricted competition from the large European MNCs. The transformation countries would need a decisive western market opening, especially for East European agriculture, where unskilled labor migration propensity and structural unemployment are highest

(ii)   the Union will even work towards eliminating the agricultural trade surpluses of individual CEEC nations

(iii)   the massive capital inflow to the new member states will be especially destabilizing for national development in the long run, because as yet there is no real network of established firms, banks, entrepreneurs, and national upper and middle classes, to confront the competition of Western countries

(iv)   land acquisition will become a sensitive issue

(v)   the degree of foreign penetration will render many measures of national adjustment policy practically useless

(vi)   migration will be a brain-drain of skilled people, whose activities will be missing in the modernization and adaptation process

(vii)   huge transfers in the wake of membership will lessen the capacity for problem solving (the Greece-effect), so that 'expensive adjustment' will set in

(viii)   coalition-building among the EU-'have-nots' will lead towards a de-motivation of the 'haves' and towards increased protectionism in the EU relations with the rest of the world

On the other hand, the internal European Union development blocks (see below) create a situation, were Union enlargement brings one of the few dynamizing effects for the Union itself. Whether or not Poland (HDI 0.802) and the other accession countries will be able to follow the more dynamic paths of Ireland (HDI 0.900) or Spain (HDI 0.894), which today has a similar *human development index* as Germany (HDI 0.906) or Austria (HDI 0.904), is of course open to question. But social scientific experience tells us that Poland will become rather a sort of Greece (HDI 0.867) in the enlarged Union, with long-term slow growth, high unemployment, a large negative current account, a high dependence from labor migration, and high debt ratios (UNDP, HDR 1999. The *Human Development Indices*, HDI, are calculated in this report according to a new methodology, based on natural logarithms of the income component).

Europe must come to terms with the contradictions of the process of the aging of democracies, especially phenomena which one might term sclerosis bruxelliana and sclerosis Europea

There is a growing awareness in labor-oriented and 'social movement' circles around the world that state expenditures are, more often than not, directed towards the rich and even the crooks benefit from them by subvention and customs fraud, while the poor are marginalized. Neo-liberal theory created the concept of distribution coalitions: people, who by political pressure or worse cut out their slice from the market which otherwise would not have been as big. Just to name a few figures from the current international press: the shadow economy now comprises up to 45% of Polish GNP; and fraud and other criminal practices determine that up to 5% of the EU yearly budget end up in the pockets of gangsters. A recent Reuters Business Briefing report by the *BBC Monitoring Service* put the situation like this:

27Apr2000 POLAND: New report prepared on public security, police.
Source: `Gazeta Wyborcza', Warsaw, in Polish 25 Apr 00
The Ministry of Internal Affairs has drawn up a new report on the growth of crime in Poland over the last decade and on proposed measures to counteract present trends and threats. Reported crime in 1999 had risen by 104.8 per cent as compared with 1989. The following is the text of a report by Polish newspaper `Gazeta Wyborcza' on 25th April:

The year 1999 saw the highest number of crimes in the entire decade. Public security in Poland is to come up for discussion at a cabinet session after Easter. The Ministry of Internal Affairs and Administration [MSWiA] has drawn up a report that will, for the first time, not only list threats, but also proposals how to combat those threats. The 400-page report consists of two parts. The first one discusses crime growth over the last decade and diagnoses the present situation in this respect. The diagnosis is catastrophic: as many as 1.121m crimes were recorded in 1999. In comparison with 1989, which was when we began our transition, it was 104.8 per cent more! Law-enforcement agencies managed to identify the culprits of a mere 45 per cent of all crimes. In criminal cases the resolution rate was lower than at any other time in the 1990's - only 40.3 per cent.
What will be the biggest threat in the near future? According to the MSWiA, these will be the following:
- Dynamically growing hard drugs trafficking, involving primarily cocaine from South America.
- Expansion of Asian and Russian-speaking criminal groups, including the Russian Mafia in the United States, which will want to subordinate Polish gangs to itself by force.
- Concentration of the activity of criminal groups in small towns and border areas, in which they may take control of local business and social life.
- The overlapping of criminal and business activity oriented toward money laundering. In the criminal sphere there will be more crimes against property: burglaries, car thefts, bank robberies, attacks on convoys and petrol stations, etc.

The other part of the report presents primarily proposals of specific organizational and legislative changes to facilitate efforts to combat these threats. In most cases the ministry adds information on who is working on the changes and how much money that is going to take.

Here are the proposals included in the report. It is necessary to do the following:

- Abandon the obligatory institution of proceedings into petty criminal cases, such as petty thefts where losses do not exceed the value of three minimum [monthly] wages. According to the MSWiA, the duty of starting proceedings in these cases burdens large numbers of policemen with unnecessary paperwork: the entire procedure is launched even though it is known all along that in most of these investigations the chances of catching the culprit are next to none. The ministry estimates that such investigations are launched in approximately 200,000 cases of this kind every year. In line with the MSWiA proposal, instead of starting a formal investigation, policemen would only register the offence reported to them. The investigation proper would only be launched after it became possible to identify the culprit. This requires amendments to the criminal procedure code.

- Develop the Central Bureau of Investigation [CBS] along with units that would specialize in combating gangs and the drugs business. The units, coordinated centrally, would operate all over Poland. The CBS was established last February.

- Reform the police pay system. The present pay system does not motivate functionaries to work better and to improve their qualifications. The service bonus, which might encourage policemen to do that, is only 8 per cent of the salary. It should increase to 15 per cent this year and rise further in the following years. To begin with, the salary structure would change in the case of policemen combating the drugs business and *organized crime*, prevention functionaries with special achievements, as well as policemen on criminal cases who work long hours. This would require spending 25m zlotys of the targeted reserve. On 1st July 2000 a generalized new pay system would come into effect. The report proposes allocating 60m zlotys for that purpose.

- Take countermeasures to prevent road accidents by installing the so-called photo radars.

- Modernize police equipment. This includes computerizing police command centres in big cities, upgrading communications equipment, and organizing a central database for dactyloscopic identification. The estimated cost of this project exceeds 1bn [over the period] until 2004.

- Introduce new regulations to broaden the operational powers of the police. This includes access to phone billings and information protected by banking, revenue, insurance, or trade secret regulations; the right to conduct sting operations, even in the case of small bribes; the right to use blackmail to force criminals to work with the police (under the control of prosecutors).

- Introduce the so-called contract service in police prevention units. This would make it possible for young men to serve there instead of doing regular military service.

- Employ career functionaries in the Border Guard [SG] and modernize this service. The SG would gain operational powers similar to those of police. It is also necessary to build new guard posts and have more functionaries working in the structure.

- Appoint a general financial inspector in the Ministry of Finance. The inspector would take measures to prevent introducing money from illegal or unrevealed sources into the financial system.

- Authorize, or even oblige, the Securities Commission to identify the source of the capital that is to be used to purchase 20-50 per cent of shares of companies quoted on the stock exchange. The commission would have to have access to secret and confidential information about parties willing to buy the shares.

- Establish town courts and a national court register.

The British Broadcasting Corporation 27/04/2000.

Distribution coalitions block, while new market opportunities dynamize the social system of the European Union. The message of this Chapter is thus simple: the European Union has very powerful internal distribution coalitions at work, that threaten to make its whole policy-set up non-competitive in the world economy (see, amongst others, Nollert, 1997; Nollert and Fiedler, 1996; as to the argument about European law and democracy by two Austrian diplomats, Thun-Hohenstein and Cede, 1996; also, from an Austrian Green perspective, Voggenhuber, 1995). Without enlargement, the Union is doomed even more to stagnation. Enlargement is a great opportunity and chance to realize a socio-liberal model on a European scale. Without question, the future of the European project of integration is of vital importance for the perspectives of the forces of change in the other regions of the world economy (Amin, 1997). With the dominating

Wall Street counter-project of financial and economic globalization in full swing, the European project - that could start out from a still significant share of global economic resources - is seen by many as the only and last realistic chance to transform the world economy. The race to the bottom, US-style, will never be the perspective of European Labor. But suppose, the eurocrats with their strange mixture of monetarist dogma and interventionist expenditures for narrow distribution coalitions and consultants were right, what would follow from this? Clearly, if the Union were to be an instrument of world economic ascent and growth (as the euro-crats would have us believe, for - why else - should we have the Union at all), then the countries most integrated into the system should be the *real tigers* of the world. The very geographical center of the Union, Belgium (then a haven of growth, and freedom from scandals and corruption), with the Union capital Brussels, would have to be on an equal growth footing with Hong Kong before 1997, and the founding member nations, like Germany, France and Italy should have unemployment rates well below the outsiders, like Switzerland, Iceland, Malta, Estonia or Norway. But average EU unemployment stood at 8.8% by 1995 (Le Monde, *Bilan du Monde* 2000). Looking at the figures of unemployment in the 1980s and 1990s of the European Union and the OECD countries, one has to arrive at the depressing conclusion that unemployment in the OECD region now stands at 6.4%, while in the EU it reaches 8.8% *(Le Monde,* Bilan du Monde, 2000). As a comparison of key social indicators for Belgium (the EU country with the highest Human Development Index) with Canada, Norway, USA, Japan, Australia, Iceland and Switzerland, the OECD competitors and non-EU-members with a similar high level of development of productive forces shows, there is an **under-achievement of the EU** human development **leader** in terms of **life expectancy** (lowest among the 8 compared countries), **reduction of functional illiteracy** (18.4%, second highest after Switzerland), **public expenditure for education** (3.2%, lowest among the 8 compared countries) and **unemployment reduction** (9%, second highest after Canada) (UNDP, HDR 1999, our own compilations from the original sources). But **Belgium** was the **leader** - among the compared nations - in **terms of corruption** *(Transparency International:* http://www.gwdg.de/~uwvw/). Belgium scored rank 29 in the world scale, Greece 36 and Italy 38 among 99 ranks of freedom from corruption. Authors as divergent as Andre Gunder Frank, Giovanni Arrighi and Erich Weede would predict further European relative decline in the global economy. The harsh critique by the growing number of eurosceptics among professional social scientists now precisely is, that the Union, as it is structured, is not the answer to the problems, but the very reason for them. The neo-liberal German social scientist Erich Weede put it like this:

> Essential to all scenarios of renewed European greatness is European unity, i.e., a unity that overcomes bickering about agricultural subsidies, and who pays for them, and replaces it by a unity of political purpose and a unified, but purely European(rather than NATO) military structure. It is quite certain that this transcendence is not going to happen within a decade. It is uncertain whether it will ever happen, or whether even a unified Western Europe will be sufficient in the 2020s. Although I am very skeptical about European readiness to unite politically and militarily, another reason why I cannot imagine European hegemony is that a **unified Europe is likely to decline even faster than a Europe of nation-states.**
>
> (...)
>
> In principle, a united Europe on the one hand and limitedgovernment, private property rights and market exchange at freely established scarcity prices on the other could be compatible with each other. Observation of political practice makes one suspicious, however. The common agricultural policy is still the most costly endeavor of the European Community or Union. **It always has been an orgy of interventionism, inefficiency and injustice. By establishing miminum prices, the European Union guarantees overproduction. Price supports benefit rich farmers more than poor farmers. Simultaneously, high food prices hurt poor consumers more than rich consumers. Moreover, exports of European farm products at subsidized prices hurt American farmers and thereby burden transatlantic relations, and hurt Third World or East European farmers, thereby reducing the chances of poor countries catching up with the rich countries. In a nutshell, professional economists would be hard pressed to invent a policy doing as much harm for as little good as the European common agricultural policy.** The more general point is that the Europeanization of economic policy-making establishes the opportunity to

commit policy errors on a much grander scale than has been possible in most of European history. Politicians might exploit such opportunities. European agricultural policies are also useful to make another point. Decisions are made to serve special interest groups or distributional coalitions, not to serve anything like national, European, or cosmopolitan interests. According to Olson, aging political regimes in general, and aging democracies in particular, are likely to become prisoners of interests groups and to pursue ever less efficient economic policies. Governments intervene in the market, distort prices, transfer income - and interfere with efficient resource allocation. The older an established regime - for example, a democracy - becomes, the more it suffers from institutional sclerosis and declining economic growth. Although empirical support for this proposition has been quite weak where American states have been compared with each other, Olson's proposition received fairly strong and consistent support where industrialized democracies have been analyzed. Moreover, economic decline was further reinforced by high government revenues, expenditures, or transfer payments. Some European countries, like Britain and Sweden, suffer from being old democracies (and therefore afflicted with strong distributional coalitions) and having high government expenditures simultaneously; others suffer from at least one of these ailments. Since European nations are still fairly close to the leading edge in technology, there is also little room to boost growth rates by capturing the 'advantages of backwardness'. Thus, Europe is likely to be outperformed by more dynamic regions elsewhere. If you add slowly declining economies and a proven record of not being capable of collective action in the security field, then the prospect of European hegemony displacing American hegemony looks poor (Weede, 1995)

Wait a moment, you might say: is that really so? What is that correlation between unemployment and European Union membership on the level of the industrialized countries? The data-base is UNDP, 1997 and Federal Ministry of Labor, Health and Social Affairs of the Republic of Austria:

Country	unemployment	membership in EU/yes/no
CND	9,5	0
F	11,6	1
N	4,9	0
USA	5,5	0
NL	6,5	1
JAP	3,1	0
SF	17,1	1
NZ	6,3	0
SW	9,2	1
SP	22,7	1
BL	9,5	1
AUS	8,5	0
UK	8,7	1
CH	4,2	0
AUT	4,5	1
DK	10,1	1
GR	9,8	1
LUX	2,8	1
IRE	12,9	1
GER	9,3	1

| ITA | 12,2 | 1 |
| POR | 7,1 | 1 |

The correlation between unemployment (1) and the dummy variable Union membership (2) is +0.44; the R^2 is above a depressing 19%. That is dramatic enough. The political right in Europe, especially in German-speaking countries, has reacted to the growing (socio)liberal and left critique of the essence of the Union by disbelief and even recurrence to old slogans like *'Volksgemeinschaft'* while sectors of the political left reacted and reacts in an almost fundamentalist way by denouncing growth itself, castigating it as *Wachstumswahn and Wachstumsfetischismus.*

We move to the very center of the EU debate in its present form - is the Union an engine of capitalist ascent? The political project of transformation from communism in Europe is not only endangered by the contradictions, globalization creates in its host countries, it is also threatened by certain negative developments in the European 'anchor economy'. Almost all the big issues, like agriculture reform, institution reform, structural funds, let alone a real strengthening of the Third Pillar against transnational crime, more rights for the European Parliament, a real common foreign policy, reform of the institutions of the EU, are blocked, and there seems no way out. And the real existing Union, with all its deficits, and without a profound reform, won't be able to absorb a 15 + 5 + 1 membership, let alone millions of extra agricultural producers.

We concentrate here on these issues, which have a long-term strategic and theoretical relevance for the policy formulation in the new Europe. **In order to provide a valid strategy to its member countries, the Union has to be an association of world economic ascent and not a club for joint world economic decline.** Very early on, a group of European policy planning and development researchers, headed by the late Dudley Seers, challenged head-on the reigning visions of the development strategy of the Commission in Brussels towards the Third World and towards the European periphery (Seers, 1978; de Bandt *et al.,* 1980). This theoretical challenge, still worthwhile reading today, was the first *real and systematic question mark* behind the policies of the Commission since 1958. The authors of that critique were a European-wide group of committed students of development and committed Europeans at the same time. Its leader, Dudley Seers, as one of the doyen of development and distribution theory among the world-wide profession of economists, having influenced the course of Keynesian economics over the whole post-war years in Britain, and above all a passionate Scotsman, took up the issue of the center-periphery relationship that characterizes the South, Northwest and eastbound relationship of the Union (Seers, 1978). Several authors, most notably Inotai and Malcolm, developed these arguments from a later, liberal perspective. With its emphasis on structural protection, Inotai maintains, the Union increases rather than decreases the long-term cleavages between the centers and the peripheries inside and outside the boundaries of Europe. Today, it is no secret, that 90% of all EU expenditure, union-wide, must be categorized as subventions. With each expansion to semi-peripheral regions, the protective element increases. Simple, as the diagnosis might sound, it strikes at the very heart of the conventional Union wisdom on matters of external economic relations. A good part of professional economists the world over, liberal and radical social scientists alike, have later taken up this theme. They maintain that the Union, by its market protecting arrangements with the outer rim of its orbit of influence leads to a secular negative balance of trade of the periphery regions with the Union, and thus prolongs structural underdevelopment (amongst others such divergent authors as Hickman, 1994; Inotai, 1993; Kennedy, 1993; Amin, 1994). The arguments of such Union critics cannot be dismissed *a-priori* and out of hand. Western Europe lost in terms of world market shares in a secular trend *vis-à-vis* the countries of the Pacific; the dynamics of growth in the world economy seemed to work to the detriment of the old European centers. *Le crash,* 1997 - we still have to wait and see. Asia's *'basics'* are healthier than expected, and the tide might still turn to the detriment of the Europeans, when the initial positive effects of European Monetary Union fade away and transnational capital flows again to the Pacific region.

The European Union shortcomings *vis-à-vis* the Pacific in terms of world export markets for manufactured goods, in terms of comparative labor costs, in terms of technological and scientific development and in terms of employment are all too obvious and were described in the literature in all detail, the crash of 1997 notwithstanding (for a debate on these issues see Inotai, 1993; Kennedy, 1993; Tausch and Prager, 1993, IFRI 1998). I strongly agree with Andre Gunder Frank's recent book (1998): it is the first time in world economic history, that an economic crisis *began* in a center outside Europe or the United States. The fundamentals of the European Union still reflect the realities of the late 1950s and still comprise the following sectors (i) the coal and steel community (ii) agricultural self-sufficiency (iii) the customs union. The new international division of labor, that characterizes the world economy since the late 1960s, is the prime challenge to the logic of the Union, built around and evolving from the Franco-German alliance of the late 1950s (Inotai, 1993). Precisely these sectors are most seriously affected by world economic and technological changes. The annual cost of the common agricultural policy of the Union is now estimated to be 44.4% of the total budget (EURO 40.4 thousand million; Fischer Weltalmanach 1999), more than 10% of this is believed to be paid to criminal channels (Malcolm, 1995: 57). Of the 27448 reports, that are stored in the *Reuters Business Briefing* information system over the last 5 years, dealing with the word *'Mafia'*, 10652, i.e. more than 38%, were dealing with events in countries of the European Union. The agricultural subvention system, an invitation to kleptocracies of all sorts, dominates the Union's external trade policy, and is distorting the world market and preventing the poor countries from exporting.

A major problem, which has to resolved first and foremost, is Germany's apparent inability to comprehend and play its role as a highly developed Mexico in the world economy. Similar in population size to that of Mexico, and with a share of roughly only 8% of world GNP, Germany's first and foremost role would be that of a highly specialized trade and current account surplus economy in the heart of a Europe, oriented towards the West and towards the Atlantic and the Pacific, still the major centers of the world economy. Germany is estimated - via its share of Brussels expenditures - to have spent up to $bn 30 thousand million alone to prop up in vain - in concert with the other Europeans - the Italian Lira on Black Friday, 1993. In that disaster year, Germany poured another 9.1 thousand million $ down another sink - this time German aid to Russia. Insiders estimate, that only 10% of Western aid to Russia reached its targets. How Germany projected in vain her dreams to become a democratic *'Weltmacht'* (world power) is to be judged from the fact, that it took over 43.7% of the burden of reconstruction of former communism - from Frankfurt at the Oder to Wladiwostock during the period 1990-1993. *If Lohengrin only were to be an economist, after all:* Germany's official and private Eastern flows amounted to 32.7 thousand million $, out of a total of 74.8 thousand million $ (our own compilations from OECD, GD (95) 41: *'Aid and other resource flows to the Central and Eastern European countries and the new independent states of the former Soviet Union in 1992 and 1993', Paris 1995)*. But the foundations of Germany's dreams to become a *Weltmacht* were shaky indeed, as the meager position of Germany's transnational corporations *vis-à-vis* their international competitors, and the losses of even companies like Mercedes-Daimler-Benz to the tune of more than 1 thousand million $ and the economic malaise in the middle of 1990s all too clearly showed. Only of lately, German transnationals could recover some of their positions *(Le Monde, Bilan du Monde,* 2000). Add to this the disaster of the Mercedes *Smart* car, developed at great costs, but practically knocked off from the market by a single test series of an automobile magazine in Sweden. $bn 700 for German unification, DEMbn 160 for Russia's pullout from East Germany - enough is enough. For the transformation countries nearer to the European center, such economic mismanagement means lost opportunities to stabilize democracy at a vital moment of world history: the Polish GNP amounted to just 75 thousand million $ in 1992 and is today $bn 157.0 (UNDP, 1995; Malcolm, 1995; *Business Central Europe,* April 2000), viz. about five times the sum that Germany lost in the casino of world finances in 1993. Germany with its current account balance of $bn - 13.8 in 1996, $bn - 4.0 in 1997 $bn - 4.2 in 1998, $bn - 1.1 in 1999 and $bn +2.6 in 2000 is in a too weak position to be the European 'growth engine' anymore *(Le Monde, Bilan du Monde,* 2000):

Graph 9.7b: current account balances in the world system, 1996/97, in millions of $

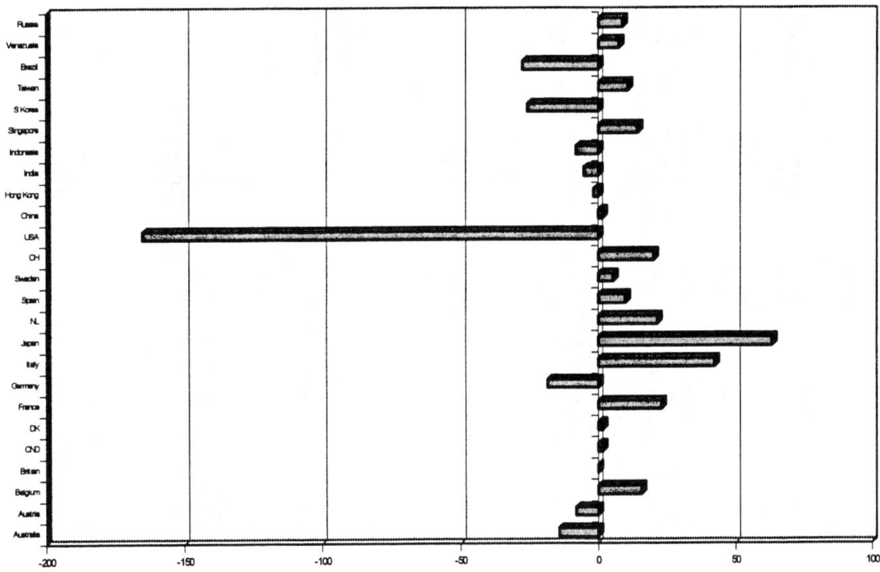

Legend: current account balances in the world system, 1996/97, in millions of $; compiled from the international press

Graph 9.7c: the structure of world trade (in % of total world trade; for the 'triad' of Asia, North America, and Europe: percentage of regional per total trade of the 'triad' countries)

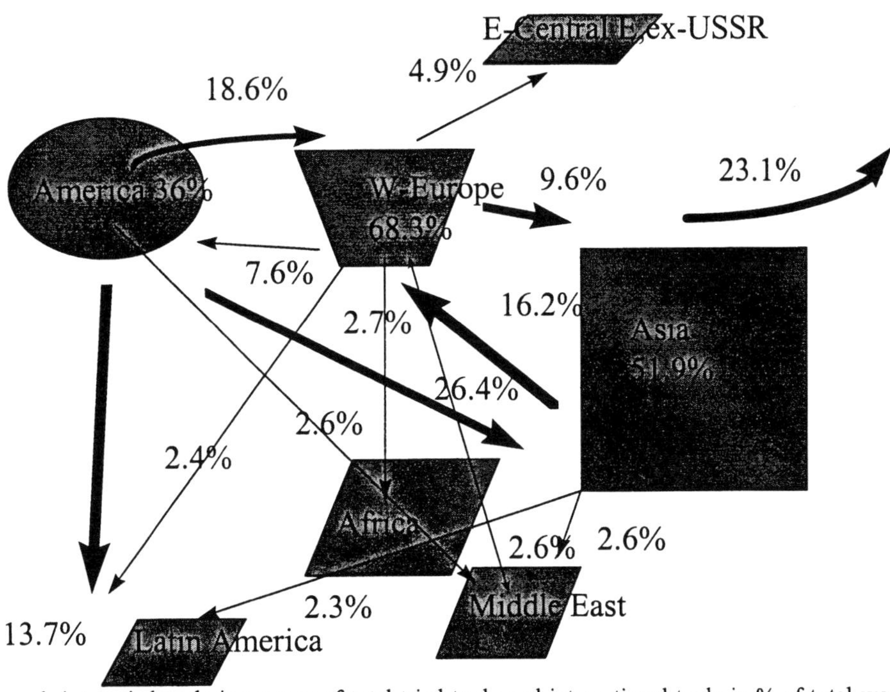

Legend: intra-triad trade in percent of total triad trade and international trade in % of total world trade. Sources for the above graphs: current Account Balances, 1997. Compiled from Economist, June 7th - 13th 1997, and world trade statistics in Le Monde, 1998: *Le Bilan du Monde.* Paris: *Le Monde*

Several authors, including Chase-Dunn and Podobnik, and Chase Dunn and Hall, are also fairly pessimistic in this context about the future trajectory of the United States of America. They cite international capital investment abroad in those countries, where profit rates are highest, as the main reason, why the 'internationalized capitalists' in the core no longer have a vested interest in their home economy. Capital investment abroad becomes, the argument goes, the driving force for hegemonic decline (Chase-Dunn and Hall, 1997). **America's** *current account balance* as a percentage of GDP performed in the following way over the years:

1961-73	+0.4%
1974-80	+0.0%
1981-90	-2.0%
1993	-1.5%
1994	-2.2%
1995	-2.0%
1996	-2.2%
1997	-2.3%
1998	-2.4%
1999	-3.7%
2000	-4.2%

Source: IFRI, 1998, and *Le Monde, Bilan du Monde,* 2000

The hegemonic decline of the USA will most probably set in slowly, cushioned by the present weaknesses of Japan and of the European competitors. **In Europe, economic stagnation and unemployment will significantly rise after 2000, or 2001 due to rising interest rates and rent-seeking that is enhanced by the way European institutions are built at the present. In terms of the environment, government subventions to declining productive branches (36.8% of the budget of the EU are for the structural funds) will increase technological backwardness and preserve transport intensity, and hence, pollution.** Economic inequalities threaten to increase with such a structure, and in turn will form a block of its own against world economic ascent. The expenditure for research and development, and trans-european networks (TEN) in the Union budget 1998 was just 6.3% (Fischer Weltalmanach, 1999). Long-term data about the EU budget indicate, that general and professional education receive less than 1% of the total Union expenditures; the energy sector, EURATOM and the environment under 1%, while expenditure for agricultural subventions consumes more than 40% and structural policies for regions, for (big) agriculture, traffic systems and fisheries more than 30% of the total budget (our own compilations from Fischer Weltalmanach, 1995-1999). Not only the internal set-up needs urgent reform, also the relationship to the outside world.

Inexorably, the centers of gravity of the world economy are shifting towards the LDCs, here most notably during the 1970s and 1980s to the countries of the Pacific, and after the Asian currency crisis 1997, most likely to India and China. The effect of the *Europe-agreements* between the EU and the countries of Eastern Europe seem to repeat the experience of Lomé and can be summarized in one word: a massive positive balance of trade in favor of the Union and to the detriment of the partners in the East, that leads to political and economic friction (Hickman, 1994; Inotai, 1993). A growing number of academic critics of present Union economic policy maintain that the EU-approach to foreign trade and relations with the semi-periphery and the periphery is based on two fatally erroneous assumptions. **First, the gradualism of trade liberalization; second, the protectionist answer to the current economic *malaise* in Western Europe.**

Samir Amin (1994, 1997) puts a heavy blame on the Europeans for prolonging the underdevelopment and stagnation of their own 'backyards'. The experience of East and Southeast

Asia during its heyday has precisely shown, that *ceteris paribus* three conditions for successful capitalist development hold (i) the existence of a reliable anchor economy (ii) substantial net transfers (iii) free market access to exports (Inotai, 1993). The failure to realize such a strategy *vis-à-vis* the CEFTA-countries results in the growing trade balance problems of the transformation region (Hickman, 1994). By enlarging the Union to the South, the protective tendencies precisely in those sectors, which are also important for the semi-periphery and the periphery, have grown. The effect of this was a growing world economic inefficiency (Nuscheler, 1993). The most visible result of this is the high unemployment in many Union countries (17 to 18 million people in the late 1990s, last time that the Union had less than 8% unemployment was in 1990); in the **Eastern European** countries **most likely still to join the Union** (CEEC 5 + Slovakia) early on, another **2.9 million unemployed persons** would have to be provided with jobs. Austria, Finland and Sweden, which joined the Union on January 1st 1995, are not free from employment problems themselves and added roughly another million unemployed persons of their own to the army of European unemployment (UNDP, 1997-99). To put the proportions of unemployment in even more drastic words: **the unemployed workers of the EU -** *excluding* **their families - would already be the 6th biggest state in the Union with more than 18.2 million inhabitants - bigger than each of the 10 smaller European Union countries. The up to 40 million persons, affected by unemployment (i.e. the unemployed and their families), probably would form the 5th biggest state in Western Europe, only surpassed in size by Germany, the UK, France, and Italy. With around 40 million inhabitants, like Spain, this 'country' should play a major role in the EU and should one day be in a position to take up at least the EU-Presidency...**

Globalization affected to a differing degree the 21 most developed and still relatively stable long-term democracies of the world, Australia, Austria, Belgium, Canada, Denmark, Finland, France, Germany, Iceland, Ireland, Israel, Italy, Japan, Luxembourg, New Zealand, Norway, Sweden, Switzerland, the Netherlands, the UK, and the United States of America. Of course, the term *'stable democracy'* is only relative. In future, the increase of new populist or neo-fascist parties in Europe will become an even more significant phenomenon, while old parties disappear. On average, populists drum up 7.4% of West European votes; neo-fascists 2.2%. Countries with well-known populist phenomena are Austria (23%), Denmark (16%), Italy (21%) and Norway and France (both at 12%), while neo-fascists are strongest in Italy (14%) (Taggart, 1995: 45). Regionalism and other centrifugal tendencies will increase in other parts of the continent.

The (in)efficiency of the European Union at the level of stable western democracies

Nollert (1996) has shown that the efficiency of an interest group at the Union level is largely determined by the age of an interest group, by the relative efficiency of internal decision making mechanism, by the low number of members, restricted to Union countries, and by the 'Unionization' of the central policy concern of the respective interest group. The basic democracy deficit of the Union, that is evident in the powerlessness of the European Parliament, actively enhances the power of these narrow distribution coalitions. Among the most powerful ones, the European Roundtable of Industrialists emerged, closely linked to Etienne Davignon, the long-term EU Commissioner for the Internal Market, linked to key Western capital groups like Rockefeller, Standard Oil, Asea-Brown-Bovery, Deutsche Bank, Fiat, Volvo, Renault, Societé General, Unilever, and later on also to the Trilateral Commission (Nollert and Fielder, 1997). The case of the Roundtable shows, that European capital integration is far more advanced than that of its countervailing power, organized labor. Johannes Voggenhuber, an Austrian member of the European Parliament for the Green Party, and an impassioned - if perhaps not always error-free critic of the 'real existing Union' - , has summarized the development blocks that the Union faces as follows:

'The law-makers of the European Union are organs of the Executive. Laws are being passed in the Council, that is to say, by Government representatives of member states. Exclusively the

Commission holds the right for law-initiatives, which is a non-elected (...) administrative body. Its suggestions can be altered by the Council only unanimously. Even that, the Commission can prevent this, by simply withdrawing its proposal (...) Laws are deliberated and passed under the exclusion of the public (...) Two Hundred Years after the French Revolution, laws again go into effect in Europe, which were not passed by an elected, lawmaking assembly' (Voggenhuber, 1995, our translation)

The very center-piece of the European Union is its agricultural policy, which, throughout the ups and downs of European integration, swallowed more than 50% of its budget. 6% of grain producers produce 60% of Union grain; 15% of milk-producing entities produce more than 50% of total production. 10% of cattle breeders possess 50% of all cattle in the Union. 20% of producing units receive 80% of all subventions.

Such a monopolistic system, Voggenhuber correctly argues, has its heavy economic price: stagnation. 50 million poor people, three million homeless, millions of unemployed, a threatening and recurring tendency towards a growing gap between the rich and the poor regions. Over the last years, there has been a certain shift in real wealth from the North to the South, aided by a policy of soft currencies in countries like Italy or Spain, thus counterbalancing the inherent internal tendencies of the Union. One of the main arguments for the *EURO* was that it will rule out once and for all such a world economic adjustment; the wage rate, or worse, if that is inflexible, the unemployment rate or migration will be the only adjustment mechanism left open for the European *mezzogiorno* after introduction of the Euro.

We now start our multivariate analysis of the basic problems of the European Union (as to the variables used, see Appendix, Variable list). The basic equation can be expanded in the following fashion:

equation (9.7) **stagnation and development blocks in western democracies** (lack of economic growth; inflation; lack of human development; unemployment) = constant + b_1 * **age of democracy** + b_2 * **state sector influence** (like state sector expenditures per GDP), t_{n-1} (+ b_3 * **years of European Union membership** (like state sector expenditures per GDP))

The original data for a repetition of Weede's original exercise (i.e. the terms age of democracy and state sector strength, see his quotation above), based on stable world politically guaranteed boundaries, were:

equation (9.8)

Sweden	48	28	1,7
Israel	17	44	1,7
USA	61	19	1,7
Finland	48	24	2,5
Belgium	20	39	2
Denmark	20	33	2,2
Ireland	42	33	3,3
Austria	10	30	2,1
New Zealand	86	31	0,7
Norway	20	35	2,3
Australia	73	20	1,6
Italy	20	30	2,2
United Kingdom	47	32	2,6

	age of democracy by 1965	central state sector strength 1972	economic growth 1980-1991
Germany	16	24	2,2
Netherlands	20	41	1,6
Switzerland	93	13	1,6
Canada	67	20	2
Japan	13	13	3,6
France	20	32	1,8
Iceland	17	44	1,7
Luxembourg	20	41,3	3,5

equation 9.8 (cont.) economic stagnation as a consequence of the interaction between a strong state sector and an aging democracy

	age of democracy 1965	central state sector strength 1972	constant
basic equation	-0,029841372	-0,017474418	3,661178511
economic growth	0,017359935	0,006306644	
	0,300811182		
	3,872059412	18	
	-1,7189795	**-2,770794915**	T-Test

Legend: as in all EXCEL 5.0 outprints in this work, first row: unstandardized regression coefficients, second row: standard errors, last row: t-Test. The values immediately below the standard errors are R^2 (third row, left side entry), F, and degrees of freedom (fourth row).

Economic growth is blocked by the interaction between a strong state and growing democratic age: the European predicament, all the European attempts at advances in the field of human development, sustainable agriculture, environmental protection, and gender empowerment notwithstanding.

The empirical results now show the **effects of years of European membership on growth** with relatively new data, relating state sector expenditures not to the preceding, but to the current measurement period of economic growth. Results, which are significant at the level of 10%, are printed in indented type, and results, significant at the 5% level, are printed in bold type[1] . Some

---

[1]* for the following degrees of freedom the subsequent critical values of the *t-test* hold at the one-tailed 10% and 5%-level according to Kriz, 1973:

df.	10%-level	5%-level
10	1.372	1.812
11	1.363	1.796
12	1.356	1.782
13	1.350	1.771
14	1.345	1.761
15	1.341	1.753
16	1.337	1.746
17	1.333	1.740
18	1.330	1.734

of the reform needs of the Union are omnipresent. The longer you stay inside, the more rent-seeking, and stagnant your economy and society could become in comparison to the other Western democracies. Human development is influenced in a negative, but not significant fashion by membership years, while inflation - as part of the still existing 'social partnership' in Europe - is somewhat lower than in other OECD democracies. Old democracies tend to have lower inflation rates, while a high state sector influence increases inflation rates:

equation (9.9) 21 stable OECD democracies (before the Union enlargements 1981, 1986, 1995)

	age of democracy 1980	state sector strength	years of membership in the European Union (93)	constant
growth 80-91	0,005957107	-0,031878483	-0,016183125	3,840249096
	0,00999156	0,018006481	0,006778025	0,78650603
	0,315131817			
	2,607431627	17		
	0,596213893	**-1,770389437**	**-2,387587165**	
Human Development Index 1992	-0,000122587	-0,000610284	-3,87854E-05	0,938652952
	0,000181832	0,000327691	0,00012335	0,014313245
	0,259690135			
	1,987785794	17		
	-0,674180237	**-1,862375606**	-0,314433415	
inflation 1980-91	-0,620613252	1,213851255	-0,069484856	-14,2296436
	0,253153083	0,456224654	0,171732728	19,92746094
	0,412664429			
	3,981423697	17		
	-2,451533457	**2,660643708**	-0,404610449	

Legend: as in all EXCEL 5.0 outprints in this work, first row: unstandardized regression coefficients, second row: standard errors, last row: t-Test. The values immediately below the standard errors are R^2 (third row, left side entry), F, and degrees of freedom (fourth row).

Variables:

- *democratic age within stable world political boundaries by 1980 (Source: Weede; Tausch, 1993a)*
- *central government expenditures 1972 (Source: World Bank, 1990, Fischer Weltalmanach, current issues)*

Readers should compare the results for the European Union also with the 5% level: most of our results are also significant at the 5%-level

- *years of Union membership by 1993 (Die Presse, 1. 11. 1993)*
- *economic growth (GNP per cap.) 1980-91 (UNDP, 1994)*
- *human development index (UNDP, 1994)*
- *yearly rate of inflation, 1980-91*

Our following analysis is a scenario for the effects of EU-enlargement. Several newly stabilized democracies, like Greece (1981) Spain and Portugal (1986) have entered the European arena, and processes ever since their democratic transformation suggest that these countries must be considered as stable as the 'old' core of the European Union. In addition, Germany's globally recognized borders have shifted after the fall of the Berlin Wall, thus suggesting that we have to consider Germany in the new borders as a relatively young democracy, that leaves behind many of the characteristics of the old Federal Republic.

Our enlargement scenario now shows, that - under proper control for the effects of the 'socio-liberal' policy variable 'human development index', - the negative **significant** growth effects of Union membership years **disappear**, and although the negative **direction** of the effects on growth does **not disappear**, the Union contributes **positively** towards **stabilizing inflation** and towards **decreasing the level of absolute poverty**. The positive development experience of countries like Spain, Portugal and Ireland after Union integration must be mentioned here. Significant transfers, intensified trade and economic restructuring, along with a well-designed policy of economic management and human development in these three nations, have flattened the European North-South social divide considerably, while Greece's record must be regarded as rather mixed.

Economic growth and employment creation continue to be the darker, negative sides of the present European constellation. The 10% significant stagnation effects against growth and pro higher unemployment brought about by state sector expenditures and by years of Union membership must give pause for thought in Brussels:

equation (9.10) European Union enlargement scenario

	EU-years	age democr	state sector	HDI	Constant
growth 80-93	-16,67395356	-0,008067547	-0,007537608	0,003530399	18,19605658
	11,33207653	0,017241946	0,005600134	0,011328545	10,60696527
	0,276294457				
	1,813442886	19			
	-1,471394366	-0,467902368	*-1,34596917*	0,311637443	T-Test
	EU-years	age democr	state sector	HDI	Constant
male unempl	91,28143425	0,136673824	0,038181667	0,008593515	-83,86218196
	67,04769418	0,102014202	0,033133917	0,067026799	62,75747977
	0,227294323				
	1,397230625	19			
	1,36144032	*1,339752911*	1,152343903	0,128210142	T-Test
	EU-years	age democr	state sector	HDI	Constant
gender power	1,435177878	0,00081657	0,000828903	-0,001253021	-0,778160859

	EU-years	age democr	state sector	HDI	Constant
	1,727293234	0,002628106	0,000853601	0,001726755	1,616768056
	0,190393063				
	1,117044588	19			
	0,830882591	0,310706792	0,971066104	-0,725651022	
	EU-years	age democr	state sector	HDI	Constant
inflation	-103,9963046	0,062262777	-0,035317665	-0,048076406	100,9789444
	36,01225964	0,054793263	0,017796693	0,036001037	33,70792514
	0,539872064				
	5,573215836	19			
	-2,887802812	1,136321768	**-1,984507211**	*-1,335417274*	T-Test
	EU-years	age democr	state sector	HDI	Constant
female unemp	109,00827	0,199525396	-0,029795743	0,024086249	-96,99876663
	87,10316755	0,132528944	0,043045017	0,087076022	81,52965352
	0,204267371				
	1,219341748	19			
	1,251484568	*1,505523169*	-0,692199576	0,276611726	T-Test
	EU-years	age democr	state sector	HDI	Constant
% not surviving to age 40	-20,48743614	0,001519878	0,005628924	0,000142796	21,93027679
	9,672780251	0,014717299	0,004780136	0,009669766	9,053843214
	0,211899239				
	1,277148095	19			
	-2,118050406	0,103271538	1,177565564	0,014767307	

Legend: as in all EXCEL 5.0 outprints in this work, first row: unstandardized regression coefficients, second row: standard errors, last row: t-Test. The values immediately below the standard errors are R^2 (third row, left side entry), F, and degrees of freedom (fourth row).

Variables:

- *democratic age within stable world political boundaries by 1997 (Source: Weede; Tausch, 1993a. Note the effects of German unifaction)*
- *central government expenditures, mid 1980s (Source: World Resources Institute, UNEP, UNDP, 1992)*
- *years of Union membership by 1997 (Die Presse, 1. 11. 1993)*
- *economic growth (GNP per cap.) 1980-93 (UNDP, 1994)*
- *human development index (UNDP, 1997)*

- *yearly rate of inflation, 1993 (UNDP, 1997)*
- *people not expected to survive to age 40, by 1990 (poverty indicator, UNDP, 1997*
- *male unemployment rate, 1993 (UNDP, 1997. For Sweden, the national average of 9.2% unemployment)*
- *female unemployment rate, 1993 (UNDP, 1997. For Sweden, the national average of 9.2% unemployment)*
- *gender empowerment (UNDP, 1997. For the missing values for Iceland, the average of the Scandinavian countries)*

Without enlargement, the negative internal European Union blocks against capitalist development would even increase, thus turning the tide further in favor of the original equation. **Union enlargement, new world political borders or a new political order for a nationally organized society at home would take away some of the most detrimental effects of distribution coalition building.** The basic reason for such results is the **emergency support philosophy of the Commission, that strengthens the euro-wide rent-seeking mentality.** Our results also show how a socio-liberal project of reform and enlargement might still dynamize the Union.

Looking back at the experience of enlargement of the European Union towards the South in the 1980s, one should admit that, together with NATO, it stabilized the young democracies of the Mediterranean, rapidly improved the ranking of the European South in the hierarchy of international human development, and finally even brought about a significant transfer of economic activities and financial reserves from the North to the South and European West (Ireland). Spain and Ireland, perhaps, stand out as the most positive examples, what enlargement can bring about for European semi-peripheral democracies. And here, an argument comes in that speaks very much in favor of the European semi-periphery both in the East and the South, and against the ideology of a *'fortress Europe'*: any serious indicator analysis will show that the social distance between the European center and the East European periphery is smaller than usually pretended, and yet that there are important tasks ahead. For our empirical analysis, we used the following indicators:

- *Human development shortfall (UNDP 1997; ((1 - Human Development)*100)*
- *Gender related development shortfall (UNDP 1997; ((1 - Gender Development)*100)*
- *Gender empowerment shortfall (UNDP 1997; ((1 - Gender Empowerment)*10)*
- *Lack of modern communication (UNDP 1997; ((Swedish (record) value for main telephone lines per 100 people (=68.3) - main telephone lines per 100 people in the country)/2)*
- *Unemployment (conventional labor office data taken from Bundesministerium fuer Arbeit, Gesundheit und Soziales, Vienna (EU countries), UNDP, 1997 (Eastern Europe), Globale Trends, 1998 (Eastern Europe))*
- *Early Death (percentage of people not expected to survive age 40; UNDP, 1997)*
- *< Grade 5 (children not reaching grade 5 in school; UNDP, 1997)*
- *< 1 $ a day (percentage of population living from an income which is equal to or lower than 1 $ expressed in real purchasing power parity rates a day, UNDP, 1997)*

Calculating simple unweighted means from these indicator series, we get the final results for our poverty indicator:

	Poverty
S	4,13
DK	5,76
France	6,04
SF	6,05
A	6,16
ITA	6,82
LUX	7,07
GER	7,12
GRE	7,16
CYP	7,2
NL	7,43
UK	8,06
CZ	8,48
BLG	8,84
POR	9,8
SLO	10,02
HUN	10,48
SLK	10,64
ESP	11,42
IRE	12,19
PL	12,76
BUL	16,04
EST	16,72
LAT	17,52
ROM	18,13
LIT	19,13

Source: our own calculations from the sources, mentioned above

The most important reason, why the North America-Pacific triangle gained ground in the world market, was the pattern of specialization based on co-operation with less-developed partners that significantly cut production costs (Inotai, 1993).

Globalization, East European reconstruction and the fatal conceit of euro-centrism

29 countries with a Pacific coast now already control over 53% of the world GNP, and the Pacific rim-lands tended to be the countries with the highest growth-rates in the world economy. This 'earthquake' has set free powerful forces of change on the European landmass, both East and west of the Iron Curtain, while the power of the world depression during the 1980s and beyond brought new centers of gravity of the world economy to the fore. At the same time and by the very same process, the new international division of labor restructured the old industrial centers and created new conflicts. The share of the industrial labor force in total employment in East Asia (excluding China) is now 34% and is thus higher than in the established industrial countries.

The moment of *victory over communism* in Europe became, before the Asian crash, the moment of the *fundamental weakness of both Europe and North America in a changing world economy*. But at the same time, there was a dramatic southward shift of European productive potential, that could be threatened under a strong *'Euro'*, that could ruin the European *mezzogiorno's* export capacity that grew over the last years. The following materials, calculated from *Le Monde, Bilan du Monde 2000* show this very clearly:

	current account EU	current account Germany	implicit current account non-German EU
1996	83,7	-13,8	97,5
1997	118,5	-4	122,5
1998	83,1	-4,2	87,3
1999	27,5	-1,1	28,6
2000	22,8	2,6	20,2

Faced with a growing trilateral competition between economic power blocs (Japan + Pacific/USA/Europe), that could even one day become a bilateral competition between the Pacific and an expanded Europe, the danger arises, that the losers in the trilateral economic power struggle are unable to provide their *'spheres of influence'* with the kind of advantageous economic relationships, that would be necessary to be able to break the deadlock of semi-peripherization and partial underdevelopment in regions like Latin America, Africa and Eastern Europe. Germany in particular will assert with all means possible its own backyard *'sphere of influence'* in East Central Europe.

Instead of letting 'them' participate in global welfare, the **power blocs** - and not the vicissitudes of the 'East' or 'South Europeans' or 'Latin Americans' or 'Asians' or 'Africans' will increase corruption and crime in the East and South of the world system.

	Exploitation - Concept 1 - Monopoly of Capital: Current Account Balance in $bn, 1997	Exploitation - Concept 2 - Unequal Exchange, gains or losses in $bn, 1995	Net position in the chain of the two exploitation structures	Freedom from Corruption Index - Transparency International
Japan	94,354	521,396	615,75	6
USA	-155,375	442,244	286,869	7,5
Germany	**-2,774**	**240,994**	**238,22**	**8**
France	39,474	95,305	134,779	6,6
Italy	33,424	64,502	97,926	4,7
NL	21,985	64,97	86,955	9
UK	10,304	61,565	71,869	8,6
Belgium	13,939	35,533	49,472	5,3
Switzerland	23,714	20,254	43,968	8,9
South Korea	-8,167	44,382	36,215	3,8
Spain	2,486	29,423	31,909	6,6
Sweden	7,301	15,456	22,757	9,4
Canada	-9,261	28,433	19,172	9,2
Singapore	14,803	3,42	18,223	9,1
Austria	-4,996	19,367	14,371	7,6
Australia	-12,591	19,945	7,354	8,7
Ukraine	-1,335	-0,87	-2,205	2,6
Slovakia	-1,359	-1,247	-2,606	3,7
Bulgaria	0,427	-6,077	-5,65	3,3
Hungary	-0,982	-6,684	-7,666	5,2
Greece	-4,86	-3,722	-8,582	4,9

Argentina	-9,429	-1,049	-10,478	3
Romania	-2,338	-9,869	-12,207	3,3
Turkey	-2,679	-16,478	-19,157	3,6
Czech R	-3,271	-18,399	-21,67	4,6
Poland	-5,744	-19,885	-25,629	4,2
Russia	2,569	-32,563	-29,994	2,4
Philippines	-4,351	-25,73	-30,081	3,6
Nigeria	0,522	-49,717	-49,195	1,6
Brazil	-33,84	-24,095	-57,935	4,1
India	-5,811	-56,231	-62,042	2,9
Malaysia	-4,792	-61,967	-66,759	5,1
Thailand	-3,024	-63,968	-66,992	3,2
Mexico	-7,454	-84,11	-91,564	3,4
Indonesia	-4,89	-98,668	-103,558	1,7
China	29,718	-351,811	-322,093	3,4

Legend: Unequal exchange is - according to Gernot Koehler - defined here in the following fashion:

In order to determine the relative value of one currency in comparison with another, two conflicting concepts and measurement procedures exist, namely:

(1) currency exchange rates between two countries (i.e., the rates at which units of one currency are exchanged for units of another currency; e.g., how many dollars do I get for 100 rupees; how many rupees do I get for 100 dollars? etc.); and

(2) purchasing power parity rates (PPP rates) between two countries (i.e., the ratio of the purchasing power of money in countries A and B; e.g., how much money do I need in order to buy a pair of shoes in country A; and how much money do I need in order to buy an equivalent pair of shoes in country B?).

The proposed estimation method is, as follows: (a) calculate the distortion factor d (see above, exchange rate deviation index); and (b) apply it to the volume of trade, giving (c) the loss or gain due to unequal exchange, according to the formula:

$$T = d*X - X$$

where:
T = magnitude of unrecorded transfer (loss or gain) due to unequal exchange
X = volume of exports from a low-wage country to high-wage countries, and
d = the distortion factor (i.e. the deviation of the nominal exchange rate from the PPP rate, also known as ERD)
*The formula means, in words, that the unrecorded transfer (T) resulting from unequal exchange is equal to the difference between the fair value of the export (d * X) and the unfair (actual) value of the export (X). For low-wage countries this magnitude T is a loss. For high-wage countries the same magnitude T is a gain.*

Sources: our own compilations from World Bank, World Development Report, 1999; Gernot Koehler and Arno Tausch (2000); and Transparency International - Corruption Perception Index, from their Internet Website: *http://www.transparency.de/*

We fully agree here with recent analyses in *Le Monde Diplomatique,* April 2000 (especially Guilhem Fabre) who states that dirty money is already 1 to 5% of global gross domestic product in the world. Both the over-exploiters as the exploited ones suffer from corruption, bribery and crime, and the world economy has an unhalting tendency towards *'criminal capitalism'.* The UNDP HDR 1999 states, that **organized crime** already has a turnover of **1.5 trillion $ a year** (UNDP, HDR, 1999: 5). Corruption, - the *World Development Report 2000,* to appear in July 2000, will state, - is a means to redistribute from the poor to the rich in the countries of the world system - yes, but *transnational* crime is a very efficient method to re-distribute from the *poor to the rich countries:*

Exploitation and corruption

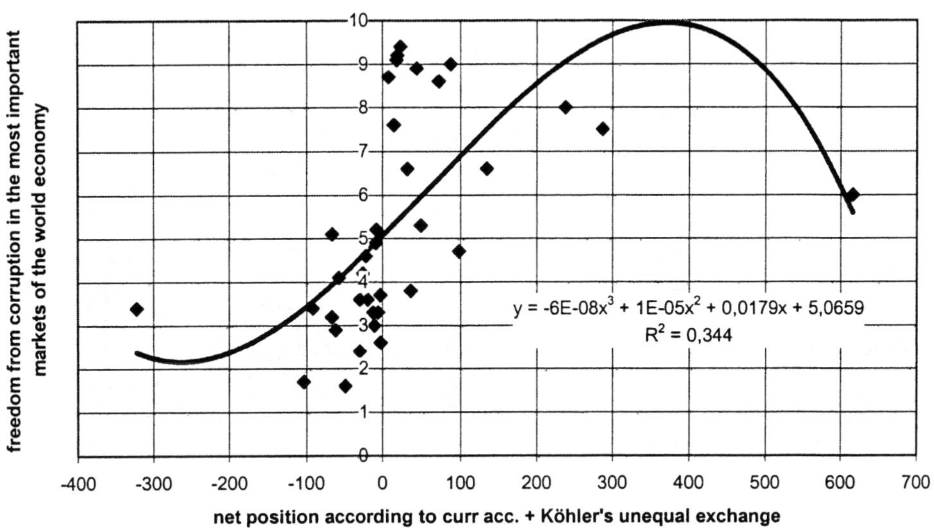

Source: compiled from the above materials

For Europe, faced with the danger to fall behind in the global power race, the temptation is great to increase unequal exchange with its own 'backyard' in Africa and Eastern Europe (Amin, 1994). And in Europe itself, the North will try to shift to the South the burden of negative current account balances again. 1988, the year before the Berlin Wall fell, old Federal Germany had still a current account surplus of 60.3 thousand million $. More and more, Germany's role will also depend on its ability to impose and to prolong the structures of unequal exchange in East Central Europe.

Secular negative trends in the trade and current account balances of nations are seen to be very strong motivations for international conflict. The rise of nationalism, anti-Westernism and anti-Germanism could receive a powerful ammunition by the ongoing post-transformation economic performance of the reform countries of Eastern Europe, dominated by the inability to find a (legal) export-oriented growth model, which is the underlying cause of the official negative current account balance. The balance of trade of the reform countries clearly demonstrates this:

Table 9.10: Trade balances and current accounts in Eastern Europe

	1993	1994	1995	1996	1997	1998	Total
current account			0,379	-11,7	-14,7	-17,25	-43,271
trade balance	-12,038	-10,481	-15,938	-26,86			-42,798

Source: our own calculations from Vienna Institute for International Economic Comparisons, Bank Austria and Business Eastern Europe

Even the integration of the 'Near European East' - that is to say, EU 5 + 1 extension, will be a painful process. For a long time to come, the balance of trade and the balance on current account will be negative, a powerful force in the motivation of economic and political nationalism against the West. The *'extractive economy'* (Tausch and Prager, 1993) is a term used to describe a situation, when exorbitant energy consumption is used to produce a shrinking or stagnating, or at least not very rapidly growing amount of welfare. Our hypothesis is that Poland and other former or continuously communist countries (like Belarus) play precisely such an 'extractive role' in the emerging cycle of the world economy.

The East, unable to reap the benefits of technical progress and being forced to export what there is, is thrown back to the old patterns of the extractive economy. No major advances in the energy/income balance are in sight. We witness a heavy or even increased reliance of the export sector on the extractive branches of the economy, and the inability to change the price mechanism, partially because losses in the terms of trade and the 'scissors' of lagging (legal) exports and rising imports dictate that the urban and rural poor cannot pay higher energy bills. The result is one more reason for a possible rising tide of nationalism.

Research and technology should be at the center of a development path, **together** with savings creation and (legal) exports. Savings and (legal) exports in Eastern Europe are small compared to the 'tigers' of Asia during the heyday of their development 1955-95. Poland, whose struggle contributed so much to the downfall of communism, found itself left alone in a peripheral position in the hour of victory. This is at least, what nationalists will assert, and hard economic and social data about societal development in the post-1989 world unfortunately have to support their lamentable assertion.

Transnational integration and national disintegration - a 134 nation study and a further note on EU-enlargements

The emergence of dozens of nations after 1989 makes cross-national development research in the world of today an especially difficult task. Yet in the name of intellectual honesty and political foresight, such an attempt must be made, integrating the development lessons and experiences of Eastern Europe and the former USSR in our now truly globalized economy. Unfortunately, the lack of appropriate data severely limited the analytical possibilities of this investigation. Nevertheless, some important conclusions can be drawn in the light of our earlier debate. How 'general' is the 'particular', and how 'particular' is the 'general' path of world development from the 1980s onwards? Arrighi wrote in 1995:

> 'Partial as the current revival of a self-regulating world market has actually been, it has already issued unbearable verdicts. Entire communities, countries, even continents, as in the case of sub-Saharan Africa, have been declared 'redundant', superfluous to the changing economy of capital accumulation on a world scale. Combined with the collapse of the world power and territorial empire of the USSR, the unplugging of these 'redundant' communities and locales from the world supply system has triggered innumerable, mostly violent feuds over 'who is more superfluous than whom', or, more simply, over the appropriation of resources that were made absolutely scarce by the unplugging' (Arrighi, 1995: 330)

On the other hand, it is clear that:

> Antigua, Botswana, China, Cyprus, Dominica, Hong Kong, Maldives, Mauritius, Saint Kitts, Saint Vincent, Singapore, South Korea, Thailand

had a GNP per capita growth rate of 4.5% or more per annum during 1980-93. The prediction of most world system theories for the future long-term prospects of the capitalist system are gloomy. Chase-Dunn and Hall cite especially population growth with its consequence on natural resources and pressures for migration as the elements that will ultimately cause systemic decline (Chase-Dunn and Hall, 1997: 199). Our reading of the post-1980s tendencies of world development is now in at least some accordance with hypotheses, put forward by Amin. For Samir Amin (1997), ascent and decline is largely being determined in our age by the following *'five monopolies'*

(i)   the monopoly of technology, supported by military expenditures of the dominant nations
(ii)   the monopoly of control over global finances and a strong position in the hierarchy of current account balances
(iii)   the monopoly of access to natural resources
(iv)   the monopoly over international communication and the media
(v)   the monopoly of the military means of mass destruction

Performance over the last 1 ½ decades teaches us an important lesson about the evolving mechanisms of the future Kondratieff cycle, that began - our reasoning went - in the mid-1980's. Let us recall, that for dependency and world system theory in the tradition of Samir Amin (1975), there are four main characteristics of the peripheral societal formation

(i)   the predominance of agrarian capitalism in the 'national' sector
(ii)   the formation of a local bourgeoisie, which is dependent from foreign capital, especially in the trading sector
(iii)   the tendency of bureaucratization
(iv)   specific and incomplete forms of proletarization of the labor force

In partial accordance with liberal thought, (i) and (iii) explain the tendency towards low savings; thus there will be

(a) huge state sector deficits and, in addition, their 'twin'
(b) chronic current account balance deficits

in the peripheral countries. High imports of the periphery, and hence, in the long run, capital imports, are the consequence of the already existing structural deformations of the role of peripheries in the world system, namely by

(i)   rapid urbanization, combined with an insufficient local production of food
(ii)   excessive expenditures of the local bureaucracies
(iii)   changes in income distribution to the benefit of the local elites (demonstration effects)
(iv)   insufficient growth of and structural imbalances in the industrial sector
(v)   and the following reliance on foreign assistance

The history of periphery capitalism, Amin argues, is full of short-term 'miracles' and long-term blocks, stagnation and even regression. Our graph shows the dramatic decline, measured in real GDP per capita in 1987 $ for Eastern Europe during the world economic crisis of the 1980s (a crisis, which it shared with the Arab nations, Latin America and Sub-Saharan Africa); Latin America recovered more rapidly, however, while East Asia, South Asia and South-East Asia forged ahead from 1960 to 1994, with East and South-East Asia thrown into a crisis in 1997:

Graph 9.8: income polarization in world capitalism - 1960 - 1994

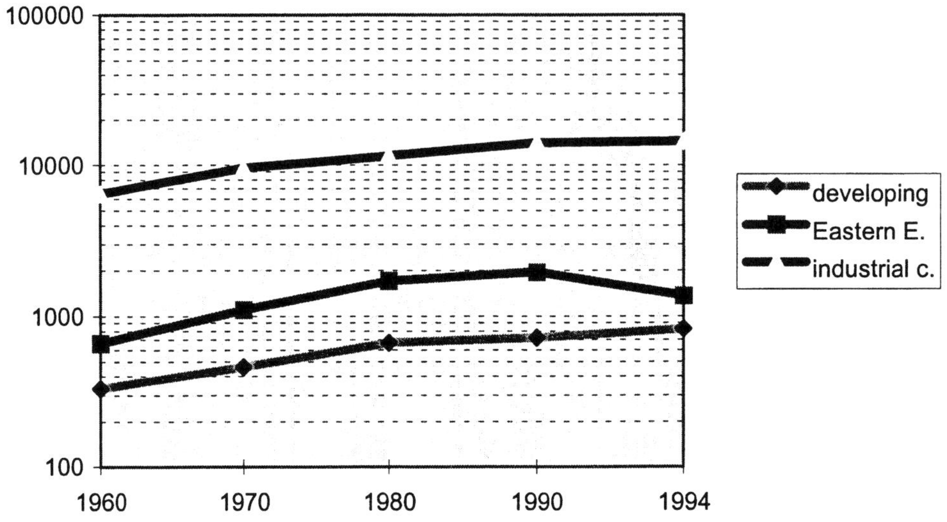

Legend: real income, measured in real GDP per capita in 1987 during the world economic crisis of the 1980s and beyond (semi-log-scale). Our own compilations from UNDP, 1997. The data are:

	SubSAfrica	Eastern E.	Arab States	East Asia	Latin America	South Asia	SE Asia+Pac
1960	495	658	989		1122	193	282
1970	598	1108	1893		1435	229	370
1980	634	1701	2757	2379	1965	363	575
1990	514	1954	1740	4674	1793	462	756
1994	507	1370	1595	5759	1931	514	935

Dependency has, according to Amin, a commercial, financial and technological aspect. *'Rent seeking'* - originally a neo-liberal concept, interpreted here from the viewpoint of dependency theory, has its basis in big landholding, which throughout the periphery was introduced, supported and upheld by colonial and post-colonial structures. Profitable investments in many periphery countries are - in part - constrained by the (emerging) unequal income distribution, which again determines, that the local 'surplus' is being squandered by luxurious consumption, transferred abroad in the form of capital flight, or being used for speculation. Just to illustrate Amin's point: in the newly capitalist countries of Eastern Europe, only the Czech Republic ($bn 15.6), Hungary ($bn 19.7), Poland ($bn 38.9) and Russia attracted $bn 10.0 or more foreign direct investment. Foreign direct investment in Russia in late 1999 was just $bn 10.3 ($bn 7.5 in 1998), while poverty data on Russia are just alarming. Russia concentrates within its borders around half the income poor of the entire region, numbering in all 60 million poor Russians (poverty is defined here as $4 or less a day). Another 60 million Russians work in the shadow economy or live from crime, that now controls 45% of Russian GNP: and these are statements by the government, and not by Radio Liberty ... (former Interior Minister Kulikov, quoted in *Agence France Press, 2nd July 1997).*

In the entire region of Eastern Europe, income poverty increased at an alarming speed between 1988 and 1994 - from 4% to 32% of the total population. 62% of all Russian children and 34% of the aged are poor; the suicide rate increased by more than 50% and the homicide rate more than doubled against 1989. 29.7% of all people are not expected to survive to age 60, 50% of Russians are living below the World Bank poverty line of 14.40 $ a day, and the Human Development Index is 0.747 (UNDP, 1999). 22.1% of all Russians live below the 50% median income OECD/EU poverty threshold. Materials from the World Development Report 2000, which are already available from the World Bank's Website (http://www.worldbank.org/wdr/2000/fullreport.html) indicate the following poverty trends and projections for the entire region:

Poverty in Eastern Europe and the former USSR

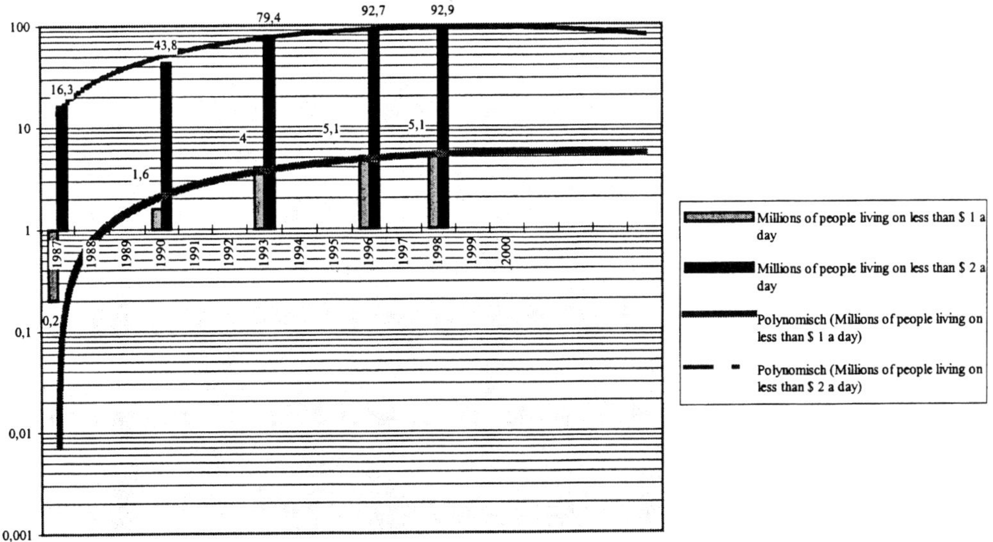

Legend: our own compilations and projections from World Bank, WDR 2000 (July 2000)

The poorest 20% have an income of 881 $ per capita and year in terms of real purchasing power, while the richest 20% have 12804 $ per capita and year (UNDP, 1999). Our next Graph now shows the twin deficits, that neoclassical economists and dependency authors like Samir Amin alike so much associate with underdevelopment:

Graph 9.9: twin deficits in the newly capitalist countries of Eastern Europe

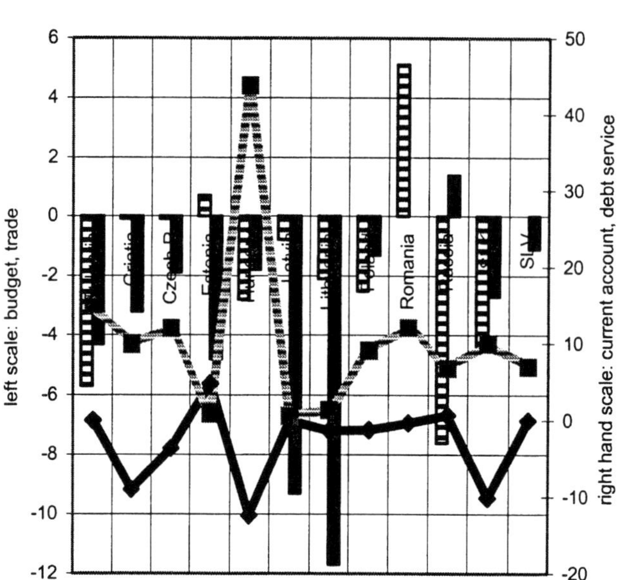

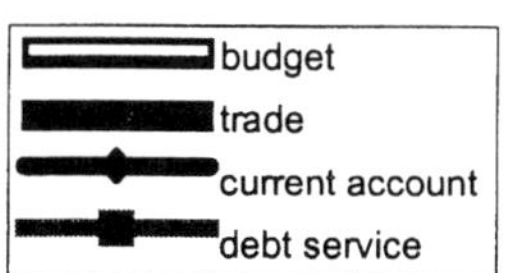

Legend: See inscriptions on the axes. Sources: our own compilations from Business Central Europe, May and June 1997

Past and present foreign domination and colonialism cause long term structural imbalances. Countries as far apart as large parts of Africa and Asia, just as Poland from 1795 - 1918, were no national state during the important era of the Industrial Revolution. Their economies were geared to the needs of others, i.e. their colonizers. The structural heterogeneity between the different economic sectors on the one hand and the 'modern', export oriented sector, the medium sector and the 'traditional sector' in agriculture, industry and services, became the main reason for the unequal income distribution in the countries of the periphery. Colonial trade, foreign investment in the 19th Century, import substitution in the first half of the 20th Century, and the new international division of labor that we observe from the middle of the 1960s onwards did not really change the structures of inequality in the world system. While mass demand and agricultural structures (Elsenhans, 1983) were responsible for the transition from the tributary mode of production in Western Europe to capitalism from the Long 16th Century onwards, periphery capitalism was and is characterized by the following main tendencies (Amin, 1973 - 1997):

(i)   regression in both agriculture and small scale industry characterizes the period after the onslaught of foreign domination and colonialism

(ii)   unequal international specialization of the periphery leads to the concentration of activities in export oriented agriculture and or mining. Some industrialization of the periphery is possible under the condition of low wages, which, together with rising productivity, determine that unequal exchange sets in (double factorial terms of trade < 1.0; see Raffer, 1987)

(iii)   these structures determine in the long run a rapidly growing tertiary sector with hidden unemployment and the rising importance of rent in the overall social and economic system

(iv) the development blocks of peripheral capitalism (chronic current account balance deficits, re-exported profits of foreign investments, deficient business cycles of the periphery, that provide important markets for the centers during world economic upswings)

(v) structural imbalances in the political and social relationships, *inter alia* a strong *'compradore'* element and the rising importance of state capitalism and an indebted state class

What tendencies, then, do emerge from the multivariate analysis of international development for the decade of Casino-capitalism in 134 countries with fairly consistent and complete data? Is Arrighi's hypothesis about the *'deregulatory logic'* of post-1980 capitalism confirmed by the data? And what about the other hypotheses of 'world system research'?

The results are fairly consistent with earlier research findings. First of all, **MNC penetration** (UNCTAD measure, 1985) significantly **lowers the human development index,** and **increases -** *ceteris paribus* **- infant mortality, and - as we show below, is also related to early death (percentage of people dying before age 40).** Under inclusion of the world of former 'real' socialism, the curve-linear effect of the development level on subsequent **economic growth** is partially taken over by variables, pertaining to the **employment structure.** Both the saturation effects of 'mature capitalism' with a high labor force participation rate as well as periphery capitalism's blocked rural transformation are responsible for slow economic growth. Again, only the statistically significant effects, that cannot be explained by simple random, are being taken into account. Countries with a large labor force participation ratio (the saturation effect of mature capitalism), and hence, a relatively smaller industrial de-facto **reserve army** of employment, grow **slower** than countries at the middle income level with a still larger industrial reserve army. Neoclassical theory would mention here wage flexibility in the urban sector as one of the main underlying processes. But on the other hand, **predominantly rural societies** at the present stage of globalization are being negatively affected by the ongoing **urban bias in world development** (M. Lipton).

Seen from the perspective of Third World development, it is amazing to see how some European countries repeat the experience of what Armando Cordova and Samir Amin once called **'structural heterogeneity'** and what development sociologists today call structural disarticulation. Especially those countries, that were once or still are characterized by big landholding and or extensive agriculture, implanted in the world system during the Long 16th Century, like most of the nations of the world's East and South, are still doomed to slow economic growth, slow human development, and relatively higher infant mortality rates. In terms of measurement, it boils down to the same effect: disarticulation, urban bias, structural heterogeneity - they all happen, whenever agriculture has a much larger share in national labor than in national product, reflecting the relative discrimination of the rural sector in society. The world map of structural disarticulation looks like the following:

Map 9.2: The urban bias of world development

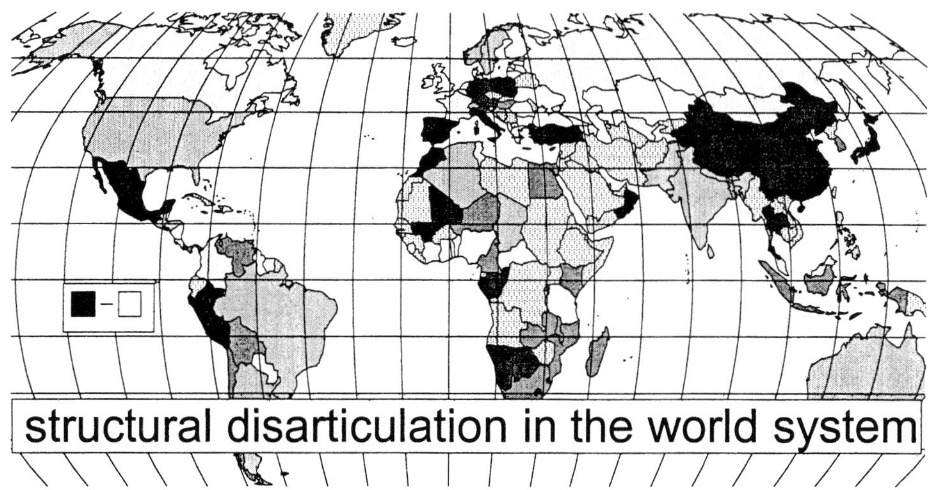

Legend: the darker, the stronger the urban bias in development. Urban bias is measured in terms of the income difference, that separates the rural sector from the rest of society, and is calculated by the share of the agriculturally active population per total employment, divided by the share of agriculture in total GDP. An urban bias factor of 4.5 thus means, that the average monetary income of the rural population is 4.5 times lower than the national average.

Some of the most surprising data from this comparison about the urban bias on a world level are:

Austria	4.0
Brazil	2.09
Germany	4.0
India	2.06
Israel	1.33
Japan	3.5
NL	1.25
New Zealand	1.11
Poland	4.5
UK	1.0
USA	2.14

Legend: employment share of agriculture, divided by product share of agriculture. For the ongoing debate about this 'urban bias', 'structural heterogeneity' or 'disarticulation' see Huang, 1995; Rothgeb, 1995, Wickrama and Mulford, 1996, as well as the earlier theoretical advances by Amin, 1976; Cordova, 1973, and Lipton, 1977. Our data analysis is based on EXCEL 7 and UNDP, 1996

Hence also the negative effect of agricultural employment on growth. **Redistribution** of incomes is significantly affected by the 'Kuznets curve', by the **labor supply** rate, and hence, population growth, and by the **power status** of a **nation** in the world economy (market size). **Katzenstein's small state theory is only partially vindicated here.** The process of **bourgeoisie nation formation** (Amin does not use the term 'nation building') before the First World War is a crucial determinant of today's growth and development chances in the world system. Those nations, that were founding members of the UN in 1945 - and hence have a high UN membership age - **disproportionately reap the benefits of economic growth today.** The **international system** indeed seems to work like a single, huge, **distribution coalition - or to put in Samir Amin's words - the international system favors at least some of the five monopolies.** Economic **growth disproportionately favors** countries with a **long-established record of UN-membership.** Participation in the 'distribution coalition' of world power allows for a better access to the distributed goods, while the predominantly rural or semi-rural societies of the 'Fourth' and 'Fifth' World, but also of the 'East' are being excluded from the benefits. Those, that have access in the established networks of distribution coalitions, accumulate even more economic power. And Deutsch's pessimistic stability theory is again vindicated; mainly because a strong state sector role in the economy and low initial *exposure* to 'modernization' (high population growth) still dampen war intensity, while *modernization under way* (high mean years of schooling) increase conflict intensity.

State sector size affects growth in a way, as predicted by both conventional and radical economic theory. But - contrary to Amin's expectations - **the economic burden of the military sector** today also significantly and **negative affects** economic growth at the level of the 134 nations under analysis. Amin's own wider theory would allow for such a hypothesis: the state class, and bureaucracies all block against development; militarization, first and foremost, is bureaucratization; while only a handful of nations might reap (if at all?) the benefits of militarily controlling the globe. **The effect of militarism** must be further qualified: **growth is hampered by high military expenditures, and employment is hampered by state sector expenditures.** Thus Amin's hypotheses, derived from his theory, must be qualified: there is a negative employment, and a negative growth effect of monopoly number five in the world system, state capitalism and militarism. Further research should also look into the current account balance effects of militarism and world power political status. High military expenditures are closely linked to the conflict zones of this world, as measured by the indicator War Years from 1990 to 1995.

But some results from earlier research are partially contradicted here. Small states do not tend, in Katzenstein's sense, towards redistribution but towards a higher income inequality; but the economic burden of international power is seen in the negative correlation between absolute GNP and economic growth; or to put it in reverse, **small markets have a partially optimistic growth perspective.** Their growth will tend to be fast, but not egalitarian. Thus Katzenstein's old hypotheses are updated in a way. **Former communist countries could grow rapidly**, but often stagnate, not because they are former communist nations, but because their peripheral state is too bureaucratic and too big, because their reserve army is too small, because their military burden rate is too high, and because their **rural populations are being discriminated against.** But *per se,* the tendencies of world society after 1980 during the new cyclical set-up seem to suggest, that a world political experience as a **former communist** nation **does not block against** subsequent economic **growth.** Again: absolute market size is not a precondition of subsequent economic growth anymore, as successful island nations like Mauritius show impressively. Our equation determines **46.6% of economic growth** from 1980 onwards; the F-statistic for the whole equation is 8.05, with 120 degrees of freedom. What flexible specialization has to offer to the *megalomania* of current European center thinking, would be open for a debate.

Human development, on the other hand, is positively determined by a **high agricultural share,** and hence the absence of what Michael Lipton once called the 'urban bias of world development'. It is being negatively determined by a high ratio of **foreign direct investment penetration.** Thus, findings of earlier cross-national development research, most notably Huang (1995) are being confirmed anew. Our two statements are very well compatible with the essence of dependency theories. A development, that is dependent to a large extent on foreign capital, is socially polarizing and regionally exclusive. The rural regions stagnate relatively, while the rich urban centers are receiving disproportionate shares of the newly created wealth. But *ceteris paribus*, it also emerges, that a concerted effort in only one area of human capital formation - education - without the proper health policy effort can also be negatively affecting human development. Poland comes to my mind here: education data for Poland are still better than health data, where the need for reform is especially dramatic. Highly repressive totalitarian communist regimes - in the past - had a relatively good quantitative record in the education sector, that was connected with **severe deficits in other areas of social policy.** This same effect also holds for the determination of **infant mortality rates.** A policy of high labor force participation ratios, and hence, **full employment, less urban bias** and chances for rural employment all **reduce infant mortality** rates significantly, while **communist power** experience, **foreign capital penetration** and a **one-sided human capital policy,** concentrated on schooling, and neglecting health, all **contributed significantly to higher infant mortality** rates. **Employment** - here labor force participation, is being determined by a **Kuznets-type non-linear process.** And employment is the one instance, where neo-liberal theories are vindicated in an important way. Foreign direct investment penetration pushes up the labor force participation rate, while human rights violations, state sector expenditures and past communist experience all determine the labor force participation rate - and hence employment - downward. The effect is of course significant, with an F-value of 8.13 and 42.3% of total variance explained.

The **war experience of a nation** is only weakly determined in our model (14.9%); yet, the most significant results are achieved by the state sector and low social mobilization (high population growth), working against a prolonged war experience, while military expenditures and mean years of schooling enhance the conflict potential: the **state neutralizes violence potential, while modernization and social mobilization increase it.** Finally, **income inequality** is being determined - in an almost brutal Wallersteinean sense - (41.3%) - by the **Kuznets curve, population growth, and by the absence of a position of power in the international system** (absolute GNP).

Table 9.11 and Graph 9.10: towards an age of de-regulation? Bivariate and multivariate analyses

a) determinants of growth

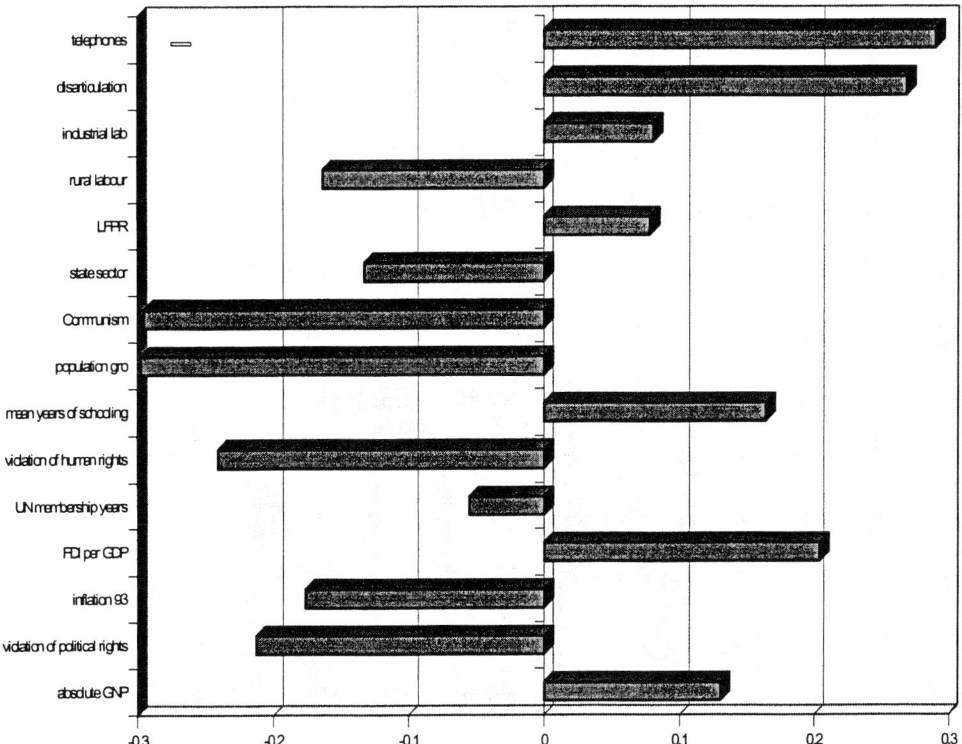

Legend: Pearson-Bravais correlation coefficients of economic growth with different predictor variables (see inscriptions) for the countries of the world system

b) determinants of human development

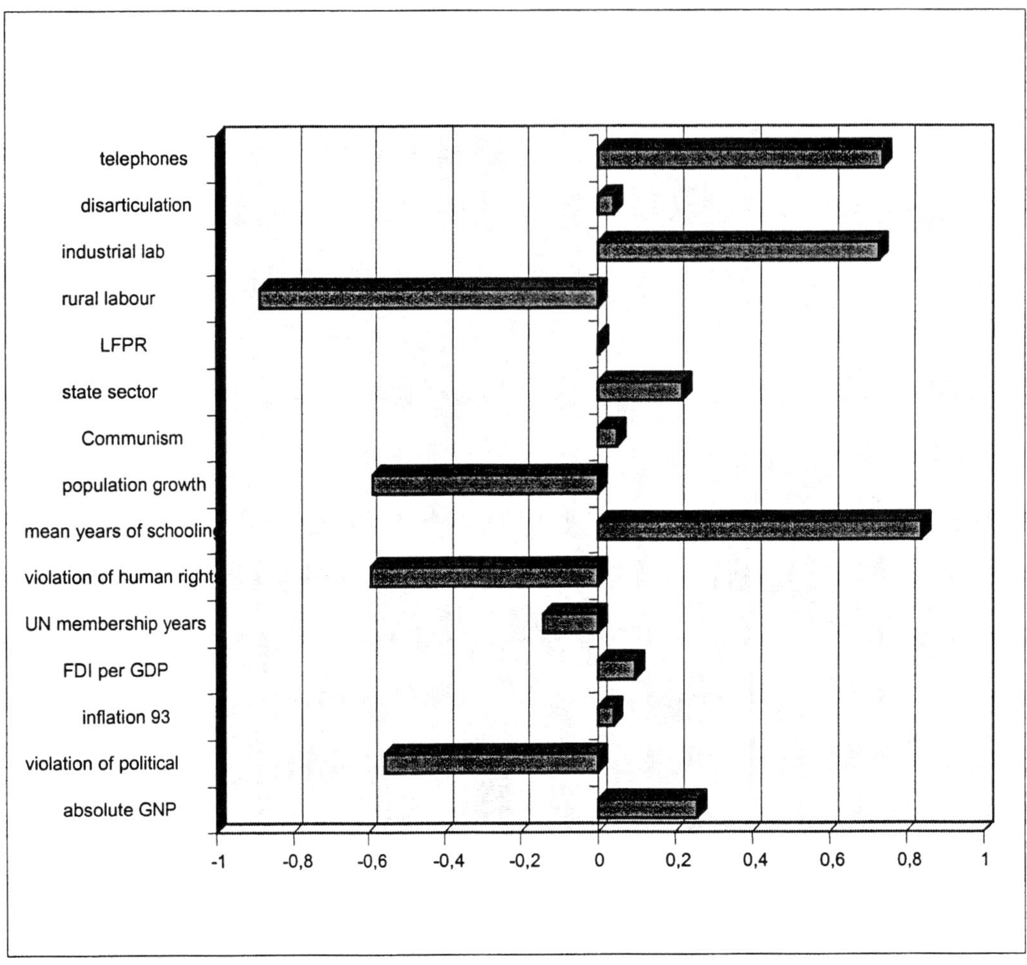

Legend: Pearson-Bravais correlation coefficients of the human development index with different predictor variables (see inscriptions) for the countries of the world system

a) Growth in the period 1980 - 94

UN memb.y	mean y scho	absolute GNP	FDI per GDP	Years of Comm	popula-tion gr	state sector	%labor force	%lf agric.	%lf industry	agr.share GP	MILEX	HDI	constant
10,213	0,27658	-0,0449	-0,0038	0,04683	0,04623	-0,0412	-0,9458	-0,0299	-0,0034	1E-04	-0,372	-0,0035	-4,1729
2,44484	0,09678	0,02556	0,03757	0,02002	0,03517	0,01661	0,25246	0,01213	0,01112	0,0003	0,13	0,01406	3,1815
0,466													
8,04862	120												
4,177	**2,858**	**-1,755**	-0,1006	**2,339**	1,31457	**-2,481**	**-3,746**	**-2,463**	-0,308	0,33523	**-2,861**	-0,2517	t-test

b) The human development index

UN memb.y	mean y scho	absolute GNP	FDI per GDP	Years of Comm	popula-tion gr	state sector	%labor force	%lf agric.	%lf industry	agr. shareGP	MILEX	constant
-0,0017	-0,0042	-6E-05	-0,003	-0,0018	-0,0002	-0,0134	0,00027	0,00053	-7E-06	0,02086	-0,0001	0,86611
0,0036	0,00087	0,0014	0,00069	0,0013	0,00062	0,00931	0,00045	0,00041	1,1E-05	0,00445	0,00052	0,08829
0,88												

74,1983	121											
-0,4828	-4,78	-0,0435	-4,383	-1,3488	-0,3169	-1,4343	0,59058	1,29988	-0,6638	4,691	-0,2103	t-test
UN memb.y	mean y scho	absolute GNP	FDI per GDP	Years of Comm	popula-tion gr	state sector	%labor force	%lf agric.	%lf industry	agr.shar eGP	MILEX	constant

c) Employment

mean y scho	absoluteG NP	FDI per GDP	Years of Comm	popula-tion gr	state sector	viol hum rites	ln PPP	ln PPP^2	agr.share GP	MILEX	constant
-0,1821	-0,0119	3,2941	-55,631	-0,0743	-0,0998	-1,8049	0,108	0,0249	-5E-05	0,1234	281,05
0,2493	0,0652	0,5025	8,4382	0,4299	0,0415	0,6148	0,0275	0,0256	0,0008	0,3029	36,372
0,423											
8,1294	122										
-0,7305	-0,183	6,555	-6,593	-0,1728	-2,402	-2,936	3,922	0,9727	-0,0601	0,4073	
mean y scho	absoluteG NP	FDI per GDP	Years of Comm	popula-tion gr	state sector	viol hum rites	ln PPP	ln PPP^2	agr.share GP	MILEX	constant

d) Infant mortality

UN memb.y	mean y scho	absolute GNP	FDI per GDP	Years of Comm	popula-tion gr	state sector	%labor force	%lf agric.	%lf industry	agr.shar eGP	MILEX	constant
0,02855	0,32736	-0,2226	0,5792	0,53384	0,11911	2,52969	-0,2306	-0,1964	0,00208	-4,1766	0,0939	13,9921
0,83446	0,20233	0,32428	0,16052	0,30125	0,14331	2,16057	0,10451	0,0953	0,00256	1,03204	0,12131	20,4932
0,811												
43,3413	121											
0,03421	1,618	-0,6864	3,608	1,772	0,83112	1,17084	-2,206	-2,061	0,81363	-4,047	0,77406	t-test
UN memb.y	mean y scho	absolute GNP	FDI per GDP	Years of Comm	popula-tion gr	state sector	%labor force	%lf agric.	%lf industry	agr.shar eGP	MILEX	constant

e) War years, 1990-1995

viol pol rites	mean y scho	absolute GNP	FDI per GDP	Years of Comm	populati on gr	state sector	%labor force	%lf agric.	%lf industry	agr.shar eGP	MILEX	HDI
-13,4614	0,83461	0,04328	0,15409	0,11675	-0,33473	-0,17015	-0,16198	-0,09705	-0,01932	-0,00094	1,7409	0,66349
12,1148	0,48782	0,12636	0,18622	0,09847	0,17369	0,08252	1,27292	0,0601	0,05313	0,00147	0,65095	0,63394
0,149												
1,61588	120											
-1,11115	1,7109	0,34251	0,82748	1,18565	-1,927	-2,062	-0,12725	-1,61495	-0,3636	-0,63412	2,6744	1,0466
viol pol rites	mean y scho	absolute GNP	FDI per GDP	Years of Comm	populati on gr	state sector	%labor force	%lf agric.	%lf industry	agr.shar eGP	MILEX	HDI

constant
12,9576
15,742

f) Income inequality

Income inequality	ln PPP	(ln PPP)^2	mean y scho	absolute GNP	FDI per GDP	Years of Comm	popula-tion gr	state sector	%labor force	%lf agric.	%lf industry	agr. shareGP
	-0,2335	-0,1353	-0,0849	-0,1051	0,01724	-0,0049	3,23042	-0,0236	0,00432	-6E-05	-0,3733	-0,5457
	0,25144	0,06956	0,09698	0,05241	0,10312	0,04445	0,64893	0,03575	0,02768	0,00079	0,3202	0,61236
	0,413											
	6,50195	120										
	-0,9286	**-1,946**	-0,8756	**-2,004**	0,16716	-0,111	**4,978**	-0,6614	0,15599	-0,0814	-1,1657	-0,8911
	ln PPP	**(ln PPP)^2**	mean y scho	**absolute GNP**	FDI per GDP	Years of Comm	**populati on gr**	state sector	%labor force	%lf agric.	%lf industry	agr.share GP

MILEX	constant
6,41566	36,2921
10,3385	47,0594

0,62056	0,7712
MILEX	constant

g) Life expectancy

	e-function	pi-function	mean y scho	viol pol rites	FDI per GDP	Years of Comm	population gr	state sector	constant
LEX	-0,0002	-0,0079	0,0007	0,0002	0,0004	0,0165	-5E-06	0,6557	-1,303
	0,0004	0,0053	0,0002	0,0002	0,0028	0,0028	4E-07	0,028	0,078
	0,955								
	328,65	125							
	-0,6104	-1,4894	**2,741**	0,6657	0,1386	**5,997**	-13,04	**23,46**	-16,71
	e-function	pi-function	**mean y scho**	viol pol rites	FDI per GDP	**Years of Comm**	population gr	**state sector**	constant

Legend: War years (as of December, 1995) are calculated from D. Smith, 1997. Income inequality data are estimated from World Bank, WDR 1996, UNDP HDR 1996 and Moaddel, 1994. The existing data were augmented by averages of non-linear, second-order polynomial trend-line estimates of existing income inequality data projected onto the countries with missing data, with labor force participation rates and mean years of schooling serving as the two predictors. The choice of the predictors was made by calculating the highest linear correlation coefficients of income inequality data with the main variables of the model. The original war data were coded by subtracting the year, in which a war began, from the final year of a war (if unfinished, then 1995). Wars, which lasted less than a year, are coded as '1'. Source: our EXCEL 5.0 and 7.0 calculations from UNDP and other data sources, quoted above. As in all EXCEL 5.0 outprints in this work, first row: unstandardized regression coefficients, second row: standard errors, last row: t-Test. The values immediately below the standard errors are $R^{\wedge 2}$ (third row, left side entry), F, and degrees of freedom (fourth row).

In terms of employment policy and future labor force participation rates, Europe is not in a very lucky constellation right now. We have again and again stated this throughout this work: low population growth, a strong urban bias, high overall educational levels, combined with a high employment share of industry and a run-down of military expenditures all would suggest a future lowering of the labor force participation rates, while in some European countries there is still a high agricultural employment share, which works as an additional constraint against a higher labor force participation ratio. The urban bias of European development, in the end, could become the major stumbling block of the European Union. This explosive mix of problems is made all the worse by faltering economic growth, determined downward by high state sector ratios, a dried-up reserve army of labor, and too high military expenditures, that, under the inflexibilities of really existing capitalism, are often the only way out to prop up employment.

These results are all the more deplorable, since in terms of internal redistribution, the European Union has been more efficient than other existing trade blocks around the world. The Union policy of redistribution to the Mediterranean South could have been more efficient, would it not have been accompanied by the above mentioned high social structural disarticulation rates in Mediterranean agriculture, which are, if we again correctly follow Samir Amin, nothing but the consequence of the expansion of capitalism east- and southward during the Long 16th Century, made all the worse by the effects of heavily subsidized agricultural exports from the Union. Millions and millions of ECU have reached since the mid 1980s the poorer regions of Europe's South, thus homogenizing Europe's economic regions to a great extent. Our empirical measurement of these phenomena starts out from the assumption, that the *Human Development Indicator* is indeed the single best measurement scale for the analysis of the social conditions of states in world society. We compare here the EU 12, and samples of the kernel of the ASEAN states with complete data, EFTA, APEC, NAFTA, and the EU associated countries since the 1980s. Our analysis can only be tentative, since there are problems of missing data and, above all, also shifting and overlapping memberships, that had to be taken care of. Nevertheless, we think that our choice of states to be analyzed with complete data is relatively balanced and fair. In each case, we compare the standard deviation of the different integrative units and their relative predecessors or processes in the making for 1980, 1992, and 1994, and arrive at the following Graph by putting the 1980 value at 100 each. For comparison, the original values about HDI standard deviations and mean values of HDIs from 1980 onwards are given in the following graph:

Graph 9.11: The redistribution effect within integrative units. EU12 compared (standard deviations of Human Development Indices in the trade blocks by 1980 are set at 100 each)

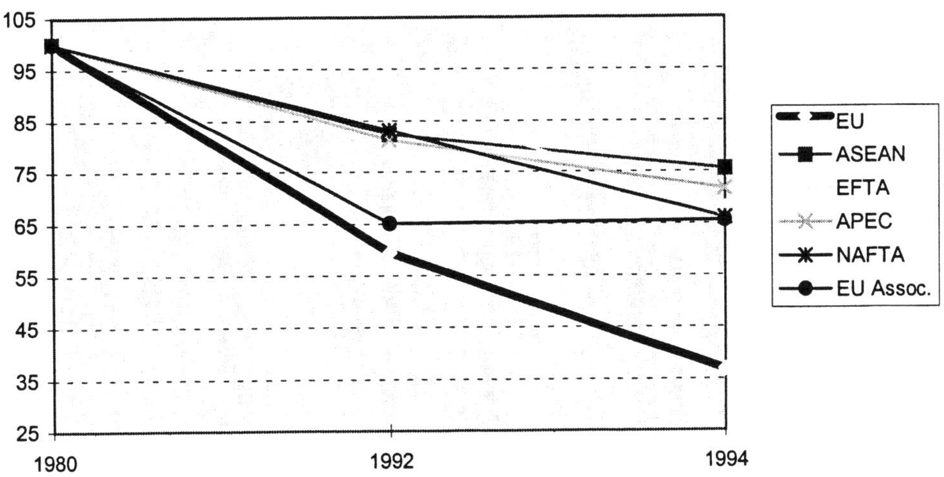

Legend: standard deviations of HDIs (human development indices) in the different trade blocks of the world economy. As to the samples and original data for this graph, see Appendix.

Graph 9.12: The absolute values of the average Human Development Indices and their standard deviations in each trade block since 1980

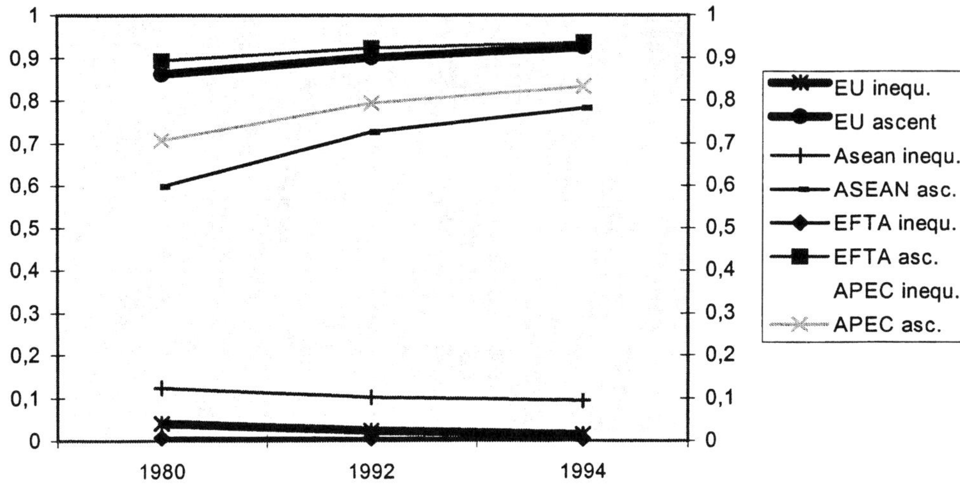

Legend: absolute values of average Human Development Indices per trade block (lines above, right hand scale) and standard deviations of HDIs within each trade blocks (lines below, left-hand scale). The thick lines symbolize the European Union.

The Rotten Heart of Europe? A technical note on EMU and the rise of world-wide narco capitalism

The above mentioned positive redistribution effect on a European scale between the North and the South (and later on, between the West and the East) could be endangered by the long-term effects of *EMU*. The proponents of *EMU* maintained all along, that it will be an engine of political and economic unification on the continent. We fear, that the long-term effect of the project in its present, neo-monetarist form will be an increasing nationalism and a cultural conflict along the old cultural frontier, the *Limes,* between the Latin and the Germanic Europe, between the wine and the beer culture, between the olive oil consumers and the sausage eaters. This is not a Chapter against the *EMU,* it is a Chapter against Euro-monetarism. An increasing number of scholars propose an alternative course of action, that stresses the political and social cohesion in Europe as the main pillars of a true European Monetary Union (Rothschild, 1997). There is the danger, that Euro-monetarism will accelerate the tendency of the world system on its path towards financial speculation, narco-capitalism, and the shifting of resources away from the Atlantic region towards the Pacific. On the other hand, it is evident that Europe's long-term ascent from the Long 16th Century onwards from the state of a former periphery of the world system to a center (Arrighi, 1995; Amin, 1975), which was based on agrarian reform and mass demand, is now threatened to be reversed by the application of monetary orthodoxy.

The neo-liberal Maastricht orthodoxy is characterized by the following basic fallacies: **Fallacy number one: by high unemployment you can control inflation.** At the outset of this technical appendix, we would thus like to state **that unemployment, first of all, is an enormous waste of economic resources.** For 18 western democracies with complete UNDP (or Federal Ministry of Labor of the Republic of Austria) data for 1995, we have:

Graph 9.13: Unemployment is a waste of resources

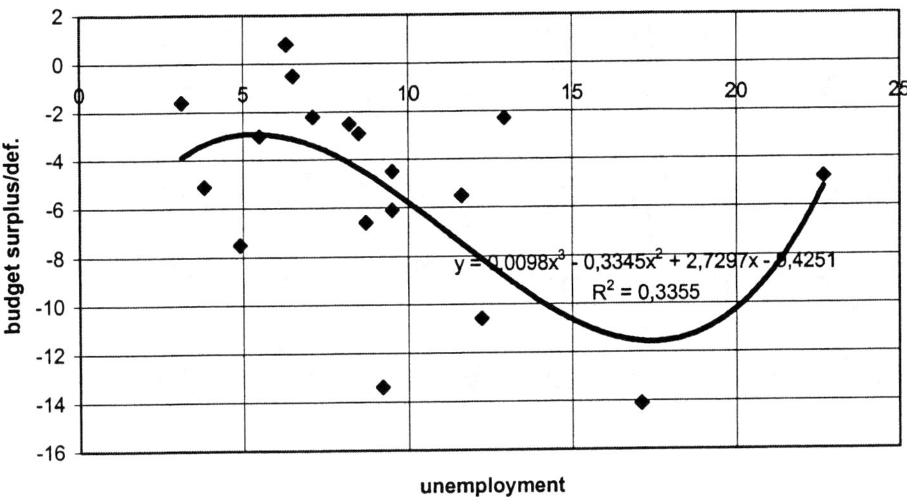

Legend: unemployment rates (x-axis) and budget balances (y-axis, per GDP) in OECD countries. Compiled from data series, published in the international press, 1998

Thus, only at very small and at very high levels of already existing unemployment, a *'shock therapy'* might work to flatten out budget deficits. But else, there is an across the board **negative correlation between unemployment and budget surplus**, i.e. increasing **unemployment still increases deficits**. Saving has limits. And here, the story of Euro-'monetarism' begins (the hyphens are to indicate, that the relationship between real monetarist theory of the Milton Friedman type to contemporary European applications is far from certain; see also Friedman's excellent essay on the *EURO*, 1997):

'Jacques Rueff, fierce 1950s critic of American monetary hegemony, once said: 'Europe will be built through a currency or it will not be built at all'. What the ERM story shows is quite the opposite: trying to lock countries like France and Germany together via their currencies does not forge one nation; instead it turns domestic monetary questions into international political conflicts' (Connolly, 1995: 1995)

Milton Friedman all along has been very outspoken about the real dangers of the concept. In his interview with Radio Australia on July 17th, 1999 he said:

I think it's a big gamble and I'm not optimistic. Unfortunately, the Common Market does not have the features that are required for a common currency area. A common currency area is a very good thing under some circumstances, but not necessarily under others. The United States is a common currency area. Australia is also a common currency area. The characteristics that make Australia and the United States favourable for a common currency are that the populations all speak the same language or some approximation to it; there's free movement of people from one part of the country to the other part, so there's considerable mobility; and there's a good deal of flexibility in prices and to some extent in wages. Finally, there's a central government which is large relative to the local state governments so that if some special circumstances affect one part of the country adversely, there will be flows of funds from the centre which will tend to offset that.
If you look at the situation in the Common Market, it has none of those features. You have countries with people all of whom speak different languages. There's very little mobility of people

from one part of the Common Market to another. The local governments are very large compared to the central government in Brussels. Prices and wages are subject to all sorts of restrictions and control.

The exchange rates between different currencies provided a mechanism for adjusting to shocks and economic events which affected different countries differently. In establishing the common currency area, the Euro, the separate countries are essentially throwing away this adjustment mechanism. What will substitute for it?

Perhaps they will be lucky. It may be that events, as they turn out in the next 10 or 20 years, will be common to all the countries; there will be no shocks, no economic developments that affect the different parts of the Euro area asymmetrically. In that case, they'll get along fine and perhaps the separate countries will gradually loosen up their arrangements, get rid of some of their restrictions and open up so that they're more adaptable, more flexible.

On the other hand, the more likely possibility is that there will be asymmetric shocks hitting the different countries. That will mean that the only adjustment mechanism they have to meet that with is fiscal and unemployment: pressure on wages, pressure on prices. They have no way out. With a currency board, there is always the ultimate alternative that you can break the currency board. Hong Kong can dismantle its currency board tomorrow if it wants to. It doesn't want to and I don't think it will. But it could. But with the Euro, there is no escape mechanism.

Suppose things go badly and Italy is in trouble, how does Italy get out of the Euro system? It no longer has a lira after whatever it is - 2000 or 2001 - so it's a very big gamble. I wish the Euro area well; it will be in the self-interest of Australia and the United States that the Euro area be successful. But I'm very much concerned that there's a lot of uncertainty in prospect. (M. Friedman, http://abc.net.au/money/vault/extras/extra5.htm)

It is time to stress the fundamental weaknesses of the present neo-liberal vision of the *EMU* project from the viewpoint of world system theory. Up to now, Europe does not form an integrated economic region with truly European transnational corporations; Europe forms only a preferential market (Amin, 1997). Secondly, Europe does not have a continental **societal project,** that would integrate such areas as research and development, public markets, and would have a joint commercial and corporate law, and as yet does not integrate the vital sectors of film and TV production. **Trade union and other social law would have to be integrated, and Europe does not have as yet a joint project of external relations with the other regions of the world economy (Amin, 1997; Friedman, 1997).** The *EMU* project should facilitate a truly common market, the free movement of capital and stable external exchange rates. As the critics of the project have shown all along, the project could only function if **there is a parallel economic and social policy in the member states of *EMU*; that means harmonization of tax and expenditure systems, the integration at the level of corporate policy, and the harmonization of trade union policy at the European level.** There would have to be a coordinated European policy not only of the internal, but also of the external opening of markets - **especially regarding foreign investment and capital inflows from third countries (Amin, 1997).** The repeated attempts by the United States to push through a *Mutual Agreement on Investment (MAI)* run counter to the very spirit of a European social area; as Jadwiga Staniszkis, as a lone preacher in the desert, has repeated in Poland. On the real agenda would be a European social space, with a European Monetary Union at the service of continental and global Keynesianism (Kohler/Tausch, 2000).

We all know by today the Maastricht criteria (Rothschild, 1997):

a)   in the examination year an inflation rate no more than 1.5 percent above the average of the three EU states with the lowest price rises

b)   a long-term rate of interest within two percentage points of the average of the three 'best' countries

c)   a national budget deficit (covering national, federal and local governments) less than 3 percent of GDP

d)   a public debt ratio which does not exceed 60 percent of GDP

e)   a currency for two years within the normal band of EMS

Fallacy number two now arises: that economic theory fully supports a neo-liberal design of the *EURO*. Academic economists found 24 main arguments against the neo-liberal design of the *EURO*:

(i)   external changes and shocks will not be answered anymore by changes in the external exchange rate. Since the exchange rate is not anymore a factor of economic policy regulation, either migration, wage flexibility, fiscal policy or economic transfers from other countries will become the main regulatory mechanisms in the new, monetarily united Union (Friedman, 1997; see also Klaus, 1997; Beirat 1996; Stephen Roach from Morgan Stanley Dean Witter, Neue Zuercher Zeitung, Monday, 16th of June, 1997: 16)

(ii)   but labor is not that flexible; so the result will be - in all probability - economic transfers within the *EMU* countries. Economic transfers are the inevitable result of monetary union (a contradiction, perhaps spelt out most clearly by the neo-liberal former acting Czech Premier and neo-liberal economist Vaclav Klaus, 1997). This scenario will lead to the inevitable result of a loss of autonomy of national fiscal policies (Klaus, 1997). Such a scenario is all the more likely since there is no convergence in the productivity of labor in the *EMU* countries themselves. Without a financial transfer system from the rich to the poor regions, *EMU* will prove to be not operational, anywhere up to \$bn 1000 DM will have to be transferred (Borchert, Sueddeutsche Zeitung, 1st March, 1997: 25; Watzal, 1997), thus repeating the experience of the integration of the *New Laender* into the Federal Republic

(iii)   the problems of the classic 'euro-monetarist' Maastricht package are compounded by the fact that not governments, but parliaments decide on fiscal policy in European democracies - thus making the signatures of heads of governments or foreign ministers under treaties of stability liable to parliamentary control - or worse - Maastricht would have led to the gradual erosion of the role of the national parliaments in favor of the executive branch

(iv)   according to the textbooks, the function of financial markets is the transfer of savings into the financing of real economic investments (Beirat, 1996). On a global scale, European and Atlantic region savings in general will be transferred to real economic investments in East Asia, formerly the most dynamic region of the capitalist world economy (Arrighi, 1995), to be succeeded today possibly by China, and India. Gross domestic savings in the European Union are only 20%, and gross domestic investment only 19% of GDP. In the US, savings (15%) and investments (16%) are even lower. Before Fall 1997, the international system seemed to work in a very simple way: **international debts financed the Asian/US economic compound.** On a global scale, East Asia achieved an investment boom (39% investments per GDP), followed by South-East Asia and the Pacific region (37%), while Eastern Europe and the CIS and South Asia stood at 23% investment, Latin America and the Caribean at 20% and Sub-Saharan Africa at 19% (UNDP, 1998). Only Sub-Saharan Africa has a similar or lower investment rate than the EU (19%) and the USA (16%). At the heart of the 'euro-monetarist' Maastricht prescriptions against the European ills now lies the assumption, **that monetary policy will influence only prices, but not output and employment.** The *EMU*-optimists hope that the single currency will be an ideal instrument for Europe to sustain in international economic competition. But a 'hard' *EURO* will be of a negative influence on trade-, and hence, on European current account balances with the rest of the world, since European exports will become more expensive and European imports will become cheaper internationally. Until now, de-valuations were a proper economic policy instrument of the weaker European economies to balance their negative current accounts, as the example of Spain and Italy over the last years amply demonstrates. This instrument would now be absent; only **migration,** the **wage rate, transfers** and or **unemployment** would be the only options left for the European *mezzogiorno* under *EMU* (see above, and

Boyer, 1996, Friedman, 1997). A sinister argument could even be, that the motives for the neo-liberal version of the *EMU* project could be rather inner-European competition. A 'hard' *EURO* comprising the European *mezzogiorno,* would ruin exporters in the South (that made important headway against the dominance of the German work bench in Europe over recent years) while cementing the position of German and a few other multinationals - banks and companies - on an increasingly protected European home market. Then, indeed, the European Union would become what Samir Amin has contemptuously called (although we do not agree with him here) - the **democratic** *'Fourth Reich'* (Amin, 1997)

(v)   on the other hand, the 'euro-monetarist' package against future inflation under *EMU,* that solely relies on 5 monetary criteria, overlooks the very plausible role of encompassing trade unions in combating inflation - an argument, originally also conceded by neo-liberal economic theory. Furthermore, the 'euro-monetarist' Maastricht strategy, as envisaged by around 1995-1997, would have brought about a monetary union between only those EU countries that already are in the upper ¼ or 1/3 of stability on the European continent - with uncertain implications for the unfortunate rest (Beirat, 1996). The annual rate of inflation in EU-Europe is the minor problem: the real problem is massive European unemployment and the massive social disintegration of the European cities

(vi)   the Kohl/Waigel strategy would have relied on the European North, and not on the South. The political backlash against *Euro-monetarism, Frankfurt (Franc fort?)-*style, is only too well understandable, considering the high social costs that French society in particular would have had to bear. Dramatic words are being used by European politicians nowadays: the *EURO* should guarantee peace on the European continent *et cetera.* But: **it creates the very conflicts between a 'hard' and a 'soft' European economic zone.** But a 'weak' Euro' would, most probably, also be no alternative: restructuring of ailing European enterprises will be postponed; with capital markets most probably reacting by pushing up interest rates (Neue Zuercher Zeitung, 16th of June, 1997: 9), thus prolonging the vicious downward cycle of the European political economy. The only real alternative would be to follow a socio-liberal flexible growth path, combined with the measures of harmonization, described above, as the basis of an EMU project compatible with global and European social reform

(vii)   the problem of the Italian economy merits special attention in the EURO zone (Beirat, 1996). The performance of austerity of the Italian economy over the last years was remarkable in capitalist terms, and unemployment has declined from the 1996/97 record of 12.1% to 11.9% (IFRI, 1998). But the arithmetic of the EU Council provides the real answer to the now resolved question of Italian EMU membership: the 10 countries which fulfilled two, three or four Maastricht criteria by 1996 (Belgium, Germany, Finland, Netherlands, France, Austria, Luxembourg, Denmark, Ireland, United Kingdom) would have had 55 votes on the EU council, while the *'outs'* (Sweden and the European *'mezzogiorno')* would have had enough votes (32) to block voting in the Council, so it was decided to take on board the *'weaklings'* except Greece (Beirat, 1996; our own calculations from Weixner and Wimmer, 1997). This perspective could have also blocked the project of extending Europe eastward; but the price will now be a more vulnerable Euro. Another plausibility, though, could be a an increased massive inflow of capital, including laundered one, into Europe during the first years of the *EURO,* to be followed by a crisis of the US $ in 2001/2002/2003. The harshest times of the *EURO* would come, when Asia surges upward

(viii)   All this will lead to a 'deficit' of democracy in the Union; in accordance with the liberal doctrine that the weakening of democracy is - *inter alia* - the result of the geographical distance between the locality, where decisions are taken, and the citizens, who are the subject of these decisions (Klaus, 1997)

(ix)   1996, Portugal, Spain, Italy and Greece did not meet any of the first four criteria; Sweden missed three criteria; Germany and Austria two; and the rest of the Union at least one of the criteria (Weixner and Wimmer, 1997). Only Luxembourg met all the five Maastricht criteria (Weixner and Wimmer, 1997; Rothschild, 1997)

(x)   on 'Black Friday', July 30th 1993, the Bundesbank had to buy foreign currencies to the tune of $bn 30 DM under the old EMS (Weixner and Wimmer, 1997). Now, the political conflict lines in Europe would suggest: either a 'weaker' *EURO* against the Dollar and the Yen, which is good for the European export industries and the European South on the world markets; an option that will end in the inevitable flight into real estate and the Dollar by the accumulated wealth in Germany (and, to a minor extent in the other countries) to the tune of over DMbn 4000 to DMbn 5000 as the immediate consequence. Maastricht is realized at the cost of transforming the European East and South into a mirror-picture of the process of the integration of the New Laender into Germany after 1989. The vast size of accumulated savings in Germany, together with the savings of the European shadow economy, are an immense pool of potential speculative money, should the *EURO* project get into real trouble. Anything can happen: transfers into US $, real estate, Yen, Swiss Francs, Swedish Crones. European Central Bank official currency reserves were in February 2000 at $bn 383.8 EURO; while the EURO's main competitors had the following international reserves in $bn: Japan 222.4; USA 146.0; China 152.8; Taiwan 94.2. Seen in such a way, parts of the political class that rules Germany knew well enough, why it insisted all along on a 'hard *EURO*' - to the detriment of European export industries. But you cannot expect banking capital to rule against banking capital. In a real battle over international finances, the European strategic currency reserves are small compared to the Asian reserves, brought about by the enormous accumulated current account balances over the years - even after the crash in 1997. In 1997, shortly before the crash, Taiwan alone had currency reserves to the tune of $bn 88.0; Japan 218.2; China 114.0; Hong Kong 69.6, Singapore 77.3; while Switzerland had 35.3; and the USA only 56.2, with the big European economies like France, Spain, the Netherlands and Italy holding reserves to the tune of around 25 to 60 billion $ each. Well-established German financial institutes more and more propagate Dollar savings accounts - a clear sign how real the transfer of German savings into US $ already has become, only temporarily halted by the currency crisis in Asia. It is significant, that the European *mezzogiorno* states Spain (60.6) and Italy (45.4) had increased their foreign currency reserves by about $bn 30 in the late 1990s, and together already have larger reserves than the Federal Republic of Germany

(xi)   public opinion in the richer countries of the Union is mostly against the whole project, with rejection rates in 1996 already ranging from 46% in Austria to 64% in Denmark (Weixner and Wimmer, 1997)

(xii)   the erosion of the *EMU*-project found its counterpart in the erosion of the state of public finances in the Federal Republic of Germany. The economic consequences of Mr. Theo Waigel were very clear to judge: he presided over the doubling of Germany's public sector debt to $bn 1259 during his record tenure as Germany's longest-serving finance minister. His 'defiant alchemism' in his bitter dispute with the Bundesbank over German gold reserves was but the last straw in a long chain of events *(Financial Times,* Weekend, May 31st, June 1st, 1997)

<table>
<tr><td>(xiii)</td><td>the shadow economy will partially have to come out from the darkness, most probably increasing the already existing capital flight into the Dollar, the Yen, the Stock Exchange, and into real estate</td></tr>
<tr><td>(xiv)</td><td>the Maastricht criteria will prove to be an instrument of anti-Keynesian global governance (Raffer, 1997). But the reception of neo-liberal economics by the EU-Commission and the Maastricht heads of governments was highly selective: while they seem to imply the importance of 5 monetary criteria, the Union overlooks day by day other neo-liberal prescriptions in important policy areas - from human capital policy over trade policy to agriculture</td></tr>
<tr><td>(xv)</td><td>if General Motors, AT & T, and individual households had been required to balance their budgets in the manner applied to the Federal Government (which in the US is under similar pressures as the governments in Europe), there would be no corporate bonds, no bank loans, and many fewer automobiles, telephones and houses (Vickrey, 1996). The Maastricht criteria are part and parcel of the 15 fatal fallacies of financial fundamentalism</td></tr>
<tr><td>(xvi)</td><td>a more useful arrangement than Maastricht would have been to achieve first a certain degree of European political cohesion in order to arrive at a more consensual democratic and better enforceable economic framework (Rothschild, 1997; Amin, 1997)</td></tr>
<tr><td>(xvii)</td><td>there are fundamental differences between the 'freedoms' for capital and labor - the first can be moved without having to learn a language and without leaving behind friends and a familiar environment - labor even when organized in a union cannot threaten to transfer as to another firm or country. The freedom of labor does not present a countervailing power to the bargaining power obtained by business through the complete liberalization of capital movements; on the contrary; that bargaining power is strengthened by the uninhibited possibility of attracting workers from low-wage EU countries (Rothschild, 1997). The basic policy approach of Maastricht and the Commission overlooks this important fact</td></tr>
<tr><td>(xviii)</td><td>real outcomes in economic life, such as growth, employment, productivity, development, income distribution, do not figure at all in the so-called convergence criteria (Rothschild, 1997)</td></tr>
<tr><td>(xix)</td><td>full employment is a good precondition against inflation</td></tr>
<tr><td>(xx)</td><td>the harmonization of social conditions in the Union remains one of the most important tasks for an effective, real monetary union, because this would lay down the conditions for a convergence in the real welfare conditions of the countries concerned (Rothschild, 1997)</td></tr>
<tr><td>(xxi)</td><td>with the Maastricht criteria, Kalecki's prediction, dated 1943, about a political business cycle with the entrepreneurs losing any real interest in full employment would come true (Rothschild, 1997; Raffer, 1997)</td></tr>
<tr><td>(xxii)</td><td>the institutionalized acceptance of neo-classical economics, inherent in the Maastricht criteria, is only one-sided. The Free Market optimism which had been developed on the assumptions of atomistic competition between powerless firms is transferred to a world of oligolopolies and mammoth corporations (Rothschild, 1997).</td></tr>
<tr><td>(xxiii)</td><td>the negative attitude to special protective treatment for the poorer regions and their development is the more astonishing in view of the fact that the Union is not opening its own economic frontiers world-wide (Rothschild, 1997)</td></tr>
</table>

(xxiv)   the conflict between the North and the South would increase instead of decrease under a scenario of a strict implementation of the Maastricht criteria. But the eastward extension of the Union would be more important than monetary union (Amin, 1997). Maastricht-style monetary union would, especially for the new members of the Union in the East, mean a two-class type of European integration. For that reason alone, monetary union plus eastward extension for the European East are a chance, not to be missed (Koehler/Tausch, 2000).

Fallacy number three now consists in the assumption, that you can exclude the shadow economy and its accumulated savings from the *EURO* debate. A new currency will mean for the gangsters: open the money suitcases and try to exchange or place any bill that is not yet placed. The battle over the *EMU*-project now unfolds on the international financial markets. On paper, the USA face the same current account balance trends as Germany faced them - to be weighted at any rate by the role of the $ in international transactions. 'Their' American-Asian-Pacific economic space attracts - mainly via the Japanese bank - a large percentage of the surplus capital of the world, partly also, because both legal and illegal funds, flow to that region. Japan's high official current account balance pointed in a downward direction, but currency reserves went up - a clear indicator for the hypothesis, that both legal and illegal world surplus capital flows into Japan. Only experience will be able to tell us, how the currency crisis in East Asia was connected to major possible 'tectonical shifts' in international crime, international finance and surplus flows.

It is entirely possible that the briefer strength period of the European currencies in the run-up to the *EURO*, is now followed by a renewed Asian-oriented flow. Let us not underestimate especially the economic power of the Japanese *Yakuza,* the richest criminal organization in the world. The profit opportunities for the international speculators are enormous - 1997: rock the boat in Asia, jump in profits number one. Method: lending of local overvalued currencies, selling it into $ or European currencies. Pay back calmly your credits in local currencies, which are severely down. Now, 1998-2001: perhaps rock the boat in Europe. Method: lending of Lira or Euro, selling it into $ or Asian currencies. Pay back calmly your Lira or Euro credits, which are worth nothing anymore. Now, 2000, 2001 or 2002: rock the boat in America: Method: lending of $, selling it into Asian currencies. Pay back calmly your $ credits, which are worth nothing anymore as Asia recovers and the Arrighi cycle of financial transfers from the Atlantic to the Pacific nears its finish; America then stumbles, because of its negative current account (see also Guilhem Fabre, *Le Monde Diplomatique,* April 2000).

On a world level, it is absolutely unrealistic to overlook the power of international drug cartels and other criminal groups. 20 'narco states' (soft on drugs, according to the US State Department terminology, US State Department, 1996) had a considerable power over international reserves. **The leading 'drug countries' with comparable data (see list at the end of the graph) controlled already $bn 324.137 currency reserves, while the 10 leading western industrial democracies and financial places (Japan, USA, Germany, France, United Kingdom, Italy, Spain, Austria, Switzerland, Sweden) still controlled $bn 739.707.** After the three-fold rock the boat strategy around the globe is finished, the gangsters and speculators will have been able to shift then this relationship decisively, to perhaps $bn 500 to 500 or even worse. Already today, an alarming proportion of OECD country currency reserves also stem from the proceeds of money laundering, as the comparison between current account balances and international reserves suggests:

Graph 9.14: International reserves of 20 *narco* states and 10 leading western democracies

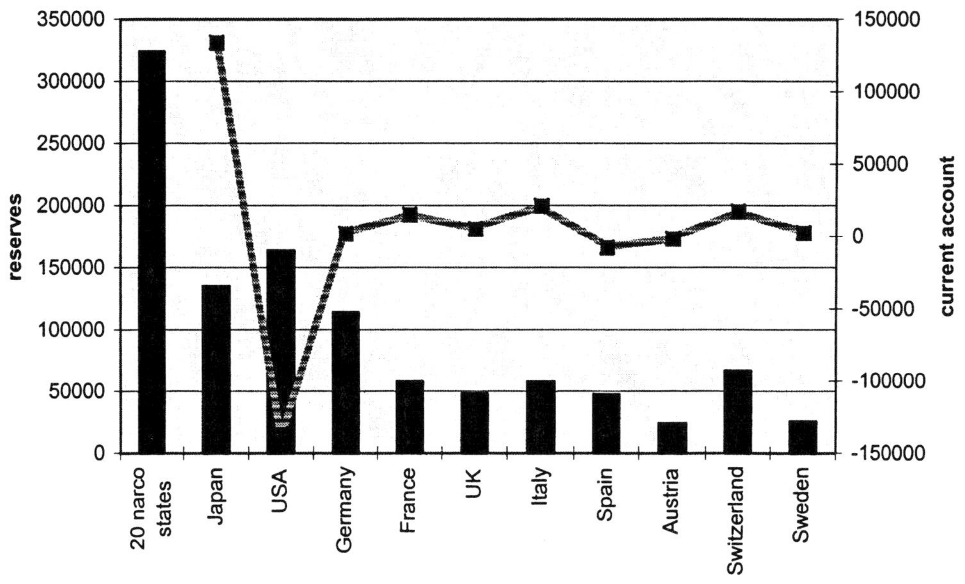

Legend: international reserves - bars, left-hand scale; current accounts - dotted line, right-hand scale in 1000 $. The currency reserves of the narco states in millions of $ are the following:

Bolivia	793
Brazil	38492
Taiwan	97653
China	57781
Dom R	259
Ecuador	2003
Guatemala	943
India	24221
Colombia	7862
Lao PDR	68
Lebanon	4210
Malaysia	26339
Mexico	6441
Myanmar	518
Nigeria	1649
Pakistan	3716
Paraguay	1030
Peru	7420
Thailand	30280
Venezuela	12459

| 20 narco states | 324137 |

Definition: A narco state is understood as a country, figuring on the *list of statements of explanation* by the US Department of State International Narcotics Control Strategy Report, 1996

Even the most powerful capitalist nations are - due to the mechanisms of international financial markets, practically at the mercy of the currency reserves accumulated in the 20 leading narco states of the South (international reserves):

Graph 9.15: The share of *narco* states in international reserves of the main world financial centers

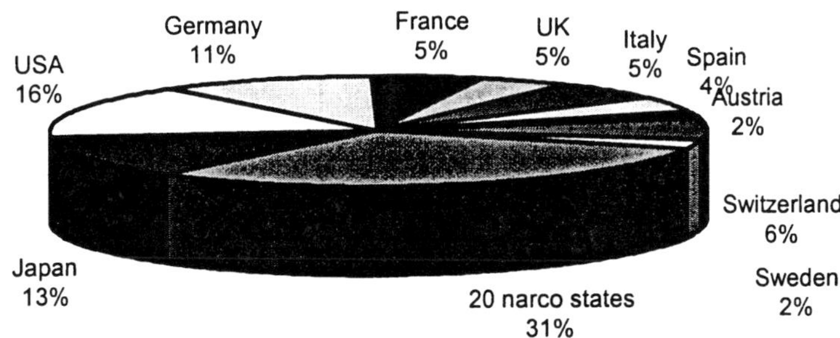

Legend: the share of different groupings in world-wide currency reserve holdings, end-1997. Our own calculations from Fischer Weltalmanach and the international press.

In the direct comparison between Japan, the US and Germany, we also see the basic weakness of the *Deutschmark* against the main contenders:

Graph 9.16: currency reserves and current account balances since 1990 in the world system - Germany, Japan and the USA compared

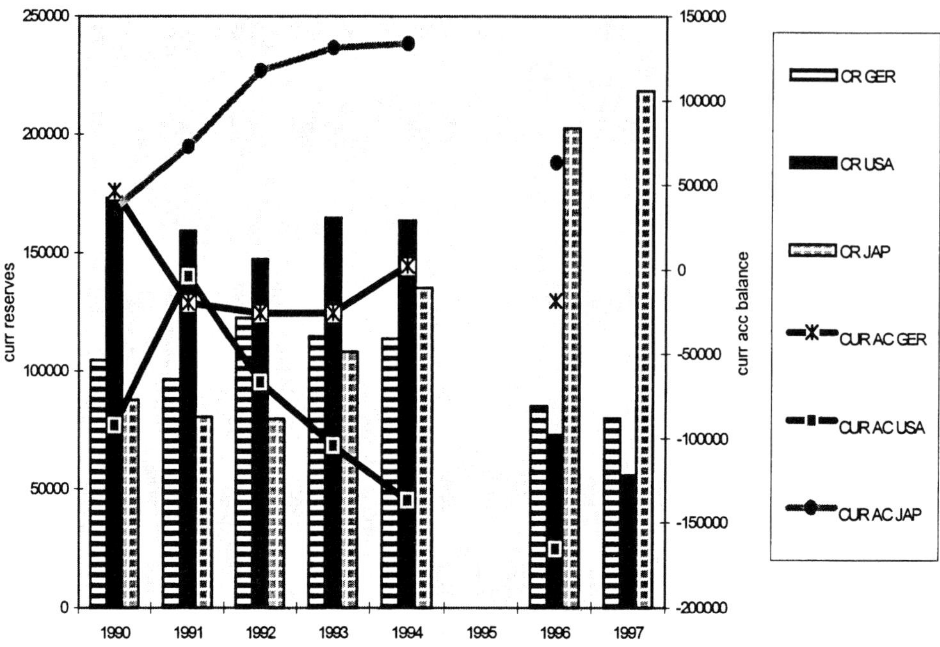

Legend: current account balances: columns (right-hand scale); currency reserves: lines (left-hand scale)
Legend: data and projections on the current account balances of Germany, Japan, and the United States of America from 1990 onwards

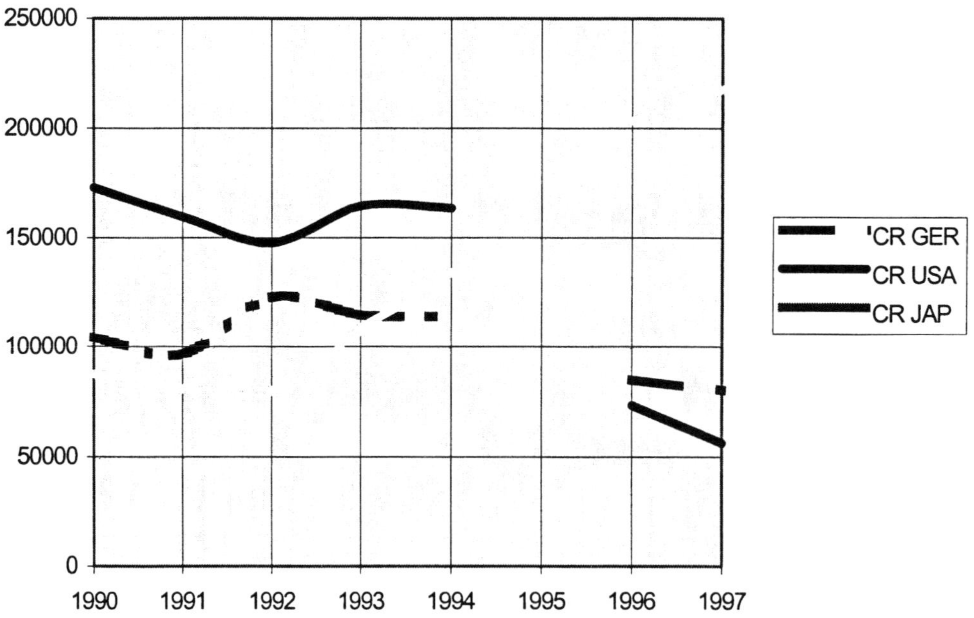

Legend: currency reserves in the major capitalist centers from 1990 onwards

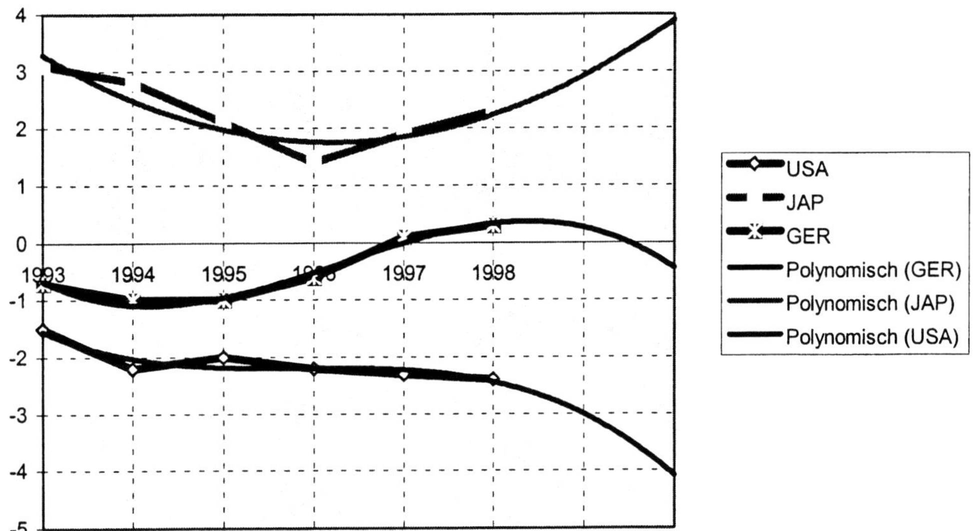

Legend: current account balances per GNP; and projections about their future development. Sources: Data for the last Graph are IFRI (1998), the other data were from Fischer Weltalmanach and *Economist:*

	CR GER	CR USA	CR JAP	**CUR AC GER**	CUR AC USA	CUR AC JAP
1990	**104547**	173094	87828	**46800**	-92160	35870
1991	**96657**	159273	80626	**-19497**	-3690	72905
1992	**122686**	147526	79697	**-25563**	-66380	117640
1993	**114822**	164620	107989	**-25563**	-103925	131510
1994	**113841**	163591	135145	**2327**	-136484	133900
1995						
1996	**85300**	73200	202700	**-18500**	-165100	63400
1997	**80200**	56200	218200			

Asia's hour will still come, while Maastricht tries to achieve a stability that it can never achieve.

One of the real reasons of financial instability on a global scale is - as we already explained - to be found in the ever-larger share of drug money in international reserves and savings. **The annual financial volume of organized crime - at $bn 1500 - is much larger than the $bn 400 world direct foreign investments and approximately five times the size of the currency holdings of the European Central Bank. The drug lords could ruin not only the EURO, but the entire international financial system.** Maastricht walks another path - that of financial austerity, to bring about financial stability. America tried another strategy: that of supply-side upswing. The waving 'working poverty' US cycle (under Bush more poverty than work uder Clinton), on the other hand, will also definitely come to a halt. World system theory argues, that hegemonic capital leaves the hegemonic centers during eras of the de-legitimatization of the world system, after the period of world hegemony, lasting one Kondratieff cycle, came to an end (Chase-Dunn and Hall, 1997).

Another fallacy, fallacy four, of the Maastricht process is that it excludes the option of full employment. UNDP-data 1996 show that labor force participation rates and inflation rates in the highly developed countries had quite a negative correlation with each other which flattens off only at very high levels of employment, thus indicating certain limits of the 'NAIRU' debate *('non-accelerating inflation rate of unemployment')*(Beirat, 1996). Maastricht policy brings about not only short-term, but also middle range and long-term unemployment; which - in the long run - is a very costly strategy, even increasing the very inflation process.

Graph 9.17: unemployment, labor force participation rate and inflation in developed capitalism

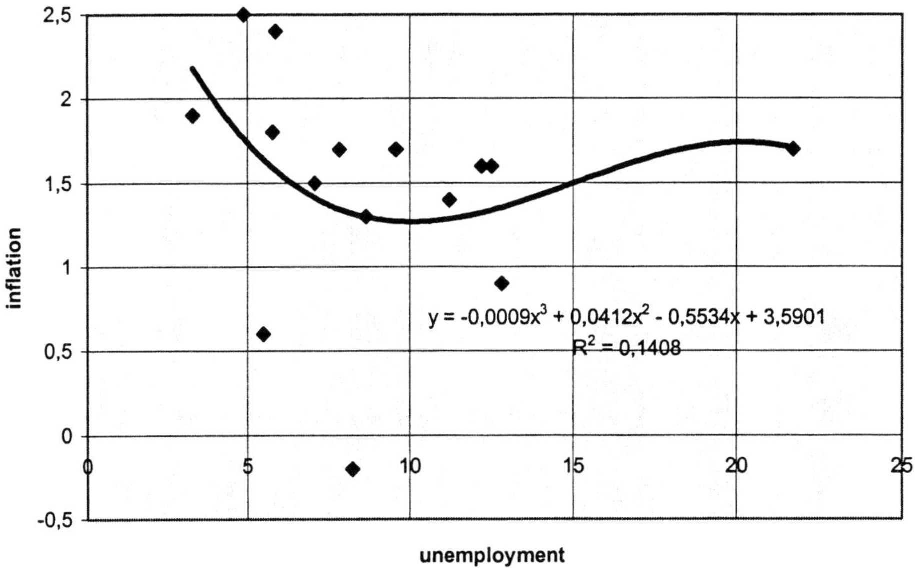

Legend: unemployment (x-axis) and inflation (y-axis) in developed OECD democracies. Data: our own compilations from Fischer Weltalmanach, *The Economist,* and other international media.

Since official unemployment statistics tell us only half the story about unemployment, the negative influence of labor force participation rates on inflation are telling indeed:

9.17 (continued)

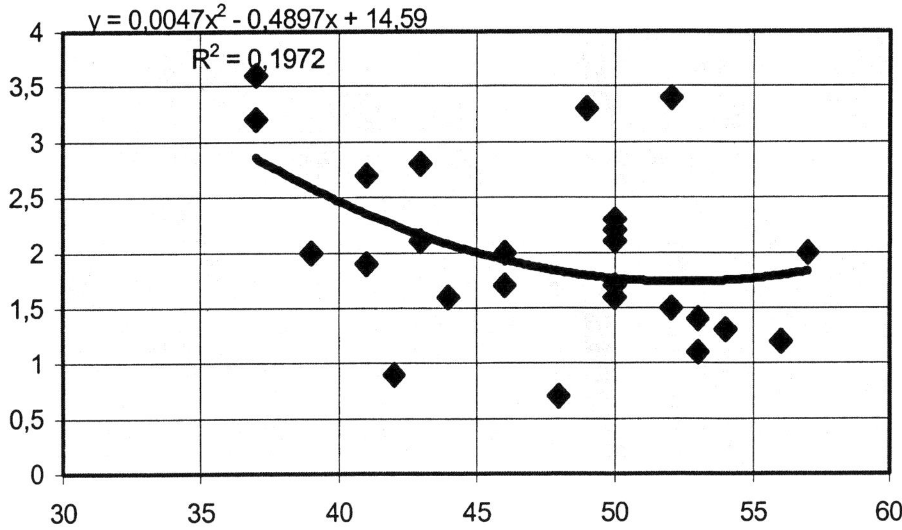

Legend: employment rates (x-axis) and inflation rates (y-axis). Sources: the following UNDP 1996 data were used:

	LFPR	inflation
Canada	53	1,4
USA	50	1,7
Japan	52	3,4
NL	46	1,7
NOR	50	2,2
SF	52	1,5
France	44	1,6
Iceland	56	1,2
Swed	54	1,3
Spain	41	2,7
Australia	50	1,6
Belgium	41	1,9
Austria	46	2
NZ	48	0,7
CH	53	1,1
UK	50	2,3
DK	57	2
GER	50	2,1
IRE	37	3,6

ITA	43	2,1
GRE	42	0,9
ISR	39	2
LUX	43	2,8
MAL	37	3,2
POR	49	3,3

Fallacy five consists in overlooking what a 'hard' *EURO* will mean for the European exporter. Like in the former GDR, it would mean an enormous upward push in the price of export goods on world markets. This analysis maintains all along, that factors, like the position in the world economy, are far more important variables than mere monetary aggregates. So why should Germany push for a 'hard *EURO*'? The hypothesis, that German corporations and banks, by a policy of a hard *EURO*, rather tend towards eliminating present and future unwelcome competitors from the closed European home market, instead of providing the European backbone in the trilateral competition between Asia, America, and Europe, finds further support by a look at the current account balances of the world's leading industrial nations, in comparison with the EU, by around end 1996:

Graph 9.18: European current account balances by international comparison

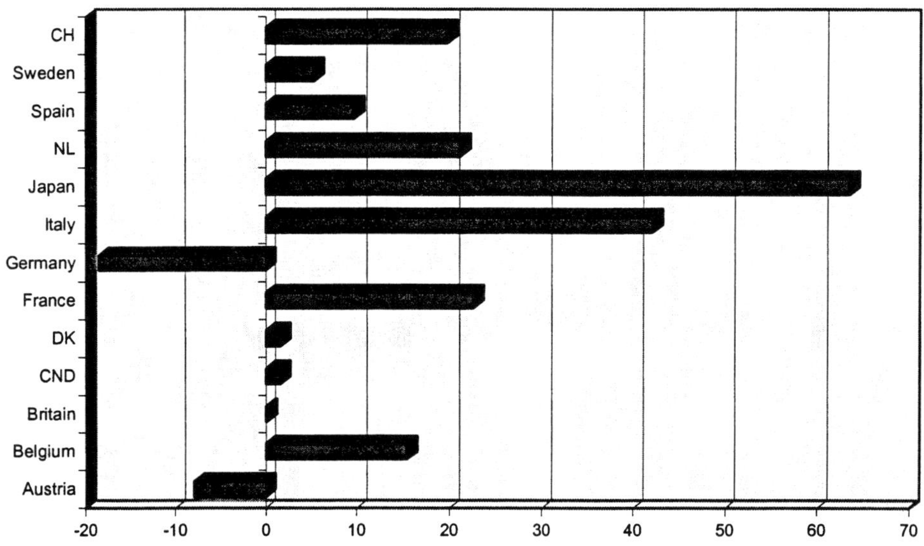

Legend: current account balances in OECD democracies. Sources: for this and the following graphs, we used *Fischer Weltalmanach* and *Economist* data

When proponents of a hard *EURO* in Germany (and Austria) maintained that it will mean a welcome future exclusion of competitive de-valuations, this argument overlooks the fact, that hundreds of countries can still competitively de-value, while the less than a dozen member countries of *EMU* cannot. Faced with an ever stiffer competitive pressure from the world markets, Germany and her northern European partners indeed seem to be inclined to a policy of monetarily regulating, if not dominating, the chances for export of the European continent. **Only a 'hard' *EURO* would prevent profoundly enough the unwelcome low-value-currency-driven competition from the European *mezzogiorno* countries, a competition, which is, *nota bene*,**

partly the result of the run-away of the very German (and other Northern European) productive capital abroad under present-day social and policy regulations. A third path would be to 'recycle' German and other northern European savings into real transfers towards the Mediterranean EU countries, and later, the East. But it would be politically unthinkable in the long run. The story of exchange rates over 1996/97 is quite different from what politicians sometimes pretend. The strength of the Deutschmark was a myth, just as the EURO revealed it's weaknesses after 1998:

Graph 9.19: trade-weighted exchange rates since 1990

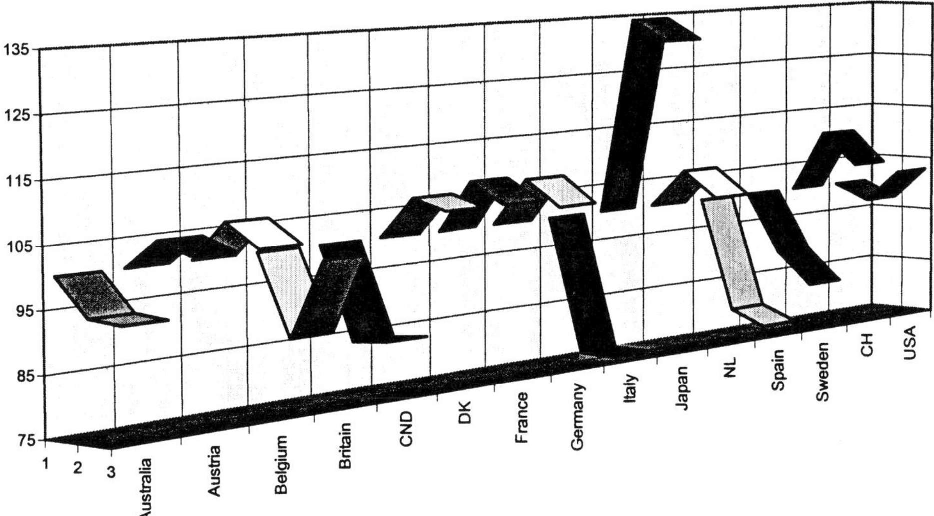

Legend: trade-weighted exchange rates of major OECD currencies since 1990 (=100). Our own compilations from the Dialog-archive *(http://www.dialogselect.com)*

Fallacy six consisted in overlooking the real weakness of the D-Mark, that led to the real weakness of the EURO, and it also consists in overlooking that this trend will continue. Short of direct speculation, the following swings could be tentatively interpreted, without maintaining any rigor from that first inspection of the empirical data:

Graph 9.20: The projected rise of the $ and the fall of major currencies

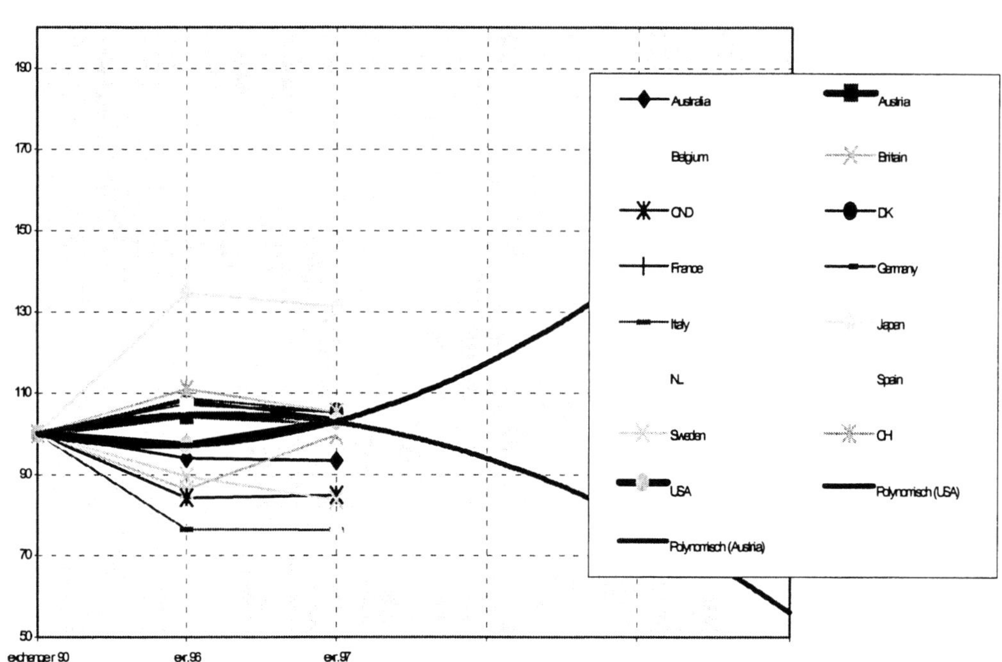

Legend: our own compilations about trade-weighted exchange rates (1990=100); see above

Already, in more analytical terms, the following cross-national analyses from the ups and downs of the exchange rates were possible in 1997/98, using the data base of the *'Economist'* newsmagazine (Economic Indicators, comprising GDP growth, unemployment, inflation, current account balance per GDP, growth rate of broad money supply (M2), interest rates (banks prime rate), foreign reserves) for 12 leading economies in the world. I reprent these results without further comments here - a true prophesy needs no alteration. In the website discussion version of this book, I said in 1998:

Available data series also show, that the obsession with inflation should give way to an obsession with economic growth. ***The ups and downs of the exchange rate are determined primarily by economic growth ('the basics'), and not by monetary aggregates.*** *Since I am not a monetary economist, such a heterodoxy does not bother me at all. Thus, we expect an underlying, basic strength of the US $ for 1997 and 1998, since America will have a stronger growth than Europe:*

Table 9.12: the determinants of the 1996/97 exchange rate rise or fall

interest r	**dyn gdp**	inflation	current acc	constant
-0,194708194	3,906341351	0,198525086	0,651907557	-11,13735669
0,492759217	1,853312658	1,037989266	0,555292814	4,812306156
0,571097567				
3,32883147	10			

-0,395138614	**2,107761653**	0,191259286	1,173988824	t-Test

dyn m2	**dyn gdp**	inflation	current acc	constant
-0,581775269	3,836251645	-0,436197965	0,43290356	-7,733318113
0,416297207	1,848356602	0,95437895	0,348103742	3,066290195
0,57734929				
3,415049808	10			

-1,397499812	**2,075493246**	-0,457049021	1,243605017	t-Test

Legend: as in all EXCEL 5.0 outprints in this work, first row: unstandardized regression coefficients, second row: standard errors, last row: t-Test. The values immediately below the standard errors are R^2 (third row, left side entry), F, and degrees of freedom (fourth row).

The case for reflating Europe's economies can even be stated in a provocative fashion:

Graph 9.21: growth, consumer price rises (1997 in %) and changes in the trade-weighted exchange rate, 1996/97

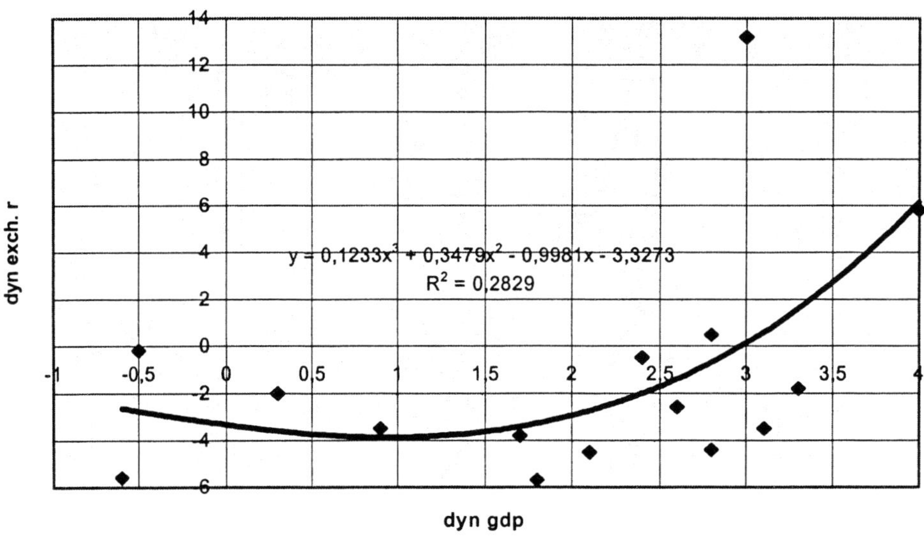

Legend: economic growth (x-axis) and growth of the value of the exchange rate (y-axis) in major OECD democracies. Our own compilations from Economist and Dialog archive.

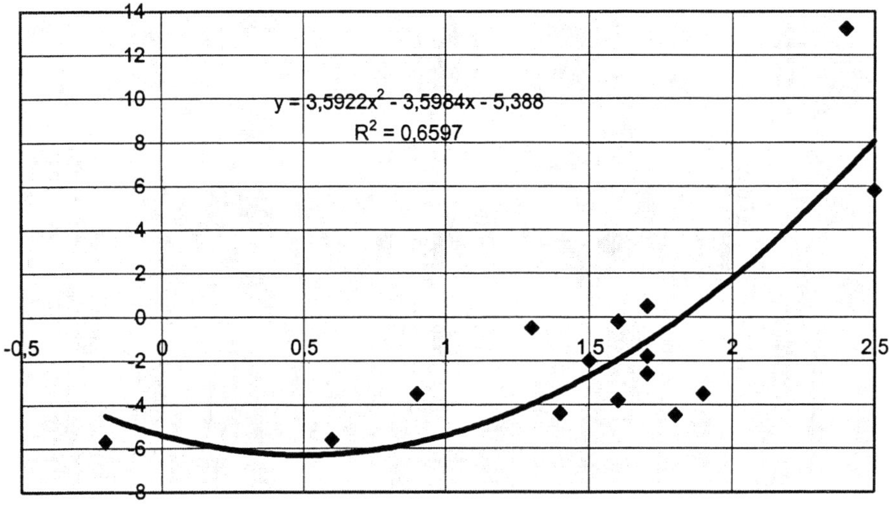

Legend: inflation (x-axis) and exchange rate dynamism (y-axis); see above

Post-hoc predictions from an **anti-shock-strategy model** for the real observable data 1996-97 show, that the Graph above strikingly corresponds to realities:

dyn exchange rate	trend dyn exchange rate 1997	
-0,5	-4	Australia
-2	-2,7	Austria
-3,8	-1,9	Belgium
13,2	6,7	Britain
0,5	-1,1	CND
-1,8	-1,1	DK
-3,5	-5,7	France
-4,4	-3,4	Germany
-0,2	-1,9	Italy
-3,5	0,7	Japan
-4,5	-0,2	NL
-2,6	-1,1	Spain
-5,7	-4,5	Sweden
-5,6	-6,3	CH
5,8	8,1	USA

One consequence of this **empirical relationship between inflation and upward movements in the trade-weighted exchange rates** is a prediction of the behavior of the major currencies on the world markets in 1998. The prediction was based on the Economist's prediction of inflation in Europe and in the major other economies of the world in 1998

Economist predictions of inflation for 1998

predicted inflation 98	
2,9	Australia
2,3	Austria
2,1	Belgium
3,2	Britain
2,1	CND
2,7	DK
1,9	France
2,1	Germany
2,6	Italy
1,2	Japan
2,6	NL
2,6	Spain
1,7	Sweden
1,4	CH
3,1	USA

The consequence of this assumption then would be the prediction of the exchange rate dynamics for 1998:

trend dyn exchange rate 1998	
-3,9	Australia
-2,6	Austria
-1,85	Belgium
6,77	Britain
-1,02	CND
-1,02	DK
-5,62	France
-3,29	Germany
-1,85	Italy
0,85	Japan
-0,12	NL
-1,02	Spain
-4,44	Sweden
-6,16	CH
8,18	USA

I said in 1998: If you want to invest your money in Sterling or US $, do it. Do not go in for Swiss Franks, Deutschmark, Swedish crowns, or French Francs, or Lira:

Graph 9.22: $ and Sterling - superstars 1998. Predicted exchange rate dynamics, 1998 in %

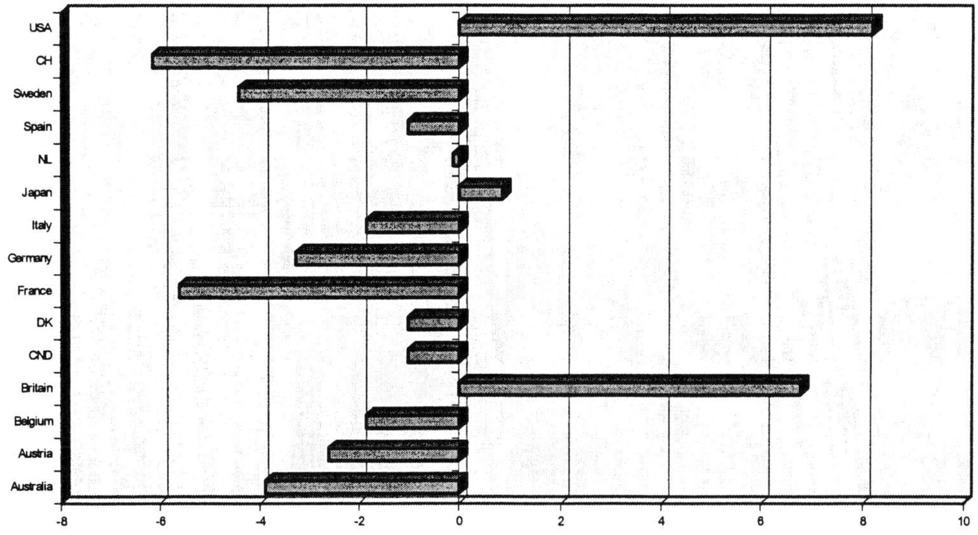

Legend: our predictions for the 1998 exchange rate dynamism

Fallacy seven is equally important as the six previous ones. It consists in overlooking the effects of illegal money on Europe's poorer East. A hard *EURO* would attract an enormous amount of illegal Eastern capital to Western Europe, while the crooks will not hesitate to change their partially existing D-Mark wealth into $ or other non-*EURO* currencies, should the need arise. Market imperfections and the peripheral position of Eastern Europe in the world economy cause a tendency towards a secular current account balance deficit in most of the new democracies (at least those with historical records of big landholding and a weak national state), that can only be closed by the shadow economy, including illegal migration and money laundering:

Table 9.13: economic performance in Central and Eastern Europe, 1997:

	GDP	budget	unemployment	inflation	current acc	reserves	debt
Bulgaria	11,6	-12	16,3	1972,5	0	0,5	10,3
Croatia	18,8	-0,9	16,7	4,4	-1,5	2,2	4,1
Czech R	52,7	0,5	3,9	6,7	-4,5	12	18,1
Estonia	4,2	0,2	4,5	9,2	-0,4	0,6	0,4
Hungary	44,4	-1,4	11	18,8	-0,5	9,7	27,6
Latvia	5,4	0	7,5	8,8	-0,3	0,7	0,4
Lithuania	7,7	-2,3	6,2	7,3	-0,4	0,7	1,2
Poland	115,7	-0,9	13	15,3	-1,1	21,1	40,7
Romania	35,5	-0,1	7,2	176,8	-0,2	1	6,9
Russia	450,7	-6,8	9,7	15,1	1,6	11,3	122,8
Slovakia	18,8	-0,5	13,4	6,5	-0,2	3,5	7,8
Slovenia	18,4	-0,4	14,5	8,2	0	2,4	4

GDP, current account, reserves and debt are given in $bn, budget is given as percent of GDP, unemployment and inflation are the usual percent rates. Our own compilations from *Economist,* 1998, current issues

Strict financial discipline indeed brings about less unemployment and not more, by international cross-national comparison. But rising unemployment pushes inflation up, and not down.

Graph 9.23: stability criteria and economic performance in the transformation countries

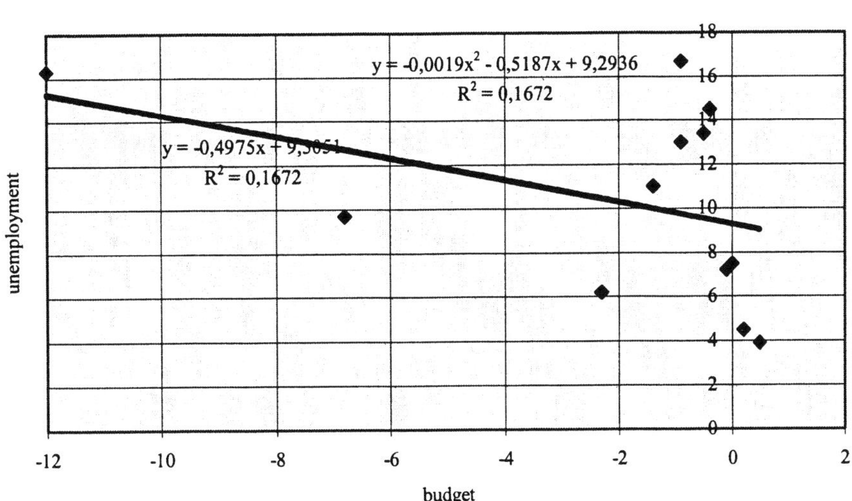

Legend: government budget balance (x-axis) and unemployment (y-axis). Data: *Economist,* 1998

**Graph 9.24: unemployment and inflation - the evidence from Eastern Europe
and the former USSR**

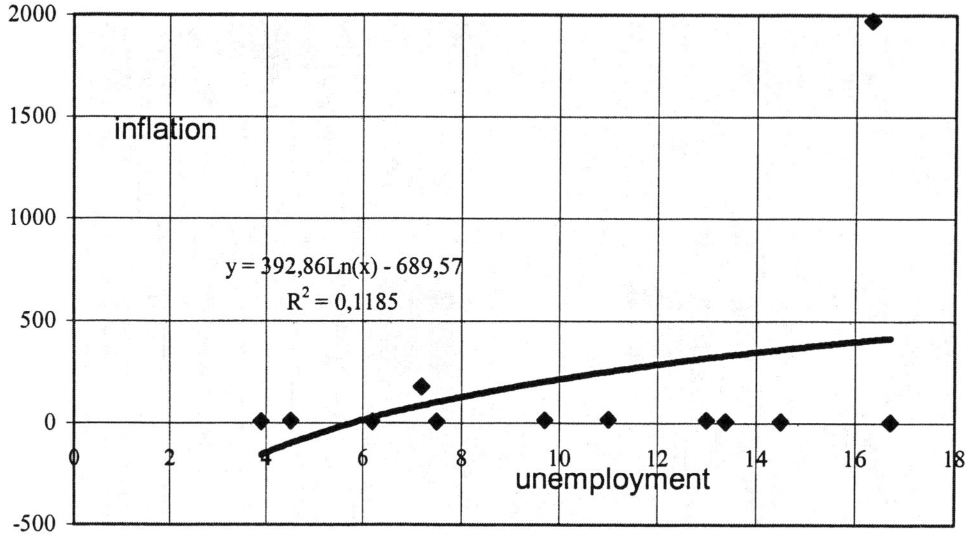

Legend: unemployment (x-axis) and inflation (y-axis). Data: *Business Central Europe,* current issues

Thirdly, current account balances determine only to a certain extent international reserves, and indeed, excess reserves are a good signal for money-laundering processes taking place in the economy, but such excess reserves dampen inflation. The transformation economy, successor to peripheral socialism 1945 - 1989, Nazi occupation 1938/39 - 1945 and peripheral capitalism 1450 - 1939, is characterized, as Amin teaches us, by a secular current account balance deficit, that has to be closed by almost any means - including imports of 'illegal savings'. Like all wealth-owning capitalist classes, the crooks of Eastern Europe become very interested in financial stability and the canon of 'property rights', once their illegal money is parked. The right-hand upper outlayers in our following graph - the Czech Republic, Hungary, Poland, Slovakia, all have nowadays a much higher proportion of foreign currency reserves to their GDP as one might expect from the current account balance. Only the first, rising parts of our curves - or the straight fitting line - correspond to economic wisdom, while much of the rest is due to the global casino of money laundering and capital flight:

Graph 9.25: reserves and current account balances in the world system

1) Eastern Europe

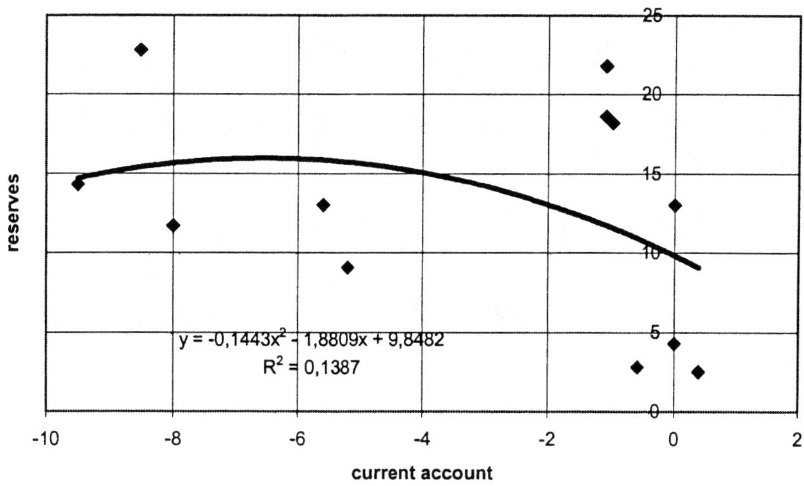

Legend: current account balance (in $ bn) (x-axis) and currency reserves (in $ bn) (y-axis). Data: *Business Central Europe,* current issues

2) developed western democracies

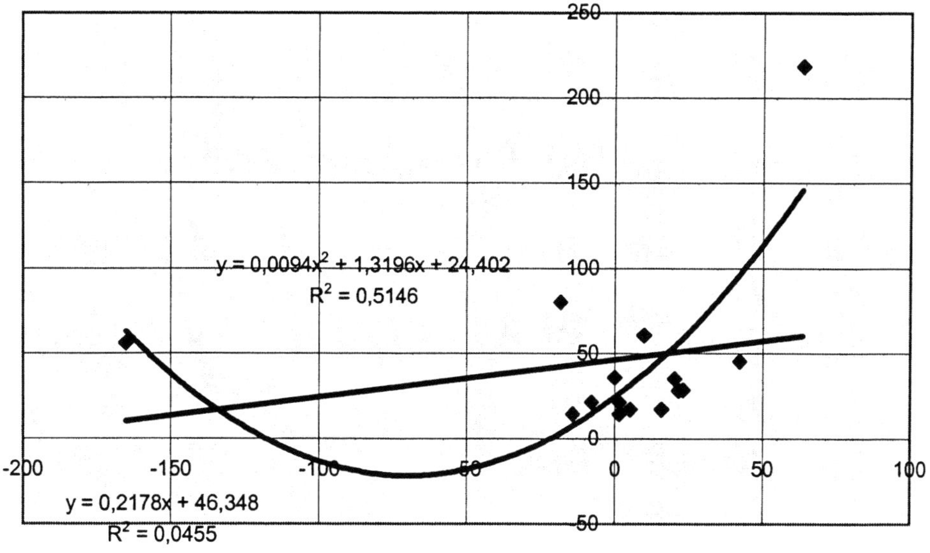

Legend: see above; source: Fischer Weltalmanach and UNDP

3) developing countries

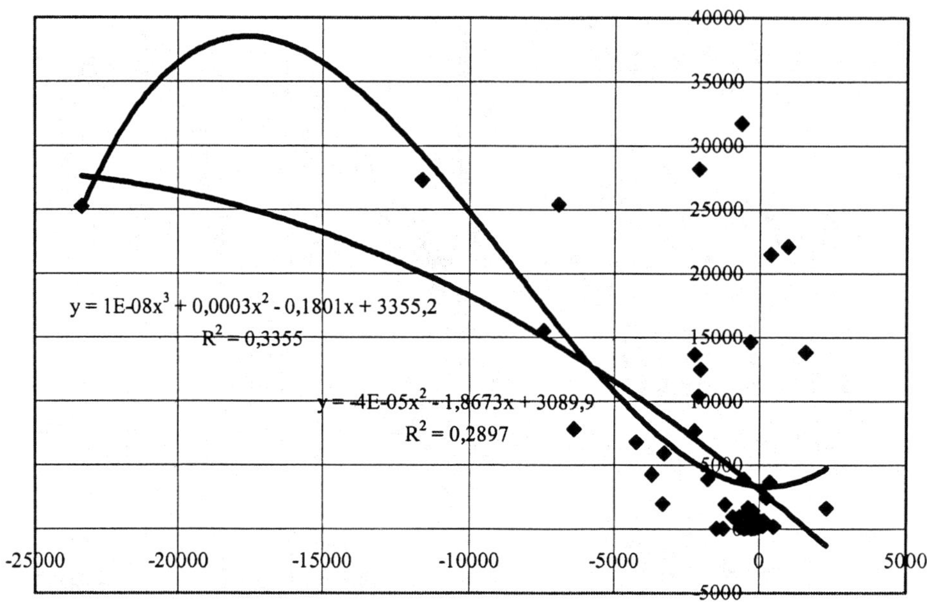

Legend: see above.

Eastern European inflation, to a great part, is also linked to the problem of illegal capital inflows that boost reserves in excess of the available current account balances, contributing to a dampening of the inflation process in the semi-periphery:

Graph 9.26: 'excess reserves' (money-laundering) and inflation

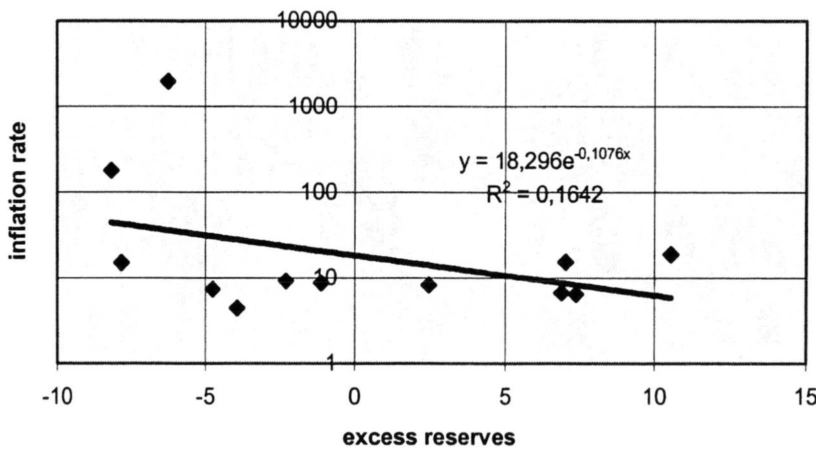

Legend: regression residuals from Graph 9.25 1), above (x-axis) and the inflation rate (y-axis). As to the data sources, see 9.25; plus EXCEL non-linear trend-line projections and residual value calculations. Put in simple terms: the more 'unaccounted' and 'strange' reserve currency inflows, the lower is the inflation rate.

Thus, one might say, that the stability of the East European exchange rates depends on these very same huge semi-legal and illegal reserves, that were accumulated by the opening of the twin Pandora's boxes of open borders and liberalized world financial markets:

Table 9.14: stability conditions of Eastern currencies

inflation	current acc	**reserves**	debt	growth	constant
-177,34449	-36,68374	204,515725	15,3515777	0,35514332	-1558,1171
117,86279	41,2055865	104,321881	129,842067	1,40047248	850,153922
0,60849828					
1,86512062	6				
-1,504669	-0,8902613	**1,9604298**	0,1182327	0,25358822	T-test
inflation	current acc	**reserves**	debt	growth	constant

Legend: as in all EXCEL 5.0 outprints in this work, first row: unstandardized regression coefficients, second row: standard errors, last row: t-Test. The values immediately below the standard errors are $R^{\wedge 2}$ (third row, left side entry), F, and degrees of freedom (fourth row).

But dependency becomes decisive, when long-term growth perspectives of East and Central European economies are being determined. There are indeed 'the balance of payments constraints' on economic growth: **not only the stability of the Eastern currency,** *but also short-term Eastern economic growth becomes largely dependent on the import of 'narco' and other laundered money, that neatly shows up in the international reserves statistics* (see also Chapter 8 for the results on a more long-term basis at the level of the world system).

**Table 9.15: the balance of payments constraint on economic growth
in the transformation states**

budget	unemployment	inflation	current acc	**reserves**	constant
0,04146493	0,04189921	0,00122375	0,15937235	1,42604392	2,90491826
0,13145571	0,24323974	0,00246502	0,19867407	0,43335864	2,98086477
0,86923249	2,40001513				
7,97659149	6				
229,728731	34,5604357				
0,31542889	0,17225476	0,49644786	0,80217993	**3,29067843**	0,97452199
budget	unemployment	inflation	current acc	**reserves**	constant

Legend: as in all EXCEL 5.0 outprints in this work, first row: unstandardized regression coefficients, second row: standard errors, last row: t-Test. The values immediately below the standard errors are $R^{\wedge 2}$ (third row, left side entry), F, and degrees of freedom (fourth row).

One plausibility is, of course, that the Central and East European economies, sandwiched by the process of negative current account balances and the march of the shadow-economy, will return to a process of arms manufacturing and arms exporting, which was one of the backbones of their economies in the 1980s and before. A time-series analysis of US ACDA data shows this hypothesis to be not without foundations:

**Graph 9.27: towards a resumption of the arms exporting mechanisms
in Eastern Europe? - The Polish case re-considered**

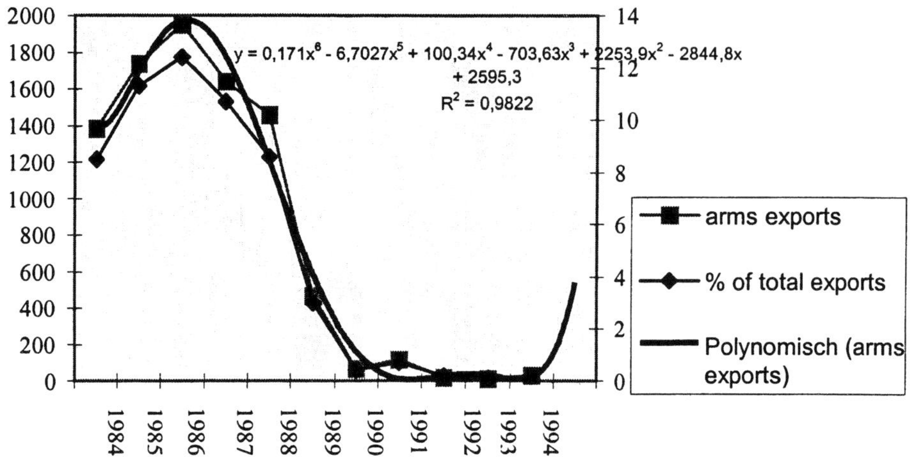

Legend: total arms exports (in constant US $, 1987) and the share of arms exports per total exports
(right-hand scale), as well as the polynomial function fitted by the EXCEL program to the data
series (trend-line). The function leaves less than 2% of arms exports unaccounted for. Our own
compilations from the US ACDA web-site.

Fallacy eight is to overlook that in the long run, the stability of the capitalist system needs
labor as an organized, countervailing power, that the very *EURO* process, as it is now underway, is
about to put into question. In the developed capitalist countries, the empirical relationships suggest
a new, labor-oriented approach to stabilization policy. Our Aristotelean message of a middle
course is: at least a medium-level unionization rate and earnings growth rate will be necessary to
stabilize capitalism, while at the same time the empirical support for a shortening of the weekly
working hours as a way out of the crisis is rather weak.

Chapter 4

MIGRATION AND GLOBALIZATION

Arno Tausch
Associate Visiting Professor, Department of Political Science,
Innsbruck University, Austria

10) MIGRATION AND GLOBALIZATION

A number of authors from the dependency/world system tradition observed dramatic shifts in the location and organization of international production since the mid 1960s. While the traditional division of labor between the center and the periphery implied industrial production in the centers and raw material production in the peripheries, linked to each other via the mechanism of unequal exchange and oligopolistic competition, these structures began to change, the argument of Froebel *et al.* and Ross goes, in favor of global shifts of the sites and organization of production: the old, classic working class of the centers is 'substituted' by a) the re-location of industrial production to the semi-periphery and b) by the massive process of migration of peripheral labor that set in North America and Western Europe since the 1960s. Although there are quite a number of systematic studies on the impact of capital penetration on the host countries in the periphery, the impact of migration on the development process of the sending and recipient countries has been less at the center of attention of world-system and dependency-oriented development research.

Mass migration, as Amin (1997) reminded us, is part and parcel of this process of transnational capitalism. The market economies of western Europe first imported labor; now, with the transfer of production away from the European central zones, second generation foreigners become increasingly marginalized. In the inner cities of countries like France, Germany, and Britain, real *'ghettos'* develop, a process that began in the United States of America three or two decades ago. Women also have to suffer from these tendencies, as their jobs are being exported away to the still much-lower paid labor power of the periphery and the semi-periphery (Stiftung Entwicklung und Frieden, 1993). Migration is even part of the *five pillars of international inequality* (Amin, 1997, see also Chapter 9):

(i)	unequal exchange: the gaps in wages are much greater than the gaps in productivities
(ii)	capital flight from the peripheries to the centers
(iii)	selective migration from the peripheries into the centers
(iv)	the monopoly position of the centers in the international division of labor
(v)	the control of the centers over the earth's natural resources

Following research contributions, which linked the patterns of international migration to the overall patterns of the center-periphery relationship, we try to develop here some hypotheses. The impact of migration on the sending countries under such conditions will be increasing the patterns of unequal exchange and the peripheral role in the world economy. It might be, that income distribution will become perhaps less unequal under the impact of the absence of millions of unskilled laborers from their home countries, but many other phenomena of peripheral development will be intensified; such as the deficient structures of agriculture, the environmental crisis (due to the intensification of traffic), and - in the end - the dependent character of accumulation, leading to slower economic growth and increased capital imports. World system oriented empirical research on migration confirmed, by and large, such a somber perspective (Amankwaa, 1995; Arrighi/Silver, 1984; Boehning and Schloeter-Paredes, 1994; Elsenhans, 1978; Parnreiter, 1994; Stalker, 1994; Stark and Taylor, 1991; Tausch, 1997).

Semi-peripheral and peripheral decision makers, largely representing the import-dependent, urban elites, - and here there is no basic difference between the Philippines and Poland - demand semi-peripheral or peripheral access to the labor markets of the centers, but they overlook the dire sociological implications of mass migration on the sending countries (Tausch, 1997, with a detailed debate about mainly ILO research). Econometric models, reviewed by Breuss (1997), could show that, in the case of EU-recipient countries with relatively high rigidities, immigration leads to higher unemployment, lower wage growth, but also a slightly lower inflation rate. Wage *'dumping'* indeed is a problem on a European scale, made all the worse by present-day and future dispositions to migrate (see also the empirical survey in Poland, the Czech Republic, Hungary, Slovakia, and Slovenia by the Gallup Institute and the Austrian Academy of Science, reported in Fassmann/Hintermann, 1997). These tendencies could even increase after EU-accession, basically because the problem of millions of small-scale peasants in East-Central Europe is unresolved. Unimpeded competition by high-tech and high-subvention Western agriculture will ruin millions of jobs in the peripheral rural structures of the East (Tausch, 1997).

In the centers, inequality will increase under the impact of mass migration, while at the same time, mass demand and technical progress, the 'twin engines' of auto-centered development, will suffer under the impact of the evolution of a 2/3-society in the center countries.

Our dire prediction, based on the systematic study of 'hard' data about world development in the 1990s is that there is hardly any 'mobility' in the international system; and that in particular, mass migration is not a strategy of ascent for the semi-periphery and periphery. How can we maintain such a hypothesis? Arrighi (1995) indicated, that, the Asian crisis of fall 1997 notwithstanding, the basic movement of the capitalist world economy during the 1980s and 1990s is the geographical shift away from the Atlantic region towards the Pacific. 'Hard' data about international capital movements support Arrighi's hypothesis. Our basic thesis is, that West European capital flows out, partially to Eastern Europe, but also to the United States and the Pacific theater, while the long-term tendency for the balance between outflows and inflows in both North America and Japan decreases, indicating the international productive capital shifts to the Pacific region, the more short-term shifts of the fall 1997 notwithstanding. At the same time, the rise of China as a haven for transnational capital continues. The share in world GDP of the different regions of the world has changed considerably since the 1960s: however, not all changes reflected faster growth; some, like for the European Union, **were rather the consequence of enlargement; i.e. integration as a reaction mechanism towards decline.** The four blocs were: the European Union, USA, Japan, the remaining OECD countries, and the rest of the world. Our results are:

Graph 10.1a: shares in world GDP, 1960 - 1994

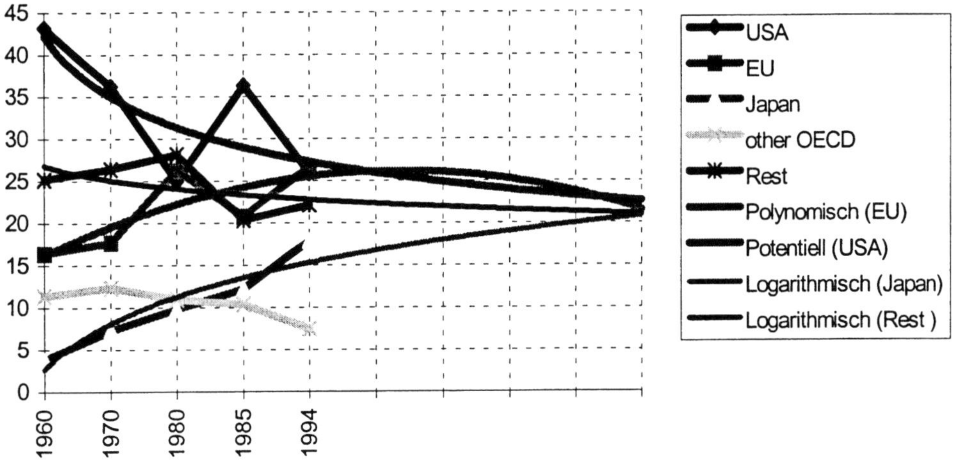

Legend: shares in world GNP. Source: our own calculations from Stiftung Entwicklung und Frieden, 1998: 152. The data for the EXCEL projections were:

	USA	EU	Japan	other OECD	Rest	Total
1960	43,2	16,4	3,8	11,4	25,2	100
1970	36,2	17,7	7,3	12,4	26,4	100
1980	24,9	26,2	9,8	11	28,1	100
1985	36,3	20,8	12,2	10,4	20,3	100
1994	25,9	26,6	17,9	7,5	22,1	100

The transnational world-wide market economy has expanded tremendously since the early 1980s. A look at transnational investment flow statistics shows this process in all clarity:

Table 10.1a: Global patterns of foreign direct investments, 1975-1995, in billions of $:

	OECDinflows	OECDoutflows	LDCinflows	LDCoutflows	CEEinflows	CEEoutflows
1990	169,8	222,5	33,7	17,8	0,3	0,04
1991	114	201,9	41,3	8,9	2,45	0,04
1992	114	181,4	50,4	21	3,77	0,1
1993	129,3	192,4	73,1	33	5,59	0,2
1994	132,8	190,9	87	38,6	5,89	0,55
1995	203,2	270,5	99,7	47	12,08	0,3

	EU inflows	EU outflows	EU balance	US+CND infl.	US+CND out.	US+CND bal.	Jap inflows	Jap outflows	Jap balance
1984-89	37702	62641	**24939**	48656	21511	**-27145**	81	20793	**20712**
1990	97387	132959	**35572**	55773	31900	**-23873**	1753	48024	**46271**
1991	77715	106842	**29127**	24760	39111	**14351**	1730	42619	**40889**
1992	79812	108716	**28904**	22097	42613	**20516**	3490	21916	**18426**
1993	74467	91488	**17021**	46125	74803	**28678**	234	15471	**15237**
1994	64017	101070	**37053**	55803	50421	**-5382**	908	18521	**17613**
1995	111920	132285	**20365**	71418	100291	**28873**	39	21286	**21247**

Source: our own compilations from Bailey, Parisotto and Renshaw, 1993, and UNCTAD, 1996

Acquisitions of foreign assets by US residents slowed sharply, and total net capital inflows of $43.1 thousand million were recorded in the first quarter of 1996. Apart from the USA, European countries and the LDCs - especially in East and South Asia and the Americas - became the major investment areas of the international order (with shifts between Western and Eastern Europe being likely). In 1997, the following rank scale of major net foreign direct investment flows in $bn could be observed:

USA	90,7
China	45,3
UK	36,9
France	18,3
Brazil	16,3
Belgium	12,6
Mexico	12,1
Singapore	10

Source: our own calculations from UNDP HDR, 1999

Argentina (6.3), Russia (6.2), Chile (5.4), Indonesia (5.3) Poland (5.0) and Hungary (2.1) are major locations for foreign investments in the future. Thus, Eastern Europe could become again a contested zone of influence - in between the eastward expansion of west European, Asian and North American capital and a newly asserted Russian power projection. Graph 10.1 now shows the volume of center exports and imports and the balances for the different trade blocs in the world economy. It should be kept in mind, that Russia's energy-export-driven positive current account balance still biases the picture for Eastern Europe.

Graph 10.1b: world trade between the major power blocs

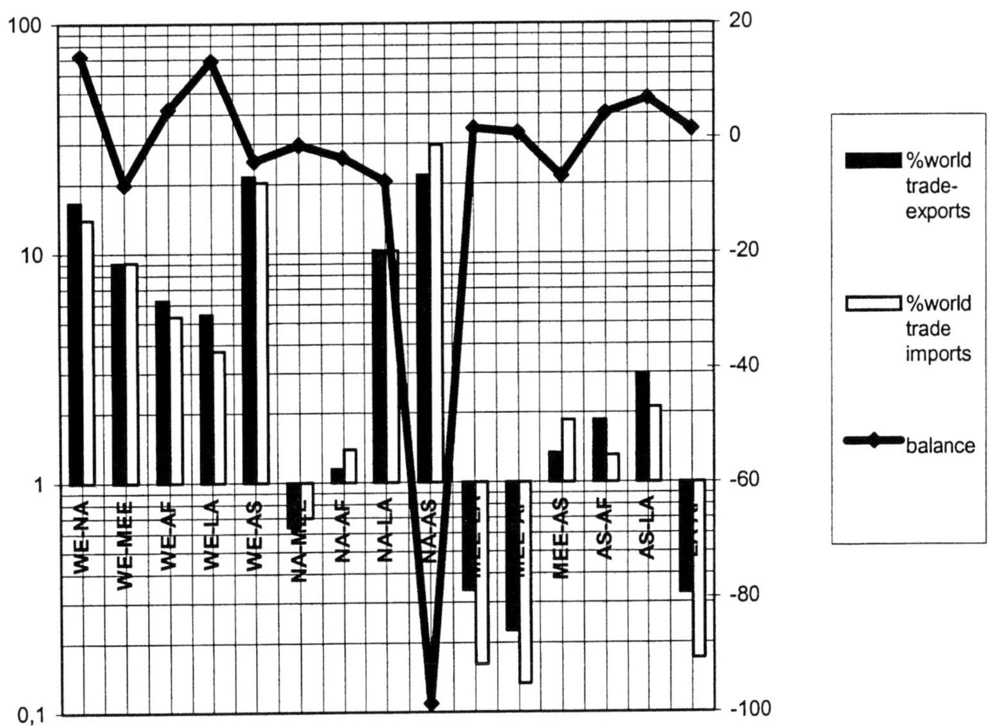

Legend: left hand, logarithmic scale: columns, percent of the regions exports (imports) to other world regions in % of total world exports (imports). Line (right hand scale) is the trade balance of the exporting/importing region. The WTO raw data were:

Region	%world trade-exports	%world trade imports	balance
(WE-NA) Western Europe-North America	16,68	14,02	14,3
(WE-MEE) Western Europe-Eastern Europe and former USSR	9,06	9,12	-8
(WE-AF) Western Europe-Africa	6,28	5,32	5
(WE-LA) Western Europe-Latin America	5,46	3,75	13,5
(WE-AS) Western Europe-Asia	21,62	20,32	-4
(NA-MEE) North America-Eastern Europe+former USSR	0,64	0,7	-1,2
(NA-AF) North America-Africa	1,14	1,39	-3,5
(NA-LA) North America-Latin America	10,29	10,21	-7,5
(NA-AS) North America-Asia	21,77	29,43	-98,5
(MEE-LA) Eastern Europe-Latin America	0,34	0,16	1,6

(MEE-AF) Eastern Europe-Africa	0,23	0,13	0,8
(MEE-AS) Eastern Europe-Asia	1,34	1,86	-6,6
(AS-AF) Asia-Africa	1,85	1,31	4,2
(AS-LA) Asia-Latin America	2,99	2,11	6,8
(LA-AF) Latin America-Africa	0,33	0,17	1,4

Source: our own compilations from WTO data, as quoted in Zeitpunkte, 1/1997: 12

Western Europe could be tempted, in order not to fall behind China, to overexploit Latin America and Africa, and to try to shift the present favorable East European and former Soviet balance in its favor, while North America's negative balance with Asia is also an expression of the dramatic shifts in the production of multination US corporations.

Outward foreign direct investment stock of western European countries increased dramatically its share in West European gross domestic product, as one of the most visible signs of the process of globalization:

Graph 10.2a: the share of outward foreign direct investment stock in gross domestic product from 1980 - 1994 of major economic power groups in the world system

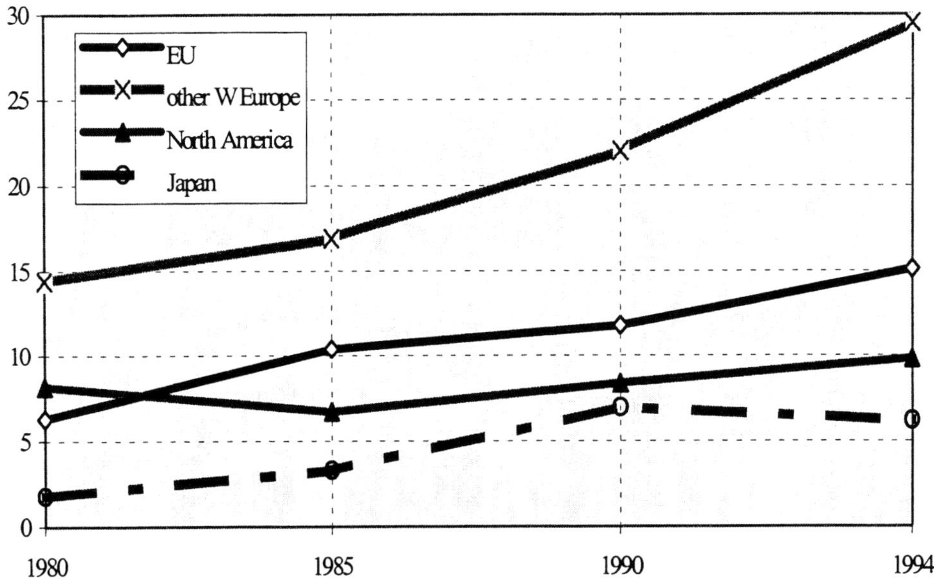

Legend: the share of outward foreign direct investment stock in gross domestic product from 1980 - 1994 of major economic power groups in the world system. Source: our own compilations from UNCTAD, 1996

It is to be expected, that world capitalism is on its way towards an anti-egalitarian, and de-regulatory phase which will do away with many of the social advances that characterized the corporatist economic cycle of the post-World-War-II period. An analysis by Deininger and Squire compares the evolution of the GINI-coefficients of inequality in the different regions of the world from 1960 onwards and comes to the following results:

Graph 10.2b: inequality from 1960 onwards in the world system

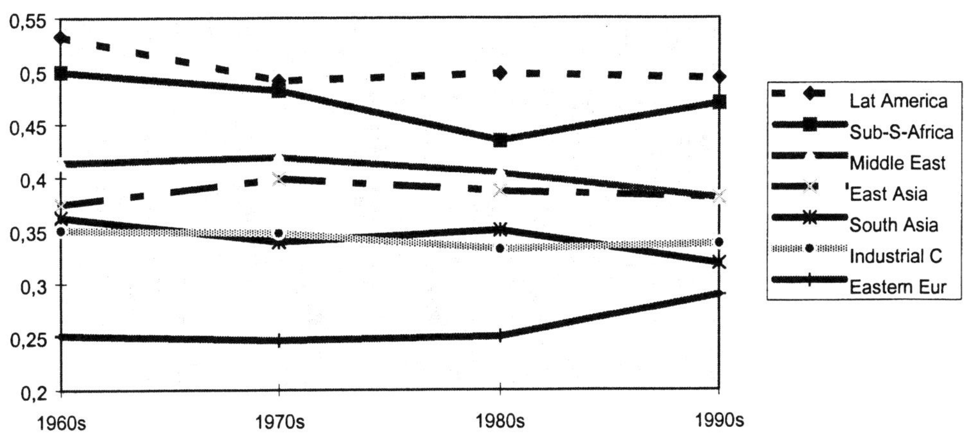

Legend: The Gini coefficient of income inequality in the different regions of the world system from 1960 onwards. The Gini coefficient ranges from 0 (maximum equality) to 1 (maximum inequality). Source: our own compilation from Deininger and Squire.

From these data it is also possible to arrive at the following projections of inequality until the year 2000. South Asia's and Latin America's inequality will decline, while in Sub-Saharan Africa, in the industrialized countries, and in Eastern Europe inequalities will increase considerably, and in the Middle East and North Africa there will be only a slight reduction of inequality rates:

Graph 10.2c: The future of world inequality

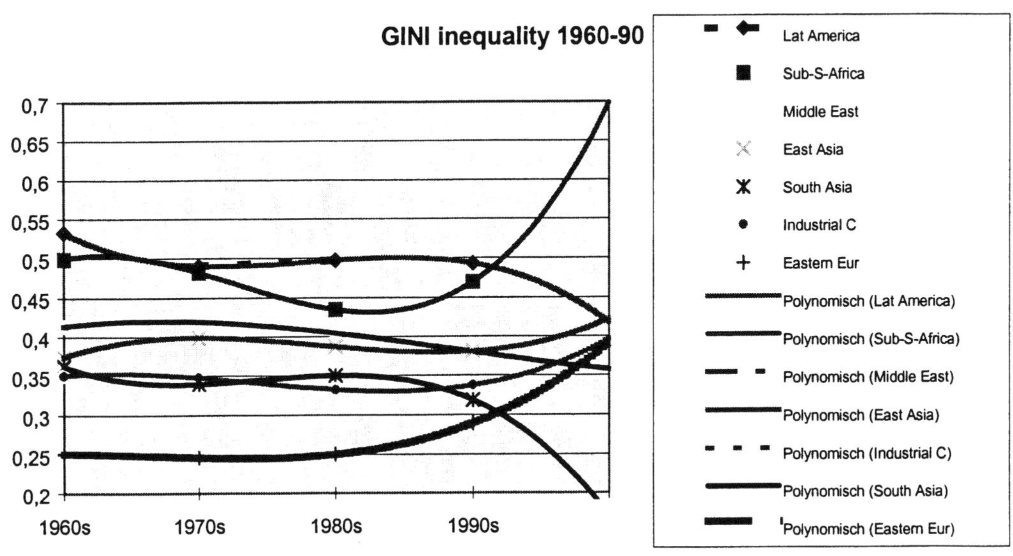

Legend: see above. Source: our own EXCEL projections from Deininger and Squire, 1997

The growth of inequality in Eastern Europe, in Sub-Saharan Africa and in the industrial countries might herald the advent of a 'Latin-American'-style capitalism of the 1960s and 1970s, that goes hand in hand with mass migration, the growth of transnational corporations penetration, short-term spurts of growth and long-term stagnation, and protected markets and economic distortions. The imperative of *'balanced budgets'*, *'financial markets'* and *'de-regulation'* might, in the end, undermine the very logic of economic growth that the anti-Keynesianism of the 1990s maintained to uphold. Comparative data for the 1980s and 1990s show, that inequality - as in the past - has no positive relationship to economic growth, and that, rather, the opposite is true. Because of the limitations of income inequality data, we test this important relationship also with other indicators of inequality:

Graph 10.3: inequality measures and economic growth

income inequality (x-axis) and economic growth (y-axis) in the world system

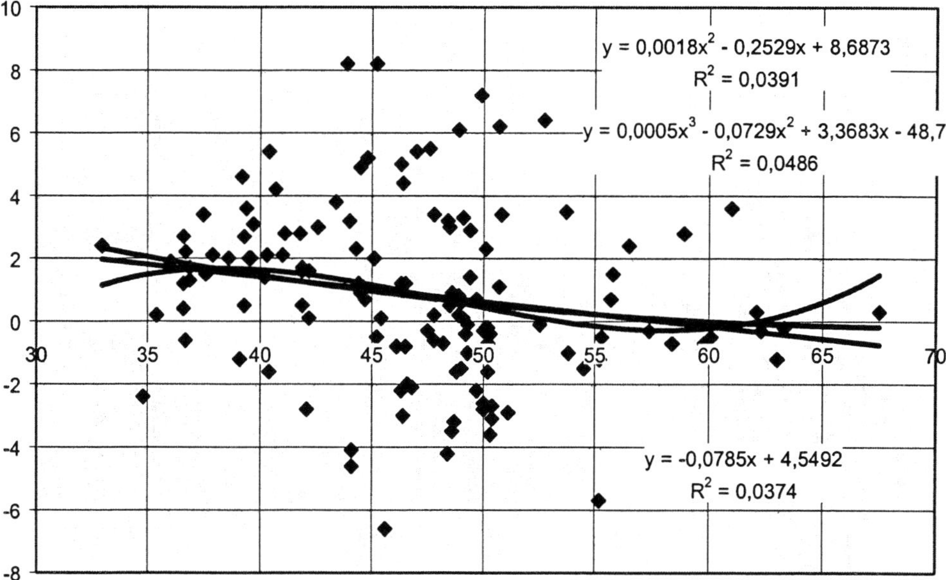

Human development index (x-axis) and economic growth (y-axis) in the world system

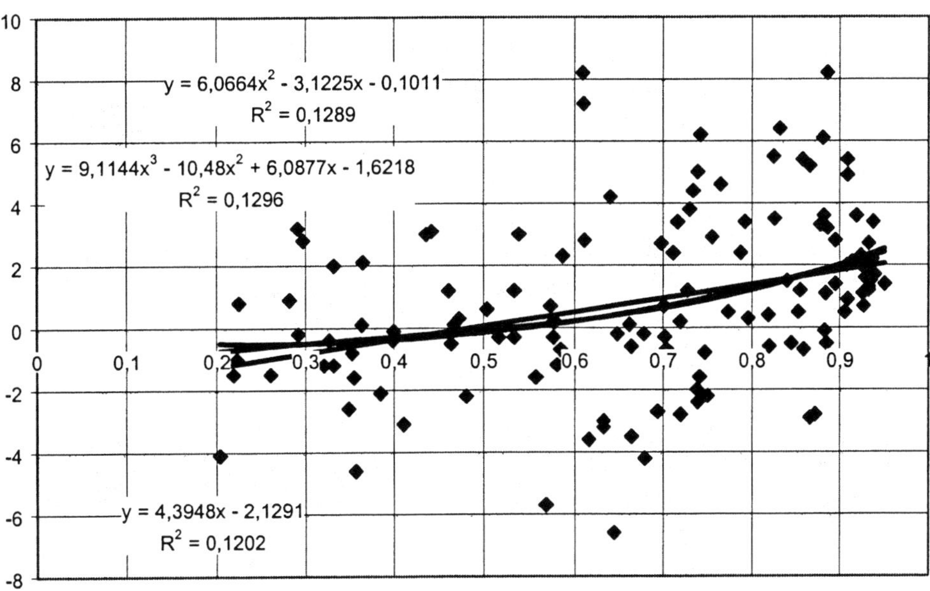

Infant mortality (x-axis) and economic growth (y-axis) in the world system

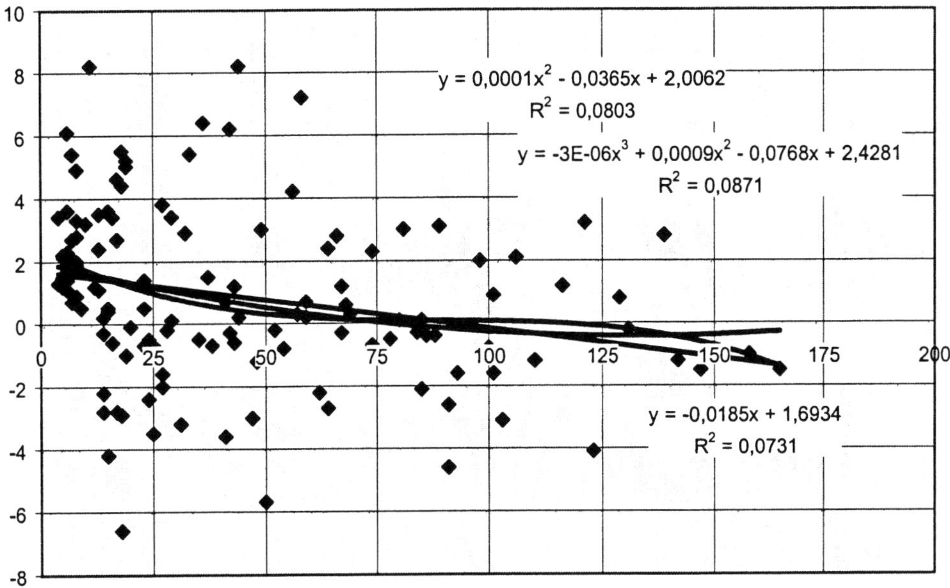

Human capital formation (mean years of schooling) (x-axis) and economic growth (y-axis) in the world system

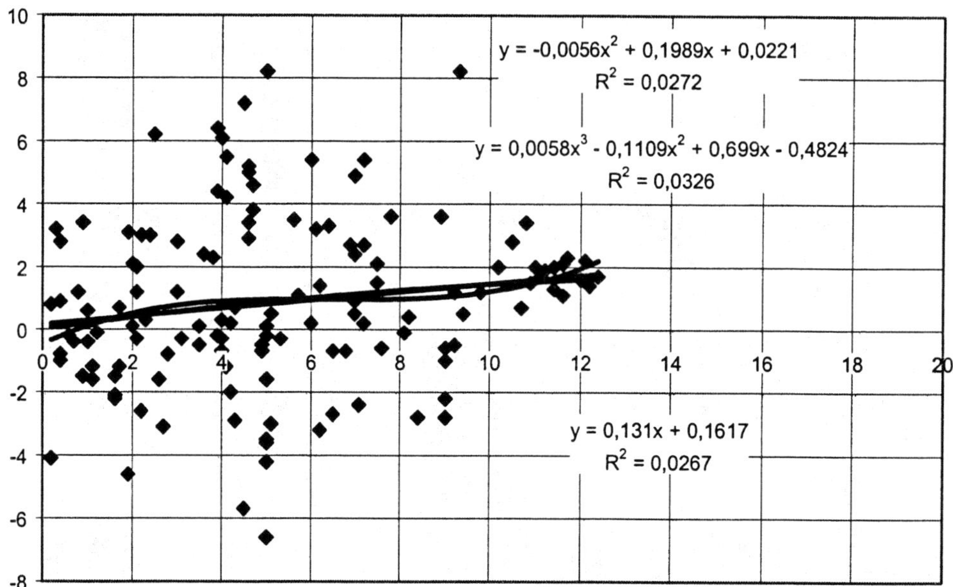

Sources: income inequality data from UNDP, Moaddel and WDR Human Development Report, 1996; other variables: UNDP. All test series at least show that equality is not detrimental to economic growth on a global scale

Samir Amin and Giovanni Arrighi most vocally proclaim today the idea that there has never been any *'catching up'* of the semi-peripheries and peripheries, and that there is a fairly constant real gap between the rich and the poor regions in the world system. Thus, the *'Asian crises'* are not an accident, but part and parcel of the structure of the transnational system that tends to petrify the system of inequality.

Apart from that dire enough fact, matters are - Amin's argument goes - made worse by adhering to neo-conservative strategies in precisely those countries that would need a new political project. Passive, selective migration increases, rather than decreases the wealth gap between rich and poor lands.

Such a socio-liberal interpretation of dependency theories also receives qualified support from a careful analysis of existing UNDP data about the determinants of absolute income growth from 1960 onwards. 58 nations experienced an absolute, not only relative, decline, of their real per capita incomes in the 1980s (Nohlen, 1991). While the monopoly position in the international system, as expressed by years of membership in the UN, together with the social security effort are a significant positive contribution to growth, human rights violations and population density rates are significantly blocking long-run economic growth. The second equation listed in Table 10.1 even more optimistically mentions social security expenditures, mean years of schooling and the Human Development Index as a precondition of absolute income growth. In between them, our predictor variables account for over 80% of the real, absolute income growth in the world system between 1960 and 1990. To avoid severe problems of collinearity, the Matthew's effect was dropped from the equations, substituted by political and human rights or mean years of education and the Human Development Index.

Table 10.1b: the *absolute real income increase from 1960 to 1990* in the world system

	Violations of Political Rights	Violation of Civil Rights	Population Density^0,5	Terms of Trade	MNC PEN73	Government Consumption
growth in the sense of Arrighi's and Amin's theory	-387,6044339	-335,5309726	-38,35553994	-159,3658871	-2,142065598	-38,08417293
	147,1946027	756,8905041	14,7393743	773,404945	18,01237032	28,8547924
	0,80679169					
	29,78709404	107				
t-Test	**-2,633278848**	-0,443301866	**-2,602250215**	-0,206057497	-0,118921916	-1,319856071

Trade Dependency	social security effort	UN membership years	% Women in Parliament	Women % Labor Force	ethno-linguistic fractionalization
3,383706329	353,0850466	14,16819598	58,90557906	-2,079932631	-8,378867087
16,17414266	42,82585478	6,800556167	44,53034007	1,379485421	14,31186935
0,209204679	**8,244670153**	**2,083387833**	1,322818981	-1,507759777	-0,585448825

public investment	ln(MPR+1)(military personnel)	Fertility Rate	constant
24,90210293	-166,5370259	137,2074945	3642,23847
7,916573906	280,3858807	209,1100071	2191,222144
3,145565649	-0,593956534	0,656149825	

Legend: as in all EXCEL 5.0 outprints in this work, first row: unstandardized regression coefficients, second row: standard errors, last row: t-Test. The values immediately below the standard errors are R^2 (third row, left side entry), F, and degrees of freedom (fourth row).

216 Arno Tausch

Alternatively, one might also express:

	MNCP85	Govexpenditures	Trade Dependency	social security	UN-member years	Women in Parliament	Women % LF	mean years of schooling	HDI	ln(MPR+1)	Fertility Rate	Constant
absolute	-0,1024	-313,04	1145,54	304,721	14,0635	-33,038	-15,546	336,965	28,15	-25,605	-6,937	-907,19
growth	195,851	697,948	1775,06	146,832	17,3298	27,872	15,0547	43,5687	5,40439	15,8157	12,008	1882,33
	0,80028											
	40,4342	111										
t-Test	-0,0005	-0,4485	0,64535	**2,07531**	0,81152	-1,1853	-1,0326	**7,73411**	**5,20873**	-1,6189	-0,5777	

Legend: As in all EXCEL 5.0 outprints in this work, first row: unstandardized regression coefficients, second row: standard errors, last row: t-Test. The values immediately below the standard errors are R^2 (third row, left side entry), F, and degrees of freedom (fourth row). Absolute real income increase is understood to be the difference between PPP \$ income in 1990 to PPP \$ income in 1960

Since for Arrighi and Amin the international hierarchy is an international hierarchy of wealth, the **relative** distances of poor to rich countries is of enormous relevance at a given time-point in the international system. The real purchasing power income of the richest country in 1960 and 1990, the United States, is put at 100 in each case; relative mobility is defined as the difference between the position in 1990 (USA PPP \$ income = 100) from the position in 1960 (USA PPP \$ income = 100). The socio-liberal variables: mean years of schooling, the already existing position in the international power networks (years of UN membership) and the Human Development Index enhance international mobility, while MNC penetration and a costly social security system work against international mobility:

Table 10.2: mobility in the international system

	MNCP85	Govex	Trade Dep	social sec	UN-membery	Women Parl	Women %LF	mean years schooing	HDI	ln(MPR+1)	Fertility Rate	Constant
international mobility	-1,9435	3,40219	1,91357	-1,3193	0,16456	-0,1978	-0,103	1,19691	0,11091	-0,0914	-0,0754	6,86977
	0,8866	3,15955	8,03555	0,66469	0,07845	0,12617	0,06815	0,19723	0,02447	0,0716	0,05436	8,52114
	0,57749											
	13,7925	111										
t-Test	**-2,1921**	1,0768	0,23814	**-1,9848**	**2,09762**	-1,5679	-1,5109	**6,06857**	**4,53334**	-1,2767	-1,3862	

Legend: as in all EXCEL 5.0 outprints in this work, first row: unstandardized regression coefficients, second row: standard errors, last row: t-Test. The values immediately below the standard errors are R^2 (third row, left side entry), F, and degrees of freedom (fourth row). Relative mobility is defined as the difference between the position in 1990 (USA PPP \$ income = 100) from the position in 1960 (USA PPP \$ income = 100)

The international system in the 1990s is characterized, as Arrighi correctly remarks, by two tendencies

(i)   the growing international competition between the three power blocs, US, Japan and the European Union

(ii)   the relative stability in the international hierarchies

For Arrighi, the GNP per capita at current exchange rates is the best available measurement of the goods and services that the residents of different countries command on the world markets (Arrighi *et al.*, 1996a). Personally, I have no doubt about Arrighi's results, based on such a methodology, although the implementation of his research program into empirical tests, based on polynomial regressions, might be surprising to some observers. The international system is characterized by the stability of distribution between peripheries, semi-peripheries and centers: that is Arrighi's main research result. To control Arrighi's results, we use a slightly different methodology. For us, the international hierarchy of the 123 countries of the world with fairly complete UNDP data about the social and economic system (listed in descending order of their UNDP Human Development Index) is also a stable hierarchy of real purchasing power parity rates (PPP $) in relation to the USA, the country with the highest PPP $ value in both 1960 and 1990 (USA = 100). The exponential regression lines for 1960 and 1990 show, that the 'band spread' of international distribution has widened, and that a considerable number of states even experienced a relative downward-mobility, while less than half of the states in the world system experienced an upward mobility, as evidenced by the two exponential trend lines and their cutting point:

Graph 10.4: aspects of international income distribution, 1960-1990

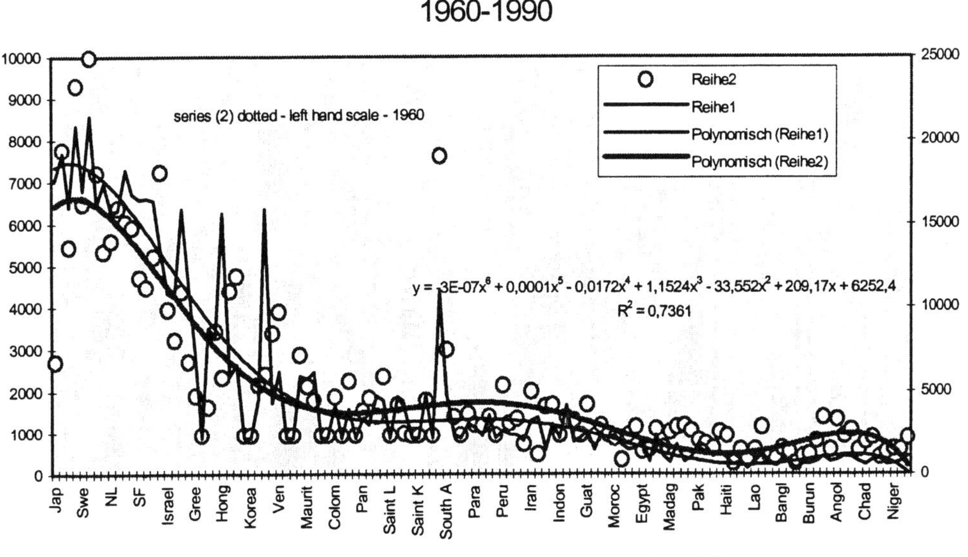

Legend: real income per capita in purchasing power parity rates and constant US $, 1960 (left hand scale) and 1990 (right hand scale), ranging from the highly developed nations to the poorest countries. Put in simple terms: there is a trend, that the poorest countries lose in relative terms.

At closer inspection, the trend lines in the above graph show the following characteristics and moved in the following direction:

1960-1990

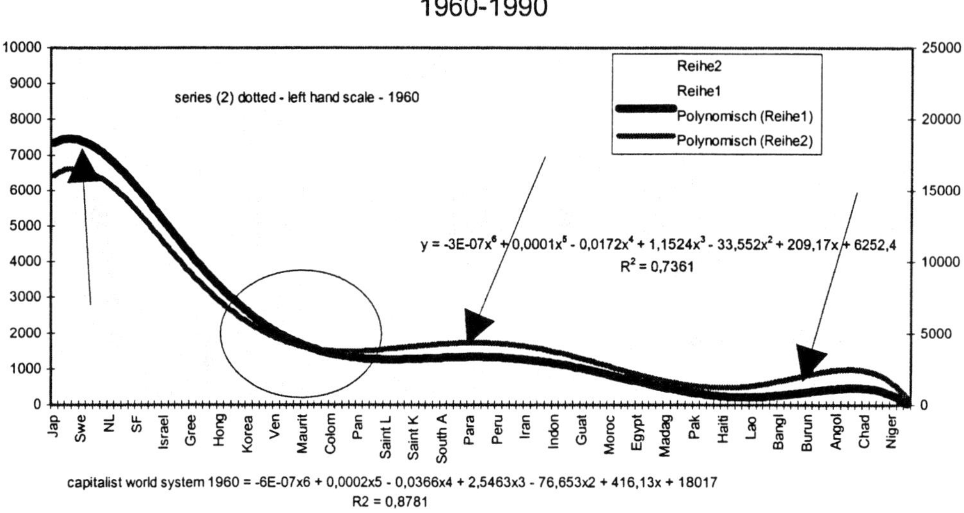

$$y = -3E\text{-}07x^6 + 0{,}0001x^5 - 0{,}0172x^4 + 1{,}1524x^3 - 33{,}552x^2 + 209{,}17x + 6252{,}4$$
$$R^2 = 0{,}7361$$

capitalist world system 1960 = $-6E\text{-}07x6 + 0{,}0002x5 - 0{,}0366x4 + 2{,}5463x3 - 76{,}653x2 + 416{,}13x + 18017$
$$R2 = 0{,}8781$$

Legend: see above.

Some observers might contend, that an exponential trend line and not a polynomial regression best reflects the underlying values. To satisfy such arguments, we include here the following results:

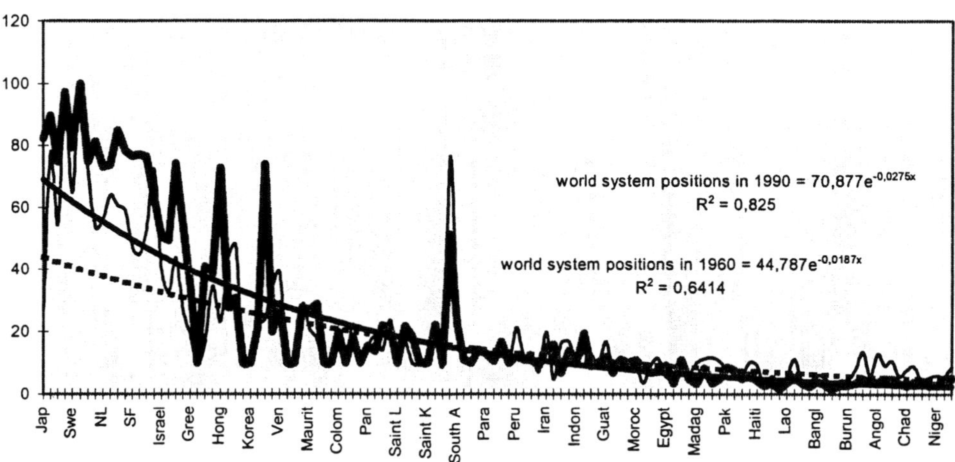

Legend: see above. The difference between the two Graphs above is the mathematical formulation of the trend lines. The relative polarization effect appears clearly visible in both formulations (polynomial expression versus exponential trend line).

Alternatively, Arrighi's own peculiar methodology can also be applied:

Graph 10.5: Arrighi's hypothesis of the constancy of international inequality

1960

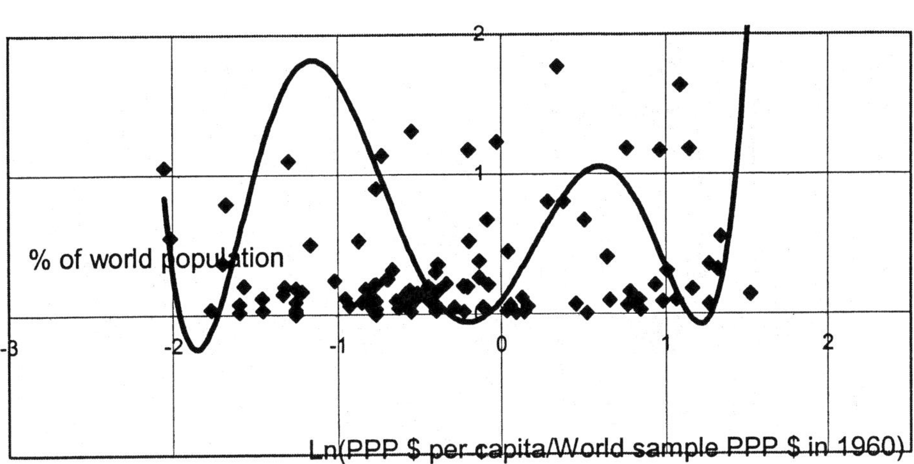

1990

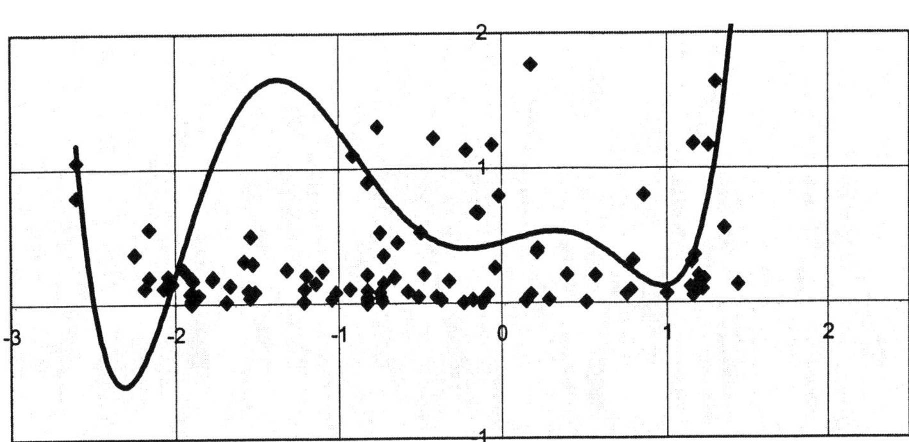

Legend: Giovanni Arrighi developed the following method to measure world development polarization: on the x-axis you have the logarithm of the per capita income for each country of the world, divided by the world per capita income of the respective period; on the y-axis you have the share, that each country of the world system has in total world population. Our own calculations from UNDP, HDR, current issues.

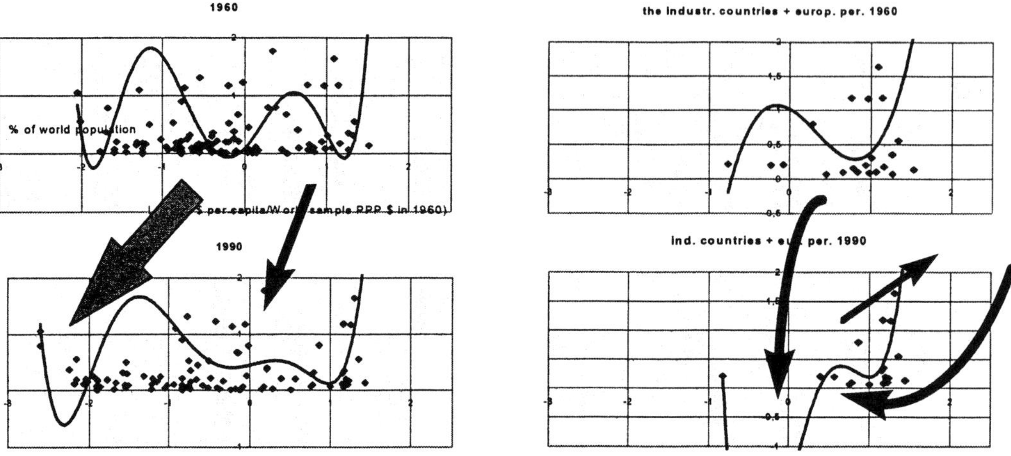

Legend: results according to our methodology as compared to the results, based on Arrighi's method, based on the following regression analysis:

(10.1) % of world population = a_0 + b_1 * (ln (GNP per cap/World GNP per capita)) +-b_2 * (...)^2 +- b_3 * (...)^3 ....

We used here, like Arrighi (1996a), a polynomial regression of the 6th degree (Arrighi, 1996a; pages 11 and Figure 7

Whatever methodological preference we have, our analysis confirms the shape of distribution, expected for the dependency model of global polarization, and certainly not the modernization hypothesis, which clearly would expect a closing of the gaps. Our results also show, that the W-shaped distribution with strong semi-peripheries, expected by the world system approach (Arrighi, 1996a), has become weaker over time, resembling more and more the distribution, expected by classic dependency theory.

Thus, international mobility in the age of globalization is a myth. Asian, Russian or Mexican crashes are not accidents, but part and parcel of the very structure of the system, that crushes in periodical regularity the material progress of working generations in the semi-periphery countries and wipes out their dreams of catching-up one day with the center.

Our analysis also shows the effects, that transnational migration has on the sending and on the receiving countries in the context of overall dependency mechanisms across long cycles. The hope of many semi-periphery and periphery nations to change their weak position in the world-wide structure of the division of labor by mass migration to the developed countries is also not realistic. These findings could have an implication not only for the social scientific, but also for the political debate in Europe. At present, 'green', 'alternative' and socialist-left-wing groups claim that Western Europe should allow more immigration from the South and the East. But migration greatly increases inequality in the migration recipient countries, without really solving the long-run weak position of the sending countries in the international economy. If the 'migration industry' were right, then Jordan, Mexico, Jamaica, ex-Yugoslavia, Greece, Portugal and other highly migration-dependent countries would be 'economic miracles'. In the migration recipient countries, environmental decay, as measured by the UNDP greenhouse index, increases as one of the main consequences of the process of international migration, due to mass traffic and the consumption model that mass migration induces. For us, migration is - above all - an expression of a peripheral position in the world economy. At first sight, migration has practically no positive or negative effect on economic growth, as is to be shown in the following graph:

**Graph 10.6: migration, economic growth, inequality, the greenhouse-index
and human development**

migration and economic growth

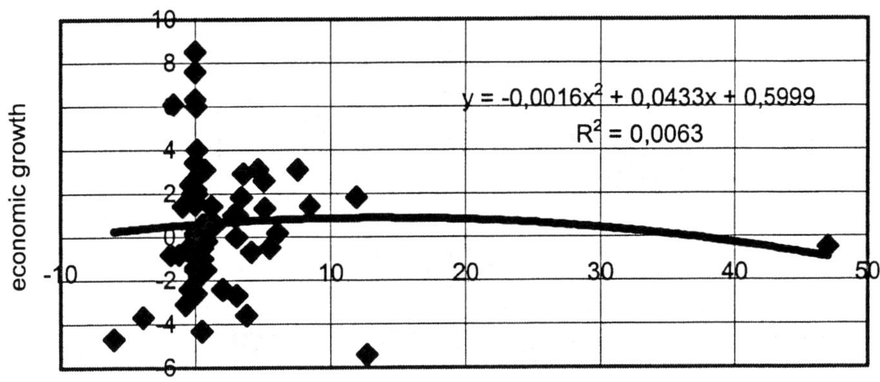

Legend: balance of worker remittances per GDP (x-axis) and economic growth (y-axis)

migration and inequality

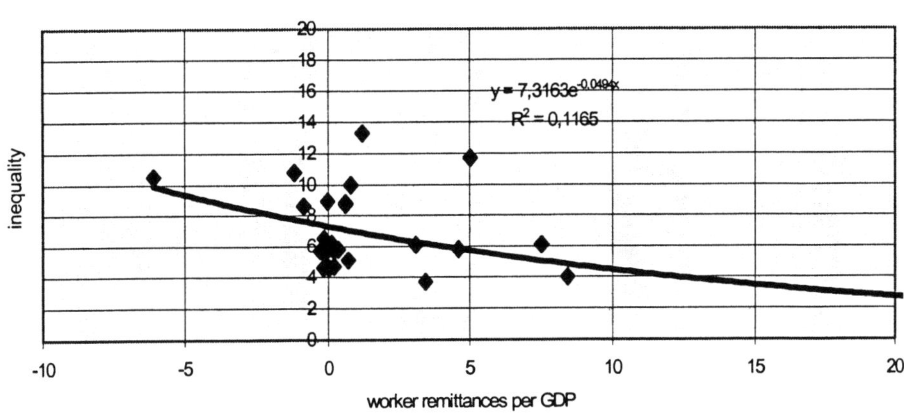

Legend: balance of worker remittances per GDP (x-axis) and economic inequality (ratio of the
income of the top 20% to the income of the bottom 20%)(y-axis)

migration and human development

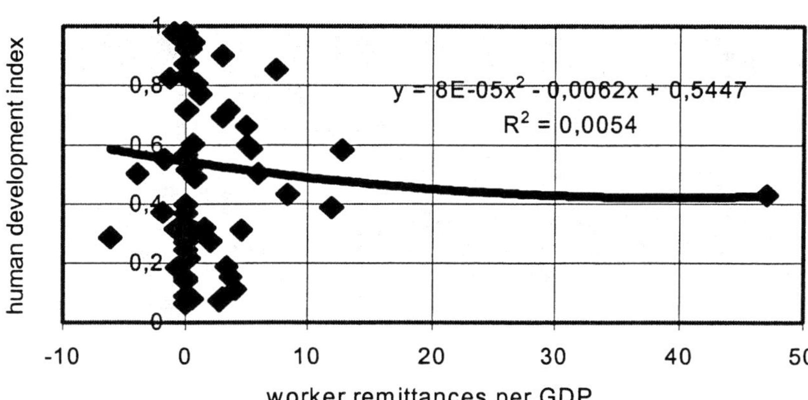

Legend: balance of worker remittances per GDP (x-axis) and the human development index (y-axis). Sources: our own compilations from UNDP data

The **dominant countries, like Japan or the United States, send their managers abroad, but never their workforce**. It is a sign of world economic weakness to be a net exporter of labor force. Poor and peripheral countries, like Jordan, Pakistan, Ireland, Portugal, or nowadays Poland, send their workers abroad, and import their managers, and never the other way around. In the old colonial days, priests and soldiers were imported, timber, ivory, copper, slaves and bananas were exported. Still, the structure exists, but at a much higher level, with a lot of *'soft body'* components as well. Interestingly enough, the effect of government size on growth becomes significantly and highly negative, once we consider the effect of migration on development. Introducing the variable: *'worker remittances per total GNP'* into the above equations, we achieve for the countries with complete data on worker remittances the following results:

Table 10.3: The Pearson-Bravais-correlations of worker remittances per GDP with variables of economic growth

	correlation with migration remittances
Govex (government expenditures)	0,26
war/internal war	0,24
government consumption	0,19
aid per capita	0,18
public investment	0,17
refugees per population	0,15
violation of political Rights	0,14
MPR (military personnel ratio)	0,14
violation of civil rights	0,09
deforestation	0,05
LEX 1990 (life expectancy)	-0,03

SIPE-Index (Social Insurance Programme Experience Index)	-0,07
HDI (Human Development Index)	-0,07
GNP growth 80-92	-0,07
mean years of schooling	-0,09
gender empowerment	-0,11
reserves per GDP	-0,13
social security expenditures	-0,14
years of female voting	-0,17

Source: our own calculations from worker remittances and other UNDP structural data for n = 123 countries of the world system, bivariate correlations according to EXCEL 5.0

Table 10.4: International dependency and its effects on growth and adjustment, allowing for the influence of the migration process

	MNC PEN73	Govex	Trade Dep	social sec	UN-membery	Women Parl	Women %LF	ln PCI	ln PCI^2	ln(MPR+1)	Fertility Rate	migration	constant
adjust ment	-0,143	-1,13	0,525	0,589	-11,5	-0,018	-0,033	-0,05	0,115	-0,02	-0,02	-0,004	60,89
	0,049	0,207	1,195	0,404	6,05	0,026	0,05	0,027	0,081	0,017	0,036	0,003	22,69
	0,56	2,072											
	5,402	51											
	278,4	219											
t-Test	**-2,897**	**-5,452**	0,439	1,456	**-1,901**	-0,671	-0,667	-1,852	1,426	-1,191	-0,552	-1,278	

	MNC PEN73	Govex	Trade Dep	social sec	UN-membery	Women Parl	Women %LF	ln PCI	ln PCI^2	ln(MPR+1)	Fertility Rate	migration	constant
growth	-0,119	-1,42	1,832	0,42	-9,152	-0,01	-0,008	-0,041	0,063	-0,019	-0,017	-3E-04	53,4
	0,046	0,194	1,12	0,379	5,671	0,025	0,047	0,025	0,076	0,016	0,034	0,003	21,27
	0,614	1,943											
	6,767	51											
	306,4	192,5											
t-Test	**-2,569**	**-7,307**	**1,636**	1,108	**-1,614**	-0,407	-0,179	**-1,637**	0,827	**-1,166**	-0,51	-0,113	

Legend: As in all EXCEL 5.0 outprints in this work, first row: unstandardized regression coefficients, second row: standard errors, last row: t-Test. The values immediately below the standard errors are $R^{\wedge 2}$ (third row, left side entry), F, and degrees of freedom (fourth row). The above results were achieved by inserting international migration remittances data (remittances per GDP) into our cross-national growth and development equations. Only countries with complete data were used.

Migration conserves economic structures that inhibit world economic adjustment. The greatest proponents of mass migration from the semi-periphery and periphery are in reality those very social strata, **that represent the powerful urban power monopolies at home: instead of bringing their monopolies under the discipline of the market and allowing their agricultural**

regions to prosper under a system of export-led growth and mass-demand at home, they are inclined to send a considerable part of their talented work-force abroad so that it does not constitute any threat to the elites' privileged social position at home. State sector expenditures and a reliance on foreign aid will be part and parcel of a such a migration-driven development model. The state sector effect described above is significant at the 12.5% level and narrowly misses the 10% mark. **61.4% of economic growth are explained by our migration-centered equation.** Although small and open economies - especially in Europe (like Austria) - tended towards higher economic growth ratesduring past cycles, it stands out very clearly, that under due consideration for the effects of migration on growth, the critique of the **state sector** and **excessive social security** burdens becomes all the more relevant.

As already predicted by Rostow and others, migration is closely connected to the tendencies of the Kondratieff cycle, as is to be seen from the following Graph:

Graph 10.7: migration balances and the Kondratieff cycle

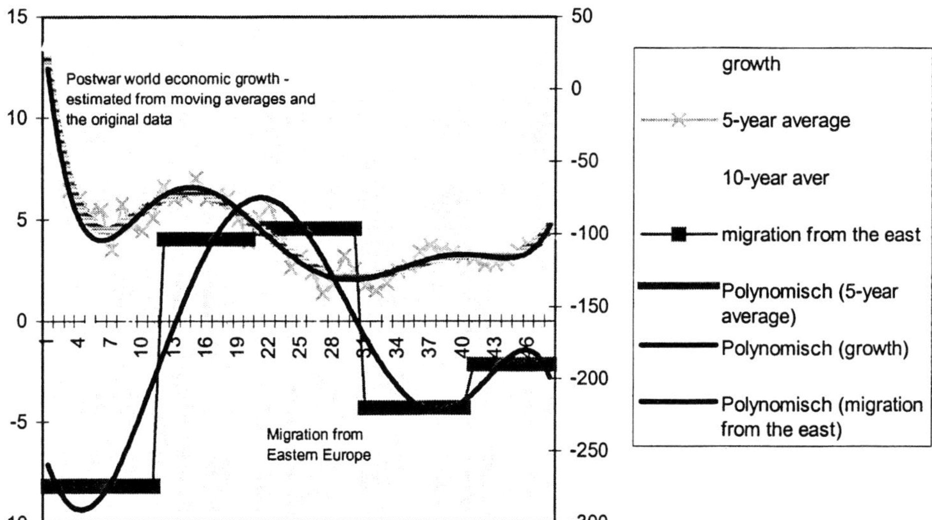

Legend: economic growth (left hand scale) and migration balances from Eastern Europe (right hand scale) during the Kondratieff cycle from 1950 onwards. Slowly, Eastern Europe's outward migration potential recedes, as the countries will become immigration regions themselves, like Southern Europe before

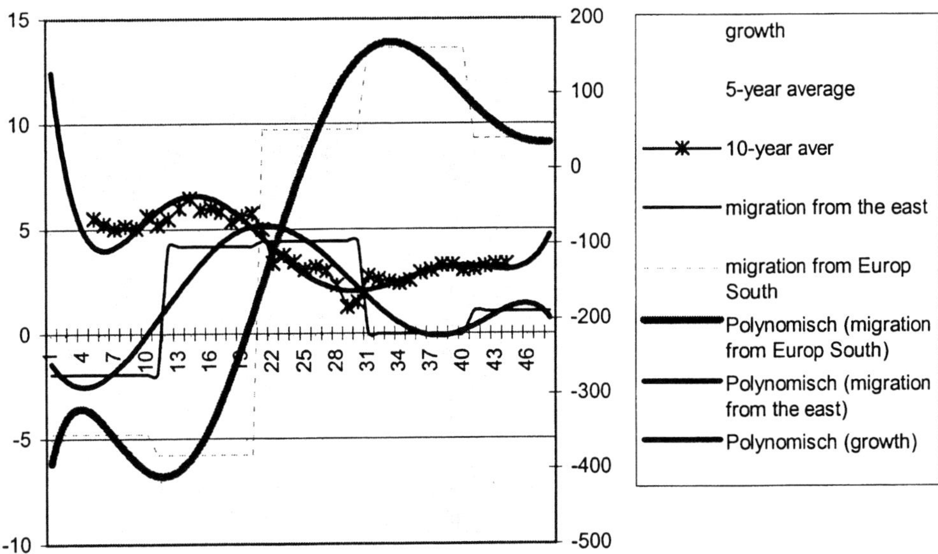

Legend: This graph compares the results from the above graph (economic growth, left-hand scale) with the migration balances in Eastern and Southern Europe (right hand scale). Southern Europe became an immigration region long ago, and tightened its borders, as East Central Europe will most probably tighten its own borders.

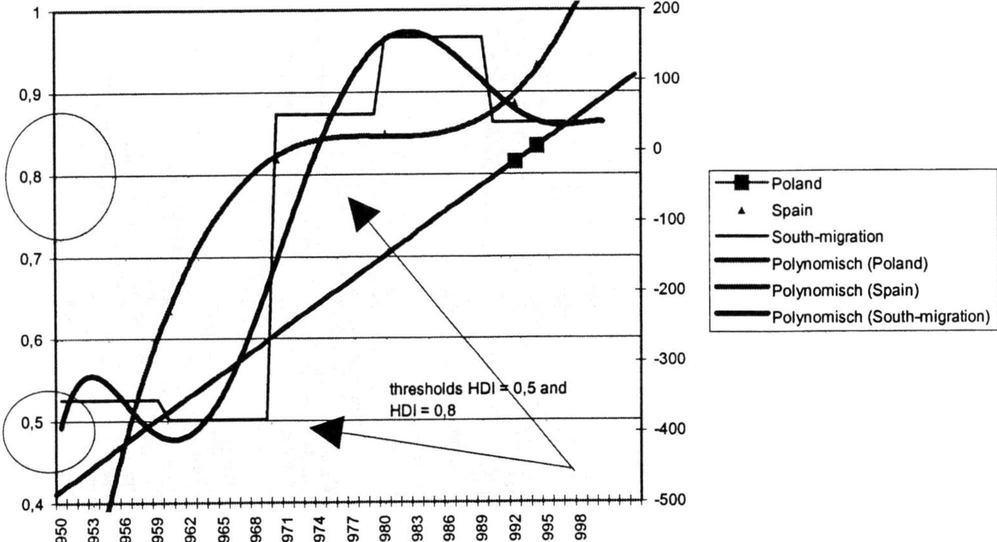

Legend: human development index (left hand scale) and outward migration balance (right hand scale). The darker non-linear trend line ('polynomial, south-migration') indicates migration balances for Europe's South, while lighter trend line ('polynomial, Spain) indicates the human development experience of Spain since 1960 (left-hand scale). The straight trend line is the probable course of Polish human development. It reaches the 0.900-human-development-threshold for migration in the not too distant future (last UNDP HDR 1999 figure - with the new methodology, based on logarithms of income levels, life expectancy, and education - **0.802**; the European South became a net importer of labor after reaching these human development levels). The graph, as before, combines data from Chapter 3 of this study and data about the globalization of migration from IFRI (1998). The economic cycle in Eastern Europe is time-lagged in comparison to the world economic cycle. Southern Europe becomes a major immigration region; whose importance grows with the downswing of the world economic cycle. During an upswing, immigration to Europe's South will decline. The data series again starts with 1950. The last graph compares the migration balance in the European South with the evolution of Spain's UNDP Human Development Index since 1960 according to the old methodology, based on income levels, life expectancy and education. The graph shows the two migration policy thresholds of HDI = 0.500 and HDI = 0.800 and compares the Spanish HDI performance over time with the UNDP figures for Poland. Not before long, Poland will become - according to this reasoning - a net immigration country, reaching a human development index of 0.900.

It can also be shown, that the propensity to migrate is a function of the Human Development Index of a society, and that migration is connected to the redistribution struggles in world society, described in this Chapter (equation 10.1). Two data series are used here to test this hypothesis. In Graph 10.8 we show the trade-off between the Human Development Index and migration propensity in 49 Polish voivodships (provinces):

**Graph 10.8: The trade-off between migration and human development
in 49 Polish voivodships**

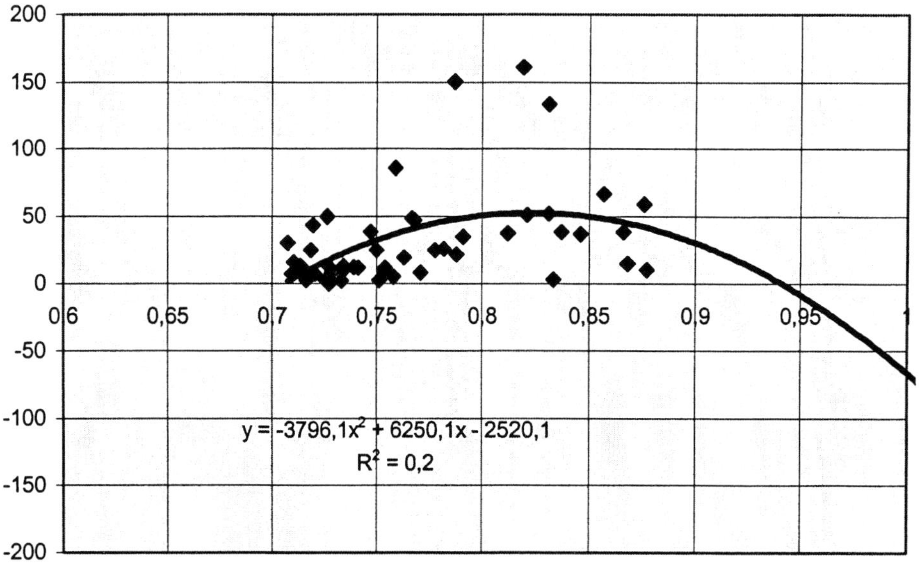

Legend: Polish voivodship migration propensity (y-axis) is being explained by the human development index of a voivodship (x-axis). Migration propensity of a province is measured by the migration balance of a province * 100 divided by the number of inhabitants of the province (thousands). Migration balance data: Polish Central Statistical Office; Human Development Index: UNDP Poland (1996).

With the rise of the Polish Human Development Index, migration propensity will decrease, and the country will become a net importer of labor.

Our following analysis now shows the relationship between the three-layer-structure of the world system in the sense of Arrighi's theory and the structure of transnational migration. Far from being a strategy of world economic ascent, mass migration is a phenomenon at the periphery, and the poorer and richer semi-periphery level. Graph 10.9 shows the trade off between migration dependence of a society (as measured by the balance of worker remittances per GDP) and the development level (PPP GDP per capita in % of the European Union average) (a) and the Human Development Index (b), again supporting our above hypotheses:

Graph 10.9: migration propensity and development on a world scale:

a) PPP GDP per capita in % of the European Union average (x-axis) and balance of worker remittances (y-axis)

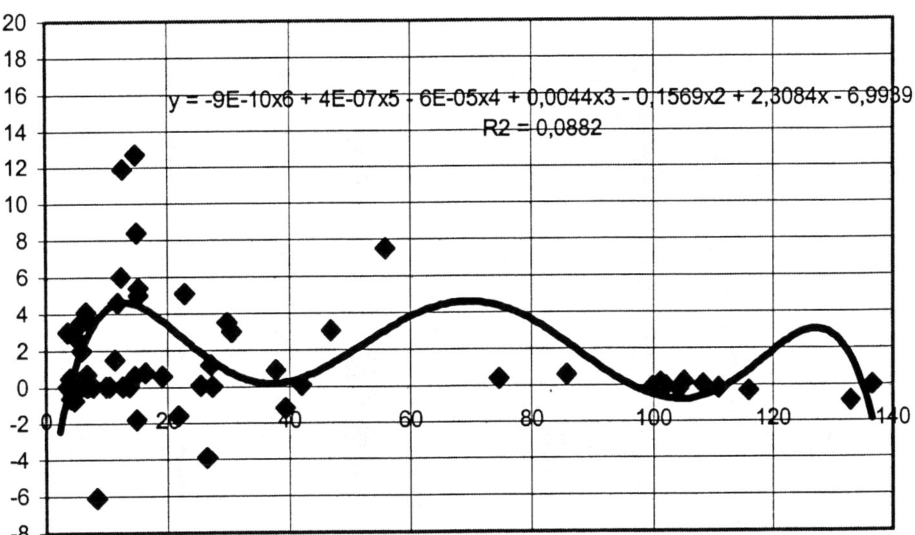

Legend: real purchasing power of a country in percent of the European Union average real purchasing power (each measured in PPP $) (x-axis) and the balance of worker remittances per GDP in % (y-axis). Source: our own compilations and calculations from UNDP Human Development Report. Note the three-layer structure that is similar to Graph 10.4 and 10.5 with three summits.

b) human development and migration

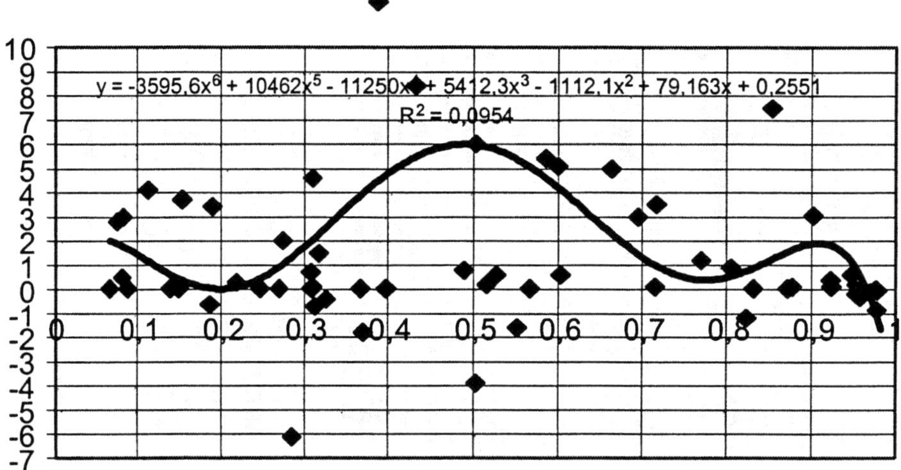

Legend: x-axis: the Human Development Index of a country of the world system. Else: see above. Note again the three-layer structure that is similar to Graph 10.4 and 10.5 with three summits.

The application of GDP or GDP PPP data alone could be very misleading in determining *'migration policy thresholds'*, viz. the negotiations between the (East) Central European accession countries and the European Union. **The Human Development Index by far better reflects the overall social situation of a country than the mere application of real purchasing power parity rate GDP data.** We look therefore at the historic trajectory of human development in the world's main sending countries. Poland becomes a country beyond the 0.800 human development threshold, and in future will become a migration target country:

Graph 10.10a: human development in migration societies - HDI according to the old methodology

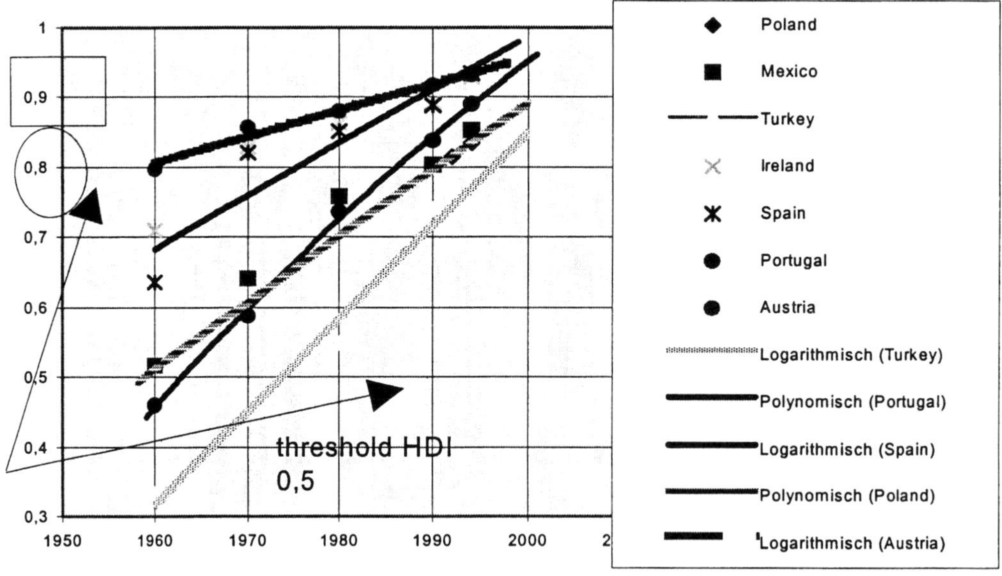

Legend: data analysis and projections about the human development trajectory of migration societies in the world system since 1990. Y-axis: the Human Development Index, according to the old methodology (income, life expectancy, education). Source: our own compilations from UNDP HDR, 1997 and IFRI, 1998. The number of people who emigrated from these countries were (millions of people)

Mexico	7.1
Bangladesh	5.0
Philippines	4.5
Afghanistan	4.2
Pakistan	2.9
Vietnam	2.2
Algeria	1.8
Egypt	1.5
Poland	1.4

Poland already achieved a development level (measured in terms of GNP per capita and also by the new human development index, based on logarithmic measurements of income levels, life expectancy, and education) that corresponds to the levels of Austria in the late 1960s and early 1970s, Spain and Portugal in the 1970s and 1980s:

	A	PL	P	SPA	GR	I	IRL
1965	1270		460	690	710	1260	970
1966	1390		500	790	780	1390	1040
1967	1490		570	880	850	1530	1130
1968	1610		650	960	950	1670	1220
1969	1760		700	1050	1060	1830	1290
1970	1950		790	1100	1170	1990	1350
1971	2170		890	1220	1300	2140	1520
1972	2580		1050	1470	1500	2430	1830
1973	3360		1400	1930	1860	3050	2250
1974	4360		1720	2520	2140	3700	2660
1975	5150		1910	3000	2590	4020	3020
1976	5560		2040	3180	2760	4180	2930
1977	6160		2120	3370	2890	4430	3190
1978	6980		2200	3730	3340	4980	3680
1979	8850		2500	4620	4080	6380	4570
1980	10660		2900	5660	4660	8010	5690
1981	10400		2980	5770	4590	8220	6060
1982	9590	1490	2830	5220	4230	7710	5710
1983	8770	1680	2480	4500	3760	7140	5100
1984	8630	1960	2220	4230	3620	7230	5000

1985	8740	2020	2220	4200	3490	7480	4990
1986	9980	**2060**	2700	4980	3720	8770	5640
1987	12790	1980	3630	6540	4270	11340	7280
1988	16860	2010	4830	8640	5250	14870	9050
1989	17980	1990	5410	9770	5630	16050	9720
1990	19310	1730	6100	11100	5960	17360	11030
1991	20470	1840	7000	12420	6490	18810	11700
1992	23170	1970	8630	14140	7350	21050	13010
1993	23510	2260	9130	13590	7390	19840	13000

Legend: our own compilation from: World Bank; http://www.ciesin.org/

Seen in such a way, there is reason to believe that the tide of migration from Poland already reached its climax in the 1980s and early 1990s during the double crisis of the socialist regime after 1980 and the transformation, and that from now on, Poland will slowly become a net-immigration country:

Graph 10.10b: human development in migration societies - HDI according to the new methodology (logarithm of income, life expectancy, education), and the GNP per capita gap in a historical perspective

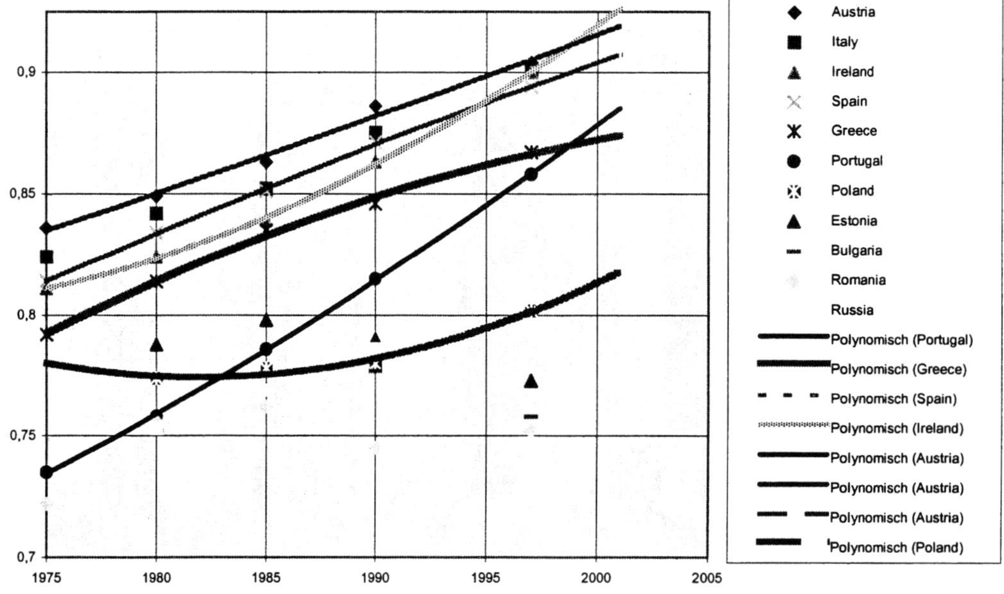

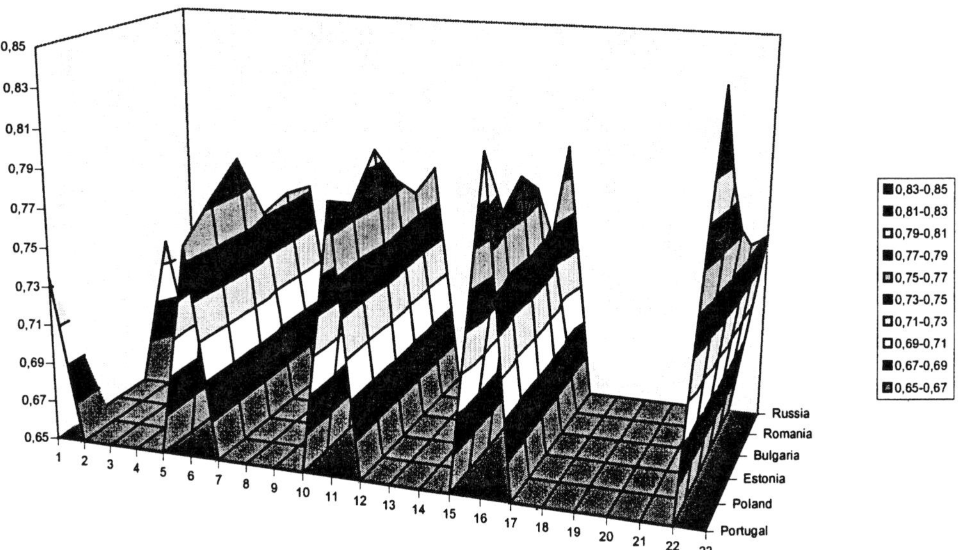

Legend: x-axis in the Graph below: number of years since 1975

GNP per capita in Europe

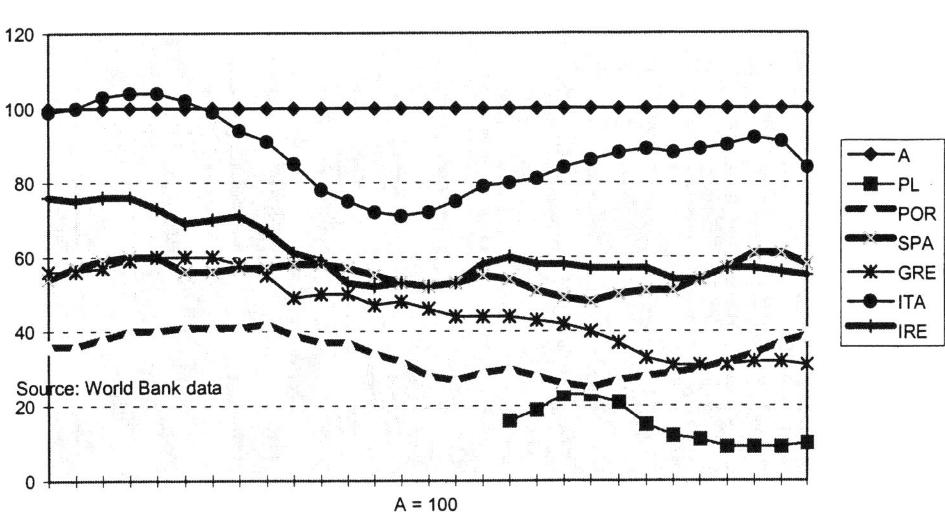

Legend: GNP per capita at current exchange rates. Source: World Bank; our own compilations from: http://www.ciesin.org/

Eastern Europe's relative backwardness in terms of the HDI and in terms of GNP per capita is a consequence of the severity of the transformation depression. Without doubt, migration propensity is highest at a human development level that corresponds to the value 0.6 to 0.5 of the HDI (Human Development Index); i.e. countries like the Ukraine, the Philippines, Indonesia, Mongolia, Albania, Armenia, China, Egypt, El Salvador, Morocco, Vietnam. This hypothesis would also correspond to the every-day experience of any migration official around the world.

Countries in the vicinity of HDI = 0.80 or more, like Portugal, Chile, Singapore, Italy, or Greece, cease to be the source of mass migration. The three-layer structure corresponds also to careful interpretation of different migration 'waves': the migration of rural laborers, the migration of industrial workers, the migration of service-personnel, and the migration of intellectuals at all three phases. Instead of leveling-off international hierarchies, migration is indeed, as Samir Amin foresees it, one of the 5 pillars of international inequality, cementing the unequal positions in the world system instead of leveling them off. Map 10.1 summarizes the tendencies of human development on a European scale. We selected here the following method in order to show the potentials and risks of the accession process. Western Europe's human development is measured in Map 10.1a) by the year 1980, before the EU last wave of expansion, while the candidate countries' human development is measured by the year 1994, the last year with available data. It is to be shown, that a large number of today's accession candidates already fulfill the conditions of the West European countries by 1980, while today's **Croatia, Latvia, Lithuania, Moldova, Romania and Ukraine** are at the level of **Portugal 1980, Bulgaria, Poland, and Turkey** reach the level of **Greek** and **Spanish** human development in 1980, while **Hungary and Slovakia** are already at the level of **Austria**, Belgium, Finland, **Ireland** and Italy in 1980. **Slovenia** and the **Czech Republic** reach already a level of human development that is equal to that of **Denmark, Germany, and the Netherlands** in 1980. Map 10.1b) shows the human development gaps of today on an actual scale. Without EU enlargement, these pan-European differences would have been much greater:

Map 10.1: human development in Europe before EU accession processes

a) comparison: Western Europe (1980), accession countries (1994)

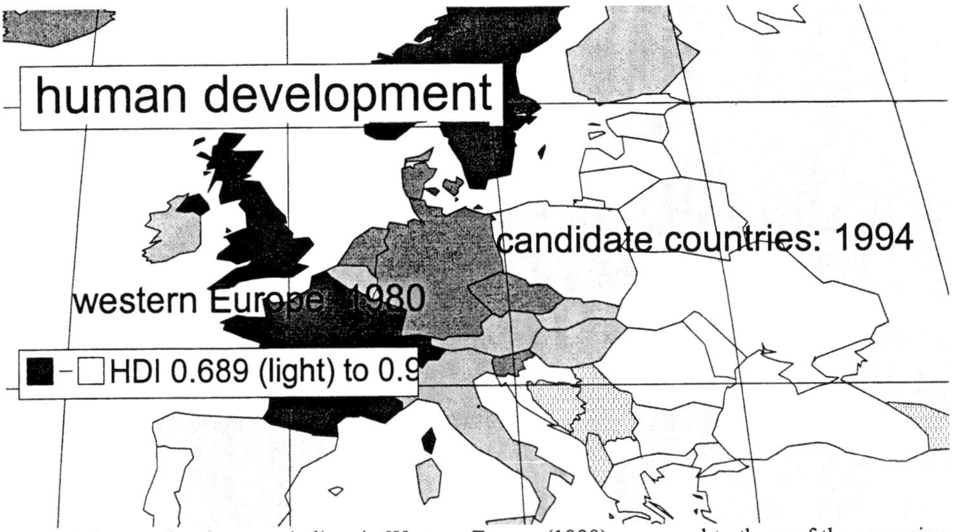

Legend: human development indices in Western Europe (1980) compared to those of the accession countries, 1994. Our own compilations from UNDP Human Development Report, 1997, and the EXCEL map system.

actual comparison (1994)

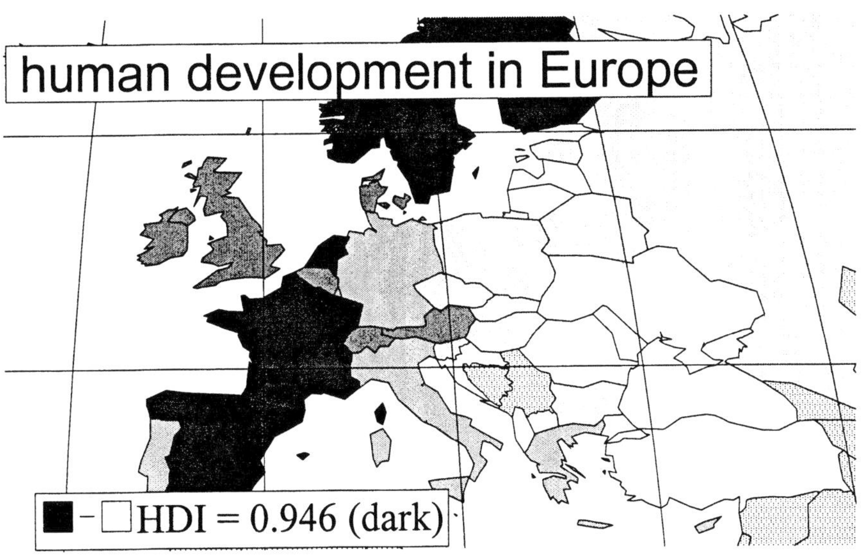

Legend: the contemporary human development differences (old UNDP HDR methodology) in Europe range from France = 0.946 to Albania = 0.655. Thus, they are as large as those between, say, USA (0.942) and Peru (0.717). Sources: see above

At any rate, it would be naive to assume that aid can be a substitute for structural policy to overcome the migration propensity of a society, which, in the end, is nothing but the reaction of a semi-periphery or a periphery to the ups and downs of three-layer structure of the international system in the Arrighian sense. In fact, aid recipients tend to be migratory labor exporters; and aid seems to be unable to reduce long-term migration propensity; on the contrary. The weak trade-off (R^2 = only 4.4%) between aid and migration propensity is the following:

Graph 10.11: aid per capita received and migration propensity

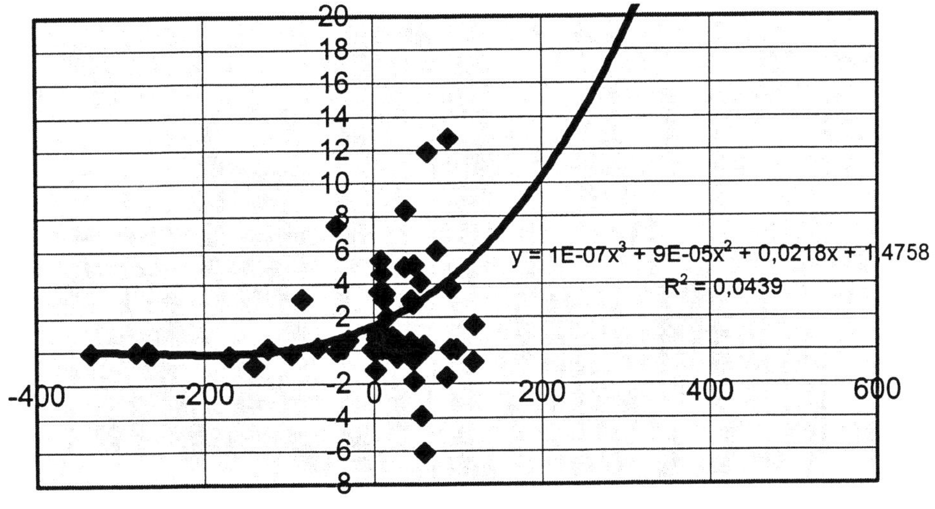

Legend: aid per capita (x-axis) and balance of worker remittances per GDP (y-axis) in the countries of the world system. A negative figure for aid per capita means, that a country is a net donor

country. Source: our own compilations from UNDP HDR, various years. The graphical
presentation excludes the out-layer Lesotho. Aid does not prevent migration.

Both in demographic as well as in sociological terms, much of West European fears about
East European migration at least conceal the real issues of the future migration processes. An
analysis of world population growth trends shows that **Africa, West Asia and Southeast-Asia**
become the real future sending countries, while the demographic structure of East Central Europe
more and more resembles the countries of Western Europe. We try to show this hypothesis in the
following map:

Map 10.2: demographic pressure and future migration trends in the 21st Century

Legend: the share of people aged 0-15 years per total population. The darker, the higher is the share
of the young population per total population. Source: EXCEL map system.

Schengen, in a way, is likely to control these migration flows for some years. But after? It is
entirely possible, that outward migration pressure from Sub-Saharan Africa and West, Central and
Southeast Asia in turn will have long-lasting effects on the countries of Eastern Europe, Turkey,
and the Arab countries. To the degree, that Western Europe effectively seals its borders via the
Schengen system, and Eastern Europe develops, migration pressures will be re-directed in the
following way:

Map 10.3: migration pressure and the Schengen accords

Legend: the darker, the greater the age-structure-determined migration potential

For that reason, East Central Europe already by now should be integrated in a pan-European system of migration reception from third countries, that could be modeled around the present-day Canadian immigration system (candidates with skills, which are still scarce on a more flexible European labor market, receive the permission to stay and to look officially for work for a given time period; if the candidate successfully can settle; asylum strictly limited to circumstances of severe human rights violations; one centralized European asylum application process; redistribution of asylum seekers around the entire European Union to avoid the overburdening of up to now soft, popular countries or countries, neighboring conflict centers). To close the borders completely, that is to say, to practice Schengen alone without any positive attempts at 'Canadization' of the immigration process, will lead to more and more conflicts and even bloodshed. The East Central European accession countries must be early on brought into this system of selective immigration and border management, because else the end-result could be the following process:

Map 10.4: the breakdown of the Schengen system, 2010?

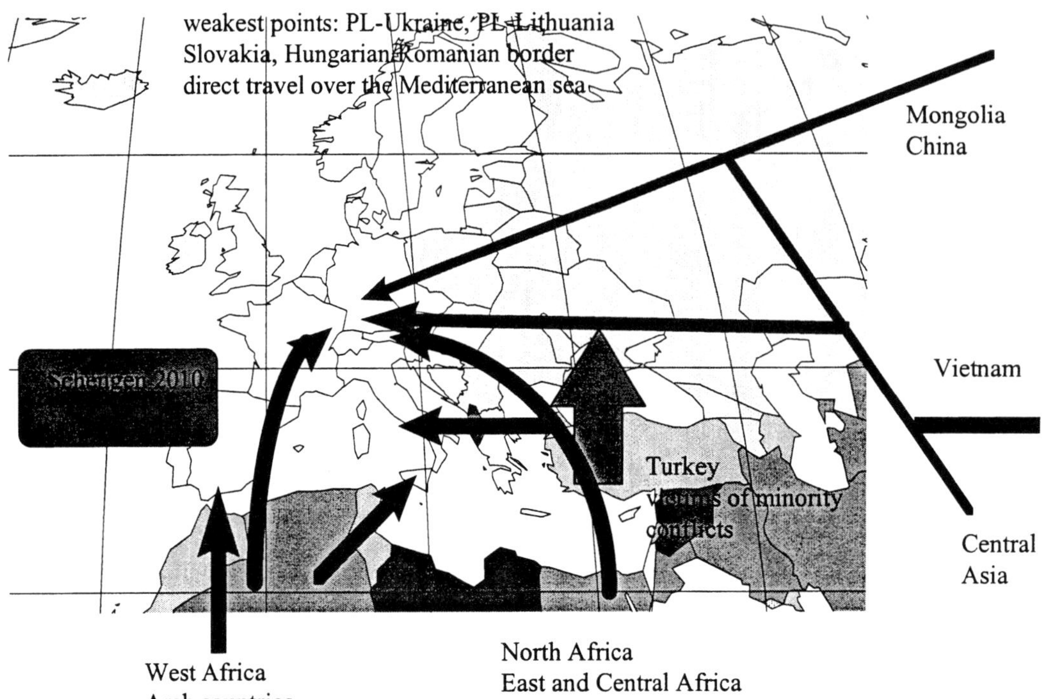

Legend: this scenario would assume, that Western Europe makes no or no decisive efforts to integrate the accession countries into the European Union early on, and does not decisively contribute to a pan-European system of migration management.

Finally, we think that mass migration, especially illegal migration, is closely inter-linked with the changing structure of the elites in the capitalist world system away from 'legal' to 'semi-legal' and 'illegal' business undertakings. Extraction and protection money, forced prostitution, all belong nowadays to a structure, which will increasingly affect the reform countries of East and Central Europe, when they themselves will become targets of mass migration. Just take this article from the *'Washington Post'* as an example of the evolving structures:

Organized Crime Goes Global While the U. S. Stays Home

The Washington Post
May 11, 1997
Edition: FINAL
By: John F. Kerry

Most Americans still refuse to believe just how well-organized global crime has become. Such groups as the Russian mafia and the Chinese triads exist only in the slick fantasy world of television, movies and thriller novels.

Like the dark and powerful men of the "Godfather" trilogy, they may thrill us or chill us, but we don't recognize them as a serious, unprecedented threat. But a new criminal order is being born, more interconnected, violent and powerful than the world has ever seen. To fight it, we have to make fundamental changes in our legal and law enforcement structure, and encourage other nations to do the same.

In strategy, sophistication and reach, the criminal organizations of the late 20th century function like transnational corporations and make the gangs of the past look like mom-and-pop operations. Today's criminal cartels use high-speed modems and encrypted faxes; they buy jet airplanes three or four at a time and even have stealth-like submersibles in their armadas. They hire the finest minds to provide the kind of complex accounting procedures any multi-billion-dollar empire requires.

In one sense, this phenomenon can best be understood as part of the same great process of change that is transforming nearly all aspects of modern life. As **Harvard's Rosabeth Moss Kanter has said, "The world century is beginning. " And, I would add, the century of world crime. Crime has been globalized along with everything else -- except our response to it.**

America is the great prize for criminals, the prime market for imported narcotics, weapons and vice. For that, Americans are, in part, responsible: We create the demand for these products. Individuals must be held accountable when they buy cocaine, guns and the services of prostitutes.

But we must also recognize that the temptation to purchase is now enhanced by sophisticated organizations totally focused on the global marketing of vicious products and violent services, and capable of the wholesale corruption of governments and societies to protect these enterprises.

As the former director of the CIA, James Woolsey, testified before my committee: "When international organized crime can threaten the stability of regions and the very viability of nations, the issues are far from being exclusively in the realm of law enforcement; they also become a matter of national security." A decade ago, my committee investigators and I began to uncover portions of a common international infrastructure for crime. We interviewed criminals inside various U. S. prisons and found that they had remarkable access to political figures in countries.all over the world. This work led me to the drug network of Manuel Noriega and eventually to the place he laundered his money, the Bank of Credit and Commerce International (BCCI). During the dozens of hearings I held, I was able to expose a lot about this hidden world. But I felt that in the day-to-day headlines, some of the scope of what I was seeing had yet to be adequately described.

The new global criminal axis is composed of five principal powers in league with a host of lesser ones. The Big Five are the Italian Mafia, the Russian mobs, the Japanese yakuza, the Chinese triads and the Colombian cartels.

They coordinate with smaller but highly organized gangs with distinct specialties in such countries as **Nigeria, Poland, Jamaica and Panama**, which remains a significant transshipment and money-laundering point even after the arrest of General Noriega. Various alliances among these groups are still in the formative stage, but all indications are that those relations are rapidly becoming more complex and coordinated.

For instance, in the summer of **1992 the leaders of the Russian and Italian mobs held a series of secret summits in Prague, Warsaw and Zurich. Our intelligence on these kinds of gatherings is woefully inadequate, but we can tell much from the results. They decided that rather than compete in the drug trade, they would form a strategic alliance: The Sicilians now provide the know-how to acquire and market the drugs, and the Russians provide security for transit routes and distribution networks throughout the former Soviet empire.**

To see where these interconnections can lead, consider such cases as the contract hit man who flew in from Moscow to kill an uncooperative store owner in New York, on behalf of the Organizatsiya. He got his fake papers by supplying the Sicilian Mafia with Soviet Army surplus ground-to-air missiles to smuggle into the Balkans to supply the Bosnian Serbs with the firepower to take on U. N. security forces.

As French journalist Roger Faligot documented in his recent book on Chinese crime, "The Invisible Empire," Chinese, Japanese and Colombian criminals are working together in the drug trade: "The Colombian cartels produce the cocaine, the Chinese take it in exchange for heroin that can then be smuggled into the U. S. The triads bring cocaine to Japan and distribute it with the help of the yakuzas. Then the Asian mafiosi launder their drug money in Europe. " The triads also have spun out extortion and loan-sharking operations to major British cities such as London, Manchester and Glasgow; heroin trafficking to Rotterdam; prostitution, gambling, robbery and contract murder to Germany; money laundering to Prague; weapons trafficking to Romania, and alien smuggling to Moscow.

In 1995, Italian officials uncovered a sophisticated joint venture between the Camorra crime group and the Russian mafia. The Russians received counterfeit $100 bills in exchange for giving the Italians property, possibly including a large bank, and significant arms shipments. The Italians also buy large quantities of the synthetic narcotics that are becoming a major industry in Russia.

There is evidence that the American mafia, perhaps in an effort to modernize and rejuvenate, is striking similar alliances. Anthony "Gaspipe" Casso, the former acting boss of the Lucchese crime family in New York, has told investigators about New York mobsters taking part in scams developed by the Russians, especially gasoline tax frauds and gasoline bootlegging.

"The Russians supplied the brains and the Mafia supplied the hit men," one investigator said.

America must lead the world in the fight against these private criminal enterprises just as we led the world in the fight against public criminal governments. But we cannot fight alone; we need to create a new international alliance to meet the threats, like the alliances that defeated fascism, communism and Saddam Hussein. We need a revolution in the way we conceive of every aspect of the law, from jurisdiction to punishment. We need to move beyond traditional notions of national sovereignty when those notions benefit only the bad guys.

When a Dominican hit man comes to the United States and engages in a contract killing that winds up also taking the lives of innocent bystanders, he knows he's scot-free if he can reach Dominican soil before the United States grabs him. The same is true if he is Panamanian, Costa Rican, Russian or, for all practical purposes, French. When a Colombian drug trafficker in a Honduran-flagged boat enters French or Dutch waters off the Caribbean island of St. Martin, he knows the pursuing U. S. Coast Guard vessel will have to stop at the three-mile limit.

We have to recognize that the world's patchwork quilt of legal systems is as much an anachronism as carbon paper. A working system of laws to combat transnational crime must be hammered out among nations of good will. These would include:

* Minimum standards of international law. Nations must agree both on a consistent system of laws and a consistent system of punishment. As matters now stand, money laundering is not a crime in Turkey or Russia; extradition is constitutionally banned in Colombia; **and illicit financial dealings still account for too much of the business of banking systems in countries like Switzerland and Austria.**

* Crackdown on money laundering. The dozen or so countries, such as the Cayman Islands, Cyprus and Vanuatu, that have become centers for laundering and sheltering money must be made to desist. The United States has the power: We could refuse to allow pirate financiers to move currency through the U. S. , or impose customs limitations on their trade and search all their cargoes, or forbid Americans to do business there.

* Controls on electronic money. We must insist that the electronic movement of capital be regulated far more strictly. The technology is available to monitor all electronic money transfers. But bankers, although they pretend otherwise, aren't doing all they can to identify the sources of money crossing their threshold. We need to make sure they understand their obligations as key players in enforcement efforts.

* Global asset forfeiture laws. The personal holdings of criminals are often located in any number of foreign lands -- yachts in the Caribbean, homes in the south of France. Each country should have laws allowing domestic and foreign law enforcement to seize and share the property of convicted criminals.

* Transnational courts. In partnership with friendly nations, we need to experiment with a system of special courts to try at home cases involving victims abroad. In such cases, which would be accepted only by agreement between both nations, trials could take place wherever the evidence and witnesses were located, applying the laws of the country where the crime took place.

* More U. S. law enforcement officers abroad. As FBI director Louis J. Freeh wrote recently, "If the FBI operates only in the United States, there is no way we can cope with crime threats of foreign origin that suddenly arrive full-blown in the United States. " We should add 1,000 officers to the 2,000 already stationed abroad. Every U. S. embassy should have a law enforcement team.

The damage done by international crime is rarely as specific and dramatic as that of a terrorist attack, but in fact it is greater. We cannot see the billions of dollars hemorrhaging out of our economy. We cannot directly feel the violation of our sovereignty and territorial integrity by the smugglers of narcotics and human beings. We cannot easily envision the harm to our national security through the failure of countries that once bravely struggled for the dignity of freedom.

If, however, we prove unable to connect the drive-by shooting with the jungle laboratory and the numbered account, we will fail to understand the world we live in. Worse, we will fail to meet our challenge at a critical junction in human history.

Sen. John Kerry (D-Mass.) chaired the Senate Subcommittee on Terrorism, Narcotics and International Operations. This article is adapted from his book, "The New War," to be published next month by Simon & Schuster.

On that somber note, we would like to conclude our analysis.

Chapter 5

A Europe of the Social Movements

Peter Herrmann
Department of Applied Social Studies,
University of Cork, Ireland

Cunning of Reason or Is There a Chance for a Democratic and Social Perspective for Europe and its Role as Global Actor? - The Process of Globalisation Reviewed in a Theoretical Perspective

QUESTIONS FROM A WORKER WHO READS

who built thebes of the seven gates?
in the books you will find the names of kings.
did the kinds haul up the lumps of rock?
and babylon, many times demolished
who raised it up so many times? in what houses
of gold-glittering lima did the builders live?
where, the evening that the wall of china was finished
did the masons go? great rome

is full of triumphal arches. who erected them? over whom
did the caesars triumph? had byzantium, much praised in song
only palaces for its inhabitants? even in fabled atlantis
the night the ocean engulfed it
the drowning still bawled for their slaves.

the young alexander conquered india.
was he alone?
caesar beat the gauls.

did he not have even a cook with him?
philips of spain wept when his armada
went down. was he the only one to weep?

> *frederick the second won the seven years' war. Who*
> *else won it?*
>
> *every page a victory.*
> *who cooked the feast for the victors?*
> *every ten years a great man.*
> *who paid the bill?*
>
> *so many reports.*
> *so many questions.*
>
> *(Brecht)*

*****

During the course of this last chapter of our introductory and study textbook we attempt to set the ideas we developed up to here and the evidence as given by the empirical data in a theoretical framework. This will contribute to the debate of four wider clusters, namely
* the theory of modernisation and modernity
* the theory of globalisation and finally
* the theory of international integration, here the European integration.
We are well aware that these reflections are only tentative, aiming on the development of the debate on these issues. Especially, the class-analytical implications and the implications for a theory of the state need further and thorough investigation. If nothing else, the limited space just at the end of this textbook does not allow us any more.

*****

From whichever angle we approach those facts as we presented them above, we will not arrive at a contemplative picture. This is the case seen from both the countries which are – without having been systematically prepared and without having had the opportunity to do it on their own – teared into the process of globalisation and for those countries that are basically the moving forces. Starting from here, we cannot even attempt to draw a picture for a better world. Nevertheless – and without approaching the matter by putting the gloss over –, there is a glimmer of hope at the end of the tunnel. This is based on two momentums.
* The one is the predicament, which arises for the so-called developed countries and especially for the member countries of the European Union. Up to a certain point it had been possible to build national success stories – under headings as economic growth, wealth, social market economy, social justice but as well cultural diversity, tolerance, advanced education and training and others – on the foundation of the exploitation of the countries of the so-called third world. It had been very simple "exchange" – success here paid by systematically withholding opportunities of development for the other countries. However, it is getting increasingly obvious that this strategy reached the limits. Externalisation of costs, striving for economic success on the back of others is not getting morally reprehensible. Moreover, the western world is now challenged by consequences of the own – intended and unintended – action. This advantage of "unrecognised export of social issues" tips now over into the requirement to repay for the shortcoming and carelessness of the past.
This is most visible in regard of migration. The patterns of migration reflect very much the past strategies – to some extent just turning previous trends back; to some extent continuing these trends in a different setting. Portugal is an example for both these trends – turning back and continuation. A recent article, which looks at Portugal's shift from being a country of emigration to becoming a country of immigration, mentions four momentums that characterise the pattern of immigration.

* ◆ The lack of highly qualified migrants coming into the country – surely not least a reflection of the history and the politics to keep Portugal as one of the rural backyards of Europe.[1]
* ◆ A high share of migrants is coming from previous Portuguese colonies.
* ◆ The ongoing absence of migrants coming from the near regions of North Africa – Muslims stay away and continue in a specific way their resistance against the early Portuguese conquest.
* ◆ The settlement of the migrants in only a few large urban areas – a reflection of the general urban pattern of capitalist development *(see for qualitative data on the migration flows in Portugal Schmidt-Fink, 2000: 17 f.).*
* * Second, we are working in an extremely contradictious field – and here we are concerned with fundamental antagonisms of the process of modernisation rather than with "single issue" contradictions. Speaking of fundamental contradictions is on the one hand concerned with those inherent in capitalist development, but moreover it is at the very same time employing the contradiction of modernisation and modernity. To mention the most important of these contradictions we want briefly point at the following.
* ◆ Even if class relationships never had been as easy as they had sometimes been interpreted, this is today even more the case. Social class interests are still the basis for the structuration of current societies. However, in the context here we are concerned with the national classes, the same classes in different countries and the different classes in different countries. This complex multi-layered pattern – which is permanently present, even if at times dormant – makes it easily possible to play interests around nationality off against class interests.
* ◆ Another contradiction – to some extent just an expression of the one mentioned before – is the one between actions against different horizons in regard of time – medium and long term interests are more and more taken consciously into consideration as part of developing economic and political strategies.
* ◆ A crucial challenge exists in balancing the contradictious field of regional, namely EUropean interests versus the monopolistic, worldwide oriented interests of the capitalist block, as it is represented by the TNCs. Even in political terms the later take always part in the negotiations. However, this is both the contradiction between regional and truly international interests and between economic and political interests. Interestingly, the representatives of the economic block are reaching further in regard of the political dimension – they are global players on the foundation of being "global thinkers". One could now formulate the other point of view from the parliamentary perspective – far reaching political approaches and limited economic power and as well limited global impetus are characterising the politicians' views.
* ◆ Especially the current economic status is characterised by the contradicting interests of productive capital on the one hand side and capital in the sphere of circulation on the other side. The latter is divided in – on the one hand – the financial capital and – on the other side – the interest in services. The latter, again, is especially tricky and contradictious in itself insofar as explicitly not-for-profit aspects, common goods and the like are included. This causes special problems either for the service providers – if they agree upon the fact to produce market goods under non-market conditions – or it causes problems for the users of some services as far as they are forced to accept non-market services as market-commodities.
* ◆ Another important aspect is concerned with the ever increasing integration of the structures of acquiring the existing knowledge; on the other hand the capabilities of action are getting increasingly negatively effected by processes of differentiation, which undermine the development of complex and strategically elaborated action.

We have to take these – and other – momentums against the background of the idea which *Frederick Engels* spelled out so well in his letter to *J. Bloch* in Königsberg: 'According to the materialist conception of history, the *ultimately* determining element in history is the production and reproduction of real life. Other than this neither Karl Marx nor I have ever asserted. Hence if

---

[1] Of course, there had been other aspects involved that caused the reserve to develop Portugal faster.

somebody twists this into saying that the economic element is the *only* determining one, he transforms that proposition into a meaningless, abstract, senseless phrase. The economic situation is the basis, but the various elements of the superstructure – political forms of the class struggle and its results, to wit: constitutions established by the victorious class after a successful battle, etc., juridical forms, and even the reflexes of all these actual struggles in the brains of the participants, political, juristic, philosophical theories, religious views and their further development into systems of dogmas – also exercise their influence upon the course of the historical struggles and in many cases preponderate in determining their *form*. There is an interaction of all these elements in which, amid all the endless host of accidents (that is, of things and events whose inner interconnection is so remote or so impossible of proof that we can regard it as non-existent, as negligible), the economic movement finally asserts itself as necessary. Otherwise the application of the theory to any period of history would be easier than the solution of a simple equation of the first degree.' (Engels, 1890)

*****

That we are, in fact, employed by the fundamental contradiction of modernisation and modernity is especially relevant for and from a EU-perspective. The member countries of this entity took up on the world agenda as "inventors of modernisation and modernity". Of course, this has to be qualified, namely in two regards

* Modernisation stands in these countries in a very specific context which is not just a contemporary "statutory ideology". Instead, popular movements during the recent history of these countries employ the topic of modernisation. Basically, we can go back to the emancipative impetus of the bourgeois enlightenment and the – especially French – revolution. Of course, all the movements reflect and many of these movements mirror and reproduce the class conflict of capitalist societies and it might even be asked how far modernisation had been systematically split into two halves. Furthermore it can be asked if and in which sense modernisation had been basically a concept of capitalisation – the political and ideological superstructure of the capitalist mode of production. Nevertheless, even if this question would have to be answered affirmatively, it does not make any difference to the fact of the connection to the bourgeois movement.

* Of course, it has to be admitted as well that EUrope is not alone in claiming the originality of modernisation. There had been and is a way of modernisation in the American Society as well. However, the specific understanding in Western Europe had always been against this economistic and "world gendarme role", and instead more based on the philosophy of enlightenment. Thus, in a generalised way we can say that the European understanding is more concerned with "personal", psychological elements.

Thus, departing from this wider context, we are challenged (and have the opportunity) to work on a theory of globalisation that takes into account not simply the processes on the surface but recognises this – by real actors made – process in its very real-dialectical nature. There are the following three sides of a kind of sequence that have to be considered.

1) globalisation as process of externalisation of "costs" from the so-called developed into the so-called underdeveloped countries;

2) globalisation as process of enforcement of the reimbursement of the previously externalised costs;[2]

3) globalisation as chance of enhanced integration *(cf. Herrmann, 1999)*.

This corresponds with

1) the worsening of the situation of the peripheral countries and some groups of the population respectively;

2) the enforcement of concessions; and

---

[2] En passent, this is – seen from many of the economists and politicians of the world-economy and world-development institutions – connected with avoiding additional, future costs.

3) the real inclusion and setting up an world-inclusive process of emancipation and development. As such, we can back the analysis of these developments by the classical dialectical methodology with thesis (1) anti-thesis, (2) and syntheses (3). Furthermore and again in theoretical terms now, taking more recent terminology of system-theory into account, we can see this as sequence of differentiation, de-differentiation and finally integration.

*****

Just while writing on this last chapter, we are – once again – stumbled on the complexity of the real process behind the development – October the 17th is the annual *International Day for the Eradication of Poverty*. This aims – according to the information entailed in a background and information package – on the following:
* to commemorate victims of extreme poverty.
* to bear witness to their suffering, courage and struggle.
* to affirm the conviction that extreme poverty is not inevitable.
* to find and give support, sing, pray, meet and unite in the common goal of eradicating poverty.
* to allow children's and young people's inherent sense of justice lead the way towards overcoming poverty and exclusion.
* to commit ourselves to act all year long against extreme poverty, learning how to do this in partnership with the poorest.' *(http://www.nscentre.org/english/opening.htm – 2000-10-15)*

It is not without a specific curiosity that this – and here especially the role of the actors, the non-governmental forces – is put (back) on our minds just at the end, after compiling the bulk of empirical work in regard of describing poverty and social exclusion, after analysing these phenomena in the context of the world system of political and more particularly economic relations and after elaborating the connection of exclusion between processes of exclusion of countries and in countries. The latter could easily be highlighted by looking at countries of the so-called Middle East or – as some of them are called as well – the countries in transition. It is only now, at the very end, that our attention is lead on the NGOs – as they are a last resort in history they are a last resort as well only in investigation on the subject.

To speak of these actors as a last resort has to be understood in a twofold way. They are those whose voice is heard in the last instance, who have only at the end of a long process the opportunity to contribute their experience and knowledge into the process of policymaking. And, second, they are the last resort insofar that they are suggested as actors only when the traditional actors fail in their role of facing the challenges and, in addition recognise the pressing need to (re)act.

Of course, it has to be qualified when we just said that *the traditional actors fail* because it is questionable who can be seen as traditional actors. Finally, the state in its current form as nation state is – historically – a very recent in(ter)vention. In other words, speaking of NGOs as subsidiary is not only addressing their nearness to the lower aggregative levels of societies, just referring to something what we might call originality; rather it is concerned as well with an originality in historical terms, in terms of the development of societies. Actually, these organisations had been in existence before the state stepped onto the stage. Later, they redefined their role by becoming intermediaries. That, however, does not change their character as original entities. Seen in this perspective the recent and current debate cannot be other than the re-socialisation of tasks, which had been and are taken out of society. This is not (primarily) employed by the idea of the sociological approach of bureaucracy. Rather, the remark links up to the *Marxist* approach, which sees the state and its single sub-institutions as institutions of the bourgeois class-society, institutions that gained a seemingly independent status.[3]

*****

---

[3] Of course, we are well aware of the problems – limitations and even dangers – which have to be considered in connection with these organisations in question. However, we cannot look into details in this regard and we do not even want to think about the justification and limitation of these organisations here.

Before we look at this process of "bringing society back to the fore", we have to consider briefly some general questions of the process, which is commonly referred to as globalisation. We have to get aware of the implicitly underlying fact of the previous remarks that globalisation, as we are concerned with in the current political debate is not necessarily new in generic terms. Moreover, it is not a process, which is in any way threatening the current systems both "here" and "there". Largely, moreover, we are confronted with '"Globalization" as a myth' *(Hoffmann/ Hoffmann, 1997: 7)*. The authors point on four momentums for this argument.

'Firstly: The term "globalization" does *not* denote a new, historically *unusual* expansion of the volume of world trade on a global scale which has supposedly not already been noted in the debate on internationalization that has taken place over the last few decades. ...

Secondly: Similarly, increased *direct investment* abroad, which is likewise held out as proof of the pressure of globalization, can *not* be accounted for by the globalization of the economy and – embedded therein – by the wage cost argument; instead it serves as a dynamo of globalization. ...

Thirdly: In Europe, in the background of the economic developments outlined here, there can by no means be said to be excessively high wage costs when viewed in "global" terms; indeed there has been a demonstrably *favourable* development of *unit labor costs* for companies – i.e. the connection between overall wages and productivity. ...

Fourthly: Similarly, the employment crisis in Western Europe can hardly be accounted for primarily by the "globalization" of world trade, in which ... the EU's export share is only 8 %, or by the decentralization strategies facing multinational companies.' *(ibid.: 7-9; Italic in the original; cf. for a discussion of these and similar issues: the contributions by Fligstein, 2000 and Pierson, 2000)*[4]

Nevertheless, even if the process is not entirely new there is some new impetus inherent. One has not to desert to the idealist camp to accept that one important strand of these new momentums is the increasing knowledge about the process not only of impoverishment and neglecting human rights but of the interconnection between the different levels and forms of action. In other words, even if in one or the other way much of what is happening today happened already since decades it is nowadays not anymore going on in isolation. Rather, connections, which had been unknown before, become known, unintended actions have become accepted side effects – and both is not a matter of establishing theoretical links. Instead, the knowledge becomes part of everyday and everybody's life. What is more is that the real imbalance of power is coming to the fore as well as the potential power of those who had been – and still are – excluded of decision making *(cf. Herrmann, 1999)*.

---

[4] Conversely, they point at the following aspects of '"Globalization" as reality.

Firstly: With the formation of Eurodollar markets following US indebtedness resulting from the Vietnam War, with the collapse of the Bretton Woods global currency system, with the subsequent flexibility of exchange rates, with the global debt crisis of the 1980s, and with the development of offshore banking centres, enormous, free-floating financial and speculative assets have accumulated on the back of government borrowing. ...

Secondly: A decisive factor for the emerging dramatic changes in the business culture in the countries of "Rheinish capitalism" in Europe is the trend for a growing number of companies, instead of taking capital out capital loans and using interest rates, to acquire the capital they need via the stock exchange, where they are increasingly confronted in their business policy with the short-term interests and calculations of shareholders. ...

Thirdly: Through the use of modern information and communications technologies, transnational companies (TNCs) in particular, and companies in general, can switch their production to a new level of policy of cross-border "external flexibility" as part of strategies of "lean production" and "new production concepts". ...

Fourthly: With the internationalisation of money capital and the international investment strategies of "global players" ..., *nations* and regional groups of nations... increasingly become *competitors* for this capital, try to keep budget, to economize additionally under the pressure of high interest rates on government debt.' *(ibid.: 11-13)*

Another important point is that these imbalances of power are occurring across social borders, to some extend lay themselves over the traditional power structures. In other words, those who have had power up to recently see that these powers evaporate. Even if this process can be named – power of the state is transferred to power of TNCs, political power is replaced by economic power – it is legitimate to speak of evaporation. The reason is that we are not really concerned by a simple transfer of power. Instead, what is behind it is the creation of new powers and new power structures. I.e. economic power does not "influence" political power, it builds up to a new political-economic-social-cultural power. The regulation theory mentions the systemic character by introducing terms as accumulation regimes etc.

In regard of the nation state, this has been discussed for many times over the recent years – the loss of power, thus the loss of opportunities to act by the state. What is part of this is that actually the nation ceases to some extent to exist – borders are abrogated, they evaporate. Again, even if it can be made out "where they are going", there is no point to get hold of them.

This calls for new alliances – and we can link this interpretation back to original interpretations of the ideas of enlightenment insofar as the perspective of the actors change. What had been previously the extension of their own, "personal"[5] horizon of action begins to tip over into fetters.

Underscoring the political economy of the process of soci(et)al development *Karl Marx* formulated 'In the social production of their life, men enter into definite relations that are indispensable and independent of their will, relations of production which correspond to a definite stage of development of their material productive forces. The sum total of these relations of production constitutes the economic structure of society, the real foundation, on which raises a legal and political superstructure and to which correspond definite forms of social consciousness.

The mode of production of material life conditions the social, political and intellectual life process in general. It is not the consciousness of men that determines their being, but, on the contrary, their social being that determines their consciousness.

At a certain stage of their development, the material productive forces of society come in conflict with the existing relations of production, or – what is but a legal expression for the same thing – with the property relations within which they have been at work hitherto. From forms of development of the productive forces these relations turn into their fetters.

Then begins an epoch of social revolution.' *(Marx, 1859)*

For our context here this means that we have to analyse the continuities and discontinuities of power structures.

*****

We want to discuss this now in the theoretical perspective of society-(re-)building and in this context arising opportunities for action. Here we take up the term from above, i.e. "bringing society back to the fore". To analyse the contradiction of modernisation and modernity we refer to a shift of the power of disposal over the means of social production and appropriation. We can summarise this idea by pointing at the development of a large and still increasing body of increasing social control mechanisms, growing social knowledge, enhanced instruments and means on the social level to intervene; but at the same time personal control and even social control of how to use these advancements and enhancements are neither developed to the same degree nor are they in any way socially equitable; in other words, the individual and soci(et)al capacity of appropriation increases while the individual and soci(et)al control does not keep pace or – even worse – decreases *(cf. Herrmann, 1993 b; 1994)*. This is closely linked to the soci(et)al re-structuration in regard of what *Nobert Elias* called "long chains of action" *(see Elias, 2000)* and what is in more recent sociological terms debated under differentiation.

The question of economic power and its mono-dimensional orientation versus the political power and its more multidimensional orientation involves at least the questions around the

---

[5] Personal here is not only concerned with individual; rather it includes the space of action for the social group to which the individual belongs.

limitation of (previously and seemingly well established) existing power – it is the politicians, who fear to loose their privileges. This turns out as an extremely outspoken trend in the European Parliament's Report in regard of the Multilateral Agreement on Investment *(Kreissl-Dörfler, 1998)*. This document states that 'these are times of dramatic change in the world economy, which is becoming a globalized, transnational, deregulated, virtual world of markets in which political freedom of action and national sovereignty are gradually being yielded to the multinationals, the international banks and powerful international organizations … This is not to deny that flexibly regulated markets can promote productivity and prosperity. This is not however true of totally deregulated markets, since market forces alone are not capable of regulating matters which lie outside the laws of the economy, such as social justice, environmental protection or human rights. … In this context it is unacceptable that the MAI should place the multinationals on virtually the same political footing as the individual states … .' *(13)* – Admittedly the report shows in depth the contradictory character of the argument – fear of loosing own power and the will to broaden power, the will to overcome economically backed power of monopolist capital and holding on to a concept of the market economy, backed by the unspecified interpretation of a social market economy.[6] But contradictory means just this – that there are two sides, standing unresolved side by side. In other words, the threat under which the political system currently is put by losing power and opportunities for action opens the system and its representatives to other forces – to the forces of the "market economy", as they are forinstance accepted in the social democratic statement on the Third Way *(Blair/Schroeder, 1999)*, but as well to democratic forces.

Actually, it is to some extent the basis for mutual understanding and action. It involves the question if and in which sense it might be necessary to reconsider the theory of the state.

This institutionalised contradiction between classes is at the same time a means to bridge at least some of the contradictions of the process of modernisation. Modernisation, as *Norbert Elias* pointed out in his excellent study on *The civilizing process,* is a process of a very specific structuration of social relationships, which connects the individual with the social character of being. As such, it is concerned with processes of increasing appropriation by – at the same time – limiting the direct, abrupt control by the individuals. The individual capacities are being socialised – access to a much wider field of being has been established via exchange – but for the price of limiting the immediate reach of action. Again, we have to remember his writing on establishing and maintaining long chains of action. We can observe this process over an extremely long period, happening in some form of revolutionary changes as well as by the interstitial process of at the respective time nearly unrecognised development *(cf.Mann, 1986)*. What is important is the translation of this process of establishing, developing and maintaining such long chains of action in changing power and thus class structures – actually on its own an interesting process of balancing change and stability/persistence, dynamic and static elements of structuration. *Karl Marx* and *Frederick Engels* as well as their later scholars worked on this matter, showing the objective foundation of this structuration and allowing to elaborate their dialectical-material and historical terms. A closed term at what they called formation is surely worthwhile. Even if this seems to be a different issue, concerned with international class relationships rather then with the process of globalisation as process of general modernisation it is important, indeed, to emphasise this dimension of the contradicting character. What actually happens is the prolongation and "mirroring" of what we mentioned before – in the words of *Karl Marx* – in regard of the political economy and what we can find now as well in the political system. Borrowing – and at the same time changing – the words of *Marx* we can say that *at a certain stage of its development, the differentiation of the political system of society come in conflict with the existing relations of strategic powers. From forms of development of the freedom of action and opportunity to intervene in regard of soci(et)al relations these relations turn into their fetters.*

---

[6] *Cf. Deutscher Bundestag, 2000*

In other words up to a certain point in history the ever increasing differentiation of the political system, therein subsequently the division of labour and the partial diffusion and even renunciation of power worked out as a means of integration of the whole system. There is, however, a limit in regard of gains by this process – decision making is getting more and more concerned with trying to control unintended consequences of previous action; freedom of action and opportunities for action are abolished and localised or regionalised – a question of space, but as well one of time and "sociality" *(cf. Ferge, 1999).*

*****

History never repeats itself. However, what happens is a kind of reinforcing reintegration which makes place for at least part of the previously – and still suppressed, excluded and disadvantaged parts of the world. This is concerned with the spatial regional, namely the integration of the interest of countries of the so-called Third World. Furthermore, it is concerned with the inclusion of social groups and interests in political action. We are concerned with a process of regaining capability of action. Of course, this is a very painful process because some groups will loose power or will have less power than they currently have. Thus, it is a contradictious process. – As *Frederick Engels* highlighted 'We make our history ourselves, but, in the first place, under very definite assumptions and conditions. Among these the economic ones are ultimately decisive. But the political ones, etc., and indeed even the traditions which haunt human minds also play a part, although not the decisive one.' *(Engels, 1890)*[7]

In regard of theory of modernisation this means that we are confronted with another – in a sense revolutionary – leap of extending the chain of action and reuniting capabilities to act und possibilities to intervene on a higher level.

Necessarily we have to come back now on the previous remarks on NGOs – the last resort of action. Since and insofar the prevailing economic and political systems are not in the position to resolve the conflicts – simply because they lost ground and are fetters for further action – they have to give power away. This is what we mentioned as process of bringing society back to the fore. Citizenship, civil action are gaining a pronounced meaning – as we said above *decision making is getting more and more concerned with trying to control unintended consequences of previous action; freedom of action and opportunities for action are abolished and localised or regionalised – a question of space, but as well one of time and "sociality".'* What there had been set up as a process of loss of control means here a gain of control. By including localities, regions, social groups, "local times" etc. in the process of decision making this is an answer on the pressing loss of control. The chain of action, which had been broken, is reunited; the alienation is overcome not by adaptation but by the process of the dialectically two sided process of *Aufhebung,* keeping and maintaining, but as well abolishing.

Actually, the whole process is a paradox shift of control. If we look back we see that the state (had been) established (itself) as institution to control civil society. Civil society was not capable to resolve the problems of living together – for this one does not have to accept *Hobbes'* theses. One problem, which was in no way connected with this *Hobbesian* battle all against all had been the long chains of action, as we mentioned them already for several times. People lost the control over their immediate surrounding and the whole system at the same time.[8] Thus, "the state" became essential and actually a consequence of the parallel process of "internalising control", as *Elias* described it. In a second historical step it turned out necessary that the state itself had to be controlled – civil society changed its role and became to some extent a counterforce, a mechanism, which controlled partly the power, which became more and more independent from "real life". In addition they worked against some of the consequences of this detachment. However, the long

---

[7] Of course, we have to consider in a more detailed study the resistance of the aristocracy and the specific alliance between bourgeoisie and aristocracy on the one hand, on the other side the alliance between bourgeoisie and working-class.

[8] These statements can well be fit into a *Marxist* theory of the state.

chains of action had been not effected – they remained the underlying pattern – and actually only their existence made this civilisation of politics possible – and necessary. Even if this process was already a kind of weakening of the statutory system it was really not more than said before: *civilisation of politics.* Only in a third step it might be possible – we cannot say more yet because we are currently in the middle of this process – that the civilisation of politics is driven further and it is possible to establish *civilised politics.* As such, we would reach at a point where direct control is at least part – and a central part – of the overall political structuration. We might support – and extend – in this way the idea of *Mary Kaldor,* who writes 'Whereas, the classical definitions [of society, the authors] presupposed the existence of a state, the contemporary concepts can be described as a move away from state centred approaches, both in a societal sense – more concern with individual empowerment and personal autonomy – and in a geographical sense – a territorial restructuring of social relations resulting from intensifying interconnectedness.' *(Kaldor, 2000: page 4)*

Some support of such a thesis can be gained by what one of the current authors called occasionally *(e.g. Herrmann, 1998 b: passim)* "politics surrounding the nation state".

*****

This is – up to here – a very abstract rapprochement. Nevertheless, it is neatly mirrored in the current development and the difficulties and juggle with the world powers.

In the current setting the traditional dichotomous approach of "developed" and "underdeveloped" world cannot be used anymore[9] to conceptualise world development. It cannot be used either to establish the role of individual actors. Here it does not matter if we are concerned with individuals – the "great men of history" – or with social groups or with nation states. What matters, then again, is the pressure from the totality of the conditions. The connection between actions all over the world in combination with (a) the knowledge of the dependencies and (b) the increasing capabilities to re-act[10] respectively enforce the consideration of "the other" in the own action. – It is remarkable when *James Wolfensohn,* president of the World Bank, says 'Outside these walls young people are demonstrating against globalisation. I believe deeply that many of them are asking legitimate questions, and I embrace the commitment of a new generation to fight poverty. I share there passion and their questioning. Yes, we all have a lot to learn.' *(Wolfensohn, 2000: 18)*[11] According to the same source he stated that 'poverty is about more than inadequate income or even low human development; it is also about lack of voice, lack of representation. It is about vulnerability to abuse and to corruption. It is against violence against women and fear of crime. It is about lack of esteem.' The cold shower of reality follows by the commentator who states that 'if they are to help, global institutions must have a focused understanding of their objectives and appropriate means. Mr Wolfensohn hardly provides this. ... Alas, a development institution that believes poverty is about all this will collapse under its imperial overstretch.' *(ibid.; cf. Brittan, 2000: 19)* As we all know, this harsh reality is still a major driving force – Multilateral Agreement on Investment (MAI), General Agreement on Trade and Services (GATS), General Procurement Agreement (GPA) and the like are opposing any glimmer of hope. Even if for example the MAI could not succeed in the envisaged way the underlying strategic attitude is still the same. It claims for many times that there is a border, a demarcation line between *The We*

---

[9] Actually it is a question if it had been a legitimate concept at whichever time.

[10] And it does not matter what kind of reaction we find here; it might even the re-action of an increasing number of refugees who cross the borders and represent seemingly a threat for the Western societies of Europe.

[11] Without doubt, there will be much ideology and trimming in such a statement. On the other hand, despite lip-service there will be some grain of honesty in it, as well. In any case, we have to be careful with such statements because they can easily be used (a) to shift the issue on a subjective level and water down the objective problems and (b) even to accuse the victims.

and *The Others,* of course celebrating the first as the better, if not the best of all worlds and peoples.[12]

However, in a way remarks as that of *Wolfensohn* might be at least an embryonic form of the cunning of reason. We remember, *G.F.W. Hegel* wrote that 'the special interest of passion is thus inseparable from the active development of a general principle: for it is from the special and determinate and from its negation, that the Universal results. Particularity contends with its like, and some loss is involved in the issue. It is not the general idea that is implicated in opposition and combat, and that is exposed to danger. It remains in the background, untouched and uninjured. This may be called the *cunning of reason,* – that it sets the passions to work for itself, while that which develops its existence through such impulsion pays the penalty and suffers loss. For it is *phenomenal* being that is so treated, and of this, part is of no value, part is positive and real. The particular is for the most part of too trifling value as compared with the general: individuals are sacrificed and abandoned. The Idea pays the penalty of determinate existence and of corruptibility, not from itself, but from the passions of individuals.' *(Hegel, 1837)*

*****

To talk of a shift and re-structuration is by no means coupled with the abolishment of the class conflict. Openness and transparency the interests of national propria, the interests of nation states and the institutionalised coverage of these vested interests. Furthermore, of ongoing meaning is the process of playing the national working classes off against the workers in other countries – we just see this confirmed again and again in the negotiations where employees renounce – allegedly in the interest of "national competitiveness" – on their share. The signing of national agreements indicate this as their failure in practice does indicates it at the same time. Contemporary Ireland is a classic example for this. What takes place, nevertheless, is a re-definition of the "nation state" and its "best interest".

And in this context it is interesting – we can mention it only en passant – that innernational and international exploitation are in fact just the different sides of one single coin. According to the recent report of the *UNDP* the difference in income between the richest and the poorest fifth quintile of the world population increased from 30:1 in 1960 to 7:1 in 1997. We do not draw an immediate parallel and renounce an exact empirical evaluation. However, fact is that the gap between the rich and poor increased as well in the so-called developed world.

Just for curiosity it should be mentioned that modernisation in the way as we mean it is just the opposite of modernisation as it had been developed as ideology especially during the middle of the last century in the United States of America. Rather than being a gospel for the countries of the so called Third World, where the peculiarities of inhabitants had only been accepted as *"cuteness of the Sarotti golliwog",*[13] a responsible use of the term, linking it back to the epoch of enlightenment, underscores the empowering dimension. This generic European interpretation interlinks individualisation with socialisation, and in fact sees them as complementing features. Between individualisation and socialisation we do not find a "either-or"- and a "despite"-relation respectively. What we find is a relationship of causality in both directions: because of the high level of individualisation a high level of socialisation is possible and necessary and at the very same time: because of the high level of socialisation a high level of individualisation is possible and necessary. To ask if individualisation or socialisation had been there in the first place is like the well-known egg-hen-question. In regard of the search for answers it is more important, anyway, to ask how it had been possible that the chicken came into the egg.

Anyway, coming back to the main line of the argument it has to be clear that what is needed is a positive identity which goes beyond the borders of the nation state – and opening consciousness

---

[12] This refers as well to several paragraphs in our own previous analysis. In regard of the so-called Third-World-countries as well as in regard of the countries of real socialism our elaboration simply adopted this argument, thus neglecting very much the strength of the countries.

[13] As an at the time famous and actually very popular advertisement in Germany promoted.

for a European identity could be well a basic step to develop as well an openness for global connections.

What is interesting in this context is a seeming paradox – the complementary relationship between global and local orientation. 'An unexpected consequence of the globalization and universalization of identity ... is that this process may simultaneously reinforce small-scale particularistic attachments as well. This is because universalism comprises and affirms the right to one's own culture, in other words, the right to be particularistic.' *(Kohli, 2000: 129; with reference to Robertson, 1992 and Soysal, 1997)*

Thus, what we are dealing with when reflecting European Integration in the context of globalisation is actually nothing less then the development of a new citizenry.

*****

We talked during the previous parts of the book – in one or another way – about the globalisation of a process lead by the international capital, by multinational trusts and enterprises and not least increasingly by the free floating resources on financial markets. We talked as well – departing from the included inequality on market based developments about developmental aid. There is – as far as the mainstream is concerned – nothing wrong with this. However, European integration in the context of globalisation is a multilayered process, where different levels of action and actors influence each other. Moreover, given these conditions, development can not be maintained in the way it had been used up to now. Actually, the concept has been employed in the empirical context in a rather American-Euro-centric way – assuming that the rest of the world is simply under-developed. In other words, such a concept still suggests that the development of the capitalist world is basically the only acceptable way of development, only lacking some justice in regard of distribution and redistribution. We are back to all these concepts which had been used against communism and socialism during the years of the cold war, looking for a better capitalism but not for an alternative – and thus better – society. But the search for a real alternative is by far not redundant after the capitalist overrule-policy succeeded. Instead, it is more important than ever.

Marx and *Engels* focussed on this, characterising it as a field of tensions, with two – complementing – remarks. The one says that human beings make their history themselves, but emphasises that they do so under specific historic circumstances. The other says that such a process has to be understood as a dialectic one, realising development as process of *Aufhebung* – keeping and maintaining as well as abolishing.

Taking the *Marxist* point of view as interim step we have to redefine our question. Then it does not read anymore *How can we make the current path of development be shaped in a way, which is more just? How can we increase its legitimacy?* Rather we have to ask *What kind of development are we concerned with?* And: *Can we sustain the assumptions of this pathway?*

*****

Concluding this introductory and study textbook we only want to make a brief comment on this issue. Especially we will highlight what we called above the last resort and go a little bit beyond the issue of NGOs to ask *if we are on the way to any kind of a globalised citizenship or a responsible and sustainable[14] European citizenship?* – Asking these questions – and attempting to give answers – implies already some optimism. We are strongly suggesting that such optimism is not based on a voluntaristic worldview. Rather this is an optional worldview, taking into account the fact that is behind the *Marxian* quote given above; i.e. it is the people who make their history; but we have to be well aware of the limits of power.[15]

We find empirical evidence for an increasing importance of globality not just in regard of markets but as well in regard of citizenship or responsibility. Even if it is a contradictory process,

---

[14] Here, the term sustainability is not meant in the way as it is originally developed, thus including the human being with its social dimension as point of departure rather then reducing sociality as by-product or point for influencing behaviour.

[15] The limits of growth are, in fact, nothing else than the limits of power.

we can see this development in connection with two issues. The one is – to some extent at least – a top-down process. The United Nations and the Council of Europe are a kind of classical examples in this regard – they have an extensive strategy of including nongovernmental organisations in their policy development processes. Besides the usual openness for lobbying procedures we find a formally elaborated system of accreditations, negotiations and decision making structures. The institutions of the European Union, in particular the European Commission is as well concerned with enhancing and signalling openness for the interests of civil society organisations. Hearings, open fora, specialised "NGOs" (or supporting selected NGOs in an extensive way), established from above and act as mediators (as for example EAPN, the Platform of social NGOs and others) have to be mentioned here *(cf. Herrmann, 1998 a).*[16] To mention just one other incidence which is relevant here we point on the Report on Equal Opportunities, which stresses the importance of including women's and gender questions respectively in the fight for Human Rights *(cf. European Commission, 2000: 26 ff.; in general see Deacon, 1999; Salamon, 1994; Salamon/Anheier, 1999; as well Herrmann/Lorenz, 1997; finally:* http://www.lse.ac.uk/Depts/global/Default.htm*).*

The second evidence of the development of a kind of global citizenship is concerned with the development of the idea and practice of some kind of global citizenship *consciousness*. It has to be said that this is – as a bottom-up process – well in line with the tradition of enlightenment. Inclusion, empowerment, reason are mentionable as guiding principles *(see for the development in the EU-context again Herrmann/Lorenz, 1997)* even if in many instances distracted by settings of current policy making procedures.[17]

In both cases, this brings us to the issue of multidimensionality as it draws attention to the necessity of acting in various – connected – dimensions, namely

a) the inherent injustices of capitalism.

b) the price of the Western lifestyle, including not least

◆ the commodification as it is especially currently visible in the trend[18] to a "service based society" respectively the dominance of service providing industries

◆ "depowerment" of people, actually an unintended effect, which counteracts modernisation by its own means – we described it as breaking apart of capacities of appropriation (increasing knowledge etc.) and decreasing opportunities to utilise it.

c) the social and cultural resources of the so-called Third World.

Anyway, we should not overlook the dangers. Surely, civil society is part of the solution; but we should not forget that they are part of the problem as well: they are in many cases based on social inequality (acting with the aim to reproduce it) and in many cases they succeed in doing so – in fighting in an elitist way for particularistic interests. Furthermore, they are part of the problem as they enforce and enhance processes of differentiation in the bad sense of disguising class conflicts, increasing soci(et)al complexity, making sustainable action nearly impossible.

They are part of the problem insofar that they look (only) for answers rather than posing questions – thus reproducing the system.

*****

EUROPEAN PATHWAY OF POLITICS IN A GLOBALISING WORLD

To conclude: *Berthold Brecht* once raised the *Questions from a worker who reads*. During the period of modernisation and globalisation, which was widely not scrutinised anymore, we have

---

[16] What is of special relevance here is the – attempted – utilization of these organisations as service providers respectively the – attempted – steering of these organisations to act and argue as service providers. This is a marked difference compared with the UN and Council of Europe.

[17] Of course, we have to be well aware that the danger exists that this just reproduces again the traditional patterns – socially defined as class-stratification and regionally defined as Eurocentrism.

[18] By the way, it is a renewed trend – during the 50^s/60^s and another time during the 70^s it had been high on the agenda, already.

had questions concerned not so much with the actors. Rather than issuing power relationships, questions had been employed by looking for justice of (re-)distribution – even if many people had been aware of the limits of this direction and that it leaves the question of power unanswered. Anyway, the questions – pressing at that time as they still are pressing today – are posed in the *'summary of the world'*, which reads as follows.

> *If we could shrink the Earth's population to a village of precisely 100 people. With all existing human ratios remaining the same, it would look like this:*
>
> *There would be 57 Asians, 21 Europeans, 14 from the Western Hemisphere (North and South) and 8 Africans.*
>
> *51 would be female; 49 would be male, 70 would be non-white; 30 white.*
>
> *70 would be non-Christian; 30 Christian.*
>
> *50% of the entire world's wealth would be in the hands of only 6 people and all 6 would be citizens of the United States. 80 would live in substandard housing. 70 would be unable to read. 50 would suffer from malnutrition.*
>
> *1 would be near death , 1 would be near birth. Only 1 would have a college education. No one would own a computer.*
>
> *When one considers our world from such an incredibly compressed perspective, the need for both tolerance and understanding becomes glaringly apparent........*
>
> *This was forwarded to me by a friend. If it makes sense to you, forward it to a friend.*

First: Nevertheless, as pressing as these questions are we have at least to redefine there overall meaning. Questions today have to raise again the distribution of power. At the same time this has to be widened. We have to look for a way where economic power fulfils four requirements
* Economic (redistributive) justice;
* Freedom of action in the sense of control over the own life;
* Opportunity to translate economic power into political power and vice versa (considering the first aspect);
* Translating into a set of mutually interwoven economic, political and social rights.[19]

---

[19] The reduction on the three dimensions of economic, political and social rights, however, does not suggest a strategy, which is reduced on these rights without considering other rights that have to be enforced. However, we think that other rights as they are currently suggested for additional inclusion – for instance, environmental rights should be seen as part and parcel of the three other sets. Furthermore, even if *Marshall* on whom this distinction goes back *(Marshall, 1950/1992)* is basically right in regard of the development of distinct sets of rights two points have to be kept clear:
(a) the development has always been one of alternation, economic rights made political and social rights possible and in turn lead to increasing economic rights and so forth. Thus, the distinct phases are only a kind of analytical tool and one for the purpose of presenting a kind of modelled development.

This is a crucial element of what we want to develop here as *European Pathway of politics in a globalising world.* It is concerned with what we elaborated before as citizenship.

Second: Such a concept of citizenship and its foundation on a wider understanding of rights[20] has a twofold meaning for nongovernmental organisations.

On the one hand, they have to take over a role in which they materialise as the cunning of reason. This is, of course, very different to the current threats and the tendency of many NGOs to give in the "requirement" to act as service providing organisations, first in addition to statutory services, then replacing statutory services and later again in competition with market forces. At least this is the threat given by national governments *(cf. Blair, 1999, Department of Social, Community and Family Affairs, 2000),* the European Union *(NGO-dialogue website http://europa.eu.int/comm/secretariat_general/sgc/ong/en/index.htm)* and by the strategies of the MAI and the GATS. These agreements strive for shifting social services away from their special status and establishing them as tradable goods instead *(for the complex of the meaning of MAI and GATS for social services see Staub-Bernasconi, 2000).* Rather than following this trend these organisations – individually and as "sector" – have to be aware of the fact that their real strength is given in their action as advocates and enhancing especially, but not only, local democracy and the realisation of citizenship and enforcing alternative pathways. Lending *Habermas'* terms they are challenged to realise life world and utilise the system world for its improvement rather than integrating life world into the system world and changing the latter on the surface.

The latter is the expression of the second meaning of NGOs. They are – as far and soon the respective conditions are realised – guarantors of citizenship, they implement it by giving it a framework. What they are striving for in the first instance is what they can realise in the second instance.

Third: This formulation shows already that we are in no way employed by the idea that NGOs can play in any way a role of replacing statutory functions. Instead, what is required is an expanded social sector – we would not have any problem to call it social economic sector or social economy even if these terms are predefined and suggest a strong emphasis of the economic dimension. As we will see later *(and already commented a long time ago – s. Herrmann, 1993 a and later again in different documents)* there is in no way any sense in posing an economic against a social dimension. Instead, we are indeed strongly committed to a socio-economic approach where economy is part of the social and vice versa. By social we mean here the very basic feature of living together, of relationships between people. These relations are based and arranged through and founded on exchange; but at the same time they are more than just exchange relations and comprise the whole life. To refer to a social economic sector in this sense means to speak of social quality *(cf. Beck /van der Maesen /Walker [Eds.], 1997),* of the quality of life, where "services" are not "flanking" any economic dimension – as it is conceptualised in mainstream EU-thinking. Instead, a well-developed economy flanks services. Thus, a complex field of relations – commodified or not – defines their character.

Fourth: In this context, the so-called *Services of General Interest* could and should play a crucial role. However, this depends on a reinterpretation of the approach that the Commission of the European Union takes. Instead of taking them as providers of infrastructural mechanisms and means it would be necessary, to integrate them in the wider concept of quality. Thus, they would not be concerned with services in the conventional sense. The services of general interest, we are talking about, are instead connecting or even integrating links of the idea of general rights with

---

(b) It is questionable if we can adhere at today's stage of development to any kind of distinction between different "types" of rights at all. Instead as more as the idea of enlightenment is realised as a democratic reality we have to refer to universal human rights of which economic, political and social are just "subgroups on equal foot".

[20] In discussing the development of rights-based strategies we can learn a lot from the history of France and her current way of dealing with social policy issues, making human rights a matter of everyday life.

their realisation via the micro-level. Thus, economy or to be more precise: economic activities gain the character of realising soci(et)al access, of empowering the actors and being a means of appropriation. They enhance control, make it possible to dispose of one's own life and shape it in accordance with the social setting.

Fifth: The economic sphere is fundamental for further European integration, indeed. However, this is not only concerned with a strategy of enhancing competitiveness. Since in our "pathway" economy is part of a wider social framework, a "European economic model" would include cohesion, diversity and sustainability as original and essential elements. Even if established on the foundation of long chains of action, control over the social and natural environment by the actors must be established as core of the economic activities. This control is only possible as a careful balance of individual and social interests, of satisfying immediate needs and taking care of long-term interests, of small-scale, craftsmen-like activity and large-scale production and finally between local economy and orientation on a large-scale process of exchange. – Thus, the "long chains" are actually means to (re-)gain a higher level of individual and social control.

The EUropean politics are by no means straightforward as far as we aim on a classification between regulation and deregulation. In principle we cannot take them easily as de-regulation; instead we would have to speak at best of a regulated de-regulation – the mechanisms set in place to de-regulate certain aspects of the economy and soci(et)al life are highly tuned systems of regulation. Furthermore, even EU politics are not only focussing on the single set of goals "de-regulation/flexibilisation". We find approaches for non-de-regulative economic activities – even if they had been mentioned in the last instance they have to be seen as the core of such a pathway. Several elements in the framework of the ESF have to be mentioned. As well the so-called *Delors-White Paper (European Commission, 1993)* contains a variety of regulative elements. And with them it is thoroughly in line with classical *Keynesianism.* If these elements are strong enough to hold out against opposing strategies has to be shown by the pudding's proof, i.e. the eating. Tendencies against the development of any kind of orientation on regulation exist, without doubt. They do so inside of the EUropean institutions and outside. Thus, it is even more important to support anti-de-regulative forces from outside. The working group *Alternative Economic Policy for Europe (European Memorandum-Group) (http://www.barkhof.uni-bremen.de/kua/memo/europe/euromemo/indexmem.htm)* or the *attack-Group,* which works for the Tobin-tax *(http://attac.org/)* are just two examples.

In any case, the challenge is that what is required is at least to some extent paradox. It is a *local Keynesianism* – the combination of building up local power structures and at the same time a global system of planning – going much further than simple co-ordination and mediation of different interests.

Sixth and finally our pathway, so-far sketched by reference on

* Citizenship,
* NGOs as alternative forces,
* Social Quality
* Services of general interests as specific mechanism of empowerment and enhancing control over one's life,
* widening the understanding of economic activities

links up to world economy by providing needed facilities, but as well opening space for the enhancement of citizenship, personal development, enhancing personal cultural identity. Only part of this is strictly exchange-oriented – but on the back of a strong own economy which is a resource for third parties rather than using them as a space to which externalities can be transferred.

Above, we stated that *taking the Marxist point of view as interim step we have to redefine our question. Then it does not read anymore How can we make the current path of development be shaped in a way, which is more just? How can we increase its legitimacy? Rather we have to ask*

What kind of development are we concerned with? And: Can we sustain the assumptions of this pathway? We can continue from here and reformulate the question again. For this we take the words of *Mary Kaldor,* who states 'In my view, a reversal of globalization is no longer a viable option. ... Rather, what is at issue is the future direction of globalization. Can we anticipate the continuation of what has been up to now an anarchic and unequal process, accompanied by growing conflict and fundamentalist reactions, or is it possible to envisage a taming of globalization, a global "civilizing" process?' *(Mary Kaldor, ibid.: 1f.)*

Following this approach consequently further we come to the conclusion that speaking of empowerment of NGOs and enhancing politics by "civilising the policy process" on the one hand and – on the other side – empowering the so called Third-World-countries has to go hand in hand. In fact, we are employed by two sides of a single coin. Conversely, this has drastic consequences for the two dimensions already mentioned. On the one hand the idea of civil-society-organisations has to be developed as understanding them as entities with a specific focus,[21] nevertheless permanently in a conscious, intended communication, mediation and tuning with their immediate social setting as well as with society in general. On the other hand – with view on the developing world – they have to be included as "countries" rather than as "states". In other words, it has to be guaranteed that participation and empowerment is not reduced on the elite of these countries and thus refurbishes national – economic, social and political – inequalities and extends unproductive tensions.

This is the main consequence for the European Pathway as we propose it here – linking the regional EU and the global development together. If this shall be successful, the condition is, however, to base this strategy on an enlightenment-based understanding of modernisation. Thus, a European pathway combines developing own, "internal" strength with an approach of integration not as absorption and not at all as subordination. Instead, integration of others is nothing less than an expression and enhancement of own openness.

REFERENCES:

Beck, Wolfgang/van der Maesen, Laurent/Walker, Alan (Eds.), (1997) The Social Quality of Europe; The Hague/London/Boston

Blair, Tony (1999) Speech on the NVCO-conference, 21.1.1999 –http://www.number-10.gov.uk/news.asp?NewsId=328 – 3.11.2000

Blair, Tony/Schroeder, Gerhard (1999) The Third Way http://www.labour.org.uk/lp /new/labour/docs/PMSPEECHES/THIRDWAYPURPLEBOX.HTM – 2000-10-29

Brecht, Bertholt, questions from a worker who reads; http://www.geocities.com/Area51 /1256/POEMS1.HTM#workerreads – 2000-10-29

Brittan, Samuel (2000) Protest against the protesters; in: Financial Times; September 28th

Deacon, Bob (1999) Socially Responsible Globalization: A Challenge for the European Union; Helsinki: Ministry of Social Affairs and Health

Department of Social, Community and Family Affairs (2000) Supporting Voluntary Activity. A white paper on a framework for supporting voluntary activity and for developing the relationship between the state and the community and voluntary sector – http://www.dscfa.ie/dept/reports/volact.htm – 3.11.2000

Deutscher Bundestag (2000) Answer by the Federal Government on the main question by the MPs Klaus-Juergen Hedrich u.a. and the Parliamentary Party CDU/CSU. An international social market economy as basic model for the global structural and societal contract policy – Opportunities and risks of the globalisation of the world economy for the developing countries (Antwort der Bundesregierung auf die Grosse Anfrage der Abgeordneten Klaus-Juergen Hedrich u.a. und der Fraktion der CDU/CSU. Eine internationale Soziale Marktwirtschaft als Grundmodell

---

[21] Finally they are in many cases and often in a specific way single-issue-organisations.

für eine globale Struktur- und Ordnungspolitik –Chancen der Globalisierung der Weltwirtschaft für die Entwicklungsländer; Bundestagsdrucksache 14/3967 – 2.8.2000

Elias, Norbert, (2000) The civilizing process : sociogenetic and psychogenetic investigations; translated by Edmund Jephcott with some notes and corrections by the author ; edited by Eric Dunning, Johan Goudsblom, and Stephen Mennell; Oxford, UK ; Malden, Mass. : Blackwell Publishers

Engels, Frederick (1890) Letter to J. Bloch in Koenigsberg; Written: September 21-22, 1890; Source: Historical Materialism [Marx, Engels, Lenin], p. 294 – 296; Publisher: Progress Publishers, 1972; Translated: from German; Online Version: marxists.org 1999; Transcription/Markup: Brian Basgen –http://www.marxists.org/archive/marx/letters/ engels/90_09_21-ab.htm – 2000-10-29

European Commission (1993) White paper on growth, competitiveness, and employment: The challenges and ways forward into the 21st century; COM(93) 700 final; Brussels, 5 December 1993 – http://www.europa.eu.int/en/record/white/c93700/contents.html –3.11.2000

European Commission (2000) Equal Opportunities for Women and Men in the European Union, 1999. Report to the Council, the European Parliament, the Economic and Social Committee of the Regions. Brussels: COM [2000] 123 fin., 8/3/2000

Ferge, Zsuzsa 1999 The changing functions of the state – a virtuous or vicious circle?, in: Herrmann (ed.) 1999

Fligstein, Neil (2000) Is globalization the cause of the crisis of welfare states in: Globalization, European Economic Integration and Social Protection; Conference, March 11-12, 1999, organised by Martin Rhodes in Collaboration with the European Commission, DG V; Florence: European University Institute

Hegel, G.F.W. (1837) The philosophy of history; Translated by J. Sibree; http://www.ets.uidaho.edu/mickelsen/texts/Hegel%20-%20Philosophy%20of%20History.htm – 2000-10-29

Herrmann, Peter (1993 a) Social Problems in the View of a Dedifferentiating Modernisation – Social Intervention in the Process of EC-Integration [Soziale Probleme in der Perspektive entdifferenzierender Modernisierung – Sozialintervenierendes Handeln im Prozeß der EG-Integration); in: Neue Praxis. Zeitschrift für Sozialarbeit, Sozialpädagogik und Sozialpolitik]; Neuwied: Luchterhand, Issue 1+2/1993: pp. 147 ff.

Herrmann, Peter (1993 b) Society and Organisation. Sociological Theory of Organisations [Gesellschaft und Organisation. Zur soziologischen Theorie von Organisationen]; Egelsbach/New York: Hänsel-Hohenhausen

Herrmann, Peter (1994) The Organisation. An analysis of the Modern Society [Die Organisation. Eine Analyse der modernen Gesellschaft]; Rheinfelden/Berlin: Schäuble

Herrmann, Peter (1998 a) Cultures of Participation in the European Union. Nongovernmental Organisations in EU-member states [Partizipationskulturen in der Europäischen Union. Nichtregierungsorganisationen in EU-Mitgliedstaaten]; Rheinfelden/Berlin: Schäuble Verlag

Herrmann, Peter (1998 b) European Integration between Institution Building and Social Process. Contributions to a Theory of Modernisation and NGOs in the Context of the Development of the EU; New York: Nova Science

Herrmann, Peter (1999) Re-defining centrality and Differentiation, in: Herrmann [ed.] (1999)

Herrmann, Peter [ed.] (1999) Challenges for a global welfare system; New York: Nova Science

Herrmann, Peter/Lorenz, Walter (1997) Towards a European Welfare State – A European Welfare Regime by Design or Default?; in: The Politics of Social Policy in Europe; Maurice Mullard/Simon Lee (Eds.); Cheltenham: Edward Elgar Publishing Ltd: pp. 12 – 29

Hoffmann, Jürgen/ Hoffmann, Reiner (1997) Globalization. Risks and opportunities for labor policy in Europe. Brussels: European Trade Union Institute; (undated) [DWP 97.04.01 – E]

Kaldor, Mary (2000) "Civilizing" Globalization? The Implications of the "Battle in Seattle" – http://www.lse.ac.uk/Depts/global/MarySeattle.htm – 2000-11-03

Kohli, Martin (2000) The battlegrounds of European Identity; in: European Societies 2, 2; 2000: 113-137

Kreissl-Dörfler, Wolfgang (1998) Report containing Parliament's recommendations to the Commission on the negotiations in the framework of the OECD on a multilateral agreement on investment [MAI]. European Parliament: 26.2.1998 – A4-0073/98

Mann, Michael (1986) The Sources of Social Power, Vol. I/II; Cambridge: Cambridge University Press

Marshall, T.H. (1950) Citizenship and social class; in: Marshall, Tom H./Bottomore, Tom: Citizenship and social class; London; Concord/Mass. 1950/1992

Marx, Karl (1859) Preface to A Contribution to the Critique of Political Economy http://www.marxists.org/archive/marx/works/1850/pol-econ/preface-abs.htm – 29.10.2000)

Pierson, Paul (2000) Post-industrial pressures on the mature welfare states in: Globalization, European Economic Integration and Social Protection; Conference, March 11-12, 1999, organised by Martin Rhodes in Collaboration with the European Commission, DG V; Florence: European University Institute

Robertson, R. (1992) Globalization; London: Sage

Salamon, Lester M. (1994) The Rise of the Nonprofit Sector; in: Foreign Affairs; 73/July/August 1994

Salamon, Lester M./Anheier, Helmut K. (1999): The Nonprofit Sector: A new global force; in: Herrmann [Ed.]

Schmidt-Fink, Ekkehart (2000) A reverse "reconquista"? aid. Ausländer in Deutschland; Saarbruecken, 3-2000: 17 f.

Soysal, Y. (1997) Identity, rights and claims-making: changing dynamics of citizenship in postwar Europe; paper presented to the 3rd European Conference of Sociology; Colchester, UK

Staub-Bernasconi, Silvia (2000) The WTO as task for the management or Globalisation of Social Work [Die WTO als Managementaufgabe oder die Globalisierung deer Sozialen Arbeit]; to be published in: Socialmanagement. Zeitschrift fuer Sozialwirtschaft; Baden-Baden: Nomos Verlagsgesellschaft; 2000 – issue 1-2/2000

Wolfensohn, James 2000: quoted from: Protesters for Poverty; in: Financial Times; September 28th, 2000: 18

APPENDIX

SAMPLES AND DATA

List of variables

The general model of world development, based on 123 nations

Indicators of globalisation:

- **aid dependency** (UNDP, 1994) net per capita aid in $. Donor countries are listed according to their donations per capita and are recorded as (-)
- **export processing zones** (Bailey et al., 1993). The variable codes the number of export processing zones per country at the beginning of the 1990s
- **migration dependency** (UNDP, 1993) net worker remittances per GNP/GDP at the beginning of the 1990s
- **MNC penetration** index: penetration by transnational capital, weighted by population and capital stock, mid - 1970s (Bornschier/Heintz, 1979, based on OECD)
- **share of outward FDI stock in gross domestic product in 1985** (UNCTAD, 1996. For a very small number of countries, regional averages had to be taken to substitute for the few, missing values)
- **terms of trade index** 1987 - 90 (UNDP, 1994, Weltalmanach, 1994, based on UN)
- **trade dependency** index: exports plus imports as % of GDP 1990 (UNDP, 1993/94)
- vulnerability of a nation in terms of the expansion of the new international division of labor, 1990 (**share of women in the national labor force**) (UNDP, 1993/94)

Indicators for the institutional environment:

- **ethno - linguistic fractionalization** index, mid - 1960s (Bornschier/Heintz, 1979, based on Taylor/Hudson). Ethnic discrimination is thought to be the purest form of a 'distribution coalition'
- **government consumption** per GDP, 1990 (UNDP, 1993/94)
- **government expenditures** per GNP, 1991 (UNDP, 1993/94; UNICEF, Regional Monitoring Report, 1, 11, 1993, see Cornia, 1993; World Resources Research Institute)
- **public investment** in the preceding Kondratieff cycle (Bornschier/Heintz)
- total area in thousands of square kilometers (World Bank, WDR, 1994. This variable measures the role, that territory and resources could play for attracting foreign capital)
- *violation of civil rights*, 1991 (Stiftung, 1993/94, based on Freedom House, combining freedom of religion, the press, freedom of assembly and association, freedom of trade unions, the right to property and equality before the law)

- *violation of political rights index*, 1991 (Stiftung, 1993/94, based on Freedom House, combining free elections, role of the elected parliament in political decision making, party competition, protection of minorities)
- world political threats to a country, to be measured by the percentage of **armed forces per population**. Some neo - liberals maintain that world political threats increase the growth potential of a nation. Due to the skewness of the indicator, the natural logarithm *ln (MPR+1)* has to be taken (calculated from UNDP, 1993/94; see also: Weede, 1985)
- **years of membership in the United Nations** (coded from Weltalmanach, 1995)

Indicators for the social policy approach:

- *human development* index (UNDP, 1994) as an indicator for the quality of past social policy
- **increase/decrease of fertility rates** 1960 - 90 (UNDP, 1993/94)
- *life expectancy* at birth as an indicator for the quality of past social policy, 1990 (UNDP, 1993/94 and World Bank, WDR, 1994)
- share of **women in the membership of national legislature** (lower house) (UNDP, 1993/94)
- **social security** benefits expenditure as % of GDP in the era of the evolving contemporary Kondratieff cycle, 1985 - 90 (UNDP, 1994). Social security benefits expenditures include here the compensations for the loss of income for the sick and the temporarily disabled; payments to the elderly, the permanently disabled and the unemployed; they also include family, maternity and child allowances and the cost of welfare services. The UNDP data collection is based on ILO sources
- *total fertility* rate (UNDP, 1993/94)
- total number of inhabitants, divided by the surface area of a country (**population density**). Due to the skewness of the indicator, the squared root (population density$^{\wedge .50}$) had to be taken (calculated from UNDP, 1993/94)
- *violation of civil rights, 1991* (Stiftung, 1993/94, based on Freedom House)
- *violation of political rights index, 1991* (Stiftung, 1993/94, based on Freedom House)

The dependent variables of the general models

- absolute income growth (growth in the sense of Arrighi's and Amin's theory) 1960-1990. This measure is the simple difference between real purchasing power parity rate per capita incomes in US $ 1990 and 1960 (UNDP, 1993 ff.)
- **adjustment** 1965/80 - 80/93(calculated from UNDP, 1993/94/96). Adjustment is calculated by a simple, standard linear regression model of growth 1965-80 predicting growth in the period 1980/93. The residuals from this regression are the 'adjustment scores'
- **capability poverty measure** (CPM - value) (UNDP, 1996. The measure weights unattended births, underweight children, and female illiteracy. It is regarded by the UNDP as a direct measure of absolute poverty)
- **deforestation rate** (UNDP, 1993 - 95; World Bank, 1995; World Resources Research Institute). The index measures annual rates of deforestation in the 1980s in %. Because of missing data, a number of countries had to be coded by the LDC average or the OECD average
- **destabilization index** (coded according to Weltalmanach, 1995. The indicator codes all those countries as '1' (destabilized), that have entries about serious armed internal or external conflict in 1994. The rest is coded as '0'
- **employment** (UNDP, 1994) labor force as % of total population

- **ethno - warfare** (Gurr, 1994) magnitude of ethno - political conflict. The scores are country sums of the squared roots of the deaths (in 10s of thousands) from ethno - political conflict 1993 - 94 plus refugees (in 100s of thousands). Countries with no entries according to Gurr's main research results, 1994, are coded as '0'
- **forest area per total land area** (UNDP, 1993 - 95). In contrast to the above indicator, that measures flows, this measure rather captures stocks of already existent forest destruction. Agricultural land per total land area has to be taken into consideration as an independent variable, because else the regression equations would be biased by a desert - factor
- **gender empowerment measure** (UNDP, 1995. The index weights seats held by women in parliament, the percentage share of women and managers, the share of women in the professional and technical workforce, and the share of women in total earned income
- **gender - related development index** (GDI) (UNDP, 1995) - dimension female life chances. This index was developed by the UNDP especially for the 1995 women's conference in Beijing. The index weights the share of earned income for females and males, the gender - specific life expectancies, the gender - specific adult literacy rates, and the gross primary, secondary and tertiary enrollment ratios. It ranges theoretically from 0.0 to 0.999, with Sweden (0.919) at the top of the international scale, and Afghanistan (0.169) at the bottom. Since there unfortunately no were no data for Dominica, Grenada, Antigua, Seychelles, Saint Lucia, Saint Vincent, Saint Kits, Belize, South Africa, Oman, Jordan, Gabon, Solomon Islands, Sao Tome, Congo, Rwanda, Bhutan, Angola, Mauritania, Somalia, Gambia, Germany and Israel, we had to substitute these missing values with averages for the socio - economic groups concerned: a) the industrialized democracies (gender development index average 0.87) b) developing countries with a Human Development Index above 0.6 (in our 123 nations analysis: Barbados to Tunisia, gender development index average 0.721) c) developing countries with a Human Development Index from 0.599 to 0.389 (Oman to Egypt, gender development index average 0,542) d) developing countries with a Human Development Index under 0.388 (except for the very least developed countries; Kenya to Sierra Leone; gender development index average 0.33) and e) the very least developed countries Benin, Guinea Bissau, Chad, Mali, Niger, Burkina Faso and Sierra Leone with a gender development index of 0.2. This procedure can be regarded only as a first approximation and should be substituted in future research
- GNP per capita **growth** (1965 - 1980 and 1980 - 90/1980 - 92, 1980 - 93) (UNDP, 1993/94/95/96; Fischer Weltalmanach) - dimension growth
- **greenhouse index**, 1989 (greenhouse index per 10 million people, UNDP, 1994. The greenhouse index measures the net emissions of three major greenhouse gases: carbon dioxide, methane and chlorofluorocarbons. The index weights each gas according to it's heattrapping quality in carbon dioxide equivalents and expresses them in metric tons of carbon per capita) - dimension environmental quality/degradation
- **human development index** (HDI) (UNDP, 1994)
- **income distribution (Moaddel, 1994. The measure focuses on the share of the top 20% in total incomes in over 80 countries. Wherever possible, Moaddel's data were updated by World Bank WDR, 1994, 1995 and 1996). For the calculation of the relationship with income distribution, a reduced sample ofthe n = 123 world sample with complete data was taken**
- **increase in life expectancy** 1960 - 90 (calculated from UNDP, 1993/94 via a regression procedure, predicting 1990 life expectancy on 1960 life expectancy, and then taking the residuals as growth rates) - dimension redistribution and human development
- **mean years of schooling of the population aged 25 and > (UNDP, 1993 and 1994)**

- mobility in the international system (calculated from UNDP, 1993 ff.) This indicator is the difference in relative positions of a country on the PPP $ per capita income scale in 1990 (USA = 100) vis-à-vis 1960 (USA = 100)
- **violation of civil rights**, 1991 (Stiftung, 1993/94, based on Freedom House) - dimension democracy
- **violation of political rights index**, 1991 (Stiftung, 1993/94, based on Freedom House) - dimension democracy
- mobility in the international system (calculated from UNDP, 1993 ff.) This indicator is the difference in relative positions of a country on the PPP $ per capita income scale in 1990 (USA = 100) vis-à-vis 1960 (USA = 100)

The models based on 134 countries

- % **labor force participation** ratio (UNDP, 1996)
- % of the **labor force** in **agriculture** (UNDP, 1996; Fischer Weltalmanach, 1996)
- % of the **labor force** in **industry** (see: labor force agriculture)
- **absolute GNP** (UNDP, 1996)
- absolute income growth (growth in the sense of Arrighi's and Amin's theory) 1960-1990.
- **agricultural share** in GDP (UNDP, 1996; Fischer Weltalmanach, 1996)
- **average population growth** (UNDP, 1996)
- **economic growth 80 - 93**, pc. and year (UNDP, 1996)
- **EU membership years** (Fischer Weltalmanach, 1995, 1996)
- **FDI per GDP** (UNCTAD, 1996; Business Central Europe, 1996)
- **human development index** (UNDP)
- income distribution: share of top 20% in total incomes (World Bank WDR 1996; UNDP 1996; Moaddel 1994; the few missing cases were substituted with the means from linear trendline estimates, based on the countries with complete data, using mean years of schooling and population growth as predictor variables)
- infant mortality rates, 1993 (UNDP, 1996)
- **inflation 93** (UNDP, 1996)
- **main telephone lines** per 100 population (UNDP, 1996)
- mean **years of schooling**, population aged >25y
- **military expenditures per GDP** (UNDP, 1996)
- **state sector size** (gov. expenditures per GDP; UNDP 1996; Weltalmanach, 1995, 1996; World Resources Institute)
- **structural heterogeneity** (labor force share in agriculture divided by product share of agriculture; see labor force data)
- **total fertility rate** (UNDP, 1996)
- **UN membership years** (Weltalmanach, 1996, 1995)
- **violation of political rights** (1, democracy, to 7, dictatorship) (Stiftung Entwicklung und Frieden, 1996, based on Freedom House)
- **violations of civil rights** (see political rights)
- war years (from D. Smith, 1997)
- **years of Communist Rule** (Autorenkollektiv; Weltalmanach)

Development as a function of the Human Development Index

As to the variable definitions, see above and elsewhere in this Appendix.

world econ. adjustment

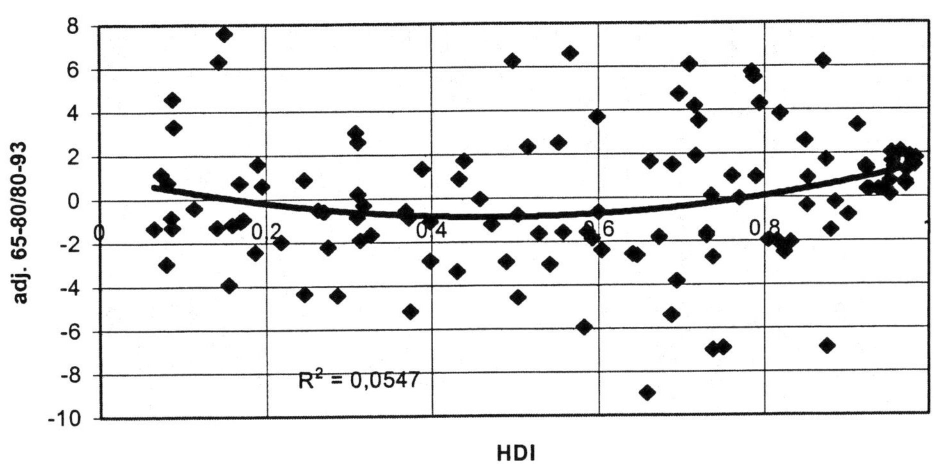

economic growth

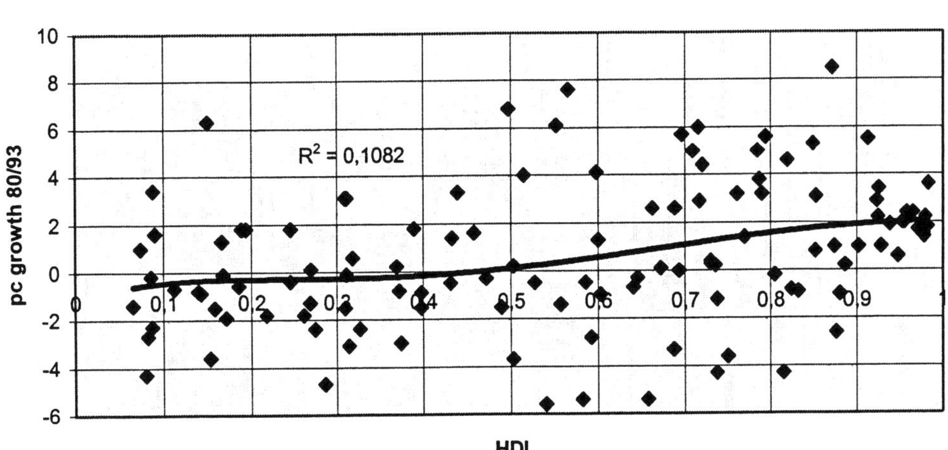

Dyn Life Expectancy

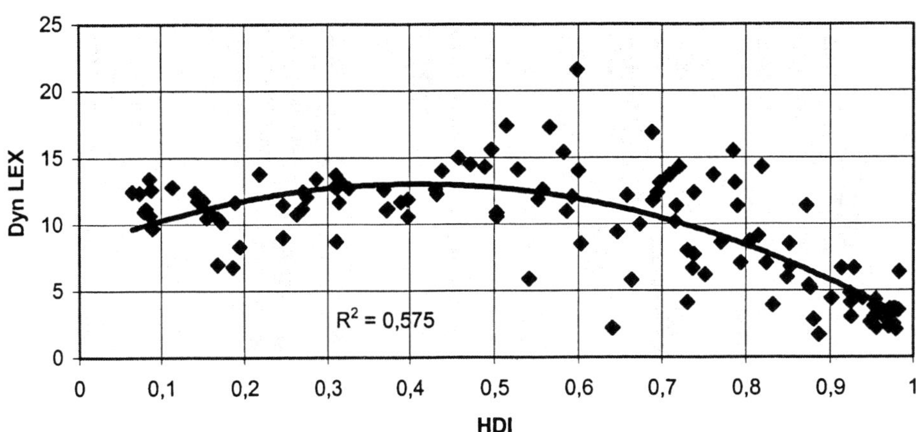

greenhouse index

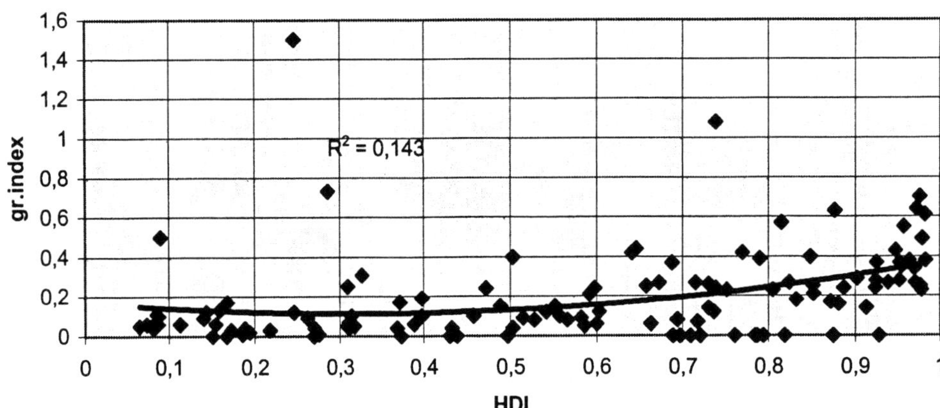

political rights violations

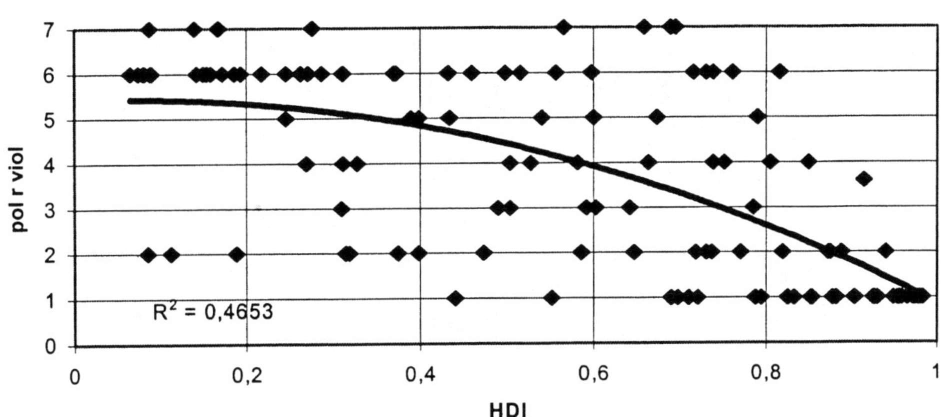

civil rights violations

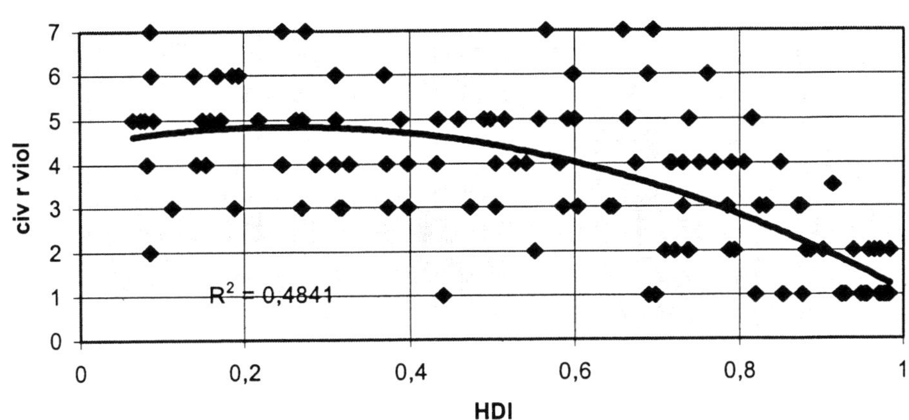

gender development

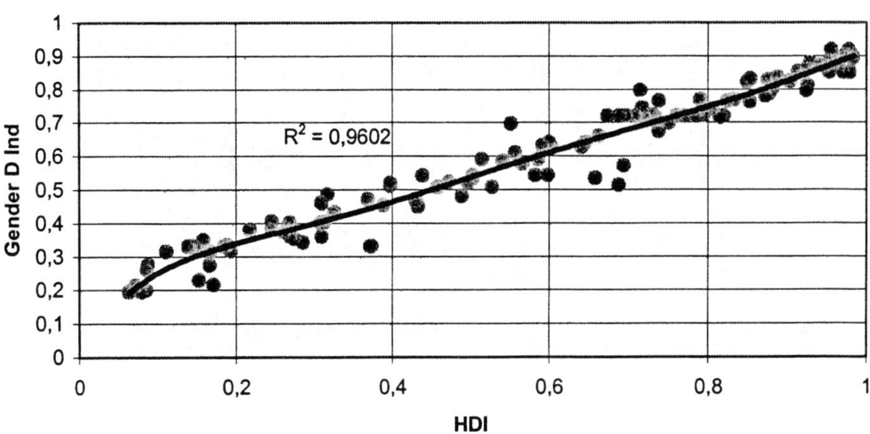

gender empowerment

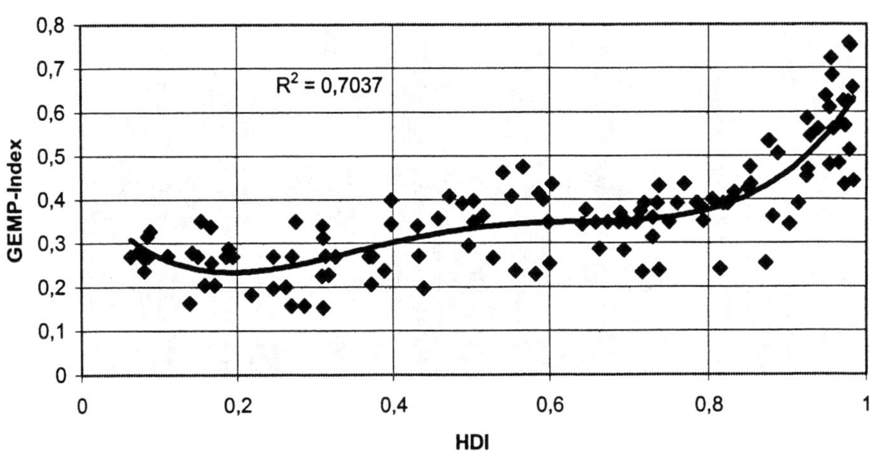

life expectancy

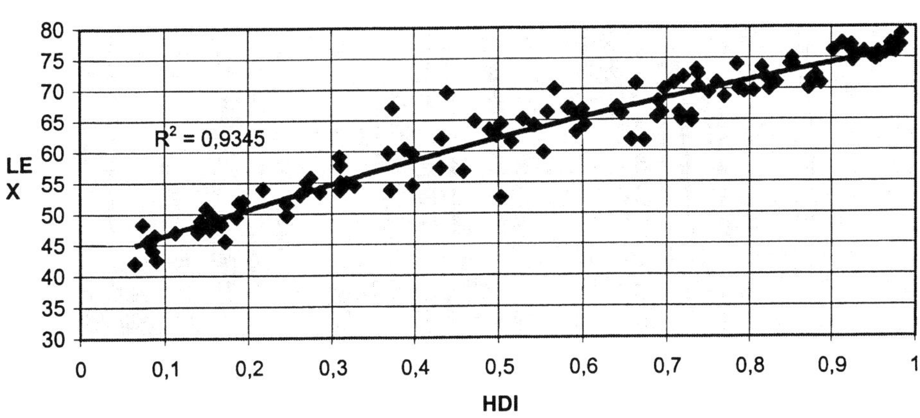

maternal mortality

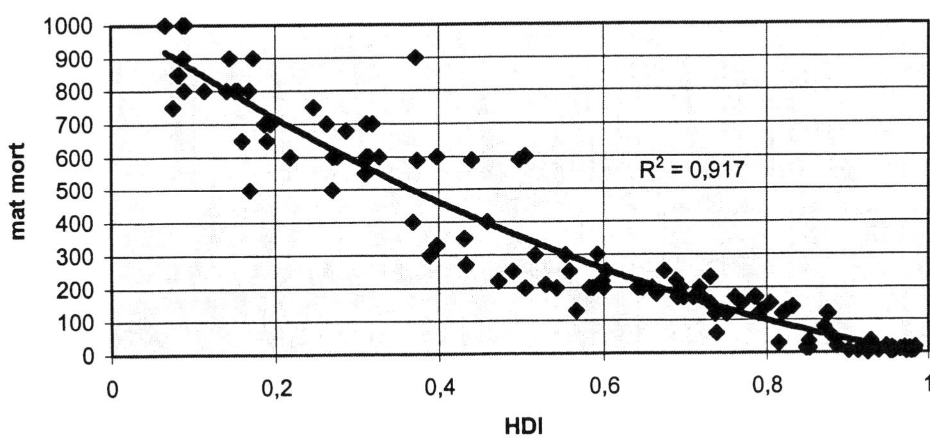

% people in poverty

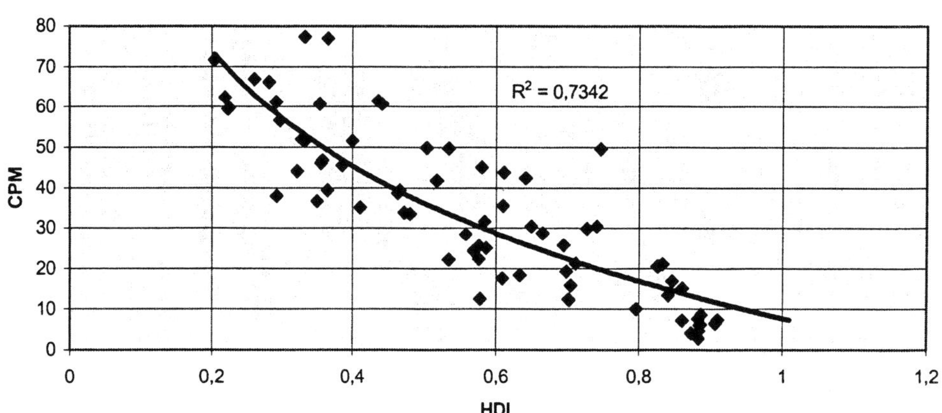

income concentration

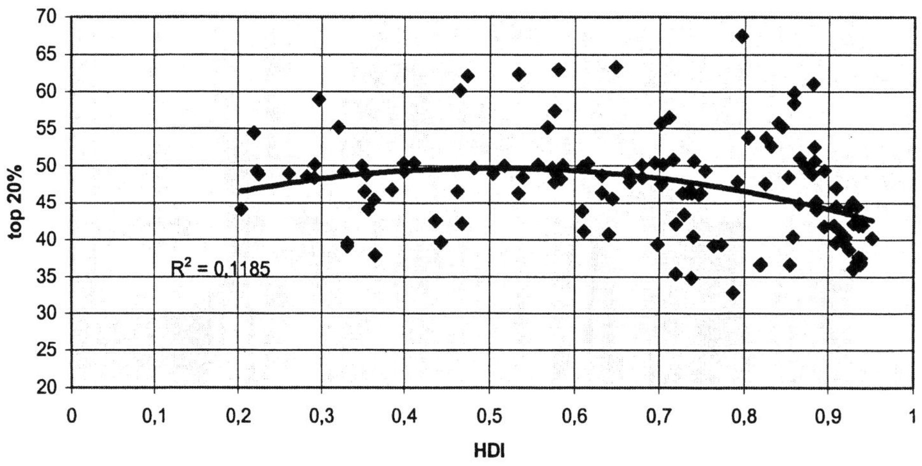

political refugees

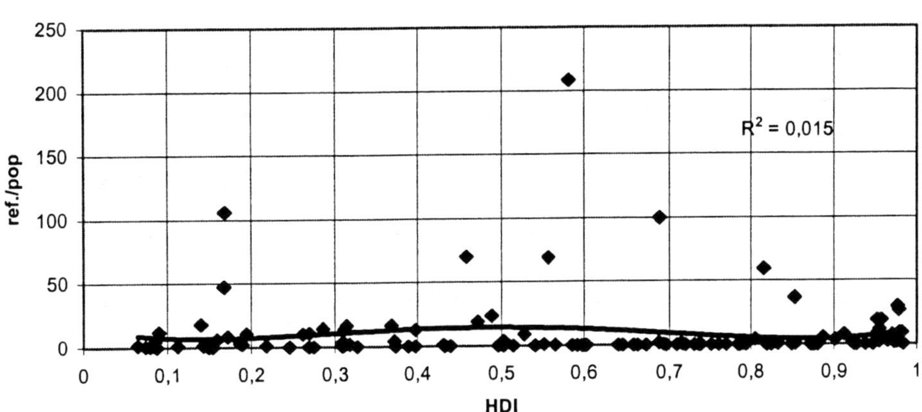

destabilization/war

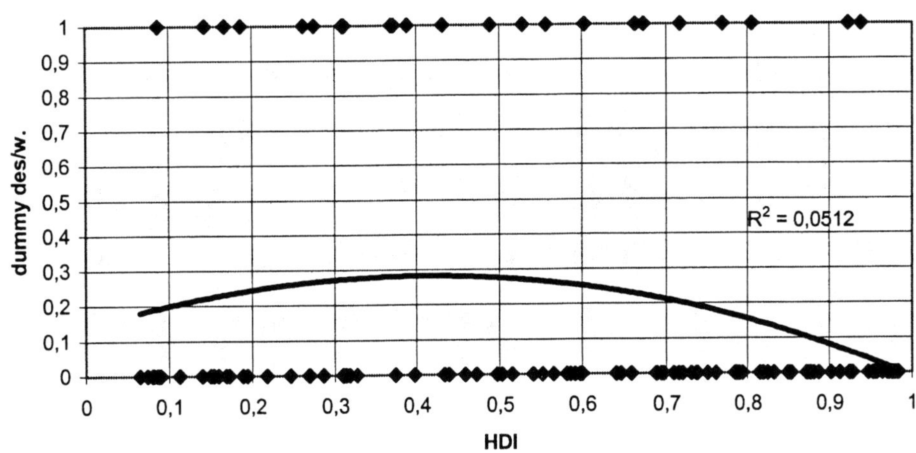

ethno-warfare

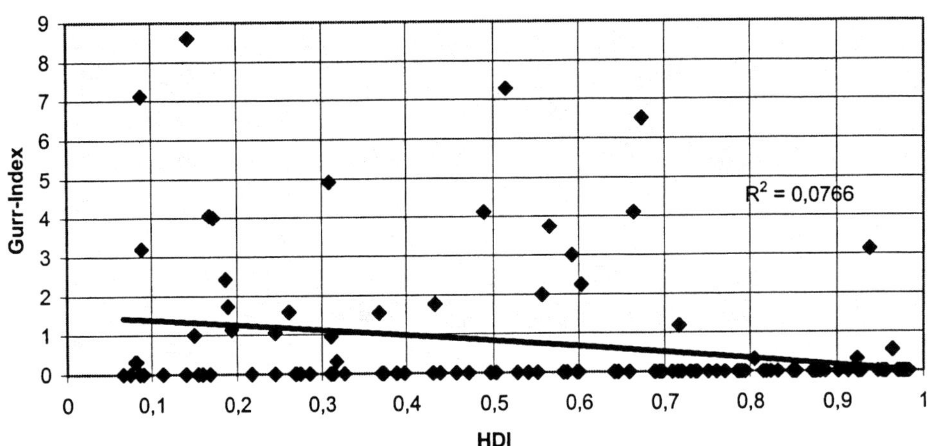

deforestation process

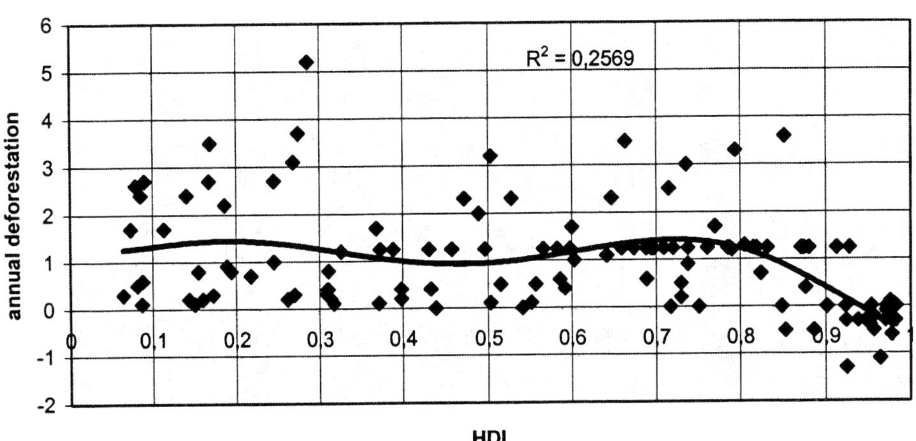

forest area

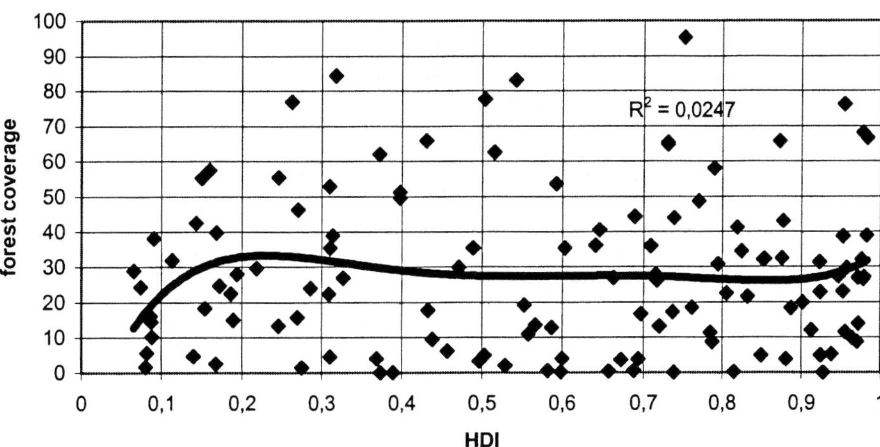

The instability model based on 99 countries

Sample: determined by data availability from Gurr (1994: ethno-political strife score), World Bank (1994: transfers per capita) and UNDP HDR (1993: social data)

- adult literacy rate (UNDP, HDR, 1993)
- ethno-political strife (Gurr, 1994)
- failure of demographic transition (fertility rates at the end of the 1980s are explained in a standard linear OLS regression by fertility rates around 1960. The residuals from that regression, viz. fertility rates still above the world-wide trends of fertility reduction, are interpreted as the failure of demographic transition. Original data from UNDP, HDR, 1993)
- historical fertility rate (fertility rate in 1960; UNDP, HDR, 1993)
- human development index (UNDP, HDR, 1993)
- mean years of schooling (UNDP, HDR, 1993)
- natural logarithm of of per capita income, squared; ln PCI^2 (UNDP, HDR, 1993)
- natural logarithm of of per capita income; ln PCI (UNDP, HDR, 1993)
- political rights violations (Stiftung Entwicklung und Frieden, 1993, based on Freedom House)
- population density^0.50 (UNDP, HDR, 1993)
- repressiveness of the security apparatus (civil rights violations are predicted in a standard linear OLS regression by political rights violations. The residuals from that regression, viz. civil rights violations in excess of political rights violations, are interpreted as the repressiveness of the security apparatus. Original data from Stiftung Entwicklung und Frieden, 1993, based on Freedom House)
- transfers per capita (calculated from World Bank World Development Report, 1994)

Corruption levels in 47 countries

From the 52 countries of the Transparency International study (Polityka, 32, 1998: 34 - 35, Warsaw) we used only those nations that had fairly complete predictor variables for our n = 134 world sample. The sample and the data thus was defined as follows:

Country	absence of corruption level
Canada	9,1
USA	7,61
Japan	6,57
NL	9,03
NOR	8,92
SF	9,48
France	6,66
Nigeria	1,76
Swed	9,35
Spain	5,9
Australia	8,86
Belgium	5,25
Austria	7,61
NZ	9,1
CH	8,61
UK	8,22
DK	9,94
GER	8,23
IRE	8,28
ITA	5,03
GRE	5,35
ISR	7,97
LUX	8,61
India	2,75
POR	6,97
HUNG	5,18
Pakistan	2,53
POL	5,08
RUS	2,27
Costa Rica	6,45
Uruguay	4,14
Chile	6,5
Singapore	8,66
ROM	3,44
Mexico	2,66
Colombia	2,23
Thailand	3,06
Malaysia	5,01
China	2,88
Indonesia	2,72
Philippines	3,05
ALB	2,81
Turkey	3,21
Hong Kong	7,28
Brazil	3,56

Venezuela	2,77
S-Korea	4,29

The models based on 49 Polish voivodships

variables taken from the Polish Central Statistical Office and from the daily Polish Press:

- big estates (> 25 ha) per total land
- percent employment in agriculture
- percent employment in foreign capital enterprises per total employment
- percent employment in mixed enterprises per total employment
- external migration per total population
- female excess infant mortality rates (based on regression residuals of male on female infant mortality rates in the different voivodships of the country). Voivodships are said to have an excess female infant mortality, when the regression residual is positive
- human development index
- industrial employment
- industrial waste
- private land per total land
- real GDP per capita
- religious practice
- urbanization
- voting data on a voivodship level for all the elections and referenda since 1993
- wage level

Excess mortality in the Polish provinces

Original data: Stat. Yearbooks, Poland

- Column (1) male infant mortality rate per voivodship
- Column (2) female infant mortality rate per voivodship
- Column (3) female infant mortality, predicted by linear ordinary least square regression on male infant mortality rates, all per voivodship
- Column (4) implicit 'excess female infant mortality': real female infant mortality minus predicted female infant mortality rate per voivodship

male inf mor	fem inf mor	mor trend va	excess	
1485	1195	1206,3	-11,3	Warszawa
1672	1076	1292	-216	bialpodlas
1335	1404	1137,6	266,4	bialystock
1496	1287	1211,4	75,6	bielski
1984	1838	1435	403	Bydg.
2021	1670	1451,9	218,1	chelm
2011	1112	1447,3	-335,3	ciech
1444	1121	1187,6	-66,6	czesto
1334	963	1137,2	-174,2	elblas
1572	1064	1246,2	-182,2	gdan
1991	1433	1438,2	-5,2	gorzo

1629	1290	1272,3	17,7	jelen
1926	1692	1408,4	283,6	kalis
1715	1473	1311,7	161,3	kato
1335	1065	1137,6	-72,6	kiele
1579	1195	1249,4	-54,4	konin
1521	1127	1222,8	-95,8	kosza
1620	1099	1268,2	-169,2	krak
1350	1342	1144,5	197,5	krosn
1733	1288	1320	-32	legni
1752	1315	1328,7	-13,7	leszcz
1509	1259	1217,3	41,7	lubel
1506	1523	1216	307	lomzy
1830	1331	1364,4	-33,4	lodz
1361	1135	1149,5	-14,5	nowosad
1399	912	1167	-255	olszt
1741	1683	1323,6	359,4	opol
1678	1195	1294,8	-99,8	ostrol
1329	1533	1134,9	398,1	pilsk
1362	1226	1150	76	piotrk
1794	1413	1347,9	65,1	plock
1290	1228	1117	111	pozn
1568	1278	1244,4	33,6	przem
1330	1354	1135,3	218,7	radom
1443	1225	1187,1	37,9	rzesz
1379	1148	1157,8	-9,8	siedle
1335	984	1137,6	-153,6	sierad
1374	899	1155,5	-256,5	skiernie
1835	1234	1366,7	-132,7	slupsk
1730	995	1318,6	-323,6	suwal
1688	1055	1299,4	-244,4	szczec
1472	1146	1200,4	-54,4	tarnbrzes
1699	1074	1304,4	-230,4	tarnow
2054	1392	1467	-75	torun
1726	1274	1316,8	-42,8	walbrz
1557	1797	1239,3	557,7	wlocl
1751	1188	1328,2	-140,2	wroc
1346	696	1142,7	-446,7	zamoj
1432	1294	1182,1	111,9	zielono

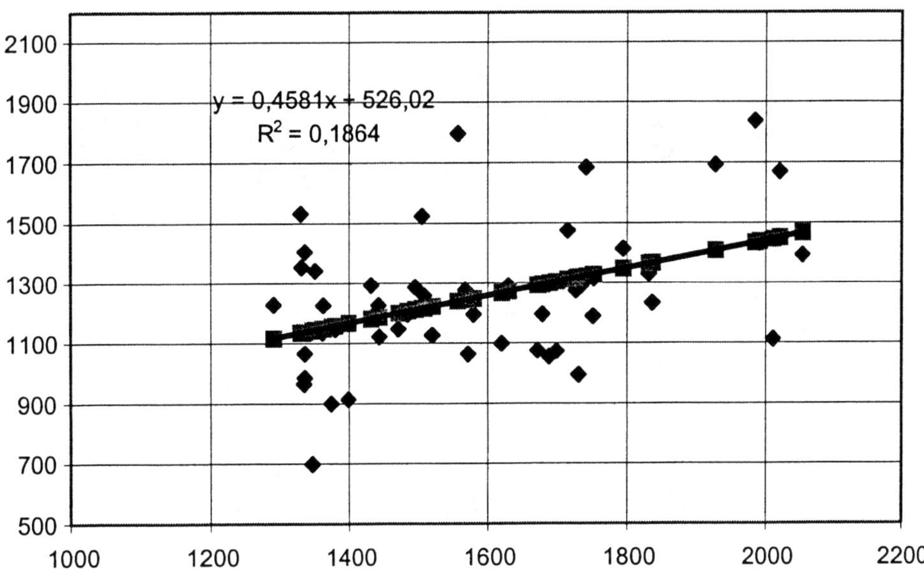

Legend: male infant mortality per 100000 (x-axis), female infant mortality per 100000 (y-axis) per Polish voivodships, and the trend-line

life expectancy in Poland per region

lodz	69,67
kato	69,72
wlocl	70,07
elblas	70,08
szczec	70,22
jelen	70,32
zielono	70,49
slupsk	70,53
pilsk	70,54
torun	70,59
kosza	70,66
gorzo	70,72
legni	70,73
Bydg.	70,76
pozn	70,76
opol	70,81
walbrz	70,81
gdan	70,87
ciech	70,88
czesto	70,94
piotrk	70,98
plock	71
konin	71,1

wroc	71,13
olszt	71,16
skiernie	71,16
kalis	71,23
radom	71,29
leszcz	71,36
Warszawa	71,43
przem	71,54
sierad	71,57
chelm	71,58
bielski	71,7
suwal	71,7
lubel	71,8
kiele	71,81
krak	71,85
ostrol	71,85
bialpodlas	71,98
siedle	72,08
nowosad	72,12
zamoj	72,12
tarnbrzes	72,17
krosn	72,25
tarnow	72,28
lomzy	72,35
rzesz	72,5
bistock	72,81

The effect of years of European Union membership on developed stable democracies before Union enlargements 1981-95

Countries of analysis

Sweden
Israel
Belgium
Denmark
Ireland
Austria
Norway
Australia
Italy
UK
Germany
Netherlands
Switzerland
Canada
Japan
France
Iceland
Luxembourg

Variables:

- democratic age within stable world political boundaries by 1980 (Source: Weede; Tausch, 1993a)
- central government expenditures 1972 (Source: World Bank, 1990, Fischer Weltalmanach, current issues)
- years of Union membership by 1993 (Die Presse, 1. 11. 1993)
- economic growth (GNP per cap.) 1980-91 (UNDP, 1994)
- human development index (UNDP, 1994)
- yearly rate of inflation, 1980-91

European Union enlargement scenario

Countries of analysis

CND
France
NOR
USA
Ice
NL
Jap
SF
NZ
Swd
Sp
Aut
Blg
Aus
UK
CH
Ire
DK
Ger
Gre
It
Isr
Lux
Port

Variables:

- democratic age within stable world political boundaries by 1997 (Source: Weede; Tausch, 1993a. Note the effects of German unifaction)
- central government expenditures, mid 1980s (Source:World Resources Institute, UNEP, UNDP, 1992)
- years of Union membership by 1997 (Die Presse, 1. 11. 1993)
- economic growth (GNP per cap.) 1980-93 (UNDP, 1994)
- human development index (UNDP,1997)
- yearly rate of inflation, 1993 (UNDP, 1997)
- people not expected to survive to age 40, by 1990 (poverty indicator, UNDP, 1997

- male unemployment rate, 1993 (UNDP, 1997. For Sweden, the national average of 9.2% unemployment)
- female unemployment rate, 1993 (UNDP, 1997. For Sweden, the national average of 9.2% unemployment)
- gender empowerment (UNDP, 1997. For the missing values for Iceland, the average of the Scandinavian countries)

Kondratieff cycle data:

For the calculations of Kondratieff cycles, I used J. Goldstein's classic (1988), plus the following data (estimates) for world (and or OECD) growth 1975 - 1997, based on IMF, IFRI, UN ECE, and Fischer Weltalmanach:

year	growth rate	5-year aver.	9-year aver.
1741	-4,8		
1742	10,1		
1743	-4,6	2,16	
1744	14,3	4	
1745	-4,2	2,8	1,81
1746	4,4	5,34	3,73
1747	4,1	0,26	2,61
1748	8,1	3,6	3,12
1749	-11,1	2,72	1,94
1750	12,5	1,9	2,02
1751	0	1,02	1,94
1752	0	2,54	0,3
1753	3,7	0,78	-0,16
1754	-3,5	-1,36	1,08
1755	3,7	-0,56	-0,74
1756	-10,7	-1,3	-0,74
1757	4	-1,38	-0,21
1758	0	-2,12	-0,62
1759	-3,9	0,98	-0,67
1760	0	0,18	-0,18
1761	4,8	-0,6	1,01
1762	0	1,8	2,21
1763	-3,9	1,8	2,21
1764	8,1	3,8	2,29
1765	0	3,8	3,02
1766	14,8	3,94	2,14
1767	0	3,64	2,14
1768	-3,2	3,02	3,66
1769	6,6	0,06	2,1
1770	-3,1	2	1,41
1771	0	1,46	0,13
1772	9,7	-1,1	0,5
1773	-5,9	0,18	1,2

1774	-6,2	0,84	0,81
1775	3,3	-0,48	0,5
1776	3,3	1,32	0,5
1777	3,1	1,38	-0,92
1778	3,1	0,72	1,89
1779	-5,9	-0,56	2,28
1780	0	2,7	2,22
1781	-3,1	1,54	3,96
1782	19,4	3,28	4,11
1783	-2,7	7,06	4,01
1784	2,8	8,58	4,43
1785	18,9	5,14	6,61
1786	4,5	5,26	6,76
1787	2,2	8,62	4,81
1788	-2,1	4,48	5,92
1789	19,6	3,96	4,1
1790	-1,8	4,98	2,43
1791	1,9	2,68	2,57
1792	7,3	-0,46	3,11
1793	-13,6	1,04	2,42
1794	3,9	2,08	1,26
1795	5,7	-1,04	3,49
1796	7,1	3,5	3,9
1797	-8,3	6,38	2,5
1798	9,1	6,36	4,63
1799	18,3	3,88	4,34
1800	5,6	6,66	4
1801	-5,3	5,1	3,5
1802	5,6	1,96	4,56
1803	1,3	1,36	3,96
1804	2,6	2,66	1,39
1805	2,6	2,28	1,04
1806	1,2	1,06	2,58
1807	3,7	1,04	2,58
1808	-4,8	2,22	1,72
1809	2,5	3,1	1,56
1810	8,5	1,08	1,39
1811	5,6	2,26	2,49
1812	-6,4	1,98	2,08
1813	1,1	2,5	2,61
1814	1,1	1,38	4,56
1815	11,1	2,66	2,69
1816	0	6,44	2,07
1817	0	4,56	2,78
1818	20	2,34	3,67
1819	-8,3	2,34	4,47

1820	0	4,16	3,23
1821	0	1,82	4,09
1822	9,1	3,48	3,29
1823	8,3	5,02	2,78
1824	0	3,58	4,44
1825	7,7	4,84	3,76
1826	-7,2	4,52	5,23
1827	15,4	3,28	4,22
1828	6,7	4,4	2,64
1829	-6,2	5,84	4,03
1830	13,3	1,58	3,8
1831	0	2,74	5,19
1832	-5,9	5,1	4,59
1833	12,5	3,5	2,83
1834	5,6	5,5	4,63
1835	5,3	4,86	4,17
1836	10	4,36	4,17
1837	-9,1	5,06	4,82
1838	10	4	2,97
1839	9,1	2	2,83
1840	0	2,98	3,63
1841	0	1,86	3,34
1842	-4,2	2,54	4,36
1843	4,4	4,02	2,86
1844	12,5	4,02	3,03
1845	7,4	4,16	3,03
1846	0	5,42	3,03
1847	-3,5	2,92	4,58
1848	10,7	1,44	5,07
1849	0	3,38	4,57
1850	0	5,84	4,3
1851	9,7	5,3	4,82
1852	8,8	6,3	6,22
1853	8	7,24	4,8
1854	5	7,12	4,8
1855	4,7	4,94	5,51
1856	9,1	3,34	5,1
1857	-2,1	3,62	4,12
1858	0	3,88	1,98
1859	6,4	2,06	2,37
1860	6	0,22	2,5
1861	0	1,92	1,69
1862	-11,3	1,82	3,53
1863	8,5	0,98	3,36
1864	5,9	3,88	3,54
1865	1,8	5,82	3,38

1866	14,5	5,74	3,07
1867	-1,6	5,46	5,3
1868	8,1	4,54	5,56
1869	4,5	3,4	4,77
1870	-2,8	5,88	4,57
1871	8,8	4,02	2,68
1872	10,8	3,12	3,28
1873	-1,2	3,18	2,51
1874	0	2,18	2,28
1875	-2,5	0,26	2,84
1876	3,8	0,98	2,77
1877	1,2	1,44	2,16
1878	2,4	3,56	3,07
1879	2,3	3,86	3,49
1880	8,1	5,02	3,47
1881	5,3	5,3	2,93
1882	7	4,3	3,43
1883	3,8	2,48	4,06
1884	-2,7	2,56	4,27
1885	-1	2,76	4,33
1886	5,7	2,84	4,31
1887	8	5,12	3,69
1888	4,2	6,34	3,42
1889	8,7	5,48	3,36
1890	5,1	4,16	3,86
1891	1,4	2,66	4,28
1892	1,4	1,62	3,67
1893	-3,3	2,5	3,73
1894	3,5	2,72	3,79
1895	9,5	3,4	4,04
1896	2,5	5,9	3,94
1897	4,8	6,68	4,22
1898	9,2	4,88	5,48
1899	7,4	5,16	5,33
1900	0,5	5,8	4,32
1901	3,9	4,4	5,18
1902	8	3	5,16
1903	2,2	4,94	4,46
1904	0,4	5,08	2,72
1905	10,2	4,06	3,74
1906	4,6	1,98	4,1
1907	2,9	3,84	3,4
1908	-8,2	3,22	4,13
1909	9,7	2,64	4,62
1910	7,1	3,82	2,5
1911	1,7	6,42	2,33

1912	8,8	2,7	2,86
1913	4,8	1,9	3,86
1914	-8,9	3,08	2,12
1915	3,1	1,48	0,41
1916	7,6	-0,66	0,87
1917	0,8	-0,54	-1,68
1918	-5,9	0	0,29
1919	-8,3	-4,34	1,86
1920	5,8	0	2,16
1921	-14,1	2,22	2,21
1922	22,5	5,04	2,49
1923	5,2	5,5	3,88
1924	5,8	8,98	5,31
1925	8,1	5,8	5,48
1926	3,3	5,68	5,68
1927	6,6	5,98	1,71
1928	4,6	1,9	-0,47
1929	7,3	-1,4	0,29
1930	-12,3	-5,6	0,63
1931	-13,2	-4	1,57
1932	-14,4	-3,22	2,24
1933	12,6	1,58	2,86
1934	11,2	6,76	0,89
1935	11,7	11,66	4,14
1936	12,7	7,06	6,43
1937	10,1	8,22	10,19
1938	-10,4	7,36	10,64
1939	17	8,7	10,94
1940	7,4	10,02	9,08
1941	19,4	14,88	4,26
1942	16,7	10,46	1,48
1943	13,9	2,84	4,03
1944	-5,1	-4,02	2,98
1945	-30,7	-4,84	2,38
1946	-14,9	-6,12	1,74
1947	12,6	-4,7	0,84
1948	7,5	4,18	-0,43
1949	2	8,88	0,96
1950	13,7	6,84	4,37
1951	8,6	6,82	7,34
1952	2,4	6,42	6,49
1953	7,4	6,06	6,02
1954	0	5,32	5,51
1955	11,9	5,5	5,24
1956	4,9	3,5	5,02
1957	3,3	5,76	5,16

1958	-2,6	4,7	5,07
1959	11,3	4,44	5,63
1960	6,6	5,1	5,22
1961	3,6	6,64	5,5
1962	6,6	6,02	6,01
1963	5,1	6,18	6,47
1964	8,2	7,04	5,91
1965	7,4	6,02	6
1966	7,9	6,26	5,83
1967	1,5	6,1	5,32
1968	6,3	5,04	5,62
1969	7,4	3,86	5,72
1970	2,1	5,12	4,99
1971	2	5,68	3,38
1972	7,8	4,36	3,74
1973	9,1	2,62	3,46
1974	0,8	3,18	3,09
1975	-6,6	2,36	3,19
1976	4,8	1,36	3,01
1977	3,7	1,8	2,31
1978	4,1	3,2	1,27
1979	3	2,54	1,49
1980	0,4	1,74	2,77
1981	1,5	1,48	2,61
1982	-0,3	1,86	2,49
1983	2,8	2,46	2,41
1984	4,9	2,68	2,56
1985	3,4	3,42	2,92
1986	2,6	3,72	3,06
1987	3,4	3,48	3,29
1988	4,3	3,34	3,29
1989	3,7	3,18	3,04
1990	2,7	3,06	3,12
1991	1,8	2,74	3,24
1992	2,8	2,82	3,31
1993	2,7	3,02	3,32
1994	4,1	3,46	
1995	3,7	3,78	
1996	4		
1997	4,4		

1975	-6,6 (-0,7)
1976	4,8
1977	3,7
1978	4,1
1979	3

1980	0,4
1981	1,5
1982	-0,3
1983	2,8
1984	4,9
1985	3,4
1986	2,6
1987	3,4
1988	4,3
1989	3,7
1990	2,7
1991	1,8
1992	2,8
1993	2,7
1994	4,1
1995	3,7
1996	4
1997	4,4
1998	
1999	

These data yield the following graphical results:

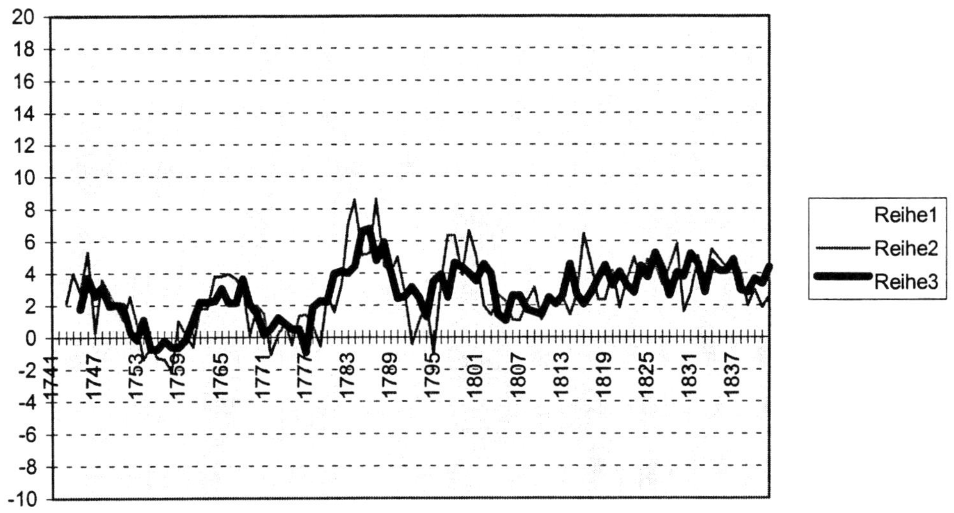

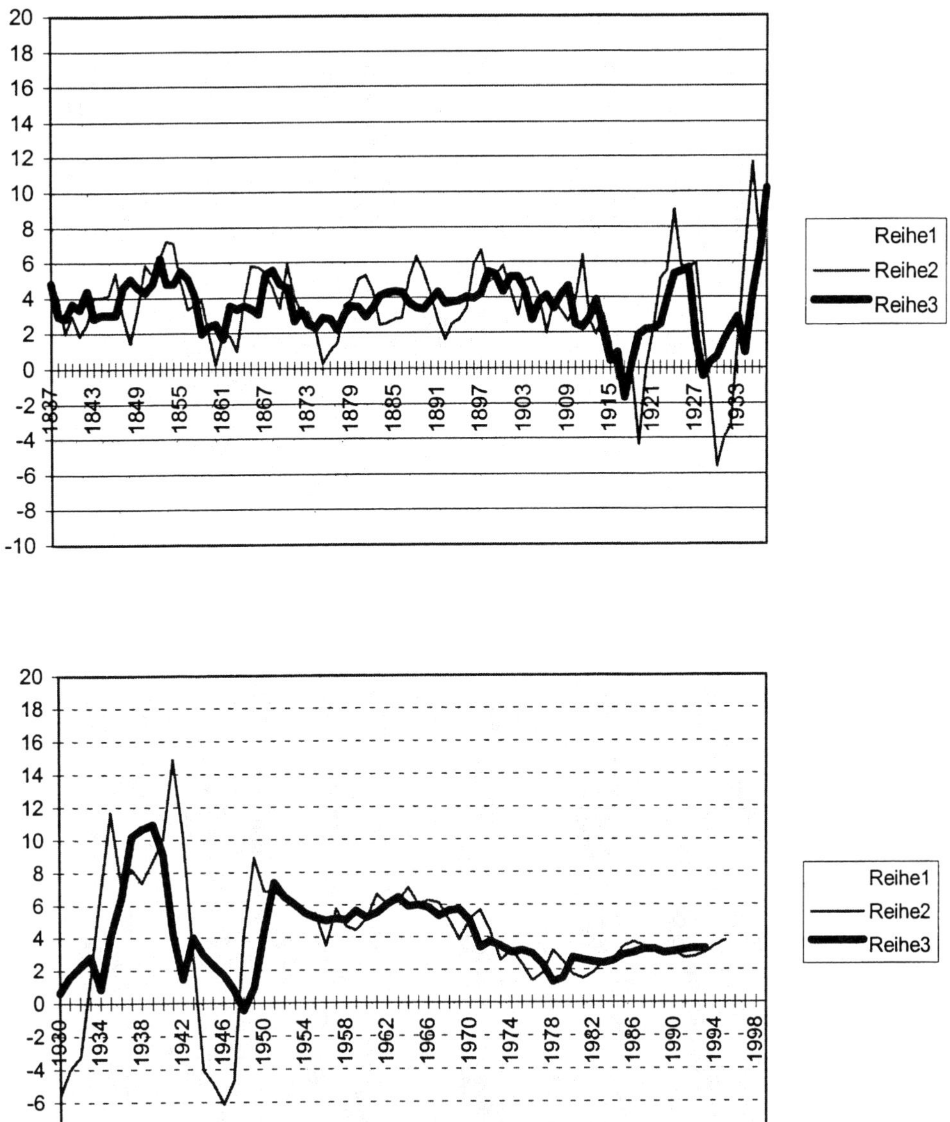

Legend: the darker and thicker line are 9-year moving averages, the lighter and thinner lines are 5-year moving averags

TNC Penetration and Transformation Country Development

The transformation success or failure 1989-95

	gdp (1989=100)	privatization	Pol Rights Violations 1991	urbanization	ln (GNP)	ln(GNP)^2	HDI
CS	85	70	2	65	7,9047039	62,484344	0,872
SLOK	84	60	2	57	7,5755847	57,389483	0,872

H	86	60	2	63	8,1167156	65,881073	0,856
PL	97	60	2	63	7,7231201	59,646584	0,855
RU	81	40	5	54	7,0387835	49,544474	0,703
BUL	75	45	2	69	7,0387835	49,544474	0,796
ALB	75	60	4	36	5,8289456	33,976607	0,739
EST	74	65	2	72	8,0326849	64,524026	0,862
LAT	54	60	2	72	7,60589	57,849563	0,857
LIT	42	55	2	70	7,185387	51,629787	0,769
ARM	37	45	5	68	6,4922398	42,149178	0,715
AZE	35	25	5	55	6,5930445	43,468236	0,696
BRU	54	15	4	68	7,9620673	63,394516	0,866
GEO	17	30	6	57	6,3630281	40,488127	0,709
KAZ	44	25	5	58	7,3524411	54,05839	0,798
KYR	43	40	5	39	6,7452363	45,498213	0,717
MOL	42	30	5	49	6,9660242	48,525493	0,755
RUS	49	55	3	75	7,7579062	60,185109	0,849
TAD	40	15	5	32	6,1527327	37,85612	0,643
TUR	63	15	6	45	7,237059	52,375023	0,731
UKR	43	35	3	69	7,7007478	59,301517	0,842
UZB	82	30	6	41	6,8772961	47,297201	0,706
		privatization	Pol Rights	urbanization	ln (GNP)	ln(GNP)^2	HDI

Sources: Osteuropa-Institute Munich, Working Paper 186 (GDP growth, privatization); Stiftung Entwicklung und Frieden (Political Rights Violations, based on Freedom House); UNDP, 1995 (urbanization, Human Development Index); Fischer Weltalmanach (GNP per capita)

Inequality, savings, taxes, and social expenditure. Evidence from Eastern Europe by cross-national comparison

	Share of the top 20% in total incomes	dom. savings rate per GDP	tax revenue per GNP	% expenditures social services
transformation countries:				
Lao PDR	40.2%	-	-	-
China	43.9%	44%	2.6%	3.3%
Moldova	41.5%	0%	-	-
Kazakstan	40.4%	20%	-	-
Bulgaria	39.3%	21%	29.3%	36.3%
Romania	34.8%	25%	26.5%	46.9%
Lithuania	42.1%	11%	18.3%	-
Ukraine	35.4%	-	-	-
Belarus	32.9%	27%	30.8%	57.2%
Slovak R	31.4%	23%	-	-
Latvia	36.7%	25%	25.3%	52.8%
Poland	**36.6%**	**17%**	**37.9%**	-
Russia	53.8%	29%	19.1%	54.1%
Estonia	46.3%	28%	29.1%	56.4%
Czech R.	37.4%	20%	38.0%	60.6%
Hungary	36.6%	15%	-	-

Slovenia	37.9%	25%	-	-
by comparison:				
Austria	-	26%	33.7%	70.1%
Finland	37.6%	20%	29.6%	59.3%
Netherlands	36.9%	24%	44.7%	69.3%
Sweden	36.9%	17%	31.7%	56.8%
Norway	36.7%	26%	37.0%	55.6%
Denmark	38.6%	21%	33.3%	53.5%
Japan	37.5%	32%	17.8%	59.2%
Indonesia	40.7%	30%	16.3%	14.4%
Thailand	52.7%	35%	17.0%	35.4%
Hong Kong	47.0%	33%	-	-
Singapore	48.9%	51%	17.1%	35.9%

Source: our compilations from World Bank, 1996, WDR

Gini-Index of income inequality in the formerly socialist or quasi-socialist countries

Country	GINI inequality	pol rights violations	civil rights violations	GNP per capita	growth 85-94
Tanzania	0,381	6	5	140	0,8
Vietnam	0,357	7	7	200	
G-Bissau	0,562	6	5	240	2,2
Lao PDR	0,304	7	6	320	
Nicaragua	0,503	4	5	340	-6,1
China	0,376	7	7	530	7,8
Moldova	0,344	5	5	870	
Kazakstan	0,327	6	4	1160	-6,5
Bulgaria	0,308	2	2	1250	-2,7
Romania	0,255	4	4	1270	-4,5
Lithuania	0,336	1	3	1350	-8
Algeria	0,387	7	6	1650	-2,5
Ukraine	0,257	4	4	1910	-8
Belarus	0,216	5	4	2160	-1,9
Slovak R	0,195	3	4	2250	-3
Latvia	0,27	3	3	2320	-6
Poland	0,272	2	2	2410	0,8
Russia	0,496	3	4	2650	-4,1
Estonia	0,395	3	2	2820	-6,1
Turkmenistan	0,358	7	7		
Czech R	0,266	1	2	3200	-2,1
Hungary	0,27	1	2	3840	-1,2
Slovenia	0,282	1	2	7040	

Country	GINI inequality	pol rights violations	civil rights violations	GNP per capita	growth 85-94

Country	GINI inequality	pol rights violations	civil rights violations	FCAPPen
Tanzania	0,381	6	5	1,3
Vietnam	0,357	7	7	1,9
G-Bissau	0,562	6	5	6
Lao PDR	0,304	7	6	12,1
Nicaragua	0,503	4	5	10,8
China	0,376	7	7	17,9
Kazakstan	0,327	6	4	3
Bulgaria	0,308	2	2	0,6
Romania	0,255	4	4	1,8
Lithuania	0,336	1	3	1,7
Algeria	0,387	7	6	2,9
Slovak R	0,195	3	4	3,2
Latvia	0,27	3	3	8,5
Poland	0,272	2	2	5,3
Estonia	0,395	3	2	26,5
Czech R	0,266	1	2	9,9
Hungary	0,27	1	2	15,6

Country	GINI inequality	pol rights violations	civil rights violations	GNP per capita	FCAPPen	Unemployment
Bulgaria	0,308	2	2	1250	0,6	10,4
Romania	0,255	4	4	1270	1,8	7,1
Lithuania	0,336	1	3	1350	1,7	7
Moldova	0,344	5	5	870	1,5	1,6
Ukraine	0,257	4	4	1910	0,7	1
Belarus	0,216	5	4	2160	0,2	3,7
Slovak R	0,195	3	4	2250	3,2	12,1
Latvia	0,27	3	3	2320	8,5	7
Poland	0,272	2	2	2410	5,3	14,3
Russia	0,496	3	4	2650	0,9	3,6
Estonia	0,395	3	2	2820	26,5	2,2
Slovenia	0,282	1	2	7040	2,2	13,2
Czech R	0,266	1	2	3200	9,9	2,8
Hungary	0,27	1	2	3840	15,6	10,6
Slovenia	0,282	1	2	7040	2,2	13,2

Source: our own compilations from UNDP, 1996; World Bank, WDR, 1996; UNCTAD, 1996; Stiftung (1996, for the Freedom House data series); Polish Central Statistical Office, Poland Quarterly Statistics, 4, 2, 1996: 52 (unemployment figures)

economic growth =

Gini inequality	political repr.	civil rights violations	ln (GNP)	$(ln(GNP))^2$	constant
10,91358546	-162,8188826	-0,722897795	0,116576987	-11,0941545	607,4708743
2,711016139	39,90219401	0,98220757	0,764921232	10,11245772	148,4162944

0,6951136					
4,103838325	9				
4,025643853	**-4,080449376**	-0,735992897	0,152403911	-1,097077962	t-test
Gini inequality	**political repr.**	civil rights violations	ln (GNP)	(ln(GNP))^2	constant

GINI income inequality =

pol rights violations	civil rights violations	**FCAPPen**	lnGNPpc	lnGNP^2	constant
-0,018992718	0,176971676	**0,004611249**	-0,020469912	0,006726173	0,061751233
0,025122747	0,324494352	0,002916141	0,028052902	0,020223575	1,016901378
0,504766872					
2,24235225	11				
-0,755996872	0,545376754	**1,581284635**	-0,729689648	0,332590687	
pol rights violations	civil rights violations	**FCAPPen**	lnGNPpc	lnGNP^2	

unemployment rate =

GINI inequality	pol rights violations	civil rights violations	GNP per capita	FCAPPen	constant
-0,218971053	0,000392913	-1,528791364	-0,907559915	-17,56078807	19,53812103
0,183471851	0,000686046	2,166180602	1,418759587	14,50565314	6,935047266
0,56989396					
2,385014466	9				
-1,193485827	0,572720543	-0,705754341	-0,639685485	-1,210616847	T-test
GINI inequality	pol rights violations	civil rights violations	GNP per capita	FCAPPen	

Legend: as in all EXCEL 5.0 outprints in this work, first row: unstandardized regression coefficients, second row: standard errors, last row: t-Test. The values immediately below the standard errors are R^2 (third row, left side entry), F, and degrees of freedom (fourth row).

Source: our own calculations from the above Tables with EXCEL 5.0 multiple regression routine.

foreign aid, aggregate resource flows per GNP and economic growth in the transformation countries

	Aid 94	**Growth 95**	**Resource flow**
Albania	7,8	6	9,1
Bulgaria	1,6	3	0,1
Croatia		2	0,3
Czech R.	0,4	5	7,8
Hungary	0,5	2	7,3
Macedonia		-4	-2,4

Poland	2	7	3,8
Romania	0,5	7	4,3
Slovak R	0,6	7	6,6
Slovenia		5	2,4
Armenia	6,9	7	7
Azerbaijan	4	-17	3,7
Belarus	0,6	-12	1,6
Estonia	0,9	4	5,5
Georgia	8,4	-5	9
Kazakstan	0,3	-9	4,4
Kyrgyz R	5,8	-6	5,9
Latvia	0,9	1	5,2
Lithuania	1,4	3	1,8
Moldova	1,4	2	5,1
Russia	0,5	-4	0,8
Tajikistan	3,2	-12	11,5
Turkmenistan	0,1	-5	1
Ukraine	0,4	-12	0,9
Uzbekistan	0,1	-2	0,2
China	0,6	10,2	9,6
Mongolia	22,5	6,3	14,4
Vietnam	5,2	9,5	6,5

Legend: our own compilations from World Bank, WDR, 1996

The external conditions of the transformation and the World Bank's liberalization index:

net flows per GNP	development assistance per GNP	present value of external debt per GNP	liberalization Index	
7,8	0,4	28	9,3	CS
6,6	0,6	30	8,5	SLOK
7,3	0,5	66	9	H
3,8	2	37	9	PL
4,3	0,5	17	7,1	RU
0,1	1,6	100	6	BUL
9,1	7,8	45	7,5	ALB
5,5	0,9	4	9,3	EST
5,2	0,9	6	8,2	LAT
1,8	1,4	7	8,5	LIT
7	6,9	8	6	ARM
3,7	4	3	4,5	AZE
1,6	0,6	5	4,8	BRU
9	8,4	56	6	GEO
4,4	0,3	14	5,9	KAZ
5,9	5,8	13	8,3	KYR
5,1	1,4	12	6,8	MOL
0,8	0,5	23	6,9	RUS

11,5	3,2	25	3,8	TAD
1	0,1	1	2,1	TUR
0,9	0,4	6	5,9	UKR
0,2	0,1	5	5,3	UZB
NET FLOWS	DEV ASS	NET DEBT	Liberalization	

Source: our own compilations from World Bank, WDR, 1996

economic recovery in Eastern Europe and the former USSR:

privati-zation	Pol Rights Violations	ln (GNP)	ln(GNP)^2	HDI	NET FLOWS	DEV ASS	Liberali-zation	Constant
0,536737	-6,757594	-0,988263	-4,253716	18,634372	-274,6279	4,6616276	0,932771	1024,9646
5,2836872	2,9991756	1,9402744	167,95219	13,84864	197,52304	5,844472	0,6182559	727,345
0,5709663								
2,1625809	13							

privati-zation	Pol Rights Violations	ln (GNP)	ln(GNP)^2	HDI	NET FLOWS	DEV ASS	Liberalization
0,1015838	**-2,253151**	-0,509342	-0,025327	1,3455741	-1,390359	0,7976131	*1,5087134*

Legend: as in all EXCEL 5.0 outprints in this work, first row: unstandardized regression coefficients, second row: standard errors, last row: t-Test. The values immediately below the standard errors are R^2 (third row, left side entry), F, and degrees of freedom (fourth row).

Source: our calculations from the above Tables on the basis of the EXCEL 5.0 multiple regression program

EU-eastward expansion - a synopsis of the conditions, prevailing in the European periphery:

	current account balance per GNP 1994	CO2 emissions in millions of tons 1994	government surplus or deficit per GNP 1994	political repression 1993	civil rights violations 1993
Greece	-6,3	73,9	-15,6	1	3
Portugal	-1,9	47,2	-2,2	1	1
Spain	-1,5	223,2	-4,8	1	2
Ireland	2,3	25,1	-2,3	1	2
Italy	2,5	407,7	-10,6	1	3
Bulgaria	1,9	54,4	-4,5	2	2
Romania	-1	122,1	-2,5	4	4
Lithuania		22		1	3
Slovak R	5,8	37		3	4
Latvia		14,8	-4,4	3	3
Poland	-3,1	341,9	-2,4	2	2
Croatia	0	16,2	1,7	4	4
Estonia	-1,7	20,9	1,2	3	2
Czech R	0	135,6	0,9	1	2
Hungary	-9,4	59,9		1	2
Slovenia	3,9	5,5		1	2

Sources: (1), (2), (3) World Bank, WDR, 1996; (4) and (5) Stiftung Entwicklung und Frieden, 1996, based exclusively on Freedom House

the weighted averages of the economic and political indicators of European periphery countries

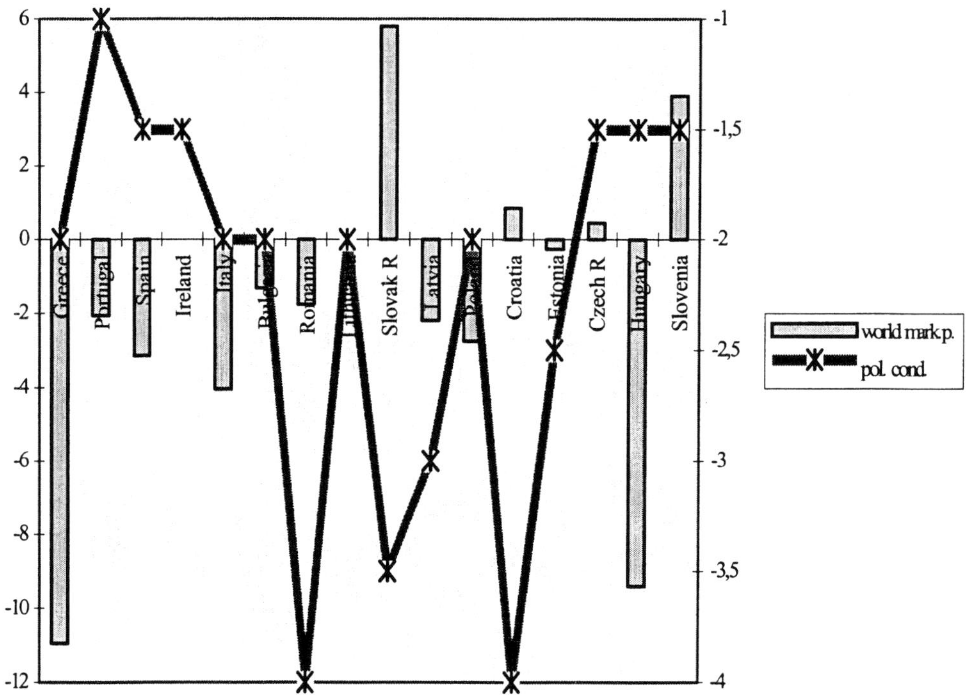

Legend: columns, left-hand scale: average of the 'double deficits' in the current account and in the budget; right-hand scale, dotted line: average of political and civil rights violations. Best value: - 1; worst value: - 7.

Effects of the European Union before and after the enlargementsof 1981, 1986, 1995

	age dem 80	state sector	y Union (93)	growth 80 - 91	HDI	inflation 80-91
sw	63	28	0	1,7	0,928	7,4
is	32	44	0	1,7	0,9	89
us	76	19	0	1,7	0,925	4,2
sf	63	24	0	2,5	0,911	6,6
bl	35	39	35	2	0,916	4,2
dk	35	33	20	2,2	0,912	5,2
ir	57	33	20	3,3	0,892	5,8
at	25	30	0	2,1	0,917	3,6
nz	101	31	0	0,7	0,907	10,3
no	35	35	0	2,3	0,928	5,2
as	88	20	0	1,6	0,926	7
it	35	30	35	2,2	0,891	9,5
uk	62	32	20	2,6	0,919	5,8
ge	31	24	35	2,2	0,918	2,8

	age dem 80	state sector	y Union (93)	growth	HDI	inflation 80-91
nl	35	41	35	1,6	0,923	1,8
ch	108	13	0	1,6	0,931	3,8
cn	82	20	0	2	0,932	4,3
jp	28	13	0	3,6	0,929	1,5
fr	35	32	35	1,8	0,927	5,7
ic	32	44	0	1,7	0,914	30
lux	35	41,3	35	3,5	0,908	4,2

Effects of the European Union after enlargements

EU-years	age democr	state sector	HDI	
0	99	22,2	0,96	CND
39	52	43,7	0,946	France
0	52	43,4	0,943	NOR
0	93	23,5	0,942	USA
0	49	27,5	0,942	Ice
39	52	53,9	0,94	NL
0	45	16,3	0,94	Jap
2	80	30	0,94	SF
0	118	44,7	0,937	NZ
2	80	41,3	0,936	Swd
11	**20**	**33,6**	**0,934**	**Sp**
2	42	39,1	0,932	Aut
39	52	50,1	0,932	Blg
0	105	27,5	0,931	Aus
24	79	35,6	0,931	UK
0	125	21	0,93	CH
24	**74**	**52,4**	**0,929**	**Ire**
24	52	38,3	0,927	DK
39	7	30,4	0,924	Ger
16	**23**	**40,1**	**0,923**	**Gre**
39	52	46,8	0,921	It
0	49	48	0,913	Isr
39	52	41,3	0,899	Lux
11	**22**	**41,9**	**0,89**	**Port**
EU-years	age democr	state sector	HDI	

	growth	UNDP surv	growth -91	male unemploy	gender power
CND	1,4	3,1	2	11,8	0,7
France	1,6	4	1,8	10	0,452
NOR	2,2	2,7	2,3	6,6	0,795
USA	1,7	4	1,7	7,1	0,671

	growth	UNDP surv	growth -91	male unemploy	gender power
Ice	1,2	2,6	1,8	3,6	0,757
NL	1,7	2,5	1,6	6	0,66
Jap	3,4	2,2	3,6	2,4	0,465
SF	1,5	3,1	2,5	19,5	0,719
NZ	0,7	4,3	0,7	10	0,718
Swd	1,3	2,7	1,7	9,2	0,784
Sp	**2,7**	**3**	**2,8**	**9,9**	**0,542**
Aut	2	3,7	2,1	6,7	0,667
Blg	1,9	3,5	2	9,7	0,591
Aus	1,6	3,5	1,6	11,5	0,659
UK	2,3	2,6	2,6	12,4	0,543
CH	1,1	3,4	1,6	4,4	0,642
Ire	**3,6**	**2,9**	**3,3**	**18,8**	**0,521**
DK	2	3,4	2,2	11,3	0,728
Ger	2,1	3	2,2	8	0,661
Gre	**0,9**	**3,8**	**1,1**	**6,4**	**0,391**
It	2,1	3	2,2	8,1	0,573
Isr	2	2,8	1,7	8,5	0,475
Lux	2,8	3,8	3,5	1,5	0,631
Port	**3,3**	**4,7**	**3,1**	**4,6**	**0,556**

	growth	UNDP surv	growth -91	female unpl.r	gender power	inflation 93
CND	1,4	3,1	2	10,6	0,7	1,1
France	1,6	4	1,8	13,7	0,452	2,2
NOR	2,2	2,7	2,3	5,2	0,795	1
USA	1,7	4	1,7	6,5	0,671	2
Ice	1,2	2,6	1,8	5,4	0,757	2,9
NL	1,7	2,5	1,6	7,3	0,66	1,6
Jap	3,4	2,2	3,6	2,6	0,465	0,8
SF	1,5	3,1	2,5	15,7	0,719	2,3
NZ	0,7	4,3	0,7	8,9	0,718	0,9
Swd	1,3	2,7	1,7	9,2	0,784	2,6
Sp	**2,7**	**3**	**2,8**	**23,8**	**0,542**	**4,4**
Aut	2	3,7	2,1	6,9	0,667	3,6
Blg	1,9	3,5	2	17,4	0,591	4,4
Aus	1,6	3,5	1,6	10,1	0,659	1,1
UK	2,3	2,6	2,6	7,5	0,543	3,4
CH	1,1	3,4	1,6	4,7	0,642	2,1
Ire	**3,6**	**2,9**	**3,3**	**19,5**	**0,521**	**3,6**
DK	2	3,4	2,2	13,7	0,728	1,2
Ger	2,1	3	2,2	8,4	0,661	3,9
Gre	**0,9**	**3,8**	**1,1**	**15,2**	**0,391**	**12,6**
It	2,1	3	2,2	17,3	0,573	4,4
Isr	2	2,8	1,7	12,1	0,475	11
Lux	2,8	3,8	3,5	1,9	0,631	6,2

Port	3,3	4,7	3,1	6,5	0,556	7,4
	growth	UNDP surv	growth -91	female unpl.r	gender power	inflation 93

Our data and trade block compositions were:

EU-12	Human Development Index		
	1980	1992	1994
France	0,895	0,927	0,946
NL	0,888	0,923	0,94
SP	0,851	0,888	0,934
Blg	0,873	0,916	0,932
UK	0,892	0,919	0,931
Ire	0,862	0,892	0,929
DK	0,888	0,912	0,927
Ger	0,881	0,918	0,924
Gre	0,839	0,874	0,923
Ita	0,857	0,891	0,921
Lux	0,869	0,908	0,899
Port	0,736	0,838	0,89
standard dev.	0,041240066	0,024517001	0,015200512
average HDI	0,860916667	0,9005	0,924666667

Asean	Human Development Index		
	1980	1992	1994
Indonesia	0,418	0,586	0,668
Malaysia	0,687	0,794	0,832
Philippines	0,557	0,621	0,672
Singapore	0,78	0,836	0,9
Thailand	0,551	0,798	0,833
Brunei			
Vietnam			
standard dev.	0,124364947	0,102496829	0,09393189
average HDI	0,5986	0,727	0,781

EFTA	Human Development Index		
	1980	1992	1994
Iceland	0,89	0,914	0,942
Norway	0,901	0,928	0,943
Switzerland	0,897	0,931	0,93
Austria	0,88	0,917	0,932
Sweden	0,899	0,928	0,936
standard deviation	0,007657676	0,006770524	0,0052
average HDI	0,8934	0,9236	0,9366

NAFTA	Human Development Index		
	1980	1992	1994

CND	0,911	0,932	0,96
USA	0,905	0,925	0,942
Mexico	0,758	0,804	0,853
standard deviation	0,070753092	0,058759396	0,046778438
average HDI	0,858	0,887	0,918333333

EU-Assoc.	Human Development Index		
	1980	1992	1994
Bulgaria			
Estonia			
Israel	0,862	0,9	0,913
Lithuania			
Latvia			
Malta	0,802	0,843	0,887
Morocco	0,383	0,549	0,566
Poland			
Romania			
Slovakia			
Czech Republic			
Turkey	0,549	0,739	0,772
Tunesia	0,499	0,69	0,748
Hungary			
Cyprus	0,844	0,873	0,907
standard deviation	0,186958774	0,121742442	0,122490022
average HDI	0,6565	0,765666667	0,798833333

APEC	Human Development Index		
	1980	1992	1994
Indonesia	0,418	0,586	0,668
Malaysia	0,687	0,794	0,832
Philippines	0,557	0,621	0,672
Singapore	0,78	0,836	0,9
Thailand	0,551	0,798	0,833
Australia	0,89	0,926	0,931
Chile	0,753	0,848	0,891
Japan	0,906	0,929	0,94
CND	0,911	0,932	0,96
USA	0,905	0,925	0,942
Mexico	0,758	0,804	0,853
S-Korea	0,666	0,859	0,89
New Zealand	0,877	0,907	0,937
Papua-NG	0,348	0,408	0,525
China	0,475	0,644	0,626
Hong-Kong	0,83	0,875	0,914
standard deviation	0,18081897	0,146817276	0,129612343
average HDI	0,707	0,79325	0,832125

Values for other member countries were missing (as well). Our analysis makes the assumption of a 'pipeline effect', i.e. that integration is a long-term process, already affecting countries before actual joining or founding the trade block takes place, viz. Spain before full membership of the EU, NAFTA before it came into being etc.

Data provided by the Austrian Federal Ministry of Labor (1997, Bericht ueber die soziale Lage) show the following connection between social security expenditures and poverty in the countries of the European Union:

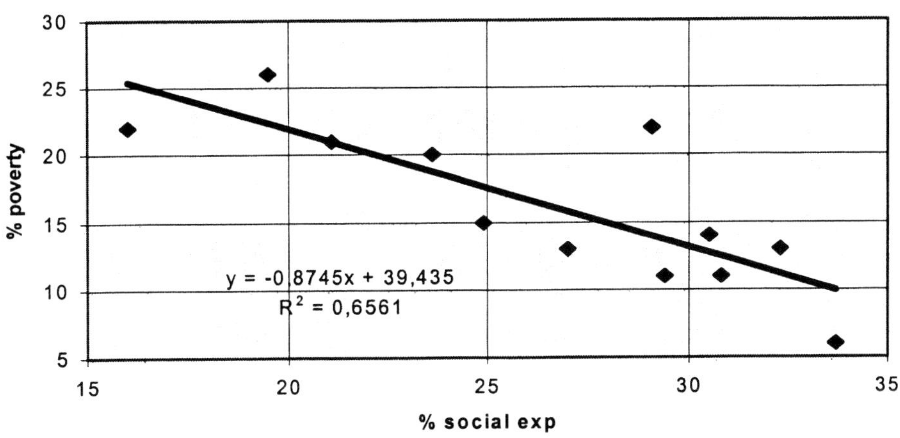

Legend: social expenditures per GDP, 1994; percent of the total population endangered by poverty, 1993. Compiled by the Austrian Federal Ministry of Labor.

BIBLIOGRAPHY

1. Achen Ch. H. (1982), *'Interpreting and Using Regression'* Beverly Hills: Sage University Papers.

2. Adamczyk F et al. (1992), *'Rynek Oracy w Polsce'* Warsaw: Fundacja 'Promocja'.

3. Addo H. (1986), *'Imperialism: the permanent stage of capitalism'* Tokyo: United Nations University.

4. Afheldt H. (1994), *'Wohlstand fuer niemand? Die Marktwirtschaft entlaesst ihre Kinder'* Munich: Kunstmann.

5. *Agence France Press English Wire*, Dialog - online.

6. Aghion Ph. and Williamson J. G. (1998), *'Growth, Inequality and Globalization. Theory, History and Policy'* Cambridge: at the University Press

7. Ahluwalia M.S. (1974), 'Income Inequality: Some Dimensions of the Problem' in *'Redistribution with Growth'* (Chenery H.B. *et al.* (Eds.)), pp. 3 - 37, New York and Oxford: Oxford University Press.

8. Akerman J. (1936) *'Economic Progress and Economic Crises'* London and Basingstoke: Macmillan.

9. Almond G. (1991), 'Capitalism and Democracy' *PS. Political Science and Politics,* 24, 3, September: 467 - 474.

10. Althaler A. and Hohenwarter A. (Eds.)(1992), *'Torschluss. Wanderungsbewegungen und Politik in Europa'* Vienna: Verlag fuer Gesellschaftskritik.

11. Amankwaa A. A. (1995), 'The World Economic System and International Migration in Less Developed Countries: An Ecological Approach' *International Migration,* 33, 1: 93 - 114.

12. Amato G. and Batt J. (1999), *'Final Report of the Reflection Group on The Long_term Implications of EU Enlargement: The Nature of the New Border'* The Robert Schuman Centre for Advanced Studies, European University Institute and The Forward Studies Unit, European Commission (mimeo)

13. Amin S. (1973), *'Le developpement inegal. Essai sur les formations sociales du capitalisme peripherique'* Paris: Editions de Minuit.

14. Amin S. (1976), *'Unequal Development: An Essay on the Social Formations of Peripheral Capitalism'* New York: Monthly Review Press.

15. Amin S. (1984), 'Was kommt nach der Neuen Internationalen Wirtschaftsordnung? Die Zukunft der Weltwirtschaft' in *'Rote Markierungen International'* (Fischer H. and Jankowitsch P. (Eds.)), pp. 89 - 110, Vienna: Europaverlag.

16. Amin S. (1992), *'Empire of Chaos'* New York: Monthly Review Press.

17. Amin S. (1994), 'Die neue kapitalistische Globalisierung - die Herrschaft des Chaos' *Starnberger Forschungsberichte,* 3, 4, May: 7 - 26.

18.   Amin S. (1997), *'Die Zukunft des Weltsystems. Herausforderungen der Globalisierung. Herausgegeben und aus dem Franzoesischen uebersetzt von Joachim Wilke'* Hamburg: VSA.

19.   Amin S. (2000), 'Not a happy ending' *Al Ahram Weekly,* 462, Cairo, electronic edition at http://www.ahram.org.eg/weekly/

20.   Ammon G. (1994), *'Das Europa der Regionen'* Munich: Eberhard.

21.   Ammon G. and Eberhard Th. (Ed.)(1993), *'Kultur, Identitaet, Kommunikation. 2. Versuch'* Munich: Eberhard.

22.   Amnesty International (current issues), *'Jahresbericht'* Frankfurt a.M.: Fischer TB.

23.   Amsden A.H. et al. (1994), 'From Pseudo - Socialism to Pseudo - Capitalism: Eastern Europe's First Five Years' *Internationale Politik und Gesellschaft. International Politics and Society (Friedrich Ebert Foundation),* 2: 107 - 116.

24.   Angresano J. (1994), 'Evolving Socio - economic Conditions in Central and Eastern Europe: A Myrdalian View' *Development Policy Review,* 12: 251 - 275.

25.   Apter D. (1987), *'Rethinking Development: Modernization, Dependency and Post - Modern Politics'* Newbury Park, CA.: Sage.

26.   Ardelt R. and Haas H. (1975), 'Die Westintegration Oesterreichs nach 1945' *Oesterreichische Zeitschrift fuer Politikwissenschaft,* 3: 379 - 399.

27.   Arnold E. (1991), 'German foreign policy and unification' *International Affairs,* 67, 3: 453 - 471.

28.   Arrighi G. (1989), *'The Developmentalist Illusion: A Reconceptualization of the Semiperiphery'* paper, presented at the Thirteenth Annual Political Economy of the World System Conference, University of Illinois at Urbana - Champaign, April 28 - 30.

29.   Arrighi G. (1991), *'World Income Inequalities and the Future of Socialism'* Fernand Braudel Centre, State University of New York at Binghamton.

30.   Arrighi G. (1995), *'The Long 20th Century. Money, Power, and the Origins of Our Times'* London, New York: Verso.

31.   Arrighi G. (1999) 'The Global Market' Journal of World-Systems Research, 5, 2 electronic journal at World Systems Archive, University of Colorado, at: http://csf.colorado.edu/jwsr/

32.   Arrighi G. and Silver, B. J. (1984), 'Labor Movements and Capital Migration: The United States and Western Europe in World - Historical Perspective' in *'Labor in the Capitalist World - Economy'* (Bergquist Ch. (Ed.)), pp. 183 - 216, Beverly Hills: Sage.

33.   Arrighi G. et al. (1991), *'The Rise of East Asia. One Miracle or Many?'* State University of New York at Binghamton: Fernand Braudel Centre.

34.   Arrighi G. et al. (1996a), *'Modelling Zones of the World-Economy: A Polynomial Regression Analysis (1964-1994)'* State University of New York at Binghamton: Fernand Braudel Center.

35.   Arrighi G. et al. (1996b), *'The Rise of East Asia in World Historical Perspective'* State University of New York at Binghamton: Fernand Braudel Center.

36.   Arrighi G. et al. (1996c), *'Beyond Western Hegemonies'* State University of New York at Binghamton: Fernand Braudel Center.

37.   Aslund, A. (1992), 'The Soviet Economy After the Coup', *Problems of Communism,* 40, Nov. - Dec.: 44 - 52.

38.   Austrian Central Statistical Office (current issues), *'Statistische Nachrichten'.* Vienna: Austrian Central Statistical Office.

39.   Austrian Federal Ministry for Foreign Affairs (current issues), *'Austrian Foreign Policy Yearbook'* Vienna: Manzsche Buchdruckerei.

40.   Austrian Federal Ministry for Foreign Affairs (current issues), *'Jahrbuch der oesterreichischen Aussenpolitik. Aussenpolitischer Bericht'* Vienna: Manz'sche Buchdruckerei.

41. Austrian Federal Ministry of Labor and Social Affairs (1994), *'Austria's Labor Market Policy'* Vienna: Federal Ministry of Labor and Social Affairs.

42. Austrian Federal Ministry of Labor and Social Affairs (1997), *'Bericht ueber die soziale Lage. Analysen und Ressortaktivitaeten, 1996'* Vienna: Federal Ministry of Labor and Social Affairs.

43. Austrian Federal Ministry of Labor, Vienna (current issues), *'Arbeitsmarktdaten'* Vienna: Federal Ministry of Labor and Social Affairs.

44. Austrian Federal Ministry of Labor, Vienna (current issues), *'Statistik ueber die bewilligungspflichtig beschaeftigten Auslaender'* Vienna: Federal Ministry of Labor.

45. Autorenkollektiv (1981), *'Laender der Erde. Politisch - oekonomisches Handbuch'*. Koeln: Pahl Rugenstein Verlag.

46. Axtmann R. (1995) 'Kulturelle Globalisierung, kollektive Identitaet und demokratischer Nationalstaat' *Leviathan,* 1: 87 - 101.

47. Bablewski Z. (1995), 'Development studies and the changes in Eastern *Europe' Afryka, Azja, Ameryka Lacinska (Warsaw),* 73: 17 - 32.

48. Bailey P.; Parisotto A. and Renshaw G. (1993*), 'Multinationals and Employment. The Global Economy of the 1990s'* Geneva: International Labor Office.

49. Baldwin R. E. et al. (1997), *'The Costs and Benefits of Eastern Enlargement: The Impact on the EU and Central Europe'* Economic Policy, April (quoted from the typescript).

50. Balibar E. (1991), 'Es gibt keinen Staat in Europa: Racism and Politics in Europe Today' *New Left Review,* March/April, 186: 5 - 19.

51. Bandt J. de et al. (Eds.)(1980), *'European Studies in Development. New Trends in European Development Studies'* Basingstoke and London: Macmillan.

52. *Bank Austria East - West Report. Business Information for the Central European Investor* (current issues), Vienna: Z - Laenderbank Bank Austria AG.

53. *Bank Austria Report* (current issues), Vienna: Z - Laenderbank Bank Austria AG.

54. Baran P. A. (1957), *'The Political Economy of Growth'* New York: Monthly Review Press.

55. Barnes S.H. *et al.* (1979), *'Political Action. Mass Participation in Five Western Democracies'* Beverly Hills: Sage.

56. Barro R. (1996), *'Getting It Right. Markets and Choices in a Free Society'* Cambridge, Mass.: MIT Press.

57. Barro R. and Grilli V. (1994) *'European Macroeconomics'* Basingstoke and London: Macmillan

58. Barro R. and Sala-i-Martin X. (1991) 'Convergence across States and Regions' *Brookings Papers on Economic Activity,* 1: 107-182

59. Barro R. and Sala-i-Martin X. (1995/98) *'Wirtschaftswachstum (Economic Growth)'* München: Oldenbourg (McGraw Hill, New York).

60. Barta V. and Richter S. (1996), *'Eastern Enlargement of the European Union from a Western and an Eastern Persepctive'* Research Reports, 227, Vienna Institute for Comparative Economic Studies.

61. Bauboeck, R. (1991a), 'Migration and citizenship', *New Community,* 18, 1: 27 - 48.

62. Bauboeck, R. (1991b), 'Einwanderungs - und Minderheitenpolitik. Ein Plaedoyer fuer neue Grundsaetze' *Oesterreichische Zeitschrift fuer Soziologie,* 16, 3: 42 - 56.

63. Bauer Th. and Zimmermann, K. F.(1999) *'Assessment of Possible Migration Pressure and It's Labour Market impact Following EU Enlargement to Central and Eastern Europe.'* A Study for the Department for Education and Employment, London, 1999

64. Bayer K. and Kreisky P. (1987), 'Die oesterreichische Gemeinwirtschaft nach dem Debakel bei VOEST - Alpine' *Das Argument,* 162: 200 - 209.

65. *BBC World Service* (current news broadcasts) short - wave, 31 - m - band.

66. Beaud M. (1990), *'Histoire du capitalisme de 1500 à nos jours'* 4e édition revue et corrigée en 1990, Paris: Éditions du Seuil.

67. Beck N. (1991), 'The Illusion of Cycles in International Relations' *International Studies Quarterly,* 35: 455 - 476.

68. Beck W./van der Maesen L. /Walker A. (Eds.), (1997) *The Social Quality of Europe;* The Hague/London/Boston.

69. Becker G. (1993), 'Europe Wastes Its Human Capital' *The Wall Street Journal Europe,* 18 - 19 June: 10.

70. Beckerman W. (1992), *'Economic Development and the Environment. Conflict or Complementarity?'* World Bank Policy Research Papers, WPS 961, Washington D.C.: The World Bank.

71. Behan T. (1996), *'The Camorra'* London: Routledge.

72. Beirat fuer Gesellschafts-, Wirtschafts- und Umweltpolitische Alternativen (Beigewum) (1996), *'Was hat der Euro mit den Arbeitslosen zu tun?'* Vienna: Department of Economics, Economics University, Vienna.

73. Bello W. (1989), 'Confronting the Brave New World Economic Order: Toward a Southern Agenda for the 1990s' *Alternatives,* XIV, 2: 135 - 168.

74. Benard Ch. and Schlaffer E. (1985), *'Die Grenzen des Geschlechts. Anleitungen zum Sturz des Internationalen Patriarchats'* Reinbek: rororo Sachbuch.

75. Bergesen A. (1983a), '1914 Again? Another Cycle of Interstate Competition and War' in *'Foreign Policy and the Modern World - System'* (Mc Gowan P. and Kegley Ch.W. Jr. (Eds.)), pp. 255 - 273, Beverly Hills: Sage.

76. Bergesen A. (1983b), 'Modeling Long Waves of Crisis in the World - System' in *'Crisis in the World System'* (Bergesen A. (Ed.)), pp. 73 - 92, Beverly Hills: Sage.

77. Berman R.A. (1987), 'The Vienna Fascination' *Dialog,* 3, 8: 173 - 204.

78. Bernal - Restrepo S. *Societas Jesu* (1991), 'Katholische Soziallehre und Kapitalismus' in *'Veraendert der Glaube die Wirtschaft? Theologie und Oekonomie in Lateinamerika'* (Fornet - Betancourt R. (Ed.)), pp. 21 - 38, Freiburg im Breisgau: Herder.

79. Bernhard M. (1996), 'Civil Society After the First Transition. Dilemmas of Postcommunist Democratization in Poland and Beyond' *Communist and Post - Communist Studies,* 29, 3: 309 - 330.

80. Berry A. et al. (1981), *'The Level of World Inequality: How Much Can One Say?'* Document 38, Laboratoire d'Economie Politique, CNRS, 45, rue d'Ulm, F - 75230 Paris Cedex 05.

81. Berry B. J. L. (1991), *'Long Wave Rhythms in Economic Development and Political Behavior'* Baltimore: John Hopkins University Press.

82. Berry W.D. and Feldman S. (1985), *'Multiple Regression in Practice'* Beverly Hills: Sage University Papers.

83. Berryman, Ph. (1987), *'Liberation Theology: The Essential Facts about the Revolutionary Movement in Latin America and Beyond'* New York: Pantheon Books.

84. Betz J. and Bruene St. (1995), *'Jahrbuch Dritte Welt 1995'* Munich: C.H. Beck.

85. Betz J. and Matthies V. (Eds.)(1992), *'Jahrbuch Dritte Welt 1992'* Munich: C.H. Beck.

86. Bhaduri A. and Laski K. (1996), *'Lessons to be drawn from main mistakes in the transition strategy'* Paper, presented at the 'Colloquium on Economic Transformation and Development of Central and Eastern Europe', OECD, Paris, 29/30 May 1996.

87. Bhagwati J.N. (1989), 'Nation States in an International Framework: An Economist's Perspective' *Alternatives,* XIV, 2: 231 - 244.

88. Birdsall N. (1993), *'Social Development is Economic Development'* Policy Research Working Papers, WPS 1123, Washington D.C.: The World Bank.

89. Blaas W. (1984), *'Stabilisierungspolitik. Zur politischen Oekonomie marktwirtschaftlicher Instabilitaet'* habilitation thesis, Vienna Technical University.

90. Blair, Tony (1999) Speech on the NVCO-conference, 21.1.1999 – HYPERLINK "http://www.number-10.gov.uk/news.asp?NewsId=328" http://www.number-10.gov.uk/news.asp?NewsId=328 – 3.11.2000.

91. Blair, Tony/Schroeder, Gerhard (1999) The Third Way HYPERLINK "http://www.labour.org.uk/lp/new/labour/docs/PMSPEECHES/THIRDWAYPURPLEBOX.HTM" http://www.labour.org.uk/lp/new/labour/docs/PMSPEECHES/THIRDWAYPURPLEBOX.HTM– 2000-10-29.

92. Blank S. (1994), 'Russia and the Baltic States. Is There a Threat to European Security?' Carlisle, Pennsylvania: Strategic Studies Institute, US Army War College.

93. Boehring W.R. and Schloeter - Paredes M.L. (1994), 'Aid in place of migration?. A World Employment Programme Study' Geneva: International Labor Office.

94. Boff C. and Boff L. (1984), 'Salvation and Liberation: In Search of a Balance between Faith and Politics' Maryknoll, NY: Orbis Books.

95. Boff L. (1979), 'Liberating Grace' Maryknoll, NY: Orbis Books.

96. Boff L. (1985), 'Kirche: Charisma und Macht. Studien zu einer streitbaren Ekklesiologie' Duesseldorf: Patmos - Verlag.

97. Boff L. and Boff C. (1988), 'Introducing Liberation Theology' Trans. Paul Burns. Maryknoll, NY: Orbis Books.

98. Boli J. (1983), 'The Contradictions of Welfare Capitalism in the Core: The Role of Sweden in the World System' in 'Foreign Policy and the Modern World System' (Mc Gowan P. and Kegley Ch.W.Jr. (Eds.)), pp. 187 - 221, Beverly Hills: Sage.

99. Bollen K. A. (1980), 'Issues in the Comparative Measurement of Political Democracy' American Sociological Review, 45: 370 - 390.

100. Bornschier V. (1976), 'Wachstum, Konzentration und Multinationalisierung von Industrieunternehmen' Frauenfeld and Stuttgart: Huber.

101. Bornschier V. (1988), 'Westliche Gesellschaft im Wandel' Frankfurt a.M./ New York: Campus.

102. Bornschier V. (1992), 'The Rise of the European Community. Grasping Towards Hegemony or Therapy against National Decline in the World Political Economy?'. Vienna: paper, presented at the First European Conference of Sociology, August 26 - 29.

103. Bornschier V. (1995), 'Hegemonic Decline, West European Unification and the Future Structure of the Core' Journal of World Systems Research, 1, 5 electronic journal at World Systems Archive, University of Colorado, at: http://csf.colorado.edu/jwsr/

104. Bornschier V. (1996), 'Western society in transition' New Brunswick, N.J. : Transaction Publishers.

105. Bornschier V. (1997), 'European Porcesses and the State of the European Union' Paper, distributed at the European Sociological Association Conference, University of Essex, 27-30 August

106. Bornschier V. (Ed.) (1994), 'Conflicts and new departures in world society' New Brunswick, N.J. : Transaction Publishers.

107. Bornschier V. and Chase - Dunn Ch. K (1985), 'Transnational Corporations and Underdevelopment' N.Y., N.Y.: Praeger.

108. Bornschier V. and Heintz P., reworked and enlarged by Th. H. Ballmer - Cao and J. Scheidegger (1979), 'Compendium of Data for World Systems Analysis' Machine readable data file, Zurich: Department of Sociology, Zurich University.

109. Bornschier V. and Nollert M. (1994); 'Political Conflict and Labor Disputes at the Core: An Encompassing Review for the Post - War Era' in 'Conflicts and New Departures in World Society' (Bornschier V. and Lengyel P. (Eds.)), pp. 377 - 403, New Brunswick (U.S.A.) and London: Transaction Publishers, World Society Studies, Volume 3.

110. Bornschier V. and Suter Chr. (1992), 'Long Waves in the World System' in *'Waves, Formations and Values in the World System'* (Bornschier V. and Lengyel P. (Eds.)), pp. 15 - 50, New Brunswick and London: Transaction Publishers.

111. Bornschier V. *et al.* (1980), *'Multinationale Konzerne, Wirtschaftspolitik und nationale Entwicklung im Weltsystem'* Frankfurt a.M.: Campus.

112. Boswell T. (1989), *'Revolutions in the World System'* Greenwich CT: Greenwood.

113. Boswell T. (1995), 'Hegemony and Bifurcation Points in World *History' Journal of World Systems Research,* 1, 15, electronic journal at World Systems Archive, University of Colorado, at: http://csf.colorado.edu/jwsr/

114. Boswell T. and Dixon W.J. (1990), 'Dependency and Rebellion: A Cross - National Analysis' *American Sociological Review,* 55, August: 540 - 559.

115. Boswell T. and Sweat M. (1991), 'Hegemony, Long Waves, and Major Wars: A Time Series Analysis of Systemic Dynamics, 1496 - 1967' *International Studies Quarterly,* 35, 2: 123 - 149.

116. Botz G. (1987), *'Krisenzonen einer Demokratie. Gewalt, Streik und Konfliktunterdrueckung in Oesterreich seit 1918'* Frankfurt a.M.: Campus.

117. Bourdieu P. (1998) 'The essence of neoliberalism: Utopia of endless exploitation', *Le monde diplomatique,* December 18, 1998; online: http://www.monde-diplpmatique.fr/en/1998/12/08bourdieu.html

118. Bourdieu P. (1999), *'The Weight of the World: Social Suffering in Contemporary Societies'* Stanford: Stanford University Press

119. Boyer M. (1996), 'Seid vernuenftig, vertagt den Euro!' *Zeit-Punkte, (Hamburg),* 4: 60 - 62.

120. Brackley D. SJ (1996), *'Divine Revolution. Salvation and Liberation in Catholic Thought. Foreword by Jon Sobrino'.* Maryknoll, New York: Orbis.

121. Bradshaw Y. (1987), 'Urbanization and Underdevelopment: A Global Study of Modernization, Urban Bias, and Economic Dependency' *American Sociological Review,* 52: 224 - 239.

122. Bradshaw Y. and Huang J. (1991), 'Intensifying Global Dependency. Foreign Debt, Structural Adjustment, and Third - World Underdevelopment' *Sociological Quarterly,* 32, 3: 321 - 342.

123. Brecht, Bertholt, questions from a worker who reads; HYPERLINK "http://www.geocities.com/Area51/1256/POEMS1.HTM#workerreads" http://www.geocities.com/Area51/1256/POEMS1.HTM#workerreads – 2000-10-29.

124. Brenner R. (1977), 'The Origins of Capitalist Development: A Critique of Neo - Smithian Marxism' *New Left Review,* 104: 25 - 92.

125. Breuss F. (1996), 'Die Osterweiterung der EU: Oekonomische Auswirkungen auf Oesterreich' *Die Union. Oesterreichische Zeitschrift fuer Integrationsfragen,* 4: 17 - 26.

126. Breuss F. (1997), 'Macht die Agenda 2000 bisherige Kosten-Nutzen-Schaetzungen der EU-Osterweiterung obsolet?' *Europa-Institut der Universitaet des Saarlandes, Vortraege, Reden und Berichte,* 50, Dezember 1997.

127. Brill H. (1996); 'Dimensionen der Sicherheitspolitik aus geopolitischer Sicht nach dem Ende des Ost - West - Konfliktes.' *Oesterreichische Militaerische Zeitschrift,* 5: 519 - 528.

128. Brittan, Samuel (2000) Protest against the protesters; in: Financial Times; September 28th.

129. Brown J.F. (Ed.), (1994), 'The Politics of Intolerance' *RFE/RL Research Report,* 3, 16, 22 April 1994 (special issue).

130. Brown L.R. *et al.* (1992), *'Zur Lage der Welt - 1992. Worldwatch Institute Report'* Frankfurt a.M.: Fischer TB.

131. Bruno M. and Sachs J. D. (1985), *'Economics of Worldwide Stagflation'* Cambridge, MA.: Harvard University Press.

132. Buckley, K. D. and Wheelwright E. L. (1988) *'No paradise for workers: capitalism and the common people in Australia, 1788 - 1914'* Melbourne; New York: Oxford University Press.

133. Bulletin of Electoral Statistics and Public Opinion Research Data (1994), 'Parliamentary Elections in Poland' *East European Politics and Society,* 8, 2: 369 - 379.

134. Bullock B. and Firebaugh G. (1990), 'Guns and Butter. The Effect of Militarization on Economic and Social Development in the Third World' *Journal of Political and Military Sociology,* 18, 2: 231 - 266.

135. Bundeskanzleramt der Republik Oesterreich (1992), *'Bericht ueber Oesterreichs Massnahmen fuer die Zentral - und Osteuropaeischen Reformstaaten (ZOR)'.* Vienna: Bundeskanzleramt, IV/1.

136. Bundesministerium fuer Arbeit und Soziales (1993), *'Von Ausgrenzung bedroht. Struktur und Umfang der materiellen Armutsgefährdung im österreichischen Wohlfahrtsstaat der achtziger Jahre'* Vienna: BMAS.

137. Bundesministerium fuer Arbeit und Soziales (current issues), *'Auslaenderbeschaeftigung'* (monthly) Vienna: BMAS.

138. Bundesministerium fuer Arbeit und Soziales (current issues), *'Bericht ueber die soziale Lage'* Vienna: BMAS.

139. Bundesministerium fuer Arbeit und Soziales (current issues), *'Statistik ueber die bewilligungspflichtig beschaeftigten Auslaender'* Vienna: BMAS.

140. Bundesministerium fuer Finanzen (1987), *'Staatliche Verteilungspolitik in Oesterreich'* Vienna: Bericht des Bundesministers fuer Finanzen an den Nationalrat.

141. Bundesministerium fuer Landesverteidigung, Landesverteidigungsakademie Wien (1993), *'Militaer - Strategisches Umwelt - und Konfliktbild (Synopse)'* Vienna: Bundesministerium fuer Landesverteidigung.

142. Bunzl J. and Marin B. (1983), *'Antisemitismus in Oesterreich. Sozialhistorische und soziologische Studien'* Innsbruck: Inn - Verlag.

143. Burant St.R. (1993), 'International Relations in a Regional Context: Poland and Its Eastern Neighbours - Lithuania, Belarus, Ukraine' *Europe - Asia Studies,* 45, 3: 395 - 418.

144. Bush K. (1992), 'The Disastrous Last Year of the USSR' *RFE/RL Research Report,* 12, 20 March: 39 - 41.

145. Business Central Europe (1996) *'Europe's Emerging Markets, 1997'* London: The Economist Group.

146. *Business Central Europe* (current issues).

147. Butterwege Ch. (1991), 'Rechtsruck in Ostdeutschland? Neofaschismus, Rassismus und Auslaenderfeindlichkeit nach der Wiedervereinigung' *Zukunft,* Oktober: 25 - 29.

148. Caporaso J. A. (1978), 'Dependence, Dependency, and Power in the Global System: A Structural and Behavioral Analysis' *International Organization,* 32: 13 - 43.

149. Cardoso F.H. (1969), *'Mudancas sociais na América Latina'* Sao Paulo: DIFEL.

150. Cardoso F.H. (1972), *'O Modelo Politico Brasileiro, e outros ensaios'* Sao Paulo: DIFEL.

151. Cardoso F.H. (1973), 'Associated - Dependent Development. Theoretical and Practical Implications' in *'Authoritarian Brazil. Origins, Policies and Future'* (Stepan A. (Ed.)), New Haven and London: Yale University Press.

152. Cardoso F.H. (1977), 'El Consumo de la Teoria de la Dependencia en los Estados Unidos' *El Trimestre Economico,* 173, 44, 1, Enero: 33 - 52.

153. Cardoso F.H. (1979), *'Development under Fire'* Mexico D.F.: Instituto Latinoamericano de Estudios Transnacionales', DEE/D/24 i, Mayo (Mexico 20 D.F., Apartado 85 - 025).

154. Cardoso F.H. and Faletto E. (1971), *'Dependencia y desarrollo en América Latina'* Mexico D.F.: editorial siglo XXI.

155. *Central European Quarterly* (current issues). Vienna: Creditanstalt.

156. Central Statistical Office of the Polish Republic (1993a), *'Historia Polski w Liczbach. Ludnosc. Terytorium'* Warsaw: Glowny Urzad Statystyczny (CSO).

157. Central Statistical Office of the Polish Republic (1993b), *'Border Crossings'* Warsaw: CSO, unpublished data outprint.

158. Central Statistical Office of the Polish Republic (1994), *'Economic History of Poland in Numbers'* Warsaw: Glowny Urzad Statystyczny (CSO).

159. Central Statistical Office of the Polish Republic (current issues), *'Rocznik Statystyczny'* Warsaw: CSO.

160. Central Statistical Office of the Polish Republic (current issues), *'Maly Rocznik Statystyczny'* Warsaw: CSO.

161. Central Statistical Office of the Polish Republic (current issues), *'Research Bulletin'* Warsaw: CSO.

162. Central Statistical Office of the Polish Republic (current issues), *'Rocznik Statystyczny Wojewodztw'* Warsaw: CSO.

163. Central Statistical Office of the Polish Republic (current issues), *'Kosciol Katolicki w Polsce 1918 - 1990. Rocznik Statystyczny'* Warsaw: CSO.

164. Central Statistical Office of the Polish Republic (current issues), *'Statistical Bulletin'* Warsaw: CSO.

165. Central Statistical Office of the Polish Republic (current issues), *'Information on Social and Economic Situation in Poland'* Warsaw: CSO.

166. Central Statistical Office of the Polish Republic (current issues), *'Poland Quarterly Statistics'* Warsaw: CSO.

167. Central Statistical Office of the Polish Republic (current issues), *'Polen in Zahlen'* Warsaw: CSO.

168. Central Statistical Office of the Polish Republic (current issues), *'Quarterly Report on the Employment Situation'* Warsaw: CSO (in Polish).

169. Central Statistical Office of the Polish Republic (current issues), *'Aktywnosc Ekonomiczna Ludnosci Polski'* Warsaw: CSO.

170. Central Statistical Office of the Polish Republic (current issues), 'Unemployment in Poland' Warsaw: CSO.

171. Chaloupek G. (1977), 'Die Verteilung der persoenlichen Einkommen in Oesterreich' *Wirtschaft und Gesellschaft,* 3, 1: 9 - 21.

172. Chaloupek G. and Swoboda H. (1975), 'Sozialpartnerschaft und Wirtschaftsentwicklung in den fuenfziger und sechziger Jahren' *Oesterreichische Zeitschrift fuer Politikwissenschaft,* 3: 333 - 343.

173. Chase - Dunn Ch. and Podobnik, B. (1995), 'The Next World War: World-System Cycles and Trends' *Journal of World Systems Research,* 1, 6 electronic journal at World Systems Archive, University of Colorado, at: http://csf.colorado.edu/jwsr/

174. Chase - Dunn Ch. K. (1975), 'The Effects of International Economic Dependence on Development and Inequality: a Cross - national Study' *American Sociological Review,* 40: 720 - 738.

175. Chase - Dunn Ch. K. (1983), 'The Kernel of the Capitalist World Economy: Three Approaches' in *'Contending Approaches to World System Analysis'* (Thompson W.R. (Ed.)), pp. 55 - 78, Beverly Hills: Sage.

176. Chase - Dunn Ch. K. (1984), 'The World - System Since 1950: What Has Really Changed?' in *'Labor in the Capitalist World - Economy'* (Bergquist Ch. (Ed.)), pp. 75 - 104, Beverly Hills: Sage.

177. Chase - Dunn Ch. K. (1991), *'Global Formation: Structures of the World Economy'* London, Oxford and New York: Basil Blackwell.

178. Chase - Dunn Ch. K. (1992a), 'The National State as an Agent of Modernity' *Problems of Communism,* January - April: 29 - 37.

179.	Chase - Dunn Ch. K. (1992b), 'The Changing Role of Cities in World Systems' in *'Waves, Formations and Values in the World System'* (Bornschier V. and Lengyel P. (Eds.)), pp. 51 - 87, New Brunswick and London: Transaction Publishers.

180.	Chase - Dunn Ch. K. (Ed.), (1982), *'Socialist States in the World System'* Beverly Hills and London: Sage.

181.	Chase - Dunn Ch. K. and Grimes P. (1995), 'World - Systems Analysis' Annual Review of Sociology, 21: 387 - 417.

182.	Chase - Dunn Ch. K. and Hall Th. D. (1997), *'Rise and Demise. Comparing World - Systems'* Boulder, Colorado: Westview Press.

183.	Chase - Dunn Ch. K. and Podobnik B. (1995), 'The Next World War: World - System Cycles and Trends' *Journal of World Systems Research* 1, 6 (unpaginated electronic journal at world - wide - web site of the World System Network: *http://csf.colorado.edu/wsystems/jwsr.html).*

184.	Choucri N. and North R.C. (1989), 'Roots of War: The Master Variables' in *'The Quest for Peace'* (Vaerynen R. et al. (Eds.)), pp. 204 - 216, London, Beverly Hills: Sage.

185.	Clad J.C. (1994), 'Slowing the Wave' *Foreign Policy,* 95: 139 - 150.

186.	Clark R. (1992), 'Economic Dependency and Gender Differences in Labor - Force Sectoral Change in Non - Core Nations' *Sociological Quarterly,* 33, 1: 83 - 98.

187.	Clark R. et al. (1991), 'Culture, Gender, and Labor - Force Participation. A Cross - National Study' *Gender and Society,* 5, 1: 47 - 66.

188.	Clarke D.L. (1993), 'Europe's Changing Constellations' *RFE/RL Research Report,* 2, 37: 17 September: 13 - 15.

189.	Clauss G. and Ebner H. (1978), *'Grundlagen der Statistik. Fuer Psychologen, Paedagogen und Soziologen'* Berlin: Volk and Wissen.

190.	Cline M. (1992), 'Political Parties and Public Opinion in Poland' *RFE/RL Research Report,* 1, 43, 30 October: 66 - 69.

191.	Cline M. (1993), 'The Demographics of Party Support in Poland' *RFE/RL Research Report,* 2, 36, 10 September: 17 - 21.

192.	Clinton B. (1993), *'National Drug Control Strategy'* Washington D.C.: Report by the President of the United States of America to Congress.

193.	Cohen R. (1991), 'East - West and European migration in a global context' *New Community,* 18, 1: 9 - 26.

194.	Cohn - Bendit D. (1993), 'Europe and its borders: the case for a common immigration policy' in *'Towards a European Immigration Policy'* (Ogata S. et al.), pp. 22 - 31, London: Philip Morris Institute for Public Policy Research.

195.	Commission of the European Communities (1995); *'White Paper. Preparation of the Associated Countries of Central and Eastern Europe for Integration into the Internal Market of the Union'* Brussels, 10.05.1995, Com (95) 163, final.

196.	Commission of the European Communities (current issues), *'Employment Observatory Central and Eastern Europe'* Brussels: EU, DG Employment, Industrial Relations and Social Affairs.

197.	Connolly B. (1995*), 'The Rotten Heart of Europe. The Dirty War for Europe's Money'* London and Boston: Faber and Faber.

198.	Cordova A. (1973), *'Strukturelle Heterogenitaet und wirtschaftliches Wachstum'* Frankfurt a.M.: edition suhrkamp.

199.	Cordova A. and Silva - Michelena H. (1972), *'Die wirtschaftliche Struktur Lateinamerikas. Drei Studien zur politischen Oekonomie der Unterentwicklung'* Frankfurt a.M.: edition suhrkamp.

200.	Cornia G.A. (Ed.)(1993), *'Economies in Transition Studies, Regional Monitoring Report, 1'* Firenze: UNICEF.

201. Cornia G.A. (Ed.)(1994), *'Economies in Transition Studies, Regional Monitoring Report, 2'* Firenze: UNICEF.

202. Crenshaw E. (1991), 'Foreign Investment as a Dependent Variable: Determinants of Foreign and Capital Penetration in Developing Nations, 1967 - 1978' *Social Forces,* 69, 4: 1169 - 1182.

203. Crenshaw E. (1992), 'Cross - National Determinants of Income Inequality: A Replication and Extension Using Ecological - Evolutionary Theory' *Social Forces,* 71: 339 - 363.

204. Crough, G. J. and Wheelwright E. L. (1982), *'Australia, a client state'* Ringwood, Vic., Australia: Penguin Books Australia; New York, N.Y.: Penguin Books.

205. Dadush U. and Brahmbhatt M. (1995), 'Anticipating Capital Flow Reversals' *Finance and Development,* December: 3 - 5.

206. Dallinger A. et al. (1975), 'Auslaendische Arbeitnehmer in Oesterreich' Vienna: Bundesministerium fuer Arbeit und Soziales.

207. Daly M. (1973*), 'Beyond God the Father: Toward a Philosophy of Women's Liberation'* Boston: Beacon Press.

208. Datta A. (1993), 'Warum fluechten Menschen aus ihrer Heimat?' in *'Die Neuen Mauern. Krisen der Nord - Sued - Beziehungen'* (Datta A. (Ed.)), pp. 31 - 46, Wuppertal: P. Hammer.

209. David A. and Wheelwright T. (1989), *'The Third Wave. Australia and Asian Capitalism'* Sutherland, New South Wales: Left Book Club Cooperative Ltd.

210. Deacon B. (1992a),'East European Welfare: Past, Present and Future in Comparative Context' in *'The New Eastern Europe. Social Policy Past, Present and Future'* (Deacon B. (Ed.)), pp. 1 - 31, London and Newbury Park: Sage.

211. Deacon B. (1992b),'The Future of Social Policy in Eastern Europe' in *'The New Eastern Europe. Social Policy Past, Present and Future'* (Deacon B. (Ed.)), pp. 167 - 191, London and Newbury Park: Sage.

212. Deacon, Bob (1999) Socially Responsible Globalization: A Challenge for the European Union; Helsinki: Ministry of Social Affairs and Health.

213. Delacroix J. and Ragin Ch. (1981), 'Structural Blockage: A Cross - National Study of Economic Dependency, State Efficacy, and Underdevelopment' *American Journal of Sociology,* 86, 6: 1311 - 1347.

214. Department of Social, Community and Family Affairs (2000) Supporting Voluntary Activity. A white paper on a framework for supporting voluntary activity and for developing the relationship between the state and the community and voluntary sector – HYPERLINK   "http://www.dscfa.ie/dept/reports/volact.htm" http://www.dscfa.ie/dept/reports/volact.htm – 3.11.2000.

215. Deshingkar G. (1989), 'Arms, Technology, Violence and the Global Military Order' in *'The Quest for Peace'* (Vaerynen R. et al. (Eds.)), pp. 260 - 274, London, Beverly Hills: Sage.

216. Deutsch K. W. (1960), 'Ansaetze zu einer Bestandsaufnahme von Tendenzen in der vergleichenden und internationalen Politik' in *'Political Science. Amerikanische Beitraege zur Politikwissenschaft'* (Krippendorff E. (Ed.)), Tuebingen: J.C.B. Mohr.

217. Deutsch K. W. (1966), *'Nationalism and Social Communication. An inquiry into the foundations of nationality'* Cambrigde, Massachusetts and London: M.I.T. Press.

218. Deutsch K. W. (1978), *'The Analysis of International Relations'* Englewood Cliffs, N.J.: Prentice Hall.

219. Deutsch K. W. (1979), *'Tides Among Nations'* New York: Free Press.

220. Deutsch K. W. (1982), 'Major Changes in Political Science' in *'International Handbook of Political Science'* (Andrews W.G. (Ed.)), pp. 9 - 33, Westport, Con.: Greenwood Press.

221. Deutscher Bundestag (2000) Answer by the Federal Government on the main question by the MPs Klaus-Juergen Hedrich u.a. and the Parliamentary Party CDU/CSU. An international social market economy as basic model for the global structural and societal

contract policy –Opportunities and risks of the globalisation of the world economy for the developing countries (Antwort der Bundesregierung auf die Grosse Anfrage der Abgeordneten Klaus-Juergen Hedrich u.a. und der Fraktion der CDU/CSU. Eine internationale Soziale Marktwirtschaft als Grundmodell für eine globale Struktur- und Ordnungspolitik –Chancen der Globalisierung der Weltwirtschaft für die Entwicklungsländer; Bundestagsdrucksache 14/3967 – 2.8.2000.

222. Dialog (current issues) (electronic archive, containing practically the entire English-language world press, the main international news agencies and newsletters and the Social Science Citation and Arts and Humanities Index, as well as the possibility to order on-line or fax copies from the international social science journals at *http://www.dialogselect.com)*

223. *Die Presse* (current issues) (free electronic archive at *http://www.diePresse.at)*

224. Dietz R. and Havlik P. (1995), *'Auswirkungen der EU-Ost-Integration auf den oesterreichischen und den EU-Osthandel'* Reprint Series, 161, Vienna Institute for Comparative Economic Studies.

225. Dixon W. J. (1984), 'Trade Concentration, Economic Growth and the Provision of Basic Human Needs' *Social Science Quarterly,* 65: 761 - 774.

226. Dixon W. J. and Boswell T. (1996), 'Dependency, Disarticulation, and Denominator Effects. Another Look at Foreign Capital Penetration' *American Journal of Sociology,* 102, 2: 543 - 562.

227. Doran Ch. F. (1983), 'Power Cycle Theory and the Contemporary State System' in *'Contending Approaches to World System Analysis'* (Thompson W.R. (Ed.)), pp. 165 - 182, Beverly Hills: Sage.

228. Dubiel I. (1983), *'Der klassische Kern der lateinamerikanischen Entwicklungstheorie. Ein metatheoretischer Versuch'* Munich: Eberhard.

229. Dubiel I. (1993), 'Andere Zeiten - Andere Wirtschaftstheorien. Elemente einer oekonomischen Theorie von morgen' in *'Kultur - Identitaet - Kommunikation. 2. Versuch'* (Ammon G. and Eberhard Th. (Eds.)), pp. 81 - 124, Munich: Eberhard - Verlag.

230. Dunn J. F. (1992), 'Hard Times in Russia Foster Conspiracy Theories' *RFE/RL Research Report,* 1, 46, 20 November: 24 - 29.

231. Durkheim E. (1997), *'Suicide: A Study in Sociology'* New York: Free Press.

232. Dussel E. (1981), 'A History of the Church in Latin America, Colonialism to Liberation (1492 - 1972)' Grand Rapids, MI: Eerdmans.

233. Economist (1994), 'Against the grain. A survey of Poland' *The Economist (London),* April 16 - 22: Survey 1 - 22.

234. *Economist Intelligence Unit,* Dialog - online.

235. Ehrlich S. (1981), 'The Rationality of Pluralism' *The Polish Sociological Bulletin,* 54, 2: 27 - 38.

236. Eklund K. (1980), 'Long Waves in the Development of Capitalism?' *Kyklos,* 33 (3): 383 - 419.

237. *El Pais (Madrid)* (current issues) (free electronic archive at *http://www.elpais.es)*

238. Elias, Norbert, (2000) The civilizing process : sociogenetic and psychogenetic investigations; translated by Edmund Jephcott with some notes and corrections by the author ; edited by Eric Dunning, Johan Goudsblom, and Stephen Mennell; Oxford, UK ; Malden, Mass. : Blackwell Publishers.

239. Ellacuria I. *Societas Iesu* (1989), 'Utopia y profetismo desde América Latina. Un ensayo concreto de soterología historica' *Revista Latinoamericana de Teología (San Salvador, El Salvador),* 6, 17: 141 - 84.

240. Ellacuria I. *Societas Iesu* (1990, posth.), *'Teólogo mártir por la liberación del pueblo'* Madrid: editorial nueva utopía.

241. Ellacuria I. *Societas Iesu* (1990b, posth.), *'Filosofía de la realidad historica'* San Salvador: Universidad Centroamericana Editores.

242. Ellacuria I. *Societas Iesu* (1991), *'Veinte anos de historia en El Salvador (1969 - 1989): escritos politicos'* 1. ed. San Salvador, El Salvador: UCA Editores.

243. Ellacuria I. *Societas Iesu* and Sobrino J. *Societas Iesu* (1993), *'Mysterium liberationis: Fundamental Concepts of Liberation Theology'* Maryknoll, NY: Orbis Books.

244. Elsenhans H. (1983), 'Rising mass incomes as a condition of capitalist growth: implications for the world economy' *International Organization,* 37, 1: 1 - 39.

245. Elsenhans H. (1992), *'Equality and development'* Dhaka, Bangladesh: Centre for Social Studies: Distributor, Dana Publishers.

246. Elsenhans H. (1996),' *State, class, and development'*. New Delhi: Radiant Publishers.

247. Elsenhans H. (Ed.), (1978), *'Migration und Wirtschaftsentwicklung'* Frankfurt a.M.: Campus.

248. Engelbrekt K. (1994), 'Sharp Rise in Drug Trafficking and Abuse in Former East Bloc' *RFE/RL Research Report,* 3, 9, 4 March: 48 - 51.

249. Engels, Frederick (1890) Letter to J. Bloch in Koenigsberg; Written: September 21-22, 1890; Source: Historical Materialism [Marx, Engels, Lenin], p. 294 – 296; Publisher: Progress Publishers, 1972; Translated: from German; Online Version: marxists.org 1999; Transcription/Markup: HYPERLINK "mailto:brian@marxists.org" Brian Basgen. HYPERLINK "http://www.marxists.org/archive/marx/letters/engels/90_09_21-ab.htm" http://www.marxists.org/archive/marx/letters/engels/90_09_21-ab.htm – 2000-10-29.

250. Ernst A. *et al.* (1987), *'Sozialstaat Oesterreich. Bei Bedarf geschlossen'* Vienna: Orac.

251. Ernst D. (1973), 'Wirtschaftliche Entwicklung durch importsubstituierende Industrialisierung?' *Das Argument,* 79, July, p. 332 ff.

252. Esping - Andersen G. (1985), *'Politics against markets. The social democratic road to power'* Princeton: Princeton University Press.

253. European Commission (1993) White paper on growth, competitiveness, and employment: The challenges and ways forward into the 21st century; COM(93) 700 final; Brussels, 5 December 1993 – HYPERLINK "http://www.europa.eu.int/en/record/white/c93700/contents.html" http://www.europa.eu.int/en/record/white/c93700/contents.html –3.11.2000.

254. European Commission (2000) Equal Opportunities for Women and Men in the European Union, 1999. Report to the Council, the European Parliament, the Economic and Social Committee of the Regions. Brussels: COM [2000] 123 fin., 8/3/2000.

255. Evans P. B. and Timberlake M. (1980), 'Dependence, Inequality, and the Growth of the Tertiary: A Comparative Analysis of Less Developed Countries' *American Sociological Review,* 45: 531 - 552.

256. Eyal G. and Townley E. (1995), 'The social composition of the Communist nomenklatura: A comparison of Russia, Poland and Hungary' *Theory and Society,* 24: 723 - 750.

257. Farmer P. (1996), 'On Suffering and Structural Violence: A View from Below' Daedalus, 4: 261 - 283.

258. Fassmann H. and Hintermann Ch. (1997), 'Migrationspotential Osteuropa. Struktur und Motivation potentieller Migranten aus Polen, der Slowakei, Tschechien, und Ungarn' Vienna: Austrian Academy of Sciences

259. Fassmann H. and Muenz R. (1992), *'Einwanderungsland Oesterreich? Gastarbeiter - Fluechtlinge - Immigranten'* Vienna: Oesterreichische Akademie der Wissenschaften und Bundesministerium fuer Unterricht und Kunst.

260. Fassmann H. and Muenz R. (1993), 'Oesterreich - Einwanderungsland wider Willen' *Migration. A European Journal of International Migration and Ethnic Relations,* 1, 17: 11 - 38.

261. Fassmann H. and Muenz R. (1995), *'Einwanderungsland Oesterreich?* Vienna: Jugend und Volk.

262. Feder E. (1972), *'Violencia y despojo del campesino: el latifundismo en América Latina'* Mexico D.F.: siglo XXI.

263. Ferge, Zsuzsa (1999) The changing functions of the state – a virtuous or vicious circle?, in: Herrmann (ed.) 1999.

264. Fiala R. (1992), 'The International System, Labor Force Structure, and the Growth and Distribution of National Income, 1950 - 1980' *Sociological Perspectives,* 35, 2: 249 - 282.

265. *Financial Times,* Dialog - online.

266. Fink G. (1989), 'Die verplante Planwirtschaft. *Perestroijka* und das Problem der Kapitalverwertung im 'Arbeiterstaat'' *Akzente (Vienna),* 9/10: 11 - 14.

267. Finnish EU-Presidency (1999*), 'The Future of Social Security'* http://www.vn.fi/stm/english/tao/publicat/financing/scherman.htm

268. Firebaugh G. (1992), 'Growth Effects of Foreign and Domestic Investment' *American Journal of Sociology,* 98: 105 - 130.

269. Firebaugh G. (1996), 'Does Foreign Capital Harm Poor Nations? New Estimates Based on Dixon and Boswells Measures of Capital Penetration' *American Journal of Sociology,* 2, 102: 563 - 575.

270. Fischer - Lexikon (1975), *'Das Grosse Fischer - Lexikon in Farbe'* 20 vols., Frankfurt a.M.: Fischer Taschenbuch Verlag.

271. Fischer - Welt - Almanach (current issues), *'Der Fischer Welt - Almanach. Zahlen, Daten, Fakten'* Frankfurt a.M.: Fischer Taschenbuch Verlag.

272. Flechsig St. (1987), 'Raul Prebisch - ein bedeutender Oekonom Lateinamerikas und der Entwicklungslaender' *Wirtschaftswissenschaft,* 35, 5: 721 - 741.

273. Flechsig St. (1994), 'Raúl Prebisch (1901 - 1986) - ein bedeutendes theoretisches Vermaechtnis oder kein alter Hut' *Utopie kreativ,* 45/46, Juli/August: 136 - 155.

274. Fligstein, Neil (2000) Is globalization the cause of the crisis of welfare states in: Globalization, European Economic Integration and Social Protection; Conference, March 11-12, 1999, organised by Martin Rhodes in Collaboration with the European Commission, DG V; Florence: European University Institute.

275. Forrester J.W. (1978), 'A Great Depression Ahead?' *The Futurist,* December: 379 - 385.

276. Foxley A. (1982), 'Experimentos neoliberales en América Latina' *Estudios CIEPLAN (Santiago de Chile),* 7.

277. Foye St. (1994), 'The Armed Forces of the CIS: Legacies and Strategies' *RFE/RL Research Report,* 3, 1, 7 January: 18 - 21.

278. Frank A. G. (1978), *'Dependent accumulation and underdevelopment'* London: Macmillan.

279. Frank A. G. (1978), *'World accumulation, 1492 - 1789'* London: Macmillan.

280. Frank A. G. (1980) *'Crisis in the world economy'* New York: Holmes & Meier Publishers.

281. Frank A. G. (1981), *'Crisis in the Third World'* New York: Holmes & Meier Publishers.

282. Frank A. G. (1983), 'World System in Crisis' in *'Contending Approaches to World System Analysis'* (Thompson W.R. (Ed.)), pp. 27 - 42, Beverly Hills: Sage.

283. Frank A. G. (1990), 'Revolution in Eastern Europe: lessons for democratic social movements (and socialists?),' *Third World Quarterly,* 12, 2, April: 36 - 52.

284. Frank A. G. (1992), 'Economic ironies in Europe: a world economic interpretation of East - West European politics' *International Social Science Journal,* 131, February: 41 - 56.

285. Frank A. G. (1998), *'ReORIENT. Global Economy in the Asian Age'* Berkeley: University of California Press'.

286. Frank A. G. and Frank - Fuentes M. (1990), *'Widerstand im Weltsystem'* Vienna: Promedia.

287. Frank A. G. and Gills B. (Eds.)(1993), *'The World System: Five Hundred or Five Thousand Years?'* London and New York: Routledge, Kegan&Paul.

288. Friedman M. (1997), 'Monetary Unity, Political Disunity' *Transitions,* December: 32 - 33.

289. Friedrich-Ebert-Stiftung (current issues) *'FES-Analysen'*. FES. Bonn. Albrecht.Koschuetzke@fes.de

290. Froebel F. *et al.* (1977a), 'Internationalisierung von Kapital und Arbeitskraft' in *'Armut in Oesterreich'* (Junge Generation der SPOe Steiermark und Erklaerung von Graz fuer Solidarische Entwicklung (Eds.)), pp. 12 - 46, Graz: Leykam.

291. Froebel F. *et al.* (1977b), *'Die neue internationale Arbeitsteilung. Strukturelle Arbeitslosigkeit in den Industrielaendern und die Industrialisierung der Entwicklungslaender'* Reinbek: rororo aktuell (English translation: Cambridge University Press).

292. Froebel F. *et al.* (1984), 'The Current Development of the World Economy: Reproduction of Labor and Accumulation of Capital on a World Scale' in *'Transforming the World Economy? Nine Critical Essays on the New International Economic Order'* (Addo H. (Ed.)), pp. 51 - 118, London and Sydney: Hodder & Stoughton.

293. Froebel F. *et al.* (1986), *'Umbruch in der Weltwirtschaft'* Reinbek: rororo aktuell (English translation: Cambridge University Press).

294. Fuest C. (1996), 'Die finanzielle Last der EU - Ausgaben. Bleibt Europa noch finanzierbar?' *Die Neue Gesellschaft. Frankfurter Hefte,* 43, 7: 594 - 598.

295. Fukuyama F. (1991), 'Liberal Democracy as a Global Phenomenon' *PS: Political Science and Politics (Washington D.C.),* 24, 4: 659 - 664.

296. G - 24 (1992), *'G - 24 Assistance Poland'* Brussels: EU Commission and G - 24, Data discette.

297. Gabrisch H. et al. (1992), *'Depression and Inflation: Threats to Political and Social Stability. The Current Economic Situation of the former CMEA Countries and Yugoslavia'* Vienna: *Forschungsberichte,* 180, Vienna Institute for Comparative Economic Studies.

298. Gaechter A. (1991), 'Illusionen einer Einwanderungspolitik' *Oesterreichische Zeitschrift fuer Politikwissenschaft,* 4: 351 - 366.

299. Galganek A. (1992), *'Zmiana w globalnym systemie miedzynarodowym. Supercycle i wojna hegemoniczna'* Poznan: Uniwersytet im. Adama Mickiewicza w Poznanie, Seria Nauki Polityczne, 13 (entire).

300. Galtung J. (1971), 'A Structural Theory of Imperialism' *Journal of Peace Research,* 8, 2: 81 - 118.

301. Gardawski J. (1992), *'Robotnicy 1991. Swiadomosc ekonomiczna w czasach prelomu'* Warsaw: *Polityka ekonomiczna i spoleczna,* 25, Fundacja im. Friedricha Eberta w Polsce.

302. Gartner R. (1990), 'The Victims of Homicide: A Temporal and Cross - National Comparison' *American Sociological Review,* 55, February: 92 - 106.

303. Gerlich P. *et al.* (1988), 'Corporatism in Crisis: Stability and Change of Social Partnership in Austria' *Political Studies,* 36: 209 - 223.

304. Geschwender J.A. (1982), 'The Hawaiian Transformation: Class, Submerged Nation, and National Minorities' in *'Ascent and Decline in the World - System'* (Friedman E. (Ed.)), pp. 189 - 226, Beverly Hills: Sage.

305. Gibellini R. (1987), *'The Liberation Theology Debate'* Trans. John Bowden. Maryknoll, NY: Orbis Books.

306. Gierus J. (1998), *'Russia's Road to Modernity'* Warsaw: Instytut Studiow Politycznych, Polskiej Akademii Nauk.

307. Gilpin R. (1989), 'International Politics in the Pacific Rim Era' *The Annals of the American Academy of Political and Social Science,* 505, September: 56 - 67.

308. Goble P. (1989), 'Ethnic Politics in the USSR' *Problems of Communism,* 38, 4: 1 - 14.

309. Goedings S. (1997), *'The Expected Effect of the Enlargement of the European Union with Central and Eastern European Countries in the Area of the Free Movement of Workers'* Study for the European Commission, DG V, Amsterdam: International Institute of Social History

310. Goedings S. (1999), *'EU Enlargement to the East and Labour Migration to the West'* International Institute of Social History Amsterdam, Research Paper 36

311. Goldfrank W. (2000), *'Hegemonic Transition via World War? Repetition, Variation, and Transmutation as Scenarios for the 21st Century'* Introductory paper, to be published in the Political Economy of the World System Annual

312. Goldfrank W.L. (1978), 'Fascism and the World Economy' in *'Social Change in the Capitalist World Economy'* (Kaplan B.H. (Ed.)), pp. 75 - 117, Beverly Hills: Sage.

313. Goldfrank W.L. (1982), 'The Soviet Trajectory' in *'Socialist States in the World - System'* (Chase - Dunn Ch. K. (Ed.)), pp. 147 - 156, Beverly Hills: Sage.

314. Goldfrank W.L. (1990), 'Fascism and the Great Transformation' in *'The Life and Work of Karl Polanyi'* (Polanyi - Levitt K. (Ed.)), Montreal: Black Rose (quoted from the author's typescript).

315. Goldstein J.S. (1985a), 'Kondratieff Waves as War Cycles' *International Studies Quarterly,* 29, 4: 411 - 444.

316. Goldstein J.S. (1985b), 'Basic Human Needs: The Plateau Curve' *World Development,* 13, 5: 595 - 609.

317. Goldstein J.S. (1988), *'Long Cycles. Prosperity and War in the Modern Age'* New Haven and London: Yale University Press.

318. Goldstein J.S. (1994), *'Introduction to the Japanese Edition of Long Cycles'* Tokyo: Tsuge Shobo (quoted from the author's manuscript).

319. Goldstein J.S. (1996), *'International Relations'* New York, N.Y.: Harper Collins, College Publishers, 2nd edition.

320. Golinowska S. et al. (1996), *'Children in Diffcult Circumstances in Poland'* UNICEF: Innocenti Occasional Papers, Economic Policy Series, Number 57, Spedale degli Innocenti, Firenze, Italia.

321. Golinowska St. (1995), 'Migration Processes in Poland' and 'Main problems of employment transfer in Central and Western Europe' in *'Migration processes in Central and Eastern Europe'*, pp. 66-79 and 165-182 (Wachowicz R. (Ed.)), Warsaw: Ministry of Labour and Social Policy

322. Gonzales Casanova P. (1973), *'Sociología de la explotación'* Mexico D.F.: Siglo XXI.

323. Gore A. (1994), *'Wege zum Gleichgewicht. Ein Marshallplan fuer die Erde'* Frankfurt a.M.: Fischer (*'Earth in the Balance. Ecology and Human Spirit'* Boston, New York: Houghton Mifflin Company).

324. Gourevitch P.A. (1989), 'The Pacific Rim: Current Debates' *The Annals of the American Academy of Political and Social Science,* 505, September: 8 - 23.

325. Gower J. (1996), 'EU Enlargement to Central and Eastern Europe: Issues for the 1996 IGC' *Die Union. Oesterreichische Zeitschrift fuer Integrationsfragen,* 4: 85 - 93.

326. Gray C.S. (1990), 'The Soviet Threat in the 1990s' *Global Affairs,* 5, 2: 25 - 44.

327. Griffin K. (1987), *'World Hunger and the World Economy. And Other Essays in Development Economics'* London, Basingstoke and New York: Macmillan/Saint Martin's Press.

328. Griffin K. (1996), *'Studies in Globalization and Economic Transitons'* Basingstoke and New York: Macmillan/Saint Martin's Press.

329. Griffin K. and Gurley J. (1985), 'Radical Analyses of Imperialism, the Third World, and the Transition to Socialism: A Survey Article' *Journal of Economic Literature,* 23, September: 1089 - 1143.

330. Griffin K. and Knight J. (Eds.)(1990), *'Human Development and the International Development Strategy for the 1990s'* London and Basingstoke: Macmillan.

331. Grosser I. (1992), *'Szenarien des Uebergangs zur Marktwirtschaft in ehemaligen RGW - Laendern Europas'* Studie im Auftrag des Beirats fuer Wirtschafts - und Sozialfragen, Vienna: Vienna Institute for Comparative Economic Studies.

332. Gurr T. R. (1991), 'America as a Model for the World? A Skeptical View' *PS: Political Science and Politics (Washington D.C.)*, 24, 4: 664 - 667.

333. Gurr T. R. (1994) *'Ethnic conflict in world politics'* Boulder: Westview Press.

334. Gurr T. R. (1994), 'Peoples Against States: Ethnopolitical Conflict and the Changing World System' *International Studies Quarterly*, 38: 347 - 377.

335. Gutierrez G. (1987), *'On Job: God - Talk and the Suffering of the Innocent'* Trans. Matthew J. O'Connell. Maryknoll, NY: Orbis Books.

336. Gutierrez G. (1988), *'A Theology of Liberation: History, Politics and Salvation'* Trans. and ed. Sister Caridad Inda and John Eagleson. Rev. edition, Maryknoll, NY: Orbis Books.

337. Gutierrez G. (1991), *'The God of Life'*. Trans. Matthew J.O'Connell. Maryknoll, NY: Orbis Books.

338. Haas E. B. (1989), 'War, Interdependence and Functionalism' in *'The Quest for Peace'* (Vaerynen R. et al. (Eds.)), pp. 108 - 126, London, Beverly Hills: Sage.

339. Hadden K. and London B. (1996), 'Educating Girls in the Third World. The Demographic, Basic Needs, and Economic Benefits' *International Journal of Comparative Sociology*, 37, 1 - 2: 31 - 46.

340. Haeusler W. (1988) 'Wege zur Oesterreichischen Nation' *Roemische Mitteilungen*, Oesterreichische Akademie der Wissenschaften und Historisches Institut beim oesterreichischen Kulturinstitut in Rom), 30: 380 - 411.

341. Haller M. et al. (1985), 'Patterns of careers: mobility and structural positions in advanced capitalist societies: a comparison of men in Austria, France and the United States' *American Sociological Review*, 50, 5: 579 - 603.

342. Hallett A.J.H. (1994), 'The Impact of EC - 92 on Trade in Developing Countries' *The World Bank Research Observer*, 9, 1, January: 121 - 146.

343. Handelman St. (1994), 'The Russian 'Mafiya'' *Foreign Affairs*, 73, 2: 83 - 95.

344. Hausner J. (1992), *'Populist Threat in Transformation of Socialist Society'* Warsaw: *Economic and Social Policy Series, 29*, Friedrich Ebert Foundation.

345. Hausner J. and Owsiak St. (1992), *'Financial crisis of a state in transformation: The Polish case'* Warsaw: *Economic and Social Policy Series, 26*, Friedrich Ebert Foundation, Poland.

346. Havlik P. (1996), *'Exchange Rates, Competitiveness and Labour Costs in Central and Eastern Europe'* Research Reports, 231, Vienna Institute for Comparative Economic Studies.

347. Hegel G.F.W. (1837) The philosophy of history; Translated by J. Sibree; HYPERLINK "http://www.ets.uidaho.edu/mickelsen/texts/Hegel%20-%20Philosophy%20of%20History.htm" http://www.ets.uidaho.edu/mickelsen/texts/Hegel%20-%20Philosophy%20of%20History.htm –2000-10-29.

348. Herrmann P. (1993 a) Social Problems in the View of a Dedifferentiating Modernisation – Social Intervention in the Process of EC-Integration [Soziale Probleme in der Perspektive entdifferenzierender Modernisierung – Sozialintervenierendes Handeln im Prozeß der EG-Integration); in: Neue Praxis. Zeitschrift für Sozialarbeit, Sozialpädagogik und Sozialpolitik]; Neuwied: Luchterhand, Issue 1+2/1993: pp. 147 ff..

349. Herrmann P. (1993 b) Society and Organisation. Sociological Theory of Organisations [Gesellschaft und Organisation. Zur soziologischen Theorie von Organisationen]; Egelsbach/New York: Hänsel-Hohenhausen.

350. Herrmann P. (1994) The Organisation. An analysis of the Modern Society [Die Organisation. Eine Analyse der modernen Gesellschaft]; Rheinfelden/Berlin: Schäuble.

351. Herrmann P. (1998 a) Cultures of Participation in the European Union. Nongovernmental Organisations in EU-member states [Partizipationskulturen in der Europäischen Union. Nichtregierungsorganisationen in EU-Mitgliedstaaten]; Rheinfelden/Berlin: Schäuble Verlag.

352. Herrmann P. (1998 b) European Integration between Institution Building and Social Process. Contributions to a Theory of Modernisation and NGOs in the Context of the Development of the EU; New York: Nova Science.

353. Herrmann P. (1999) Re-defining centrality and Differentiation, in: Herrmann [ed.] (1999).

354. Herrmann P. [ed.] (1999) Challenges for a global welfare system; New York: Nova Science.

355. Herrmann P./Lorenz, Walter (1997) Towards a European Welfare State – A European Welfare Regime by Design or Default?; in: The Politics of Social Policy in Europe; Maurice Mullard/Simon Lee (Eds.); Cheltenham: Edward Elgar Publishing Ltd: pp. 12 – 29.

356. Hertoghe A./Labrousse A. (1990), *'Die Koksguerilla'* Berlin: Rotbuch - Verlag.

357. Hesoun J. (Ed.), (1993), *'Bericht ueber die soziale Lage. Taetigkeitsbericht des Bundesministeriums fuer Arbeit und Soziale Lage'* Vienna: Federal Ministry of Labor.

358. Hettne B. (1983), 'The Development of Development Theory' *Acta Sociologica,* 26, 3 - 4: 247 - 266.

359. Hettne B. (1989), 'Three Worlds of Crisis for the Nation State' in *'Crisis in Development'* (Bablewski Z. and Hettne B. (Eds.)), pp. 45 - 77, Goeteborg: United Nations University: European Perspectives Project 1986 - 87, Peace and Development Research Institute, Gothenburg University, P.A.D.R.I.G.U Papers.

360. Hettne B. (1994), 'The Political Economy of Post - Communist Development' *The European Journal of Development Research,* 6, 1, June: 39 - 60.

361. Hettne B. (1995a), *'International political economy: understanding global disorder.'* Halifax, N.S. : Fernwood Pub.; Cape Town: SAPES SA ; Dhaka : University Press Ltd. ; London ; Atlantic Highlands, N.J. : Zed Books.

362. Hettne B. (1995b), *'Development theory and the three worlds: towards an international political economy of development'* 2nd ed. Essex, England : Longman Scientific & Technical ; New York, NY. Copublished in the United States by John Wiley.

363. Hickmann Th. (1994), 'Wenn Ost und West zusammenwachsen sollen...' *Osteuropa - Wirtschaft,* 39, 2, Juni: 115 - 127.

364. Hilferding R. (1915), 'Europaer, nicht Mitteleuropaer' *Der Kampf (Vienna),* 8, 11 - 12: 357 - 365.

365. Hillgenberg H. (1994), 'Fluechtlinge als Herausforderung fuer Europa. Ansaetze fuer eine Politik der Schutzgewaehrung an Kriegs - und Buergerkriegsfluechtlinge' *Europa - Archiv,* 18: 537 - 544.

366. Hinnells J. (Ed.), (1984), *'The Penguin Dictionary of Religions'* London: Penguin Books.

367. Hintjens H.M. (1992), 'Immigration and Citizenship Debates: Reflections on Ten Common Themes' *International Migration,* 30, 1: 5 - 16.

368. Hirschman A. O. (1980), *'National Power and the Structure of Foreign Trade'* Berkeley, CA: University of California Press.

369. Hoell O. (Ed.), (1983), *'Small States in Europe and Dependence'* Vienna/ Boulder CO.: W. Braumueller/Westview Press.

370. Hoell O. and Kramer H. (1986), 'Internationalization and the Position of Austria: Problems and Current Development Trends of a Small State' in *'Security for the Weak Nations. A Multiple Perspective'* (Farooq Hasnat S. and Pelinka A. (Eds.)), pp. 201 - 230, Lahore: Izharsons.

371. Hoensch J.K. (1990), *'Geschichte Polens'* Stuttgart: Ullmer, 2nd edition.

372. Hoffmann, Jürgen/ Hoffmann, Reiner (1997) Globalization. Risks and opportunities for labor policy in Europe. Brussels: European Trade Union Institute; (undated) [DWP 97.04.01 – E].

373. Holst J.J. (1993), *'A Changing Europe: Security Challenges of the 1990's'* Warsaw: *Occasional Papers,* 35, Polish Institute of International Affairs.

374. Holtbruecke D. (1996), 'Oekonomische Voraussetzungen und Folgen einer Osterweiterung der Europaeischen Union' *Osteuropa*, 46, 6: 537 - 547.

375. Holy Bible (1958 edition), King James Version. London and New York: Collins Clear Type Press.

376. Hopkins T.K. (1982), 'The Study of the Capitalist World - Economy. Some Introductory Considerations' in *'World Systems Analysis. Theory and Methodology'* (Hopkins T.K. and Wallerstein I. et al.), pp. 3 - 38, Beverly Hills: Sage.

377. Hopkins T.K. and Wallerstein I. et al. (1982), 'Patterns of Development of the Modern World System' in *'World Systems Analysis. Theory and Methodology'* (Hopkins T.K. and Wallerstein I. et al.), pp. 41 - 82, Beverly Hills: Sage.

378. Huang J. (1995), 'Structural Disarticulation and Third World Human Development' *International Journal of Comparative Sociology*, 36, 3 - 4: 164 - 183.

379. Huber P. (1999a), *'Wirtschaftliche und soziale Folgen der Erweiterung der EU'* in *'Zukunft ohne Grenzen'* Wien: Institut für den Donauraum und Mitteleuropa

380. Huber P. (1999b), *'Labour Market Adjustment in Central and Eastern Europe: How Different?'* Vienna: WIFO

381. Huber Peter, Pichelmann K. (1998) 'Osterweiterung, struktureller Wandel und Arbeitsmärkte' in: *Wirtschaftspolitische Blätter* 4

382. Huebner K. (1994), 'Wege nach Nirgendwo: Oekonomische Theorie und osteuropaeische Transformation' *Berliner Journal fuer Soziologie*, 3: 345 - 364.

383. Huntington S.P. (1991), *'The Third Wave: Democratization in the Late Twentieth Century'* Norman, Oklahoma: University of Oklahoma Press.

384. Huntington S.P. (1993), 'The Clash of Civilizations?' *Foreign Affairs,* Summer: 22 - 49.

385. Huntington S.P. (1996) *'The clash of civilizations and the remaking of world order'* New York: Simon & Schuster.

386. ICMPD (1998), *'Auswirkungen der EU-Osterweiterung auf die Zuwanderung in die Europäische Union unter besonderer Berücksichtigung Österreichs'* Studie im Auftrag des Bundeskanzleramtes, Sektion IV, Wien (3 volumes): ICMPD

387. IFRI (Institut Francais des relations internationales) (1998), *'Ramses 98. Rapport Annuel Mondial sur le Système Economique et les Stratégies'* Paris: Dunod

388. ILO (current issues) 'Key Indicators of the Labour Market' *http://www.ilo.org/public/english/60empfor/polemp/kilm/*

389. ILO (current issues) *'Social Security Africa'* *http://www.ilo.org/public/english/protection/socsec/techmeet/haracp1.htm*

390. ILO (current issues) *'Social Security Russia'* *http://www.trud.org/ilo_conf/ilo_conf11_eng.htm*

391. *ILO World Labor Yearbook* (current issues).

392. Inglehart R. and Carballo M. (1997), 'Does Latin America Exist? (And is there a Confucian Culture?): A Global Analysis of Cross - Cultural Differences' PS: Political Science & Politics, 30, 1, March: 47 - 52.

393. Inoguchi T. (1989), 'Shaping and Sharing Pacific Dynamism' *The Annals of the American Academy of Political and Social Science,* 505, September: 46 - 55.

394. Inotai A. (1993), 'Central and Eastern Europe' in *'Reviving the European Union'* (Austrian National Bank and IMF (Eds.)), pp. 139 - 176. Washington D.C. and Vienna: IMF and Austrian National Bank.

395. Institut fuer Fremdenverkehr, Warsaw *(current issues),* *'Polen. Fremdenverkehr in Zahlen'* Warsaw: Amt fuer Koerperliche Kultur und Tourismus, ul. Merliniego 9, PL - 02511 Warsaw.

396. Institute of Labor and Social Studies (1995) 'Social Policy in 1993 - 1994: Main Problems in Transition Period' *Occasional Papers,* 6, 1995.

397. Institute of Labor and Social Studies (current issues), *'Occasional Papers'* Warsaw: Institute of Labor and Social Studies, Ministry of Labor and Social Policy.

398. International Labor Office and United Nations Centre on Transnational Corporations (1988), *'Economic and social effects of multinational enterprises in export processing zones'* Geneva: ILO.

399. International Labor Office Geneva (1995), *'World Labor Report'* Geneva: International Labor Office.

400. *Internationale Politik* (current issues).

401. IOM (1999), *'Migration Potential in Central and Eeastern Europe'* Geneva: IOM

402. Jackman R.W. (1975), *'Politics and Social Equality: A Comparative Analysis'* New York: Wiley.

403. James E. (1995), 'Averting the Old - Age Crisis' *Finance and Development*, June: 4 - 7.

404. Janacek K. (1992), 'Poland: Survey of Major Trends in 1991' *RFE/RL Research Report*, 1, 12, 20 March: 31 - 32.

405. Janos A.C. (1994), 'Continuity and Change in Eastern Europe: Strategies of Post - Communist Politics' *East European Politics and Societies*, 8, 1: 1 - 31.

406. Janowska Z. et al. (1992), 'Female Unemployment in Poland' Warsaw: *Economic and Social Policy Series*, 18, Friedrich Ebert Foundation, Poland.

407. Jenkins R. (1987), *'Transnational Corporations and Uneven Development: The Internationalization of Capital and the Third World'* London and New York: Methuen.

408. Jodice D.H. *et al.* (1980), *'Cumulation in Social Science Data Archiving. A Study of the Impact of the two World Handbooks of Political and Social Indicators'* Koenigstein: Anton Hain.

409. John Paul II, Pope (1988), 'Sollicitudo Rei Socialis' *Origens*, 17, 38: 641 - 60.

410. John Paul II, Pope (1991a), *'Vor neuen Herausforderungen der Menschheit. Enzyklika 'Centesimus annus' Papst Johannes Pauls II. Kommentar von Walter Kerber'* Freiburg im Breisgau: Herder.

411. John Paul II, Pope (1991b), 'Redemptoris missio' *Catholic International*, 2, 6, March, 16 - 31.

412. Juchler J. (1992a), 'Zur Entwicklungsdynamik in den sozialistischen bzw. postsozialistischen Laendern' *Schweizerische Zeitschrift fuer Soziologie*, 17, 2: 273 - 307.

413. Juchler J. (1992b), 'The Socialist Societies: Rise and Fall of a Societal Formation' in *'Waves, Formations and Values in the World System'* (Bornschier V. and Lengyel P. (Eds.)), pp. 145 - 174, New Brunswick (USA),: Transaction Publishers.

414. Juchler J. (1995), 'Kontinuitaet oder Wende? Polen seit dem Wahlsieg der 'Postkommunisten'' *Osteuropa*, 45, 1: 65 - 76.

415. Kabashima T. (1984), 'Supportive Participation With Economic Growth: The Case of Japan' *World Politics*, 36, 3: 309 - 338.

416. Kaldor M. (1986), 'The Global Political Economy' *Alternatives*, 11, 4: 431 - 460.

417. Kaldor N. (1957), 'A model of economic growth' *The Economic Journal*, 67: 591 ff.

418. Kaldor N. (1974), 'Model of Distribution' in *'Growth Economics'* (Sen A. K. (Ed.)), Harmondsworth: Penguin Modern Economics Readings.

419. Kaldor, Mary (2000) "Civilizing" Globalization? The Implications of the "Battle in Seattle" – HYPERLINK http://www.lse.ac.uk/Depts/global/MarySeattle.htm; http://www.lse.ac.uk/Depts/global/MarySeattle.htm – 2000-11-03.

420. Kalecki M. (1972), *'The Last Phase in the Transformation of Capitalism'* New York: Monthly Review Press.

421. Kalecki M. (1979), *'Essays on Developing Economies. With an Introduction by Professor Joan Robinson'* Hassocks, Sussex: The Harvester Press.

422. Karatnycky A. (1994), 'Freedom in Retreat' *Freedom Review*, 25, 1: 4 - 9.

423. Kasarda J.D. and Crenshaw E.M. (1991), 'Third - World Urbanization. Dimensions, Theories and Determinants' *Annual Review of Sociology*, 17: 467 - 501.

424. Katzenstein P.J. (1984), *'Corporatism and Change. Austria, Switzerland and the Politics of Industry'* Ithaca and London: Cornell University Press.

425. Kawato A. (1990), 'The Soviet Union: A Player in the World Economy?' in *'Perestroika: Soviet Domestic and Foreign Policies'* (Hasegawa T. and Pravda A. (Eds.)), pp. 122 - 140, London: Sage.

426. Kay C. (1989), *'Latin American Theories of Development and Underdevelopment'* London and New York: Routledge, Kegan and Paul.

427. Kay C. (1991), 'Reflections on the Latin American Contribution to Development Theory' *Development and Change*, 22, 1: 31 - 68.

428. Keman H. *et al.* (1987), *'Coping with the Economic Crisis'* London: Sage Publications.

429. Kennedy P. (1989), *'The Rise and Fall of the Great Powers. Economic Change and Military Conflict from 1500 to 2000'* New York: Vintage Books, paperback edition.

430. Kennedy P. (1993), *'In Vorbereitung auf das 21. Jahrhundert'* Frankfurt a.M.: S. Fischer TB.

431. Kent G. (1984) *'The political economy of hunger: the silent holocaust'* New York: Praeger.

432. Kent G. (1991) *'The politics of children's survival'* New York: Praeger. .

433. Kent G. (1995) *'Children in the international political economy'* Houndmills, Basingstoke, Hampshire: MacMillan Press LTD, New York, N.Y.: St. Martin's Press.

434. Kent N. J. (1990), 'The End of the American Dream: A Break in Political Economy' *Occasional Papers in Political Science, Manoa Campus: University of Hawaii, Department of Political Science*, 3, 3, Jan.: 93 - 107.

435. Keuschnigg C. and Kohler W. (1999), *'Eastern Enlargement to the EU: Economic Costs and Benefits for the EU Present Member States?'* Study XIX/B1/9801, European Commission

436. Keynes J.M. (1936), *'The General Theory of Employment, Interest and Money'* London and Basingstoke: Macmillan.

437. Khoury A. Th. (1991), *'Was its los in der islamischen Welt? Die Konflikte verstehen'* Freiburg, Basel, Vienna: Herder.

438. Kidron M. and Segal R. (1996), *'Der Fischer Atlas zur Lage der Welt'* Frankfurt a.M.: Fischer Taschenbuch Verlag.

439. Kiljunen K. (1985), *'Towards a Theory of International Division of Labor'* Helsinki: Helsinki University, Department of Political Science Publications, Sarja A, 69.

440. Kiljunen K. (1992), *'Finland and the new international division of labor'* Houndmills, Basingstoke, Hampshire : Macmillan Press.

441. Kirkpatrick J. (1987), 'Ethnic Antagonism and Innovation in Hawaii' in *'Ethnic Conflict. International Perspectives'* (Boucher J. et al. (Eds.)), pp. 298 - 316, Newbury Park: Sage.

442. Klaus V. (1996), 'Europaeische Waehrungsunion - ihre ordnungspolitischen und fiskalpolitischen Konsequenzen' Alpbach, 28. August 1996: European Forum Alpbach (Tyrol)

443. Klecatsky H. and Morscher S. (1993), *'Die oesterreichische Bundesverfassung. Bundes - Verfassungsgesetz in der gegenwaertigen Fassung mit wichtigen Nebenverfassungsgesetzen'* Vienna: Manzsche Verlags - und Universitaetsbuchhandlung.

444. Kleinknecht A (1987) *'Innovation patterns in crisis and prosperity: Schumpeter's long cycle reconsidered'* New York: St. Martin's Press.

445. Kleinknecht A. (1987), *'Innovation Patterns in Crisis and Prosperity: Schumpeter's Long Cycle Reconsidered'* London and Basingstoke: Macmillan.

446. Kleinknecht A. et al. (Eds.) (1993), *'New Findings in Long - Wave Research'* New York: Saint Martin's Press.

447. Klitgaard R. and Fedderke J. (1995), 'Social Integration and Disintegration: An Exploratory Analysis of Cross - Country Data' *World Development*, 23, 3: 357 - 369.

448. Koehler   G.   (1998a),   'Unequal   Exchange   1965-1995' *http://csf.colorado.edu/wsystems/archive/papers/Köhler/Köhler3.htm*

449. Koehler G. and Tausch A. (2001), *'Studies in Unequal Exchange. Superexploitation on a Global and a European Level'* Huntington, N.Y.: Nova Science.

450. Koehler G.: (1998b), 'The Structure of Global Money and World Tables of Unequal Exchange' *Journal   of   World   Systems   Research,*   4,   2,   Fall   1998 *http://csf.colorado.edu/wsystems/jwsr.htm*

451. Kohli, Martin (2000) The battlegrounds of European Identity; in: European Societies 2, 2; 2000: 113-137.

452. Komlosy A. and Hofbauer H. (1992), 'Gemeinsames Haus Europa' *Forum,* 39, 465 - 467, 10.11.1992: 34 - 39.

453. Kondratieff N.D. (1926), 'Die langen Wellen der Konjunktur' *Archiv fuer Sozialwissenschaft und Sozialpolitik,* 56, 3: 573 - 609.

454. Kondratieff N.D. (1928), 'Die Preisdynamik der industriellen und landwirtschaftlichen Waren (Zum Problem der relativen Dynamik und Konjunktur),' *Archiv fuer Sozialwissenschaft und Sozialpolitik,* 60, 1: 1 - 84.

455. Korbonski A. (1996), 'How Much Is Enough? Excessive Pluralism as the Cause of Poland's Socioeconomic Crisis' *International Political Science Review,* 17, 3: 297 - 306.

456. Korcelli P. (1992), 'International Migrations in Europe: Polish Perspectives for the 1990s' *International Migration Review,* 26, 2, Summer: 292 - 304.

457. Koronkiewicz A. (1996), *'The Polish Health Care Reform Programme. Description worked out for Members of the World Bank Mission'* Ministry of Health and Social Welfare, Warsaw, Republic of Poland, Ministry of Health and Social Welfare: 23 October 1996.

458. Korpi W. (1985), 'Economic growth and the welfare state: leaky bucket or irrigation system?' *European Sociological Review,* 1, 2: 97 - 118.

459. Korpi W. (1996), 'Eurosclerosis and the Sclerosis of Objectivity. On the Role of Values Among Economic - Policy Experts' *Economic Journal,* 106, 439: 1727 - 1746.

460. Kothari R. (1986), 'Masses, Classes and the State' *Alternatives,* XI, 2: 167 - 183.

461. Kowalewski A.T. (1994), *'We Are Doing Less Than Nothing'* Warsaw: Polish Institute of International Affairs.

462. Koydl W. (1994), 'Kehren die Kommunisten zurueck? Gefahren fuer Mittel - und Osteuropa' *Europa - Archiv,* 5: 141 - 148.

463. Kreisky B. (posth., 1992), *'Stellungnahmen Bruno Kreiskys zum Asylproblem'* Vienna: Bruno - Kreisky Archive, August 18, 1992.

464. Kreissl-Dörfler, Wolfgang (1998) Report containing Parliament's recommendations to the Commission on the negotiations in the framework of the OECD on a multilateral agreement on investment [MAI]. European Parliament: 26.2.1998 – A4-0073/98.

465. Kreissler F. (1980), *'La Prise de Conscience de la Nation Autrichienne 1938 - 1945 - 1978'* Paris: Presses Universitaires de France.

466. Kriz J. (1978), *'Statistik in den Sozialwissenschaften'* Reinbek: rororo studium.

467. Krzysztofiak M. and Luszniewicz A. (1979), *'Statystyka'* Warsaw: PWE.

468. Kueng H. (1968), *'The Church'* New York: Sheed and Ward.

469. Kurth J.R. (1989), 'The Pacific Basin versus the Atlantic Alliance: Two Paradigms of International Relations' *The Annals of the American Academy of Political and Social Sciences,* 505, September: 34 - 45.

470. Kurz R. (1991), 'Die Krise, die aus dem Osten kam. Wider die Illusion vom Sieg des Westens und seiner Marktwirtschaft' *Basler Magazin,* 44, 2, 11.6.1991: 6 - 7.

471. Kuznets S. (1940), 'Schumpeter's Business Cycles' *The American Economic Review,* 30, 2: 257 - 271.

472. Kuznets S. (1955), 'Economic Growth and Income Inequality' *The American Economic Review,* 45, 1: 1 - 28.

473. Landesmann M. (1996), *'Emerging Patterns of European Industrial Specialization: Implications for Labour Market Dynamics in Eastern and Western Europe'* Research Reports, 230, Vienna Institute for Comparative Economic Studies.

474. Landesmann M. and Burgstaller J. (1997), *'Vertical Product Differentiation in EU Markets: the Relative Position of East European Producers'* Research Reports, 234a, Vienna Institute for Comparative Economic Studies.

475. *Landesverteidigungsakademie Zentraldokumentation Informationshefte* (current issues). Vienna: National Defense Academy, Federal Ministry for Defense of the Republic of Austria.

476. Lange O. (1970), *'Ensayos sobre planificación económica'* Esplugues de Llobregat, Barcelona: Ediciones Ariel.

477. Lapid Y. (1989), 'The Third Debate: On the Prospects of International Theory in a Post - Positivist Era' *International Studies Quarterly,* 33, 3: 235 - 254.

478. Laughland J. (1998), *'The Tainted Source. The Undemocratic Origins of the European Idea'* London: Warner Books, Little, Brown and Company.

479. Launer E. (1992), *'Datenhandbuch Sued - Nord'* Goettingen: Lamuv.

480. Layard R. et al. (1994), *'East-West Migration: The Alternatives'.* Cambridge Ma.: MIT Press

481. *Le Monde* (1998), *'Le Bilan du Monde'* Paris: Le Monde.

482. *Le Monde* (current issues).

483. Leggett J. (Ed.)(1991), *'Global Warming. Die Waermekatastrophe und wie wir sie verhindern koennen. Der Greenpeace - Report'* Munich and Zurich: Piper.

484. Lengauer R. et. al. (1999), *'Arbeitsmarkt und Osterweiterung'* IOS-Management, A-1010 Wien, Babenbergerstraße 1

485. Lepingwell J.W.R. (1994a), 'The Soviet Legacy and Russian Foreign Policy' *RFE/RL Research Report,* 3, 23, 10 June: 1 - 8.

486. Lepingwell J.W.R. et al. (1994b), 'Russia: A Troubled Future' *RFE/RL Research Report,* 3, 24, 17 June: 1 - 12.

487. Lernoux P. (1980), *'Cry of the People'* Garden City, NY: Doubleday.

488. Lernoux P. (1989), *'People of God: The Struggle for World Catholicism'* New York: Viking Press.

489. Levy - Pascal E. (1976), *'An Analysis of the Cyclical Dynamics of Industrialized Countries'* Washington D.C.: U.S. Central Intelligence Agency Staff Report PR 76 10009. .

490. Levy J.S. (1983), 'World System Analysis: A Great Power Framework' in *'Contending Approaches to World System Analysis'* (Thompson W.R. (Ed.)), pp. 183 - 201, Beverly Hills: Sage.

491. Lewis - Beck M.S. (1980), *'Applied Regression. An Introduction'* Beverly Hills: Sage University Paper.

492. Lewis Sir W.A. (1978), *'The Evolution of the International Economic Order'* Princeton N.J.: Princeton University Press.

493. L'Express (1992), 'En Couverture. Elle Envahit la France et l'Europe' *L'Express,* 4/12: 24 - 35.

494. Liemt G. van (1992), *'Industry on the move. Causes and consequences of international relocation in the manufacturing industry'* Geneva: International Labor Office.

495. Linder S. B. (1986), *'The Pacific Century. Economic and Political Consequences of Asian - Pacific Dynamism'* Stanford, CA.: Stanford University Press.

496. Linnemann H. and Sarma A. (1991), 'Economic Transformation in Eastern Europe: Its Genesis, Adjustment Process, and Impact on Developing Countries' *Development and Change*, 22, 1: 69 - 92.

497. Lipset S.M. (1994), 'The Social Requisites of Democracy Revisited. 1993 Presidential Address' *American Sociological Review*, 59, February: 1 - 22.

498. Lipton M. (1977), *'Why Poor People Stay Poor: Urban Bias in World Development'* Cambrige, MA: Harvard University Press.

499. Lipton M. and Ravallion M. (1993), *'Poverty and Policy'* Policy Research Working Papers, WPS, 1130, Washington D.C.: The World Bank.

500. Lisiecki M. (1993), *'Obrona i ochrona granicy panstwowej Polski jako element bezpieczenstwa panstwa'* Warsaw: *Studia i Materialy*, 60, Polish Institute of International Affairs.

501. Loeffelholz H. D., und G. Koepp (1998), *'Ökonomische Auswirkungen der Zuwanderungen nach Deutschland'* Berlin: Duncker und Humblot

502. Loeschnak F. (1993), *'Menschen aus der Fremde. Fluechtlinge, Vertriebene, Gastarbeiter'* Vienna: Holzhausen.

503. London B. (1987), 'Structural Determinants of Third World Urban Change: An Ecological and Political Economic Analysis' *American Sociological Review*, 52: 28 - 43.

504. London B. and Robinson Th. D. (1989), 'The Effect of International Dependence on Income Inequality and Political Violence' *American Sociological Review*, 54: 305 - 308.

505. London B. and Ross R. J. S. (1995), 'The Political Sociology of Foreign Direct Investment: Global Capitalism and Capital Mobility, 1965 - 1980' *International Journal of Comparative Sociology*, 36, 3 - 4: 198 - 218.

506. London B. and Smith D. A. (1988), 'Urban Bias, Dependence, and Economic Stagnation in Noncore Nations' *American Sociological Review*, 53: 454 - 463.

507. London B. and Williams B. A. (1988), 'Multinational Corporate Penetration, Protest, and Basic Needs Provision in Non - Core Nations: A Cross - National Analysis' *Social Forces*, 66, 3: 747 - 773.

508. London B. and Williams B. A. (1990), 'National Politics, International Dependency, and Basic Needs Provision. A Cross - National Analysis' *Social Forces*, 69, 2: 565 - 584.

509. Longerich et al. (1993), *'Der neue alte Rechtsradikalismus'* Munich: Piper.

510. Luif P. (1988), *'Neutrale in die EG? Die westeuropaeische Integration und die neutralen Staaten'* Vienna: Oesterreichisches Institut fuer Internationale Politik, W. Braumueller.

511. Luttwack E. (1999), *'Turbo-Capitalism. Winners and Losers in the Global Economy'*. New York: HarperCollins.

512. Luxemburg R. (1905/without year) *'Kirche und Sozialismus. Kosciol a Socjalism*. Mit einer Einfuehrung von Dorothee Soelle und Klaus Schmidt' Frankfurt a.M.: Stimme-Verlag.

513. Luza R. (1984), *'The Resistance in Austria, 1938 - 1945'* Minneapolis: University of Minnesota Press.

514. Lynch A. (1994), Postcommunist Political Dynamics: Ex Uno Plura' *RFE/RL Research Report*, 3, 1, 7 January: 1 - 8.

515. Maerz E. (1983), *'Joseph Alois Schumpeter - Forscher, Lehrer und Politiker'* Vienna: Verlag fuer Geschichte und Politik.

516. Magenheimer H. (1994), 'Neue Bedrohungen und Konflikte. Herausforderungen und Konsequenzen' *Oesterreichische Militaerische Zeitschrift*, 4: 357 - 366.

517. Malcolm N. (1995) 'The Case Against 'Europe'' *Foreign Affairs*, March, April: 52 - 68.

518. Mandel E. (1973), *'Der Spaetkapitalismus'* Frankfurt a.M.: edition suhrkamp.

519. Mandel E. (1980), *'Long Waves of Capitalist Development'* Cambridge: at the University Press.

520. Mann, Michael (1986) The Sources of Social Power, Vol. I/II; Cambridge: Cambridge University Press.

521. Marin B. (1983), 'Organizing Interests by Interest Organizations. Associational Prerequsites of Corporatism in Austria' *International Political Science Review*, 4, 2: 197 - 216.

522. Maritain J. (1936), *'Freedom in the Modern World'* Trans. Richard O'Sullivan. New York: Charles Scribner's Sons.

523. Maritain J. (1944), *'Christianity and Democracy'* Trans. Doris C. Anson. New York: Charles Scribner's Sons.

524. Maritain J. (1959), *'Distinguished to Unite: Or, The Degrees of Knowledge'* Trans. Gerald B. Phelan et al. London: Geoffrey Bles.

525. Maritain J. (1973), *'Integral Humanism: Temporal and Spiritual Problems of a New Christiandom'* Trans. Joseph W. Evans. Notre Dame, IN: University of Notre Dame Press.

526. Marshall D. D. (1996), 'Understanding Late 20th Century Capitalism. Reassessing the Globalization Theme' *Government and Opposition*, 31, 2: 193 - 215.

527. Marshall, T.H. (1950) Citizenship and social class; in: Marshall, Tom H./Bottomore, Tom: Citizenship and social class; London; Concord/Mass. 1950/1992.

528. Martin K. (1994), 'Central Asia's Forgotten Tragedy' *RFE/RL Research Report*, 3, 30, 29 July: 35 - 48.

529. Martin P. (1992), 'Rising Unemployment in Czechoslovakia' *RFE/RL Research Report*, 1, 17 January: 38 - 42.

530. Marx K. and Engels F. (posth.), *'Werke'* Berlin: Dietz.

531. Marx, Karl (1859) Preface to A Contribution to the Critique of Political Economy HYPERLINK "http://www.marxists.org/archive/marx/works/1850/pol-econ/preface-abs.htm" http://www.marxists.org/archive/marx/works/1850/pol-econ/preface-abs.htm – 29.10.2000).

532. Mc Sweeny B. (1987), 'The Politics of Neutrality. Focus on Security for Smaller Nations' *Bulletin of Peace Proposals*, 18, 1: 33 - 46.

533. Meier G.M. and Seers D. (Eds.) (1984), *'Pioneers in Development'* New York and Oxford: Oxford University Press.

534. Metz J.B. (1981), *'The Emergent Church: The Future of Christianity in a Postbourgeois World'* Trans. Peter Mann. New York: Crossroad.

535. Michelsen G. (Ed.)(current issues), *'Der Fischer Oeko - Almanach'* Frankfurt a.M.: Fischer TB.

536. Michna W. (1992), *'Poland's Food Security and Agricultural Policy at the Turn of the 20th and 21st Centuries'* Warsaw: *Economic and Social Policy Series*, 23, Friedrich Ebert Foundation, Poland.

537. Microsoft Excel (1992), *'Microsoft Excel. Verzeichnis der Funktionen'* Microsoft Corporation.

538. Mihalka M. (1994), 'German and Western Response to Immigration from the East' *RFE/RL Research Report*, 3, 23, 10 June: 36 - 48.

539. Millard F. (1992), 'Social Policy in Poland' in *'The New Eastern Europe. Social Policy Past, Present and Future'* (Deacon B. (Ed.)), pp. 118 - 143, London, Newbury Park: Sage.

540. Mittelman J. (1994); 'The Globalization of Social Conflict' in *'Conflicts and New Departures in World Society'* (Bornschier V. and Lengyel P. (Eds.)), pp. 317 - 337, New Brunswick (U.S.A.) and London: Transaction Publishers, World Society Studies, Volume 3.

541. Mizgala J.J. (1994), 'The Ecology of Transformation: The Impact of the Corporatist State on the Formation and Development of the Party System in Poland, 1989 - 93' *East European Politics and Societies*, 8, 2: 358 - 368.

542. Moaddel M. (1994), 'Political Conflict in the World Economy: A Cross - national Analysis of Modernization and World - System Theories' *American Sociological Review*, 59, April: 276 - 303.

543. Mock A. (1994), 'Religionsfriede durch Dialog' *Salzburger Nachrichten,* Neujahrsbeilage, 31. 12. 1994: X.

544. Modelski G. (1983), 'Long Cycles of World Leadership' in *'Contending Approaches to World System Analysis'* (Thompson W.R. (Ed.)), pp. 115 - 139, Beverly Hills: Sage.

545. Modelski G. (1987), *'Long Cycles in World Politics'* Basingstoke: Macmillan.

546. *Monatsberichte des Oesterreichischen Instituts fuer Wirtschaftsforschung* (current issues).

547. Moon B.E. and Dixon W.J. (1992), 'Basic Needs and Growth Welfare - Trade Offs' *International Studies Quarterly,* 36, 2: 191 - 212.

548. Morawetz R. (1991), *'Recent foreign direct investment in Eastern Europe: Towards a possible role for the Tripartite Declaration of Principles concerning Multinational Enterprises and Social Policy'* Geneva: International Labor Office, Multinational Enterprises Programme, Working Paper 71.

549. Morawska E. (2000) *'International Migration and Consolidation of Democracy in East Central Europe: A Problematic Relationship in a Hostorical Perspective'* University of Pennsylvania, emorawsk@as.upenn.edu

550. Moreira A. F. (2000), *'Saint Francis and Modernity'* Universidade Sao Francisco, Avenida Sao Francisco de Assis, 218 CEP 12.900-000, Caixa Postal 163, Fax 011 404 1825 - Brazil, Braganca Paulista, Sao Paulo, Brazil (appeared in Mueller et al. (2000)).

551. Mueller A. et al. (Eds.) (2000) *'Global Capitalism, Liberation Theology and the Social Sciences: An Analysis of the Contradictions of Modernity at the Turn of the Millenium'* Huntington, New York: Nova Sciences

552. Mueller G.P. (1988, with Volker Bornschier) *'Comparative World Data. A Statistical Handbook for Social Science'* Frankfurt a.M., Baltimore and London: Campus/John Hopkins University Press.

553. Muller E. N. (1988), 'Democracy, Economic Development, and Income Inequality' American Sociological Review, 53: 50 - 68.

554. Muller E. N. (1995), 'Economic Determinants of Democracy' *American Sociological Review,* 60, 6: 966 - 982.

555. Muller E. N. and Seligson M. (1987), 'Inequality and Insurgency' *American Political Science Review,* 81, 2: 425 - 452.

556. Munoz O. (1982), 'La economía mixta como camino al pleno empleo. Lecciones de un cuarto de siglo' *Estudios CIEPLAN (Santiago de Chile),* 9: 107 - 138.

557. Myrdal G. (1956/1974), *'Oekonomische Theorie und unterentwickelte Regionen. Weltproblem Armut'* Frankfurt a.M.: Fischer TB.

558. Myrdal G. (1972), *'Politisches Manifest ueber die Armut in der Welt'* Frankfurt a.M.: suhrkamp TB.

559. Myrdal G. (1984), 'International Inequality and Foreign Aid in Retrospect' in *'Pioneers in Development. A World Bank Publication'* (Meier G.M. and Seers D. (Eds.)) pp. 151 - 165. New York and Oxford: Oxford University Press.

560. Nederveen-Pieterse J. (1997), 'Equity and Growth Revisited: A Supply-Side Approach to Social Development' *The European Journal of Development Research,* 9, 1, June: 128-149.

561. Nelson D.N. (1994), 'Waffen im Ueberfluss. Ruestungsgueter des Warschauer Paktes und ihre Verbreitung' *Europa - Archiv,* 6: 179 - 186.

562. *Neue Zuercher Zeitung* (current issues).

563. Nikolinakos M. and Nikolaou, K. (1969), *'Die verhinderte Demokratie: Modell Griechenland'* Frankfurt a.M.: edition suhrkamp.

564. Nohlen D. (1991), *'Lexikon Dritte Welt'* Reinbek: rororo.

565. Nollert M. (1990), 'Social Inequality in the World System: An Assessment' in *'World Society Studies. Volume 1'* (Bornschier V. and Lengyel P. (Eds.)), pp. 17 - 54, Frankfurt and New York: Campus.

566. Nollert M. (1994a), 'Ressourcenmangel, Soziooekonomische Ungleichheit und Delinquenz: Ein internationaler Vergleich' *Schweizerische Zeitschrift fuer Soziologie, 20*, 1: 127 - 156.

567. Nollert M. (1994b), 'World Economic Integration and Political Conflict in Latin America' in *'Conflicts and New Departures in World Society'* (Bornschier V. and Lengyel P. (Eds.)), pp. 159 - 179, New Brunswick (U.S.A.) and London: Transaction Publishers, World Society Studies, Volume 3.

568. Nollert M. (1996), 'Verbandliche Interessenvertretung in der Europaeischen Union: Einflussressourcen und faktische Einflussnahme' *Zeitschrift fuer Politikwissenschaft (vormals Jahrbuch fuer Politik), 6*, 3: 647 - 667.

569. Nollert M. and Fielder N. (1997), *'Lobbying for a Europe of Big Business: the European Roundtable of Industrialists'* Department of Sociology, University of Zurich, Research paper (Raemistrasse 69, CH-8001, Zurich).

570. Nolte H.H. (1982), *'Die eine Welt. Abriss der Geschichte des internationalen Systems'* Hannover: Fackeltraeger.

571. Nolte H.H. (1989), *'Tradition des Rueckstands. West - Ost - Technologietransfer in der Geschichte'* Department of History, University of Hannover, FRG.

572. Nowotny I. (1991), 'Auslaenderbeschaeftigung in Oesterreich. Die Gesamtproblematik und aktuelle Situation' *WISO (Chamber of Workers and Employees, Linz), 14*, 1: 38 - 63.

573. Nowotny Th. (1985), *'Bleibende Werte - Verblichene Dogmen. Die Zukunft der Sozialdemokratie'* Koeln, Graz and Vienna: Hermann Boehlaus Nachfolger.

574. Nowotny Th. (1994), *'The Politics of Unemployment'* Vienna: paper, presented for the Bruno Kreisky Commission, 21 - 22 March.

575. Nuscheler F. (1993), 'Nach dem Fall von Mauern und Grenzen in Europa' in *'Die Neuen Mauern. Krisen der Nord - Sued - Beziehungen'* (Datta A. (Ed.)), pp. 13 - 30, Wuppertal: P. Hammer.

576. O'Leary Ch. J. (1995), 'Performance Indicators: A management tool for active labour programmes in Hungary and Poland' *International Labour Review, 134*, 6: 729 - 751.

577. O'Neill H. (1997), 'Globalisation, Competitiveness and Human Security: Challenges for Development Policy and Institutional Change' *The European Journal of Development Research, 9*, 1, June: 7-37.

578. Odom W. (1990), 'Only Ties to America Provide the Answer' *Orbis*, Fall: 483 - 504.

579. OECD (1999) *'The Future of the Global Economy. Towards a Long Boom?'* Paris: OECD

580. Oesterreichischer Arbeiterkammertag (current issues), *'Wirtschafts - und Sozialstatistisches Taschenbuch'* Vienna: Verlag der Arbeiterkammer Vienna.

581. Okolski M. (1992) 'Anomalies in Demographic Transition in Poland' *Geographia Polonica (Warsaw), 59*: 41 - 53.

582. Olbrich E. (1993), 'Polityka Spoleczna w Austrii' *Polityka Spoleczna* (Institute for Labor and Social Affairs, Ministry of Labor and Social Policy, Republic of Poland), 11/12: 19 - 21.

583. Olson M. (1982), *'The Rise and Decline of Nations'* New Haven and London: Yale University Press.

584. Olson M. (1986), 'A Theory of the Incentives Facing Political Organizations. Neo - Corporatism and the Hegemonic State' *International Political Science Review, 7*, 2, April: 165 - 89.

585. Olson M. (1987), 'Ideology and Economic Growth' in *'The Legacy of Reaganomics. Prospects for Long - term Growth'* (Hulten Ch.R. and Sawhill I.V. (Eds.)), pp. 229 - 251, Washington D.C.: The Urban Institute Press.

586. *OMRI Research Institute Prague, Daily digest* (e - mail).

587. Opitz P. J. (1988), *'Das Weltfluechtlingsproblem. Ursachen und Folgen'* Munich: C.H. Beck.

588. Opp K.D. and Schmidt P. (1976), *'Einfuehrung in die Mehrvariablenanalyse. Grundlagen der Formulierung und Pruefung komplexer sozialwissenschaftlicher Aussagen'* Reinbek: rororo studium.

589. Orenstein M. (1996), 'The Failures of Neo - Liberal Social Policy in Central Europe' *Transition*, 28 June 1996.

590. Orlowski L. T. (1995), 'Preparations of the Visegrad Group countries for admission to the European Union: monetary policy aspects' *Economics of Transition*, 3, 3: 333-353.

591. Orlowski L. T. (1995), 'Social Safety Nets in Central Europe: Preparation for Accession to the European Union?' *Comparative Economic Studies*, 37, 2, Summer: 29-48.

592. Orlowski L. T. (1996*), 'Fiscal Consolidation in Central Europe in Preparation for Accession to the European Union'* Center for Social and Economic Research, Bagatela 14, PL-00-585 Warsaw, Studies and Analyses, 77.

593. Österreichische Gesellschaft für Europapolitik (1999), *'Die EU-Erweiterung aus der Sicht der Österreicher und seiner Nachbarn'* Wien: Österreichische Gesellschaft für Europapolitik

594. Papademetriou D.G. (1992), 'Contending Approaches to Reforming the U.S. Legal Immigration System' *Migration. A European Journal of International Migration and Ethnic Relations*, 4, 16: 5 - 54.

595. Parnreiter Ch. (1994), *'Migration und Arbeitsteilung. Auslaenderbeschaeftigung in der Weltwirtschaftskrise'* Vienna: promedia.

596. Passel J.S. and Fix M. (1994), 'Myths about Immigrants' *Foreign Policy*, 95: 151 - 160.

597. Pelinka A. (1985), *'Windstille. Klagen ueber Oesterreich'* Vienna: Medusa - Verlag.

598. Pelinka A. (1990), *'Zur oesterreichischen Identitaet. Zwischen deutscher Vereinigung und Mitteleuropa'* Vienna: Ueberreuter.

599. Pelinka A. (1993), *'Der Westen hat gesiegt - hat der Westen gesiegt?'* Vienna: Picus.

600. Pelinka A. (1995), *'Europa 1996: Mitbestimmen, Menschenrechte und mehr Demokratie'* Vienna: Verlag Osterreich: Osterreichische Staatsdruckerei.

601. Pelinka A. (1996) *'Austro - corporatism: past, present, future'* New Brunswick, NJ: Transaction Publishers.

602. Pelinka A. (1997), *'Austrian historical memory & national identity'* New Brunswick: Transaction Publishers.

603. Pelinka A. *et al.* (1994), *'Ausweg EG? Innenpolitische Motive einer aussenpolitischen Umorientierung'* Vienna, Koeln, Graz: Boehlau.

604. Petrella R. (1995), 'Europe between competitive innovation and a new social contract' *International Social Science Journal*, 143: 11 - 23.

605. Petrella R. (1995), 'Europe between competitive innovation and a new social contract' *International Social Science Journal*, 143: 11 - 23.

606. Pfister U. and Suter Chr. (1991), 'Politische Regimes und Staatsentwicklung in der Dritten Welt: Peru seit den 1950er Jahren' *Schweizerische Zeitschrift fuer Soziologie*, 17, 2: 343 - 374.

607. Pierson, Paul (2000) Post-industrial pressures on the mature welfare states in: Globalization, European Economic Integration and Social Protection; Conference, March 11-12, 1999, organised by Martin Rhodes in Collaboration with the European Commission, DG V; Florence: European University Institute.

608. Pilsudski J. (1936), *'Erinnerungen und Dokumente. Von Josef Pilsudski dem Ersten Marschall von Polen, persoenlich autorisierte deutsche Gesamtausgabe. Mit einem Geleitwort von Ministerpraesident Hermann Goering'* Essen: Essener Verlagsanstalt.

609. Piore M. (1990), 'Work, labor and action: Work experience in a system of flexible production' in *'Industrial Districts and Inter - Firm Cooperation in Italy'* (Pyke F. et al. (Eds.)), pp. 52 - 74, Geneva: International Institute for Labor Studies.

610. Podkaminer L. et al. (1996), *'Continuing Improvements in Central and Eastern Europe - Russia and Ukraine Have Not Yet Turned the Corner'*, Research Reports, 225, February 1996, Vienna Institute for Comparative Economic Studies.

611. Podolec B. (1992) *'Household Budgets in Poland 1979 - 1991'* Warsaw: *Economic and Social Policy Series,* 15, Friedrich Ebert Foundation, Poland.

612. Polanyi, K. (1944/1957), *'The Great Transformation'* Boston: Beacon.

613. Polanyi, K. (1979), *'Oekonomie und Gesellschaft'* Frankfurt a.M.: suhrkamp taschenbuch wissenschaft.

614. Polish Institute of International Affairs (1993), *'Report on the State of National Security - External Aspects'* Warsaw: Polish Institute of International Affairs.

615. Polish Labor Statistical Yearbook (1996), Central Statistical Office, Warsaw (in Polish).

616. Pollack M. (1991), 'Zurueck in die Vergangenheit. Der Nationalitaetenhader im verschwindenden Osteuropa' *Kursbuch,* 102, Dezember: 54 - 64.

617. Pollins B. M. (1996), 'Global Political Order, Economic Change, and Armed Conflict: Coevolving Systems and the Use of Force' *American Political Science Review,* 90, 1: 103 - 117.

618. Popper Sir K. (1991), 'The Best World We Have Yet Had. George Urban Interviews Sir Karl Popper' *Report on the USSR,* 3, 22, May 31: 20 - 22.

619. Poulantzas N. (1977), *'Die Krise der Diktaturen. Portugal, Griechenland, Spanien'* Frankfurt a.M.: suhrkamp.

620. Prader H. (1974), 'Ziele und Resultate kooperativer Gewerkschaftspolitik im Wiederaufbau nach 1945' *Oesterreichische Zeitschrift fuer Politikwissenschaft,* 3: 345 - 366.

621. Prader H. and Unterleitner M. (1976), 'Das 'Trade Union Recovery Program' der amerikanischen Gewerkschaften im Westeuropa und Oesterreich der Nachkriegszeit' *Oesterreichische Zeitschrift fuer Politikwissenschaft,* 1: 89 - 106.

622. Prader Th. (Ed.)(1992), *'Moderne Sklaven. Asyl - und Migrationspolitik in Oesterreich'* Vienna: Promedia.

623. Pradetto A. (1991a), 'Internationale Politik osteuropaeischer Staaten. Grundlegende Bedingungen und Tendenzen' *Oesterreichische Osthefte,* 33, 4: 663 - 678.

624. Pradetto A. (1991b); 'Politik und Oekonomie im postkommunistischen Polen' *Osteuropa,* 41, 10: 941 - 952.

625. Pradetto A. (1994), 'Europaeisierung oder Renationalisierung. Europa nach dem Ende des Ost - West - Konflikts' *SWS - Rundschau,* 33, 1: 5 - 21.

626. Prebisch R. (1983), 'The crisis of capitalism and international trade' *CEPAL Review,* 20, August: 51 - 74.

627. Prebisch R. (1984), 'Five Stages in My Thinking on Development' in *'Pioneers in Development. A World Bank Publication'* (Meier G.M. and Seers D. (Eds.)), pp. 175 - 191. New York and Oxford: Oxford University Press.

628. Preston P.W. (1987), *'Rethinking Development. Essays on development and Southeast Asia'* London and New York: Routledge & Kegan Paul.

629. Przeworski A. (1991), *'Democracy and the Market. Political and Economic Reforms in Eastern Europe and Latin America'* Cambridge: at the University Press.

630. Przeworski A. (1996), 'Public Support for Economic Reforms in Poland' *Comparative Political Studies,* 29, 5: 520 - 543.

631. Rabinbach A. (1985), *'Austrian Social Democracy 1918 - 1934: The Socialist Experiment and Its Collapse'* Boulder, CO: Westview.

632. Radio Free Europe and Radio Liberty Research Institute (current issues), *'RFE/RL Research Reports'* Munich: Radio Free Europe/Radio Liberty.

633. Radio Free Europe/Radio Liberty (current issues), *'News Briefs'* Munich: Radio Free Europe/Radio Liberty.

634. *Radio Free Europe/Radio Liberty, electronic files* (world - wide - web: *http://www.rferl.org).*

635. Raffer K. (1987), *'Unequal Exchange and the Evolution of the World System Reconsidering the Impact of Trade on North - South Relations'* London, Basingstoke and New York: Macmillan/Saint Martin's Press.

636. Raffer K. (1989), *'Sovereign Debts, Unilateral 'Adjustment', and Multilateral Control: The New Way to Serfdom'* (Singer H.W. et al. (Eds.)), New Delhi: Ashish Publishing House (quoted here from the author's typescript).

637. Raffer K. (1992), *'The Least developed and the oil - rich Arab countries: dependence, interdependence, or patronage?'* New York, N.Y.: St. Martin's Press.

638. Raffer K. (1993), *'Trade, transfers, and development: problems and prospects for the twenty - first century'* Aldershot, Hants, England; Brookfield, Vt., USA: E. Elgar Pub. Co.

639. Raffer K. (1995a), 'Oesterreichs Entwicklungshilfe: Ein trauriges Kapitel' *Oesterreichisches Jahrbuch fuer Internationale Politik,* 1995: 21 - 47.

640. Raffer K. (1995b), 'Lo que es bueno para los Estados Unidos debe ser bueno para el mundo. Propuesta de una Declaración Universal de Isolvencia' *Persona y Sociedad, Instituto Latinoamericano de Doctrina y Estudios Sociales ILADES,* 9, 2, Septiembre: 64 - 73.

641. Raffer K. (1997), 'Is a Revival of Keynesian Ideas Likely?' in *'John Maynard Keynes: Keynesianism into the 21ˢᵗ Century'* (Sharma S. (Ed.)), Cheltenham-Lyme: Edward Elgar (quoted here from the author's typescript).

642. Raffer K. and Singer H.W. (1996), *'The Foreign Aid Business. Economic Assistance and Development Cooperation'* Cheltenham and Borookfield: Edward Alger.

643. Ragin C.C. and Bradshaw Y.W. (1992), 'International Economic Dependence and Human Misery, 1938 - 1980. A Global Perspective' *Sociological Perspectives,* 35, 2: 217 - 247.

644. Rahr A. (1993), 'Russia: The Struggle for Power Continues' *RFE/RL Research Report,* 2, 6, 5 February: 1 - 5.

645. Rahr A. (1994), 'The Implications of Russia's Parliamentary Elections' *RFE/RL Research Report,* 3, 1, 7 January: 32 - 37.

646. Raith W. (1994a), *'Das neue Mafia - Kartel: wie die Syndikate den Osten erobern'* Berlin : Rowohlt.

647. Raith W. (1996a), *'The red mafia: the Eastern European mob'* New York : Four Walls Eight Windows.

648. Raith W. (1994b), 'Mafia als Lehrstueck. Die Behandlung als exotisches Fremdgewaechs lenkt vom Problem der organisierten Kriminalitaet ab' *Gewerkschaftliche Monatshefte,* 4: 240 - 247.

649. Raith W. (1996b) *'Organisierte Krminilatitaet'* Reinbek: rororo aktuell.

650. Ray J.L. (1983), 'The 'World System' and the Global Political System: A Crucial Relationship?' in *'Foreign Policy and the Modern World - System'* (Mc Gowan P. and Kegley Ch.W. Jr. (Eds.)), pp. 13 - 34, Beverly Hills: Sage.

651. Reich R. B. (1992), *'The Work of Nations. Preparing Ourselves for 21ˢᵗ - Century Capitalism'* New York: Random House, Vintage Books Edition.

652. *Reports and Summaries* (current issues). Vienna: Austrian National Bank.

653. Republic of Poland, Ministry of Health and Social Welfare (1996), *'Health Care System in Transition (HiT) Profile Poland'* Ljubljana: The World Health Organization Conference on European Health Care Reforms.

654. Research Centre for Economic and Statistical Studies of the Central Statistical Office and the Polish Academy of Sciences (current issues), *'Research Bulletin'* Warsaw: Central Statistical Office.

655. *Reuters Textline,* Dialog - online.

656. Riggs F. (1990), *'Presidentialism in the USA A Comparative Perspective'* Honolulu: Department of Political Science, University of Hawaii at Manoa.

657. Ringel E. (1987), *'Zur Gesundung der oesterreichischen Seele'* Vienna: Europaverlag.

658. Robertson, R. (1992) Globalization; London: Sage.

659. Robinson J. (1947), *'An Essay on Marxian Economics'* London: Basil and Blackwell.

660. Robinson T.D. and London B. (1991), 'Dependency, Inequality, and Political Violence. A Cross - National Analysis' *Journal of Political and Military Sociology,* 19, 1: 119 - 156.

661. Rode R. (1991), 'Deutschland: Weltwirtschaftsmacht oder ueberforderter Euro - Hegemon?' *Leviathan,* 2: 229 - 246.

662. Roehrich W. (1979) 'Sozialgeschichte politischer Ideen. Die buergerliche Gesellschaft' Reinbek: rororo wissen.

663. Rogers R. (1992), 'The Politics of Migration in the Contemporary World' *International Migration,* 30, Special Issue: Migration and Health in the 1990s: 30 - 55.

664. Rosecrance R. (1987), 'Long cycle theory and international relations' *International Organization,* 41, 2: 283 - 301.

665. Ross R.J.S. and Trachte K.C. (1990), *'Global Capitalism: The New Leviathan'* Albany: State University of New York Press.

666. Rostow W.W. (1978), *'The World Economy: History and Prospects'* London and Basingstoke: Macmillan.

667. Roth J. (1995) *'Der Sumpf: Korruption in Deutschland'* Munchen: Piper.

668. Rothgeb, Jr. J. M. (1995), 'Investment Penetration, Agrarian Change, and Political Conflict in Developing Countries' Studies in Comparative International Development, 30, 4: 46 - 62.

669. Rothschild K. W. (1944), 'The Small Nation and World Trade' *The Economic Journal,* April: 26 - 40.

670. Rothschild K. W. (1963), 'Kleinstaat und Integration' *Weltwirtschaftliches Archiv,* 90, 2: 239 - 275.

671. Rothschild K. W. (1966), *'Marktform, Loehne, Aussenhandel'* Vienna: Europa - Verlag.

672. Rothschild K. W. (1984), *'Politische Oekonomie in Oesterreich seit 1945'* Roma: Instituto A. Gramsci, 10 - 11.5 (mimeo).

673. Rothschild K. W. (1985), 'Felix Austria? Zur Evaluierung der Oekonomie und Politik in der Wirtschaftskrise' *Oesterreichische Zeitschrift fuer Politikwissenschaft,* 3: 261 - 274.

674. Rothschild K. W. (1993a), *'Employment, wages, and income distribution: critical essays in economics'* London; New York: Routledge.

675. Rothschild K. W. (1993b), *'Ethics and economic theory: ideas, models, dilemmas'* Aldershot, Hants., England; Brookfield, Vt.: E. Elgar.

676. Rothschild K. W. (1997), *'Some Considerations on the Economics and Politics of the EU and the Maastricht Treaty'* Vienna: quoted from the author's typescript

677. Rubinson R. (1976), 'The World - Economy and the Distribution of Income within States: A Cross - National Study' American Sociological Review, 41: 638 - 659.

678. Rummel R. R. (1994), 'Power, Genocide and Mass Murder' *Journal of Peace Research,* 31, 1: 1 - 10.

679. Rummel R. R. (1995), 'Democracy, Power, Genocide, and Mass Murder' *The Journal of Conflict Resolution,* 39, 1, March: 3 - 26.

680. Russett B. (1967), *'International Regions and the International System. A Study in Political Ecology'* Westport, Con.: Greenwood Press.

681. Russett B. (1978), 'The marginal utility of income transfers to the Third World' *International Organization,* 32, 4: 913 - 928.

682. Russett B. (1983a), 'International Interactions and Processes: The Internal versus External Debate Revisited' in *Political Science: The State of the Discipline'* (Finifter A. (Ed.)), pp. 541 - 68, Washington D.C.: American Political Science Association.

683. Russett B. (1983b), 'The Peripheral Economies. Penetration and Economic Distortion, 1970 - 75' in *Contending Approaches to World System Analysis'* (Thompson W.R. (Ed.)), pp. 79 - 114, Beverly Hills: Sage.

684. Russett B. (1994), 'The Democratic Peace' in *Conflicts and New Departures in World Society'* (Bornschier V. and Lengyel P. (Eds.)), pp. 21 - 43, New Brunswick (U.S.A.) and London: Transaction Publishers, World Society Studies, Volume 3.

685. Sabbat - Swidlicka A. (1994a), 'Local Elections Redress Political Imbalance in Poland' *RFE/RL Research Report,* 3, 27, 8 July: 1 - 8.

686. Sabbat - Swidlicka A. (1994b), 'Pawlak Builds Up Peasant Power' *RFE/RL Research Report,* 3, 24, 17 June: 13 - 20.

687. Sabbat - Swidlicka A. (1994c), 'Poland: The End of the Solidarity Era' *RFE/RL Research Report,* 3, 1, 7 January: 81 - 86.

688. Sachs J. (1993), *'Poland's Jump to the Market Economy'* Cambridge MA: MIT Press.

689. Saffioti H.B. (1978), *'Women in Class Society'* New York and London: Monthly Review Press.

690. Salamon, Lester M. (1994) The Rise of the Nonprofit Sector; in: Foreign Affairs; 73/July/August 1994.

691. Salamon, Lester M./Anheier, Helmut K. (1999): The Nonprofit Sector: A new global force; in: Herrmann [Ed.].

692. Salt J. (1996), *'Current trends in international migration in Europe'* Council of Europe, 6th Conference of European Ministers responsible for migration affairs, MMG - 6 (96) 3 E, Warsaw, 16 - 18 June 1996.

693. Salt J. et al. (1999): *'Assessment of Possible Migration Pressure and Its Labour Market Impact Following EU Enlargement to Central and Eastern Europe'.* Migration Research Unit, Department of Geography, University College, London

694. *Salzburger Nachrichten* (current issues).

695. Scandella L. (1998), *'Le Kondratieff. Essai de théorie des cycles longs économiques et politiques'* Paris: Economica, Economie poche

696. Schade W. (1991), 'Das Parteienspektrum in der Republik Polen' *Osteuropa,* 41, 10: 953 - 962.

697. Scharpf F.W. (1987), *'Sozialdemokratische Krisenpolitik in Europa'* Frankfurt and New York: Campus.

698. Scharsach H.H. (1992), *'Haider's Kampf'* Munich: Wilhelm Heyne.

699. Schmidt M.G. (1983), 'The Welfare State and the Economy in Periods of Economic Crisis: A Comparative Study of Twenty - three OECD Nations' *European Journal of Political Research,* 11, 1: 1 - 26.

700. Schmidt M.G. (1986), 'Politische Bedingungen erfolgreicher Wirtschaftspolitik. Eine vergleichende Analyse westlicher Industrielaender (1960 - 1985),' *Journal fuer Sozialforschung,* 26, 3: 251 - 273.

701. Schmidt P.G. (1990), 'Soziale Marktwirtschaft als wirtschaftspolitisches Leitbild' *Wirtschaftswissenschaft,* 7: 961 - 997.

702. Schmidt-Fink, Ekkehart (2000) A reverse "reconquista"? aid. Ausländer in Deutschland; Saarbruecken, 3-2000: 17 f..

703. Schock K. (1996), 'A Conjunctural Model of Political Conflict. The Impact of Political Opportunities on the Relationship Between Economic Inequality and Violent Political Conflict' *Journal of Conflict Resolution,* 40, 1: 98 - 133.

704. Schoppa M. (1992), 'Der Wandel in Europa und die Sicherheit Polens' *Hamburger Beitraege zur Friedensforschung und Sicherheitspolitik,* 61 (January).

705. Schulz B. (1995), 'Germany, The United States and Future Core Conflict' *Journal of World Systems Research*, 1, 13 electronic journal at World Systems Archive, University of Colorado, at: http://csf.colorado.edu/jwsr/

706. Schumpeter J.A. (1942/50), *'Kapitalismus, Sozialismus und Demokratie'* Munich: A. Francke, 5th printing, 1980 ('Capitalism, Socialism and Democracy' New York: Harper and Brothers).

707. Seager J. and Olson A. (1986), *'Der Frauenatlas'* Frankfurt a.M.: Fischer TB.

708. Seers D. (Ed.)(1978), *'Underdeveloped Europe'* Hassocks: Harvester Press.

709. Segbers K. (1991), 'Migration and Refugee Movements from the USSR: Causes and Prospects' *Report on the USSR*, 3, 46: 6 - 14.

710. Segundo Montes J. L. (1992), *'The Liberation of Dogma'* trans. Phillip Berryman, Maryknoll, N.Y.: Orbis Books.

711. Sell R. R. and Kunitz St.J. (1987), 'The Debt Crisis and the End of an Era in Mortality Declines' *Studies in Comparative International Development*, 21: 3 - 30.

712. Senghaas D. (1985), *'The European Experience: A Historical Critique of Development Theory'* Leamington Spa, Dover: Berg.

713. Senghaas D. (1989), 'Transcending Collective Violence, the Civilizing Process and the Peace Problem' in *'The Quest for Peace'* (Vaerynen R. et al. (Eds.)), pp. 3 - 18, London, Beverly Hills: Sage.

714. Senghaas D. (1994) *'Wohin driftet die Welt?: uber die Zukunft friedlicher Koexistenz'* Frankfurt am Main: Suhrkamp.

715. Senghaas D. (1994), *'Wohin driftet die Welt?'*. Frankfurt a.M.: edition suhrkamp.

716. Shafik N. and Bandyopadhyay S. (1992), *'Economic Growth and Environmental Quality. Time Series and Cross - Country Evidence'* Policy Research Working Papers, WPS, 904, Washington D.C.: The World Bank.

717. Shaw T. M. (1984), 'The Non - Aligned Movement and the New International Economic Order' in *'Transforming the World - Economy? Nine Critical Essays on the New International Economic Order'* (Addo H. (Ed.)), pp. 138 - 162, London: Hodder and Stoughton.

718. Shaw T. M. (1994), *'The South at the end of the twentieth century: rethinking the political economy of foreign policy in Africa, Asia, the Caribbean, and Latin America'* New York: St. Martin's Press.

719. Shaw T. M. (1995), 'Globalisation, Regionalisms and the South in the 1990s: Towards a New Political Economy of Development' *The European Journal of Development Research*, 7, 2, Dec.: 257 - 275.

720. Sheahan M. D. (1995), *'Aspects of Health Policy in Poland'* Public Health Reports, May (available to the author only without pagination).

721. Shlaes A. (1994), 'Germany's Chained Economy' *Foreign Affairs*, 73, 5: 109 - 124.

722. Sideri S. (1999), 'Globalisation's Dilemma: Economic Blocs or Global Economic Apartheid?' *The European Journal of Development Research*, 11, 2, December: 141 - 175

723. Sik E. (1998), *'Migration Potential in Contemporary Hungary'* Starsbourg: Strategic Task Force for European Integration, WG 10

724. Sikorski R. (1996), 'How We Lost Poland' *Foreign Affairs*, September/October, 75, 5: 15 - 22

725. Silver B. J. (1994); 'Cycles of Hegemony and Labor Unrest in the Contemporary World' in *'Conflicts and New Departures in World Society'* (Bornschier V. and Lengyel P. (Eds.)), pp. 339 - 359, New Brunswick (U.S.A.) and London: Transaction Publishers, World Society Studies, Volume 3.

726. Simatupang B. (1991), *'The Polish Economic Crisis of 1979 - 1982. Background, Circumstances and Causes'* Universiteit van Amsterdam: Academisch Proefschrift.

727. Singer P.I. (1971), *'Dinámica de la población y desarrollo'* Mexico D.F.: Ed. Siglo XXI.

728. Singer P.I. (1981), 'O feminino e o feminismo' in *'Sao Paulo: O povo em movimento'* (Singer P.I. *et al.* (Eds.)), pp. 109 - 142, Petropolis, Rio de Janeiro: Editora Vozes.

729. SIPRI (1993), *'SIPRI Report'* Goettingen: Lamuv.

730. Slater W. (1994), 'Russia: The Return of Authoritarian Government?' *RFE/RL Research Report*, 3, 1, 7 January: 22 - 31.

731. Slay B. (1992), 'Poland: The Rise and Fall of the Balcerowicz Plan' *RFE/RL Research Report*, 31 January: 40 - 57.

732. Slay B. (1993), 'Evolution of Industrial Policy in Poland since 1989' *RFE/RL Research Report*, 2, 2, Jan. 8: 21 - 28.

733. Slay B. (1994a), 'The Polish Economy under the Post - Communists' *RFE/RL Research Report*, 3, 33, 26 August: 66 - 76.

734. Slay B. (1994b), 'The Macroeconomics of Transition in Eastern Europe' *RFE/RL Research Report*, 3, 1, 7 January: 139 - 143.

735. Smith D. (1997), *'Der Fischer Atlas. Kriege und Konflikte'.* Frankfurt a.M.: Fischer Taschenbuch Verlag.

736. So A. Y. (1990), *'Social Change and Development. Modernization, Dependency, and World - System Theories'* Newbury Park, CA.: Sage Library of Social Research, 178.

737. Sobrino J. SJ and Ellacuria I. SJ (posth.) (1996), *'Systematic Theology. Perspectives from Liberation Theology'.* Maryknoll, New York: Orbis.

738. Socher K. (1996), 'Die Waehrungsunion - eine kritische Buerteilung politischer und oekonomischer Aspekte' *Finanznachrichten*, 24, 13. Juni 1996: 1 - 8.

739. Soysal, Y. (1997) Identity, rights and claims-making: changing dynamics of citizenship in postwar Europe; paper presented to the 3rd European Conference of Sociology; Colchester, UK.

740. Srubar I. (1994), 'Variants of the Transformation Process in Central Europe. A Comparative Assessment' *Zeitschrift fuer Soziologie*, 23, 3, Juni: 198 - 221.

741. Stalker P. (1994), *'The Work of Strangers: A Survey of international labor migration'* Geneva: International Labor Office.

742. Staniszkis J. (1985), *'Poland: Self-Limiting Revolution'* Princeton: Princeton University Press.

743. Staniszkis J. (1991), *'The Dynamics of Breakthrough'* San Francisco: University of California Press.

744. Staniszkis J. (1992), *'The Ontology of Socialism'* Oxford: Oxford University Press.

745. Staniszkis J. (1994a), *'Ontology, Context and Change'* Cambridge, MA.: Minda de Ginzburg Center of European Studies, Working Paper, Harvard University.

746. Staniszkis J. (1998), *'Prolegomena to the theory of transition in Eastern Europe'* Warsaw: Instytut Studiow Politycznych, Polskiej Akademii Nauk (typescript)

747. Staniszkis J. (Ed.) (1994b), *'W Poszukiwania Paradygmatu Transformacji'* Warsaw: Instytut Studiow Politycznych, Polskiej Akademii Nauk.

748. Stankovsky J. (1992), 'Direktinvestitionen Oesterreichs in den Oststaaten' *Monatsberichte des oesterreichischen Instituts fuer Wirtschaftsforschung*, 8: 415 - 420.

749. Stankovsky J. (1993), 'Marktstellung in Ost - Mitteleuropa bedroht Oesterreichs Osthandel 1992' *Monatsberichte des oesterreichischen Instituts fuer Wirtschaftsforschung*, 6 (quoted from the author's typescript).

750. Stark O. and Taylor J.E. (1991), *'Relative Deprivation and Migration. Theory, Evidence and Policy Implications'* World Bank Policy, Research and External Affairs Working Papers, WPS 656, Washington D.C.: The World Bank.

751. Staub-Bernasconi, Silvia (2000) The WTO as task for the management or Globalisation of Social Work [Die WTO als Managementaufgabe oder die Globalisierung deer Sozialen Arbeit]; to be published in: Socialmanagement. Zeitschrift fuer Sozialwirtschaft; Baden-Baden: Nomos Verlagsgesellschaft; 2000 – issue 1-2/2000.

752. Stauffer R. B. (1982) *'Losing hegemony: U.S. TNCs and the global capitalist crisis'* Sydney: Transnational Corporations Research Project, University of Sydney.

753. Stauffer R. B. (1983) *'The Manila - Washington connection: continuities in the transnational political economy of Philippine development'* Sydney: Transnational Corporations Research Project.

754. Stauffer R. B. (1985a) *'Transnational corporations and the state'* Sydney: Transnational Corporations Research Project, University of Sydney.

755. Stauffer R. B. (1985b), *'The Marcos Regime: Failure of Transnational Developmentalism and Hegemony - Building from Above and Outside'* Transnational Corporations Research Project, Faculty of Economics, The University of Sydney, Research Monograph no. 23.

756. Stauffer R. B. (1986) *'The Philippines under Marcos: failure of transnational developmentalism'* Sydney: Transnational Corporations Research Project, University of Sydney.

757. Stauffer R. B. (1990), 'Capitalism, 'Development', The Decline of the Socialist Option, and the Search for Critical Alternatives' *Occasional Papers in Political Science, Department of Political Science, University of Hawaii at Manoa,* 3, 3, Jan.: 29 - 43.

758. Steger H. A. (1989), *'Weltzivilisation und Regionalkultur. Wege zur Entschluesselung kultureller Identitaeten'* Munich: Eberhard.

759. Steger H. A. (1990), *'Europaeische Geschichte als kulturelle und politische Wirklichkeit. Hornruf von der anderen Seite des Limes.'* Munich: Eberhard.

760. Steger H. A. and Morell R. (1988), *'ein Gespenst geht um ...: MITTELEUROPA'* Munich: Eberhard.

761. Stephens J. D. (1989), 'Democratic Transition and Breakdown in Western Europe, 1870-1939: A Test of the Moore Thesis' *American Journal of Sociology,* 94, 5, March: 1019-77.

762. Stephens J. D. (1991), 'Industrial Concentration, Country Size, and Trade Union Membership' *American Political Science Review,* 85, 3, September: 941 - 949.

763. Stiftung Entwicklung und Frieden (1993), *'Globale Trends 93/94. Daten zur Weltentwicklung'* Frankfurt a.M.: Fischer Taschenbuch Verlag.

764. Stiftung Entwicklung und Frieden (1996), *'Globale Trends 1996. Fakten Analysen Prognosen'* Frankfurt a.M.: Fischer Taschenbuch Verlag.

765. Stokes R.G. and Andreson A. (1990), 'Disarticulation and Human Welfare in Less Developed Countries' *American Sociological Review,* 55, February: 63 - 74.

766. Stpiczynski T. (1992), *'Polacy w swecie'* Warsaw: Central Statistical Office.

767. Sunkel O. (1966), 'The Structural Background of Development Problems in Latin America' *Weltwirtschaftliches Archiv,* 97, 1: pp. 22 ff.

768. Sunkel O. (1972/3), 'Transnationale kapitalistische Integration und nationale Desintegration: der Fall Lateinamerika' in *'Imperialismus und strukturelle Gewalt. Analysen ueber abhaengige Reproduktion'* (Senghaas D. (Ed.)), pp. 258 - 315, Frankfurt a.M.: suhrkamp. English version: 'Transnational capitalism and national disintegration in Latin America' *Social and Economic Studies,* 22, 1, March: 132 - 76.

769. Sunkel O. (1973), *'El subdesarrollo latinoamericano y la teoria del desarrollo'* Mexico: Siglo Veintiuno Editores, 6a edicion.

770. Sunkel O. (1978a), 'The Development of Development Thinking' in *'Transnational Capitalism and National Development. New Perspectives on Dependence'* (Villamil J.J. (Ed.)), pp. 19 - 30, Hassocks, Sussex: Harvester Press.

771. Sunkel O. (1978b), 'Transnationalization and it's National Consequences' in *'Transnational Capitalism and National Development. New Perspectives on Dependence'* (Villamil J.J. (Ed.)), pp. 67 - 94, Hassocks, Sussex: Harvester Press.

772. Sunkel O. (1980), *'Transnacionalizacion y dependencia'* Madrid: Ediciones Cultura Hispanica del Instituto de Cooperacion Iberoamericana.

773. Sunkel O. (1984), *'Capitalismo transnacional y desintegracion nacional en America Latina'* Buenos Aires, Rep. Argentina : Ediciones Nueva Vision.

774. Sunkel O. (1990), *'Dimension ambiental en la planificacion del desarrollo.* English The environmental dimension in development planning ' 1st ed. Santiago, Chile : United Nations, Economic Commission for Latin America and the Caribbean.

775. Sunkel O. (1991*), 'El Desarrollo desde dentro: un enfoque neoestructuralista para la America Latina'* 1. ed. Mexico: Fondo de Cultura Economica.

776. Sunkel O. (1994), *'Rebuilding capitalism: alternative roads after socialism and dirigisme'* Ann Arbor, Mich.: University of Michigan Press.

777. Suter Ch. (1994); 'Genesis and Dynamics of Populist Regimes at the Periphery' in *'Conflicts and New Departures in World Society'* (Bornschier V. and Lengyel P. (Eds.)), pp. 181 - 207, New Brunswick (U.S.A.) and London: Transaction Publishers, World Society Studies, Volume 3.

778. Suter Ch. *et al.* (1990), 'External public debt of the periphery. A recurrent problem of world society' in *'World Society Studies. Volume 1'* (Bornschier V. and Lengyel P. (Eds.)), pp. 237 - 271, Frankfurt and New York: Campus.

779. Sweezy P. M. (1971), *'Theorie der kapitalistischen Entwicklung'* Frankfurt a. M.: edition suhrkamp.

780. Swoboda H. (1973), 'Sozialstaat und kapitalistische Entwicklung' *Oesterreichische Zeitschrift fuer Politikwissenschaft,* 4: 333 - 353.

781. Szelenyi I. and Kostello E. (1996), 'The Market Transition Debate. Toward a Synthesis' *American Journal of Sociology,* 101, 4: 1082 - 1096.

782. Szlajfer H. (1977), 'Nachzuholende Entwicklung unter den Bedingungen des Weltmarktes: Das Beispiel der polnischen Entwicklung' *Probleme des Klassenkampfes,* 7, 27: 7ff.

783. Szlajfer H. (1979), *'Economic surplus and surplus - value: an attempt at comparison'* Dar es Salaam: Economic Research Bureau, University of Dar es Salaam.

784. Szlajfer H. (1984), *'The Faltering economy: the problem of accumulation under monopoly capitalism'* New York: Monthly Review Press.

785. Szlajfer H. (1985), *'Modernizacja zaleznosci: kapitalizm i rozwoj w Ameryce Lacinskiej'* Wroclaw: Zaklad Narodowy im. Ossolinskich.

786. Szlajfer H. (1990), *'Economic nationalism in East - Central Europe and South America: 1918 - 1939 = Le Nationalisme economique en Europe du Centre - Est et en Amerique du Sud'* Geneve: Librairie Droz.

787. Szlajfer H. (1993), 'Dezintegracja prestrzeni eurazjatyckiej a bezpieczenstwo Europy Srodkowej i Wschodniej' *Studia i Materialy,* 65, Polish Institute of International Affairs, Warsaw.

788. Szlajfer H. (1995), *'From the Polish underground: selections from Krytyka, 1978 - 1993'* University Park, Pa. : Pennsylvania State University.

789. Szylko - Skoczny M. (1992), *'Spoleczne skutki bezrobocia w wymiarze lokalnym. Raport z badan empirycznych'* Warsaw: Polityka ekonomiczne i spoleczna, Fundacja im. Friedrich Eberta w Polsce.

790. Tabatabai H. and Fouad M. (1993), *'The incidence of poverty in developingcountries. An ILO compendium of data'* Geneva: ILO.

791. Taggart P. (1995), 'New Populist Parties in Western Europe' *West European Politics,* 1: 34 - 51.

792. Talos E. (1981), *'Staatliche Sozialpolitik in Oesterreich. Rekonstruktion und Analyse'* Vienna: Verlag fuer Gesellschaftskritik.

793. Tatur M. (1994), ''Corporatism' as a paradigm of transformation' in *'W Poszukiwania Paradygmatu Transformacji'* (Staniszkis J. (Ed.)), pp. 93 - 130, Warsaw: Instytut Studiow Politycznych, Polskiej Akademii Nauk.

794. Tausch A. (1972) 'Der Nahostkrieg in der westdeutschen Presse' *Publizistik. Vierteljahreshefte fuer Kommunikationsforschung*, 17, 4: 117-118 (Review Article)

795. Tausch A. (1973a) 'Zur Analyse politischer Systeme in Lateinamerika' *Zeitschrift fuer Lateinamerika*, Wien, 5: 40 - 56

796. Tausch A. (1973c) 'Rassenbeziehungen in den USA' *Oesterreichische Zeitschrift fuer Politikwissenschaft*, 2, 2: 203 - 207 (Review Article)

797. Tausch A. (1974) 'Statistische Auswertung: Medienforschung in Oesterreich' in *'Medienforschung in Oesterreich'* (Fabris H.H./ Firnberg H. (Eds.) Springer, Vienna, New York: 44-80

798. Tausch A. (1976a) *'Die Grenzen der Wachstumstheorie'* Ph.D. dissertation, Department of Political Science, Paris-Lodron-Universitaet Salzburg, published by the Vienna Institute for Development (2 volumes)

799. Tausch A. (1976b coll. in.:/ Fabris H.H./ Kreuzhuber H.) *'Das Internationale Jahr der Frau 1975 und die Darstellung von Frauenthemen in den oesterreichischen Massenmedien'* Bundesministerium fuer Soziale Verwaltung, Staatsdruckerei L 61 33 3 37/F/F/O, Vienna: 69-73

800. Tausch A. (1977a) 'Ist der Kapitalismus tot? Zur Verelendung in Oesterreich' in *'Armut in Oesterreich'* (JG in der SPOe Steiermark/Erklaerung von Graz fuer solidarische Entwicklung (Eds.)) Leykam, Graz: 66-100

801. Tausch A. (1977b) 'Neuere Literatur zur Verteilungstheorie' *Oesterreichische Zeitschrift fuer Politikwissenschaft*, 6, 3: 355-358

802. Tausch A. (1978a) 'Nicht nur der Artikel 7' *Mladje-Literatura in Kritika*, 29: 58-90 http://thing.at/ejournal/litprim/renltz1.html

803. Tausch A. (1978b) 'Politische Systeme und Abhaengigkeit. Ein faktorenanalytisches Modell' *Internationale Entwicklung*, I + II: 54 - 62

804. Tausch A. (1979a) 'Weltweite Armut' in *'Christliche Markierungen'* (Dotter F. et al. (Eds.)) Europa, Vienna: 137-170

805. Tausch A. (1979b) *'Armut und Abhaengigkeit. Politik und Oekonomie im peripheren Kapitalismus'*. Studien zur österreichischen und internationalen Politik, Bd. 2 (Eds. P. Gerlich und A. Pelinka) W. Braumueller, Vienna

806. Tausch A. (1980a, together with O. Hoell) 'Austria and the European Periphery in *'European Studies of Development'* (J. de Bandt et al. (Eds.)) Macmillan, London: 28-37

807. Tausch A. (1980b) *'Gierek-Dengisme'* in *'Transfert de Technologie et Developpement: Un Debat'* (Masini J. (Ed.)) Institut d'Etude du Developpement Economique et Social- Universite de Paris I- Pantheon Sorbonne: 82-84

808. Tausch A. (1980c) 'Sozialwissenschaftliche Revolutionsforschung - Revolutionstheorien. Eine Auswahlbibliographie' in *'Revolution und Gesellschaft'* (Reinalter H. (Ed.)) Inn, Innsbruck: 223-228 (Bibliography)

809. Tausch A. (1980d) 'Ruestung und peripherer Kapitalismus' in *'Aktuelle Beitraege zur Entwicklungspolitik'* (Raffer K./Kopeinig M. (Ed.)) Oesterreichischer Informationsdienst fuer Entwicklungspolitik: 73-120

810. Tausch A. (1981a) 'Waffenschmiede Oesterreich?' *Zukunft*, 12: 22-24

811. Tausch A. (1981b) 'Burgermark - Der Burgerstimmenanteil auf Gemeindeebene und Bezirksebene' *Journal fuer Sozialforschung*, 21, 3: 265-283

812. Tausch A. (1982a) 'Ruestung und Lebensbedingungen in der Dritten Welt' in *'Ruestung und Oekonomie'* (Sonntag Ph. (Ed.)) Haag und Herchen, Frankfurt a.M.: 176-188

813. Tausch A. (1982b) 'Gleicher als die Anderen?' *Oesterreichischer Forschungsalmanach*: 200-212

814. Tausch A. (1982c) *'Aggregate Data Set Eastern Europe.'* Cologne: Koelner Zentralarchiv fuer empirische Sozialforschung, MRDF + Codebook, ZA Study 1159

815. Tausch A. (1982d) 'Das Ruestungszahlenspiel' *Fortschrittliche Wissenschaft*, 4: 83-85

816. Tausch A. (1982e) 'Hunger und Ruestung: Das fatale Ein Drittel - Zwei Drittel - Bild' *KSOe-Nachrichten und Stellungnahmen der Katholischen Sozialakademie Oesterreichs*, 15, 04. 09: 7-8

817. Tausch A. (1983a) 'Neueste Tendenzen im internationalen Waffenhandel' *Zukunft*, 5: 14-16

818. Tausch A. (1983b) 'Wie die Industrielaender die Dritte Welt ausbeuten' *Arbeit und Wirtschaft*, 37, 4: 24-28

819. Tausch A. (1983c) 'Atompolitik oder menschliche Entwicklung?' *Freie Argumente*, 4: 18-35

820. Tausch A. (1983d) 'Erzwungene Technologie - Abhaengigkeit, Ruestung und Konsum in Osteuropa. Reflexionen ueber Intelligence Research und die amerikanische Aussenpolitik' *Oesterreichische Zeitschrift fuer Politikwissenschaft*, 4: 452-467

821. Tausch A. (1983e) 'German Language Research about Brazil' *Latin American Research Review*, 3: 261-263 (Review Article)

822. Tausch A. (1984a) 'Zur kubanischen Entwicklungseffizienz' *Zeitschrift fuer Lateinamerika, Wien*, 25: 33-44

823. Tausch A. (1984b) 'Zentrum, Peripherie, strukturelle Gewalt und Superruestung. Unterwegs zu einem politometrischen Modell' *Dialog*, 1, 1: 72-106

824. Tausch A. (1984c) 'Umverteilen vor dem Wachstum? Umverteilung, Geburtenpolitik und langfristige Entwicklung in China' *China-Report*, 77-78: 52-66

825. Tausch A. (1985a) 'Development, Social Justice, and Dependence in Poland' *Occasional Paper, 9, Transnational Corporations Research Project, Faculty of Economics, University of Sydney* (N.S.W.)

826. Tausch A. (1985c) 'Tendenzwende im Vatikan' *Zukunft*, Jaenner: 10-11

827. Tausch A. (1986a) 'Costa Rica im System der internationalen Stratifikation' in *'Costa Rica'* (Maislinger A. (Ed.) Innverlag, Studien zur Politischen Wirklichkeit, 3: 197-207

828. Tausch A. (1986b) 'Entwicklungsmodell realer Sozialismus? - Eine politometrische Untersuchung zu Verteilung, Wachstum und Humanentwicklung in Weltmarkt-abgekoppelten Systemen' *Reader Politikwissenschaft*, Haag und Herchen, Frankfurt a.M.: 60-103

829. Tausch A. (1986c) 'Rezension: Weltentwicklungsbericht 1984' *Koelner Zeitschrift fuer Soziologie und Sozialpsychologie*, 1: 164-167 (Review Article)

830. Tausch A. (1986d) 'Was bleibt von der Dependenztheorie?' *Journal fuer Entwicklungspolitik*, 3: 84-90

831. Tausch A. (1986e) 'Austria. Shadows from the Past' *Economic and Political Weekly (Bombay)*, 21, 52, Dec. 27: 2264

832. Tausch A. (1986f) 'Positions within the Global Order, Patterns of Defense Policies, and National Development: Austria and Pakistan Compared' in *'Security for the Weak Nations. A Multiple Perspective. A Joint Project of Pakistani and Austrian Scholars'* (S. Farooq Hasnat/Pelinka A. (Eds.)) Izharsons, Lahore: 245-255

833. Tausch A. (1986g) 'Windstille' *The Jerusalem Journal of International Relations*, 4: 147 - 148 (Book Review)

834. Tausch A. (1986h) "Die Aufgabe in Richtung gegen das Slawentum' Zur NS-Reichsidee der Waldheim-Dissertation 1944' *Alternative (Bolzano)*, 5, 6: 9. 06. 1986: 7

835. Tausch A. (1987a) 'Geburtenrate und Weltentwicklung. Die Bedeutung der Bevoelkerungsentwicklung fuer Lebensqualitaet, Wachstum und Verteilung und die krichlichen Nord - Suedbeziehungen' *Dialog*, 8, 1: 239-273

836. Tausch A. (1987b) 'Transnational Corporations and Underdevelopment' *Acta Sociologica*, 30, 1: 118-121 (Review Article)

837. Tausch A. (1987c) 'Waldheim jaka itaevaltaa' *Ydin (Helsinki)*, 6: 22-25

838. Tausch A. (1987d) 'Schumpeter Mannes - Bild' *Emanzipation und Partnerschaft*, 14, 2: 11-18

839. Tausch A. (1987e) 'Lebensqualität und Entwicklung - Ein quantitatives Modell' in '1. *Umwelttag der Universität Innsbruck 1987'* Veröffentlichungen der Universität Innsbruck, 162, 64 (V)

840. Tausch A. (1989a) 'Stable Third World Democracy and the European Model. A Quantitative Essay' in *'Crisis in Development'* (Z. Bablewski and B. Hettne (Eds.), The European Perspectives Project of the United Nations University, University of Gothenburg, PADRIGU-Papers: 131-161

841. Tausch A. (1989b) 'Noricum und kein Ende' Zukunft, 9: 17-19

842. Tausch A. (1989c) 'Bichi, Bomzhi und Brodyagi' *Zukunft,* 12: 33-36

843. Tausch A. (1989d) 'Armas socialistas, subdesarrollo y violencia estructural en el Tercer Mundo' *Revista Internacional de Sociologia, CSIC, Madrid,* 47, 4: 583-716 (appeared 1991)

844. Tausch A. (1990a) 'Bruno Kreisky' *Economic and Political Weekly (Bombay),* 25, 33, August 18: 1826

845. Tausch A. (1990b) 'Bundesheer abschaffen? Von der Destruktion österreichischer Neutralitätspolitik durch die 'grüne' Programmatik' *Akzente - Der sozialistische Akademiker (Vienna),* 3, September: 24-25

846. Tausch A. (1991a) 'Der Krieg am Golf' *Zukunft,* 4: 44

847. Tausch A. (1991b) 'Amerikanisiert die Universitäten. Die Hochschulreform bleibt auf der politischen Tagesordnung' *Zukunft,* 8: 5-9

848. Tausch A. (1991c) 'UdSSR: Fahrkarte nach Beirut?' *Zukunft,* 2: 32-36

849. Tausch A. (1991d) *'Jenseits der Weltgesellschaftstheorien. Sozialtransformationen und der Paradigmenwechsel in der Entwicklungsforschung'.* Grenzen und Horizonte (Eds. G. Ammon et al.) Eberhard, Munich (second printing)

850. Tausch A. (1991e) *'Rußlands Tretmühle. Kapitalistisches Weltsystem, lange Zyklen und die neue Instabilität im Osten'.* Eberhard, Munich

851. Tausch A. (1992) 'Leise stirbt die Alma Mater. Die Reformpläne Buseks' *Zukunft,* 2: 5 - 6

852. Tausch A. (1993a) *'Produktivkraft soziale Gerechtigkeit? Europa und die Lektionen des pazifischen Modells'.* Eberhard, Munich

853. Tausch A. (1993b; coauthor: Fred Prager) *'Towards a Socio-Liberal Theory of World Development'.* Basingstoke and New York: Macmillan/St. Martin's Press

854. Tausch A. (1993c) ''Kanadisierung' der Einwanderungspolitik. Die Grundlage der oesterreichischen 'Auslaenderpolitik'' *Zukunft,* 12: 15 - 19

855. Tausch A. (1997) *'Schwierige Heimkehr. Sozialpolitik, Migration, Transformation, und die Osterweiterung der Europaeischen Union'* Munich: Eberhard

856. Tausch A. (1998a) *'Transnational Integration and National Disintegration.'* Electronic publication at the World Systems Archive Working Paper Series (Coordinator: Christopher K. Chase-Dunn, Johns Hopkins University), http://csf.colorado.edu/wsystems/archive/papers.htm

857. Tausch A. (1998b*) 'Globalization and European Integration'* Electronic book publication at the World Systems Archive (Coordinator: Christopher K. Chase-Dunn, Johns Hopkins University) http://csf.colorado.edu/wsystems/archive/books/tausch/tauschtoc.htm

858. Tausch K. (1993), *'Frauen in Peru. Ihre literarische und kulturelle Praesenz'* Munich: Eberhard, Schriften zu Lateinamerika, Band 5.

859. Taylor Ch.L. and Jodice D.H. (1983), *'World Handbook of Political and Social Indicators III.'* Machine readable data file, University of Michigan: ICPSR.

860. Teague E. (1994), 'The CIS: An Inpredictable Future' *RFE/RL Research Report,* 3, 1, 7 January: 9 - 12.

861. Tedstrom J. (1989), 'Recent Trends in the Soviet Economy: A Balance Sheet on the Reforms' *Radio Liberty Report on the USSR,* 1, 5, February 3: 10 - 19.

862. The Times, Dialog - online.

863. Thee M. (1993), *'Armament and Disarmament in the Post - Cold - War Period'* Warsaw: *Occasional Papers,* 36, Polish Institute of International Affairs.

864. Thee M. (1994), 'Armaments and Disarmament in the Post - Cold War Period: The Quest for a Demilitarized and Nuclear - Free World' in *'Conflicts and New Departures in World Society'* (Bornschier V. and Lengyel P. (Eds.)), pp. 61 - 91, New Brunswick (U.S.A.) and London: Transaction Publishers, World Society Studies, Volume 3.

865. Therborn G. (1985), *'Arbeitslosigkeit. Strategien und Politikansaetze in OECD - Laendern'* Hamburg: VSA.

866. Therborn G. (1986), 'Karl Marx Returning. The Welfare State and Neo - Marxist, Corporatist and Statist Theories' *International Political Science Review,* 7, 2, April: 131 - 164.

867. Thompson W.R. (1983a), 'The World - Economy, the Long Cycle, and the Question of World - System Time' in *'Foreign Policy and the Modern World System'* (Mc Gowan P. and Kegley Ch.W.Jr. (Eds.)), pp. 35 - 62, Beverly Hills: Sage.

868. Thompson W.R. (1983b), 'Cycles, Capabilities and War: An Ecumenical View' in *'Contending Approaches to World System Analysis'* (Thompson W.R. (Ed.)), pp. 141 - 163, Beverly Hills: Sage.

869. Thun-Hohenstein Ch. and Cede F. (1995), *'Europarecht'* Vienna: Manz.

870. Thygesen N. et al. (1991), *'Business Cycles: Theories, Evidence, and Analysis'* London and Basingstoke: Macmillan.

871. Tibi B. (1992), 'Kreuzzug oder Dialog? Der Westen und die arabo - islamische Welt nach dem Golfkrieg' in *'Kreuzzug oder Dialog. Die Zukunft der Nord - Sued - Beziehungen'* (Matthies V. (Ed.)), pp. 107 - 120, Bonn: J.H.W. Dietz Nachfolger.

872. Tilton T.A. (1979), 'A Swedish Road to Socialism: Ernst Wigforss and the Ideological Foundations of Swedish Social Democracy' *American Political Science Review,* 73, 2: 505 - 20.

873. Timberlake M. and Kantor J. (1983), 'Economic Growth: A Study of the Less Developed Countries' *Sociological Quarterly,* 24: 489 - 507.

874. Timberlake M. and Williams K.R. (1984), 'Dependence, Political Exclusion, and Government Repression: Some Cross - National Evidence' *American Sociological Review,* 49: 141 - 46.

875. Timberlake M. and Williams K.R. (1987), 'Structural Position in the World - System, Inequality and Political Violence' *Journal of Political and Military Sociology,* 15: 1 - 15.

876. Toekes R.L. (1992), 'From Visegrad to Krakow: Cooperation, Competition, and Coexistence in Central Europe' *Problems of Communism,* 40, Nov. - Dec.: 100 - 114.

877. Tolz V. (1992), 'Russia: Westernizers Continue to Challenge National Patriots' *RFE/RL Research Report,* 1, 49, 11 Dec.: 1 - 9.

878. Tracy M. A. and Tracy M. B. (1996), 'The Impact of Market - Economy Transition on Social Security and Social Welfare in Poland' *Journal of Sociology and Social Welfare,* 23, 1: 23 - 39.

879. *Transition* (current issues) OMRI Prague.

880. Treiman D.J. and Roos P.A. (1983), 'Sex and earnings in industrial society: a nine - nation comparison' *American Journal of Sociology,* 89, 3: 612 - 650.

881. Tyson L.D'A. (1986), 'The debt crisis and adjustment responses in Eastern Europe: a comparative perspective' *International Organization,* 40, 2: 239 - 285.

882. Ulrich Ch.J. (1994), 'The Growth of Crime in Russia and the Baltic Region' *RFE/RL Research Report,* 3, 23, 10 June: 24 - 32.

883. United Nations Centre on Transnational Corporations (1983), *'Transnational Corporations in World Development'* New York: United Nations.

884. United Nations Children Fund (1998) *'Kinderarbeit. Zur Situation der Kinder in der Welt'.* Frankfurt a.M.: Fischer TB

885. United Nations Conference on Trade and Development (1996), 'World Investment Report 1996. Investment, Trade and International Policy Arrangements' New York and Geneva: United Nations.

886. United Nations Department of International Economic and Social Affairs, Statistical Office (current issues), *Compendium of Social Statistics* New York: United Nations.

887. United Nations Development Programme (1998a) *'Overcoming Human Poverty'*. UN New York, UNDP

888. United Nations Development Programme (1998b) *'The Shrinking State'* UN New York, UNDP

889. United Nations Development Programme (current issues), *'Human Development Report'* New York and Oxford: Oxford University Press.

890. United Nations Development Programme (current issues), Internet access to global, national and regional *Human Development Reports* at: *http://www.undp.org/hdro/*

891. United Nations Development Programme Warsaw (current issues), *'Human Development Report Poland'* Warsaw: UNDP Poland: Split Trading Publishing House, and current subsequent issues.

892. United Nations Development Programme, Bratislava Office (1999) *'Transition 1999. Human Development Report for Europe and the CIS'* New York: United Nations

893. United Nations Economic and Social Council (1978), *'Transnational Corporations in World Development: A Re - examination.'* New York: United Nations.

894. United Nations Economic and Social Council (1993), *'International Migration Flows Among ECE Countries, 1991'* New York: United Nations, CES/778, 27 May.

895. United Nations Economic Commission for Europe (1994) *'International Migration: Regional Processes and Responses'* Geneva: UN ECE Economic Studies, 7 (entire)

896. United Nations Economic Commission for Europe (1996); *'International Migration in Central and Eastern Europe and the Commonwealth of Independent States'* Geneva: UN ECE Economic Studies, 8 (entire)

897. United Nations Economic Commission for Europe (1998), *'In-Depth Studies on Migration in Central and Eastern Europe: The Case of Poland'* Geneva: UN ECE Economic Studies, 11 (entire)

898. United Nations Economic Commission for Europe (current issues), *'Economic Survey of Europe'* New York: United Nations.

899. United Nations High Comissioner for Refugees, Warsaw Liaison Office (1993), unpublished data on the refugee situation in Eastern Europe.

900. United States Arms Control and Disarmament Agency (current issues), *'World Military Expenditures and Arms Transfers'* Washington DC.: US Government Printing Office.

901. United States Central Intelligence Agency, National Foreign Assesment Center (1980), *'Developed Country Imports of Manufactured Products from LDC's. A Research Paper'* Washington D.C.: US - CIA, ER 80 - 10476.

902. United States Commission on Immigration Reform (1994), *'U.S. Immigration Policy: Restoring Credibility'* Washington D.C.: US Government Printing Office.

903. United States Department of State (curent issues), *'International Drug Control Strategy Report'* Washington D.C.: US Government Printing Office.

904. United States Department of State (current issues), *'Country Reports on Human Rights Practices'* Washington D.C.: US Government Printing Office.

905. Vaerynen R. (1987), 'Global Power Dynamics and Collective Violence' in *'The Quest for Peace. Transcending Collective Violence and War among Societies, Cultures and States'* (Vaerynen R. et al. (Eds.)), pp. 80 - 96, London: Sage.

906. Van Rossem R. (1996), 'The World System Paradigmas General Theory of Development: A Cross - National Test' *American Sociological Review,* 61, June: 508 - 527.

907. Vickrey W. (1996), 'Fifteen Fatal Fallacies of Financial Fundamentalism. A Disquisition on Demand Side Economics' New York: Columbia University, Web-Site: http://www.columbia.edu/dlc/wp/econ/vickrey.htm.

908. Vinton L. (1992a), 'Poland: Government Crisis Ends, Budget Crisis Begins' *RFE/RL Research Report,* 1, 3, 17 January: 14 - 21.

909. Vinton L. (1992b), 'Poland's Governing Coalition: Will the Truce Hold?' *RFE/RL Research Report,* 1, 31, 31 July: 34 - 40.

910. Vinton L. (1992c), 'Poland's Government Crisis: An End in Sight?' *RFE/RL Research Report,* 1, 30, 24 July: 15 - 25.

911. Vinton L. (1992d), 'Polish Government Proposes Pact on State Firms' *RFE/RL Research Report,* 1, 42, 23 October: 10 - 18.

912. Vinton L. (1992e), 'Sejm Approves New Law on Radio and Television' *RFE/RL Research Report,* 1, 43, 30 October: 32 - 34.

913. Vinton L. (1993a), 'Walesa Applies Political Shock Therapy' *RFE/RL Research Report,* 2, 24: 11 June: 1 - 11.

914. Vinton L. (1993b), 'Poland's New Election Law: Fewer Parties, Same Impasse?' *RFE/RL Research Report,* 2, 28, 9 July: 7 - 17.

915. Vinton L. (1993c), 'Dissonance: Poland on the Eve of New Elections' *RFE/RL Research Report,* 2, 33, 20 August: 1 - 7.

916. Vinton L. (1993d), 'Poland's Political Spectrum on the Eve of the Elections' *RFE/RL Research Report,* 2, 36, 10 September: 1 - 16.

917. Vinton L. (1994), 'Power Shifts in Poland's Ruling Coalition' *RFE/RL Research Report,* 3, 11, 18 March: 5 - 14.

918. Voggenhuber J. (1995), 'Die EU reformieren!' in *'Oesterreichisches Jahrbuch fuer Politik 1994'* (Khol A. et al. (Eds.)), pp. 379 - 412, Munich, Oldenbourg - Verlag.

919. Vogt W. (Ed.) (1973), *'Seminar: Politische Oekonomie. Zur Kritik der herrschenden Nationaloekonomie'* Frankfurt a. M.: suhrkamp taschenbuch wissenschaft.

920. Vranitzky F. (1992a), 'Aufbruch in das Europa der Zukunft' *Akzente,* 1, Februar: 5 - 10.

921. Vranitzky F. (1992b), *'Die russisch - oesterreichischen Beziehungen. Entwicklungen und Perspektiven in einem neuen Europa'* Moskau: Vortrag von Bundeskanzler Dr. Franz Vranitzky im Institut fuer Internationale Beziehungen, Moskau, 1. April 1992 (mimeo).

922. Wade L. L. et al. (1995), 'Searching for Voting Patterns in Postcommunist Poland Sejm Elections' *Communist and Post - Communist Studies,* 28, 4: 411 - 425.

923. Wallerstein I. (1974), *'The Modern World System I. Capitalist Agriculture and the Origins of the European World - Economy in the Sixteenth Century'* New York: Academic Press.

924. Wallerstein I. (1976), 'Semi - Peripheral Countries and the Contemporary World Crisis' *Theory and Society,* 4: 461 - 483.

925. Wallerstein I. (1979a), *'The Capitalist World Economy'* Cambridge, England: Cambridge University Press.

926. Wallerstein I. (1979b), 'Underdevelopment and Phase B: Effect of the Seventeenth - Century Stagnation on Core and Periphery of the European World - Economy' in *'The World - System of Capitalism: Past and Present'* (Goldfrank W.L. (Ed.)), pp. 73 - 85, Beverly Hills: Sage.

927. Wallerstein I. (1982), 'Socialist States: Mercantilist Strategies and Revolutionary Objectives' in *'Ascent and Decline in the World - System'* (Friedman E. (Ed.)), pp. 289 - 300, Beverly Hills: Sage.

928. Wallerstein I. (1983a), 'Crises: The World Economy, the Movements, and the Ideologies' in *'Crises in the World - System'* (Bergesen A. (Ed.)), pp. 21 - 36, Beverly Hills: Sage.

929. Wallerstein I. (1983b), *'Historical Capitalism'* London: Verso.

930. Wallerstein I. (1984), *'Der historische Kapitalismus. Uebersetzt von Uta Lehmann - Grube mit einem Nachwort herausgegeben von Hans Heinrich Nolte'* Westberlin: Argument - Verlag.

931. Wallerstein I. (1986), "Krise als Uebergang' in *'Dynamik der globalen Krise'* (Amin S. and associates), pp. 4 - 35, Opladen: Westdeutscher Verlag.

932. Wallerstein I. (1989), *'The National and the Universal: Can There Be Such a Thing as World Culture?'.* Fernand Braudel Centre for the Study of Economies, Historical Systems, and Civilizations, Binghamton, New York: Suny Binghamton.

933. Wallerstein I. (1990), *'America and the World: Today, Yesterday, and Tomorrow'* Fernand Braudel Centre for the Study of Economies, Historical Systems, and Civilizations, Binghamton, New York: Suny Binghamton.

934. Wallerstein I. (1991a), *'Who Excludes Whom? or The Collapse of Liberalism and the Dilemmas of Antisystemic Strategy'* Fernand Braudel Centre for the Study of Economies, Historical Systems, and Civilizations, Binghamton, New York: Suny Binghamton.

935. Wallerstein I. (1991b), *'The Concept of National Development, 1917 - 1989: Elegy and Requiem'* Fernand Braudel Centre for the Study of Economies, Historical Systems, and Civilizations, Binghamton, New York: Suny Binghamton.

936. Wallerstein M. (1989), 'Union Organization in Advanced Industrial Democracies' *American Political Science Review,* 83, 2, June: 481 - 501.

937. Walterskirchen E./Dietz R.(1998): *'Auswirkungen der EU-Osterweiterung auf den österr. Arbeitmarkt'* Studie im Auftrag der Bundesarbeiterkammer - WIFO, 1998.

938. Walton J. and Ragin Ch. (1990), 'Global and National Sources of Political Protest: Third World Responses to the Debt Crisis' *American Sociological Review,* 55: 876 - 890.

939. Ward K.B. (1985), 'The Social Consequences of the World Economic System. The Economic Status of Women and Fertility' *Review,* 8, 4, Spring: 561 - 93.

940. Washington J. M. (1986), *'A Testimony of Hope: The Essential Writings of Martin Luther King'* San Francisco: Harper and Row.

941. Watzal L. (1997), 'Die Europaeische Union vor der Einfuerhung des Euro' *Europaeische Rundschau,* 4: 15-25.

942. Weber R.Ph. (1983), 'Cyclical Theories of Crises in the World - System' in *'Crises in the World - System'* (Bergesen A. (Ed.)), pp. 37 - 55, Beverly Hills: Sage.

943. Weede E. (1985), *'Entwicklungslaender in der Weltgesellschaft'* Opladen: Westdeutscher Verlag.

944. Weede E. (1986a), 'Catch - up, distributional coalitions and government as determinants of economic growth or decline in industrialized democracies' *The British Journal of Sociology,* 37, 2: 194 - 220.

945. Weede E. (1986b), 'Verteilungskoalitionen, Staatstaetigkeit und Stagnation' *Politische Vierteljahresschrift,* 27, 2: 222 - 236.

946. Weede E. (1990), *'Wirtschaft, Staat und Gesellschaft'* Tuebingen: J.C.B. Mohr.

947. Weede E. (1992), *'Mensch und Gesellschaft. Soziologie aus der Perspektive des methodoligischen Individualismus'* Tuebingen: J.C.B. Mohr.

948. Weede E. (1994), 'Determinanten der Kriegsverhuetung waehrend des Kalten Krieges und danach: Nukleare Abschreckung, Demokratie und Freihandel' *Politische Vierteljahresschrift,* 35, 1: 62 - 84.

949. Weede E. (1995), 'Future Hegemonic Rivalry between China and the West?' *Journal of World Systems Research,* 1, 14, electronic journal at World Systems Archive, University of Colorado, at: http://csf.colorado.edu/jwsr/

950. Weggel O. (1994), 'Die Internationalisierung der chinesischen Mafia' *Europa - Archiv,* 11: 325 - 332.

951. Weidenfeld W. and Hillenbrand, O. (1994a), 'EG - Einwanderungspolitik: Herausforderungen - Optionen - Folgen' *Internationale Politik und Gesellschaft. International Politics and Society (Friedrich Ebert Foundation)*, 1: 31 - 39.

952. Weidenfeld W. and Hillenbrand, O. (1994b), 'Wie kann Europa die Immigration bewaeltigen? Moeglichkeiten und Grenzen eines Einwanderungskonzepts' *Europa - Archiv*, 1: 1 - 10.

953. Weil F.D. (1985), 'The variable effect of education on liberal attitudes: a comparative - historical analysis of antisemitism using public opinion survey data' *American Sociological Review*, 50, 4: 458 - 474.

954. Weixner B. and Wimmer M. (1997), *'Stichwort EURO'* Munich: Wilhelm Heyne.

955. *Weltgeschehen* (current issues), Sankt Augustin: Siegler&Co. Verlag fuer Zeitarchive.

956. Weydenthal J.B. (1992), 'The Realignment of Polish Foreign and Military Policies' *RFE/RL Research Report*, 1, 30, 24 July: 40 - 42.

957. Weydenthal J.B. (1993a), 'Poland on Its Own: The Conduct of Foreign Policy' *RFE/RL Research Report*, 2, 2, 8 January: 1 - 4.

958. Weydenthal J.B. (1993b), 'Economic Issues Dominate Poland's Eastern Policy' *RFE/RL Research Report*, 2, 10, 5 March: 23 - 26.

959. Weydenthal J.B. (1994), 'Poland's Eastern Policy' *RFE/RL Research Report*, 3, 7, 18 February: 10 - 13.

960. Wheelwright E. L. (1974) *'Radical political economy: collected essays'* Sydney: Australia & New Zealand Book Co.

961. Wheelwright E. L. (1980) *'Australia and world capitalism'* Ringwood, Australia; New York: Penguin Books.

962. Wheelwright E. L. (1991) *'Oil & world politics: from Rockefeller to the Gulf War'* Sydney: Left Book Club.

963. Wheelwright E. L. (1994), 'Book Review: Richard Cocket *'Thinking the Unthinkable: Think - Tanks and the Economic Counter - Revolution'*, London, 1994' *Journal of Australian Political Economy*, 34: 128 - 135.

964. Wickrama K. A. S. and Mulford Ch. L. (1996), 'Political Democracy, Economic Development, Disarticulation, and Social Well - Being in Developing Countries' *The Sociological Quarterly*, 37, 3: 375 - 390.

965. Wieczorek P. (1993), *'Polski przemysl obronny w kontekscie nowego modelu sil zbrojnych'* Warsaw: Polish Institute of International Affairs, *Studia i Materialy, 9*.

966. Wiehn E.R. (1993), *'Ghetto Warschau. Aufstand und Vernichtung 1943 fuenfzig Jahre danach zum Gedenken'* Konstanz: Hartung Gorre Verlag.

967. WIIW (1999): *'Potential size of migration from Poland after joining the EU'* WIIW monthly report, 2

968. WIIW and EcoGI (1999) 'Hungary's Accession to the EU. State and prospects of Hungarian Austrian relations. Bilateral Synthetic report. Vienna and Budapest: WIIW and Economic Growth Institute

969. Wilkiewicz Z. (1996) 'Arbeitslosigkeit und ihr Stellenwert in der polnischen Sozialpolitik' *Osteuropa*, 46, 1, 1996: 64 - 79.

970. Williamson J (1998), *'Real Wages and Relative Factor Prices in the Third World 1820 - 1940: The Mediterranean Basin'*. Discussion Paper 1842, Harvard Institute of Economic Research

971. Williamson J. (1996), 'Globalization, Convergence and History' *The Journal of Economic History*, 56, 2: 277 - 306.

972. Williamson J. (1997) 'Globalization and Inequalities, Past and Present' *The World Bank Research Observer*, 12, 2, August: 117-135.

973. Williamson J. A. (1998), Harvard Institute of Economic Research, Internet site (with link-up to the data base on wages in the world periphery 1820-1940): *http://www.economics.harvard.edu/~jwilliam/*

974. Wimberley D. W. (1990), 'Investment Dependence and Alternative Explanations of Third World Mortality: A Cross - National Study' *American Sociological Review,* 55: 75 - 91.

975. Wimberley D.W. and Bello R. (1992), 'Effects of Foreign Investment, Exports and Economic Growth on Third - World Food Consumption' *Social Forces,* 70, 4: 895 - 921.

976. Winckler G. (Ed.), (1992), *'Central and Eastern Europe. Roads to Growth'* Washington D.C.: International Monetary Fund and Austrian National Bank.

977. Winters A. (1993), 'The Europe Agreements: with a little help from our friends' in *'Trade, Transfers and Development. Problems and Prospects for the Twenty - First Century'* (Murshed S. M. and Raffer K. (Eds.)), pp. 196 - 209, Aldershot, UK: Edward Elgar.

978. Wippermann W. (1983), *'Europaeischer Faschismus im Vergleich (1922 - 1982)'.* Frakfurt a.M.: edition suhrkamp.

979. Wishnevsky J. (1992), 'Antidemocratic Tendencies in Russian Policy - Making' *RFE/RL Research Report,* 1, 45, 13 November: 21 - 25.

980. Wistrich R.S. (Ed.)(1992), *'Austrians and Jews in the Twentieth Century. From Franz Joseph to Waldheim'* Basingstoke and New York: Macmillan and Saint Martin's Press.

981. Wlodarczyk C. and Mierzewski P. (1991), 'From words to deeds: health service reform in Poland' *International Social Security Review,* 44, 4: 5 - 8.

982. Woehlcke M. (1987), *'Umweltzerstoerung in der Dritten Welt'* Munich: C.H. Beck.

983. Woehlke M. (1993), *'Der oekologische Nord - Sued - Konflikt'* Munich: C.H. Beck.

984. Wolf J. (1996), 'Pluralitaet statt Uniformitaet. Werthaltungen der polnischen Buerger' *Soziale Welt,* 47, 2: 202 - 222.

985. Wolf K.D. (1991), 'Das neue Deutschland - eine Weltmacht?' *Leviathan,* 2: 247 - 260.

986. Wolfensohn, James 2000: quoted from: Protesters for Poverty; in: Financial Times; September 28th, 2000: 18.

987. Wolffsohn M. (1991), 'Deutschland: eine verwirrte und verwirrende Nation' *Europa - Archiv,* 7: 211 - 214.

988. Wolfgruber E. (1994), 'Parteipolitischer Diskurs und Strategien in der Auslaender/innen/politik in Oesterreich 1989 bis 1993' *Oesterreichische Zeitschrift fuer Politikwissenschaft,* 23, 3: 299 - 313.

989. Wollenberg J. and Friedrich J. (1987), *'Licht in den Schatten der Vergangenheit'* Stuttgart: Ullstein.

990. Wood A. (1994), *'Structural Unemployment in the North: Global Causes, Domestic Cures'* Vienna: Kreisky Commission Symposion, 21 - 22 March.

991. World Bank (1991a), *'Staff Appraisal Report Poland. Employment Promotion and Services Project'* Washington D.C.: World Bank, Country Department IV, Report 9408 - POL.

992. World Bank (1991b), *'Managing Development: The Governance Decision'* Washington D.C.: World Bank.

993. World Bank (1993), *'Social Indicators of Development 1993'* Baltimore and London: The John Hopkins University Press.

994. World Bank (1994), *'Poverty in Poland'* Washington D.C.: Country Operations, Central Europe Department, Europe and Central Asia Region (in two volumes).

995. World Bank (1995), *'Understanding Poverty in Poland'* Washington D.C.: The World Bank.

996. World Bank (current issues), *'World Development Report'* Washington D.C.: World Bank and Oxford University Press.

997. World Economy Research Institute Warsaw (current issues), *'Poland International Economic Report'* Warsaw: Warsaw School of Economics.

998. World Economy Research Institute Warsaw and International Centre for Economic Growth, San Francisco (current issues), *'Transforming the Polish Economy'* Warsaw: Warsaw School of Economics.

999. World Reporter (1997 ff.) *World Reporter,* in conjunction with Financial Times and Dow Jones & Co, at http://dialogselect.krinfo.com

1000. World Resources Institute in collaboration with The United Nations Environment Programme and The United Nations Development Programme (1992), *'World Resources 1992 - 93'* New York and Oxford: Oxford University Press.

1001. Yasmann V.A. (1994), 'Imperiale Ideologie fuer die russische Aussenpolitik. Die Rolle von Militaer und Sicherheitsapparat' *Europa - Archiv,* 9: 248 - 256.

1002. Yotopoulos P.A. (1996) *'Exchange Rate Parity for Trade and Development. Theory, tests and case studies'* Cambridge: at the University Press

1003. *Zeitpunkte (current issues)* Hamburg: Die Zeit.

1004. Zentner Chr. (1980), *'Geschichtsfuehrer in Farbe. Weltgeschichte in Bildern, Daten, Fakten'* Berlin and Darmstadt: Deutsche Buch - Gemeinschaft and Delphin - Verlag.

1005. Zielonka J. (1991), 'East Central Europe: Democracy in Retreat?' *The Washington Quarterly,* 14, 3, Summer: 107 - 120.

1006. Zienkowski L. (Ed.), (1993), *'Polish Economy in 1990 - 1992. Experience & Conclusions'* Warsaw: Research Centre for Economic and Statistical Studies of the Central Statistical Office and the Polish Academy of Sciences.

1007. Zimmerman E. and Saalfeld Th. (1988), 'Economic and Political Reactions to the World Economic Crisis of the 1930s in Six European Countries' *International Studies Quarterly,* 32, 3: 305 - 334.

1008. Zoethout T. (1993), 'Financing Eastern Europe's Capital Requirements' *RFE/RL Research Report,* 2, 7, 12 February: 38 - 43.

1009. Zolberg A.R. (1983), "World' and 'System': A Misalliance' in *'Contending Approaches to World System Analysis'* (Thompson W.R. (Ed.)), pp. 269 - 290, Beverly Hills: Sage.

SUBJECT INDEX

A

absolute GNP, 171, 172, 262
absolute income growth, 214, 260, 262
adjustment, xvi, xxxix, xlii, l, 25, 26, 36, 37, 40, 46, 47, 60, 74, 77, 81, 144, 154, 180, 223, 260, 338
adult literacy rate, x, xi, 80, 82, 84, 261, 271
age of democracy, l, 24, 154, 155, 156
aggregate net transfers, 80, 82, 118, 119
agricultural share in GDP, 262
aid dependency, 259
Albania, 17, 54, 83, 140, 231, 233, 289
Algeria, xlvii, 15, 108, 229, 287, 288
Amnesty International, 300
Angola, xi, 17, 261
Argentina, xxxv, 10, 84, 120, 123, 162, 208, 333
Armenia, 231, 290
Arms Control and Disarmament Agency, United States Department of State, ix, 203, 204
Association of Southeast Asian Nations, ix, 177
asylum, 235
Atom Energy Agency of the European Union, 152
Australia, xxxv, xlvii, 22, 51, 52, 59, 147, 153, 154, 161, 179, 180, 191, 197, 198, 272, 276, 296, 305, 308, 341
Austria, 5, xv, xxiii, xxix, xxx, xlvi, l, 5, 10, 11, 17, 22, 27, 54, 59, 67, 72, 101, 113, 134, 145, 148, 153, 154, 161, 164, 170, 178, 182, 183, 185, 191, 192, 197, 198, 205, 224, 229, 232, 238, 272, 276, 287, 295, 301, 312, 314, 316, 318, 320, 322, 329, 335, 336
Austrian Federal Ministry for Foreign Affairs, 300
Autorenkollektiv, xiv, 262, 301
average population growth, 262

B

Bahamas, 46
Bangladesh, xlvii, 15, 49, 229, 310
Bank Austria, xxx, 5, 164, 301
Barbados, xi, 39, 46, 261
BBC World Service, 301
Belarus, xliv, xlvi, 24, 72, 105, 121, 139, 164, 286, 287, 288, 290, 305

Belgium, xlvi, l, 16, 53, 59, 101, 110, 147, 153, 154, 161, 182, 191, 197, 198, 208, 232, 272, 276
Belize, xi, 261
Benin, xi, 108, 261
Bhutan, xi, 261
big estates (> 25 ha) per total land, 273
big landholding, 125, 128, 129, 166, 169, 199
Bolivia, xlviii, 186
Bosnia, 81, 83
Botswana, 165
Brazil, xlviii, 15, 17, 22, 57, 61, 84, 119, 120, 139, 162, 170, 186, 208, 272, 305, 323, 335
Bruene St., 302
Bulgaria, ix, xxix, xxx, xlv, xlvi, xlvii, 6, 7, 8, 9, 54, 73, 86, 90, 91, 101, 106, 118, 119, 161, 199, 232, 286, 287, 288, 289, 291, 296
Bundesministerium fuer Arbeit, Gesundheit und Soziales, Vienna, 159
Burkina Faso, xi, xlviii, 261
Burundi, xlvii, 17, 52
Business Central Europe, xxxii, xlv, 8, 91, 92, 93, 102, 103, 104, 106, 118, 119, 150, 168, 200, 201, 262, 305

C

Cambodia, xlvii, 69
Canada, xlvii, 3, 22, 50, 52, 60, 61, 107, 147, 153, 155, 161, 191, 272, 276
capability poverty measure, ix, 260
Catholic Church, xiii, 25
center, xvii, xxxvi, xxxviii, li, 10, 11, 19, 25, 57, 70, 86, 93, 101, 144, 147, 149, 150, 159, 164, 171, 178, 205, 206, 208, 220
Central Africa, xlviii, 10
Central African Republic, xlviii
Central European Free Trade Area, ix
Central Statistical Office of the Polish Republic, 129, 306
Chad, xi, 261
Chile, xlviii, 22, 52, 81, 108, 120, 142, 208, 232, 272, 296, 311, 324, 333
China, xxv, xlviii, 3, 10, 11, 15, 28, 46, 48, 52, 68, 69, 70, 84, 108, 120, 136, 152, 160, 162, 165,

AUTHOR INDEX

S

Saalfeld Th., 344
Sabbat - Swidlicka A., 329
Sachs J. D., 305
Salt J., 329
Schade W., 330
Schock K., 330
Seager J., 330
Seers D., 322, 324, 327, 330
Segal R., 318
Seligson M., 323
Sell R. R., 330
Senghaas D., 330, 333
Seychelles, xi, 261
Shafik N., 330
Shaw T. M., 330, 331
Sheahan M. D., 331
Shlaes A., 331
Silver B. J., 331
Slater W., 331
Slay B., 331
Smith D., 321, 331
Smith D. A., 321
So A. Y., 331
Sobrino J. Societas Iesu, 310
Socher K., 331
Srubar I., 331
Stankovsky J., 332
Stark O., 332
Stauffer R. B., 332
Steger H. A., 332
Stephens J. D., 332
Sunkel O., 333
Swoboda H., 306, 333
Szelenyi I., 333
Szlajfer H., 333, 334

T

Tabatabai H., 334
Taggart P., 334
Tajikistan, 17, 290
Talos E., 334
Tausch A., 319, 334, 335, 336, 337
Tausch K., 337
Teague E., 337
Tedstrom J., 337
Thee M., 337
Therborn G., 337
Thygesen N., 337
Tibi B., 337
Timberlake M., 310, 338
Tolz V., 338
Townley E., 310
Tracy M. A., 338
Tracy M. B., 338

U

Unterleitner M., 326

V

Vaerynen R., 307, 308, 314, 330, 339
Van Rossem R., 339
Vickrey W., 339
Vinton L., 339, 340
Vranitzky F., 340

W

Wade L. L., 340
Wallerstein I., 316, 340
Walton J., 341
Washington J. M., 341
Weede E., 341
Weggel O., 341
Weidenfeld W., 341
Weixner B., 341
Wickrama K. A. S., 342
Wieczorek P., 342
Wilkiewicz Z., 342
Williams B. A., 321
Wimberley D. W., 342
Wimmer M., 341
Winckler G., 342
Winters A., 342
Wippermann W., 342
Wishnevsky J., 342
Wlodarczyk C., 342
Woehlcke M., 342
Wolf J., 343
Wolffsohn M., 343
Wolfgruber E., 343
Wollenberg J., 343
Wood A., 343

Z

Zielonka J., 343
Zienkowski L., 343
Zimmerman E., 344
Zoethout T., 344
Zolberg A.R., 344